ORGANIZATIONAL REALITY

Reports from the Firing Line

edited by

PETER J. FROST
University of British Columbia

VANCE F. MITCHELL
University of British Columbia

WALTER R. NORD
Washington University

Goodyear Publishing Company, Inc.
Santa Monica, California

To
Nola,
Fran
and
Ann

Library of Congress Cataloging in Publication Data
Main entry under title:

Organizational reality.

1. Organizational behavior—Addresses, essays,
lectures. I. Frost, Peter J. II. Mitchell, Vance F.
III. Nord, Walter R.
HD58.7.O74   1978   658.4   77-20503
ISBN 0-87620-654-2

Y-6542-8

Current Printing (last digit):
10 9 8 7 6 5 4 3

Printed in the United States of America

Production Editor: Linda G. Schreiber
Cover and Text Design: James van Maanen
Illustrations: Harold Funston

Preface

This book is the result of a meeting of minds one rainy day in Vancouver, British Columbia, in the spring of 1976. Like many others in the field of organizational behavior, each of us over the years has been confronted with the many discrepancies which seem to exist between what we teach about behavior in organizations and what our own and other people's perceptions tell us is "out there" in so-called real organizations. We reached a point that day where we were able to articulate our independently nurtured needs to do something constructive and to better understand some of the substance of this "other" organizational reality.

Our first step in this direction was to pool our thoughts and energies to survey what had been written on the subject in essentially nonacademic literature. We turned, therefore, to reports by keen observers of human behavior in organizational settings, to self-reports of participants in such settings, to fictionalized accounts in novels and short stories of individual and collective action and, on occasion, to academic journals. The perspectives which emerged from our excursion into this material provided the stuff of this book.

We have been struck by the many similarities in observations across many of these reports from the firing line, as we have termed them, as well as by the many differences between the "reality" which emerges and that with which we are familiar from our reading of academic texts in the area. We have been stimulated, intrigued and educated by the experience and hope that many readers likewise will find their thinking and assumptions about organizations challenged and perhaps revised as they make their way through the material in this book. We believe the reports may provide pointers to a richer understanding of behavior in organizations and that they complement the existing material which we read today in academic texts and journals in our field.

We are unanimous in our verdict that the compilation of this book has been for us one of those enviable experiences, an exploration which has been interesting, exciting and most rewarding. Our contributions have been distributed equally throughout the book, and the ordering of names on the title page represents the outcome of a random selection procedure.

No book is ever attributable solely to its authors, and this book is no exception. We wish to acknowledge the helpful comments of Craig Pinder and the efficient and enthusiastic administrative and secretarial efforts of Marilyn Logan. Also, for their invaluable assistance, our thanks go to Marcia Clagg, Kathy Raymond, Ruth Scheetz and Lesley Tucker, and Nancy Knapp. We owe a debt of gratitude to the many university and professional students in our courses whose healthy skepticism of what we teach inevitably served as a prod toward this endeavor. We thank also the many astute and articulate students of organization whose reports comprise this book. Finally, our deep thanks to Linda Schreiber, Production Editor for Goodyear, who shepherded this book through with grace, good humor and skill.

Peter J. Frost
Vance F. Mitchell
Walter R. Nord

Contents

CROSS-REFERENCE TABLE
SECTIONS IN *ORGANIZATIONAL REALITY*

SELECTED TEXTBOOKS	Section 1 Selection, Recruitment and Advancement	Section 2 Struggles Within Organizations	Section 3 Organizational Body Language
Behling, O. & Schriesheim, C. *Organizational Behavior: Theory, Research & Application* (Allyn & Bacon, 1976)	Ch. 10	Ch. 2, 5, 6, 7, 10	Ch. 4, 6, 7, 9, 11
Carroll, S. J. & Tosi, H. L. *Organizational Behavior & Management: A Contingency Approach* (St. Clair Press, 1977)	Ch. 13, 14, 15, 17	Ch. 3, 4, 5, 8, 10	Ch. 3, 4, 5, 9, 13, 16
Coffey, R. G., Athos, A. G. & Raynolds, P. A. *Behavior in Organizations: A Multidimensional View* (Prentice-Hall, 1975)	Ch. 2, 6, 7	Ch. 2, 4, 6, 8, 9	Ch. 1, 2, 3, 4, 5, 9
Filley, A. C., House, R. J. & Kerr, S. *Managerial Process & Organizational Behavior,* 2nd Edition (Scott, Foresman, 1976)	Ch. 19, 20	Ch. 6, 9	Ch. 4, 8, 10, 15
Gibson, J. L., Ivancevich, J. M. & Donnelly, J. H. *Organizations: Behavior, Structure, Processes,* 2nd Edition (Business Publications, Inc., 1976)	Ch. 5, 6	Ch. 8, 9, 10, 11	Ch. 5, 6, 7, 13, 17
Hellriegel, D. & Slocum, J. W. Jr. *Organizational Behavior: Contingency Views* (West Publishing, 1976)	Ch. 3, 9	Ch. 2, 4, 5, 7, 8	Ch. 3, 4, 6, 7, 8, 9, 11
Herbert, T. T. *Dimensions of Organizational Behavior* (Macmillan, 1976)	Ch. 13	Ch. 12, 16, 17, 19	Ch. 3, 9, 10, 13, 16
Huse, E. F. & Bowditch, J. L. *Behavior in Organizations: A Systems Approach to Managing,* 2nd Edition (Addison-Wesley, 1977)	Ch. 3	Ch. 3, 4, 6, 7	Ch. 3, 4, 5
Ivancevich, J. M., Szilagyi, A. D. Jr. & Wallace, M. J. Jr. Organizational Behavior & Performance (Goodyear, 1977)	**Ch. 14, 15, 16**	**Ch. 3, 4, 8, 9, 15**	**Ch. 3, 4, 5, 6, 7, 8, 9, 13**
Luthans, F. *Introduction to Management: A Contingency Approach* (McGraw-Hill, 1976)	Ch. 15	Ch. 13, 14	Ch. 6, 13, 14
Porter, L. W., Lawler, E. E. III & Hackman, J. R. *Behavior in Organizations* (McGraw-Hill, 1975)	Ch. 5, 11, 12, 15	Ch. 4, 6, 7, 12, 13	Ch. 1, 2, 4, 9, 10, 13, 14
Reitz, H. J. *Behavior in Organizations* (Richard D. Irwin, 1977)	Ch. 5, 21	Ch. 4, 5, 17, 18, 19	Ch. 4, 5, 6, 12, 13, 14, 15
Robbins, S. *The Administrative Process: Integrating Theory & Process* (Prentice-Hall, 1976)	Ch. 5, 22	Ch. 5, 6, 7, 16	Ch. 15, 16, 18, 21

Section 4 The Individual in the Organization	Section 5 Conflict, Resistance to Change and Control	Section 6 The Politics of Control in Organizations	Section 7 Getting Results	Section 8 Organizational Stress	Section 9 Organizational Effectiveness-Ineffectiveness
Ch. 4, 5, 6, 7, 10, 11	Ch. 5, 8	Ch. 8, 9, 12, 13, 14	Ch. 3, 4, 10, 11	Ch. 2, 3, 5, 11, 12	Ch. 8, 9, 14
Ch. 3, 4, 5, 8, 10, 13	Ch. 4, 13, 16, 17, 18	Ch. 4, 8, 11, 14, 15, 18	Ch. 3, 5, 10, 11, 12, 13, 14, 15	Ch. 3, 5, 8, 9, 13, 14	Ch. 6, 7, 16, 18
Ch. 2, 4, 7, 8, 12	Ch. 7, 10, 12, 14	Ch. 8, 9, 10	Ch. 3, 9	Ch. 2, 7, 8, 9	Ch. 3, 5, 10, 11, 12
Ch. 6, 9, 10, 15	Ch. 9, 19, 20	Ch. 6, 9, 11, 12, 14, 19, 20, 22	Ch. 8, 10, 14, 19, 21	Ch. 6, 7, 9, 10, 11, 12	Ch. 8, 9, 13, 14, 21
Ch. 3, 4, 5, 6, 7	Ch. 9, 12, 13	Ch. 8, 9, 12, 17	Ch. 6, 14, 15, 17	Ch. 3, 5, 13, 14	Ch. 2, 3, 4, 5, 13
Ch. 3, 7, 10, 11	Ch. 6, 12, 13	Ch. 8, 10, 11, 12, 13	Ch. 4, 9, 13	Ch. 3, 11	Ch. 3, 8, 11, 12, 13
Ch. 5, 6, 12, 13, 14, 15, 16, 17, 22	Ch. 17, 23	Ch. 3, 5, 7, 14, 15, 17, 18, 19, 20	Ch. 11, 12, 17	Ch. 5, 6, 12, 13, 19, 20	Ch. 3, 19, 23, 24
Ch. 3, 5, 8, 9	Ch. 6, 12, 13, 14	Ch. 6, 7, 10, 14	Ch. 3, 8, 9, 12, 14	Ch. 8, 9, 12, 13, 15	Ch. 6, 7, 10, 13, 14
Ch. 5, 6, 8, 11, 15	**Ch. 9, 16, 17**	**Ch. 9, 10, 11, 12, 16, 17**	**Ch. 5, 14, 15, 17**	**Ch. 5, 6, 10, 13, 15**	**Ch. 11, 12, 16, 17, 18**
Ch. 6, 7, 8, 13	Ch. 3, 7, 14, 15, 20	Ch. 3, 7, 14	Ch. 12, 13	Ch. 8, 10, 13	Ch. 5, 16, 17, 19, 20
Ch. 4, 10, 12, 17	Ch. 15, 16	Ch. 9, 14, 15	Ch. 10, 11, 12	Ch. 4, 7, 9, 10, 14, 20	Ch. 3, 4, 13, 14, 17
Ch. 4, 5, 11, 12, 16, 17, 19	Ch. 16, 17, 21	Ch. 16, 17, 18, 19, 20	Ch. 4, 6, 7, 21	Ch. 16, 20	Ch. 10, 16, 17, 18, 19
Ch. 17, 18, 20, 24	Ch. 5, 7	Ch. 2, 5, 6, 7, 8, 14, 19, 25	Ch. 9, 10, 17, 22	Ch. 10, 18	Ch. 5, 7, 13, 15, 22, 23, 25

Introduction

Suppose that you are a visitor to Earth from the distant planet Utopia. One of your assignments is to bring back printed materials to Utopian scholars who are attempting to understand what Earthlings call formal organizations. You have limited space so you must choose very carefully. One option you have is to bring back one or two of the leading textbooks on organizational behavior. Another option you have is to bring back selections from newspapers, business and general periodicals, and short stories and plays about life in organizations. Which would you choose to bring back?

The picture that the Utopian scholars will develop from each of these sets of materials will most likely be very different. If you were to choose the textbooks, the scholars would most likely come to understand organizations as systems which are managed in a rational manner in pursuit of certain stated goals. They would be more than likely to conclude that organizations are staffed by people who are committed to achieve these objectives. Also, it is probable that the scholars would come to believe members of organizations are oriented towards cooperation and are sincerely concerned with each other's well being. Depending on the particular textbook you brought back, however, the scholars might conclude that organizations do not in fact operate in these ways, but that through the application of a certain set of procedures, techniques, philosophies, and so on, any organization which is not operating both rationally and cooperatively could be made to do so.

By contrast, if you happened to take this book or some other collection of materials from periodicals, newspapers and other sources which have been less completely filtered by the academic mind, the picture of organizations the scholars derived would be quite different. They would be likely to decide that organizations are anything but rational, cooperative systems. They would conclude that members at all levels of the organization frequently pursue their own interests at the expense of others in the organization as well as at the expense of the achievement of the goals of a total organization. The scholars would see that organizations are frequently quite inhumane systems. Individuals experience intense stress from task demands as well as intense and often bitter conflict and rivalry with members of their own work group and with members of other work groups and organizations. One would also find that organizational participants often respond aggressively against these pressures and against whatever threatens their own interests. Furthermore, it is unlikely that the scholars would conclude that there is any discernible set of principles, techniques and philosophies which seems capable of turning most organizations into rational, cooperative systems. It is more likely that they would discover that various strategies of power, manipulation, human relations and "all out war" are used, all having varying degrees of success in giving different organizational participants different degrees of influence in organizations.

Most students in organizational behavior, introductory business and even management policy courses are exposed only to the first set of sources. In this book, we plan to provide a ready collection of the second set. We do not offer this collection as evidence that the normative views presented in most academic textbooks are totally irrelevant. In fact, we believe that the normative views are very relevant. However, it is ineffective to present them to students without complementary information about how organizations are experienced. Students readily discover that organizations as described in the textbooks are not the same as organizations they actually experience. Consequently, students and managers reject the "whole package" of organizational behavior as "soft," theoretical or irrelevant without examining the potentially relevant materials. Many students take their courses in management and organizational behavior because they are required, but turn to accounting, finance, economics, information systems and even marketing when they seek to discover what organizations really are. Other students accept the text material while in school, but never find ways to translate it into action when they become managers.

We do not propose that the following selection of readings captures the "true" essence of organizations. We do suggest, however, that current management and organizational textbooks do not capture this essence either. Moreover, it may seem that the current collection provides a very distorted, biased picture of organizations. Undoubtedly there is some bias; we did not use a random selection procedure to determine which articles would be included. However, we did not systematically seek out muckrakers. We were amazed at how many other articles we could find which make very similar points to almost all the ones we have included. Consequently, we are convinced that the contents of the book gives an accurate picture of many aspects of what people perceive to be the reality of organizations.

We ask the reader to pay careful attention to the sources of the articles included in this collection. Many of the selections come from what are normally considered as pro-business sources. Almost all come directly from mainstream publications. In particular, we have included a number of papers from *Fortune, Business Week* and the *Harvard Business Review*. Other sources include an organized labor publication, fictional works and academic texts. Still, a number of selections were written by critics of organizations and individuals who are discontent with many elements of modern life. We believe these selections, taken together, provide a useful picture of a number of aspects of modern organizations.

Of course, the reader must ultimately determine for himself or herself how realistic the picture is. Unlike the interplanetary scholars, most readers of this book will have a number of alternative sources of information about organizations as they exist on earth. In addition to academic textbooks, they will have access to personal experiences and to the reactions of others who, willingly or not, have the quality of their lives thoroughly affected by their participation in modern organizations.

I

ſELECTIOΠ, RECRUITMEΠT AΠD ADVAΠCEMEΠT

Few organizational practices have received as much attention from organizational researchers and management consultants as the key processes of selection, recruitment and advancement—processes that provide the subject matter of this section. Industrial psychology, one of the primary roots from which the field of organizational behavior has evolved, gained its early impetus and continues to give major attention to these areas. It is not surprising, therefore, that an extensive literature offers rational or normative guidance for the performance of these important functions.

However, organizational reality frequently departs widely from the guidelines offered in textbooks. In our initial reading, Crawford Greenewalt, former president of the Du Pont Company, states his belief that executive selection is an art rather than a process susceptible to a scientific approach. In a vein reminiscent of an earlier social Darwinism he further expresses the view that most people end up by getting their just deserts in the struggle for advancement. The nineteenth-century British novelist George Eliot expresses a cynical if still popular view to the contrary. Sally Quinn's reminiscences of her brief experience with CBS News illustrate what may well be a classic of haphazard and thoughtless recruitment and selection.

Ely's "Interview" adds humorous credibility to psychologists' frequent observations that while almost invariably part of the selection process, little evidence exists to support the validity of most interview techniques.

Meyer overviews some of the widely varied approaches to performance appraisal used by business and government. It is significant that efforts to deal with this function date back at least to the sixteenth century but as yet few thoughtful executives and even fewer psychologists are satisfied with the procedures being used. In the selection following, Meyer further acknowledges that although there are imperfections in appraisal systems, they are increasingly being used in tightly structured systems of salary administration.

The selections by Loving and Bennis illustrate the truly formidable problems that surround the choice of *the* appropriate candidate for a top management position. It is worth noting first that few corporations exert the effort described by Loving in "Bob Six" of Continental Airlines's search for Six's successor. Second, while universities traditionally devote extensive time, money and effort to this process, the resulting track record leaves much to be desired.

In our final selection, Gooding describes the difficult process of firing a manager, the increasing trend of terminations and some of the techniques organizations have adopted to ease the trauma for both parties.

The Uncommon Man

Crawford H. Greenewalt

. . . We have only to listen to a pianist, examine the work of an artist, or observe an actress on the stage to determine whether or not they are of outstanding rank. In other fields, there are recognized standards to aid judgment. A lawyer must pass a bar examination, a surgeon can refer you to his diploma from the American College, a ball player's batting average is published in the newspapers daily. Among executives, we can recognize competence only after long periods of observation and, even then, there are sometimes large differences of opinion. How much more difficult it is to appraise potential in advance! In this area, I am sure we have all made bad guesses, even with candidates who appeared highly promising.

It seems to me that the attributes which make a successful executive are found more than anywhere else in the intangibles. A job analysis, useful enough in other areas, falls down completely in appraising executive potential, for the duties defy classification or description.

I remember with some embarrassment a visit paid me some years ago by a young lady who was preparing a college thesis on management duties. The first thing she asked was what did I do all day. That was a fair question, but I am afraid the difficulty I had in answering it put me at the bottom of the class. The more I thought about it, the more I was impressed by the fact that, in the executive area, there is no fixed procedure, no precise pattern, no yardstick of performance which can be counted and measured.

What *did* I do in any given day? An electrician or a painter could have given a ready answer; so, presumably, could a burglar, but certainly I could not and the stature of executives in the mind of my young visitor was not enhanced. Perhaps some could do better than I, but I am inclined to doubt it and to conclude that the difficulty of description merely emphasizes the imponderables which make up the executive's daily chores.

Most studies agree that an essential quality is "leadership," and I have no doubt that leadership is, in fact, an important executive attribute. But here again, we betray the limitations of our vocabulary for, while leadership is important, I am not at all sure that it is more than a small fraction of the answer. An articulate clergyman, for example, may be an able leader of ethical thought, or a soldier may exercise great leadership entirely through courage and personal example. Neither of them need necessarily have executive talent as we conceive it.

Judgment is important. Vision is undoubtedly essential. And we could exhaust our list of virtues without reaching the core of the problem. For I have known men with leadership, with judgment, with vision, who were not in any sense of the word good executives.

The best that I can offer is to say that the basic requirement of executive capacity is the ability to create a harmonious whole out of what the academic world calls dissimilar disciplines. This is a fancy way of saying that an executive is good when he can make a smoothly functioning team out of people with the many different skills required in the operation of a modern business. His most important function is to reconcile, to coordinate, to compromise, and to appraise the various viewpoints and talents under his direction to the end that each individual contributes his full measure to the business at hand.

Perhaps the best analogy to an executive's job is that of the symphony conductor under whose hand a hundred or so highly specialized and very different talents become a single effort of great effectiveness. No conductor can play every musical instrument and no more can an executive be skilled in every talent he is called upon to supervise. There was a time when the boss prided himself on personal experience with every job in the shop. If this view ever had merit, it has long since become entirely unrealistic. Today, specific skill in any given field becomes less and less important as the executive advances through successive levels of responsibility. Today, for example, there are thousands of people in the Du Pont Company whose expertness in their special fields I can regard only with awe and admiration. And to make the sad cycle complete, I have been out of touch with my own field of chemical engineering for so long that I cannot even talk on equal terms with the young men of that profession.

One thought that I passed along to my friends from *Fortune* seemed constructive to me, but I fear that they were not impressed. This was an observation that, while executive ability cannot be catalogued or measured, it can almost invariably be recognized. I cannot say what there is about extraordinary ability which projects itself so unmistakably, but somehow it does, transcending any personal differences and defying all preconceptions.

It is my principal task to recommend candidates for our important managerial posts. I have had to do that many times and have always accompanied my recommendations with a recital of the man's virtues, much, I am afraid, in the McGuffey Reader style. I frequently encounter from my associates violent disagreement over some particular virtue which I have emphasized, but, when it comes to an over-all judgment of the man and his suitability for the post at hand, it is a very rare circumstance when the choice is not unanimous.

Achievement in the executive field is much less spectacular than comparable success in many of the professions—the scientist, for example, who wins the Nobel Prize, the headline name who is elected governor, the skillful politician, the articulate college president. In fact, the more effective an executive, the more his own identity and personality blend into the background of his organization. Here is a queer paradox. The more able the man, the less he stands out, the greater his relative anonymity outside his own immediate circle.

So, as we pass more and more away from special, measurable skills into the less definable intangible talents, it becomes clear that the selection of executives becomes more of an art and less of a science. We must rely in large measure on intuition and hope and pray that our candidate's performance will reflect our wisdom rather than our incompetence.

I am sure that all organizations have made mistakes in judgment of personnel and that the equities are sometimes compromised if not outraged by such errors. On the other side, however, I can't remember more than a very small handful of people whom I would say had not gotten their just deserts in terms of their abilities. I have worked at all levels of the Du Pont Company in 36-odd years, and I know a great many people, from wage-roll workers up. And the cases in which someone suffered an injustice are nearly negligible.

It may take time—I've often seen instances in which a man who was ready for a promotion had to wait two or three years, or perhaps four or five years, before it came. The realities of the situation were such that it couldn't be given to him at the instant in which he was ready for it. But given time he got there.

Middlemarch

George Eliot

The question whether Mr. Tyke should be appointed as salaried chaplain to the hospital was an exciting topic to the Middle-marchers; and Lydgate heard it discussed in a way that threw much light on the power exercised in the town by Mr. Bulstrode. The banker was evidently a ruler, but there was an opposition party, and even among his supporters there were some who allowed it to be seen that their support was a compromise, and who frankly stated their impression that the general scheme of things, and especially the casualties of trade, required you to hold a candle to the devil.

Mr. Bulstrode's power was not due simply to his being a country banker, who knew the financial secrets of most traders in the town and could touch the springs of their credit; it was fortified by a beneficence that was at once ready and severe—ready to confer obligations, and severe in watching the result. He had gathered, as an industrious man always at his post, a chief share in administering the town charities, and his private charities were both minute and abundant. He would take a great deal of pains about apprenticing Tegg the shoemaker's son, and he would watch over Tegg's churchgoing; he would defend Mrs. Strype the washerwoman against Stubb's unjust exaction on the score of her drying-ground, and he would himself scrutinise a calumny against Mrs. Strype. His private minor loans were numerous, but he would inquire strictly into the circumstances both before and after. In this way a man gathers a domain in his neighbours' hope and fear as well as gratitude; and power, when once it has got into that subtle region, propagates itself, spreading out of all proportion to its external means. It was a principle with Mr. Bulstrode to gain as much power as possible, that he might use it for the glory of God. He went through a great deal of spiritual conflict and inward argument in order to adjust his motives, and make clear to himself what God's glory required. . . .

The subject of the chaplaincy came up at Mr. Vincy's table when Lydgate was dining there, and the family connection with Mr. Bulstrode did not, he observed, prevent some freedom of remark even on the part of the host himself, though his reasons against the proposed arrangement turned entirely on his objection to Mr. Tyke's sermons, which were all doctrine, and his preference for Mr. Farebrother, whose sermons were free from that taint. . . .

"What line shall you take, then?" said Mr. Chichely, the coroner, a great coursing comrade of Mr. Vincy's. . . .

"I know little of either," said Lydgate, "but in general, appointments are apt to be made too much a question of personal liking. The fittest man for a particular post is not always the best fellow or the most agreeable. Sometimes, if you wanted to get a reform, your only way would be to pension off the good fellows whom everybody is fond of, and put them out of the question."

We're Going to Make You a Star

Sally Quinn

The countdown: Dick Salant, president of CBS News, was beaming. Hughes Rudd was chuckling to himself and Sally Quinn was fending off questions about her sudden rise in TV news. The setting was a luncheon at "21" in New York and the guests included members of the press, who were given an opportunity to meet and chat with the CBS correspondents who will go on the air next Monday. Salant was saying he'd love to switch the time of the *CBS Morning News* show from 7 A.M. to 8 A.M. but he'd run into opposition from the fans of *Captain Kangaroo*. "I know because I raised all my children on *Captain Kangaroo*." If the new team is a success, Salant said naturally he'd take credit for the show, but if the show bombs he said he's going to find someone to point the finger at. Who dreamed up Rudd and Quinn? he was asked. "That was Lee Townsend." Townsend, the executive producer, however, modestly disclaimed credit. "It was a group effort," he told Eye, *Women's Wear Daily*, Tuesday, July 21, 1973. . . .

When Gordon and I first discussed the job I told him I had grave reservations about his choice. I reminded him that I was controversial, opinionated, flip, open and had no intention of changing. Was he sure this was what he wanted on television? Did they really want me to say what came to my mind during the ad libs, and would they not try to turn me into a bland, opinionless, dull-but-safe marshmallow? And I wondered aloud whether, if we were supposed to be journalists, we could maintain any kind of objectivity and still express controversial opinions—or any opinions, for that matter.

"Paley wants controversy," Gordon had said. "And so does Salant. You can get away with much, much more at that hour than you ever could on the *Evening News*."

I had doubts and so did a lot of people I talked to, but I figured CBS knew what it wanted.

I also pointed out to Gordon that I had a rather unconventional life style. I had been living on weekends with Warren, I explained, and if I moved to New York I would move in with him. I would also be talking about him openly and freely in interviews. I saw nothing wrong with it, and I had no intention of hiding the fact.

I think Gordon gulped a little at that one, but he gamely said that was just fine, I could say anything I wanted to. After all, CBS was not hiring me because or in spite of my personal life.

On Friday morning, June 22nd, the first piece about me appeared in *The Washington Post*. The head ran "SHOWDOWN AT SUNRISE," and it carried pictures of me and Barbara opposite each other. I wasn't too crazy about that. It created an atmosphere of rivalry I would have preferred to avoid. But my editors laughingly pointed out that I was now a public personality and had no say in the matter. They also pointed out that it was clearly the right angle for the story. They were right.

TV critic John Carmody had written, "Although a number of her candid interviews had attracted CBS's attention, it was, ironically enough, her appearance on Miss Walters' *Not for Women Only* TV program that whetted the network's interest." He quoted Salant as saying that the format of the revamped show would "have no relationship to the *Today* Show" and would "retain the integrity of the basic news show." But also as predicting that "*Today* is ripe to be taken."

Stuart Shulberg, the producer of the *Today* Show, was quoted: "We welcome fresh competition. *Today* has led the morning field for so long that we could run the risk of growing too fat, smug and sassy. This will speed up the pace, sharpen our competitive spirit, and provide the kind of honest competition we need and relish. May the best program win."

Barbara Walters was quoted: "The only thing I can say as a woman in broadcasting is that I welcome any new member to the fold. . . . I have respect and friendship for Sally. I know her very well. And I applaud both her and CBS for a very smart choice."

And Sally Quinn said: "Barbara is a great friend of mine and one of the most professional people I've ever known. As far as competing with each other, we covered the Shah's celebration in the desert of Iran together last year and stayed in the same dormitory. That's like being in combat together, and I imagine this will be a somewhat similar situation."

And we were off. . . .

Monday, rehearsals began. Thank God. Now they were going to roll it all out for us, lay it on, let us in on all the fabulous plans for the first week of shows. And it was about time. I had begun to have doubts, but

I knew that they would disappear as soon as we got to the studio and saw what they had for us.

We were to arrive at 6 A.M. to start getting the feel of getting up early. We would watch the *Morning News*, then go into a simulation of what our anchor booth was going to look like (it wasn't nearly ready) and tape a news broadcast. We were to write it from the same wires and newspapers that John Hart had used hours earlier.

Lee Townsend was jittery. Townsend, the most even-tempered man I know, was also as irritated as I had ever seen him. He had been against the promo tour (though he didn't object violently enough) because he felt we could have better used our time rehearsing. His objections had been overridden by Blackrock, which—who? I never got the pronoun straight—had insisted that it was necessary. So Townsend was nervous and angry because we had been away and virtually co-opted by the PR department, and because it was then clear to him that we didn't have a super-duper razzle-dazzle show to put on the air in a week's time. And no real studio to rehearse in.

He had reason to be more than nervous, and we did exactly what we had done for the pilot except at greater length. We wrote a little news and a few lead-ins to film pieces, and Hughes wrote an essay. I couldn't think of anything that morning, and besides, I'm not an essayist. I'm a reporter and interviewer. Hughes would do essays, which he did marvelously, and I would do what I did best.

In front of the camera, they outfitted me with an ear-piece on a wire, called a Telex, which enables them to talk to you from the control room. They handed us mikes, rolled our copy onto the TelePromTers, and away we went. It was a disaster. There were two cameras and I didn't know which one to look at. The stage manager waved his hands around, but I hadn't a clue what he was trying to tell me. I was fumbling my words and couldn't read the prompters. They were shouting in my ear through the Telex to do this and do that, and three minutes here and twenty seconds there, and ad lib here. The ad libs were always by surprise, and I would fumble around trying to think of something clever to say about a film piece we had just seen. It might have been a bloody plane crash or a dairy farm. It BOMBED, and I was shell-shocked by the time it was over. Suddenly I *knew* this was the way it was going to be. There was nothing I could do about it. It was too late to get out of it.

I was even more upset when everyone came out of the control booth and said it was just fine and all it needed was a little smoothing out and we would be just great by the end of the week. No mention of any guests for interviews, no mention of any special film pieces that would lend themselves to interesting, informative ad libs and, most frightening of all, no mention of anything I should do to improve myself. I realized fully for the first time that I didn't know anything, and I panicked.

As we were filing down the stairs to the *Morning News* section, Jim Ganser, one of the producers, caught up with me. He was to be the only one at CBS who really tried to help me.

"Try to punch your words a little more," he sort of whispered out of the side of his mouth, as though he didn't want anyone to hear.

I fell on him. "What? How? What do you mean?" I said desperately. "Tell me, for God's sake. Tell me what I'm doing wrong."

And he told me. "You're wrong to expect anyone to give any help or guidance of any kind. You're a big star now, and people figure if you're a big star you must know what you're doing. Nobody's going to stick his neck out to help you."

I went to the ladies' room and threw up. But I had to hurry. Hughes and I were the "big stars" of a large press luncheon at the "21" Club, and we were late. . . .

We finally got into our own studio on Friday, and we rehearsed there Friday and Saturday. Nothing went right. Friday morning after John Hart's last show someone came into the Cronkites, where we were working, and said that the staff of the *Morning News* was having a farewell party for John and the old producer. I hadn't really seen John to talk to him. I like and respect him a great deal, but we had been so busy working the lobster shift (that's the night shift in newspapers) that we just hadn't had a chance to see each other.

"Oh, great, I'll go up and tell John goodbye," I said, jumping up from my chair.

"I wouldn't if I were you," someone said. "There's a great deal of hostility up there toward the new team. And the atmosphere upstairs is more like a wake than a party. I think you had better forget it."

That was the first I had heard of resentment or hostility on the home team front. It worried me because, except for Townsend, Hughes and me, the "team" was the same. There had been no staff changes. I had found that curious. If they had really wanted a whole new format, with more entertainment and a lighter mood, I thought that they would surely have tried to bring in some people who were more in the show-biz line. The *Morning News* staff was very good. But they were hard-news oriented, and Gordon had said the idea was to take on the *Today* Show.

That morning when I went in to get my makeup done for the rehearsals my hair was a mess. While I was upstairs, the woman who was doing my makeup said her friend Edith, the hairdresser for *Edge of Night*, was right down the hall and maybe she would roll my hair up on the hot rollers for me. She called Edith, and a round-faced woman in her late fifties, with reddish hair, big, wide innocent eyes, a very strong New York accent, and dyed-to-match pants, vest, blouse and shoes, came rushing in. Edith said she would be delighted. She had the lightest, most soothing touch, and the whole time she did my hair she told me how great I looked and how terrific I was going to be on the air and that she was honored to do my hair. Then she asked who my official hairdresser was.

"Hairdresser? I don't have a hairdresser." Both women were stunned. "You have to have a hairdresser," they chimed. "Every woman on television has one. You can't just go on with your hair like this every morning."

Edith asked me if she could be my hairdresser and said she was sure that if I asked they would let me have one. I told Lee and Sandy Socolow about it and they both went blank. Nobody had given my hair a thought. They okayed it right away, but it indicates how little thought went into the planning for the first woman network anchor. Edith was a godsend. She not only took care of my hair, she took care of my ego.

After the rehearsal on Saturday, I was about to leave. No interviews were lined up for me for the following week. The big interview for Monday was with Patrick Buchanan, the President's speech writer, and that would be out of Washington. I had no idea what film pieces were going to be used. They weren't sure.

I was so depressed and scared that I didn't really care. I wanted to go somewhere and hide. As we were leaving (Sunday was a free day) Lee Townsend gave me a big smile and said, in a way I couldn't decide was joking or not, "Let me know if you have any good ideas tomorrow for the show."

Sunday was the worst day of my life. I thought about ways to disappear where no one would hear from me for years and would think I had been kidnapped by some freak. I considered the possibility of having plastic surgery so I would never be recognized as Sally Quinn. I fantasized about going on the broadcast and saying, "Good morning, I'm Sally Quinn and we are not prepared to do this show and I don't know what I'm doing up here." I thought seriously about calling Salant and Manning and telling them. I came close to quitting.

The water pipes broke in our apartment and I had to go to a friend's place on West End Avenue to wash my hair.

When I got out of the shower, I put on a large white robe that was hanging on the door. I came out of the bathroom draped in that robe and I said to Warren, who had been babysitting me all day, "I really feel like one of those ancient Aztec virgins who has been chosen to be sacrificed on top of the temple of the Gods. All the other virgins are wildly jealous of her because she has this fabulous honor bestowed on her. What they don't know is that she doesn't want her heart cut out with a knife anytime by anyone. It hurts."

I went to bed at 5 P.M. It was bright and sunny outside, and I could hear the children playing on Riverside Drive and happy couples walking and chatting and laughing as they strolled in Riverside Park.

"I will never be happy again," I thought. "My life is over."
I never went to sleep. We had been coming in around 4 or 5 in the
morning that week, but it wasn't proper preparation for coming in at
1:30. The alarm went off at 1:00 A.M. Warren was waiting to walk me to
my limousine, which arrived promptly at 1:30 A.M. It was like being
escorted in a golden carriage to the guillotine.

I didn't feel too hot. I figured it must be because I hadn't slept. I
slipped into the gloamings of the enormous black car and we glided
over to Hughes' apartment, the Apthorpe, a few blocks away on West
End Avenue. He hadn't slept either. We didn't say a word. A few
minutes later we arrived at the studio and went directly back to the
Morning News area and into the Bullpen.

In front of each of us was a pile of news wire stories, the first edition
of *The New York Times* and the *Daily News*. Bob Siller, the copy editor,
was there and so was Dave Horowitz, one of the assistant producers.
They would make up the "line-up." The line-up was a sheet on which
the show was blocked out minute-by-minute. Taking all the film pieces
and counting their time, they would, along with Hughes and me and
Lee Townsend, decide what the top news stories were and allot a
certain amount of time to each, from forty-five seconds to a minute,
and then block out time for commercials (we had only network commercials for the first six weeks) and station breaks. They would leave
about a minute and a half for Hughes' essay, and what was left—
roughly five minutes—would be alloted for "ad libs."

While this was going on, Hughes and I read the papers and the wires
to get an idea of what stories we wanted to use. When we had finished,
about 3 or 3:30, Bob and Dave came back with the line-up designating
which one of us would write which stories and which lead-ins to film
pieces. If the film piece was ready, Hughes and I would try to take a
look at it so that we could write a clearer lead-in; if not, there was
generally some kind of script. Often the film piece wasn't ready.
Horowitz and Siller, with our advice or without, would figure out
which film piece seemed like the best topic for conversation and block
in a certain amount of time for ad libs after those pieces. There was
some freedom to move around, but not much. Everything we were to
say we typed out on our enormous typewriters.

We had two writers who were to do the weather, sports and late-
breaking news. Hughes was to read all the sports. We had tried to
divide it, but I didn't understand sports and kept fumbling and breaking up in the middle of the report. Hughes hated it too, but it wasn't
quite as ridiculous when he did it.

By the time Hughes and I would have read everything thoroughly,
discussed camera angles with Bob Quinn, our director, who came in
about 4, written all our news items, lead-ins and station and commercial breaks, had something to eat at our desks (it was called "lunch"

and usually came from the CBS cafeteria, known appropriately and without affection as "the Bay of Pigs"), it would be about 6 A.M.—time for Edith and Rickey, the makeup person, to arrive and get us ready.

At around 3:30 I had started to break out in a cold sweat and I became weak and dizzy and slightly nauseated. I couldn't concentrate on what I was writing. Finally I went into Townsend's office and passed out. I tried to get up about 4 A.M. and write, but I stayed at my typewriter for about twenty minutes and then went back to Townsend's office and passed out again. I thought it was probably because I was tired and nervous, but by then my throat was so sore and I was coughing so badly that I could barely talk. I had shivers and had to be wrapped up in a blanket.

Everyone piled into Townsend's office and stared at me in horror. "Do you think you can do it?" Lee asked, terrified.

"I just don't know, Lee." I didn't.

I think at that point I was more scared not to go on than to go on.

"I'll try. I'll really try. But I can't talk. And I'm so dizzy. Is there any way I could get a vitamin B shot or something to give me quick energy?"

By then it was 5:30 in the morning and I was so sick I couldn't breathe. I kept trying to sit up and I would just fall right down. I couldn't tell whether the beads of perspiration on my head were from temperature or desperation. Finally Townsend said that they had to get me to a hospital. Somebody had a car and they carried me out to the front of the building, stuffed me in the car, and drove two blocks away to Roosevelt Hospital to the emergency room. A young doctor took me back to examine me and take my temperature. I had a temperature of 102 and he said he thought I might have pneumonia. I was coughing so badly that my body was racked. "You don't understand," I practically screamed. "I'm making my television debut in an hour."

"So I've heard," he smirked.

"Well, I can't possibly go on like this. Can't you give me a vitamin B shot or something? Anything."

He said that in my condition a vitamin B shot wouldn't do any good. The only thing he could do for me was to give me a throat spray that would stop me from coughing for a few hours. But he suggested that I get to a doctor immediately afterward for proper medication.

"Anything else I could give you now," he said, "would knock you out." Oh, how I wished . . .

He left the room and came back a few minutes later with the most enormous syringe I have ever seen, with a needle a mile long.

"Forget it," I said, backing away from him.

"Don't get hysterical," he said, laughing. "This is a throat spray. I'm not going to stick the needle in you."

He stuck the needle in my mouth and sprayed a gooey liquid, which coated the inside of my throat.

Lee grabbed me, back we went into the car, and we screeched off around the corner and back to CBS as though we were bank robbers getting away.

It was a little before 6:30. Edith and Rickey were frantic, and Hughes looked as though all his blood had drained out of him. Edith rolled my hair while Rickey sponged some makeup on me. I lay down while all this was going on. The hot rollers stayed in too long and I looked like Shirley Temple when my hair was combed out. There was nothing we could do about the frizz. At about ten minutes to seven they finished on me. I was still so weak and dizzy that I could barely move, and all I can remember is a large fuzz of Warren leaning over me asking if I was all right, Townsend in a frenzy, and Hughes pulling himself together as he walked into my dressing room. "Hughes—" I tried to smile— "get me off this horse immediately." Hughes tried to smile, too, but he wasn't very convincing. "Don't worry," he growled, "you'll make it, kid."

I tried to say thank you, but the throat spray had a numbing effect, like Novocain, and I couldn't feel whether my tongue was touching the roof of my mouth or whether I was forming my words properly.

"You look beautiful, darling, just beautiful. You'll be wonderful, I know you will," Edith was murmuring.

I looked in the mirror. I was hideous. My hair was frizzy, the granny glasses looked wrong, and the only thing I owned that wasn't blue (I hadn't had the time to shop that week) was a yellow battle jacket that made me look like a dyke.

"Well," I thought, "there's no way anybody is going to accuse me of being a sex bomb this morning."

Somebody shoved a pile of telegrams in my face and I tried to read. They were all amiable, from close friends and family, but it was upsetting me. "Oh, God," I thought, "if only they knew how terrible I'm going to be."

They were screaming for me to get into the studio and I ran in, got behind the desk, had my mike adjusted, and somebody handed me my Telex, which I stuck in my ear.

"One minute," yelled the floor manager.

My mouth was dry. No possibility of talking. I looked at Hughes. He was looking at me as though we were copilots and I had just been shot. He tried to smile. I tried to smile back.

"Thirty seconds," said the floor manager.

I looked straight outside the glass partition to the newsroom and saw everyone staring.

"Five seconds," the floor manager said.

For a fleeting moment I thought maybe I would wake up and find out this wasn't happening.

An arm went out to me and a finger pointed. I gazed at the Tele-PromTer.

"Good morning," I read, "I'm Sally Quinn. . . ."

I don't remember much else about that hour. I was propped up with several pillows because I was so weak and dizzy that I couldn't sit up by myself.

I coughed a lot. I remember a swirl of sweltering bright lights, moving cameras, different noises and shouts in my ear through the Telex—"Turn to Camera 2, thirty seconds to ad-lib, five seconds till commercial, ten seconds more of interview"—hand signals, desperate and self-delirious mumblings . . . and then it was over. And when it was over I felt completely numb. Nothing. . . .

When I walked back into my office there were three bouquets. One was from Charlotte Curtis, then editor of *The New York Times'* Family, Food, Fashions and Furnishings, now editor of the op-ed page of *The Times* and probably the woman I admire most in journalism. One from Vic Gold, former Press secretary of former Vice President Spiro T. Agnew and now a columnist. And one from Connie Tremulis of "Flowers by Connie," Rockford, Illinois.

I still have their cards.

Everybody was talking at once and saying what a great show it had been and how did I ever get through it, and, boy, what a terrific start we had gotten off to, and how terrible the *Today* Show was outdoors in front of Rockefeller Center. I don't remember seeing Hughes. I remember Lee Townsend taking me by the hand and leading me outside to a taxi. I put my head back on the seat and stared out the window as we went whizzing up Central Park West. It was a beautiful day. I thought about all the people walking along the street and bicycling in the park and about how happy they looked. I thought how odd it was that my work day was over and it was only 8, and that that was going to be my life from now on. And how depressing it was. I did not think about the show. It had not happened. Nor did Lee mention it. . . .

During the first week, I had not seen or heard from Gordon. I debated whether or not to call him or leave a message, but then I figured if he wanted to see me he would have come back or sent a note. I will never understand why, after the first show, he didn't come screaming back to the *Morning News* and fire everybody, or put Hughes on with straight news, tell the world I had terminal pneumonia, and send me away to some hideaway studio in Connecticut with his trustiest producers and cameramen to work me over.

As far as I knew, nobody had seen or heard from Gordon. I waited each day for him to ask me into his office and explain gently that I needed some kind of training; that they were going to change the format, get a new set and a jazzy producer, set me up with taped interviews, get me out of reading the news, get me voice lessons, make me put on contact lenses, and demand that I grow my hair longer and cut out the ad libs.

Nothing.

The broadcast Monday was uneventful, including my first live television interview. It was—I still have a hard time believing this was the best person CBS could think of for my TV interview debut—the designer Emilio Pucci. I discovered that he was branching out from lingerie into sheets and men's wear.

Hughes did not participate. He wasn't all that anxious to, didn't particularly like to do interviews, and I'm sure he didn't have all that much to talk to Pucci about anyway, except the fact that they were both World War II pilots.

I called Gordon and left a message after the show. I was told he was out. Gordon soon became for me a Major Major Major figure from *Catch-22*. Hard to reach. . . .

My health all along had not been good. I still felt dizzy and nauseated in the early mornings, and I was constantly exhausted though there wasn't anything wrong with me as far as anyone could see.

There was, however, a major cosmetic problem.

For the first time since I was seventeen years old, I was developing acne. And it was getting bad. Rickey switched to an allergenic makeup, but it didn't help. The makeup and the bright lights must be doing it, I decided. I should have my face cleaned.

I remembered that a classmate of mine from Smith had a mother who ran an Institute of Cosmetology on East 62nd Street, which I occasionally read about in *Vogue* or *Harper's Bazaar*. Her name was Vera Falvy, and she was a Hungarian with the most beautiful complexion I had ever seen.

Mme. Falvy examined my face carefully and asked about my eating habits, health and life style. She knew I was on TV but had no idea of the hours or the pressure. She felt the breakout was caused by emotional tension. I would need regular treatment. We made another appointment and she gave me a special lotion which I was to use under, or preferably instead of, makeup.

Altogether I visited Madame six times, and the bills ran close to $300. She did her best, but the tensions kept building and my face got worse. My complexion has never been the same. I have scars on my face to show for those horrible months. . . .

That week I got a call from Barbara Howar. We chatted for a bit and Barbara, who had had her own TV shows, gave me a few pointers. She told me that I was coming along really well and shouldn't worry. Then she said, "Why don't you look at the right camera when the show is closing each day? Half the time the camera zooms out to the newsroom while you're looking straight ahead into the camera in the studio, and whenever the camera is in the studio you're looking across at the newsroom. You've got to keep your eye on the red light."

"Red light?"

"For God's sake," she screamed, "hasn't anyone told you about the red light?"

"No," I said. "What about it?"

"There's a light on the side of the camera," she said, "and when it goes on red it means that camera is on you and that's where you're supposed to look."

"Oh, no," I moaned. "No wonder. I saw that light flash on and off but I didn't know what it meant." . . .

Thanksgiving was the next day, and we never had holidays off. It was the tenth anniversary of Kennedy's assassination. When I looked at the line-up that morning, I saw that the only scheduled interview was one I had done several weeks earlier with a woman who had written a diabetic cookbook.

I couldn't believe it. Hughes complained to no avail. That seemed like the final straw. On the tenth anniversary of a president's death we were to do a mediocre (at best) taped interview with a diabetic-cookbook writer. There was no hope for any of us, or that broadcast.

Without staff meetings, there was still no coordination. Things hadn't gotten better. Usually, we didn't know who the guest was to be until we came on the program, and half the time it was someone neither of us was interested in or wanted to interview. We wrote lists of suggestions and notes, but nothing ever came of them. It is not that the people on the staff were incompetent, but just that there was zero direction, that morale was low, and that there was no coordination.

We had a rule about not accepting guests if they'd already been on the *Today* Show, and they had the same rule about our show. What that meant was that we hardly ever got any of the good people because the *Today* Show had a much larger audience and no publisher would allow his author on our show unless he couldn't get him or her on the *Today* Show.

I thought that was dumb. I thought we should take people who'd been on the other show, then try to do a better, or a different kind of interview. We were in a no-win situation.

Another problem I kept hearing about third-hand from my friends was that some of them had talked their publishers into letting them go on our program because they were friends, and then for some odd reason they were rejected. This happened to Art Buchwald and Teddy White. There would be some vague explanation; but usually there were about three people involved in setting up the interviews, and often they weren't there when I was, so I couldn't find out. It was a mini-example of the total method of functioning at CBS. It was exasperating and, in the end, useless to try to do anything about anything.

The broadcast was beginning to take on a slight death smell. I had to get out. . . .

I've often asked myself how CBS could have made so many mistakes, how they could have let me go on the air with no experience.

Part of my despair during that terrible time had stemmed from trying to fathom where I had gone wrong. The thing is, nobody really yet understands the medium. Television isn't even fifty years old. Shows go on and off every month, people are hired and fired ruthlessly, because nobody knows what will work and what won't. They don't know what terrible vibes a great-looking or -talking person may give out over the air or what good vibes a clod may transmit. So they don't want to make decisions—especially long-term ones. Therefore nobody does. It's what Sander Vanocur calls the "how-about?" school. Somebody said, "How-about-Sally-Quinn?" and there was a generalized mumble, and that was it. They hired me and nobody ever did anything about it again. Mainly because they didn't know what to do.

So much money is at stake—millions and millions of dollars in advertisements—that those who make mistakes cost their company a lot of money. If they do that too often they lose their jobs. On newspapers everything doesn't ride on one story or one series but on the long run. Everyone in television is basically motivated by fear.

And television news is run by the network. It is not really autonomous. Those in charge of entertainment have ultimate charge over the news programs. CBS News has a buffer between the management and the news division: Richard Salant. In fact, that is his primary function. He is a lawyer, not a newsman, and he is able to negotiate the vast differences of approach between the news side and Blackrock and to work out acceptable compromises. . . .

Thursday of the first week, Small asked me to come down to his office. Gordon was sitting there. I was surprised, to say the least. He hadn't told me he was coming down. He asked where I would be later in the day. He said he would call.

He called around 3:30 and asked if I could have a drink with him. I suggested he have a drink with Ben [Bradley, *Washington Post*] and me, since they were old friends.

He hedged. Then he said he could get a hotel room and stay over if I wanted him to. We could have dinner. I suggested we all have dinner. He hesitated. I couldn't figure out what he wanted. "Well, Gordon," I said finally, "what do you want?"

He mumbled something about dinner for the two of us and how he could get a hotel room. I said I thought it would be more fun with the three of us. He blew up. . . .

"Gordon," I said quietly, "I'm going to quit CBS. I'll try to be out in about six weeks. But I've got to find a job first. Just get Small to let me stay in Washington until then. I can't—won't go back to the anchor job. But I don't want to just quit and have it look like I was a total loss. I want to have a great job to go to. Will you do that much for me? Just hold them off for a while?"

He looked relieved. "I'll do it," he promised.

We walked in silence to the Watergate Terrace Restaurant and made polite conversation through dinner. Nobody ate anything. I ordered gazpacho but I couldn't swallow it. As we were leaving I asked Gordon what I had been longing to ask him since we went on the air.

"Gordon, why did you do it? Why did you hire me and then throw me on the air like that with no training? Why did you do it to me?"

"What if I had told you we wanted to make you the anchor on the *Morning News* but that you'd have to have about three to six months' training on one of our local stations first. Would you have done it?"

"Of course not."

"That's why.". . .

The morning after I quit, Hughes signed me off: "Sally Quinn is leaving CBS News for *The New York Times*—not necessarily sadder, but certainly wiser. And we hope she's happier there than she was here. For one thing, the help over there don't have to get up as early as they do here."

I thought it was touching and funny in Hughes' own gruff way.

Later that morning Richard called to say that Don Hamilton, Director of Business Affairs, wanted that day to be my last day. I pointed out that I had two film pieces to finish and that I intended to work two more weeks, that I had two further weeks of vacation coming to me, and that therefore they could count me on the payroll for another month. I wasn't to start at *The Times* until March 18.

Richard said Hamilton wouldn't buy that. I told Richard that I would call Salant or Bill Paley if I had to, and give interviews about what a cheap crumby outfit CBS was if I heard another word on the subject. Just get me the four weeks' pay. I didn't care how he did it.

Richard understood that I meant it. A half hour later he called back and said, "It's all set."

It still made me chuckle, though, that such a huge corporation would be so unbelievably cheap, especially under the circumstances. But I don't know why I was surprised, after what I had been through.

Saturday, I got a letter from Dick Salant.

Dear Sally,
In case you missed the AP story, I am attaching it. It quotes me absolutely correctly.

I am terribly sorry that things did not work out as we all expected and hoped. The fault, I honestly believe, was ours—mine.

In any event, best wishes for every sort of satisfaction and happiness. And if you can bear it, do drop in so I can say goodbye and good luck.

All the best,

Dick Salant

The AP story was enclosed. It said: "CBS News President Richard Salant said Thursday that CBS would not hold her to her contract. Asked if he considered Miss Quinn's move a slap at CBS, Salant said, 'No, not at all. She doesn't owe us a thing. We owe her a lot. And we damn near ruined her by making a mistake and pushing her too far too fast.'"

On February 7 Gordon Manning was fired from his job as news director. He was given a job as "vice president and assistant to the president of CBS News."

Gordon had been news director for nine years. His ten years were up in June and he was to receive a pension. That's why he was given that job, to hold him over so he could get his pension. He was fifty-seven in June, 1974. Somehow Gordon managed to redeem himself, partly by landing Solzhenitsyn for Walter Cronkite to interview. He stayed on after June and became a producer for the public affairs division of CBS News.

Bill Small was given Gordon's job, Sandy Socolow was given the Washington bureau. The day the change was announced Small was in Gordon's office.

Reached there, he said he was completely surprised by the promotion. "I've only been at this desk for six hours," he said. "I'm just trying to find out where the men's room is and where they keep the key to the liquor cabinet."

On February 28 Lee Townsend was fired. They had no ready title for him to assume. He was later assigned to the investigative unit. The new *Morning News* producer was the Rome bureau manager, Joseph Dembo.

The Interview

David Ely

The personnel agent was not quite what George had expected. In the first place, he was young; his round, smooth face fairly radiated inexperience. Then, too, the fellow was not only unpolished but downright graceless. He had none of that brisk, deferential manner which George had come to look for in the company's younger staff.

At first, George was annoyed at the fact that they had sent such a stripling to obtain the information necessary for the processing of his promotion. However, this irritation was soon succeeded by a tolerant amusement at the agent himself, for, while not painfully shy, the young man was obviously aware of his own awkwardness, and as a matter of fact seemed resigned to its tyranny. He proceeded along the hallway with a reluctant and foreboding air, as if he fully expected to lurch against a vase or to slip disastrously on the edge of a rug, and when he had in fact managed to reach the living room without mishap, he sank down on the sofa with a sigh of evident relief. George could not help but smile.

"Well," the agent announced cheerfully, "I guess we'd better start, if you're ready, sir." He dug with both hands into his briefcase and came up with a thick stack of mimeographed sheets through which he thumbed hastily to see if they were arranged in proper order. Evidently they were, for the agent gave a little nod of satisfaction, patted the sheaf of papers into a more orderly shape, drew a pen from his pocket and tested it on his forefinger to be sure it was working, and then cleared his throat portentously.

"Okay, sir. I guess I'm all set." In a slow, singsong voice, the young man began to ask questions concerning George's chronological record of employment—positions held, titles of immediate supervisors, descriptions of principal duties, and so forth.

George was mildly surprised. Surely the company had all this routine data in his file already. It was not as though he were seeking a position with some new firm; he was simply being processed for promotion to the parent concern, which had full access to the records of its subsidiary. But he contented himself with a shrug, assuming that Personnel had its own system to follow, with which it would be pointless to quarrel.

The interviewer completed the top set of questions and carefully put it aside. George eyed the remaining pile of sheets uneasily and glanced at his watch. It was a quarter to six. He could hear his wife in the kitchen. The children would eat early anyway, he thought, but Vera might not like it if their own dinner were delayed.

"Are you going to use all that material in the interview?" he asked.

"I think so, yes, sir," the young man answered rather doubtfully. "Except for maybe one or two—although in your case, I think, possibly not—"

"Well, it doesn't matter," George put in quickly, not wanting to risk confusing his visitor. "Go right ahead." He took comfort in the thought that the promotion would be worth any reasonable inconvenience. "Say," he added, "it's after work. How about a little drink?"

"Not for me, sir," the interviewer replied, with a short laugh that sounded embarrassed, as though George had made an improper suggestion. "I'm still working, I mean." He laughed again. "But you go ahead, sir," he said, in sudden earnestness. "Don't let me stop you."

"Well, perhaps I will, if you don't mind," said George, getting to his feet. "I don't usually drink alone, you know, but it's been a tough day. . . ."

He poured himself a stiff drink in the kitchen and warned Vera that the interview might last another hour or more. Before he returned to the living room, he took a big swallow of the whisky; immediately, he wondered why, and then realized that he had not wanted to walk back into the room with a brimming glass, for the clumsy young man did represent his employers, after all, and might make a secretive little marginal note: "Drinks to excess!"

But as soon as George had seated himself again, he thought how ridiculous such fancies were, for the agent was having a hard time handling the simple materials they had given him, and obviously was incapable of adding observations of his own.

The next two lists also dealt with ordinary matters already recorded in George's file: his educational background (schools, college) and basic family data (number and ages of his children, his wife's maiden name, etc.). George hesitated over the year of his graduation from high school. Had it been '37 or '38? The agent waited anxiously for the answer, as if the date were all-important.

"Make it '37," George said finally. "You can double-check it with my file at the company, if you like. As a matter of fact," he added, "all the rest of the information is there, too."

"Oh, really? Well, yes, of course," the young man mumbled, noting down George's answer. He appeared to be disconcerted at the thought that much more reliable answers to all the questions already reposed in a file which perhaps his superiors had not remembered to tell him about. George was annoyed at the needless duplication of effort, but he felt a kind of pity for the awkward young man, who undoubtedly was the butt of a thousand little jokes in his office.

"There's probably a good reason for getting this information a second time," George remarked soothingly. He tried to think of such a reason, and the agent waited hopefully for him to supply one. "For one thing, it's a way of cross-checking," George said. But he realized this was nonsensical; he would hardly need to be checked on the names of his children, and as for such facts as graduation years, the data in his file had been based on original records. He frowned into his drink, aware of the interviewer's disappointment. "Maybe it's this," he continued. "They may want to compare my recollection of these facts with the file itself, you see, for psychological reasons. The differences—if there are any—may be quite significant to someone who's trained to analyze these things." The agent nodded solemnly, evidently impressed by George's idea. "A man may repress or alter certain data subconsciously," George added, "and for all we know, this may provide valuable insights into his character, which the company would need to know."

"That makes sense to me," the agent declared admiringly.

Encouraged by the young man's confidence in him, George thought of yet another explanation. "It also occurs to me," he said, indicating the considerable stack of papers that remained in the agent's lap, "that the reason may be psychological in a different way." The agent blinked at him, waiting for a further revelation. "You have a lot of materials there," George explained, "and some of them are bound to deal with fairly personal matters. Possibly the routine questions you've asked me up to now are simply to prepare me—to relax me, in a sense—so that I won't be alarmed when you begin asking what they really want to know."

"Well, sir, that certainly may be true," the agent said. He shook his head wonderingly and fingered the stack of papers. "Some of these are quite personal, it's a fact," he added, "but I'm not sure—in your case, sir—if all of them—which of them, I mean . . . " He laughed, apparently in embarrassment, and shuffled the papers.

George sighed. It was odd that the company would have sent an interviewer who did not seem quite sure of what to ask and, on top of that, had no idea of the purposes underlying the interview. But of course the company undoubtedly had a good reason for it, no matter how mystifying it might seem to an outsider.

"Here we are, sir," the agent declared, having picked up the next questionnaire. He scanned the top page and pursed his lips. "You may be right, sir. This one is a bit personal. It deals with religion. May I ask your religion, sir?"

"No religion," George replied. Then, with a smile, he corrected himself, using the common phrase: "No religious preference."

"Are you sure of that?" the agent asked; but he was writing down George's answer anyway.

"Oh, yes. Of course."

The agent smiled shyly. "I didn't mean to suggest you weren't, sir. That was only the next question on the sheet. 'Are you sure of that?' I mean, it's not my question, it's theirs."

"Well, my answer's the same," George said politely. For some reason, he felt impelled to explain further. "I said 'no religion' at first, but then I decided 'no religious preference' would be better, because 'no religion' implies atheism, you see, whereas the other could well mean that I go to several different churches."

"Yes, I see," said the agent. He made a note and glanced inquiringly at George. "Well, sir, if you're sure you don't want to add anything to that . . ."

"That's all there is to say."

"No, I mean if you're Jewish or anything, you can say so. I'm Jewish, too."

"Are you really?" asked George.

The agent seemed baffled by the question. Then he ducked his head bashfully and grinned. "No, I'm not, actually," he admitted. "I'm just supposed to say so, because it makes people anxious to show that it's all right."

"To show that what's all right?"

"Anything. You see, they're sorry for me and want to make it up."

"I don't understand," said George. "Are they sorry you're a Jew?"

"Oh, no. It's just that they feel they forced me to say I'm a Jew."

"But then, you're *not* a Jew," George persisted.

The agent blushed slightly in his boyish way. "Well, I made a mistake," he conceded frankly. "I wasn't supposed to admit that I'm not a Jew. But the rest of it makes sense, doesn't it?"

His manner was so earnest that George did not want to weaken his faith in the company's peculiar psychology. "Oh, it makes good sense, I guess," George said quickly. He was puzzled by it, however, and not a little annoyed; still, he suspected that the company's tactic was probably justified, and that it merely had seemed foolish because the young agent had handled it badly. At the same time, he felt an almost paternal desire to help the young man along through the intricacies of the interview, no matter how long it might take. He glanced at the window and noticed that it had grown dark. Perhaps Vera had already put the children to bed and had eaten her meal alone. But George knew she would not really be angry, for she, too, was anxious that all the various stages leading to the promotion be carried through smoothly.

"There's certainly a lot of personal information to get," the agent remarked apologetically, after he had completed the religious questionnaire.

"That's quite all right," said George, trying to hearten his guest. "The company needs information about its senior staff. They certainly have a right to know and I'm anxious to help all I can."

"I appreciate that, sir," the agent responded formally. He eyed the next questionnaire doubtfully, as if he thought it might have slipped into his satchel by error. "This one's political, I think," he said. Then he read the first question: "Are you loyal to our form of government?"

George smiled and answered facetiously: "Oh, yes. I've only tried to overthrow it a couple of times." The agent solemnly wrote this down, and George exclaimed: "I was only kidding about that, of course."

"I understand that, sir, but we're supposed to note down everything anyway."

"Look," George said firmly, "that might cause a real misunderstanding."

"Don't worry, sir," the agent told him. "I've noted that you were merely joking." He smiled at George in a reassuring way, but George made a private resolve to keep any further pleasantries to himself.

"Next question," said the young man. "Do you feel loyal toward the company?"

"Yes, I do."

"That seems like a strange question," the agent remarked. "I mean, you would hardly admit that you *didn't* feel loyal, would you?"

"No," said George, "I suppose not."

The agent quickly jotted down his response. "I'm sorry," he said, "but that was a trick question. You see, you just admitted you might have lied."

"But I *do* feel loyal to the company," George protested.

"It isn't fair to trick you like that," the agent agreed, "but it's part of the process, you see." He put down the pen and shook his head moodily. "I can't say I like to ask trick questions, though."

The agent appeared so worried by the dubious morality of the company's questionnaire that George again sought to ease his mind. "They're really not so bad," said George. "Of course," he added, anxious on the other hand not to weaken the agent's repugnance toward what was certainly a suspect practice, "I wouldn't like to be in your shoes, having to ask questions like that."

"You think it's unprincipled?" the agent asked, with a sad expression.

"Well, yes, in a way, I think possibly so," replied George cautiously.

Once more the agent made swift notes. "I'm terribly sorry, sir," he stammered, not looking up from the papers, "but that was another of those tricks."

George was astonished. "What did you write down?"

"Well, I wrote that you felt the questions were probably unprincipled." The agent stared at his shoe tops in embarrassment. "I had to do it, sir. I hope it won't have any bad effect for you."

"Don't worry about me," said George, although he was in truth somewhat disturbed. "I'm sure I can explain everything in case the higher-ups don't like my answers."

"I sincerely hope so, sir," said the young man. He sighed and continued with the questions, which dealt with a wide range of subjects, including capital punishment, labor unions, civil rights, and foreign relations. George framed his replies with circumspection, but the trick questions that had been inserted here and there were so artfully concealed that time and again he said things which sounded absolutely foolish or dangerously subversive when the agent regretfully read them back to him. "I've got to be careful," George told himself angrily, but he was not so confident now; his hands were trembling and he kept wiping his forehead with his handkerchief, for his perspiration flowed freely.

The young man was, if anything, even more distressed than George by the turn things had taken. "Sir," he said once, "I wonder if it would be all right for me to sort of tip you off when I'm asking a trick question, by winking my eye or scratching my nose in a certain way?"

"Oh, no, that wouldn't be fair to the company," George responded firmly. Then he caught his breath. "Was that another trick?"

"Not at all, sir," the agent assured him. He pondered the matter for a few moments. "I guess you're right, sir. I couldn't very well tip you off. After all, the company is paying me to do the job the way they want it done."

George nodded. "I appreciate the thought, though," he said.

"Maybe we could start all over again," the young man said suddenly, but he quickly realized the impossibility of this suggestion, too. "No, I guess that wouldn't be fair, either."

"That's all right," George told him, with a heartiness that was more assumed than natural. "Just go ahead and don't worry about me." He forced a smile. "I've been with the company for a good many years now, and I'm sure they won't misunderstand anything I say. My feeling is, if you're fair to the company, the company will be fair to you."

"Do you really think so, sir?" The agent looked as though he would very much like to share George's opinion on the subject.

"Absolutely."

The agent gazed at George's face for a moment. "But some of these answers are going to look bad for you, sir," he insisted. "And the questions—why, they're not fair at all!" He flung his pen aside and bit his lip. "It's just not fair. It's a trick, and it's an unfair trick besides!"

Again George tried to reassure him, but the young man was bitterly indignant. "I don't see what these questions have to do with your job, sir. The company has no business to inquire into your beliefs in the first place, let alone to trick you in this way."

The agent's attitude presented a delicate problem. George felt it was absolutely necessary to answer all the questions, tricks included, in order to obtain his promotion, but he did not want to dilute the young man's apparently honest outrage at the company's knavish practices (although George remained convinced that the reasons, if he could know them, would prove to be sufficient). He sighed. It seemed almost too much trouble. He glanced at his wrist, but discovered that his watch was missing. He assumed he had left it in the kitchen. The darkness was broken only by the slanting ray of the tiny adjustable ceiling lamp which the agent had lowered so that he could read his materials more readily.

The young man was pondering the stack of questionnaires that remained in his lap. The pile seemed not to have diminished, but rather to have increased, which George found disheartening, for the interview had already taken several hours. The agent appeared downcast, too, not so much at the amount of material yet untouched as at the character of the job he had been forced to undertake. "I definitely don't like it, sir," he muttered.

George knew that he had the responsibility for finding some solution to this dilemma. He thought that perhaps he could read the questionnaires himself and write down his answers, thus relieving the agent of his unpleasant duty; but he reflected that this would probably be in violation of personnel rules, and besides, it would not really take care of the basic problem, which was essentially a question of reconciling this honest young man to the bewildering and often underhanded methods of the company.

He noticed that his visitor's face, previously so fresh and smooth, already seemed to be touched with cynicism, and he realized that he must act quickly.

"Look here, my young friend," he said with a steady smile, "we've got to keep our minds on the business at hand. The company requires certain information concerning my background and intellectual makeup, in order to assemble all the various data necessary in the matter of my promotion. Now, it's not our job to criticize the company; after all, they're the ones to decide what they need to know. The questions may seem strange to us, some of them may seem unethical, even, but this is a free country, and I have a perfect right not to answer if I don't want to. Now," George went on, feeling that he was arguing with unusual clarity, "I happen to choose—freely, of my own will—to answer these questions, not because I absolutely have to have the promotion, but because I have a real faith in the company. If there was a better way to do it, they'd do it differently. But it's clear that they have chosen this way because it suits their needs perfectly."

"That's very well put, sir," said the young man, but he still seemed reluctant to resume the interview. "I'm willing to take your word for it," he added with earnestness, and George perceived that his visitor had a really touching trust in him, which in turn gave George the premonitory sensation that all would somehow turn out for the best.

"Well, then, let's go ahead with it," said George, settling back in the chair with more composure. The house was quiet now; he decided that Vera had gone on to bed.

The agent leafed through the papers in his lap, selecting one set, then rejecting it in favor of another. "This may not be so bad," he commented hopefully. "Let's see. Have you ever been convicted of any crime?"

"No."

"Have you ever committed any immoral act?"

George stroked his jaw reflectively. "Do they provide a definition of what's immoral?"

"No," said the agent.

"Well," said George, almost cheerfully, "then my answer will have to be 'I don't know.'"

The agent protested with heartfelt distress: "But that sounds awfully bad, sir. You can't really let such an answer go into the record—"

"It's all right, my boy," George replied airily. "I know what I'm doing." He smiled reassuringly at his companion. Already he felt the beginnings of enlightenment, for he sensed what the company was driving at, and he was stirred almost to pleased laughter. The room was darker than before, but it was a velvety, comforting darkness that suited George's new, optimistic mood.

"Next question, then," said the agent. He cleared his throat self-consciously. "I don't know how this got in here. Well"—he hesitated, then stated it haltingly—"are your relations with your wife satisfactory?"

"Most of the time, yes," said George, smiling not at the question nor at the agent's awkward manner, but because he simply could not help himself.

"Are you still in love with her?" The agent whispered the question and kept his eyes on the paper in his hands.

"Yes, I would say so," said George, with a chuckle.

Now the agent blushed deeply and began to perspire. "Sir," he mumbled, "I really can't bring myself to ask the next one. It's—it's terribly personal, sir—"

"Go ahead!" George declared, thumping his fist on his knee to emphasize his willingness to hear the question.

The agent stammered in such embarrassment and confusion that George could hardly make out his words. "Sir, it—it asks how many—how many times—a week, sir—" The young man broke off in despair and bowed his head.

"I think I know what you mean," George said, not at all upset by the question, "so just put down 'once or twice' if you please."

"Yes, thank you, sir," said the agent, hurriedly jotting down the words. He dropped the pen and nervously retrieved it. "Sir, they've really got no right to ask—no right at all, sir—I don't think I can go on with it, any of it, sir—"

"Nonsense!" George boomed. "They've got a right to know, don't you see that? You've got to go on with the questions, my boy. It's a test, in a way. They're testing you and they're testing me, too." He laughed and snapped his fingers. "But it's more than that, young man. Look at that stack of papers! It's as high as it ever was. You had more than you thought you did, didn't you? Well, that just goes to show that they aren't fools, they know what they're doing—"

He paused to catch his breath. The young man was staring at him with a pitiful expression, but George was now possessed by a growing realization of the company's objectives, and continued authoritatively:

"They have their reasons! Right now I think I understand what they really want, but actually I may be quite wrong, I may be completely mistaken, but that's not the point. The point is that we must do our part faithfully and let the company handle the material in its own way."

Even as he spoke, his intuition carried his understanding forward by yet another step, and he could not repress a quick chuckle of delight. "But we can't waste our time!" he exclaimed. "We've got a long way to go! No more doubts, young man! No more soul-searchings! Just ask those questions—I'll have the answers for you!"

He found that he was on his feet, flexing his knees springily, like an athlete preparing for some contest. "Let's go!" he declared exuberantly, and the agent bent obediently over his papers, reading off more questions in a voice that George could barely understand, for it was low and trembling.

George began to pace around the room, tossing off his answers in phrases that seemed to echo resonantly from wall to wall. The agent meanwhile perspired over his papers, uttering the questions automatically, then scribbling frantically in an effort to keep up with George's rapid answers.

"You're going too fast, sir!" cried the agent, but George loftily dismissed his complaint with a quick motion of his hand. "On the contrary, my boy, not fast enough!" He laughed, but shortly, for he was determined not to waste a moment. There were too many questions left unasked, and although he felt confident of his ability to answer every one without an instant's pause, he was impatient to rush ahead. He hastened his step, as if the swifter rhythm of his marching would spur the agent to greater efforts; he snapped his fingers, too, in time with the quickening tempo of their voices.

"Faster!" he cried out eagerly, dizzied by his growing comprehension. He seemed to hear the questions almost before the agent stammered them out, and his answers came so rapidly that question and answer often overlapped. "Faster!" The agent was on the verge of exhaustion, but George pressed on at an ever-increasing rate, striding energetically to and fro, so intent on his task that he even knocked down chairs and tables in his path. The agent began to gasp with shortness of breath, and his fingers tightened painfully with cramp, requiring him to shift the pen to his other hand, but still George forced the momentum of the interview, rattling off his answers with such velocity that the agent began to lag behind in his transcription, despite desperate attempts to keep up; still George continued to accelerate his flow of words, faster and faster, so that soon their voices absolutely merged, question and answer becoming a continuous babble, punctuated by George's swiftly moving footsteps that reverberated like a lightning drum roll in all parts of the room at once.

Finally, the agent screamed out, "I can't do it!" and, with a sob, flung down the pen and slumped on the sofa, letting the stack of questionnaires cascade from his lap to the floor.

"It doesn't matter!" George shouted. He did not slacken his pace, but actually increased it, bounding now, almost floating, so quickly did he move. "You don't need to ask any more questions—I know what the company wants!" He clapped his hands together sharply and laughed. "My promotion—that's going to put me right up there with the top men, my boy, and in a position like that, it's not just services that are needed—not by a long shot!" He spread his arms wide, as if to encompass the very walls, which themselves seemed to quiver in response. "No, if I'm to become a part of the company, then they've got the right—they've got the duty—to know everything about me! And so they've got to ask all questions—all!" Then he thundered a prideful acknowledgment of the unique obligation the company had placed on him. "And I will answer all!"

He continued, calling out both questions and answers, and then dispensed with questions entirely, since the answers alone were enough. He continued even when the agent crept away and left, for he realized that his answers now were of a self-sufficient permanence that needed no recording.

On and on his voice rolled forth, his eloquence swelling ever greater. His words became song, prayer, offering. He was on his knees among the thousand sheets of paper, his arms extended toward the single feeble light. He sang aloud his dreams, his doubts, his follies, triumphs and disorders, his weaknesses and strengths.

All, all he poured forth freely, eagerly, for he knew that at last they wanted him in totality—not just his skills, as before, but his very heart and soul. Already he felt himself drawn by a new happiness toward the center of the great instrument for which he had labored faithfully for so long. Already he felt a yielding, boundless love responsive to the company's insatiable desire to know him, to possess him utterly. He cried out in his joy, for he realized, too, that he was at but the beginning of this total happiness, this total submission. The process would go on, perhaps without end. And so, even as the tiny light dulled and then darkened, and as the room grew chill in the coldness of the deepening night, he knelt happily among the mass of papers on the floor. The interview continued.

The Science of Telling Executives How They're Doing

Herbert E. Meyer

It is a universally acknowledged truth that uncertainty is bad for business. It is not so often observed that uncertainty is also bad for businessmen—bad for their health, their peace of mind, even bad for their performance as executives. And of all the uncertainties that have kept executives from sleeping peacefully at night, probably none are quite so unsettling as those related to the difficulty of figuring out their boss's real opinion of them.

It is partly—but only partly—to relieve executives of such anxieties that American business has developed a remarkable institution called "performance evaluation." Formal, regularized evaluation programs are now more or less omnipresent in large U.S. corporations. Not all corporations do it in precisely the same way, but the exercise ordinarily includes a face-to-face meeting, held at least once a year, at which each executive gets a fairly explicit judgment of his performance from his immediate superior.

Typically, this verdict has been approved at least two levels above the man or woman being judged—i.e., the executive doing the judging clears it with his own superiors. The evaluations are ordinarily recorded on special forms, which then become part of the executive's permanent employment record. At most companies, these systems are used to judge the performance of virtually all executives, from the lowest-ranking recruit up to and often including the chairman of the board (whose performance is evaluated by the directors).

Adapted from material originally appearing in the January 1974 issue of *Fortune* Magazine by special permission; © 1974 Time Inc. □ Research associate: Varian A. Knisely.

GOOD MARKS FOR THE LOSERS

While just about all corporations have adopted performance-evaluation systems, their effectiveness is still a matter of dispute. It is not always clear that the judgment delivered to executives reflects the true sentiments of their superiors. At Xerox Corp. there is a rule that no one who has been with the company for more than eight years may be fired without the approval of Chairman C. Peter McColough. In almost every instance, says McColough ruefully, he discovers that the candidate for firing has for years been rated highly in the company's evaluations.

All of which suggests that for an evaluation to be useful and meaningful it must be delivered by someone who's capable of imparting some painful truths. The worst mistake an evaluator can make is to let some executive who's barely making it leave the session harboring delusions about great prospects in his future.

At the same time, the evaluator has to be careful not to make the event too painful: he doesn't, presumably, want to crush the executive being judged under an avalanche of devastating criticisms. Finally, it is important that the judgments being delivered really do concern performance—and do not reflect the personal preferences and prejudices of the evaluator.

GETTING A LINE ON THE JUDGES

Performance evaluation is, then, something of an executive art and science in itself. Indeed, one important benefit of the system is that it helps top management to make some further judgments about the executives who judge others.

American business got into performance evaluation for several reasons. One reason, plainly, had to do with salaries: by providing the corporation with a structured, detailed record of each executive's performance during the preceding year, the evaluations made it possible to put salary administration on a rational basis. . . .

In addition, the evaluation systems are used to help identify the executives who have some real potential for moving into the higher-ranking jobs in their companies. Supervising executives often include in their evaluation reports an outline of the preparation and experience a lower-level executive requires for his next promotion. For example, a supervisor might recommend that bright executives whose experience is limited to the U.S. market be given some exposure to international operations. Or he might recommend that a production man tapped for higher things be shifted for a while into sales.

In short, performance evaluation is being linked increasingly to companies' long-range planning efforts. And quite a few chief executives these days find the time to read hundreds, even thousands, of evaluation reports in an effort to see what's going on down there among the troops. The man at the top can get a sense from the reports of where the talent is, and where it isn't, and which parts of the company are likely to need the most executive-development help in the years ahead.

The system can also be rather helpful to the executives being evaluated. For one thing, the meetings with a supervisor can provide an occasion on which it is natural and possible for an executive to get on the record some views of his own about his job and about the possibility of handling it differently. At some companies—Texas Instruments, for example—this opportunity to get an executive's own views about his situation is considered to be as important a part of performance evaluation as the delivery of the superior's judgment.

AMAZING HONESTY AT CITIBANK

At the First National City Bank one supervising executive has gone about as far as it is possible to go in giving his subordinates a chance to express themselves in performance evaluation. E. Newton Cutler Jr., a Citibank senior vice president, simply hands his subordinates their own blank evaluation forms and tells them to fill in their ratings themselves. "It's amazing how honest people are," Cutler marvels. "They put things in that are detrimental to their own progress and promotion." The procedure, which represents Cutler's own variation on the bank's evaluation system, has a built-in safeguard against things getting out of hand: Cutler himself makes a final review of the ratings.

Performance-evaluation systems also tend to protect an executive from being held back or treated unfairly. Virtually every system requires that supervisors justify their conclusions, both to their own supervisors and to the executive being evaluated; hence the chances of discrimination based on race, sex, taste in clothing, or plain old-fashioned personality conflicts are minimized.

And, of course, evaluations do a great deal to end the awful uncertainty that comes from not knowing what the boss thinks. Dr. Abraham Zaleznik, a psycho-analyst and a professor of social psychology and management at the Harvard Business School, is among those who believe that this uncertainty really is bad for businessmen. "It's important to know that your own image of yourself, and of your performance, squares with your boss's image," Zaleznik says. "Disparities between the two can lead to personal stress and do real physical damage."

IT STARTED WITH LOYOLA

Formal performance-evaluation systems are not at all unique to American business. In fact, a system remarkably similar to many being used today was developed by Saint Ignatius of Loyola some time after he founded the Society of Jesus in the sixteenth century. Saint Ignatius used a combination reporting-and-rating system that was intended to provide a comprehensive portrait of each Jesuit's activities and potential. The system consisted of a self-rating received from each member of the order, reports by each supervisor on his subordinates' performance, and special reports sent directly to the society's Father-General from any Jesuit who believed he had information relating to his or his colleagues' performance that the Father-General might not otherwise receive.

In the U.S., however, the performance-evaluation systems being used by business have been influenced mainly by some systems first developed in the federal government. In 1842 the Congress passed a law requiring the heads of executive departments to make an annual report "stating among other things whether each clerk had been usefully employed and whether the removal of some to permit the appointment of others would lead to a better dispatch of the public business."

When James Polk became President in 1845, he ordered that these annual reports be sent directly to him. During the following decades a multitude of evaluation systems were tried and then abandoned—one system developed in 1879 by Carl Schurz, for the Pension Office, attempted to measure employees' performance simply by counting the errors they made in a year.

SOME OBEYED MORE THAN OTHERS

But as the century entered its final decade, it was the military that had developed the most precise, workable, performance-rating system. In 1889, President Benjamin Harrison, impressed by what the War Department had accomplished, suggested that civilian agencies adopt similar techniques. His suggestion was generally ignored, and so Harrison issued an executive order *requiring* agencies to adopt the military system. The order was obeyed in some agencies more than others, and the inability of any President to establish a comprehensive, standard system of performance appraisals for the executive branch has continued right down to the present.

In part, the Presidents' difficulties reflect a powerful reluctance by members of Congress to let any chief executive have too much power over the presumably nonpartisan civil service. At the moment, the government's most recent task force on performance evaluation is hard at work in Washington evaluating the performance of its scores of predecessors and preparing some recommendations on how agency heads might improve their evaluation systems.

American business has proceeded with greater dispatch. Exactly which corporation was the first to develop a formal evaluation system for executives, or when, is unknown. General Motors Corp. had a formal evaluation system for its executives as early as 1918, but G.M. doesn't know if it was first. The real trend toward formal, regularized, written systems didn't begin in earnest until after World War II.

The procedures vary quite a bit from one company to another. Sometimes the evaluator doesn't put anything on paper until after the judgment has been delivered—the written record becomes, in effect, a report on the meeting with the executive being judged. At White Motor Corp., on the other hand, the supervising executive calls in his subordinate only after completing the rating form and then clearing his conclusions with his own superior. Thus when an executive is invited in for a friendly chat, the verdict on his performance has already become a matter of record.

The form presented to the White Motor executive being evaluated includes, in addition to the traditional photograph and biographical data, a series of questions the supervisor has answered regarding the executive's major strengths and weaknesses. Also, the supervisor has placed a check next to one of the following phrases: outstanding, satisfactory plus, satisfactory, marginal, or "unsatisfactory—must be replaced." At White Motor, supervisors are required to state how soon their subordinates will be ready for promotion, and to outline to each subordinate what steps should be taken to prepare for future jobs with the company.

HE SHOULD WANT TO IMPROVE

After being presented with the company's opinion of him, the executive is asked literally to sign on the dotted line. (His signature signifies awareness, not necessarily agreement.) The interview concludes with a discussion of the executive's performance; according to the White Motor Corp. supervisors' manual, he should leave the session "with a sincere desire to improve."

If an executive feels that he has been treated unfairly—more precisely, if he thinks he should be rated higher—he is encouraged to protest during the course of the interview itself. According to H. Herbert Phillips, the company's vice president for personnel and industrial relations, most differences of opinion are resolved right then. But if the executive is still not satisfied, he is entitled to appeal his rating directly to the company's personnel department. Someone will be assigned to hear both sides, then either back up the supervisor or suggest to him that the subordinate might actually have a point, and that his rating be reconsidered. "If it's the sort of personality conflict that just can't be resolved," Phillips says, "we usually wind up suggesting that the subordinate transfer to another department."

The questions dealt with on Sperry Rand Corp.'s performance-evaluation forms deal mainly with "promotability." Once a year, at evaluation time, the company's managing executives (about 1,000 in all) fill out "replacement charts," in which each supervisor lists the two or three subordinates he considers most qualified to replace him. Then, when the evaluations take place, the supervisor is supposed to be clear about any steps that must be taken to prepare these executives for their eventual promotions. The supervisor himself is rated on how well he plans the promotions.

At the heart of Sperry Rand's evaluation system is the so-called AROT column, in which four kinds of data are listed: the A refers simply to the executive's age; the R represents a performance rating (on a scale from 60 to 100); O is organizational data, e.g., the supervisor states whether the subordinate should be kept within his division or might work elsewhere in the corporation; and T stands for the time required to prepare the executive for his next promotion.

John Grela, Sperry Rand's vice president for organization and development, says the emphasis on promotions makes it easier for a supervisor to point out flaws in an executive's performance when the two sit down for the annual interview. "I knew we couldn't get people to sit down and say, 'You are bad here,' but a supervisor can deliver criticisms more easily when he's recommending a plan for future promotions." Grela says proudly, "It works."

The completed forms are shown to the executive being evaluated after they've been cleared with the supervisor's own superior. At Sperry Rand each executive's performance-evaluation forms are reviewed at least once a year by a committee consisting of the company's chairman, its president, and Grela. They meet with the supervisors to discuss the executives they've rated, and in effect rate the supervisors on how well they're doing in preparing subordinates for promotions. "We feel that part of a manager's salary is based on how well he develops people," Grela says. "If he isn't doing that, he hasn't earned that portion of his salary."

THE PEERS VOTE AT TRW

At TRW Inc., performance evaluations involve not only an executive's supervisors, but his peers as well. Before the judgments about an executive are made, his supervisor solicits the opinion of the men and women who work alongside him. "It's a regular part of our procedure," explains Stanley C. Pace, a TRW executive vice president, "but we do it informally. What happens is that at some time during the year—usually not just before the evaluations are written—I make it a point to chat with each subordinate's colleagues to see what they think about his performance. Everyone here knows that this is done and the purpose of it is to encourage teamwork. We don't want anyone around here to think he can get away with being nasty or unhelpful to everyone except his boss."

Pace believes that checking informally around the office from time to time is the sort of thing that should be done by any good manager, regardless of whether a formal, annual evaluation interview is held with each executive. "One benefit of having these annual interviews," Pace adds, "is that they force me to get off my duff and talk to people."

RATING BY THE NUMBERS

At Worthington Corp., a subsidiary of Studebaker-Worthington, Inc., the man personally in charge of performance evaluation is Chairman Edward C. Forbes. His system is about as precise and quantitative as any in existence; it actually measures an executive's performance out to the second decimal place.

Once a year, every top-echelon Worthington executive drafts a list of his objectives for the coming twelve months, then sends the list directly to Forbes. He and the executive decide how important each objective is to the company and assign numerical priorities to them, ranging from three for the highest down to one for the lowest. At the end of the year, Forbes sits down again with the list (and with the executive), decides how well the executive did on each of his various objectives, and rates the man's success in achieving each objective on a scale of one to fifteen.

Each of these scores is then multiplied by the priority previously attached to it. The resulting numbers are added together and, finally, divided by the total number of weighted objectives for the executive's numerical rating. (When events beyond the control of any executive—such as a natural disaster in a particular marketing area—render an objective meaningless during the course of the year, Forbes simply eliminates that objective from the equation.)

The number that emerges from all this arithmetic is then worked hard by salary-administration officials at Worthington. It is combined with a variety of other numbers, reflecting, for example, the division's profit, the executive's current salary grade, his position within that grade, and his age, in order to determine the future salary.

In gauging an executive's promotability, Forbes relies on a curiously (for him) unmathematical evaluation system. He calls it RUST—an R means the executive must retire within a year, U means his performance has been unsatisfactory, S stands for satisfactory, and T, which is in there for reasons more euphonic than logical, signifies a potential for promotion. The same system Forbes uses to rate his top-echelon executives is also used, by them, to rate their own subordinates. The evaluations they perform may then be reviewed by Forbes—whose judgment on all executives at Worthington is the final one.

A Computer May Be Deciding What You Get Paid

Herbert E. Meyer

Of all the questions to which thoughtful and high-minded business executives have addressed themselves over the years, few, surely, have been as exhaustively analyzed as a question about salary administration. Reduced to its essentials, which it often has been, the question is: how do you get a raise around here? The answer has typically involved all sorts of elaborate stratagems and frequently has led to explosive confrontations in the boss's office.

All this is changing now. Those stratagems are beginning to look irrelevant, and the confrontations, a staple of *New Yorker* cartoon humor for four decades, are coming to an end. Salary administration in large corporations is a far more formal and bureaucratic exercise than it used to be. There are new ways of giving and getting raises, of establishing what particular jobs are worth, and of establishing the appropriate relationships between different executives' salaries. The raises are less likely to be negotiated, more likely to be determined by tightly structured systems involving grades, ranges, midpoints, national averages, periodic reviews, detailed performance evaluations, and computer print-outs.

Furthermore, these formal systems are being extended to include salaries at the top of the corporate hierarchy. Even some chief executives' salaries are involved, e.g., Reginald H. Jones, the chairman of General Electric, is for salary-administration purposes simply "Position Level 28" in a formal system extending down to the company's lowest management levels.

Bureaucratic administration of blue-collar pay is nothing new, of course. It began early in this century and grew steadily as corporations got larger, as unions negotiated more and more industry-wide contracts, and as business was exposed to wage controls during World War II and the Korean war. The controls also encouraged many companies to extend their compensation systems to white-collar workers: it was often easier to get the War Labor Board's agreement to raises when formal salary grades had been established. (For example, the board was more likely to allow raises when the company could demon-

Adapted from material originally appearing in the November 1973 issue of *Fortune* Magazine by special permission; © 1973 Time Inc. □ Research associate: Dhun Irani.

strate that the employees involved were being promoted to higher grades.)

THE PRESSURE FROM COLC

In more recent years, several different circumstances have increased the pressure on corporations to develop and refine white-collar salary systems, and to extend these systems to executives at high levels. Wage controls have again become part of the pressure. The Cost of Living Council is now asking that its 5.5 percent limit on raises be applied to top executives and inside directors as a group—a proposal that would obviously force management to think closely about the relationships among salaries at the top.

But the main pressures for these systems today, as in the past, are those associated with growth and diversification. George Foote of McKinsey & Co. observed recently: "Without formal systems, salary administration in companies that operate around the world, with thousands of middle- and upper-level executives, would be chaotic. A formal salary system can provide a common pay language for executives in different divisions of the same company, which is particularly important for corporations growing fast through acquisitions."

Ten years ago, when Indian Head Inc. had a sales volume of $153 million, its president, then James Robison, knew all the executives well, and also knew most of the senior plant managers. He personally decided which of them would get raises, how large they would be, and when they would take effect. But now sales are over $500 million, and the company employs around 400 people it regards as executives. President Richard J. Powers says it would obviously be impossible for him to administer salaries by himself without some sort of system to ensure a measure of equity. The company is developing a formal salary program for all its top executives.

A DEMAND FOR FAIRNESS

Indian Head's concern about equity reflects another trend that is leading to the development of standardized salary programs. The sources of the trend are elusive but the fact is clear enough: Americans generally are more insistent than they used to be about getting fair treatment. So far as executives are concerned, "fairness" involves, at a minimum, compensation equal to whatever is being received by other executives performing at similar levels.

Responding to demands for fairness requires rather elaborate measures of performance and elaborate procedures for ensuring that equal work does in fact lead to equal pay. Pearl Meyer of Handy Associates, a consultant who has specialized in compensation, contends: "A well-run salary system puts the emphasis on performance over personal considerations as the basis for raises, and it provides a more direct relationship between what an individual executive contributes to the company and what he receives from it."

Another reason for the development of standardized salary systems is that they are easier to defend. More and more searching questions about salaries are being put to management these days, by nagging stockholders at annual meetings and by critical outside directors at board meetings. Company chairmen forced to explain salary decisions are finding it easier to do so when the decisions are based on guidelines previously established and approved for some visible, comprehensible salary system.

Finally, it is possible that the new systems are expanding rapidly simply because the technology to develop them has become available. Computers have been used in corporate payroll accounting for some time; it is usually a simple enough matter to use them also in systems for determining what salaries should be. In any case, computers are now used extensively to calculate raises and to keep track of executives' progress through their salary ranges.

IT'S LIKE GRADING HOMEWORK

Whatever their reasons for installing formal salary-administration systems, the companies doing so are likely to proceed in remarkably similar fashion. They begin, typically, by clarifying executive job descriptions. Each executive is interviewed about the responsibilities of his job and the executives he reports to. Management-consulting firms are often called in to oversee this process, and often the firm works with a special committee appointed by the company chairman. When the interview data have been collected, the chairman and his committee, rather like teachers grading their students' homework, review them to get a line on what each executive knows about his job and his chain of command.

One consulting firm that works extensively in this area is Edward N. Hay & Associates, of Philadelphia; its managing partner, Milton Rock, contends that even if the process were not part of establishing a new salary system, it would be useful to many corporations. "It enables the chief executive to see precisely what his people think their jobs are, and how they perceive the lines of authority. Particularly in companies that have grown swiftly, this lets management know, sometimes for the first time, just who is reporting to whom, and doing what." The most precise job descriptions, not surprisingly, are apt to be those for the least important jobs—i.e., the ones most easily categorized. Descriptions of high-level jobs are generally more flexible.

When management has got some agreement on the content of executive jobs, the next step is to establish their relative importance to the company. Perhaps the most widely used technique is one created by Hay Associates. The technique involves the assignment of points to each job, with the number of points depending on three factors.

MORE POINTS FOR A SELF-STARTER

The first factor is know-how, which Hay defines as "the sum total of every kind of skill, however acquired, required for acceptable job performance." More points, then, for a job requiring five years' experience than for one requiring three.

The second "Hay factor" is problem solving—the degree of "original, 'self-starting' thinking required by the job for analyzing, evaluating, creating, reasoning, arriving at and making conclusions." So, more points for jobs in which individuals have to set their own standards and guidelines.

The third factor is accountability, which the firm defines as "answerability for an action and for the consequences of that action . . . the measured effect of the job on end results." More points, then, for those jobs with the most direct effect on a company's profits. In assigning points, the Hay system adjusts for the size of the company—because, in general, the larger company the larger the salary in any given job.

However a company goes about evaluating its executive jobs, it will presumably end up with a list ranking the jobs in order of importance. If the company uses a forty-eight grade system, for example, the chief executive will be alone at the top grade. His chief operating officer would be at grade 47, his group vice presidents presumably at 46, whoever had the next highest number of points at 45, and so on down through the ranks to grade 1—which would, typically, encompass B.A.'s fresh off the campus.

These rankings tend to be a highly confidential matter at just about all companies, with access to the grades list provided only on a need-to-know basis. In general, executives get to know only their own grades and those of their subordinates. . . .

THE LOST HUMAN RELATIONSHIP

In an age when many Americans worry that the efficiency associated with computerized systems is being attained at the expense of human relationships, it is not surprising that many executives—including many chief executives—are concerned about the impersonality of the new salary administration. Nobody likes to feel that his own salary has been spat out of a computer. On the other hand, those human relationships that we've lost weren't all good: they included a lot of biases and bad judgments, both of which have held plenty of salaries down unfairly over the years.

Xerox Chairman [C. Peter] McColough admits quite readily that his attitude toward his own company's salary system is ambivalent. "I have a negative reaction to the rigidity," he acknowledged recently. "But on the other hand, more flexibility would mean less equity, and fairness is very important. We just don't know how to do it better."

McColough seemed to capture the attitude of many top executives when he was asked, recently, what salary administration at his company would be like without all the grades, ranges, midpoints, and evaluations. He thought about the question for a moment, then shuddered.

Bob Six's Long Search for a Successor

Rush Loving Jr.

During his tenure as chief executive, the head of a large corporation makes decisions that shape the lives of thousands. He decides whether people are hired, promoted, or fired. His policies may generate profits in the millions, or bring about huge losses. But no decision is more critical to the future of the enterprise than his selection of a successor. That decision is irrevocable, like the writing of a will bequeathing all corporate powers to a sole survivor.

When the chief executive is the man who built the company, he can be racked by great emotion. Some pioneers have chosen their successors well. But at least three founders of major U.S. airlines have chosen unwisely. At United, at Pan Am, and at American, the successors of Pat Patterson, Juan Trippe, and C. R. Smith foundered and were eventually removed by the directors.

This hard fact has haunted one of the last of the airline pioneers, Robert F. Six, head of Continental Air Lines, who presented a plan for his own succession to the company's board last month. Six was determined that what had happened at United, Pan Am, and American would not happen at Continental, and to ensure that it would not, he spent eight years seeking the right man. The search was as thoughtful and incisive as it was deliberate. Its length and depth were especially

Reprinted from material originally appearing in the June 1975 issue of *Fortune* Magazine by special permission; © 1975 Time Inc.

surprising, because it was conducted personally by Six himself, a man who has acquired a reputation as a hip-shooter.

THE DROPOUT WHO MADE GOOD

As it happens, that reputation is undeserved, but it has been fostered by Six's colorful past. Fifteen years ago, Six literally did shoot from the hip. Traveling around Colorado with a group of quick-draw artists, he gave exhibitions with handguns, hitting a bull's-eye in a fraction of a second.

As a businessman, he talks bluntly and moves fast. The men he has been able to choose among in selecting a successor all know more about running an airline than he did when he became president thirty-seven years ago. "I just started off and learned the hard way," he says. "There wasn't any criteria for it."

A six-foot-four-inch outdoorsman, son of a doctor in Stockton, California, Six was a high-school dropout who worked as a factory hand and a merchant seaman (retaining a vocabulary to match). He got hooked on airplanes in the Twenties, and barnstormed throughout California for two years. He tried to become an airline pilot, but because he had already made three crash landings, he was turned away.

Finally, in 1936, Six borrowed $90,000 from his father-in-law and bought into Varney Air Transport Inc., a tiny El Paso mail-plane operator. First as operations manager, then as president, Six built Varney into the present-day Continental. Today his airline flies 22,657 miles of routes from Miami and Chicago to the West Coast and Hawaii.

ADMIRATION FROM THE FRIENDLY SKIES

Continental bears the vivid imprint of Six's flamboyant personality. He has an instinct for what the customers want, and he has sold the airline so well that some passengers revere it with the ardor of a cult. Many Westerners will fly no airliners but Six's golden-tailed 727's and DC-10's. Edward E. Carlson, chairman of United Air Lines, Continental's biggest and toughest competitor, says: "Continental is a great success story, and Continental is Bob Six. What the public perceives of Continental is Bob Six's imagination, personality, and willingness to do the unusual."

Six has played on the fact that Continental is a little company battling competitors who are mammoth and impersonal (Continental's operating revenues of $457 million were only one-fifth of United's last year). By casting his company in the role of David, Six has created a remarkable esprit de corps and a feisty and innovative operating style. Says Joseph A. Daley, Six's vice president for public relations and one of Continental's brightest marketing minds: "We've got to be different. Six is operating a delicatessen next to a supermarket. We've got to carry the bagels and the Danish beer and deliver." Among other things, Continental delivered the first hot meals and wide seats in coach, the first economy class, and a management representative on every airplane to take care of passengers' problems.

AN EBENEZER SCROOGE WITH CHARM

Continental's compactness makes the airline relatively easy to manage. Everyone seems to know everyone else. All flight crews based in Los Angeles check in at the operations room on the second floor of the company's general offices, where they frequently run into Continental's senior officers, and even the c.e.o. himself. Six insists that the officers take their lunch in the company cafeteria, where everyone from Six on down rubs elbows with mechanics, secretaries, and pilots. "Here the officers are human beings," says one Continental newcomer. "In some companies they go out to '21' and you never see them."

Six has instilled quality and consistency in the airline by treating his employees with the affection of a father while applying the tough discipline of a Puritan schoolmaster. At the same time, he has kept the company from bankruptcy by watching costs like an Ebenezer Scrooge reincarnate.

He charms his people into putting out for Continental, largely by knowing as many as he can personally. While clipping a twenty-five-year pin on a terminal supervisor, Six interrupted the proceedings to recall how the man had been first officer on a DC-3 that had iced up one night over Lubbock, Texas. The event took place more than two decades ago.

By touring the system and prowling the hallways at headquarters with a cold eye for detail, Six keeps acquainted with just about every facet of his company. He knows that there's been a low-pressure area over the Pacific for the past week, or that the cargo business is up from San Antonio to Alaska, or that National flies its DC-10's at lower cost than Continental.

And wherever he goes, Six reminds his people that what they do reflects on them, because *they* are Continental. When he finds that the airline is falling below his standards of quality, he is outraged—and the quality soon goes up. On a recent flight to Houston, he noticed that the tenderloin steaks were being served wrapped in strips of bacon that were nearly raw. Six asked the hostess if the dinners were being prepared this way for all flights.

"I haven't seen that on your airplanes before, sir,'" she said.

"What do you mean, my airplanes? This is *your* airplane!" he roared.

When Six returned to Los Angeles, he ordered the bacon taken off and the savings used to buy bigger steaks.

Although Continental has always been highly leveraged and sparse with cash, it has managed to report a profit every year but one since Six became president. The company has one of the lowest records of customer complaints in the industry. Its on-time performance last year was second (to Western) among all the nation's trunk lines. And on six of its nine most competitive routes, Continental fills more seats per plane than its competitors.

ADVICE FROM A HEADHUNTER

To find a man who can sustain that record is a difficult task. In the early Sixties, Six thought he had such a man in Harding Lawrence, Continental's executive vice president and general manager. Six planned to retire in 1972, when he would reach sixty-five, and he intended to promote Lawrence to president, but Lawrence quit in 1964 to run Braniff. Lawrence's departure left Six with no really qualified, well-identified successor, and in 1967 he asked the advice of Henry O. Golightly, president of Golightly & Co. International Inc., a New York consulting firm.

Golightly, fifty-nine, is a soft spoken, urbane man-about-town (Truman Capote, who was living next to Golightly's summer house on Long Island when he wrote *Breakfast at Tiffany's,* named the story's main character, Holly Golightly, after him). Golightly has been Six's chief outside confidant for more than a decade, consulting mostly on marketing and organizational problems and helping to set up new operations. He also is Continental's headhunter; many of the airline's top executives were hired on his recommendation.

Six and Golightly agreed to set up a secret program to determine whether there were any qualified candidates inside Continental. Six was looking for candidates whose aptitudes fit the company's own management needs and goals. He set August, 1970, as a deadline: if no inside candidates turned up by then he would have to search outside.

THE BLACK BOOKS IN THE SAFE

On April 21, 1967, Golightly sent Six a twenty-three-page outline of their plan. Using the outline as a guide, R. Randall Irwin, Golightly's expert on selecting and evaluating executives, interviewed every officer in Continental's top management who showed any measure of presidential potential. To keep their intentions secret, the interviews were conducted under cover of "a special program for assisting in the developing of executives."

By the end of June, Golightly and Irwin had singled out and profiled nine vice presidents, including former White House Press Secretary Pierre Salinger, who was then vice president, international (he later quit to return to politics). Each profile was ten to twelve pages long and included an appraisal by Irwin and an independent evaluation by Golightly, who knew each man personally. They bound each report in a black cover and sent them to Six. The black books described each man's character, background, education, management experience, and personal aspirations.

They also provided an insight into each officer's home life, sports, social graces, and his wife, including comments on whether she would be an asset if he became president. They even explored his relationship with his children and how well he had raised them.

At the same time, Irwin wrote Six a confidential letter telling him that out of the nine, he and Golightly had selected four potential candidates. "We are greatly impressed with their caliber," Irwin wrote. "They all have high intelligence; are highly motivated; and are completely dedicated to Continental." After reading the nine black books, marking key phrases with a red-felt-tipped pen, and putting the books away in his office safe, Six told Golightly he readily concurred with their conclusions.

A GAME OF MULTIPLE CHOICE

By both their positions in the company and the initials of their last names, the four candidates composed the A, B, C, and D of Continental Air Lines.

Richard M. Adams, now fifty-six, senior vice president, operating and technical services, is a quiet engineer who enjoys good music and photography. The son of a New Jersey patent attorney, Adams has a warmth and an air of ability that have won him a staunch following among his subordinates. He moved over from Pan Am in 1962 to head Continental's maintenance division. Six soon moved Adams up, putting him in charge of flight operations as well as maintenance. Under him Continental has achieved the best records in the industry for aircraft utilization and jet safety.

Charles A. Bucks, forty-seven, senior vice president, marketing, quit college after World War II to become a baggage handler in his home town of Lubbock at an airline that was later acquired by Continental. Showing a natural talent for salesmanship, he rapidly moved up through the marketing division until, at thirty-four, he became the air-transport industry's youngest vice president. (United now has a president ten years his junior, a fact that galls Bucks no little.)

Bucks has been the brain behind some of Continental's most outlandish marketing gimmicks. In 1959, to promote flights from Chicago, he dropped a helicopter onto Wrigley Field in the middle of a game and had a crew of midgets "kidnap" the Cubs' centerfielder. Six-foot-four, silver-maned, handsome, and an outdoorsman like Six, Bucks is second only to Six in popularity among Continental's rank and file. "Mr. Bucks knows he's a sex symbol," says a hostess on the ramp at Burbank, adding emphatically: "And he has the right to know it."

G. Edward Cotter, fifty-seven, is senior vice president, legal and diversification, and the company secretary. Disarmingly frank and ambitious, cool and well ordered, Cotter was born in the China mission field, the son of an Episcopal minister. He worked for a New York law firm and was secretary of Freeport Sulphur Co. before taking over Continental's legal division in 1965. Cotter has an extraordinary conceptual grasp of such broad issues as the airline's needs for long-term growth. And he articulates these ideas with the self-confidence and orderly flow of a seasoned barrister. "I'm a goddam good lawyer," he says. "I'm a very capable guy and this company is goddam lucky to have me."

Cotter has indeed been valuable to Continental, though most employees are unaware of his achievements. Yet everyone is aware of another fact of Cotter's life: he is Six's brother-in-law. His sister, actress Audrey Meadows, has been married to Six for fourteen years.

Alexander Damm, fifty-nine, senior vice president and general manager, is Continental's moneyman. Damm (rhymes with palm) came from T.W.A. in 1959 to bolster the company's lackluster financial division. He installed tight budget controls and a monthly head count that allows Six to veto the most minute addition to the payroll. Damm and Six are opposites in personality and complement one another, but they have never forged a close personal bond.

Born in Nebraska, the son of a Burlington railroad roundhouse foreman, Damm is a serious, no-nonsense task-master. He lives by the memo, often to Six's exasperation, and insists that written communication is the best way for an executive to keep informed. Nevertheless, Damm's rigid system of controls has kept Continental out of the red. Like many good general managers, he is not well liked by employees, largely because over the years he has had to execute the austerity programs that have laid off hundreds of men and women.

Six watched each man's performance for two years. Then, in August, 1969, Golightly and Irwin presented him with an updated profile of each man. They also uncovered a fifth candidate, Dominic P. Renda, who had come to Continental eighteen months earlier as senior vice president, international. Renda, sixty-one, a tall, swarthy man who is married to a former Miss Maryland, had been senior vice president, legal, of Western Air Lines. At this point, Golightly told Six that Damm, Renda, and Adams—in that order—were the best qualified candidates, and that in an emergency Continental could turn to any one of them as a new president.

A TIME FOR GROOMING

So far as the other candidates were concerned, Cotter had shown surprising growth in the two years, tightening his grasp of the airline business and toning down his competitive spirit, though he was sometimes still abrasive. Bucks, however, was a real comer. Golightly told Six that, for the long haul, Bucks was probably the strongest presidential prospect in the entire industry. But Golightly and Six calculated that he would require five to eight more years of grooming.

For all their strengths, each of the five candidates needed more experience. Accordingly, Six decided to put off his retirement until 1976, when he would be sixty-nine. Meanwhile, he decided to broaden the younger men's duties and see how they developed. "It's been great fun," he says proudly. "I enjoy watching these guys come up."

Bucks, for instance, had headed only the sales end of the marketing division. Six exposed him to the rigors of top-level decision making by placing him in charge of the entire division. To expand Cotter's responsibilities beyond legal affairs and into operations, Six put him in charge of a small chain of hotels in the Pacific and Continental Air Services, a contract carrier serving the government and private companies in Southeast Asia.

As Six watched eagerly through the early 1970's, each of the candidates made noticeable progress. Bucks became a practiced witness at regulatory hearings and drew on his native traits of showmanship to strengthen his following among employees around the Continental system. When the women's liberation movement attacked Continental's ad slogan—"We Really Move Our Tail For You!"—Bucks turned the dispute to his advantage by getting on a TV talk show and, waving a copy of the ad in front of the camera, stealing the show—and valuable publicity.

Under Cotter's guidance, Continental Air Services outperformed its competitor, Air America, the Central Intelligence Agency's own air-transport arm. Cotter, the missionary's son, even showed a hidden marketing flair. When he opened a new hotel on Saipan for the Japanese tourist trade, he flew in three Shinto priests to bless the place.

SAVED FROM THE MONEY EATERS

Gaining experience as general manager, Damm extended his knowledge beyond his financial specialty and into operations. He became a tough inspector, and he soon recognized the untapped potential of air cargo, pestering Six and Bucks for a better, more comprehensive and competitive freight program.

Damm also was turning into a hard bargainer. As head of a Continental negotiating team, he used eleventh-hour brinksmanship to win very favorable contracts for new airplanes from McDonnell Douglas and Boeing. And while his demeanor remained very serious, he was becoming more relaxed with people.

But the most important accomplishment during the early Seventies belonged to Adams, who persuaded Damm and Six to go against all the sacrosanct dogma of the industry and sell off Continental's brand-new fleet of four 747's. Indisputably the most popular airplane now flying, the 747 can also be a money eater. While it carries twice as many passengers as the DC-10, it costs more than four times as much to maintain. By eliminating the 747, Adams saved $2 million a year in training costs alone. By substituting more of the smaller DC-10's, Continental was able to offer passengers additional flights to its destinations. Now the Continental fleet has only two basic airplane types—the 727 and the DC-10—instead of six.

FIGHTING OVER "NICKEL-AND-DIME STUFF"

With one notable exception, the five candidates worked well together, even though it was slowly dawning on all of them that they were in a race for the top. Any temptations to jockey for position were dampened by the knowledge that Six disliked office politics. The race did affect Six's relationship with Bucks, however. Since both men shared a fondness for the outdoors, they had gone off together over the years on week-long hunting trips. But, as the search for a president continued, their close companionship set off rumors that Six had anointed Bucks his heir. When Six heard the rumors, he abruptly ended their camaraderie. Unfortunately, he never explained why, and Bucks, who regards Six as something of a father, felt hurt long afterwards. He believed he must have inadvertently done something that annoyed the boss.

The one major friction among the contenders was between Cotter and Renda, both lawyers and men of strong personality. "He's very amiable," Cotter says of Renda. "A lot of people like him. I didn't like him personally. We were not compatible." The two barraged Six with a cross fire of memos, each disputing the other on some minor matter. "It was all nickel-and-dime stuff," says Six, who talked to both men and tried to make peace. Finally Six lost patience and told them he wasn't having any more to do with their bickering, but the memos kept coming in. The fight ended in 1972, when Renda left Continental to go back to Western as its executive vice president.

By May of last year, Six was beginning to realize that even though the four remaining contenders had developed, not one of them had perfected all the attributes he wanted in his successor. Adams understood financing as well as operations, but he was short on marketing expertise. Long a staff man, Cotter still lacked experience as a line officer. Damm had little of Cotter's conceptual ability, but he had developed an eye for detail and a general knowledge of marketing, operations, and scheduling. Bucks had been so busy untangling the structural intricacies of the marketing division and selling seats on Continental's highly competitive new runs to Hawaii that he still lacked experience in finance and route planning. Besides, Six complained,

Bucks was too reluctant to fire those subordinates who failed to measure up, declaring in exasperation: "Jesus, Charlie, you're the Billy Graham of the air-transport industry!"

A RETURN TO THE GOOD OLD WAYS

Since there was no single candidate with all the qualifications, Six decided to select a team of two successors. In the near term, he would move from president to chairman, a post that was vacant. One candidate would become vice chairman and another would be named president and chief operating officer. A year later, when Six stepped down, the best man would become chief executive.

To prepare for the final selection, Six and Golightly agreed they should compile an accurate measurement of the candidates' traits and have each man prepare an analysis of himself, though that would obviously be subject to some bias. "You'd do a perfect self-evaluation," said Golightly. "I'd write a glowing one," Six declared, grinning. "S - - - ! It'd be half wrong." By last February all the evaluations were in, and Six put them away with the black books in his safe.

In the middle of last winter, Bucks's standing was enhanced by one further event. A number of rulings by the Civil Aeronautics Board had restricted Continental's use of some highly promotional sales gimmicks. Bucks's employees in the marketing division felt so hamstrung that they lost some of their enthusiasm, and the airline's distinctive individualism and feistiness was beginning to evaporate. For a year and a half, Six had been agitating for a return to the good old ways, and Bucks had picked up the call. The CAB had ordered Continental either to take the popular cocktail lounges out of its DC-10's or to charge extra for them. Continental had taken the ruling to court and, last December, the board was ordered to reconsider.

Even before the legal dust had settled, Bucks sold Six on a strategy to restore the airline's old-time pizzazz. Continental would reinstall the lounges and, going a step further, would put in electronic Ping-Pong games, show free movies—old newsreels, cartoons, and Saturday afternoon serials—and sell hot dogs, hot beef sandwiches, and Coors beer. The entire venture would cost $546,000, but Bucks estimated it would generate more than $1.3 million in extra revenues this year alone. If there had been any questions about Bucks's ability to burnish Continental's image, the new lounges swept those doubts away.

HE DIDN'T WANT PATSIES

Early this year, Six organized a selection committee including himself and three outside directors—Jay A. Pritzker, a Chicago investor whose family controls Hyatt Corp. and Cerro; Thomas D. Finney Jr., a Washington lawyer who is a partner of former Defense Secretary Clark

Clifford; and David J. Mahoney, chairman and president of Norton Simon, Inc., a former Continental director who is now one of its two advisory directors (the other is Audrey Six). Six chose the outsiders with care because, as he later explained, "I didn't want a patsy f------ committee." He was to get what he bargained for. The three men were to have a major impact on the final selection.

Six wanted to stick with his decision to name a vice chairman and a president, but now he worried about the two losers. He believed all four candidates would be valuable assets to any airline, and other carriers obviously shared that belief. In recent months Damm had been mentioned for the general manager's post of Pan Am, and Bucks had rejected the top marketing job at American. Six wanted to keep his team together, and to do that he planned to restructure the company's upper echelons and give the losing candidates additional powers.

Golightly urged Six to make his selection by using a scoring grid the consultant had set up for American Airlines:

TRAITS	MAXIMUM POINTS
Leadership	30
Technical ability	
airline experience	30
non-airline experience	15
Performance	20
Growth potential	10
Age: over 55	5
45-55	10
40-45	8
under 40	5

Though Golightly pressed the suggestion, Six rejected it. "Each of these guys I personally hired," he explained. "I just can't do it that way. My heart's not in it."

Six decided that his criteria had to be based on which man could best fulfill the particular goals and future needs of Continental. Now that the company had bought and financed its new airplanes, knowledge of operations and financing would be of secondary importance for the intermediate future. The company's main challenge would be to maintain its marketing edge and sustain its esprit de corps, while wringing as near perfect a performance as possible from its crews and terminal workers.

The unions had become more militant in recent years, and dealing with them would require personal leadership and insight into the art of handling people. While Damm had more general experience and Adams knew how to deal with flight crews, in Six's mind the candidate who fitted all those requirements best was Bucks.

But Six was also aware that Continental faced a serious and less noticeable challenge stemming from its own expansion. If the airline grew much larger, it might become impersonal and difficult for one or two men to control, a problem that had overwhelmed other airlines and railroads. Only one of the four candidates grasped the strategies needed to deal with this problem. That man was Cotter.

AUDREY KEEPS HER MOUTH SHUT

By late February the tension was gnawing at Six. Normally he can keep up with three conversations at once, but when Audrey broke the evening's silence to chat about some domestic subject, Six would answer absent-mindedly with a comment about the airline. Cotter's being his brother-in-law nagged at him terribly, perhaps more than he realized.

Except for attending traditional Christmas Eve family get-togethers, Six had made it a point to avoid seeing Cotter socially. For the past year Audrey had not discussed the four candidates with Six, knowing that he was aware of her preferences. "I'm not going to jeopardize anybody's chances by opening my big mouth," she told a friend. But once or twice she did pass on her observations to Golightly, who steadfastly refrained from repeating them to Six.

The candidates had their own opinions about who ought to get Six's job. Cotter believed himself both capable and worthy of it. "I have good judgment," he told a visitor one afternoon. "There are all sorts of extremely able people, fine sales types, accounting people. But they lack the basic element called common sense."

For his part, Damm had never doubted that his position as general manager put him next in line, but neither could he believe he would actually get the promotion. Adams and Bucks, on the other hand, took a rather unpretentious stance. Although both harbored the desire to run a major airline, they believed Damm to be the best choice. They were loyal to a senior executive who had worked hard and contributed greatly to the company's success.

Early this spring, Six privately reached his own decision. He favored Cotter as vice chairman because he understood the concepts needed to run an expanding company. He wanted Damm to be president and chief operating officer because of his vast experience in finance and administration. Six left open the decision as to which of the two would become chief executive upon his own retirement.

The trouble with the choices was that neither man was particularly popular with rank-and-file employees. When asked his opinion of Cotter, for instance, a passenger-service supervisor in Phoenix replied: "Cotter? He's in charge of ramp facilities, isn't he?" But Six believed he could persuade Continental employees that his decision was the right one. "I've been selling these kids all my life," he said. "There's no reason I can't sell them on this."

Six planned to reveal his decision to the selection committee, which had agreed to meet on April 2 in New York. He decided to send each member copies of the candidates' self-analyses, his own critique of these, and an outline of each man's career drawn up by Golightly. In order to avoid any possible leaks, Six flew from Los Angeles on March 23 to Continental's former headquarters at Denver's Stapleton field, where he still keeps an office. The following day he dictated his own critiques to a trusted former secretary, Judy L. Lawrence, who once worked for the FBI and holds a government security clearance. She typed copies for each committee member, and a little after five o'clock, Six stuffed the self-analyses and his critiques into three manila envelopes. Miss Lawrence handed the extra carbons and her stenographer's notebook over to Six and watched as he tore out her notes. He then drove to his apartment near downtown Denver and burned the notes in the kitchen sink.

"IF YOU GOT RUN OVER TOMORROW"

The committee (Six, Pritzker, Finney, and Mahoney) gathered at the Waldorf Towers at 6:30 on the evening of April 2, a Wednesday, in the living room of Suite 31-H, a warm and tasteful private apartment that Norton Simon Inc. keeps for private meetings and important visitors. Six sipped a vodka and Fresca, and the others, except for the teetotaling Mahoney, nursed scotches while they spread their papers on the carpet in front of their chairs and began talking. It soon became obvious that the outside members had studied the evaluations and come to some strong conclusions.

The committee seemed impressed by the fact that the evaluations and Six's critiques had shown incontrovertibly that none of the four candidates was totally equipped for the top job at Continental. Finney suggested that Six should postpone his retirement, and Mahoney asked him if he would extend his contract for two additional years. This proposition surprised Six, but the idea of remaining until he could bring Continental's earnings—and its stock price—closer to the levels the company had enjoyed in the mid-1960's greatly appealed to him. "Under today's conditions and with the stock options I've got," he replied, "the answer is yes."

Now that he was staying on, the Cotter-Damm tandem appointment he had in mind no longer made any sense. What Continental now needed was a president and a chief operating officer who could take over if something happened to Six. Mahoney asked: "Who would you name today if you got run over tomorrow?" Surprisingly, Six had not considered the question, but he did not hesitate in replying. The committee unanimously agreed that Al Damm would be recommended to the full board as president and chief operating officer after the annual meeting in Denver on May 7.

But Damm could not be expected to run the company for long. He will be sixty-two in 1978, when Six is to step down. With that in mind, the committee set about selecting a long-term heir. As one member said later: "Our discussion was not in the context of three years; our discussion was in the context of the next fifteen years." Nearly three hours later they came to a unanimous agreement and pledged themselves to secrecy. Some of the matters they had discussed were not to appear in the minutes of their meeting and not to be reported to the full board.

NO ONE TO TALK TO

A week or so after the meeting, Mahoney called to ask sympathetically if Six had told Audrey about his decision. The answer was no. That was the worst part, not being able to talk about it. One day he had happened to sit with Bucks at lunch in the company cafeteria. "Charlie," he said, "I'm going to have to have lunch with all you fellows. I don't want to show any favorites in the cafeteria." And in the next few days he ate with Damm, Adams, and Cotter.

As May approached, Six found it harder to sleep; he woke up night after night, thinking about the decision. There still was no one to talk to about it. By this time, Mahoney was in Paris, Pritzker was involved with a troublesome acquisition, Finney was busy with his law practice, and Golightly was in London.

On the weekend before the annual meeting, Six flew to Denver, and the candidates followed a few days later. They seemed relaxed enough. Bucks sat up most of the night before the meeting playing poker. Six was asleep by 10:30 and slept well, waking only to get a drink of water and let out the dog.

The next morning Six presided over a rather uneventful annual meeting in the ballroom of the Brown Palace Hotel. After a brief luncheon he and the board filed into a small paneled meeting room on the hotel's second floor. The pine shutters were drawn against the noise of passing cars below, and a coffeepot and soft drinks were spread on a table along one wall.

After spending thirty minutes on routine business, Six excused the four candidates, who were all members of the board, and launched into his report. When he finished, Finney began reading the minutes of the Waldorf meeting. As Finney droned on, smoke from Six's cigar curled into the air and the green cloth that covered the board table began to be blanketed by a clutter of papers and empty Fresca bottles. At one point Six got up and walked out the door. "I'm just going to the boys' room, nothing big," he told two of the candidates who were waiting outside with Golightly and a half dozen vice presidents.

Without much discussion, the board voted unanimously to accept the committee's recommendations. Out in the hallway, the executives had formed a pool on how long the board would take to reach a decision. After one hour and thirty-eight minutes, Six ushered the candidates back in and Golightly pocketed $8 in winnings. Cotter pulled back his shoulders and stiffened as he walked into the room; Adams and Bucks were relaxed, but Damm was so tense he steadily avoided looking Six in the eyes. Six opened up with a bit of lightness, saying: "Sit down. I've got bad news. You guys are not going to like it. You're not rid of me yet." Damm could not seem to manage a smile. Then Six told them the board's decision: Damm was to be president, the others were elected executive vice presidents with added responsibilities, and all were named to a new profit-planning committee, which would give them experience in making top-level financial decisions. Damm was so shocked and happy he could hardly find words.

WHAT THE BOARD DIDN'T KNOW

The selection committee is to continue until 1978, when it will formally choose a new chief executive. As Six explained the executives' additional duties, it was obvious that Bucks was well in the lead. He acquired control of scheduling, which Six considers the most important function of an airline executive. Essential to maintaining a competitive edge, good scheduling requires an ability to sniff out trends and plan capacity well in advance of the market.

But what Six did not tell either the candidates or the board was that the committee already had its eye on Bucks, as that committee member said, "in the context of the next fifteen years." For one thing, at forty-seven, Bucks is by far the youngest candidate. And during the Waldorf meeting, Mahoney, joined at times by Pritzker, had urged that the top job ultimately go to a line officer. Mahoney sprinkled his argument with examples of successful line executives who had been promoted at Norton Simon, and after thirty minutes of discussion, Six was convinced. Cotter, a staff man, was virtually eliminated from contention. Adams, a line officer like Bucks, remains a backup candidate, should Bucks stumble.

Much to Six's relief, Audrey declared at the board meeting that the decision was a good one. And even Cotter seemed content. "We're a team," he told the board. "We're going to make it work together."

Searching for the "Perfect" University President

Warren G. Bennis

POINTS TO REMEMBER ON CHOOSING A COLLEGE PRESIDENT

1. *Remember that there is no single quality, trait, characteristic, style, or person that guarantees presidential capability.* A century and a half of psychological research confirms this point. An Ivy League degree or a "low profile" is not in itself going to ensure the bearer of success in dealing with an adamant board or angry students. Being from the "outside" is no talisman either. The outsider may fail if he is unable to master quickly the special terrain of his institution—fail just as dismally as the insider whose judgment is skewed by partisan loyalties held over from his pre-presidential days. There is no one presidential "type," no presidential personality. The time is past when a Stanford or a Columbia can be described as the lengthened shadow of any one man.

Many different approaches to university management have been successful in the recent past. Among possible presidential styles are:

The problem-solver/manager. Howard Johnson, the retiring president of MIT, has used this approach most successfully. Johnson's concern has been, How can I identify problems (real problems, not temporal issues) and engage the best minds and most important constituencies to work on them?

The managerial style is often confused with that of *low-profile/ technocrat*. Similarities are superficial. Instead of putting the right people to work on the right problems, the technocrat tries to find *systems* that will somehow transcend human error. The concerns of the technocrat are all pragmatic. He cuts through moral and ideological dilemmas with a callousness that soon has students and faculty aligned against him.

The leader/mediator. Based on the labor relations model, this style is just coming into its own. If one conceives of the university in terms of constituencies seeking to maximize self-interest, a place where there is no way to make decisions without pleasing some and making some angry, then this style is very effective. In fact, there may be no decent

Warren G. Bennis, "Searching for the 'Perfect' University President," *The Atlantic Monthly*, April 1971, pp. 50–52. © 1971 by the Twentieth Century Fund, New York.

alternative. A number of men from industrial relations backgrounds have become very successful presidents recently, most notably, Robben Fleming at the University of Michigan. (Howard Johnson also has a labor relations background; he first came to MIT as dean of the School of Industrial Management.) A problem that such men have is that since they cannot help making one side on any issue angry, at a certain point in time the accumulated anger overtakes the goodwill. So the tenure of such a president will be problematical unless he possesses, in addition to mediating skills, a degree of charisma that keeps him personally above conflict.

The value of labor relations experience does not seem to have escaped the Harvard Corporation, which recently named Derek C. Bok as Harvard's twenty-fifth president. Bok, who has been dean of Harvard Law School, is an authority on labor law and has been an arbitrator in several major disputes.

The collegiate manager. This is the style of the academic administrator in the strict sense of the term—the man whose primary commitment is to a scholarly discipline, who assumes the presidency as a faculty colleague rather than as a professional administrator. This man is very like a *representative* leader. The model is Parliament, with the faculty as the House of Commons and the trustees rather like the House of Lords.

Faculties have already acquired substantial influence at the great American universities. Nonacademic leaders can forget just how powerful the faculty is within these institutions. General Eisenhower, during his Columbia presidency, had to be reminded by the vice-chairman of the faculty senate that "the faculty *is* the university, sir!"

The communal-tribal or postmodern leader. Leaders of this style are emerging in many of our institutions, not just universities. The academic leader of this style usually heads a college, not a university. The tribal leader typically identifies strongly with students; he not only backs them, he often joins with them, whether on marches to Washington or on strike. He is himself an activist, and likely to be young. John R. Coleman of Haverford or Harris Wofford at Old Westbury College (he is now at Bryn Mawr, where his style may be somewhat different) are examples of this style.

The charismatic leader. John Summerskill, who preceded Robert Smith (who preceded S. I. Hayakawa) at San Francisco State, was a charismatic president, but the exemplar of this style is Kingman Brewster of Yale. Brewster's personal attractiveness makes it possible to transcend obstacles.

In addition to these more or less acceptable presidential styles, there are several other possible approaches to university governance that should be mentioned. The following styles are currently out of favor or actually undesirable, but all of us have known men who practiced them:

The law-and-order president. Hayakawa, with his tam o'shanter and megaphone, is the epitome of this style. Ronald Reagan's behavior as the self-selected head of the University of California is also fairly typical.

The absentee-pluralist. This style, rapidly losing favor, has been highly regarded in the past. The president who adopts this approach sees his primary function as raising money for buildings and other needs and appointing competent subordinates. He hires those he considers to be good deans, spends his time on ceremonial functions, and "lets things happen." This is a spectacularly effective model when the university is rich, the subalterns capable, and the students and faculty relatively homogeneous and docile. In other words, if the university is like an elite men's club or the year is 1915.

The bureaucrat/entrepreneur. This style drives faculty to despair. The academic entrepreneur *par excellence* was Millard George Roberts, who with phenomenal *chutzpah* transformed a marginal sectarian college in the Midwest into a booming financial success and a national scandal. Before the bubble burst, Roberts succeeded in running Parsons College in Fairfield, Iowa, less like an academic institution than like a railroad. A *Swiss* railroad.

When all else fails, and the search committee and board cannot reach agreement on any of the above presidential styles, there is always the *interregnum* (or Pope John) solution. Interregnum leaders often do much better than might be expected. A good secular example is Dr. Andrew Cordier, who surprised almost everybody with his able management at Columbia.

There is at least one other presidential style, that of the *Renaissance or protean man.* This is the elusive superman that so many search committees pursue, the man who is all things to all constituencies. The protean president can role-play, presenting himself as a *communal-tribal leader* on some matters, a *bureaucratic-entrepreneur* on other matters, and on still others a *problem-solver/manager.* One of these protean men can also make life excruciatingly difficult for his constituents, who never know from one day to the next exactly what to expect.

2. *Determine the university's particular metaphor, the collectively held image of what the university is or could become.* Just as there are a number of successful presidential types, there are many university metaphors. The State University of New York at Buffalo comes close, in my view, to a "labor relations" metaphor. There are many other usable metaphors: Clark Kerr's "City," Mark Hopkins' "student and teacher on opposite ends of a log," "General Systems Analysis," "Therapeutic Community," "Scientific Management," my own "temporary systems," and so on, competing with the pure form of bureaucracy.

3. *Forgo the costly hit-or-miss search and tailor the search process to the special requirements of the individual university.* Once the university's metaphor—its collective self-image or ideal self—is determined, the type of president sought is automatically less problematical.

The university's metaphor should determine not only the style of the president sought but also the composition and relative weighting of the search committee. For example, if the university requires a *collegiate manager*, an individual with strong academic qualifications and faculty identification, then faculty should have the decisive voice on the search committee.

As corollary to Number 3, it is increasingly clear that *a presidential search committee should undertake only an intelligently limited canvass, not a national quest*. When a university picked a new president every twenty years or so, it was reasonable to underwrite a far-flung search, sparing no effort or expense to screen conceivable candidates. But the national search is beginning to appear as extravagant as the elaborate inauguration.

4. *Assuming that the search committee is representative, the committee should select the president as well as screen candidates.* Demoralizing conflicts can be avoided by making sure that trustees serving on the search committee are powerful enough and numerous enough to represent the total board throughout the search. This seems to be the only sure way to avoid the enormous frustration that results when a board of trustees overrules the decision of a responsible and representative search committee.

The Art of Firing an Executive
Judson Gooding

Of all the corporate chores performed by executives, the most painful is firing other executives. The process appears to be getting more painful every year—and also more commonplace. It is sinking in on some executives, at least, that an ability to fire one's colleagues properly is an important job qualification these days.

It is, of course, the fact that they *are* one's colleagues that makes the whole process so painful. Firing production workers or low-level white-collars is unpleasant enough; but generally those who make the decisions are shielded from direct contact with the victims. Those who decide that an executive colleague must get the ax are often obliged to wield it personally.

It is principally because of the "democratization" of American business that this process is becoming more traumatic every year. When

Reprinted from material originally appearing in the October 1972 issue of *Fortune* Magazine by special permission; © 1972 Time Inc. ☐ Research associate: Ann Hengstenberg.

the boss was a remote figure in an authoritarian corporate world, his concerns about the executives who worked under him were presumably minimal. He did not deal with them on a first-name basis; he probably didn't drink with them or belong to the same country club they did; his wife certainly wasn't a friend of their wives. But in the modern corporation, increasingly dominated by humanist values and a democratic ethic, webs of personal relationships are spun endlessly. It becomes harder all the time to view one's colleagues as just names on the table of organization—which means, among other things, that it becomes harder all the time to fire them.

Firing of executives seems to be increasing, despite all the attendant traumas, because of an intensifying pressure for profits. All data about frequency of firings are necessarily rather soft, but it is clear that during the 1969-70 recession, when many large corporations found themselves under greater profit pressure than ever, executive firings soared, apparently to levels far higher than those of past economic downturns. E. A. Butler, who runs a management-consulting firm in New York, and who has spent more than twenty years talking to out-of-work executives and corporate personnel men, is persuaded that this wave of firing represented more than a cyclical phenomenon —that it also reflected a growing commitment to the kind of performance that would come down to the bottom line. Even in the present strong economy, Butler says, "the quickness to fire is much greater than it used to be."

The traumas accompanying executive firings have had a considerable influence on the way companies talk about the process. There is a strong tradition—it seems to be especially powerful when executives at the highest level are involved—requiring that public announcements characterize departures as resignations. Henry Ford's slam-bang firing of Semon Knudsen in 1969, only twenty months after he was hired as president of the Ford Motor Co., was one of the very few instances in recent times in which it was perfectly clear that the president had been fired. A far more typical scenario was the one enacted at General Foods last April.

Arthur E. Larkin, Jr., who had been president of General Foods since 1966, announced in April that he was taking early retirement at fifty-five—ten years before the company's mandatory retirement age. His departure came just after General Foods had taken a $46,800,000 write-down, most of it related to the Burger Chef fast-food operation, whose expansion Larkin had backed. C. W. Cook, the company's chairman and chief executive, who had originally hired Larkin and worked closely with him over the years, says of the reasons for the retirement that "a basic difference in management philosophy became more evident."

As a result of this difference, Cook recommended to the board that he himself "resume operating responsibility." At this point, as Cook describes the sequence, Larkin "saw that the only thing to do was to leave. He told me this, and I agreed." His request for early retirement was accepted at a meeting of the board of directors, and the retirement was noted in the General Foods annual report in one succinct sentence. Larkin himself insists that the retirement was voluntary and says that it was for "personal reasons."

Sweetening the terms of the separation is one obvious way of easing the pain associated with firings, and most large companies have gone pretty far along that road. Many corporate managements that resisted early-retirement plans because of their expense have discovered that they have at least made it a lot easier to fire executives: announcements of resignations have become more plausible and the job loss has become less painful to the executives involved. Pearl Meyer, vice president for research at Handy Associates, a management-consulting and recruiting firm, has observed that "companies nowadays are willing to pay liberally for the privilege of getting rid of people."

The blow can also be softened by getting another company to recruit the executive who is to be fired, and then, when it's clear that he has a job offer, lowering the boom. If the victim is reasonably astute, he may manage to resign before the bad news is actually delivered. Variations of this tactic now seem to be fairly widespread. Louis F. Polk Jr., a former president of Metro-Goldwyn-Mayer (he was fired in 1969), says that, as a result, "some people are afraid they're getting the ax when the headhunters come after them."

SAVING FACE IN CHICAGO

One rather special opportunity to eliminate people with a minimum of anguish arises when the company itself is planning to move its offices. Donald A. Petrie, a former Lazard Frères investment banker (he is now serving as treasurer of the Democratic National Committee), is something of an authority on this situation: at different times in his career he has been a senior executive of both Hertz and Avis—both of which moved their headquarters from one city to another.

In each case there was a compelling reason for the move, but the opportunity to get rid of unproductive executives and staff members was exploited to the full. "A move is a time to bring your organization up to date," Petrie says. In the case of Hertz, "we had 525 persons in Chicago, and we moved 125. We said to persons we were willing to lose, 'We're moving to New York, and you ought to think about whether you ought to go.' We asked questions like 'Do you want to uproot your family?' and 'Is New York the kind of place you want to live?' and 'Does it make sense to move away just three years before retirement?'"

Just about everyone seems to have got the message. Petrie recalls: "Of the 125 we wanted to keep, only three decided to stay in Chicago, and of the 400 who remained, only seven had wanted to make the move. They had a perfect out—the person who stays saves face. He can say, 'I'm a Chicagoan, I don't want to move to New York.'" When a company uses a move this way, Petrie says, "you do an enormous amount for the people, because they never had to tell their wives or their kids they were fired—the company just moved away. Some never even admitted it to themselves."

Some of these employees benefited in still another way. When other companies heard that Hertz was moving, they began raiding it. "Most people love to steal executives," Petrie says, "so we allowed anyone who wanted it the delectable pleasure of stealing those of our people who were not making the move. They took thirty this way—of whom we had wanted to keep two."

THE DOUBLE-TALK PROBLEM

There is certainly every reason for anyone firing an executive to do whatever is possible to ease the pain, and in public statements a certain amount of double-talk about "resignation" can be appropriate. Unfortunately, a good many executives also resort to double-talk in their private sessions with men who are being fired—leaving the victims in a state of confusion about where they stand with the company.

A man may be deemed fired when he gets a message telling him that he must leave—that he has no choice about the matter. The message may be verbal and explicit. It may conceivably be nonverbal but still unmistakable—e.g., when an executive returns from vacation and finds that he has no office or secretary and can't get an appointment with his boss. The elder Henry Ford occasionally had his staff members' furniture moved out of their offices overnight.

But the message should at least be clear, and the most agonizing firings of all are those in which it isn't. Something happens—e.g., a sudden exclusion from key committees—to suggest that the executive is under a cloud. Yet the underlying message remains ambiguous: Is the man being told that he can stay, with his status somewhat reduced, or is he being told that his time is limited and that he'd better start looking for another job? Or is top management itself indecisive about the executive's future?

Personnel men and consultants who've thought a lot about the process generally agree that the ambiguous message is the cardinal sin of executive firing. Anyone who is being fired is entitled to be told clearly what's going on. Efforts to avoid telling him serve to prolong and maximize his anguish; and, for that matter, they are apt to make things harder in the long run for the senior executive who can't bring himself to deliver a clear message. Yet it is apparent that many otherwise sophisticated companies continue to fire executives the hard way.

The details are indeed harrowing. Consultants who have watched the process many times at many companies cite this typical sequence: Executives suddenly find that they've been taken off the circulation list for office memos, so that they are uninformed in meetings and liable to make fools of themselves. Then they're cut off from the meetings. Later their secretaries may be taken away, they are moved to smaller offices, and their expense accounts suddenly become the object of searching questions. Some companies have office areas known as Siberia, where executives getting the treatment are herded together.

A FEELING OF GUILT

The ultimate irony about these long, agonizing firings is that they're typically perpetrated by executives who are fearful of "hurting" a colleague. Dr. Harry Levinson, the psychologist and author, formerly a Distinguished Visiting Professor at Harvard Business School who has written several books about executive stress, says that many executives obliged to fire a colleague are overpowered by feelings of guilt. The feelings may lead them to evade the issue by keeping the message ambiguous. Alternatively, Levinson says, some executives react against their feelings and behave impulsively, even angrily, like a small boy who becomes enraged at others when he feels he has done something wrong himself. "Suddenly, without warning, they tell the man to clear out his desk, and they add 'or we'll send someone to do it for you.'"

Sometimes the senior executives will remain offstage themselves but arrange for firings to be carried out by underlings. One former executive at Metromedia, a victim of a major purge there several years ago, contends that Chairman John Kluge operated through subordinates, "somehow managing to avoid running into formerly close colleagues who were getting the ax, although some of them had helped him start the company and had been allies for ten or twenty years." The general manager of one major Metromedia-owned local station was summarily fired by a headquarters executive who had never liked him. The executive flew into town, marched into the general manager's office, and announced: "You're through." He demanded and got the keys to the manager's company car and his credit cards, snapped the credit cards in half, pocketed the keys, turned around, and left.

Sudden, brutal firings can have calamitous consequences. Not long ago, an executive of a large diversified corporation in western New York state was having lunch in a restaurant frequented by executives of a company that was being acquired by his own in a merger. He spotted a department manager, walked over to the man's table, and told him, without any preliminaries, that he was being fired. The department manager stood up, suddenly white-faced, clutched at his chest, then fell down and died of a heart attack.

Less brutal, but more unscrupulous, is an approach in which companies force executives out by getting their medical departments to overstate any problems the men may have. Dr. Walter Menninger, senior staff psychiatrist at the Menninger Foundation, says that he has received reports of this practice at a number of companies. "Management will try to get the medical department to provide a basis for early retirement. They do it to avoid the discomfort of firing." The managements in question can often cite some ailment that is real enough; after all, plenty of executives do suffer from high blood pressure or various psychosomatic ailments. Nevertheless, Menninger reports, "company physicians we've spoken to are very troubled by these attempts to use executives' medical status as grounds for retirement. It's a cop-out—the physicians feel they're being used as a tool to solve what should really be an executive's problem."

THE IMPORTANCE OF TELLING WHY

Despite the numerous inept firings in American business, there is no real mystery or disagreement about how the job should be done. The basic requirements are simple: the executive being fired must be told plainly that he is leaving the company and must also be told why. It is important to tell him why in a way that allows him to preserve his self-esteem and to explain to himself and his friends and family, particularly his wife, why this has happened to him. But the need for tact should not be allowed to obscure the realities about an inadequate performance. A. Edward Miller, president of Downe Publishing, who has fired a fair number of executives in his time (he has also been publisher of *McCall's* magazine and a consultant to Curtis Publishing Co.), says, "Most people I've fired have become better friends, because I've always told *why*. When he walks out the door, he knows why it happened." Alfred J. Seaman, president of the SSC&B advertising agency, says, "There is no one way to do it—much depends on the circumstances—but if I think firm criticism of the man will do any good, I'll tell him pretty bluntly what was going wrong."

Just about everyone agrees that it is an unacceptable evasion to blame the firing on vague authorities higher up, or on the board of directors ("I really can't go into what the board said, Bill, it has to stay confidential"). The evasion allows the man doing the firing to avoid taking any responsibility, but it deprives the victim of information he may need for success in his next job. It is also likely to leave him feeling angry and frustrated over his inability to find out just *why* his career is being deflected.

It is also generally agreed that, wherever possible, the firing should be performed by the executive's direct superior. (The man who is being dismissed should, however, be allowed to talk with a higher-up if he wants to.) Delegating the job to someone who doesn't know the situation in detail is not fair to the man being fired; at the same time it gives him an opportunity to muddy the issue by developing arguments about the merits of the case that the executive charged with firing him may not know how to answer.

In addition to being told clearly that he's leaving, and why, an executive who's being fired is entitled to know about a number of other matters that are, inevitably, of some concern to him. One matter simply involves the way any announcement of his departure will be made, and to what the departure will be attributed. He will certainly want to know how much time he's got and whether, in the interim, he can use an office to arrange to have telephone messages taken, and in general conduct his job hunt with the advantage of appearing to be employed.

SPECIALISTS IN FIRING

At some companies the executive who's doing the firing is able to tell the victim that the company can offer him the service of one of the handful of organizations specializing in "outplacement." Some of these organizations offer a kind of "full-line" firing service, which takes care of everything except the session at which the bad news is actually delivered. They counsel management on what severance arrangements are appropriate and work to help the executive find a satisfactory new job.

One of these services, called THINC., is a New York-based company that has seen its list of clients grow from three to more than a hundred companies or divisions since 1969. Thomas Hubbard, its president, says, "We consult with the company before the notices are given, to help it avoid making expensive mistakes. When they tell the man he's fired, they also tell him he will get the use of our services. This helps him at a difficult moment, and shows him he is not just being thrown out—that the company cares."

A CHANCE TO VENTILATE

The THINC. consultant meets with the man right after he has got the word, sometimes in the next room. This gives the departing executive a chance to "ventilate," as Hubbard describes the process—i.e., to get things off his chest that, if blurted out, might hurt his relationship with the company he's leaving—and also hurt him in his job hunt. The consultant helps him to avoid making serious mistakes, such as setting up interviews with job prospects before he is prepared for them. "Most mistakes in job hunting are made in the first seventy-two hours after the man is fired," Hubbard says.

One of THINC.'s major assignments in recent years was its effort in 1971 for New York's Bankers Trust Co., where sixty officers and 350 other staff members were laid off to cut costs. The bank offered THINC.'s services to all the employees involved. All forty of the executives who actively sought jobs with THINC.'s assistance were placed, according to Peter Gurney, the bank's vice president for personnel.

Richard Gleason is the proprietor of another major outplacement firm, Man-Marketing Services, Inc., of Chicago. The firm began counseling job seekers in 1954. Man-Marketing prepares résumés, provides tailor-made mailing lists, teaches the applicant how to plan for job interviews, advises on salary negotiations, counsels on follow-ups after interviews, and helps the job hunter decide which offer represents the best opportunity. Gleason's client companies include Borg-Warner Corp., for which he relocated eight executives in 1970, Mead Corp., Maremont Corp., and Jos. Schlitz Brewing Co.

A CASE FOR DEADLINES

The outplacement firms say that they can often save a lot of money for companies by simply talking them out of giving fired executives overgenerous flat settlements—a full year's pay being common. Instead, the firms may suggest that the man be kept on full salary while he conducts his job search, with a specific deadline. This arrangement motivates the fired executive to make a vigorous search and also can save the company thousands of dollars on any one separation.

Another substitute for heavy severance is putting the fired executive on a partial-pay contract basis. A contract provides a graceful exit for the executive and keeps his knowledge and contacts available if needed. An additional, sometimes critical, advantage is that it may ensure a degree of loyalty to the company and minimize the danger that secrets will be divulged. That danger is occasionally a very serious matter. Not long ago a major shopping-center developer abruptly fired the executive who had been in charge of site development and leasing. The firing took place at about the time an important rental prospect was agreeing to occupy the biggest single store in a large mid-western center; his agreement was considered crucial to the leasing of other stores. The executive who had been fired, angry at his summary treatment, proceeded to tell the client about a number of shortcomings in the facilities, some of which constituted violations of the leasing agreement. It cost $250,000 to fix up the facilities. The head of the company observed later, "That was the most expensive severance settlement I've ever had to pay."

2

/TRUGGLE/
WITHIN ORGANIZATION/
/elf-protection and /elf-a//ertion

No organization has unlimited resources. Consequently it is impossible to satisfy the wishes of all participants simultaneously. What determines whose wants get the most resources devoted to satisfy them?

Few organizational behaviorists or management theorists have attempted to answer this question directly, and thus we can only surmise what their answers would be. Undoubtedly many of them would say that the most competent individuals and those who have the resources and skills which are needed to help the organization achieve its most important goals are rewarded with more of the resources the organization has to distribute than are less competent, less important people. Without doubt these factors play an important role. Other writers, particularly those who have a bent towards economic theory, would tell us that resources are distributed to individuals according to the dictates of supply and demand. This argument also has validity, although it too is only part of the process.

Suppose we ask a related question: what determines the degree of dignity and respect which members receive? Here again, modern writers have frequently left the question unasked and consequently unanswered. In fact, the various types of the human relations theory which dominate modern management theory seem to make the question irrelevant because the "effective" manager, almost by definition, treats his or her subordinates with dignity, respect and empathy.

If the answers to the two questions we have raised are descriptive of actual life in organizations, we should expect that organizations would be rather pleasant places to be. Conflict would be limited to finding better ways to achieve the goals of the total entity rather than to the protection and enhancement of individual

66

interests. Of course, this idealistic picture, which seems to us to be characteristic of most modern organizational behaviorists, is not an accurate portrayal of organizational reality. What these arguments omit, and indeed what we believe almost all organizational behaviorists have left unstudied, are the struggles of people in organizations to influence the distribution of resources and to advance their own interests. We hope that the selections which follow will stimulate the development of a grater awareness of some of the struggles of members to protect and assert themselves.

Struggles take place at all levels. Usually we tend to assume that people at the lower levels are seeking to win more resources and control from organizations while people at higher levels are relatively satisfied. The first two selections show that individuals at upper levels are not so content with their lot. Arch Patton writes about the increase in executive self-interest and Jack Golodner discusses the unionization of professionals.

Often struggles within organizations are related to certain social issues. Two articles from *Business Week*, "How to Get Along—and Ahead—in the Office" and "How Women's Lib Works in Billings, Mont.," discuss the struggles of women to be treated equally with men in organizations. The following article, "Getting Rid of 65-and-Out," points to another source of discrimination which organizational members are contesting.

The next selections describe ways people can and have successfully wrested control within organizations. Samuel Culbert's selection from his intriguing book on organization traps discusses a general strategy for winning control in organizations. The article "Machiavellian Tactics for B-School Students" describes another general strategy for exercising control. "Coming on Strong" discusses assertion training as an aid to organizational members.

The last two selections describe two specific approaches individuals and groups might employ in gaining control. "Señor Payroll," by William Barrett, describes how one group of workers successfully fought a series of rules changes. Finally, James Thurber's "The Catbird Seat" is a delightful story about one person's strategy for retaining power.

The Boom in Executive Self-Interest

Arch Patton

One of the seldom-recognized byproducts of the great industrial boom of the 50s and 60s was a devastating decline in the loyalty of the executive to his company. As a result of this change, the chief officer of a company can no longer think of himself as standing at the head of a monolithic management corps. Instead, he will find that management below the top level is increasingly concerned with what it wants for itself rather than what the company wants of it.

Before the 1950s, many generations of industry's managers almost automatically equated their career interests with the success of their employer. They might be fired, but they rarely quit to take another job once they had graduated into the executive ranks.

The almost familial loyalty of corporation executives before World War II stemmed from the historic fact that company management was largely homegrown. The "outside executive" was simply unacceptable to most company value systems. This state of mind received powerful support from the Depression of the 30s, when every employed executive fervently blessed the company that kept him on the payroll during those grim years.

Strong company loyalty on the part of executives greatly simplified the management process. The "company interest," for example, was accepted virtually without question. If a sales manager had to uproot his family and move to a new location seven times in 10 years—a not infrequent occurrence in those days—the avowed company need in arriving at such a decision so far outweighed the effect of the moves on the executive's family that the latter was rarely even considered.

THE POSTWAR EROSION

The greatest advantage flowing from strong company loyalty, however, was the discipline it generated among executives to consider the corporate interest first and to identify their own interest with that of their employer. When combined with the management stability provided by very limited executive turnover, this focus on the company interest typically produced an effective team effort.

But the two decades that followed World War II saw company loyalty eroded by a rising tide of self-interest on the part of executives. A number of factors contributed to this turnabout. Low birth rates during the Depression years led to a shortage of executives after the war. This shortage was exacerbated by the vastly increased need for management talent in industry and government.

Largely as a result of this demand-supply imbalance, hundreds of executive recruiting firms were launched to provide a marketplace where the individual executive and the job that needed filling could be brought together. Both the buyer and seller of executive talent quickly recognized that a marketplace requires some mechanism for keeping track of the changing price level of specific jobs. As a result, the executive compensation survey was born in 1951.

The executive job market expanded prodigiously in the years that followed. The number of individual recruiters actively—and exclusively—seeking out executives who might change jobs, for example, rose from a handful to perhaps a thousand. Annual turnover—exclusive of retirement — among the approximately 135,000 truly policy-level executives in U.S. industry has risen from close to zero prewar to an estimated 20,000-plus today. Furthermore, this penchant for job-hopping among policy-level managers appears to be increasing at a rate close to 20% annually. And demographic projections indicate such turnover among experienced executives will get worse before it gets better.

In this booming sellers' market, the more aggressive executives soon realized that by judiciously changing employers they could advance their fortunes much faster than by laboriously climbing the organizational ladder of a single company. In other words, company interest no longer necessarily equated with their own.

A NEW BALL GAME

Companies themselves have helped undermine the old sense of loyalty by shifting operations from one area to another, offering employees a transfer on a "take it or leave it" basis. The wave of mergers that produced today's conglomerates forced early retirement or layoff on many middle-rank executives through no fault of their own. This negated any idea that loyalty to the company would be rewarded by security and recognition.

Other factors were also at work undermining company loyalty. During these years there was a huge expansion in the number of functional jobs required to manage the bigger and more complex business and government organizations that were evolving. More and more of these technically oriented executives gave their first loyalty to their specialty, not to the organization for which they worked. They considered themselves aircraft engineers, research chemists, financial executives, or package goods marketers, and they saw their career interests revolving about their specialized backgrounds, regardless of the company or industry in which the specialty might be employed.

Indeed, one of the top graduate schools of business has recently reported that a survey of its graduates during the past 20 years indicates that more than half have no interest in accepting general management responsibility; they prefer to remain in their specialized areas.

Many once-accepted "inconveniences" of corporate life are being reexamined as executives question company decisions in the light of their own interest. In part, of course, this reflects competition among industries for talent. (Retailing, with a six-day week, has virtually been forced to accept the five-day week as a way of life.) But a majority of questions involve policies or practices once accepted as a "right" of top management, however arbitrary the decisions might have been. These included such areas as hiring, firing, transfer, pay, promotion, holidays, and job titles.

QUESTIONING AUTHORITY

The enfeeblement of corporate disciplines in recent decades, of course, has been matched by the erosion of disciplines elsewhere in our society: Children refuse to obey their parents, police are looked down upon, teachers are shown less respect, politicians are "pardoned" for their actions. Even the church and the military have difficulty continuing long-established practices.

These are the disciplines that bind a society together, that make civilized living possible. As they have weakened, however, the disciplines involving group self-interest have with equal persistence grown stronger. It is rare indeed to find a union that has discipline problems with its members even during the most outrageous strike. The same is true where trade associations, industry combines, and other self-interest groups are concerned. Where self-interest is involved, discipline is rarely a problem.

Actions involving group self-interest have shown spectacular growth across an unusually broad spectrum. The strike of doctors in California seeking more reasonable malpractice insurance is an example of group action that accepts limited disciplines to achieve a particular end. But the largest groups are what might be called the "professional unions": nurses, doctors, teachers, airline pilots, professional football players, and a host of others.

It is the power that these disciplined self-interest groups can bring to bear that poses the problem for industry management in the years ahead. Too many aggressive young executives are aware of what organized self-interest has accomplished for other groups to assume that they will long ignore this potent weapon where their own interests are at stake.

It is true, of course, that some executives are already members of a group that speaks for their career interest. However, like engineers who have moved up to become executives while retaining their engineering association membership, these groups speak loudest for their lower-level members. In other words, the self-interest factor is substantially diluted where the executive is concerned in most such groups.

Historically, the mystique involved in "being an executive" has been adequate to squelch any enthusiasm for executive unions. And it has been reinforced by the relative certainty of being passed over for promotion in the event such a nonsensical idea surfaced with your name attached.

However, this historic discipline, too, could change. For example, if the promotion rate among the lower ranks of executives should slow down substantially during the years ahead, the risk-reward relationship for the individual executive might be altered enough to tip the scale in favor of accepting the risks of organizing. Or perhaps the right of management to withhold a promotion because of the organizational activity of a junior executive might be successfully challenged.

Indeed, conditions point to both alternatives as real possibilities. In the next five years, the number of 30- to 34-year-olds will increase 24%, and by 1985 this age group will be 45% larger than it is today. This is unquestionably the biggest expansion that this "executive entry" age group has ever experienced. Hence, the chances of a promotional slowdown among younger executives appear to be almost a certainty.

On the second point, management's promotion decisions are being attacked in the courts by both women and minority groups. These suits typically maintain that management passed over the individuals for promotion because it did not weigh their ability and contributions on the same scale as those of the white male—in other words, that sex or color prejudiced the decision against them. The same general arguments could be used in support of the passed-over executive who was organizing an "association" of executives.

THE DISCONTENTED MIDDLE

Obviously, the higher the responsibility level of the executive, the less he needs an organization to further his interests. Future executive organizational efforts, therefore, are likely to occur in the middle ranks of management. It would also seem likely that, to be successful, such an organization of executives would have to embrace functions that were both numerous and important to corporate profitability. Chain-store managers, department store buyers, regional sales managers,

product managers, and key manufacturing managers fall into this category.

How such an executive union would pursue its self-interest objectives obviously depends on conditions existing at the time. However, it
seems reasonable to expect that no such union would be organized at
all unless the jobs or pay levels of those middle-management executives were threatened. A flood of cut-rate job applicants might make
jobholders uneasy. Or perhaps the promotion rate of young executives
would prove to be far below their "expectation level."

Since population trends indicate that both conditions are likely to
occur at some point during the coming decade, top management in the
not too distant future may well find itself coping with that ultimate
weapon of self-interest—collective bargaining—among its executive
personnel.

Professionals Go Union

Jack Golodner

America has been a white-collar country for some time. By 1980, it is
projected, more Americans will be employed in white-collar jobs than
in the blue-collar, farm and service categories combined.

By 1968, one segment of that white-collar group—professional and
technical people—numbered 10.3 million and exceeded the total
number of foremen and craftsmen in the labor force. Today, they comprise the third largest job classification after clerical workers and semi-
skilled operatives. By 1980 they will number 15.5 million and equal 16.3
percent of total employment. The professional group is the fastest-
growing occupational sector in the economy and will grow by 40 percent in this decade while the entire labor force grows by only 20 percent.

The category of sales people is the next fastest-growing element in
the white-collar sector—it will grow about 30 percent over the decade.

These shifts in the relative size of occupational groups mirror a very
profound change occurring in the structure of our economy.

Economists, statisticians and others who study our society com-
partmentalize economic activity in two sections — goods-producing
and service-producing. Goods-producing industries are manufactur-

From Jack Golodner, "Professionals Go Union," *American Federationist*
(October 1973), pp. 6–8. Reprinted by permission.

ing, construction, mining and agriculture. Service-producing industries include transportation, public utilities, trade, finance, health, entertainment, recreation, communications, education, computer services and government research.

In 1950, the United States began to employ a majority of its wage and salary workers in the service-producing area. It was the first country to do so and is still the only country to do so. Since 1950, the increase in the number of service-producing employes has grown to the point where today 2 of every 3 workers are engaged in providing a service rather than a product. By 1980, 70 percent of all workers will be in the service industries.

The service industries have been and are today the largest employers of white-collar people. This shift in the relative importance of industries from goods-producing to service-producing is in large measure responsible for the rising tide of white-collar workers.

But even within the goods-producing sector, another revolution is taking place. As a result of various technological changes, the relative strength in numbers of the production worker is diminishing while the number of white-collar people is increasing at an accelerating rate. In aircraft manufacturing, for example, production workers equaled 74 percent of the workforce in 1943. But in 1968, they were down to 55 percent. The same trend is evident in machinery, electrical equipment and motor vehicles.

Recently, an official of the Steelworkers commented that the decrease of production and maintenance employes in the labor force may reach a point where some day white-collar workers might outnumber production and maintenance employes in steel. "Future membership strength of the Steelworkers," he said, "depends upon more organization of office and technical workers."

This jibes with another comment by an official of an electrical union, who says "the future life and growth of the labor movement lies with the unionization of the professional, technical and white-collar salaried workers."

The fact that unions found their first roots among the blue-collar occupations when they were the predominant employe group has been interpreted by some as an indication that unions are peculiar only to these groups of workers. This is a bit of whistling in the dark by management people and by those academicians who would like unions to wither away and stop bothering their patrician view of society.

The roots of unionism grew where the people were and where the conditions were such as to provide a need for collective action among individual employes. The people are now in the white-collar fields and the conditions for unionism—the same conditions that prompted organization by blue-collar people—are developing in the white-collar fields as well.

The process by which it occurs to today's new force of white-collar workers that they, too, need a union is sometimes gradual. One New York Teachers official tells the story of the early 1960s when most of his would-be constituents thought a union was the last thing they wanted; they had just graduated from their family's blue-collar, union background and "advancing beyond the need" for unions became a status symbol for the educated professionals.

But by 1967, when the stresses of the big city, conflicts over the municipal budget and a generally tumultuous time left the teachers with low pay and without an effective voice, those same individuals began to flock to the Teachers banner.

Some of the conditions which bother professionals are susceptible to correction by management. But, by and large, many that are most crucial to the employe are beyond the means of management to change.

Among the developing conditions encouraging the growth of white-collar unions today is the growing loss of individuality by the typical white-collar employe.

Being employed in large numbers by rapidly growing and diversifying institutions or corporations means he is slowly but surely becoming removed from participation in decision-making processes. It means an individual voice—no matter how knowledgeable—no longer counts. Large areas of judgment once controlled by the individual employe are sacrificed to the logic and formalities of mass organization.

Individual bargaining power and the ability to insist on participation in the setting of salaries and working conditions is declining. When the individual white-collar worker has a share in the control of the job, the nature of the work assignment, methods and pace, his individual task can be recognized and becomes the basis for individual bargaining. Large organizations remove this control or dilute it so the individual contribution is small relative to the total enterprise. Thus, his personal stamp is obliterated.

Rationalization, specialization, and computerization all conspire to make the large employing organization both possible and necessary, but they also separate the employe from the service and from meaningful participation in the process.

In every place, in every occupation where this bureaucratization of work has occurred, there are things which management has done or is doing and must do in its own behalf which produce a counter move in the form of collective action by those who are managed.

The crafts—because they were the earliest to be affected by this process—organized into unions. We tend to forget that craftsmen of an earlier time had great status in society. Work to the pre-industrial revolution craftsman was diverse—gathering esteem by its very individuality and providing satisfaction in creative achievement. There was dignity in the act of working. But the industrial revolution brought about new institutional demands. The craftsman was subjected to the harsh disciplines of the factory. Spontaneity, exuberance, freedom to perform, identification with the product which at one time made work, play and culture virtually synonymous were lost and the status, dignity and respect of the craftsman could no longer be maintained at the work place without organization.

And in the professions, as their industries and jobs came increasingly under the control of bureaucracies, actors, musicians and other performing artists—then journalists, broadcasters, teachers, social workers and university professors—adapted the tools of unionism to their special needs. The old "Don't Tread on Me" flag was raised against management and, like the early colonists, these white-collar professionals discovered that only by organizing and uniting with others in common cause could they make this slogan meaningful.

The dignity of the worker, white collar or blue collar, faced with societal changes beyond his control, is preserved by a contract that assures him of fair treatment, rehire rights, adequate severance pay, protected pension and other retirement benefits. These are things that can only be won through unions.

A worker can be recycled by a society that makes continuing education and retraining available. The process is made possible by governments that are sensitive to the needs of men and women who are laid off because they have been caught up in the rapid changes of the time.

And, as the employing institutions have grown and as the mechanisms of the economy have become more complex, government has grown apace. Today, it, too, confronts the unorganized individual as an indifferent, impregnable fortress of modern bureaucratic control and it can only be stormed by men and women who have marshaled their collective strength through organization with their colleagues and have lengthened their shadow through alliances with others in the AFL-CIO.

Labor's lobby has served the organized blue-collar worker well. It is serving the white-collar worker as well and will serve him even more as the current trend of white-collar workers into unions continues.

Another fact of contemporary life that is leading a growing number of white-collar people to unions is the steady decline in relative and real income among the unorganized in the white-collar occupations. They must live with the lag in salary increases which come after the unionized sectors of the economy get a raise and before it's passed on to them voluntarily by management. With inflation booming ahead, these people are hurting.

Furthermore, the gap between salaries paid white-collar professionals, sales and technical people and wages paid to operatives and laborers is narrowing. And the gap in net income is further reduced by taxes. In Sweden, unionized white-collar workers are beginning to make salary demands based on net pay—after taxes—rather than on gross pay.

Even engineers and scientists—people heretofore indifferent to unions—are slowly becoming aware of the fact that they are losing economic ground. In a letter to the editor of a journal for chemists, the writer, a chemist, suggests:

"Let's compare a blue-collar carpenter with a Ph.D. chemist. . . . The carpenter serves as an apprentice (tough work and paltry wages) for three or four years. The chemist is dragged kicking and screaming through the blood, sweat and tears of technical school (sacrificing seven or eight years and up to $100,000 in collegiate expenses and lost earning power). Both are subjecting themselves to academic flagellation—but only the chemist has to buy his own whip! And the magic connotation of a professional title quickly fades the day a $15,000 Ph.D. shops for a house built by $15,000 carpenters, plumbers and electricians. . . . While true, the technical student starts out on top salarywise, this differential quickly vanishes and often reverses itself in a few years."

The myth that professional people—the so-called snobs of the white-collar field—do not join unions is evaporating. The teachers and their successes in the face of anti-union laws governing public employes remind one of the early days of our largest and strongest blue-collar unions. They are jailed, they are enjoined, they are blacklisted. But they are building a union that could become one of the AFL-CIO's largest within this decade. The college campuses are ablaze with activity.

The technicians and professionals, often highly paid, in the entertainment-arts-communications conglomerate have built strong unions in their fields and they are active in them. Professional athletes, nurses—even medical doctors—are organizing along union lines.

A major mistake that is made in the broad analysis of the "new" groups that will never join unions is in thinking of broad categories of jobs, like white-collar, as being prestigious and high-paying. They aren't—there are a lot of white-collar people who face the same frustrations and low pay that drove the craftsmen of a century ago to organize.

The Department of Labor reports that in 1970 some 21 million members of unions or employe organizations in the United States engaged in collective bargaining. Of these, nearly 22 percent, or 5 million, were in the white-collar category.

As for the myth that professional people do not join unions or engage in collective bargaining, note that nearly 3 million of the 5 million organized white-collar workers in that 1970 survey were professional and technical people. This numbers more than 20 percent of all professional and technical people in the country and approximately 40 percent of the organizable potential—that is, excluding the self-employeds, the clergy, doctors, dentists, veterinarians and judges.

A British commentator, Alan Flanders, once noted, "The value of a trade union to its members lies less in its economic achievements than in its capacity to express their dignity.

"Viewed from this angle, employes—white-collar and professional workers, no less than manual workers—have an interest in union organization, however favorable their economic circumstances or the state of the labor market, for at least two reasons:

"They are interested in the regulation of labor management because such regulation defines their rights,their status and security and so liberates them from dependence on chance and the arbitrary will of management. They are equally interested in participating as directly as possible in the making and administration of these rules in order to have a voice in shaping their own destiny."

In a world where individuals search for the strength to be a part of the action, in a society where people want again to feel important and listened to, the union has achieved new importance.

The unorganized white-collar worker of today has no voice in his destiny. A growing number of AFL-CIO unions are helping him win such a voice through collective bargaining and effective political action.

How to Get Along—and Ahead—in the Office

Lockheed Missiles & Space Co. appointed Judith A. Schliessmann manager of manufacturing engineering last month. Promptly, 30 shop employees threatened to strike and 15 engineers requested transfers. Never, they said, would they work for a woman.

Reprinted from the March 22, 1976 issue of *Business Week* by special permission. © 1976 by McGraw-Hill, Inc.

The crisis fizzled out within the day. Management stood firm, and everybody stayed put. Today, six weeks later, a warily tactful Schliessmann runs a reasonably harmonious department at Lockheed's Sunnyvale (Calif.) plant. The uproar that was set off, however, illustrates the kind of problem that can erupt as women rise into corporate ranks formerly occupied exclusively by men. The dilemmas range from who gets the promotion to who lights the cigarette and, serious or trivial, they affect both personal careers and company operations.

But slowly, case by case, pragmatic solutions are evolving. In a real sense, they constitute a series of dos and don'ts for corporate women and their male associates, falling naturally into three categories: women's status as managers, their competence as managers, and their behavior as managers.

For men executives	*For women executives*
Do	Do
Be as supportive or critical of a woman as of a man	Plan your career and take risks
Practice talking to her if you are self-conscious	Stress your ambition. Ask "What can I do to get ahead?"
Let her open the door if she gets there first	Speak at least once in every 10-minute meeting
Tell your wife casually about a woman peer	Take the chip off your shoulder
	Don't
Don't	Say "I worked on . . ." when you wrote the entire report
Make a fuss when appointing the first woman	Imitate male mannerisms—or do needlepoint at meetings
Tune her out at meetings	Hang on to the man who trained you
Say "Good morning, gentlemen—and lady"	Leap to serve coffee when someone suggests it's time for a break
Apologize for swearing	

STATUS

"Anything that assumes women are different just because they're women has to be wrong," says Irma M. Wyman, director of technical programs at Honeywell Information Systems Inc. in Waltham, Mass. Seeing women as different distorts personnel decisions, and treating women differently undermines them, which undermines their work.

In Philadelphia, a male middle manager describes the process. His female department head never gets invited to meetings upstairs, as her predecessor did, and she clearly lacks top management support, he says; she cannot even get replacements quickly. "She feels such an outsider that sometimes she backs down when she shouldn't," he says. This affects her subordinates, he says. "If your boss has no influence, your department has no influence, so why go all-out?"

Different treatment also hurts working relations, says Wyman;

"Good morning, gentlemen . . . and lady" reduces her ability to operate in a peer group.

Top executives can integrate a woman into the corporate structure instead of setting her apart, says Barbara Boyle, president of Boyle Kirkman Associates, a New York management consultant firm specializing in women. They can skip the huzzahs over naming the first woman, she says, in order to prevent antagonisms; they can clarify her place in the hierarchy to ensure that her male peers treat her as an equal; they can support her as firmly as they would a man; and they can criticize her freely, both to help her develop and to avoid creating an artificial relationship. If they feel awkward talking with her, Boyle advises practice.

Selective deafness

As unwilling experts on differentiation, most women managers fiercely resent the social slights, social confusions, and even the social courtesies they encounter as women—all signs of the special status they are trying to lose. They cite exclusion from casual gatherings, selective deafness (no suggestion is heard till a man makes it, runs the common plaint), and the maddening uncertainty about who opens the door, who leaves the elevator first, and similar questions.

The common sense answer, says Arlen H. Towsey, vice-president and manager of training and development at United California Bank in Los Angeles, is: "Whoever arrives at the door first opens it. Whoever stands in front of the elevator gets off first. A woman in a business situation absolutely opens her own car door and lights her own cigarette. Whoever does the inviting to lunch pays the tab. And men should stop making clumsy little jokes about any of these situations."

To which a chorus of women's voices adds, "Men should also stop apologizing for swearing, which just reminds everyone of the female interloper."

COMPETENCE

"Women," says the head of a Boston-based financial service institution, "tend not to be aggressive. They shrink from it. It's their biggest handicap."

"They can't even finish a two-minute brag," says management consultant Boyle, referring to a Boyle/Kirkman training technique for women moving up. "They say, 'I'm rather good at . . .' when they're the best in the department and, 'I did some work on . . .' when they wrote the report. Then they run out of steam. A mediocre man can go on bragging for hours."

Aggressiveness—vital to corporate success but "unnatural" to women because it goes against the grain of traditional upbringing—must be proved; no one takes it for granted.

"Be assertive at every business meeting," advises bank official Towsey. "That doesn't mean you dominate, but consciously claim your part. If it's a 10-minute meeting with 10 people, make sure you take up at least a minute. And prove your ambition. If there's a training workshop, sign up."

Have a plan

If the workshop does not lead to better things, says Lockheed's Schliessmann, give corporate processes a push. "Ask for your own career development. Insist that your male supervisors level with you. I've come up with stock questions that I repeatedly ask: 'How am I doing? What can I do to get ahead?' And when I sense it's time, I go in and say, 'I'm tired of this job. I've done it all. I'd like a job like yours.' That removes any doubts your boss may have about your ambition."

Because companies differ, executive success involves more than job performance, warns consultant Boyle. "A woman must learn what the rewarded behavior is in her company—community service, or playing office politics, or being at your desk at 8 o'clock."

Over all, women's biggest hindrance is the timidity that plagues them as a sexist cliché—and sometimes as a reality. "Women executives tend to be too conservative," says Gool Thakarar, manager of industrial relations at General Electric's Reentry & Environmental Systems Div. in Philadelphia. "They're less risk-taking than their male counterparts, which is not good."

Conditioned to leave the decisions to men, many women lack the self-confidence to risk failure, says a woman department head at Polaroid Corp. in Cambridge, Mass. Supportive behavior by male executives can help, she says, but with or without it, women must learn to take decision-making in stride.

They must also accept what women frequently define as ingratitude and what men consider natural growth—leaving their first mentors behind. "Most women were trained by men, and they tend to go on looking up to them," says Kenneth MacKenzie, vice-president for service operations at Jewel Food Stores in Chicago. This freezes them psychologically at a level below the men who trained them.

BEHAVIOR

"Business is essentially a sexless relationship," says Max Ulrich, president of Ward Howell Associates, a New York executive recruiter. "A woman manager should conduct herself as a person, not a female."

"Effecting a pragmatic business style involves some delicate role-playing," says a male vice-president of a service company. "It doesn't mean talking sports incessantly, but it does mean leaving the needlepoint at home." It certainly does not mean copying male mannerisms, says Jewel Food Stores' MacKenzie. He recalls a young woman who missed promotion because she swore hard to show promotability as one of the boys.

Maintaining that delicate balance can be hard work in the face of some male reactions. Men who would never call a male executive "Buddy" sometimes call her "Toots," says the woman vice-president of a Detroit ad agency.

Business contact between men and women can produce sticky situations even when the relationship is friendly. "My boss and I talk frankly," says Patricia Galton, vice-president of Boston's Gray Line Inc., "but he finds it difficult to accept criticism from me, especially in front of other men. He'll tell me afterwards, 'If you were a man, I'd punch you.' But if I were a man, he wouldn't want to."

Taking initiative

Since social tensions handicap women (the minority) more than men (the majority), it makes sense for women to take the initiative in easing them, says Pearl Meyer, executive vice-president of Handy Associates, a New York executives recruiter. She urges women to exercise social leadership even if it means talking about the weather. "You can always move on to what it's done to your golf game," she says. "He can probably take it from there."

But do not, says Meyer firmly, ease a social situation by slipping into the traditional role of handmaiden. "Women have to stop leaping up every time someone says, 'Let's have some coffee,' " she says. "If that happens, just sit there. If silence descends, look at the person nearest the door."

Other experts advise women managers to plan personally—to decide in advance, for instance, whether they will relocate for advancement. "Don't wait until the day the boss asks you to move from Los Angeles to Cleveland," says Archie C. Purvis Jr., executive vice-president of Lear Purvis Walker & Co., a Los Angeles executive recruiter specializing in women.

And Marianne T. Bachleder, assistant credit administrator with the Bank of America in Los Angeles, suggests that women establish their career commitment before they have children. "Make sure your co-workers and your bosses know you're in for the long haul before you announce you're pregnant," she says. A six-year veteran with the bank, Bachleder expects her first child shortly.

Still others suggest bluntly: Take the chip off your shoulder. "Don't expect the worst," says Towsey. " 'He wouldn't treat me that way if I were a guy' may be true some of the time," he adds, "but not always, and it blocks personal insight.

"Paranoia," he says, "is counter-productive."

How Women's Lib Works
in Billings, Mont.

"We may do it a little nicer, but we are after the same results: equal opportunities and equal successes," says Janet Trask Cox of Billings, Mont. "We don't want to be oddities because we hold certain jobs or run our own businesses."

Cox runs her own business, Exclamation Point!, the second-largest advertising agency in Billings, a city of 65,000 that serves as the state's business capital. She works at her office three days a week. Other days, if necessary, she uses the typewriter on her kitchen table and the telephone on her kitchen wall. She also bakes cookies for her seven-year-old son to take to school. Her agency employs four and generates $230,000 in annual billings.

And that is the look of Women's Lib in the business community of Billings—and in dozens of other cities across the country.

Most people expect something bolder from a movement that seeks to change women's lives. They think in terms of New York and other metropolitan centers, where women have achieved corporate posts denied them for generations, experimented with unconventional marriages that domiciled them 1,000 mi. from their husbands, and won bitter ideological wars over nuances of title and role. These women have made feminist history.

But the women of Billings and its sister cities are also making history, of a kind that harmonizes with their own way of life. It matches neither the visions of radical feminists nor the caricatures sketched by their opponents, but it is real—and important.

SEPARATE PATHS

The quiet ferment in Billings shows that women are moving into corporate life along one path in the metropolises and along a separate but parallel path in small-city America. Billings has its first all-woman law firm and its first woman stockbroker, just as Wichita, Kan., has its first woman real estate developer and Cincinnati, Ohio, its first woman steamship company executive. Five years ago Billings' Junior League (composed mainly of middle-class and upper-class young women) had only one member who earned money, a schoolteacher. Today 10% of its active membership hold jobs or own businesses.

"I am very happy to be a wife and mother and have a husband to take care of me," says Pamela Llewellyn. "But, on the other hand, I want to be free to do my own thing—which I do." Llewellyn runs a for-profit nursery school for 100 children.

"It's happening without a lot of crashing rhetoric," says Christene Cosgriffe Meyers, a reporter for the *Billings Gazette*. "But it's happening."

NEW LIFESTYLES

Like most women far from the militant feminism of the East and West Coasts and the corporate opportunities of a Chicago or Pittsburgh, Billings women are just beginning to venture into the business world. They are starting to sign up for management training (and graduate into first-line management jobs), join professional firms, open their own businesses, and even become company directors. Doris M. Poppler, a partner with Diane G. Barz in the new law firm of Poppler & Barz sits on the board of the Midland National Bank.

To some extent, these activities have changed their lifestyles. Alice Thomas and Polly Eames, new owners of a women's clothing store, never dreamed that they would leave their children to go on buying trips. But they go and love it.

To a much greater extent, however, Billings women have found ways to fit their new activities into the traditional lifestyle they still regard as normal and desirable. Marguerite H. Fink, administrative assistant for special projects at First National Bank & Trust Co., goes home at 3 o'clock in order to spend time with her children, 4, 5, and 6. A former research analyst with the Federal Reserve Board in Washington, D.C., Fink chose First National over a competing bank because it permitted her to work short hours (and offered her a management development program).

The bank made the arrangement because "we're interested in getting high-quality women," says Charles F. Cozzens, vice-president of First National. "We will make further accommodations for young mothers," adds bank president Albert F. Winegardner.

Winegardner concedes readily that the policy is a recent one. "Five years ago, perhaps, we were not as aware of women and their ability as we are now," he says. "Now we realize that we serve a mixed group of people. We had better have a woman's perspective."

RURAL ATTITUDES

Despite this changed attitude—and the enthusiasm of James Bennett, president of First Citizens Bank, for Janet Cox's light-hearted ads about "no-account bankers"—few business observers expect women to achieve quick acceptance.

"Any place in this rural world, it's going to take time," says Gale Crowley, senior partner of Crowley, Kilbourne, Haughey, Hanson & Gallagher, Billings' largest law firm. "Outside the big population areas, we still have a limited number of women in business and, until more of the public comes into contact with them, it's going to be tougher for women than for men," he says. Crowley accepts Poppler & Barz right now. "They are very good attorneys," he says.

Personally, Billings men appear proud of their working wives. "I knew Janet couldn't be just a housewife," says real estate broker Leslie C. Cox.

But if Billings' new businesswomen are not *just* housewives, they are emphatically *still* housewives. They cook, clean house (with or without outside help), arrange for child care with a babysitter, nursery school, or neighbor, and accept responsibility for the smooth functioning of their homes. Husbands contribute only occasional babysitting and a willingness to eat canned soup.

Nobody seems to object. Polly Prchal, director of the Billings Convention & Visitors Bureau, dismisses the big-city notion of a male share in homemaking to match the female share in bread-winning with the comment: "Even if some Billings couple accepted the idea, their neighbors wouldn't."

NO MS. IN BILLINGS

In general, Billings businesswomen pointedly disassociate themselves from what they conceive of as active feminism. Most recognize "Miss" or "Mrs." rather than "Ms."; in Billings, Gloria Steinem is still "Miss Steinem." Ann Teal, a mother of four who runs two clothing stores, says firmly, "I don't work because I am a woman liberated. I work because I was bored. Women's Lib caught up with me and made it O.K."

But a sociologist who contrasted the current career choices of 135 Billings junior high school girls (only one of whom wants to be a housewife) with the majority vote for housewifery recorded nationally 10 years ago might question her explanation. Liberation comes in various forms, including the freedom to confess boredom with home life. It seems likely that the same social forces that produced militant feminism in avant garde centers such as New York and San Francisco produced Billings' milder version—although publicity from New York and San Francisco probably helped it grow.

Certainly Billings women sound much like New Yorkers or San Franciscans when they talk about their business handicaps.

"You have to work harder than your male peers," says Opal R. Eggert, a broker with the investment firm of Dain, Kalman & Quail, and Montana's first woman stockbroker.

"You have to work harder and be more visible, and, given equal qualifications, a man probably will get the job anyway because you're No. 2," says Barz.

"I earn less than the man who had this job before me," says a woman manager. "But I'd jeopardize my career if I made a fuss."

"They don't sit around the Hilands Club talking about a project and ask old Janet about handling the advertising because old Janet isn't there," says Janet Cox. Billings' most prestigious country club admits women (unlike the Petroleum Club, the premier luncheon club, which bars them till 1:30 p.m.), but lightning would probably strike the first woman who dared join the businessmen who congregate there.

If anyone ever challenges the taboo, it will probably be old Janet. A former editor with McCall Corp. in New York City, she came home to Billings and founded Exclamation Point! in 1969, several years before the current upsurge in female business activity.

"For a long time, nobody took me seriously," she recalls. "People would say, 'You don't work in the summer, do you?' Can you imagine anyone saying to my husband, 'You don't work in the summer, do you?' Even now they ask me who takes care of my children. You'd think I strap them into two little chairs and go out." For the record, Cox leaves her five-year-old daughter with a neighbor when she sends her son to school.

Looking ahead, George Selover, president of the Billings Chamber of Commerce, predicts that the region's frontier heritage will ease women's entry into the corporate world. "Both sexes had to work together, sharing the load equally, and it's continued that way," he says. "I think there's a favorable feeling toward women in business."

Some women apparently inspire more favorable feelings than others. "The better-looking the woman, the better job she can get," says Mike Kuchera, president of Billings' Furniture & Appliance Corp.

BLUE-COLLARS GET THE EDGE

So far, blue-collar women appear to have benefited most from Western habits of self-reliance. Billings women drive cabs, repair cars, and work on construction crews. The area even has a female fire-fighter, a Crow Indian. Women employees at the Pierce Packing Co. plant recently won an Equal Employment Opportunity Commission case that raised their pay scales to male levels.

Billings businesswomen do not expect to linger far behind. Barz, the only woman in the Class of 1968 at the University of Montana's Law School, notes that the present 214-member class includes 30 women. Cox and Eggert report that increasing numbers of young women ask them about careers in advertising and investments. If the last five years have marked great changes, they say, the next five will mark even bigger ones.

"Oh, we won't have a woman as head of the Chamber of Commerce by then, and who knows when we'll have a woman president of a bank?" says Cox. "But I see a growing number of women going to work and going back to work. More and more women will be doing what interests them, whether it's being a lineman for the telephone company or moving up the ladder in business."

Chances are they will also be baking cookies.

GETTING RID OF 65-AND-OUT

"Mandatory retirement at age 65," says Dr. Arthur S. Flemming, former Secretary of Health, Education & Welfare, "is just a lazy man's device to avoid making a difficult personnel decision."

Flemming, 70, heads HEW's Administration on Aging, one of the fastest-growing social agencies in the federal government. Along with other organizations representing older Americans, it is pressing for abolition of the 65-and-out rule—the actuarial bedrock of corporate pension plans, health insurance, and personal careers—as No. 1 on a long list of legislative goals. Last week the House subcommittee on aging held hearings on a bill that would achieve this end by including over-65ers in the law forbidding job discrimination against the aged, a category that now spans those 45 to 65. The bill would also open up pension plans that require retirement at 65.

Although 47 congressmen joined Representative Paul Findley (R-Ill.) in sponsoring the bill, no one expects it to meet instant success. Aside from its complicating effect on benefits programs, open-ended retirement inspires mixed feelings in industry, with some companies easing employees toward early retirement while others laud the work of employees over 65. At the same time, inflation has motivated many older workers to keep working to escape the hardships of life on a shrunken pension, swelling the ranks of those who work as a matter of lifestyle.

IN THE GROOVE

"Time doesn't change our habits of self-discipline or teamwork," says Hoyt Catlin, 85, who runs Fertl Inc., a $600,000-a-year plant nursery in South Norwalk, Conn. "We've had less absenteeism and turnover than any firm of our size that I know," says Catlin, whose workers average 68 years of age.

Reprinted from the March 1, 1976, issue of *Business Week* by special permission. © 1976 by McGraw-Hill, Inc.

"I think there are some things we can learn from Fertl," says C. Richard Blundell, vice-president of personnel at General Foods Corp., which acquired the nursery in 1972. General Foods has not changed its own mandatory retirement policy, says Blundell, but "obviously, we have some thoughts about it, very much so." The big question, he believes, is whether older people would function as well in a large work environment as in the intimate 20-person Fertl.

Similar considerations apparently trouble other employers. Richard Dugdale, research director of the Mountain States Employers Council in Denver, reports a trend toward relaxation of mandatory retirement in the companies he surveys—but mainly in companies that employ fewer than 500 workers. Half of this group now has open-ended retirement, says Dugdale, compared with only 14% among companies that employ more than 500 workers. "Smaller firms are better equipped to set the retirement age on individual performance," he says.

In practice, the decision generally is mutual, says a spokeswoman for Paddock Corp., a Chicago-area newspaper publisher whose 400 employees have no mandatory retirement age. "Around the time we begin to feel that a worker is not performing up to par, it generally dawns on him that he is getting tired and is ready to leave," she says.

MATTER OF CHOICE

This issue of personal choice explains the mass support among older Americans' groups for abolishing mandatory retirement. With links to labor, the National Council of Senior Citizens might be expected to favor enabling workers to retire earlier rather than later, and so it does. But President Nelson Cruikshank, a former AFL-CIO official, emphasizes that the worker who wants to keep working past 65 should have that option.

In fact, some theorists of the movement equate mandatory retirement with racial and sex discrimination. The law forbids an employer to reject a minority or female applicant as unqualified for a job unless he proves the applicant unqualified. They say it should also forbid him from rejecting—retiring—an elderly worker unless he proves him unqualified.

Such theories have more than a theoretical importance because the people who hold them wield increasing power through organizations ranging from the militant Gray Panthers to the sedate American Assn. of Retired Persons (AARP). First mobilized during the battle for medicare, which began in 1961, the elderly have become a political force. By Flemming's estimate, more than 11 million Americans over 65 belong to national organizations, compared with 250,000 in 1961.

So far the elderly have been most effective on the local level. In Washington state they forced enactment of a law that opened up the books of nursing homes. In Chicago they helped defeat a proposed utility rate increase and persuaded some 1,000 Chicago merchants to give them discounts of 10% to 25% under a program called PRIDE (Persons Retired in Dignity & Esteem). In addition, National Tea Co. offers discounts on food and drugs. In Houston, where retirees were successful in pressuring the city into reducing their bus fares, leader Henry A. Sherman warns, "Now come the gas, telephone, and electric companies."

FULL-TIME OCCUPATION

"Retirement has become the occupation of being retired," says demographer Richard M. Scammon, coauthor of *The Real Majority*. With time on their hands, the elderly can write letters, make phone calls, organize caravans to Washington or City Hall, and stage demonstrations. President Ford reluctantly released $375 million for loans to build housing for the elderly after the Senior Citizens threw a picket line around the headquarters of the Housing & Urban Affairs Dept. last June.

Whether the elderly remember this episode with gratitude or resentment could affect Ford's election. In 1974, citizens above 65 cast 17% of the vote while making up only 14.8% of the electorate.

The two major organizations that represent them are the AARP (directed by John Martin, former commissioner of aging) and the Senior Citizens, which claim 9-million and 3.5-million members respectively. Both organizations accept recruits as young as 55 on the ground that retirement concerns begin at that age.

The Big Two of the elderly split on some issues. They back different versions of national health insurance, and the Senior Citizens regularly criticizes the AARP for its continuing ties to Philadelphia's Colonial Penn Life Insurance Co., which seems to have exclusive rights to promote its insurance in AARP publications. But both form a united front for such goals of the elderly as more health services, property tax abatement, a cost-of-living index for pensions, special transportation services, special housing, and liberalization of Social Security—especially increases in the amount that retirees can earn without losing money from their Social Security checks.

PRESSURE PAYS OFF

Increasing political pressure from these and other groups has yielded a steady stream of gains in the form of amendments to the 1965 Older Americans Act, among them the 1972 nutrition program that serves 240,000 daily free meals at an annual cost of $100 million and the recently authorized network of area agencies on aging.

Financed by federal grants passed through the states to local communities, 500 of these agencies are already assessing local needs and mobilizing facilities to meet them. They also serve as "advocates for the aging . . . unique in terms of federal, state, and community relationships," says Flemming. He notes that they have recruited many of the 52,000 volunteers for the free meal program, mainly youngsters.

"There's a real affinity between the young and the old," Flemming remarks. "They have a common enemy—the middle-aged."

A General Strategy for Getting Out of Traps

Samuel A. Culbert

THE MODEL

The model portrays a strategy for gaining greater control of our organization life, a strategy that entails a process of consciousness-raising and self-directed resocialization. In theory, this process can be broken down into five sequential stages, each of which involves a separate consciousness-raising activity. In practice, of course, these five stages can be intermingled and used out of sequence. Where possible, however, the stages should be followed in sequence because the insights developed at one stage provide the beginning points for consciousness-raising at the next stage. Learning at each stage depends on our developing skills and receiving peer group support.

Consciousness-raising can best be accomplished by focusing on a single area of organization concerns and working our way through each of the five stages of the model. Maintaining focus on a single area at a time requires discipline because insights in one area inevitably spark insights in others. Overall, the consciousness-raising process can be likened to eating an artichoke. One starts with the less meaty leaves on the periphery and progressively spirals in toward the more meaty leaves closer to the heart. Unlike eating an artichoke, however, we don't reach the heart, that is, gain control over our organization life; we merely get closer. Each insight paves the way for a meatier realization.

Experience in using this model has shown that a preliminary overview of all five stages facilitates a deeper understanding of each stage. That is the purpose of this chapter. . . .

From *The Organization Trap and How to Get Out of It,* by Samuel A. Culbert, © 1974 by Basic Books, Inc., Publishers, New York.

STAGE 1: RECOGNIZING WHAT'S "OFF"

Consciousness-raising begins with a gut experience. We develop a vague awareness that something in our organization life is "off," although we can't quite put our fingers on exactly what it is. Such feelings of incoherence are frequent occurrences in our organization life, but usually we try to forget about them. However, if we want our consciousness raised, we've got to be ready to pay attention to what seems minor. Closer scrutiny will usually show much more beneath the surface than we saw originally.

Our vague feelings of incoherence serve as clues to identifying discrepancies between our nature and the expectations of the organization system. Such discrepancies usually fall into one of two categories. The first is when the organization seems to expect something that is unnatural for us or inconsistent with our best interests. The second is when we do what comes naturally and learn afterward that it was deemed inappropriate by the system.

Transforming feelings of incoherence into a more precise statement of discrepancies requires some concepts and some emotional support. The concepts will help us pinpoint where we and the organization are in conflict, and the support will help us resist our tendency to shoulder all the blame for these conflicts.

STAGE 2: UNDERSTANDING OURSELVES AND THE ORGANIZATION

Being able to specify discrepancies may make us feel that we can now proceed to solve our problems with the organization and put our minds at ease. Usually, this proves to be a short-sighted strategy. We need to treat discrepancies for what they are, symptoms rather than problems. In practice, taking our conflicts with the organization at face value and "resolving" them can be the surest way to keep from seeing the fundamental ills of the system as we currently live it.

Treating discrepancies as symptoms, on the other hand, helps us to understand aspects of ourselves and the organization that we had not previously recognized. We have a chance to probe beneath the discrepancy by asking ourselves what human qualities and what organization attributes can produce the conflicts we're experiencing.

Transforming discrepancies into new understanding requires skills to think divergently and support to resist our inclinations to think convergently. Divergent thinking keeps us focused on the fact that a discrepancy is a symptom of some lack in basic understanding. The support we get will help us resist our impulses to converge on a solution that prematurely puts our anxieties to rest.

STAGE 3: UNDERSTANDING OUR RELATIONSHIP
WITH THE ORGANIZATION

Greater understanding of ourselves and of the organization system helps us to recognize alternatives that suit our interests and to resist external attempts to control us. We sense a new personal freedom. However, getting carried away by this "freedom" proves to be another short-term strategy for gaining control. It puts us underground, "working" the system. But eventually, those who however unwittingly influence and control us will discover that we've eluded them, and we'll be back playing cat and dog again.

In order to really improve things, we'll need, at some point, to focus directly on our relationship with the organization . The new understanding we developed in Stage 2, about ourselves and the organization, can now be transformed into a more thorough understanding of the assumptions that link us to the organization system. This requires that we learn about our conditioning in the organization and that we get assistance in doing this from people we trust. Some of our biases are so ingrained we will require tough-minded challenging to break through to them.

STAGE 4: MOVING TOWARD A MORE NATURAL LIFE
IN THE ORGANIZATION

Increased understanding of ourselves, the organization, and our relationship with the organization will give us a new sense of power; we can now formulate the types of relationships that will give us greater control over our organization life. But while we can envision more optimal relationships, we do not yet know all that we need to know in order to see whether we can formulate alternatives that express our self-interests and yet appear practical from the standpoint of organization goals.

Transforming understanding of ourselves, the organization, and the assumptions that link us to the organization into practical alternatives also requires new skills and support. We need skills in identifying tensions between assumptions the organization makes about us and the person we're discovering ourselves to be. We need support to help us reflect on personal priorities before getting caught up in our attempts to renegotiate our relationship with the organization.

STAGE 5: AFFECTING THE ORGANIZATION LIVES
OF OTHERS

Being able to envision practical alternatives gives us a great deal of control over our organization life. We derive a new sense of independence from knowing that our options are no longer limited to the best ideas that others have for us. However, as long as others in the organization are still out of control, their spontaneous actions will set off forces that oppose the mutually beneficial directions we may try to take.

Making suggestions that change and improve the organization system requires that we be mindful of the personal realities of all the people affected. To adopt a strategy where we impose our improvements on others runs counter to our reasons for wanting change in the first place. We need to think about change as if we were statesmen concerned with the well-being of all the people. We need support from a peer group that recognizes what we're trying to accomplish and that can help us maintain our focus at times when it's difficult for us to observe the effects our efforts are having.

REFLECTION

This model is applicable to most nontechnical aspects of organization life. It is one attempt to reverse the machinery of a run-away system that influences us without our knowing it.

Gaining control eventually means probing all critical areas of organization life. However, the best place to start is with the area that is currently causing the greatest discomfort. This is where you've got the energy to maintain your focus. Of course, the first area will require the greatest concentration because you'll not only be learning specific things about your organization life but you'll also be acquiring the analytic skills necessary for consciousness-raising. Thus, you can expect a cumulative effect that enables gains made in one area to shorten the work needed in another. Nevertheless, consciousness-raising is a continuing process that requires returning over and over again to the same areas.

Machiavellian Tactics for B-School Students

No doubt about it, his principles were Machiavellian: The 30-year-old hotshot New York banker was dominated by ambition and willing to take calculated risks. Though experienced only as a systems analyst, he was scheming to land a training director's job in a big New York

Reprinted from the October 13, 1975 issue of *Business Week* by special permission. © 1975 by McGraw-Hill, Inc.

bank. He would then report directly to an influential senior vice-president, whom he regarded as capable of speeding his promotions. But the young comer never got the job. He was foiled—out Machiavellied, as it were—by a 25-year-old summer intern, fresh from a controversial new seminar on Machiavellian behavior who torpedoed the banker's chances just for practice—and for fun.

"It was clear that this guy was only interested in the job so he could impress the senior v-p, and there were others far more qualified," explains the student, one of a dozen who attended the first "Machiavelli seminar" last spring at Cornell's Graduate School of Business & Public Administration.

Machiavelli, of course, was the 16th-century Florentine civil servant who wrote *The Prince* and *The Discourses*, handbooks for acquiring and keeping power that have seduced politicians for centuries. In his Seminar in Organization Theory, Cornell's Assistant Professor Arthur J. Kover defines Machiavellian behavior as the strategy of acting dispassionately in one's own self-interest. The aim of his seminar, described as a course in "extra-legitimate and Machiavellian options for organizational behavior," is to equip students not only to recognize Machiavellian behavior in others but also to practice such techniques themselves to hasten their careers.

The summer intern, for instance, had been working closely with the bank's personnel department, which put him in a position to influence promotions such as the one the hotshot young banker wanted. "But I couldn't speak right out against him because things like that have a way of getting back to a person. So when the personnel vice-president asked for my recommendation of the guy, I decided to say nothing. By saying nothing, I blocked him without making an enemy."

Professor Kover, who conceived the idea for the seminar and runs it, explains: "The reality is that power is given only grudgingly in organizations, and people often go after it—sometimes by cruel means." He stresses that Machiavellian behavior need not be cruel or crafty, although Shakespeare seems to say so in *The Merry Wives of Windsor*. "Machiavelli really was not cruel so much as rational," Kover says. "Keeping your nose clean and working hard can be part of a person's strategy, too."

TRADITION

Machiavelli's books, together with Anthony Jay's *Management and Machiavelli* and biographies of Franklin D. Roosevelt and Robert Moses, were some of the readings discussed in last spring's seminar, which Cornell is offering again this school year. The discussion helps its participants to:

• *Recognize conditions that breed the Machiavellian manager.* When a company is big and diverse and the president can no longer keep up with

every department, a power vacuum can develop. The New York banker, for example, saw the training director's job as both a vacuum and a
good place from which to build a power base. If a company is in turmoil
because of chronic losses, a reorganization, or the introduction of a new
product, someone can seize power by promising an improvement.
• *Spot Machiavellian personality traits.* The high-potential Machiavelli
has great self-esteem and great self-confidence. "Many management
consultants have Machiavellian characteristics," says second-year
student Kenneth Traugot, who took the course last spring. He is considering a career in consulting and says the seminar helped him to
understand consultants and how to deal with them. A Machiavellian is
also clear-minded and carefully weighs the risks and benefits of every
move. "And he won't automatically accept any rules or constraints but
examines each before deciding to obey or flout them," Kover says.
• *Identify and learn Machiavellian tactics.* A Machiavellian usually grabs
the heaviest responsibility for himself. He also tries to spend as much
time as possible with the powerful people in the organization. The
banker was up to this. Making alliances is also a ploy. Another
second-year student who took the seminar last spring used this on his
summer job at a California hospital. As a hospital administrator, he
was looked down upon by the medical staff, who sometimes balked at
state regulations he had to enforce. So he sought out the chief of the
medical staff, whom all the doctors respected, gained his confidence,
and worked through him.

Still another tactic, according to Kover, is to move from job to job or
company to company, even without training, as the hotshot banker
was attempting to move from systems analysis to training. A
Machiavelli seldom threatens, attacks, or overextends himself—he is
too calculating. Instead, he measures his rivals and looks for a weakness to exploit.

IS IT RIGHT?

Some B-school faculty members at Cornell who originally rejected
Kover's idea for the seminar are still less than enthusiastic. Thomas M.
Lodahl, professor of administration, still wonders whether it is really
possible to recognize Machiavellian behavior in others, and he is ap-
prehensive about the course's instilling "secretive and tricky" behavior
in students because such tactics eventually lead to a back-lash. He adds,
"If students gain personal insights, I can't see any harm."

Associate Dean David A. Thomas, who is chairman of the curriculum committee and originally a skeptic, has been converted. When
he read the description of the course, he thought it was a "real slap in
the face to businessmen, who get enough criticism for unscrupulous
behavior." Now that it has been offered, Thomas feels differently. "It is

a practical approach," he says. "It is a way to introduce reality into the business school curriculum."

Coming on Strong
Linda Bird Francke with Martin Kasindorf

Joan Lynch, a soft-voiced schoolteacher in her early 40s, couldn't say no to the demands of her principal that she make coffee for the staff. Gary Nelson, a young electrical engineer, felt intimidated by skeptical Air Force officers when he tried to sell them on his aerospace electronics designs. A middle-aged housewife didn't have the nerve to cancel her order with a big moving company, while a young coed confessed her inability to refuse to type her boyfriend's term papers. They—along with 36 other self-doubters—were the frustrated members of an "Assertion Unlimited" workshop in Los Angeles, hoping to reap poise, confidence and self-assurance as an everyday reward.

After experiencing the elitism of "est" and practicing the private mantras of Transcendental Meditation, the meek and the would-be mighty are flocking to the latest panacea of the human-potential movement—Assertiveness Training. Anxious over their inability to function effectively in an impersonal society, men and women are devouring books and crowding into workshops promising instant success in saying no, disarming anger and putting their best foot—or any foot—forward.

CONTROL

In Atlanta, assertiveness training is offered by the Unitarian Church, the Jewish Community Center and the YWCA. In San Francisco, "chutzpa workshops" have taken the Caspar Milquetoast out of several hundred wishy-washy participants. Corporations like AT&T in New York, Procter & Gamble in Cincinnati and aerospace giant TRW Systems, Inc., in Redondo Beach, Calif., are running crowded courses to teach their staffers to stand up for their rights. "People are generally becoming aware of the fact they don't really have control over their own lives," says Maria Del Drago, coordinator of continuing-education programs for women at the University of California Extension. "They don't want to be militant or pushy in a negative way, and assertiveness seems to strike the right note to them."

The message of assertiveness training is a simple one—to teach a person how to get what he or she wants with minimal harm to others. But it is the methods that are most appealing. More training than therapy, the self-assertiveness movement offers simple, practical techniques to change behavior—an approach, some critics say, that is superficial and even potentially dangerous. The techniques are aimed at correcting one's own meek behavior. To ask for a raise, for example, the employee learns literally to place himself in the boss' position, even to the point of rehearsing the dialogue by switching chairs. The subject could also use a tape recorder to modulate a quavering voice or stand in front of a full-length mirror to practice an assertive posture (stand up straight, gaze directly ahead).

The fundamental philosophy behind the behavior is the individual's "bill of rights," or what they call at Atlanta's Assertiveness Training Institute the 3 R's, the Right to Refuse, Request and Right a wrong. Equally fundamental are the exercises which enable a person to risk rejection by saying "no." One such device is the "broken record," in which the aspiring asserter repeats "no" over and over again until the aggressor gives up. Another is "delay of confrontation," asking an angry spouse to put off discussing something until you're less upset.

Assertiveness training was popularly expounded five years ago by two California psychologists, Robert Alberti and Michael Emmons, in their book "Your Perfect Right," which has sold nearly 100,000 copies, but its growth has been a beneficiary of the women's movement—a "how to" sequel to consciousness-raising groups. Women tend to outnumber men in most assertiveness workshops by two to one, and, says Chicago psychotherapist Hannah Frisch, their particular assertiveness problems include talking less than men in group situations, not expressing disagreement, not asking for clarification when confused and not elaborating on their points. "As women, we are reinforced and complimented by being non-assertive," says Karen Coburn, 34, director of counseling at Fontbonne College in St. Louis and co-author of the recently published feminist book *The New Assertive Woman*. "A man won't be admired by society if he's a pushover. It makes his image less masculine."

For living-room trainees, there is a plethora of how-to-assertyourself books popping up on the market, with such supportive titles as *Stand Up, Speak Out, Talk Back!*, *I Can If I Want To*, and *Don't Say Yes When You Want to Say No*, which was published in April and is now in its third printing. But critics warn that do-it-yourself assertiveness may be nothing more than a dangerous fad. "Not every attempt is going to succeed," says Dr. Richard Bootzin, a behavioral psychologist at

Northwestern University. "A person will either not be adequately prepared for failure or he may misapply it in some way." Psychologist Richard Farson, the former Esalen president who himself delved into TM and "est," considers assertiveness training superficial. "Generally, human beings can only be trained for unimportant things," he says. "You can learn to return a bad steak through assertiveness training, but training is not something that can solve life's problems."

TIMID

Other social scientists, however, say that assertiveness doesn't go far enough in its training. Psychologist George Bach, 55, author of *Creative Aggression: The Art of Assertive Living*, believes that the aggressive nature of human beings should be recognized and ritualized into "fair fights" (in Bach's workshops, husbands and wives fight with sponge bats). "Assertiveness is most useful for the shy and timid underdog," he says. "It's very limited because it primarily tells you how to say 'no' and 'I want.' It does not tell you how to deal with anger." Robert Ringer, author of the best-selling *Winning Through Intimidation*, is equally unmoved by the polite manipulations of the assertive crowd. "I don't think there is any such thing as right and wrong," says the ex-real-estate salesman whose book, rejected by ten publishers, has sold 165,000 hardback copies and earned him more than $1 million. "Good is what I do and bad is what you do."

That's just the kind of approach that deeply disturbs many people. "It's a new name for an old approach: how to be a dictator and rule your own block," says Bruce Danto, a Detroit psychiatrist. "The problem is to maximize a person's ability to develop genuine relationships, not to teach people how to intimidate." All that will do, Danto notes, is add up to more best sellers: books that will teach people how to deal with intimidating personalities.

Señor Payroll
William E. Barrett

Larry and I were Junior Engineers in the gas plant, which means that we were clerks. Anything that could be classified as paper work came to the flat double desk across which we faced each other. The Main

Office downtown sent us a bewildering array of orders and rules that were to be put into effect.

Junior Engineers were beneath the notice of everyone except the Mexican laborers at the plant. To them we were the visible form of a distant, unknowable paymaster. We were Señor Payroll.

Those Mexicans were great workmen: the aristocrats among them were the stokers, big men who worked Herculean eight-hour shifts in the fierce heat of the retorts. They scooped coal with huge shovels and hurled it with uncanny aim at tiny doors. The coal streamed out from the shovels like black water from a high pressure nozzle, and never missed the narrow opening. The stokers worked stripped to the waist, and there was pride and dignity in them. Few men could do such work, and they were the few.

The Company paid its men only twice a month, on the fifth and on the twentieth. To a Mexican, this was absurd. What man with money will make it last 15 days? If he hoarded money beyond the spending of three days, he was a miser—and when, Señor, did the blood of Spain flow in the veins of misers? Hence it was the custom for our stokers to appear every third or fourth day to draw the money due to them.

There was a certain elasticity in the Company rules, and Larry and I sent the necessary forms to the Main Office and received an "advance" against a man's pay check. Then, one day, Downtown favored us with a memorandum:

"There have been too many abuses of the advance-against-wages privilege. Hereafter, no advance against wages will be made to any employee except in a case of genuine emergency."

We had no sooner posted the notice when in came stoker Juan Garcia. He asked for an advance. I pointed to the notice. He spelled it through slowly, then said, "What does this mean, this 'genuine emergency'?"

I explained to him patiently that the Company was kind and sympathetic, but that it was a great nuisance to have to pay wages every few days. If someone was ill or if money was urgently needed for some other good reason, then the Company would make an exception to the rule.

Juan Garcia turned his hat over and over slowly in his big hands. "I do not get my money?"

"Next payday, Juan. On the 20th."

He went out silently and I felt a little ashamed of myself. I looked across the desk at Larry. He avoided my eyes.

In the next hour two other stokers came in, looked at the notice, had it explained and walked solemnly out; then no more came. What we did not know was that Juan Garcia, Pete Mendoza and Francisco Gonzalez had spread the word and that every Mexican in the plant was explaining the order to every other Mexican. "To get the money now, the wife must be sick. There must be medicine for the baby."

The next morning Juan Garcia's wife was practically dying, Pete Mendoza's mother would hardly last the day, there was a veritable epidemic among children and, just for variety, there was one sick father. We always suspected that the old man was really sick; no Mexican would otherwise have thought of him. At any rate, nobody paid Larry and me to examine private lives; we made out our forms with an added line describing the "genuine emergency." Our people got paid.

That went on for a week. Then came a new order, curt and to the point: "Hereafter, employes will be paid ONLY on the fifth and the 20th of the month. No exceptions will be made except in the cases of employes leaving the service of the Company."

The notice went up on the board and we explained its significance gravely. "No, Juan Garcia, we cannot advance your wages. It is too bad about your wife and your cousins and your aunts, but there is a new rule."

Juan Garcia went out and thought it over. He thought out loud with Mendoza and Gonzalez and Ayala, then, in the morning, he was back. "I am quitting this company for different job. You pay me now?"

We argued that it was a good company and that it loved its employes like children, but in the end we paid off, because Juan Garcia quit. And so did Gonzalez, Mendoza, Obregon, Ayala and Ortez, the best stokers, men who could not be replaced.

Larry and I looked at each other; we knew what was coming in about three days. One of our duties was to sit on the hiring line early each morning, engaging transient workers for the handy gangs. Any man was accepted who could walk up and ask for a job without falling down. Never before had we been called upon to hire such skilled virtuosos as stokers for handy gang work, but we were called upon to hire them now.

The day foreman was wringing his hands and asking the Almighty if he was personally supposed to shovel this condemned coal, while there in a stolid, patient line were skilled men—Garcia, Mendoza and others—waiting to be hired. We hired them, of course. There was nothing else to do.

Every day we had a line of resigning stokers, and another line of stokers seeking work. Our paper work became very complicated. At the Main Office they were jumping up and down. The procession of forms showing Juan Garcia's resigning and being hired over and over again was too much for them. Sometimes Downtown had Garcia on the payroll twice at the same time when someone down there was slow in entering a resignation. Our phone rang early and often.

Tolerantly and patiently we explained: "There's nothing we can do if a man wants to quit, and if there are stokers available when the plant needs stokers, we hire them."

Out of chaos, Downtown issued another order. I read it and whistled. Larry looked at it and said, "It is going to be very quiet around here."

The order read: "Hereafter, no employe who resigns may be rehired within a period of 30 days."

Juan Garcia was due for another resignation, and when he came in we showed him the order and explained that standing in line the next day would do him no good if he resigned today. "Thirty days is a long time, Juan."

It was a grave matter and he took time to reflect on it. So did Gonzalez, Mendoza, Ayala and Ortez. Ultimately, however, they were all back—and all resigned.

We did our best to dissuade them and we were sad about the parting. This time it was for keeps and they shook hands with us solemnly. It was very nice knowing us. Larry and I looked at each other when they were gone and we both knew that neither of us had been pulling for Downtown to win this duel. It was a blue day.

In the morning, however, they were all back in line. With the utmost gravity, Juan Garcia informed me that he was a stoker looking for a job.

"No dice, Juan," I said. "Come back in 30 days. I warned you."

His eyes looked straight into mine without a flicker. "There is some mistake, Señor," he said. "I am Manuel Hernandez. I work as the stoker in Pueblo, in Santa Fe, in many places."

I stared back at him, remembering the sick wife and the babies without medicine, the mother-in-law in the hospital, the many resignations and the rehirings. I knew that there was a gas plant in Pueblo, and that there wasn't any in Santa Fe; but who was I to argue with a man about his own name? A stoker is a stoker.

So I hired him. I hired Gonzalez, too, who swore that his name was Carrera, and Ayala, who had shamelessly become Smith.

Three days later, the resigning started.

Within a week our payroll read like a history of Latin America. Everyone was on it: Lopez and Obregon, Villa, Diaz, Batista, Gomez, and even San Martin and Bolivar. Finally Larry and I, growing weary of staring at familiar faces and writing unfamiliar names, went to the Superintendent and told him the whole story. He tried not to grin, and said, "Damned nonsense!"

The next day the orders were taken down. We called our most prominent stokers into the office and pointed to the board. No rules any more.

"The next time we hire you *hombres*," Larry said grimly, "come in under the names you like best, because, that's the way you are going to stay on the books."

They looked at us and they looked at the board; then for the first time in the long duel, their teeth flashed white. *"Si, Señores,"* they said. And so it was.

The Catbird Seat
James Thurber

Mr. Martin bought the pack of Camels on Monday night in the most crowded cigar store on Broadway. It was theater time and seven or eight men were buying cigarettes. The clerk didn't even glance at Mr. Martin, who put the pack in his overcoat pocket and went out. If any of the staff at F & S had seen him buy the cigarettes, they would have been astonished, for it was generally known that Mr. Martin did not smoke, and never had. No one saw him.

It was just a week to the day since Mr. Martin had decided to rub out Mrs. Ulgine Barrows. The term "rub out" pleased him because it suggested nothing more than the correction of an error—in this case an error of Mr. Fitweiler. Mr. Martin had spent each night of the past week working out his plan and examining it. As he walked home now he went over it again. For the hundredth time he resented the element of imprecision, the margin of guesswork that entered into the business. The project as he had worked it out was casual and bold, the risks were considerable. Something might go wrong anywhere along the line. And therein lay the cunning of his scheme. No one would ever see in it the cautious, painstaking hand of Erwin Martin, head of the filing department of F & S, of whom Mr. Fitweiler had once said, "Man is fallible but Martin isn't." No one would see his hand, that is, unless it were caught in the act.

Sitting in his apartment, drinking a glass of milk, Mr. Martin reviewed his case against Mrs. Ulgine Barrows, as he had every night for seven nights. He began at the beginning. Her quacking voice and braying laugh had first profaned the halls of F & S on March 7, 1941 (Mr. Martin had a head for dates). Old Roberts, the personnel chief, had introduced her as the newly appointed special adviser to the president of the firm, Mr. Fitweiler. The woman had appalled Mr. Martin instantly, but he hadn't shown it. He had given her his dry hand, a look of studious concentration, and a faint smile. "Well," she had said, looking at the papers on his desk, "are you lifting the oxcart out of the ditch?" As Mr. Martin recalled that moment, over his milk, he squirmed slightly. He must keep his mind on her crimes as a special adviser, not on her peccadillos as a personality. This he found difficult to do, in spite of entering an objection and sustaining it. The faults of the woman as a woman kept chattering on in his mind like an unruly witness. She had, for almost two years now, baited him. In the halls, in the elevator, even in his own office, into which she romped now and then like a circus horse, she was constantly shouting these silly questions at him. "Are you lifting the oxcart out of the ditch? Are you tearing up the pea patch? Are you hollering down the rain barrel? Are you scraping around the bottom of the pickle barrel? Are you sitting in the catbird seat?"

It was Joey Hart, one of Mr. Martin's two assistants, who had explained what the gibberish meant. "She must be a Dodger fan," he had said. "Red Barber announces the Dodger games over the radio and he uses those expressions—picked 'em up down South." Joey had gone on to explain one or two. "Tearing up the pea patch" meant going on a rampage; "sitting in the catbird seat" meant sitting pretty, like a batter with three balls and no strikes on him. Mr. Martin dismissed all this with an effort. It had been annoying, it had driven him near to distraction, but he was too solid a man to be moved to murder by anything so childish. It was fortunate, he reflected as he passed on to the important charges against Mrs. Barrows, that he had stood up under it so well. He had maintained always an outward appearance of polite tolerance. "Why, I even believe you like the woman," Miss Paird, his other assistant, had once said to him. He had simply smiled.

A gavel rapped in Mr. Martin's mind and the case proper was resumed. Mrs. Ulgine Barrows stood charged with willful, blatant, and persistent attempts to destroy the efficiency and system of F & S. It was competent, material, and relevant to review her advent and rise to power. Mr. Martin had got the story from Miss Paird, who seemed always able to find things out. According to her, Mrs. Barrows had met Mr. Fitweiler at a party, where she had rescued him from the embraces of a powerfully built drunken man who had mistaken the president of F & S for a famous retired Middle Western football coach. She had led him to a sofa and somehow worked upon him a monstrous magic. The aging gentleman had jumped to the conclusion there and then that this was a woman of singular attainments, equipped to bring out the best in him and in the firm. A week later he had introduced her into F & S as his special adviser. On that day confusion got its foot in the door. After Miss Tyson, Mr. Brundage, and Mr. Bartlett had been fired and Mr.

Munson had taken his hat and stalked out, mailing in his resignation later, old Roberts had been emboldened to speak to Mr. Fitweiler. He mentioned that Mr. Munson's department had been "a little disrupted" and hadn't they perhaps better resume the old system there? Mr. Fitweiler had said certainly not. He had the greatest faith in Mrs. Barrow's ideas. "They require a little seasoning, a little seasoning, is all," he had added. Mr. Roberts had given it up. Mr. Martin reviewed in detail all the changes wrought by Mrs. Barrows. She had begun chipping at the cornices of the firm's edifice and now she was swinging at the foundation stones with a pickaxe.

Mr. Martin came now, in his summing up, to the afternoon of Monday, November 2, 1942—just one week ago. On that day, at 3 P.M., Mrs. Barrows had bounced into his office. "Boo!" she had yelled. "Are you scraping around the bottom of the pickle barrel?" Mr. Martin had looked at her from under his green eyeshade, saying nothing. She had begun to wander about the office, taking it in with her great, popping eyes. "Do you really need *all* these filing cabinets?" she had demanded suddenly. Mr. Martin's heart had jumped. "Each of these files," he had said, keeping his voice even, "plays an indispensable part in the system of F & S." She had brayed at him, "Well, don't tear up the pea patch!" and gone to the door. From there she had bawled, "But you sure have got a lot of fine scrap in here!" Mr. Martin could no longer doubt that the finger was on his beloved department. Her pickaxe was on the upswing, poised for the first blow. It had not come yet; he had received no blue memo from the enchanted Mr. Fitweiler bearing nonsensical instructions deriving from the obscene woman. But there was no doubt in Mr. Martin's mind that one would be forthcoming. He must act quickly. Already a precious week had gone by. Mr. Martin stood up in his living room, still holding his milk glass. "Gentlemen of the jury," he said to himself, "I demand the death penalty for this horrible person."

The next day Mr. Martin followed his routine, as usual. He polished his glasses more often and once sharpened an already sharp pencil, but not even Miss Paird noticed. Only once did he catch sight of his victim; she swept past him in the hall with a patronizing "Hi!" At five-thirty he walked home, as usual, and had a glass of milk, as usual. He had never drunk anything stronger in his life—unless you could count ginger ale. The late Sam Schlosser, the S of F & S, had praised Mr. Martin at a staff meeting several years before for his temperate habits. "Our most efficient worker neither drinks nor smokes," he had said. "The results speak for themselves." Mr. Fitweiler had sat by, nodding approval.

Mr. Martin was still thinking about that red-letter day as he walked over to the Schrafft's on Fifth Avenue near Forty-sixth Street. He got there, as he always did, at eight o'clock. He finished his dinner and the financial page of the *Sun* at a quarter to nine, as he always did. It was his custom after dinner to take a walk. This time he walked down Fifth Avenue at a casual pace. His gloved hands felt moist and warm, his forehead cold. He transferred the Camels from his overcoat to a jacket pocket. He wondered, as he did so, if they did not represent an unnecessary note of strain. Mrs. Barrows smoked only Luckies. It was his idea to puff a few puffs on a Camel (after the rubbing-out), stub it out in the ashtray holding her lipstick-stained Luckies, and thus drag a small red herring across the trail. Perhaps it was not a good idea. It would take time. He might even choke, too loudly.

Mr. Martin had never seen the house on West Twelfth Street where Mrs. Barrows lived, but he had a clear enough picture of it. Fortunately, she had bragged to everybody about her ducky first-floor apartment in the perfectly darling three-story red-brick. There would be no doorman or other attendants; just the tenants of the second and third floors. As he walked along, Mr. Martin realized that he would get there before nine-thirty. He had considered walking north on Fifth Avenue from Schrafft's to a point from which it would take him until ten o'clock to reach the house. At that hour people were less likely to be coming in or going out. But the procedure would have made an awkward loop in the straight thread of his casualness, and he had abandoned it. It was impossible to figure when people would be entering or leaving the house, anyway. There was a great risk at any hour. If he ran into anybody, he would simply have to place the rubbing-out of Ulgine Barrows in the inactive file forever. The same thing would hold true if there were someone in her apartment. In that case he would just say that he had been passing by, recognized her charming house and thought to drop in.

It was eighteen minutes after nine when Mr. Martin turned into Twelfth Street. A man passed him, and a man and a woman talking. There was no one within fifty paces when he came to the house, halfway down the block. He was up the steps and in the small vestibule in no time, pressing the bell under the card that said "Mrs. Ulgine Barrows." When the clicking in the lock started, he jumped forward against the door. He got inside fast, closing the door behind him. A bulb in a lantern hung from the hall ceiling on a chain seemed to give a monstrously bright light. There was nobody on the stair, which went up ahead of him along the left wall. A door opened down the hall in the wall on the right. He went toward it swiftly, on tiptoe.

"Well, for God's sake, look who's here!" bawled Mrs. Barrows, and her braying laugh rang out like the report of a shotgun. He rushed past her like a football tackle, bumping her. "Hey, quit shoving!" she said, closing the door behind them. They were in her living room, which seemed to Mr. Martin to be lighted by a hundred lamps. "What's after you?" she said. "You're as jumpy as a goat." He found he was unable to speak. His heart was wheezing in his throat. "I—yes," he finally brought out. She was jabbering and laughing as she started to help him off with his coat. "No, no," he said. "I'll put it here." He took it off and put it on a chair near the door. "Your hat and gloves, too," she said. "You're in a lady's house." He put his hat on top of the coat. Mrs. Barrows seemed larger than he had thought. He kept his gloves on. "I was passing by," he said. "I recognized—is there anyone here?" She laughed louder than ever. "No," she said, "we're all alone. You're as white as a sheet, you funny man. Whatever *has* come over you? I'll mix you a toddy." She started toward a door across the room. "Scotch-and-soda be all right? But say, you don't drink, do you?" She turned and gave him her amused look. Mr. Martin pulled himself together. "Scotch-and-soda will be all right," he heard himself say. He could hear her laughing in the kitchen.

Mr. Martin looked quickly around the living room for the weapon. He had counted on finding one there. There were andirons and a poker and something in a corner that looked like an Indian club. None of them would do. It couldn't be that way. He began to pace around. He came to a desk. On it lay a metal paper knife with an ornate handle. Would it be sharp enough? He reached for it and knocked over a small brass jar. Stamps spilled out of it and it fell to the floor with a clatter. "Hey," Mrs. Barrows yelled from the kitchen, "are you tearing up the pea patch?" Mr. Martin gave a strange laugh. Picking up the knife, he tried its point against his left wrist. It was blunt. It wouldn't do.

When Mrs. Barrows reappeared, carrying two highballs, Mr. Martin, standing there with his gloves on, became acutely conscious of the fantasy he had wrought. Cigarettes in his pocket, a drink prepared for him—it was all too grossly improbable. It was more than that; it was impossible. Somewhere in the back of his mind a vague idea stirred, sprouted. "For heaven's sake, take off those gloves," said Mrs. Barrows. "I always wear them in the house," said Mr. Martin. The idea began to bloom, strange and wonderful. She put the glasses on a coffee table in front of a sofa and sat on the sofa. "Come over here, you odd little man," she said. Mr. Martin went over and sat beside her. It was difficult getting a cigarette out of the pack of Camels, but he managed it. She held a match for him, laughing. "Well," she said, handing him his drink, "this is perfectly marvelous. You with a drink and a cigarette."

Mr. Martin puffed, not too awkwardly, and took a gulp of the highball. "I drink and smoke all the time," he said. He clinked his glass against hers. "Here's nuts to that old windbag, Fitweiler," he said, and gulped again. The stuff tasted awful, but he made no grimace. "Really, Mr. Martin," she said, her voice and posture changing, "you are insulting our employer." Mrs. Barrows was now all special adviser to the president. "I am preparing a bomb," said Mr. Martin, "which will blow the old goat higher than hell." He had only had a little of the drink, which was not strong. It couldn't be that. "Do you take dope or something?" Mrs. Barrows asked coldly. "Heroin," said Mr. Martin. "I'll be coked to the gills when I bump that old buzzard off." "Mr. Martin!" she shouted, getting to her feet. "That will be all of that. You must go at once." Mr. Martin took another swallow of his drink. He tapped his cigarette out in the ashtray and put the pack of Camels on the coffee table. Then he got up. She stood glaring at him. He walked over and put on his hat and coat. "Not a word about this," he said, and laid an index finger against his lips. All Mrs. Barrows could bring out was "Really!" Mr. Martin put his hand on the doorknob. "I'm sitting in the catbird seat," he said. He stuck his tongue out at her and left. Nobody saw him go.

Mr. Martin got to his apartment, walking, well before eleven. No one saw him go in. He had two glasses of milk after brushing his teeth, and he felt elated. It wasn't tipsiness, because he hadn't been tipsy. Anyway, the walk had worn off all effects of the whisky. He got in bed and read a magazine for a while. He was asleep before midnight.

Mr. Martin got to the office at eight-thirty the next morning, as usual. At a quarter to nine, Ulgine Barrows, who had never before arrived at work before ten, swept into his office. "I'm reporting to Mr. Fitweiler now!" she shouted. "If he turns you over to the police, it's no more than you deserve!" Mr. Martin gave her a look of shocked surprise. "I beg your pardon?" he said. Mrs. Barrows snorted and bounced out of the room, leaving Miss Paird and Joey Hart staring after her. "What's the matter with that old devil now?" asked Miss Paird. "I have no idea," said Mr. Martin, resuming his work. The other two looked at him and then at each other. Miss Paird got up and went out. She walked slowly past the closed door of Mr. Fitweiler's office. Mrs. Barrows was yelling inside, but she was not braying. Miss Paird could not hear what the woman was saying. She went back to her desk.

Forty-five minutes later, Mrs. Barrows left the president's office and went into her own, shutting the door. It wasn't until half an hour later that Mr. Fitweiler sent for Mr. Martin. The head of the filing department, neat, quiet, attentive, stood in front of the old man's desk. Mr. Fitweiler was pale and nervous. He took his glasses off and twiddled them. He made a small, bruffing sound in his throat. "Martin," he said, "you have been with us more than twenty years." "Twenty-two, sir," said Mr. Martin. "In that time," pursued the president, "your work and your—uh—manner have been exemplary." "I trust so, sir," said Mr. Martin. "I have understood, Martin," said Mr. Fitweiler, "that you have never taken a drink or smoked." "That is correct, sir," said Mr. Martin. "Ah, yes." Mr. Fitweiler polished his glasses. "You may describe what you did after leaving the office yesterday, Martin," he said. Mr. Martin allowed less than a second for his bewildered pause. "Certainly, sir," he said. "I walked home. Then I went to Schrafft's for dinner. Afterward I walked home again. I went to bed early, sir, and read a magazine for a while. I was asleep before eleven." "Ah, yes," said Mr. Fitweiler again. He was silent for a moment, searching for the proper words to say to the head of the filing department. "Mrs. Barrows," he said finally, "Mrs. Barrows has worked hard, Martin, very hard. It grieves me to report that she has suffered a severe breakdown. It has taken the form of a persecution complex accompanied by distressing hallucinations." "I am very sorry, sir," said Mr. Martin. "Mrs. Barrows is under the delusion," continued Mr. Fitweiler, "that you visited her last evening and behaved yourself in an—uh—unseemly manner." He raised his hand to silence Mr. Martin's little pained outcry. "It is the nature of these psychological diseases," Mr. Fitweiler said, "to fix upon the least likely and most innocent party as the—uh—source of persecution. These matters are not for the lay mind to grasp, Martin. I've just had my psychiatrist, Dr. Fitch, on the phone. He would not, of course, commit himself, but he made enough generalizations to substantiate my suspicions. I suggested to Mrs. Barrows when she had completed her—uh—story to me this morning, that she visit Dr. Fitch, for I suspected a condition at once. She flew, I regret to say, into a rage, and demanded—uh—requested that I call you on the carpet. You may not know, Martin, but Mrs. Barrows had planned a reorganization of your department—subject to my approval, of course, subject to my approval. This brought you, rather than anyone else, to her mind—but again that is a phenomenon for Dr. Fitch and not for us. So, Martin, I am afraid Mrs. Barrows' usefulness here is at an end." "I am dreadfully sorry, sir," said Mr. Martin.

It was at this point that the door to the office blew open with the suddenness of a gas-main explosion and Mrs. Barrows catapulted through it. "Is the little rat denying it?" she screamed. "He can't get away with that!" Mr. Martin got up and moved discreetly to a point beside Mr. Fitweiler's chair. "You drank and smoked at my apartment," she bawled at Mr. Martin, "and you know it! You called Mr. Fitweiler an old windbag and said you were going to blow him up when you got coked to the gills on your heroin!" She stopped yelling to catch her breath and a new glint came into her popping eyes. "If you weren't such a drab, ordinary little man," she said, "I'd think you'd planned it all. Sticking your tongue out, saying you were sitting in the catbird seat, because you thought no one would believe me when I told it! My God, it's really too perfect!" She brayed loudly and hysterically, and the fury was on her again. She glared at Mr. Fitweiler. "Can't you see how he has tricked us, you old fool? Can't you see his little game?" But Mr. Fitweiler had been surreptitiously pressing all the buttons under the top of his desk and employees of F & S began pouring into the room. "Stockton," said Mr. Fitweiler, "you and Fishbein will take Mrs. Barrows to her home. Mrs. Powell, you will go with them." Stockton, who had played a little football in high school, blocked Mrs. Barrows as she made for Mr. Martin. It took him and Fishbein together to force her out of the door into the hall, crowded with stenographers and office boys. She was still screaming imprecations at Mr. Martin, tangled and contradictory imprecations. The hubbub finally died out down the corridor.

"I regret that this has happened," said Mr. Fitweiler. "I shall ask you to dismiss it from your mind, Martin." "Yes, sir," said Mr. Martin, anticipating his chief's "That will be all" by moving to the door. "I will dismiss it." He went out and shut the door, and his step was light and quick in the hall. When he entered his department he had slowed down to his customary gait, and he walked quietly across the room to the W20 file, wearing a look of studious concentration.

3

ORGANIZATIONAL BODY LANGUAGE

Unobtruſive Aſpectſ in Organizationſ

Typically, we describe what goes on in organizations in terms of their visible or easily recognizable features. For example, we look for explanations as to why workers behave in a certain fashion in the statements and direct actions of the manager, in the contents of company rules or policy directives, or, more subtly, in the way that the work itself is organized. However, there appear to be other, nonobvious, unobtrusive characteristics of organizations which have a significant impact on what people say and do. One might talk of an organizational body language which influences those who are members of the organization.

"What Does Your Office 'Say' About You?" (Preston and Quesada) provides an interesting description of how features such as the size of an office and the way its contents are arranged signal important information about the organization as well as the office incumbent. The tendency of people in organizations to chase the means while losing sight of the intended ends is the subject of "The Activity Trap" (Odiorne). Several subtle organizational influences are described in "Symptoms of Groupthink" (Janis), providing a picture of a web of pressures which can act on individuals to prevent them from behaving independently of others in organizational situations. Edward Jones provides an excellent example of the consequences of unfamiliarity with unobtrusive organizational cues in "What It's Like to Be a Black Manager."

Some of the unintended responses to covert organizational cues go beyond the errors in decision making or in job behavior described by Janis and Jones. They extend to criminal behavior of organizational members which appears to be both initiated and supported by unobtrusive organizational characteristics. Personal experiences of employees are cited by Edwin H. Sutherland in his discussion of "white collar crime." Lane Tracy, in "Postscript to the Peter Principle," suggests the existence of an "organization within an organization," a parahierarchy, hidden from view yet playing an important part in the operation of the recognized or acknowledged organizational hierarchy.

Finally, we turn to an article which links back to the first topic of this section: "The Concept of Status as Practiced in Business Organizations." Michael Mound provides a broad description of the role which status, an often unobtrusive characteristic, plays in shaping behavior in organizations.

What Does Your Office "Say" About You?

Paul Preston
Anthony Quesada

Look around you. Do you realize how much your office reveals about your attitudes, beliefs, and willingness to communicate? The way in which your office is laid out and the ways in which you use your office space tell everyone who comes into it who you are.

Your office communicates through what anthropologists call out-of-awareness communication—an unspoken but nevertheless quite powerful language. Most likely, you are aware of at least one type of unspoken language through the best-seller *Body Language*,* which described different physical—but unconscious—signals that people give out.

Serious students of "body language" (often called kinesics) have investigated the ability to communicate by motions, gestures, postures, and facial expressions. The results of Prof. R. L. Birdwhistell's and other scientists' research in this area have pointed to some important principles about out-of-awareness communication. One major conclusion, for example, is that body languages are not instinctive in human beings, but rather are learned systems of behavior that differ markedly from culture to culture. They have been learned informally and "out of awareness" so that the people of a particular culture generally remain unaware of their participation in transmitting an elaborate—and sometimes unique—system of bodily motions.

Because few of us have exactly the same backgrounds and experiences, we must keep these cultural differences in mind. It is these

*Julius Fast (New York: M. Evans and Co., 1970)—*Ed. note.*

Reprinted by permission of the publisher from *Supervisory Management*, August 1974, © 1974 by AMACOM, a division of American Management Associations.

cultural differences that may interfere with our ability to communicate with others.

For the most part, however, certain symbols and unwritten rules are fairly pervasive in western culture. Among these are the outward representations of status and achievement. Your office, for example, may tell people more about your position in the organizational hierarchy than your job title or salary would.

WHERE DO YOU STAND?

To begin with, the very existence of an office tells a great deal about its occupant—because in any organization, only a relatively small number of its members occupy offices.

An office's size, furnishings, number of windows, number of occupants—all provide information about not only the occupants but the organization itself. In a large manufacturing company, for example, an executive promoted to a new job was transferred to an office at company headquarters. The office to which he was moving had formerly housed a vice-president—although our executive's promotion was to a position lower than that of vice-president.

The new office was well furnished, including wall-to-wall carpeting, paintings, and the other amenities of a high-status business office. Before top management would let the executive occupy his new office, however, they told maintenance to cut a 12-inch strip from the entire perimeter of the carpet. Why? Because wall-to-wall carpets convey a message of position and power in this company and belong exclusively to executives of vice-presidential rank or above. With a single action, the company had put the executive "in his place" and conveyed the message to all his future visitors.

Without such signals, people may feel uncomfortable in their surroundings. Many organizations take advantage of this unwritten code to arrange desks, space, and furniture.

Next to size and furnishings, location is the chief indicator of corporate status. Corner offices—and prime window views—belong only to the top managers. And status goes up—one, two, three—with the number of windows an executive can manage to snare.

Even air-conditioning—originally intended to solve the problem of working in hot, humid weather—has contributed another status problem: Who gets the thermostat? One harassed designer admits to having planted a dummy thermostat control in a particularly insistent executive's office. "Now this guy is really happy. He gets hot or cold simply by twisting the knob in either direction," the designer reports.

The push button is another status symbol. Seated in his high-backed chair (as the back goes down, so does an executive's worth), an astronaut-like executive can operate a multitude of office conditions from his set of panel controls. He can change the quality of lighting, move curtains back and forth, slide away wooden panels to reveal movie or TV screens or chalk boards. He can electrically control the destruction of confidential papers, silently lock doors (any kind of lock denotes status), and switch music on.

PROXIMICS

The study of the relationship between space and communication is called *proximics*. Anthropologists have defined four principal zones of interaction in which people conduct different kinds of interpersonal activities. These zones, which are described by four concentric circles and vary from one culture to another, give scientists an opportunity to evaluate the effects of space on the communication that takes place within different cultures and societies.

The "intimate zone," which extends from each person to about one arm's length, is the area in which people conduct most of their sensitive communication. Only people with close relationships are allowed to enter this zone. Strangers are excluded from it.

We allow a stranger to approach only as close as our "personal zone"—which extends from one arm's length to about three or four feet from the body. It is in this area that we conduct most ordinary business and social activities. Similar to the circle in which people arrange themselves at cocktail parties or social gatherings, the arrangement of an office or work space demonstrates the use of the social zone. Most desks, for example, are wide enough to force people sitting on the opposite side to maintain a face-to-face distance of between four to eight feet.

The "public zone," which extends from eight to ten feet away from the body, is the area that most people ignore—because it is an area over which they have little personal control. People in conversational groups of about eight to ten feet apart, therefore, can effectively block out other activities taking place around them and can concentrate on the activities going on within their more comfortable personal sphere. They may even use such tactics as lowering their voices to exclude strangers or raising their voices to talk above the comments of intruders in order to protect their group's integrity.

DESK ARRANGEMENT

Since space is such an important communication vehicle and affects people in such different ways, you should become more aware of the messages sent out by the arrangement of your office. These nonverbal or out-of-awareness messages to workers, colleagues, and clients condition them to behave quite differently than they would if they were in a coffee shop. The informal messages transmitted from your office, in fact, can hinder your managerial effectiveness or help it.

The way you use your desk, for example—including its size and shape—will affect the images that people form about you. Remember the last time you entered an office? Where were you directed to sit and where did the person whom you visited sit? Your answer will be a function of your position relative to the office's occupant and the importance of your visit to him or her. . . .

OFFICE TERRITORIALITY

In a recent survey of managers in many companies throughout the United States, certain patterns of office territoriality emerged. Each respondent was asked to complete a "personal-space inventory" by indicating on a grid the basic outline of his office, the placement of his furniture and windows, and the positions in which he and his various visitors usually sat. Then each respondent was asked to discuss the reasons for such an arrangement. The results did, indeed, follow a pattern.

In the most common office arrangements, the desk was either centered in the room or touching a wall. Of the respondents, 68 percent indicated one of these two arrangements.

The desk-centered office and its variation—the Throne (see Figure 1)—revealed that the occupant preferred to maintain total control over the communication taking place in his office. They also indicated a highly structured personality—since each person entering such an office must take a chair that has all or part of the desk between him and the occupant. In one situation where the respondent indicated a "throne" arrangement, the back corners of his desk almost touched the adjacent walls—so that in order to get back into his desk, he had to go through a fairly elaborate maneuver. Once behind his "throne," however, he didn't budge until lunch or quitting time.

The desk-touching-a-wall arrangement (Figure 2, this page) signals a somewhat less rigid personality—someone who is willing to allow visitors more freedom to structure and control the communication that takes place in his office. Although chairs are usually arranged so that most of them have some desk surface falling between the visitor and

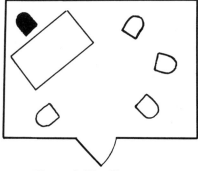

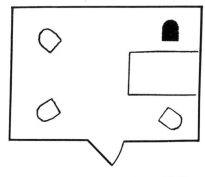

Figure 1: The Throne   **Figure 2: Desk Touching a Wall**

the occupant, the space on the non-wall side of the desk permits fairly close contact. Most of the respondents who chose this arrangement indicated that they preferred it because it left more seating room in the office—and at the same time remained "conventional" in its overall appearance.

Twenty-three percent of the respondents indicated that in some way their desks faced a wall or a window. Their reasons for choosing this arrangement were quite varied. Some of the most common ones: "It makes the office look bigger" (status considerations); "It reduces wasted space" (practical considerations); and "It removes the temptation to place a physical barrier between me and my visitors" (communication considerations). Such an arrangement does force the office occupant to make a physical effort to move from his desk in order to greet visitors.

OPEN-ENDED ARRANGEMENT

The most flexible and open arrangements for offices involve choosing a "desk surrogate" or having no desk at all. Each of these provide little in the way of a reference point either for the office occupant or for a visitor. Using something as a substitute or surrogate for a regular desk allows the office occupant almost unlimited freedom to vary seating patterns and interpersonal distances—but still allows him to maintain a hard work surface. The most common desk surrogates are coffee tables or other pieces of furniture that sit low enough on the floor to prevent an obstruction between communicators. These free-form arrangements are not widely accepted or used, however, and only 7 percent of the respondents indicated that they used a desk surrogate. Only 2 percent had no desk at all.

Almost exclusively, the people who used the no-desk arrangement were executives who used their regular or public office only for group meetings or discussions. Without exception, however, these people indicated that they maintained a smaller, private office in which they did their paperwork.

Some top executives have gone to great lengths to establish an Olympian aura. Offices have been designed with raised platforms that perch a short boss high above his visitors or with special lighting to place the "host" in a dramatic setting. One executive's floor was actually installed in reverse: It sloped downward from the door to the table desk so that the visitor seemed to grow smaller as he approached.

Since most of us are content with the more conventional types of office arrangements, we seldom give much thought to individual differences. But take a closer look. Your office may be "saying" something about who you really are.

The Activity Trap

George S. Odiorne

Most people get caught in the Activity Trap! They become so enmeshed in activity they lose sight of why they are doing it, and the activity becomes a false goal, an end in itself. Successful people never lose sight of their goals, the hoped-for outputs.

Like a design in the wallpaper which you cannot see until it is pointed out, the concept of the activity trap clarifies many things that have gone wrong and shows what we have to do to set them right. "Success is best explained by unremitting attention to purpose," stated Disraeli. The Koran advises "If you don't know where you are going, then any road will get you there."

Apparently there is a normal and natural tendency to begin with important, clear, ideal objectives but, in an amazingly short period of time, people may get so enmeshed in the activity of achieving their goals that they lose sight of them—the desired outputs—and never find them clearly again.

The most successful people are those who keep an eye on their hoped-for outputs—their objectives—while they carry on complex activities. If the objectives change, they are responsive in their behavior. The less successful people continue the same behavior, even after the goal has changed.

The purest (perhaps the only pure) act of leadership is goal-setting and getting others to accept this goal and work toward it. When John F. Kennedy in 1960 set a goal of placing a man on the moon by 1970, he was illustrating results-centered leadership. It commanded resources and activity without major complaints because it kindled the imaginations of millions of people.

Falling into the activity trap is not the result of stupidity. In fact, the most intelligent, highly educated people tend to be those most likely to become entrapped in interesting and complex activities. Having spent years mastering one class of activities, called a *profession*, they persist in practicing those activities, as learned, even when the objectives practically cry out for some other kind of behavior. The age of specialization has produced a generation of people who have learned to become *emotionally attached to irrelevancies*.

From pp. 6–9 of *Management and the Activity Trap* by George S. Odiorne. Copyright © 1974 by George S. Odiorne. By permission of Harper & Row, Publishers, Inc., and William Heinemann Ltd., Publishers, London.

The relationship between activity-fanaticism and the waste of resources is clear. Activity, especially professional activity, becomes more and more costly, consuming more and more inputs that are less and less related to any kind of output. As the activity trap enmeshes a person, he regresses to a more dependent relationship with the input-providers. "You must keep on putting in resources as long as I keep asking for them. But you are not to ask what outputs you are receiving in return for I am a professional." This attitude turns the professionals into the *irresponsibles*. "I insist that you continue to provide all my needs, without question, for I am a professional and you are not. As a professional, I am entitled to consume inputs and behave thus." The rest of society must behave as the parents of such children and provide the inputs, with ever-decreasing rights to question their use.

It is our own past generosities that have trapped us. School-teachers have flatly refused to be appraised, insisting that parents and taxpayers have no professional qualifications to judge their efforts. It is only through voting against tax increases for schools that the providers of input demonstrate their desires for different outputs.

The rise of staff departments has increased astronomically the overhead costs of doing business. Companies have gone bankrupt in times of prosperity, eaten from within by their own professionals, whose work has often been wholly unrelated to any production of visible outputs.

The activity traps also extend to supervisor-subordinate relationships. As an activity becomes entrenched, it tends to become more meaningful than the output—the position becomes more important to the holder than the reason for which the position was created. Superiors begin to enforce the activity upon subordinates for its own sake. Supervisory systems become the governance of activity rather than the direction of output. *Be active* is more important than *Produce my objectives*. Time cards, close supervision, and autocratic bosses are evidences of the grip of the activity trap. "But," wails the boss, "they have to be kept active!" Of course—but there are high-yield and low-yield activities, with the highest that which is most closely attuned to the actual product of the organization. The activity-centered supervisor is chiefly concerned with the volume of activities—looking busy is more important than being productive. He creates a network of managers through which the activities are conducted and reinforced. Of course, a set of manners for engaging in them becomes *de rigueur*.

The obsessions which follow the attachment to activity have awesome effects on the management of change. Old activities take on an air of respectability which militates against innovation. Procedures become stabilizers which assure that old activities will prevail. What started as a momentary lapse becomes a bad habit, then a procedure.

Finally, it emerges as a form of religion. The activity cult becomes the prevailing culture, and those who would press for change, for creativity, for the attainment of the brilliant possibilities of the futurist world are stopped by the activity-centered people who dominate the world.

The pervasiveness of the activity traps is formidable. It can come into existence in any institution. It affects people everywhere, with its effects often devastating; for, under hierarchical forms of organization that are activity-centered rather than result-centered, *people shrink*.

THE ACTIVITY TRAP IN BUSINESS ORGANIZATIONS

As a dominant institution in our society, the corporation has become a major influence for governing our activities and producing the activity-centered society. Products and the ways in which they are advertised embellish activity with an aura of social acceptance that is most difficult to defy or ignore. Families "go out for a ride" on Sunday afternoon; they stare endlessly at idiotic entertainment; they become enmeshed in consumer activity for its own sake. Conspicuous consumption becomes an activity in which one competes with his neighbors. Such effects upon the quality of life have been adequately described elsewhere.

But it is within the corporations themselves that the activity trap's most pernicious effects are produced, for it is there that millions of individuals find or lose satisfaction in their work. . . .

Symptoms of Groupthink Among President Kennedy's Advisers
Irving L. Janis

According to the groupthink hypothesis, members of any small cohesive group tend to maintain esprit de corps by unconsciously developing a number of shared illusions and related norms that interfere with critical thinking and reality testing. If the available accounts describe the deliberations accurately, typical illusions can be discerned among the members of the Kennedy team during the period when they were deciding whether to approve the CIA's invasion plan.

THE ILLUSION OF INVULNERABILITY

An important symptom of groupthink is the illusion of being invulnerable to the main dangers that might arise from a risky action in which the group is strongly tempted to engage. Essentially, the notion is that "If our leader and everyone else in our group decides that it is okay, the plan is bound to succeed. Even if it is quite risky, luck will be on our side." A sense of "unlimited confidence" was widespread among the "New Frontiersmen" as soon as they took over their high government posts, according to a Justice Department confidant, with whom Robert Kennedy discussed the secret CIA plan on the day it was launched:

> It seemed that, with John Kennedy leading us and with all the talent he had assembled, *nothing could stop us*. We believed that if we faced up to the nation's problems and applied bold, new ideas with common sense and hard work, we would overcome whatever challenged us.

That this attitude was shared by the members of the President's inner circle is indicated by Schlesinger's statement that the men around Kennedy had enormous confidence in his ability and luck: "Everything had broken right for him since 1956. He had won the nomination and the election against all the odds in the book. Everyone around him thought he had the Midas touch and could not lose." Kennedy and his principal advisers were sophisticated and skeptical men, but they were, nevertheless, "affected by the euphoria of the new day." During the first three months after he took office—despite growing concerns created by the emerging crisis in Southeast Asia, the gold drain, and the Cuban exiles who were awaiting the go-ahead signal to invade Cuba—the dominant mood in the White House, according to Schlesinger, was "buoyant optimism." It was centered on the "promise of hope" held out by the President: *"Euphoria reigned; we thought for a moment that the world was plastic and the future unlimited."* . . .

Once this euphoric phase takes hold, decision-making for everyday activities, as well as long-range planning, is likely to be seriously impaired. The members of a cohesive group become very reluctant to carry out the unpleasant task of critically assessing the limits of their power and the real losses that could arise if their luck does not hold. They tend to examine each risk in black and white terms. If it does not seem overwhelmingly dangerous, they are inclined simply to forget about it, instead of developing contingency plans in case it materializes. The group members know that no one among them is a superman, but they feel that somehow the group is a supergroup, capable of surmounting all risks that stand in the way of carrying out any desired course of action: "Nothing can stop us!" Athletic teams and military combat units may often benefit from members' enthusiastic confidence in the power and luck of their group. But policy-making committees usually do not. . . .

THE ILLUSION OF UNANIMITY

When a group of people who respect each other's opinions arrive at a unanimous view, each member is likely to feel that the belief must be true. This reliance on consensual validation tends to replace individual critical thinking and reality-testing, unless there are clear-cut disagreements among the members. The members of a face-to-face group often become inclined, without quite realizing it, to prevent latent disagreements from surfacing when they are about to initiate a risky course of action. The group leader and the members support each other, playing up the areas of convergence in their thinking, at the expense of fully exploring divergences that might disrupt the apparent unity of the group. Better to share a pleasant, balmy group atmosphere than to be battered in a storm.

This brings us to the second outstanding symptom of groupthink manifested by the Kennedy team—a shared illusion of unanimity. In the formal sessions dealing with the Cuban invasion plan, the group's consensus that the basic features of the CIA plan should be adopted was relatively free of disagreement.

According to Sorensen, "No strong voice of opposition was raised in any of the key meetings, and no realistic alternatives were presented." According to Schlesinger, "the massed and caparisoned authority of his senior officials in the realm of foreign policy and defense was unanimous for going ahead. . . . Had one senior advisor opposed the adventure, I believe that Kennedy would have canceled it. No one spoke against it."

Perhaps the most crucial of Schlesinger's observations is, "Our meetings took place in a *curious atmosphere of assumed consensus.*" His additional comments clearly show that the assumed consensus was an illusion that could be maintained only because the major participants did not reveal their own reasoning or discuss their idiosyncratic assumptions and vague reservations. President Kennedy thought that prime consideration was being given to his prohibition of direct military intervention by the United States. He assumed that the operation had been pared down to a kind of unobtrusive infiltration that, if reported in the newspapers, would be buried in the inside pages. Rusk was certainly not on the same wavelength as the President, for at one point he suggested that it might be better to have the invaders fan out from the United States naval base at Guantánamo, rather than land at the Bay of Pigs, so that they could readily retreat to the base if necessary. Implicit in his suggestion was a lack of concern about revealing United States military support as well as implicit distrust in the assumption made by the others about the ease of escaping from the Bay of Pigs. But discussion of Rusk's strange proposal was evidently dropped long before he was induced to reveal whatever vague misgivings he may have had about the Bay of Pigs plan. At meetings in the State Department, according to Roger Hilsman, who worked closely with him, "Rusk asked penetrating questions that frequently caused us to re-examine our position." But at the White House meetings Rusk said little except to offer gentle warnings about avoiding excesses.

As usually happens in cohesive groups, the members assumed that "silence gives consent." Kennedy and the others supposed that Rusk was in substantial agreement with what the CIA representatives were saying about the soundness of the invasion plan. But about one week before the invasion was scheduled, when Schlesinger told Rusk in private about his objections to the plan, Rusk, surprisingly, offered no arguments against Schlesinger's objections. He said that he had been wanting for some time to draw up a balance sheet of the pros and cons and that he was annoyed at the Joint Chiefs because "they are perfectly willing to put the President's head on the block, but they recoil at doing anything which might risk Guantánamo." At that late date, he evidently still preferred his suggestion to launch the invasion from the United States naval base in Cuba, even though doing so would violate President Kennedy's stricture against involving America's armed forces.

McNamara's assumptions about the invasion were quite different from both Rusk's and Kennedy's. McNamara thought that the main objective was to touch off a revolt of the Cuban people to overthrow Castro. The members of the group who knew something about Cuban politics and Castro's popular support must have had strong doubts about this assumption. Why did they fail to convey their misgivings at any of the meetings?

SUPPRESSION OF PERSONAL DOUBTS

The sense of group unity concerning the advisability of going ahead with the CIA's invasion plan appears to have been based on superficial appearances of complete concurrence, achieved at the cost of self-censorship of misgivings by several of the members. From post-mortem discussions with participants, Sorensen concluded that among the men in the State Department, as well as those on the White House staff, "doubts were entertained but never pressed, partly out of a fear of being labelled 'soft' or undaring in the eyes of their colleagues." Schlesinger was not at all hesitant about presenting his strong objections in a memorandum he gave to the President and the Secretary of State. But he became keenly aware of his tendency to suppress objections when he attended the White House meetings of the Kennedy team, with their atmosphere of assumed consensus:

In the months after the Bay of Pigs I bitterly reproached myself for having kept so silent during those crucial discussions in the Cabinet Room, though my feelings of guilt were tempered by the knowledge that a course of objection would have accomplished little save to *gain me a name as a nuisance*. I can only explain my failure to do more than raise a few timid questions by reporting that one's impulse to blow the whistle on this nonsense was simply undone by the *circumstances of the discussion*.

Whether or not his retrospective explanation includes all his real reasons for having remained silent, Schlesinger appears to have been quite aware of the need to refrain from saying anything that would create a nuisance by breaking down the assumed consensus.[1]

Participants in the White House meetings, like members of many other discussion groups, evidently felt reluctant to raise questions that might cast doubt on a plan that they thought was accepted by the consensus of the group, for fear of evoking disapproval from their associates. This type of fear is probably not the same as fear of losing one's effectiveness or damaging one's career. Many forthright men who are quite willing to speak their piece despite risks to their career become silent when faced with the possibility of losing the approval of fellow members of their primary work group. The discrepancy between Schlesinger's critical memoranda and his silent acquiescence during the meetings might be an example of this.

Schlesinger says that when the Cuban invasion plan was being presented to the group, "virile poses" were conveyed in the rhetoric used by the representatives of the CIA and the Joint Chiefs of Staff. He thought the State Department representatives and others responded by becoming anxious to show that they were not softheaded idealists but really were just as tough as the military men. Schlesinger's references to the "virile" stance of the militant advocates of the invasion plan suggest that the members of Kennedy's in-group may have been concerned about protecting the leader from being embarrassed by their voicing "unvirile" concerns about the high risks of the venture. . . .

SELF-APPOINTED MINDGUARDS

Among the well-known phenomena of group dynamics is the alacrity with which members of a cohesive in-group suppress deviational points of view by putting social pressure on any member who begins to express a view that deviates from the dominant beliefs of the group, to make sure that he will not disrupt the consensus of the group as a whole. This pressure often takes the form of urging the dissident member to remain silent if he cannot match up his own beliefs with those of the rest of the group. At least one dramatic instance of this type of pressure occurred a few days after President Kennedy had said, "we seem now destined to go ahead on a quasi-minimum basis." This was still several days before the final decision was made.

At a large birthday party for his wife, Robert Kennedy, who had been constantly informed about the Cuban invasion plan, took Schlesinger aside and asked him why he was opposed. The President's brother listened coldly and then said, "You might be right or you may be wrong, but the President has made his mind up. Don't push it any further. Now is the time for everyone to help him all they can." Here is another symptom of groupthink, displayed by a highly intelligent man whose ethical code committed him to freedom of dissent. What he was saying, in effect, was, "You may well be right about the dangerous risks, but I don't give a damn about that; all of us should help our leader right now by not sounding any discordant notes that would interfere with the harmonious support he should have."

When Robert Kennedy told Schlesinger to lay off, he was functioning in a self-appointed role that I call being a "mindguard." Just as a bodyguard protects the President and other high officials from injurious physical assaults, a mindguard protects them from thoughts that might damage their confidence in the soundness of the policies to which they are committed or to which they are about to commit themselves.

At least one other member of the Kennedy team, Secretary of State Rusk, also effectively functioned as a mindguard, protecting the leader and the members from unwelcome ideas that might set them to thinking about unfavorable consequences of their preferred course of action and that might lead to dissension instead of a comfortable consensus. Undersecretary of State Chester Bowles, who had attended a White House meeting at which he was given no opportunity to express his dissenting views, decided not to continue to remain silent about such a vital matter. He prepared a strong memorandum for Secretary Rusk opposing the CIA plan and, keeping well within the prescribed bureaucratic channels, requested Rusk's permission to present his case to the President. Rusk told Bowles that there was no need for any concern, that the invasion plan would be dropped in favor of a quiet little guerrilla infiltration. Rusk may have believed this at the time, but at subsequent White House meetings he must soon have learned otherwise. Had Rusk transmitted the undersecretary's memorandum, the urgent warnings it contained might have reinforced Schlesinger's memorandum and jolted some of Kennedy's in-group, if not Kennedy himself, to reconsider the decision. But Rusk kept Bowles' memorandum firmly buried in the State Department files.

Rusk may also have played a similar role in preventing Kennedy and the others from learning about the strong objections raised by Edward R. Murrow, whom the President had just appointed director of the United States Information Agency. In yet another instance, Rusk appears to have functioned as a dogged mindguard, protecting the group from the opposing ideas of a government official with access to information that could have enabled him to assess the political consequences of the Cuban invasion better than anyone present at the White

House meetings could. As director of intelligence and research in the State Department, Roger Hilsman got wind of the invasion plan from his colleague Allen Dulles and strongly warned Secretary Rusk of the dangers. He asked Rusk for permission to allow the Cuban experts in his department to scrutinize thoroughly the assumptions relevant to their expertise. "I'm sorry," Rusk told him, "but I can't let you. This is being too tightly held." Rusk's reaction struck Hilsman as strange because all the relevant men in his department already had top security clearance. Hilsman assumed that Rusk turned down his urgent request because of pressure from Dulles and Bissell to adhere to the CIA's special security restrictions. But if so, why, when so much was at stake, did the Secretary of State fail to communicate to the President or to anyone else in the core group that his most trusted intelligence expert had grave doubts about the invasion plan and felt that it should be appraised by the Cuban specialists? As a result of Rusk's handling of Hilsman's request, the President and his advisers remained in the curious position, as Hilsman put it, of making an important political judgment without the benefit of advice from the government's most relevant intelligence experts. . . .

DOCILITY FOSTERED BY SUAVE LEADERSHIP

The group pressures that help to maintain a group's illusions are sometimes fostered by various leadership practices, some of which involve subtle ways of making it difficult for those who question the initial consensus to suggest alternatives and to raise critical issues. The group's agenda can readily be manipulated by a suave leader, often with the tacit approval of the members, so that there is simply no opportunity to discuss the drawbacks of a seemingly satisfactory plan of action. This is one of the conditions that fosters groupthink.

President Kennedy, as leader at the meetings in the White House, was probably more active than anyone else in raising skeptical questions; yet he seems to have encouraged the group's docility and uncritical acceptance of the defective arguments in favor of the CIA's plan. At each meeting, instead of opening up the agenda to permit a full airing of the opposing considerations, he allowed the CIA representatives to dominate the entire discussion. The President permitted them to refute immediately each tentative doubt that one of the others might express, instead of asking whether anyone else had the same doubt or wanted to pursue the implications of the new worrisome issue that had been raised.

Moreover, although the President went out of his way to bring to a crucial meeting an outsider who was an eloquent opponent of the invasion plan, his style of conducting the meeting presented no opportunity for discussion of the controversial issues that were raised. The visitor was Senator J. William Fulbright. The occasion was the climactic meeting of April 4, 1961, held at the State Department, at which the apparent consensus that had emerged in earlier meetings was seemingly confirmed by an open straw vote. The President invited Senator Fulbright after the Senator had made known his concern about newspaper stories forecasting a United States invasion of Cuba. At the meeting, Fulbright was given an opportunity to present his opposing views. In a "sensible and strong" speech Fulbright correctly predicted many of the damaging effects the invasion would have on United States foreign relations. The President did not open the floor to discussion of the questions raised in Fulbright's rousing speech. Instead, he returned to the procedure he had initiated earlier in the meeting; he had asked each person around the table to state his final judgment and after Fulbright had taken his turn, he continued the straw vote around the table. McNamara said he approved the plan. Berle was also for it; his advice was to "let her rip." Mann, who had been on the fence, also spoke in favor of it.

Picking up a point mentioned by Berle, who had said he approved but did not insist on "a major production," President Kennedy changed the agenda by asking what could be done to make the infiltration more quiet. Following discussion of this question—quite remote from the fundamental moral and political issues raised by Senator Fulbright—the meeting ended. Schlesinger mentions that the meeting broke up before completion of the intended straw vote around the table. Thus, wittingly or unwittingly, the President conducted the meeting in such a way that not only was there no time to discuss the potential dangers to United States foreign relations raised by Senator Fulbright, but there was also no time to call upon Schlesinger, the one man present who the President knew strongly shared Senator Fulbright's misgivings.

Of course, one or more members of the group could have prevented this by-passing by suggesting that the group discuss Senator Fulbright's arguments and requesting that Schlesinger and the others who had not been called upon be given the opportunity to state their views. But no one made such a request.

The President's demand that each person, in turn, state his overall judgment, especially after having just heard an outsider oppose the group consensus, must have put the members on their mettle. These are exactly the conditions that most strongly foster docile conformity to a group's norms. After listening to an opinion leader (McNamara, for example) express his unequivocal acceptance, it becomes more difficult than ever for other members to state a different view. Open straw votes generally put pressure on each individual to agree with the apparent group consensus, as has been shown by well-known social psychological experiments.

A few days before the crucial meeting of April 4, another outsider who might have challenged some of the group's illusions attended one of the meetings but was never given the opportunity to speak his piece. At the earlier meeting, the outsider was the acting Secretary of State, Chester Bowles, attending in place of Secretary Rusk, who was abroad at a SEATO conference. Like Senator Fulbright, Bowles was incredulous and at times even "horrified" at the group's complacent acceptance of the CIA's invasion plans. However, President Kennedy had no idea what Bowles was thinking about the plan, and he probably felt that Bowles was there more in the role of a reporter to keep Rusk up to date on the deliberations than as a participant in the discussion. In any case, the President neglected to give the group the opportunity to hear the reactions of a fresh mind; he did not call upon Bowles at any time. Bowles sat through the meeting in complete silence. He felt he could not break with formal bureaucratic protocol, which prevents an undersecretary from volunteering his opinion unless directed to do so by his chief or by the President. Bowles behaved in the prescribed way and confined his protestations to a State Department memorandum addressed to Rusk, which, as we have seen, was not communicated to the President. . . .

During the Bay of Pigs planning sessions, President Kennedy, probably unwittingly, allowed the one-sided CIA memoranda to monopolize the attention of the group by failing to circulate opposing statements that might have stimulated an intensive discussion of the drawbacks and might therefore have revealed the illusory nature of the group's consensus. Although the President read and privately discussed the strongly opposing memoranda prepared by Schlesinger and Senator Fulbright, he never distributed them to the policy-makers whose critical judgment he was seeking. Kennedy also knew that Joseph Newman, a foreign correspondent who had just visited Cuba, had written a series of incisive articles that disagreed with forecasts concerning the ease of generating a revolt against Castro. But, although he invited Newman to the White House for a chat, he did not distribute Newman's impressive writings to the advisory group. . . .

THE TABOO AGAINST ANTAGONIZING VALUABLE NEW MEMBERS

It seems likely that one of the reasons the members of the core group accepted the President's restricted agenda and his extraordinarily indulgent treatment of the CIA representatives was that a kind of informal group norm had developed, producing a desire to avoid saying anything that could be construed as an attack on the CIA's plan. The group apparently accepted a kind of taboo against voicing damaging criticisms. This may have been another important factor contributing to the group's tendency to indulge in groupthink.

How could such a norm come into being? Why would President Kennedy give preferential treatment to the two CIA representatives?

Why would Bundy, McNamara, Rusk, and the others on his team fail to challenge this preferential treatment and accept a taboo against voicing critical opposition? A few clues permit some conjectures to be made, although we have much less evidence to go on than for delineating the pattern of preferential treatment itself.

It seems that Allen Dulles and Richard Bissell, despite being holdovers from the Eisenhower administration, were not considered outsiders by the inner core of the Kennedy team. President Kennedy and his closest associates did not place these two men in the same category as the Joint Chiefs of Staff, who were seen as members of an outside military clique established during the earlier administration, men whose primary loyalties belonged elsewhere and whose presence at the White House meetings was tolerated as a necessary requirement of governmental protocol. (Witness Secretary Rusk's unfriendly comments about the Joint Chiefs being more loyal to their military group in the Pentagon than to the President, when he was conversing privately with fellow in-group member Schlesinger.) President Kennedy and those in his inner circle admired Dulles and Bissell, regarded them as valuable new members of the Kennedy team, and were pleased to have them on board. Everyone in the group was keenly aware of the fact that Bissell had been devoting his talents with great intensity for over a year to developing the Cuban invasion project and that Dulles was also deeply committed to it. Whenever Bissell presented his arguments, "we all listened transfixed," Schlesinger informs us, "fascinated by the workings of this superbly clear, organized and articulate intelligence." Schlesinger reports that Bissell was regarded by the group as "a man of high character and remarkable intellectual gifts." In short, he was accepted as a highly prized member.

The sense of power of the core group was probably enhanced by the realization that the two potent bureaucrats who were in control of America's extensive intelligence network were affiliated with the Kennedy team. The core members of the team would certainly want to avoid antagonizing or alienating them. They would be inclined, therefore, to soft-pedal their criticisms of the CIA plan and perhaps even to suspend their critical judgment in evaluating it. . . .

The picture we get, therefore, is that the two CIA representatives, both highly esteemed men who had recently joined the Kennedy team, were presenting their "baby" to the rest of the team. As protagonists, they had a big head start toward eliciting a favorable consensus. New in-group members would be listened to much more sympathetically and much less critically than outsiders representing an agency that might be trying to sell one of its own pet projects to the new President.

Hilsman, who also respected the two men, says that Dulles and Bissell "had become emotionally involved . . . so deeply involved in the development of the Cuban invasion plans that they were no longer able to see clearly or to judge soundly." He adds, "There was so deep a commitment, indeed, that there was an unconscious effort to confine consideration of the proposed operation to as small a number of people as possible, so as to avoid too harsh or thorough a scrutiny of the plans." If Hilsman is correct, it is reasonable to assume that the two men managed to convey to the other members of the Kennedy team their strong desire "to avoid too harsh or thorough a scrutiny. . . ."[2]

Notes

1. Schlesinger's somewhat self-abasing confession about his failure to present his objections at the group meetings might be a symptom of persisting loyalty to the dead leader and to the group. He appears to be saying, in effect, "Don't put all the blame on President Kennedy or on the other leading members of our team." This theme is not apparent in other portions of Schlesinger's account of the Bay of Pigs fiasco, which level many serious criticisms against the Kennedy team and is far from a whitewash. Still, at present there is no way of knowing to what extent a protective attitude colors Schlesinger's description of how the CIA's invasion plan came to be accepted at the White House. The same problem arises, of course, for all accounts by pro-Kennedy authors, especially Sorensen (who has sought to gain political office on his record as a participant on the Kennedy team and his close personal ties with the Kennedy brothers). My only solution to the problem of subtle distortions and biased reporting is to take the position that *if* the facts reported by Schlesinger, Sorensen, and the other authors are essentially accurate, my analysis of the converging pattern of this "evidence" leads to the conclusion that the groupthink hypothesis helps to account for the deficiencies in the decision-making of the Kennedy team.

2. Bureaucratic political considerations might also have contributed to the group norm of trying to keep the two new members of the team happy. The President and his senior advisers may have realized that if they asked Dulles and Bissell too many embarrassing questions and appeared to be rejecting the work of their agency, the two chiefs of the CIA might be pushed in the direction of becoming allied with the military men in the Pentagon, who were already supporting them, rather than with the Kennedy team in the White House.

Another contributing factor might have been the President's personal receptivity to the idea of taking aggressive action against Castro. Although somewhat skeptical of the plan, Kennedy may have welcomed the opportunity to make good on his campaign pledge to aid the anti-Castro rebels. According to Sorensen, the opportunity to inflict a blow against Castro was especially appealing to the President: "He should never have permitted his own deep feeling against Castro (unusual for him) and considerations of public opinion—specifically his concern that he would be assailed for calling off a plan to get rid of Castro—to overcome his innate suspicion."

Obviously, these ancillary political and psychological factors are not symptoms of groupthink. But they may have reinforced the group norms conducive to concurrence-seeking and thus could be regarded in the same general category as biased leadership practices—that is, as conditions that foster groupthink.

What It's Like to Be a Black Manager

Edward W. Jones, Jr.

THE JOB OFFER

My story begins when I happened to bump into a recruiter who was talking to a friend of mine. On gathering that I was a college senior, the recruiter asked whether I had considered his company as an employer. I responded, "Are you kidding me—you don't have any black managers, do you?" He replied, "No, but that's why I'm here."

I did well in a subsequent interview procedure, and received an invitation for a company tour. Still skeptical, I accepted, feeling that I had nothing to lose. During a lunch discussion concerning the contemplated job and its requirements, I experienced my first reminder that I was black. After a strained silence, one of the executives at our table looked at me, smiled, and said, "Why is it that everyone likes Roy Campanella, but so many people dislike Jackie Robinson?"

I knew that this man was trying to be pleasant; yet I felt nothing but disgust at what seemed a ridiculous deterioration in the level of conversation. Here was the beginning of the games that I expected but dreaded playing. The question was demeaning and an insult to my intelligence. It was merely a rephrasing of the familiar patronizing comment, "One of my best friends is a negro." Most blacks recognize this type of statement as a thinly veiled attempt to hide bias. After all, if a person is unbiased, why does he make such a point of trying to prove it?

In the fragment of time between the question and my response, the tension within me grew. Were these people serious about a job offer? If so, what did they expect from me? I had no desire to be the corporate black in a glass office, but I did not wish to be abrasive or ungracious if the company was sincere about its desire to have an integrated organization.

There was no way to resolve these kinds of questions at that moment, so I gathered up my courage and replied, "Roy Campanella is a great baseball player. But off the field he is not an overwhelming intellectual challenge to anyone. Jackie Robinson is great both on and off the baseball field. He is very intelligent and therefore more of a threat

---

than Roy Campanella. In fact, I'm sure that if he wanted to, he could out-perform you in your job."

There was a stunned silence around the table, and from that point on until I arrived back at the employment office, I was sure that I had ended any chances of receiving a job offer.

I was wrong. I subsequently received an outstanding salary offer from the recruiter. But I had no intention of being this company's showcase black and asked seriously, "Why do you want me to work for you? Because of my ability or because you need a black?" I was reassured that ability was the "only" criterion, and one month later, after much introspection, I accepted the offer.

INITIAL EXPOSURE

I entered the first formal training phase, in which I was the only black trainee in a department of over 8,000 employees. During this period, my tension increased as I was repeatedly called on to be the in-house expert on anything pertaining to civil rights. I was proud to be black and had many opinions about civil rights, but I did not feel qualified to give "the" black opinion. I developed the feeling that I was considered a black first and an individual second by many of the people I came into contact with. This feeling was exacerbated by the curious executive visitors to the training class who had to be introduced to everyone except me. Everyone knew my name, and I constantly had the feeling of being on stage.

The next phase of training was intended to prepare trainees for supervisory responsibilities. The tension of the trainee group had risen somewhat because of the loss of several trainees and the increased challenges facing us. In my own case, an increasing fear of failure began to impact on the other tensions that I felt from being "a speck of pepper in a sea of salt." The result of these tensions was that I began behaving with an air of bravado. I wasn't outwardly concerned or afraid, but I was inwardly terrified. This phase of training was also completed satisfactorily, at least in an official sense.

At the conclusion of the training, I received a "yes, but" type of appraisal. For example: "Mr. Jones doesn't take notes and seems to have trouble using the reference material, but he seems to be able to recall the material." This is the type of appraisal that says you've done satisfactorily, yet leaves a negative or dubious impression. I questioned the subjective inputs but dropped the matter without any vehement objections.

Prior to embarking on my first management assignment, I resolved to learn from this appraisal and to use more tact and talk less. These resolutions were re-emphasized by my adviser, who was an executive with responsibility for giving me counsel and acting as a sounding board. He also suggested that I relax my handshake and speak more softly.

ON THE JOB

A warm welcome awaited me in the office where I was to complete my first assignment as a supervisor. I looked forward to going to work because I felt that subjectivity in appraisals would now be replaced by objectivity. Here was a situation in which I would either meet or fail to meet clearly defined numerical objectives.

There were no serious problems for three weeks, and I started to relax and just worry about the job. But then I had a conflict in my schedule. An urgent matter had to be taken care of in the office at the same time that I had an appointment elsewhere. I wrote a note to a supervisor who worked for another manager, asking him if he would be kind enough to follow up on the matter in the office for me.

I chose that particular supervisor because he had given me an embarrassingly warm welcome to the office and insisted that I "just ask" if there was anything at all that he could do to help me. I relied on the impersonality of the note because he was out on a coffee break and I had to leave immediately. The note was short and tactfully worded, and ended by giving my advance "thanks" for the requested help. Moreover, the office norms encouraged supervisory cooperation, so the fact that we worked under different managers did not seem to be a problem.

When I returned to the office, the manager I worked for called me in. He was visibly irritated. I sat down and he said, "Ed, you're rocking the boat." He stated that the supervisor I had asked for help had complained directly to the area manager that I was ordering him around and said he wasn't about to take any nonsense from a "new kid" in the office.

In a very calm voice, I explained what I had done and why I had done it. I then asked my manager, "What did I do wrong?" He looked at me and said, "I don't know, but whatever it is cut it out. Stop rocking the boat." When I asked why the note wasn't produced to verify my statements, he said that it "wasn't available."

I left my manager's office totally perplexed. How could I correct my behavior if I didn't know what was wrong with it? I resolved that I had no choice except to be totally self-reliant, since one thing was obvious: what I had taken at face value as friendliness was potentially a fatal trap.

The feelings aroused in this incident were indicative of those I was to maintain for some time. While I felt a need for closeness, the only option open to me was self-reliance. I felt that my manager should support and defend me, but it was obvious that he was not willing to take such a stance. Worst of all, however, was my feeling of disappointment and the ensuing confusion due to my lack of guidance. I felt that if my manager was not willing to protect and defend me, he had an increased responsibility to give me guidance on how to avoid future explosions of a similar nature.

For some months I worked in that office without any additional explosions, although I was continually admonished not to "rock the boat." During a luncheon with the area manager one day, I remember, he said, "Ed, I've never seen a guy try so hard. If we tell you to tie your tie to the right, you sure try to do it. But why can't you be like Joe [another trainee the area manager supervised]? He doesn't seem to be having any problems."

The Appraisal Incident

I directed my energies and frustrations into my work, and my supervisory section improved in every measured area of performance until it led the unit. At the end of my first six months on the job, I was slated to go on active duty to fulfill my military requirements as a lieutenant in the Army. Shortly before I left, my manager stated, "Ed, you've done a tremendous job. You write your own appraisal." I wrote the appraisal, but was told to rewrite it because "it's not good enough." I rewrote the appraisal four times before he was satisfied that I was not being too modest. As I indicated earlier, I had resolved to be as unabrasive as possible, and, even though I had met or exceeded all my objectives, I was trying not to be pompous in critiquing my own performance.

Finally, on my next to last day on the job, my manager said, "Ed, this is a fine appraisal. I don't have time to get it typed before you go, but I'll submit this appraisal just as you have written it." With that, I went into the service, feeling that, finally, I had solved my problems.

Six months later, I took several days' leave from the Army to spend Christmas in the city with my family. On the afternoon of the day before Christmas, I decided to visit the personnel executive who had originally given me encouragement. So, wearing my officer's uniform, I stopped by his office.

After exchanging greetings and making small talk, I asked him if he had seen my appraisal. He answered, "yes," but when his face failed to reflect the look of satisfaction that I expected, I asked him if I could see it. The appraisal had been changed from the one that I had originally written to another "yes, but" appraisal. The numerical results said that I had met or exceeded all objectives, but under the section entitled "Development Program" the following paragraph had been inserted:

"Mr. Jones's biggest problem has been overcoming his own impulsiveness. He has on occasion, early in his tour, jumped too fast with the result that he has incurred some resentment. In these cases his objectives have been good, but his method has ruffled feathers."

I asked the personnel executive to interpret my overall rating. He answered, "Well, we can run the business with people with that rating." I then asked him to explain the various ratings possible, and it became clear that I had received the lowest acceptable rating that wouldn't require the company to fire me. I could not see how this could be, since I had exceeded all my objectives. I explained how I had written my own appraisal and that this appraisal had been rewritten. The personnel officer could not offer an explanation; he recommended that I speak to my old area manager, who had had the responsibility to review and approve my appraisal, and ask him why I had been treated in that manner.

A Bleak Christmas

I tried to sort things out on my way to see my former area manager. My head was spinning, and I was disgusted. The appraisal was not just unfair—it was overtly dishonest. I thought of standing up in righteous indignation and appealing to higher authority in the company, but I had always resisted calling attention to my blackness by asking for special concessions and wanted to avoid creating a conflict situation if at all possible. While the 15-minute walk in the cold air calmed my anger, I still hadn't decided what I was going to do when I arrived at the area manager's office.

I walked into a scene that is typical of Christmas Eve in an office. People were everywhere, and discarded gift wrappings filled the wastebaskets. The area manager still had on the red Santa Claus suit. I looked around at the scene of merriment and decided that this was a poor time to "rock the boat."

The area manager greeted me warmly, exclaimed how great I looked, and offered to buy me a drink on his way home. I accepted, and with a feeling of disgust and disappointment, toasted to a Merry Christmas. I knew then that this situation was hopeless and there was little to be gained by raising a stink while we were alone. I had been naïve, and there was no way to prove that the appraisal had been changed.

I was a very lonely fellow that Christmas Eve. My feelings of a lack of closeness, support, and protection were renewed and amplified. It became obvious that no matter how much I achieved, how hard I worked, or how many personal adjustments I made, this system was trying to reject me.

I didn't know which way to turn, whom to trust, or who would be willing to listen. The personnel executive had told me to expect prejudice, but when he saw that I was being treated unfairly, he sent me off on my own.

"What do they expect?" I thought. "They know that I am bound to run into prejudice; yet no one lifts a finger when I am treated unfairly. Do they expect a person to be stupid enough to come right out and say, 'Get out, blackie; we don't want your type here'? This surely wouldn't happen—such overt behavior would endanger the offending person's career."

After the Christmas Eve incident, I went off to finish the remaining time in the Army. During that period, I tossed my work problems around in my mind, trying to find the right approach. The only answer I came up with was to stand fast, do my best, ask for no special favors, and refuse to quit voluntarily.

NEW CHALLENGES

When I returned to the company, I was assigned as a supervisor in another area for five or six weeks, to do the same work as I had been doing prior to my departure for the military service. At the end of this uneventful refamiliarization period, I was reassigned as a manager in an area that had poor performance and was recognized as being one of the most difficult in the company. The fact that I would be responsible for one of three "manager units" in the area was exciting, and I looked forward to this new challenge.

I walked into my new area manger's office with a smile and an extended hand, anxious to start off on the right foot and do a good job. After shaking hands, my new boss invited me to sit down while he told me about the job. He began by saying, "I hope you don't, but I am pretty sure you are going to fall flat on your face. When you do, my job is to kick you in the butt so hard that they'll have to take us both to the hospital."

I was shocked and angry. In the first place, my pride as a man said you don't have to take that kind of talk from anyone. I fought the temptation to say something like, "If you even raise your foot, you may well go to the hospital to have it put in a cast."

As I held back the anger, he continued, "I don't know anything about your previous performance, and I don't intend to try to find out. I'm going to evaluate you strictly on your performance for me."

The red lights went on in my mind. This guy was making too much of an issue about his lack of knowledge concerning my previous performance. Whom was he trying to kid? He had heard rumors and read my personnel records. I was starting off with two strikes against me. I looked at him and said, "I'll do my best."

More Appraisal Troubles

The area's results failed to improve, and John, the area manager, was replaced by a new boss, Ralph. Two weeks after Ralph arrived, he called me on the intercom and said, "Ed, John has your appraisal ready. Go down to see him in his new office. Don't worry about it; we'll talk when you get back." Ralph's words and tone of foreboding made me brace for the worst.

John ushered me into his office and began by telling me that I had been his worst problem. He then proceeded to read a list of every disagreement involving me that he was aware of. These ranged from corrective actions with clerks to resource-allocation discussions with my fellow managers. It was a strange appraisal session. John wound up crossing out half of the examples cited as I rebutted his statements. At the end of the appraisal, he turned and said, "I've tried to be fair, Ed. I've tried not to be vindictive. But if someone were to ask how you're doing, I would have to say you've got room for improvement."

Discussions with Ralph, my new boss, followed as soon as I returned to my office. He advised me not to worry, that we would work out any problems. I told him that this was fine, but I also pointed out the subjectivity and dishonesty reflected in previous and current appraisals and the circumstances surrounding them.

I was bitter that a person who had just been relieved for ineffectiveness could be allowed to have such a resounding impact on my chances in the company. My predecessor had been promoted; I had improved on his results; but here I was, back in questionable status again.

The Turning Point

About six weeks later, Ralph called me in and said, "Ed, I hope you make it on the job. But what are you going to do if you don't?"

At that moment, I felt as if the hands on the clock of life had reached 11:59. Time was running out very rapidly on me, and I saw myself against a wall, with my new boss about to deliver the coup de grâce. I felt that he was an honest and very capable person, but that circumstances had combined to give him the role of executioner. It seemed from his question that he was in the process of either wrestling with his own conscience or testing me to see how much resistance, if any, I would put up when he delivered the fatal blow. After all, while I had not made an issue of my ill treatment thus far in my career, no matter how unjustly I felt I had been dealt with, he was smart enough to realize that this option was still open to me.

I looked at Ralph and any thought about trying to please him went out of my mind. Sitting up straight in my chair, I met his relaxed smile with a very stern face. "Why do you care what I do if I don't make it?" I asked coldly.

"I care about you as a person," he replied.

"It's not your job to be concerned about me as a person," I said. "Your job is to evaluate my performance results. But since you've asked, it will be rough if I am fired, because I have a family and responsibilities. However, that's not your concern. You make your decision; and when you do, I'll make my decision." With that statement I returned to my office.

Several weeks after this discussion, a vice president came around to the office to discuss objectives and job philosophy with the managers. I noted at the time that while he only spent 15 or 20 minutes with the other managers, he spent over an hour talking with me. After this visit, Ralph and I had numerous daily discussions. Then Ralph called me into his office to tell me he had written a new appraisal with an improved rating. I was thrilled. I was going to make it. Later, he told me that he was writing another appraisal, stating I not only would make it but also had promotional potential.

After Ralph had changed the first appraisal, my tensions began to decrease and my effectiveness began to increase proportionately. The looser and more confident I became, the more rapidly the results improved. My assignment under Ralph became very fulfilling, and one of the best years I've spent in the company ensued. Other assignments followed, each more challenging than the previous, and each was handled satisfactorily.

A Theory of White Collar Crime

Edwin H. Sutherland

A complete explanation of white collar crime cannot be derived from the available data. The data which are at hand suggest that white collar crime has its genesis in the same general process as other criminal behavior, namely, differential association. The hypothesis of differential association is that criminal behavior is learned in association with those who define such behavior favorably and in isolation from those who define it unfavorably, and that a person in an appropriate situation engages in such criminal behavior if, and only if, the weight of the favorable definitions exceeds the weight of the unfavorable definitions. This hypothesis is certainly not a complete or universal explanation of white collar crime or of other crime, but it perhaps fits the data of both types of crimes better than any other general hypothesis. . . .

From *White Collar Crime* by Edwin H. Sutherland. Copyright © 1949 by Holt, Rinehart and Winston, Inc. Reprinted by permission of Holt, Rinehart and Winston.

PERSONAL DOCUMENTS

A young businessman in the used-car business in Chicago described the process by which he was inducted into illegal behavior.

When I graduated from college I had plenty of ideals of honesty, fair play, and cooperation which I had acquired at home, in school, and from literature. My first job after graduation was selling type-writers. During the first day I learned that these machines were not sold at a uniform price but that a person who higgled and waited could get a machine at about half the list price. I felt that this was unfair to the customer who paid the list price. The other salesmen laughed at me and could not understand my silly attitude. They told me to forget the things I had learned in school, and that you couldn't earn a pile of money by being strictly honest. When I replied that money wasn't everything they mocked at me: "Oh! No? Well, it helps." I had ideals and I resigned.

My next job was selling sewing machines. I was informed that one machine, which cost the company $18, was to be sold for $40 and another machine, which cost the company $19, was to be sold for $70, and that I was to sell the de luxe model whenever possible in preference to the cheaper model, and was given a list of the reasons why it was a better buy. When I told the sales manager that the business was dishonest and that I was quitting right then, he looked at me as if he thought I was crazy and said angrily: "There's not a cleaner business in the country."

It was quite a time before I could find another job. During this time I occasionally met some of my classmates and they related experiences similar to mine. They said they would starve if they were rigidly honest. All of them had girls and were looking forward to marriage and a comfortable standard of living, and they said they did not see how they could afford to be rigidly honest. My own feelings became less determined than they had been when I quit my first job.

Then I got an opportunity in the used-car business. I learned that this business had more tricks for fleecing customers than either of those I had tried previously. Cars with cracked cylinders, with half the teeth missing from the fly wheel, with everything wrong, were sold as "guaranteed." When the customer returned and demanded his guarantee, he had to sue to get it and very few went to that trouble and expense: the boss said you could depend on human nature. If hot cars could be taken in and sold safely, the boss did not hesitate. When I learned these things I did not quit as I had previously. I sometimes felt disgusted and wanted to quit, but I argued that I did not have much chance to find a legitimate firm. I knew that the game was rotten but it had to be played—the law of the jungle and that sort of thing. I knew that I was dishonest and to that extent felt that I was more honest than my fellows. The thing that struck me as strange was that all these people were proud of their ability to fleece customers. They boasted of their crookedness and were admired by their friends and enemies in proportion to their ability to get away with a crooked deal: it was called shrewdness. Another thing was that these people were unanimous in their denunciation of gangsters, robbers, burglars, and petty thieves. They never regarded themselves as in the same class and were bitterly indignant if accused of dishonesty: it was just good business.

Once in a while, as the years have passed, I have thought of myself as I was in college—idealistic, honest, and thoughtful of others—and have been momentarily ashamed of myself. Before long such memories became less and less frequent and it became difficult to distinguish me from my fellows. If you had accused me of dishonesty I would have denied the charge, but with slightly less vehemence than my fellow businessmen, for after all I had learned a different code of behavior.

A graduate student in an urban university, in order to supplement his income, took a job as an extra salesman in a shoe store on Saturdays and other rush days. He had no previous experiences as a shoe salesman or in any other regular business. He described his experience in this store thus:

One day I was standing in the front part of the store, waiting for the next customer. A man came in and asked if we had any high, tan button shoes. I told him that we had no shoes of that style. He thanked me and walked out of the store. The floor-walker came up to me and asked me what the man wanted. I told him what the man asked for and what I replied. The floor-walker said angrily: "Damn it! We're not here to sell what they want. We're here to sell what we've got." He went on to instruct me that when a customer came into the store, the first thing to do was to get him to sit down and take off his shoe so that he couldn't get out of the store. "If we don't have what he wants," he said, "bring him something else and try to interest him in that style. If he is still uninterested, inform the floor-walker and he will send one of the regular salesmen, and if that doesn't work, a third salesman will be sent to him. Our policy is that no customer gets out of the store without a sale until at least three salesmen have worked on him. By that time he feels that he must be a crank and will generally buy something whether he wants it or not."

I learned from other clerks that if a customer needed a 7-B shoe and we did not have that size in the style he desired, I should try on an 8-A or 7-C or some other size. The sizes were marked in code so that the customer did not know what the size was, and it might be necessary to lie to him about the size; also his foot might be injured by the misfit. But the rule was to sell him a pair of shoes, preferably a pair that fit but some other pair if necessary.

I learned also that the clerks received an extra commission if they sold the out-of-style shoes left over from earlier seasons, which were called "spiffs." The regular salesmen made a practice of selling spiffs to anyone who appeared gullible and generally had to claim either that this was the latest style or that it had been the style earlier and was coming back this season, or that it was an old style but much better quality than present styles. The clerk had to size up the customer and determine which one of these lies would be most likely to result in a sale.

Several years later I became acquainted with a man who worked for several years as a regular salesman in shoe stores in Seattle. When I described to him the methods I had learned in the shoe store where I worked, he said: "Every shoe store in Seattle except one does exactly the same things and I learned to be a shoe salesman in exactly the same manner you did."

Another young man who was holding his first position as a shoe salesman in a small city wrote an autobiographical statement in which he included the following instructions given him by the manager of the shoe store:

> My job is to move out shoes and I hire you to assist in this. I am perfectly glad to fit a person with a pair of shoes if we have his size, but I am willing to misfit him if it is necessary in order to sell him a pair of shoes. I expect you to do the same. If you do not like this, some one else can have your job. While you are working for me, I expect you to have no scruples about how you sell shoes.

A man who had been a school teacher and had never been officially involved in any delinquencies secured a position as agent of a book-publishing company and was assigned to public school work. He soon learned that the publishing company bribed the members of the textbook committee in order to secure adoptions of their books. With considerable shame he began to use this method of bribery because he felt it was necessary in order to make a good record. Partly because he disliked this procedure but principally because this work kept him away from home much of the time, he decided that he would become a lawyer. He moved to a large city, registered for night courses in a law school, and secured a daytime job as a claim agent for a casualty insurance company. About two years later he was convicted of embezzling the funds of the insurance company. A portion of his autobiography describes the process by which he got into this difficulty:

> Almost immediately after I got into this business I learned two things: first, the agents who got ahead with the company were the

ones who made settlements at low figures and without taking cases into court; second, the settlements were generally made by collusion with the lawyers and doctors for the claimants. Most of the lawyers for the claimants were ambulance-chasers and were willing to make settlements because they got their fees without any work. The claim agent for the insurance company got a secret kick-back out of the settlement. When I learned this was the way to get ahead in the casualty insurance business, I went in for it in a big way. Accidentally I left some papers loose in my office, from which it was discovered that I was "knocking down" on the settlements. The insurance company accused me of taking money which belonged to them, but actually I was taking money which belonged to the claimants.

The following statement was made by a young man who had graduated from a recognized school of business, had become a certified public accountant, and had been employed for several years in a respected firm of public accountants in a large city.

While I was a student in the school of business I learned the principles of accounting. After I had worked for a time for an accounting firm I found that I had failed to learn many important things about accounting. An accounting firm gets its work from business firms and, within limits, must make the reports which those business firms desire. The accounting firm for which I work is respected and there is none better in the city. On my first assignment I discovered some irregularities in the books of the firm and these would lead anyone to question the financial policies of that firm. When I showed my report to the manager of our accounting firm, he said that was not a part of my assignment and I should leave it out. Although I was confident that the business firm was dishonest, I had to conceal this information. Again and again I have been compelled to do the same thing in other assignments. I get so disgusted with things of this sort that I wish I could leave the profession. I guess I must stick to it, for it is the only occupation for which I have training.

The documents above were written by persons who came from "good homes" and "good neighborhoods" and who had no official records as juvenile delinquents. White collar criminals, like professional thieves, are seldom recruited from juvenile delinquents. As a part of the process of learning practical business, a young man with idealism and thoughtfulness for others is inducted into white collar crime. In many cases he is ordered by the manager to do things which he regards as unethical or illegal, while in other cases he learns from those who have the same rank as his own how they make a success. He learns specific techniques of violating the law, together with definitions of situations in which those techniques may be used. Also, he develops a general ideology. This ideology grows in part out of the specific practices and is in the nature of generalization from concrete experiences, but in part it is transmitted as a generalization by phrases such as "we are not in business for our health," "business is business," or "no business was ever built on the beatitudes." These generalizations, whether transmitted as such or abstracted from concrete experiences, assist the neophyte in business to accept the illegal practices and provide rationalizations for them.

Postscript to the Peter Principle

Lane Tracy

"In a hierarchy, every employee tends to rise to his level of incompetence."[1]

The arguments for accepting the Peter Principle as a serious attempt to tell us something about our own society, at least, are quite strong. The achievement orientation of Americans, our professed ideal of equality, and our high mobility, all contribute to an expectation that a man, unless he is obviously incompetent, will soon be promoted. Furthermore, men are usually promoted on the basis of faith that training and experience will develop their "potential," rather than on any hard evidence of their ability to handle the new job. It only requires a slight weakening of our faith in the powers of education to realize that sooner or later, and probably sooner, most men will come to rest in a job that is too much for them. Moreover, our eyes and ears, if not our very souls, confirm that many men have already reached that position.

The difficulty in accepting the Peter Principle at full value lies in the fact that, despite the plausibility of Peter's argument and the observed incompetence of many employees, our organizations still seem to function well. Workable decisions *are* made, orders *are* transmitted and carried out, and as often as not the product *is* delivered on time. The cynics amongst us may cite the inevitable foul-ups that occur—the Edsel, the SST, the maxiskirt—but these are the exception rather than the rule. If such mistakes were the rule, they would not provoke as much anger, chagrin, and laughter as they do. Therefore, we are faced with the question: If the Peter Principle is basically valid, why do not more things go wrong?

Peter attempts to account for the fact that much work still gets done by stating that "work is accomplished by those employees who have not yet reached their level of incompetence."[2] Somehow this argument is not convincing. The number of posts filled with such still-competent employees does not seem sufficient to account for the observed level of efficiency in our organizations. The accumulation of deadwood, particularly at the executive levels of our hierarchies, should be so great as to preclude any effective overall direction of the enterprise. Thus we have an anomaly; the evidence fails to support the principle.

If one accepts the basic validity of the arguments for the Peter Principle, such a contradiction is intolerable. The obvious conclusion is that our organizations somehow are able to retain a cadre of competent people to whom the Peter Principle does not apply. These people cannot be part of the organizational hierarchy, for there the Peter Principle operates at full force. And yet, to be in a position to carry out the necessary functions of planning, directing, and controlling the enterprise, such people must reside at all levels of the administrative hierarchy. What class of people fits this description? The obvious answer is *secretaries*.

Secretaries permeate all administrative levels of business, government, schools, nonprofit organizations, and so on, forming what I call a "parahierarchy" of administrative talent. (I define a parahierarchy as a grouping of people connected in tandem to a ranked or ordered group; or, more simply, a grouping of people in positions parallel to a hierarchy.) Whenever an executive falters, either because he has reached his level of incompetence or because he is moving up so fast that he does not have time to learn his job, his secretary is ready and waiting to take over. But what makes a secretary competent when her executive counterpart is not?

A SUBORDINATE CLASS

The answer comes from Peter's analysis that the introduction of class barriers into a hierarchy greatly retards the growth of organizational incompetence. Members of a subordinate class, restricted from entry into the higher ranks, find little opportunity to advance to a position in which they would be incompetent.

In our society, women form just such a subordinate class. No matter how competent they are, women are not expected to aspire to a position higher than the level of secretary, nurse, or elementary school teacher (at most, secondary school or women's college teacher). There is a distinct class barrier that prevents most women from rising to executive positions; thus they are expected to be satisfied to remain in, and efficiently fill, the same position year after year. Men, on the other hand, are expected to advance rapidly; and it is this cultural expectation of regular advancement for men which provides much of the motive force for the Peter Principle.

But, one may argue, there are still several ranks within the class of secretaries—file clerks, typists, stenographers, receptionists. In addition, secretaries hold levels in their parahierarchies corresponding to the hierarchical levels of the executives they serve. Does not a secretary tend to rise to her level of incompetence within her own class?

Cultural & Other Constraints

I have concluded that the answer to the preceding question is *no*, and for four reasons.

In the first place, since women are seldom permitted to take positions such as business executive, physician, engineer, or college professor, there exists a large pool of talented women from which to draw.

Second, as previously noted, there is no cultural expectation of a regular or rapid advancement for women. Women are generally assumed to be flightly, irrational, and interested only in marriage and producing babies; they are not promoted until they have proven otherwise.

Third, the pay differential between different secretarial positions is not nearly as wide as that between the corresponding executive positions. Consequently, the monetary incentive for advancement is not as great.

Finally, and most importantly, the secretarial parahierarchy is not a true hierarchy; it would not stand without the supporting structure of the executive hierarchy. A true or vertical hierarchy is always buttressed by a system of formal authority, in which each level directly bosses the level below and, indirectly, all lower levels. The motivation to move up in the hierarchy is strengthened by the desire to get one more level of authority off one's back.

But secretaries are bossed by the executives they work for, and the load gets no lighter—in fact, it may even get heavier—as they move up. Consequently, the authority structure provides no motivation to try to rise in the hierarchy.

Since secretaries have no formal authority over one another, the secretarial parahierarchy contains only one real level of authority. The secretarial parahierarchy is thus an example of a *horizontal hierarchy*. (A horizontal hierarchy may contain many positions, but they must all be on the same level of formal authority.) . . .

SIMILAR STRUCTURES

After having discovered the secretarial parahierarchy and noted its significance, I was determined to see if there were similar structures elsewhere in our organizations. I looked for positions commonly filled by members of a subordinate class. I found that women again figure prominently in medical and educational parahierarchies. Nurses are in a position to monitor and correct some of physicians' worst abuses. Primary and secondary school teachers implant the study skills with which many college students manage to learn in spite of the tutorial incompetence of their professors.

But women are not the only subordinate class members protected from the ravages of the Peter Principle. As farms have outgrown the competency of their managers, they have increasingly come to depend on the experience and skills of a cadre of black and Chicano farm workers. Mass-production industry has relied from the start on the cheap but skilled labor of ethnic and racial minority groups, particularly new immigrants. Restaurants prosper because of the efforts of foreign chefs and waiters. Hospitals are held together by a combination of refugee doctors, female nurses, and black or immigrant attendants, cooks, and laundry workers. College-trained engineers and architects rely on the skills and experience of nondegreed designers and draftsmen.

In some of these cases, the parallel linkage to the executive hierarchy is less obvious than it was for secretaries. In industry, for instance, we usually think of supervisors or foremen as being at the lower end of the executive hierarchy and, therefore, as part of the Peter progression. But there is a real barrier between the blue-collar and white-collar positions. It is not now, and never has been, common in U.S. industry to rise from the ranks into the executive hierarchy. The position of supervisor has been virtually the top of the line for a man without a college education.

Consequently, we have a large pool of experienced leaders who cannot rise to executive positions, and a group of inexperienced executives attempting to run the show. The supervisor must perform the doubly difficult task of shielding his men from the incompetence of the executives while making the necessary decisions to maintain the flow of production. Fortunately for us, he is usually equal to the task because he has not been allowed to rise to his level of incompetence.

Productive Parahierarchies

In addition to the fact that the parahierarchies just mentioned are composed of members of subordinate classes, and that they have little or no authority structure, they share one other important characteristic. They perform the productive work of their respective organizations in spite of rampant incompetence in the dominant hierarchy. For this reason, I call them "productive parahierarchies."

The old saying that secretaries really run the company, or that nurses really run the hospital, is no joke. It is such productive parahierarchies which provide the glue that holds our society together.

Without them, business, government, medicine, and education would long ago have collapsed under the weight of cumulative incompetence. . . .

What I am suggesting, then, is a general tenet which I shall call the Productive Parahierarchy Principle:

In order to survive, a dominant hierarchy must create and maintain a parahierarchy composed of members of a subordinate class to whom the Peter Principle does not apply.

Notes

1. Lawrence J. Peter and Raymond Hull, *The Peter Principle: Why Things Always Go Wrong* (New York, Bantam Books, Inc., 1969), p. 7.
2. Ibid., p.10.

The Concept of Status as Practiced in Business Organizations
Michael C. Mound

STATUS SYMBOLS

The subject of status symbols is, without question, the most fascinating aspect of the whole concept of status. As the tangible, visible, and external manifestations of a status position, status symbols are both the representation of rank incarnate and offer the most incisive and sometimes amusing glimpses into the organizational "establishment. . . ."

. . . In some situations, it is relatively easy to identify a person's status by observing the tools used to perform the assigned task (tools of the trade). Most office situations, however, do not lend themselves quite so easily to the deciphering of the symbols which reflect the underlying status structure. An interesting observation is that the more difficult it is for a casual observer to see the basis for differentia-

Michael C. Mound, "The Concept of Status as Practiced in Business Organizations," pp. 7–19, *MSU Business Topics*, Autumn 1968. Reprinted by permission of the publisher, Division of Research, Graduate School of Business Administration, Michigan State University.

tion, the more important the symbols tend to be. Anyone who has worked in a large office complex will attest to the truth of this observation.

In small companies, there is little need for such visible badges of office because all concerned know everybody in the organization and are also aware of the individual jobs and authorities. As companies increase in size, however, the search begins to enable people to differentiate between status levels in visible ways. In company manuals, models of varying degrees of complexity are set up for assigning "everything from office square footage to drapes, carpeting, carafe, telephone stand, and bookcase."[1] Some years ago, the *Wall Street Journal*[2] noted that efforts were being made to downgrade the "much maligned but omnipresent appurtenance of corporate power (the status symbol)" but evidently such efforts were not very effective. During the year 1957, the *Journal* reported that status symbols were on the rise among fifty businesses in twelve cities, thereby suggesting that the "corporate caste system was being rigidified."

The general category of executive perquisites (or "perks" as the Europeans refer to them) ranges from pedestrian to the ridiculous. One odd feature about even the most blatantly ludicrous perquisites is that few people within the organization see any humor in being deprived of these symbols. In point of fact, the less overt the differences in status and amenities may be, the more critical they are to the individual. It is tempting to joke about whether or not one has a thermo-flask on his desk, a two- or three-pen desk set, or whether the floor is rubber-tiled or carpeted; but joking among executives is strained and nervous.[3]

Titles

In most companies, titles may serve as status indicators; a "vice-president of sales" title tells that the individual is high in the formal command structure and that his chief functional capacity is as the sales executive. The term "executive" as a general sort of title, is a stepchild of the status-symbolizing culture present in most companies. There is no general agreement as to where in the corporate structure a supervisor becomes an "executive." Packard[4] notes that the term "junior executive" was invented to give marginal people the benefit of the doubt, but it is a ludicrous title to apply to older employees (some men at the junior executive level in one company were sixty-three years old). He suggests the term "semi-executive." Even at lower levels in organizations, the very morale of employees is at stake in the matter of titles, and employees are extremely sensitive to upward shifts in formal hierarchy granted to members of a lower-or peer-group status.

Status Inflation

The problem of title proliferation sometimes results in the catastrophic condition known as status inflation. As more and more people get closer to the top of the corporate "pyramid," there is sometimes a noticeable increase in the number of glowing titles bestowed by a given company. Title upgrading is a noncost incentive and is aggravated by company mergers. Consider the problem which develops when a giant corporation merges with a small company. What shall be done with the titled president of the now nonexistent company? Some companies, instead of retitling him division manager, for example, permit the "president" title to remain. Several years ago, Borg-Warner Corporation had forty presidents or chairmen, IBM had seven presidents, and Firestone Tire and Rubber had twelve presidents. Financial institutions have been noted to be especially open-handed with titles. Packard[5] puckishly observes that this not only serves as a noncost reward to the titleholder but flatters clients who feel that they are "dealing with a vice-president, not just some flunky. . . ."

Status inflation may penetrate deep into the heart of the organization from the highest executive to the lowest hourly worker. Workers become "employees," and soap salesmen become "district representatives." In the office, the clerk-typist is a "secretary," or "Gal Friday" (in Britain, an ad was run for a "Woman Friday"). The extent of title-mania in organizations has led some management experts to form the opinion that of every ten top executives, two are excellent, aggressive, and alert men, six are satisfactory, but not spectacular, and two are utter misfits. A trend in modern companies is to force early retirement upon absolute liabilities if they are within a decent neighborhood of normal retirement age. A more common solution for younger deadwood is to create titles or invent spurious assignments for them. It appears, however, that while small- and medium-sized companies will face up to the problem and fire a man, large companies tend to go to great extremes to avoid this. Some companies pride themselves on their records of never having fired anyone (people just quite for one reason or another). At times, the special and unique positions created for problem personnel become common knowledge among the rest of the employees. In these cases, the position becomes useless for other purposes because employees will be insulted if they are "promoted to the dead-end rank."

Offices

The executive symbols of status begin with the nature of office assignments; size, space, view, location and furnishings are of paramount importance in determining status levels. H. W. Herzig, manager of building and office services for Crown Zellerbach, was quoted as saying, "when we move into a new 20-story office building . . . we'll be able to arrange walls so that offices of equal rank can be built to within a square inch of one another."[6] This approach has been termed "scientific stratification." Problems of symbols result in ticklish internal situations for a company. Symbol "collectors" vie for the added extras in office furnishings. One executive had his office floor redone in pigskin tile at company expense (at $5 per square foot). Packard[7] describes the typical corporation hierarchy thusly: the top man gets the corner office with the nicest view. Because physical closeness to the center of power is evidence of powerful status, offices of subordinates branch out from his corner in descending rank. For a man "on his way up," being on the same floor with people at the head office (so that you can be seen by the powers) is important. Advancement is far more likely than if you are on another floor, building, or (worst of all) in another city. Prior to 1956, Firestone Tire and Rubber Company headquarters in Akron, Ohio, exhibited a striking example of visual status levels in offices:

> Officers were located in descending rank away from Chairman Harvey S. Firestone, Jr.'s office in progressively smaller quarters . . . as the distance increased, offices stopped being enclosed by wood and were enclosed by frosted glass that went to the ceiling . . . farther out, the glass . . . was clear. Next . . . the offices were enclosed only by clear glass rising to just above the eye level. Beyond was the open room.[8]

Union Carbide's building in Manhattan has fifteen acres of 1½-inch thick carpeting, 3,000 new desks—400 of ordinary wood (for ordinary executives) and a few of the finest teak for top management. There are fifty-three stories in the building and the important offices (for important management personnel) are arranged in ascending rank to the fifty-second floor. The "climb-to-heaven" analogy is tempting, but the fact that the top of the building (the fifty-third floor) is occupied by a water tower has a dampening effect. Another New York City corporation has such an obvious hierarchy by floors in its thirty-story headquarters that the middle management personnel likened their floor ranking system to that of Huxley's *Brave New World*: alpha = superior status, beta = above average, gamma = average, delta = below average, and epsilon = abysmally low in status.[9] The matter of windows and view is of no small importance for office status. In large buildings, offices without windows or with a one "inner-view" window carry low status. Corner locations and several windows denote high status.

Furnishings

The use of desks as rank determinants is subtle, but well known. In ascending status order, desks may be:

1) a one-drawer steel table
2) a three-drawer steel desk
3) a full-sized (30 x 60) oak desk
4) a pedestal steel desk
5) a walnut desk

6) a steel or walnut desk with a five-inch overhang
7) mahogony
8) teak (any size)
Desk complements are, in ascending rank:
1) oak mail tray (one drawer)
2) oak mail tray (two drawers), glass ashtray
3) glass desk top
4) desk blotter
5) desk pen set (one pen)
6) mahogany mail tray, phone stand
7) mahogany ashtray (1), clock
8) mahogany ashtray (2), clock-barometer, two-pen desk set
9) leather pencil holder, teak letter opener
Chairs may be important also:
1) oak chair, no arms
2) oak chair, arms
3) steel chair on rollers, no arms
4) steel chair, arms (unpadded)
5) oak chair, swivel rocker
6) steel chair, swivel rocker, padded seat
7) same as (6), but with padded arms
8) chair to match desk (wood or metal, equal in quality)
9) leather chair of choice

Executive Washrooms and Dining Rooms

Private washrooms in many companies are reserved for vice-presidents and higher. A midwestern oil company has private wash-rooms (but no toilets) for vice-presidents. Campbell's Soup Company in Camden, New Jersey, has the following washroom hierarchy: (1) president has a private washroom; (2) vice-presidents "double-up" on adjoining rooms; (3) executives below the vice-president are barred from the washroom aristocracy and must, as befits their station, walk to the regular facilities.

DuPont did away with the washroom symbol because there was a "premium on space."[10] Packard[11] described one New York company's chairman as having a water closet of carved marble. One other company has a Picasso on display in the men's room of its executive suite; another has its thick wall-to-wall carpeting continue into the executive washroom.

Executive dining room privileges are also significant perks. Dining rooms may be differentiated according to whether or not there are table cloths on the tables, and may be ranked in terms of cuisine and overall elegance.

Automobiles

As status symbols, automobile assignments are very precise measures. One study reported the following six-level system to be most widely used (prices are for 1957 cars):

1) salesmen: inexpensive Fords, Chevrolets, Plymouths ($2,200)
2) sales supervisors: better Fords, Chevrolets, Plymouths ($2,500)
3) assistant sales managers: Mercury, Pontiac, Dodge ($2,800)
4) sales managers: Oldsmobile, Buick ($3,600)
5) division managers: Chrysler, Lincoln, Cadillac ($5,100)
6) vice-presidents and up: "any kind of Cadillac they want."[12]

Secretaries

Secretaries, of course, play a key role for symbol collectors. Department heads have "executive secretaries"; inferior beings have "stenographers." Electric typewriters are only for higher level secretaries in some companies. The chief goal is to have two secretaries, but this may produce unexpected problems if they can't get along with each other. A department manager of a Pennsylvania oil company had to have a wall constructed between two feuding secretaries to solve this problem.[13] Some executives spend hours on time charts to prove that they are so busy that one secretary cannot possibly do the job; two secretaries are necessary.[14] Sommer[15] theorizes that, in a research laboratory

one good secretary is worth two good scientists. . . . Flowers on her desk, air conditioning, and electric typewriter—no expense should be spared to keep a good secretary happy. An electric typewriter will not only give her status in the eyes of her colleagues but also permit her to type faster and neater.

Sommer summarizes the law of scientific output for any laboratory:

$$Productivity = \frac{Number\ of\ secretaries \times average\ typing\ speed}{Number\ of\ Scientists}$$

An interesting feature of the equation is that productivity is infinite when the number of scientists is equal to 0.

Keys

Another of Sommer's[16] equations refers to the matter of keys as status symbols in organizations. He argues that a person's status can be gauged by the formula:

$$S = \frac{D}{K}$$

where S = status, D = the number of doors a person must open to perform his job, and K = the number of keys he carries. The higher the S number, the higher the status. If a janitor must open twenty doors and has twenty keys, he has a status of one; a secretary with one key and two doors to open has a score of two. A manager with two keys and six doors to open has a score of three. The president, of course, never has to carry keys and can get into any door, so he has a status rank of infinity. Ludicrous as this example may seem, the plain fact is that possession of single, department-master, floor-master, and grand-master keys is a definite status symbol.

Transportation Perquisites

Probably the most spectacular of all status symbols (and one which has been termed wasteful and extravagant by even devoted symbol collectors) is the private railroad car. Although this is a perquisite that is fading in popularity, some top executives still use private cars as their official means of traveling. Such an honor may cost a company in the neighborhood of $100,000 a year.[17] A more common means of conveying top executives from place to place, but only slightly less extravagant, is the company's private jet. Although use of private jets for short business trips may be realistic in terms of time saved and having the important men in the right place at the right time, indiscriminate use of the executive plane for longer trips can cost the company up to twenty times that of a first-class commercial ticket. The increased use of commercial jet travel itself has opened up new areas for status symbols; only higher ranking people are accorded first-class privileges when traveling on company business.

Other Symbols

Other perquisites include company-paid memberships to country clubs, keys to hidden lodges, use of company yachts and chauffeured cars, permission for wives to ride on company planes and accompany their husbands to spas for free medical checkups, and, in a few cases, company-owned, rent-free homes.[18]

Importance of the Wife

The role of the wife can be an extremely important factor in many of the status symbol acquisition stages. Some authors feel that the "push" of the wife is due to a desire to indicate the husband's importance when talking to her associates. It is a good deal more rewarding to boast about a free trip to a spa, the size of the office, or the number of secretaries a husband has than to openly brag about the salary he earns (which may be considered to be in poor taste); also, he may not really earn so very much. A related feature of the wife's role may be as a status symbol, herself. . . . While it is true that the amount of interest shown in a man's wife varies with the company and the geographic location, the fact is that considerable interest is shown in the wife. . . .

STATUS TENSIONS

Frequently, workers are moved (for reasons of redundant operations or bad health) to another job at the same pay but with less informal status. The resulting resentment of the displaced worker and the disrupted status situation has been called one of the common causes of strikes. In connection with status alterations and general management misconceptions, status may be lowered not only by demoting a person from one level to another, but also by indirectly lowering status of one group through taking some action to raise the relative status of another.[19] Among executives, the game of one-upmanship is played continuously. The gentle art of being a jump ahead of colleagues in acquiring a better ashtray or better air conditioner is a phenomenon that is humorous to all but the combatants.[20]

NOTES

1. V. Packard, *The Pyramid Climbers* (New York: McGraw Hill Book Company, 1962), p. 26.

2. "Status Symbols," *Wall Street Journal*, October 29, 1957, p. 1.

3. W. H. Whyte, Jr., *The Organization Man* (New York: Doubleday and Company, 1956), p. 177.

4. Packard, *The Pyramid Climbers, op. cit.*, p. 27.

5. V. Packard, *The Status Seekers* (New York: David McKay Company, 1959), pp. 205–206.

6. "Status Symbols," *op. cit.*, p. 1.

7. Packard, *The Status Seekers, op. cit.*, pp. 102–103.

8. Packard, *The Pyramid Climbers, op. cit.*, pp. 26–27.

9. E. W. Ziegler, "Payment by Status," *The Nation*, November 12, 1960, pp. 365–366.

10. "Status Symbols," *op. cit.*, p. 8.

11. Packard, *The Pyramid Climbers, op. cit.*, p. 203.

12. Packard, *The Status Seekers, op. cit.*, pp. 104–105.

13. "Status Symbols," *op. cit.*, p. 8..

14. "Executive Trappings," *Time*, January 24, 1955, p. 80.

15. R. Sommer, "Einstein's Girl Friday," *The Worm Re-Turns* (New Jersey: Prentice-Hall, 1965), pp. 13–16.

16. R. Sommer, "Keys, Kings, and Kompanies," *The Worm Re-Turns* (New Jersey: Prentice-Hall, 1965), p. 18.

17. Packard, *The Status Seekers, op. cit.*, pp. 105–106.

18. Packard, *The Pyramid Climbers, op cit.*, p. 205.

19. J. A. C. Brown, "The Informal Organization of Industry," *People and Productivity* (New York: McGraw-Hill Book Company, 1963), p. 339.

20. "Executive Trappings," *op. cit.*, p. 60.

4

THE INDIVIDUAL
IN THE ORGANIZATION

There is extensive evidence supporting the observation that for many, the organizational experience is indeed "nasty, brutish and short." In a very real sense, an alarming number of people find themselves enveloped by the organizations that employ them, manipulated by the realities of their job, dealing with callous, conniving supervisors, or literally functioning in a demeaning or even dangerous work environment.

We have chosen for this section a cross-section of snapshots of such job experiences. The first two selections, "Lilith Reynolds" and "Diane Wilson," are excerpts from Studs Terkel's book *Working*. Here the individuals relate their employment experiences with the United States government.

"The Underlife of Cabdriving" emphasizes the unpleasant and often hazardous aspects of cabdrivers' lives in the big city and the ways in which they are exploited by the public, their employers and their unions.

"Terry Mason" strips the glamor, if indeed any remains, from the occupation of airline stewardess. Once again, we see an occupation in which petty but nonetheless annoying behavior by clients and management combine to disenchant employees with their organizational experience.

The excerpt from Aronowitz's *False Promises* describes life on the assembly line at General Motors's Lordstown Plant. The physically exhausting and mentally vacuous task of staying with the line, the reactions of the workers to their jobs and management's varied approaches to the overriding problems of sustaining production are all vividly described.

Next, the few pages from "The Management Monopoly" show how rules created with the intent of providing equitable treatment can be used as weapons against the very employees whose rights they were intended to safeguard.

Finally, the selection from *Out of Their League* exposes us to some of the less visible and less savoury aspects of intercollegiate and professional football.

The reader is invited to contrast the experiences presented in this section with other materials on subjects such as job enrichment, participative management and other contemporary approaches to personnel management.

Lilith Reynolds

Studs Terkel

That's another typical thing in government. When management wants to get rid of you, they don't fire you. What they do is take your work away. That's what happened to me. He didn't even tell me what my new job would be. They sent somebody down to go through my personnel file. "My God, what can we do with her?" They had a problem because I'm a high-grade employee. I'm grade 14. The regional director's a 17. One of the deputy directors told me, "You're going to be economic development specialist." (Laughs.)

I'm very discouraged about my job right now. I have nothing to do. For the last four or five weeks I haven't been doing any official work, because they really don't expect anything. They just want me to be quiet. What they've said is it's a sixty-day detail. I'm to come up with some kind of paper on economic development. It won't be very hard because there's little that can be done. At the end of sixty days I'll present the paper. But because of the reorganization that's come up I'll probably never be asked about the paper.

It's extremely frustrating. But, ironically, I've felt more productive in the last few weeks doing what I've wanted to do than I have in the last year doing what I was officially supposed to be doing. Officially I'm loafing. I've been working on organizing women and on union activities. It's been great.

If they would let me loose a little more, I could really do something. We've got plenty of statistics to show incredible sex discrimination. Black women have the lowest average grade. White women have the next lowest. Then black men. Then white men. I'm sure these are the statistics for our whole society. We believe that in organizing women we can make changes in all directions. We've already started to do that.

There's no reason why we can't carry this to the community action agencies. Many of them deal with welfare mothers, with all kinds of households headed by women. If women knew more about their rights, they'd have an easier time. If we could get into the whole issue of law suits, we'd get real changes. My office is trying to stop us.

When you do something you're really turned on about, you'll do it off-hours too. I put more of myself into it, acting like I'm a capable person. When you're doing something you're turned off on, you don't use what talents you have. There are a lot of people in our office who are doing very, very little, simply because their jobs are so meaningless.

Some of these jobs will appear meaningful on paper. The idea of the antipoverty program is exciting. But people are stifled by bureaucratic decisions and non-decisions. When you're in the field and get into sticky situations with politicians, you can't count on your office to support you. You'll be punished—like having your job taken away from you. (Laughs.)

Since I've been doing what I want to do, my day goes much faster. When I was assistant to the regional director, an awful lot of my time was taken up with endless meetings. I spent easily twenty or more hours a week in meetings. Very, very nonproductive. Though now I'm doing what I want to do, I know it's not gonna last.

I have to hide the stuff I'm doing. If anybody walks into the office, you have to quick shove the stuff out of the way. It's fairly well known now that I'm not doing any official work, because this huge controversy has been going on between the union and the director. People are either on one side or the other. Most people who come in to see me are on the union side. I'm not hiding the fact that I'm not doing any official work.

I hide the stuff because I feel a little guilty. This is probably my Protestant upbringing. I've been work oriented all my life. I can't go on drawing a paycheck doing what I want to do—that's my conditioning. My dad worked in a factory. I was taught work is something you *have* to do. You do that to get money. It's not your life, but you must do it. Now I believe—I'm getting around to it (laughs)—you should get paid for doing what you want to do. I know it's happening to me. But I still have this conditioning: it's too good to be true.

I've had discussions with friends of mine to the right and to the left of me. The people to the left say you shouldn't take any part in a corrupt system. To give them your time and take money from them is a no-no. People to the right say you have no right to take the taxpayers' money for doing nothing. You're not doing official work, therefore you shouldn't be paid for it.

I feel much less guilty about this than I would have a year ago. I have less and less confidence that management people should be telling me what to do. They know less than I do. I trust my own judgment more. I believe that what I'm doing is important.

What would be my recommendation? I read Bellamy's *Looking Backward*, which is about a utopian society. Getting paid for breathing is what it amounts to. I believe we'd be a lot better off if people got paid for what they want to do. You would certainly get a bigger contribution from the individual. I think it would make for exciting change. It'd be great.

The reasons people get paid now are wrong. I think the reward system should be different. I think we should have a basic security—a decent place to live, decent food, decent clothing, and all that. So people in a work situation wouldn't be so frightened. People are intimidated and the system works to emphasize that. They get what they want out of people by threatening them economically. It makes people apple polishers and ass kissers. I used to hear people say, "Work needs to be redefined." I thought they were crazy. Now I know they're not.

Diane Wilson
Studs Terkel

You wish there was a better system. A lot of money is held up and the grantees want to know why they can't get it. Sometimes they call and get the run-around on the phone. I never do that. I tell the truth. If they don't have any money left, they don't have it. No, I'm not disturbed any more. If I was just starting on this job, I probably would. But the older I get, I realize it's a farce. You just get used to it. It's a job. I get my paycheck—that's it. It's all political anyway.

A lot of times the grantee comes down to our audit department for aid. They're not treated as human beings. Sometimes they have to wait, wait, wait—for no reason. The grantee doesn't know it's for no reason. He thinks he's getting somewhere and he really isn't.

They send him from floor to floor and from person to person, it's just around and around he goes. Sometimes he leaves, he hasn't ac-

From *Working: People Talk About What They Do All Day and How They Feel About What They Do*, by Studs Terkel. Copyright © 1972, 1974 by Studs Terkel. Reprinted by permission of Pantheon Books, a Division of Random House, Inc., and Wildwood House Ltd., Publishers.

complished anything. I don't know why this is so. You can see 'em waiting—so long. Sometimes it has to do with color. Whoever is the boss. If you're in the minority group, you can tell by their actions. A lot of times they don't realize that you know, but this has happened to you.

So this person was standing out there. He had come to offer something. He was from out of state. The secretary told this boss he had someone waiting. He also had someone in the office. He could've waited on the grantee and got him on his way quick. But he closed the door in the young man's face and the young man stood there. That went on for about forty-five minutes. The secretary got tired of seein' the man standin' there, so she said, could she help him? Was it somethin' he just wanted to give the man? He told her yes. She took it, so he wouldn't stand there. That was all he was gonna do, give it to him. I thought this was awfully rude. This boss does this quite often. I don't know if he does it on purpose. I know if it's an Indian or a black or a Latin he does this.

Life is a funny thing. We had this boss come in from Internal Revenue. He wanted to be very, very strict. He used to have meetings every Friday—about people comin' in late, people leavin' early, people abusin' lunch time. Everyone was used to this relaxed attitude. You kind of went overtime. No one bothered you. The old boss went along. You did your work.

Every Friday, everyone would sit there and listen to this man. And we'd all go out and do the same thing again. Next Friday he'd have another meeting and he would tell us the same thing. (Laughs.) We'd all go out and do the same thing again. (Laughs.) He would try to talk to one and see what they'd say about the other. But we'd been working all together for quite a while. You know how the game is played. Tomorrow you might need a favor. So nobody would say anything. If he'd want to find out what time someone came in, who's gonna tell 'em? He'd want to find out where someone was, we'd always say, "They're at the Xerox." Just anywhere. He couldn't get through. Now, lo and behold! We can't find *him* anywhere. He's got into this nice, relaxed atmosphere . . . (Laughs.) He leaves early, he takes long lunch hours. We've converted him. (Laughs.)

After my grievances and my fighting, I'm a processing clerk. Never a typist no more or anything like that. (Laughs.) I started working here in 1969. There was an emergency and they all wanted to work overtime. So I made arrangements at home, 'cause I have to catch a later train. Our supervisor's black. All of us are black. We'll help her get it out so there won't be any back drag on this. Okay, so we all worked overtime and made a good showing.

Then they just didn't want to give us the promotion which was due us anyhow. They just don't want to give you anything. The personnel man, all of them, they show you why you don't deserve a promotion. The boss, the one we converted—he came on board, as they call it, after we sweated to meet the deadline. So he didn't know what we did. But he told us we didn't deserve it. That stayed with me forever. I won't be bothered with him ever again.

But our grievance man was very good. He stayed right on the case. We filed a civil rights complaint. Otherwise we woulda never got the promotion. They don't want anybody coming in investigating for race. They said, "Oh, it's not that." But you sit around and see white women do nothin' and get promotions. Here we're working and they say you don't deserve it. The black men are just as hard on us as the white man. Harder. They get angry with you because you started a lot of trouble. The way I feel about it, I'm gonna give 'em all the trouble I can.

Our boss is black, the one that told us we didn't deserve it. (Laughs.) And our union man fighting for us, sittin' there, punchin' away, is white. (Laughs.) We finally got up to the deputy director and he was the one—the white man—that finally went ahead and gave us the promotion. (Laughs.) So we went from grade 4 clerk-typist to grade 5 processing clerk.

We had another boss, he would walk around and he wouldn't want to see you idle at all. Sometimes you're gonna have a lag in your work, you're all caught up. This had gotten on his nerves. We got our promotion and we weren't continually busy. Any time they see black women idle, that irks 'em. I'm talkin' about black men as well as whites. They want you to work continuously.

One day I'd gotten a call to go to his office and do some typing. He's given me all this handwritten script. I don't know to this day what all that stuff was. I asked him, "Why was I picked for this job?" He said his secretary was out and he needs this done by noon. I said, "I'm no longer a clerk-typist and you yourself said for me to get it out of my mind. Are you trying to get me confused? Anyway, I can't read this stuff." He tells me he'll read it. I said, "Okay, I'll write it out as you read it." There's his hand going all over the script, busy. He doesn't know what he's readin', I could tell. I know why he's doing it. He just wants to see me busy.

So we finished the first long sheet. He wants to continue. I said, "No, I can only do one sheet at a time. I'll go over and type this up." So what I did, I would type a paragraph and wait five or ten minutes. I made sure I made all the mistakes I could. It's amazing, when you want to make mistakes, you really can't. So I just put Ko-rect-type paper over this yellow sheet. I fixed it up real pretty. I wouldn't stay on the margins. He told me himself I was no longer a clerk-typist.

I took him back this first sheet and, of course, I had left out a line or two. I told him it made me nervous to have this typed by a certain time, and I didn't have time to proofread it, "but I'm ready for you to read the other sheet to me." He started to proofread. I deliberately misspelled some words. Oh, I did it up beautifully. (Laughs.) He got the dictionary out and he looked up the words for me. I took it back and crossed out the words and squeezed the new ones in there. He started on the next sheet. I did the same thing all over again. There were four sheets. He proofread them all. Oh, he looked so serious! All this time he's spendin' just to keep me busy, see? Well, I didn't finish it by noon.

I'm just gonna see what he does if I don't finish it on time. Oh, it was imperative! I knew the world's not gonna change that quickly. It was nice outside. If it gets to be a problem, I'll go home. It's a beautiful day, the heck with it. So twelve-thirty comes and the work just looks awful. (Laughs.) I typed on all the lines, I continued it anywhere. One of the girls comes over, she says, "You're goin' off the line." I said, "Oh, be quiet. I know what I'm doin'. (Laughs.) Just go away." (Laughs.) I put the four sheets together. I never saw anything as horrible in my life. (Laughs.)

I decided I'd write him a note. "Dear Mr. Roberts: You've been so much help. You proofread, you look up words for your secretary. It must be marvelous working for you. I hope this has met with your approval. Please call on me again." I never heard from him. (A long laugh.)

These other people, they work, work, work, work and nothing comes of it. They're the ones that catch hell. The ones that come in every day on time, do the job, and try to keep up with everybody else. A timekeeper, a skinny little black woman. She's fanatic about time. She would argue with you if you were late or something. She's been working for the government twenty-five years and she hadn't gotten a promotion, 'cause she's not a fighter.

She has never reported sick. Some days I won't come. If it's bad outside, heavy snow, a storm, I won't go. You go the next day. The work's gonna be there. She thinks my attitude is just terrible. She's always runnin', acts like she's scared of everybody. She was off *one* day. She had a dental appointment. Oh, did the boss raise hell! Oh, my goodness! He never argues with me.

The boss whose typing I messed up lost his secretary. She got promoted. They told this old timekeeper she's to be his secretary-assistant. Oh, she's in her glory. No more money or anything and she's doing two jobs all day long. She's rushin' and runnin' all the time, all day. She's a nervous wreck. And when she asked him to write her up for an award, he refused. That's *her* reward for being so faithful, obedient.

Oh, we love it when the bosses go to those long meetings, those important conferences. (Laughs.) We just leave in a group and go for a show. We don't care. When we get back, they roll their eyes. They know they better not say anything, 'cause they've done nothing when we've been gone anyhow. We do the work that we have to do. The old timekeeper, She sits and knits all that time, always busy.

I've been readin'. Everything I could on China, ever since he made that visit. Tryin' to see how people live and the ideas. It changed me a lot. I don't see any need for work you don't enjoy. I like the way the Indians lived. They moved from season to season. They didn't pay taxes. Everybody had enough. I don't think a few should control everything. I don't think it's right that women lay down and bear sons and then you have a few rich people that tell your sons they have to go and die for their country. They're not dying for their country. They're dying for the few to stay on top. I don't think that's necessary. I'm just tired of this type of thing. I just think we ought to be just human.

The Underlife of Cabdriving: A Study in Exploitation and Punishment

James M. Henslin

What is the work of the cab driver like? Many people appear to have the idea that a cabbie's work is carefree. He hops into his cab, picks up passengers at various locations, and delivers them to their destinations. In the meantime he meets interesting people from all walks of life, enjoys good conversation, and collects sizeable tips—roaming the city as a sort of modern vagabond on wheels.

Such a view does contain an element of truth. The cabbie indeed delivers people to places they want to go. He does meet many people, of whom some are interesting and a few are even fascinating. He does become involved in many conversations. And he does collect tips. But there is much more to the work of the cabbie. And not all of it is rewarding—or even pleasant. This paper emphasizes the punishments and exploitation to which the cabbie is subjected, the

Reprinted by permission of the publisher from *Varieties of Occupational Experience*, by P. L. Stewart and M. G. Cantor (eds.), pp. 67–79. © Schenkman Publishing Co., Inc., 1974. □ This is a revised version of a paper read at the annual meeting of the Midwest Sociological Society, St. Louis, Missouri, April 1970.

brutalizing elements which are built into his job and go hand in hand with driving a cab.

One must also understand the rewarding aspects of the cabbie's life if one is to have an accurate or balanced picture of the cabbie's world. These rewarding aspects of the occupation are also crucial in the cabbie's life. They also shape his identity, mold the way he thinks of himself, and structure the way he views the world. . .

This analysis of the underlife of cabdriving is based on data gathered by this participant observer who drove a cab in the City of St. Louis on a part-time basis for about a year. Neither the management nor the workers knew they were being studied. A hidden tape recorder was used to record: 1) interaction among cabbies before and after work, 2) messages transmitted over the cab's radio, 3) conversations with passengers, 4) conversations with cabbies at the cab stands, and 5) crap games which these cabbies played after work. At no time were people informed that they were being studied, nor did they indicate any awareness that they had a researcher in their midst.

Why the choice of participant observation? A major goal of many sociological researchers is to understand the subject's world from *his* point of view. This purpose goes under various names in sociology, such as verstehen, interpretative understanding, subjective interpretation, definition of the situation, uncovering underlying "background expectancies," or investigating the "socially-sanctioned-facts-of-life-that-any-bonafide-member-of-the-group-knows." . . . The assumption is that intimate familiarity with someone's world can lead to an understanding of that person's definitional process, and that we can thereby know the factors he finds important and better understand his behavior.

Those researchers who follow this goal ordinarily choose a method of research which least molests the phenomena they are studying. Participant observation is frequently chosen because it not only allows the researcher entry into the everyday world of his subjects, but also, when done correctly, minimizes disruption to interaction. Thus the researcher can have greater confidence that the data he gathers by this method is representative of the regularly occurring, ongoing interaction of the group he enters; that it is naturalistic and not an artifact of his presence. . .

If one attempts to understand life's experiences from the perspective of the other, the researcher must "get into" the symbolic system of those he is studying. He must know what members of that group consider important in any relevant situation. When he understands how the members of a culture define their situations, the researcher knows much of what goes into the decisions they make. He then has some understanding of what influences and buttresses their life style.

In this research, I entered their world as someone who knew little about cabdriving and cab drivers. Not having previously learned to accept the cab drivers' view of reality as reality led me to question fundamental aspects of their existence. I then sociologically analyzed parts of their world which they routinely and unquestioningly took for granted. . .

Not only did I gain information about the world of those I was studying, but more importantly, I directly experienced that world. I was thus able to understand the events in cabbie culture from the perspective of the members of that culture. For example, I not only learned *what* a "no-go" is (a location to which a cabbie is dispatched, but where there is no passenger when he arrives), but I also learned the *meaning* of a "no-go" for the cab driver, such things as the effect of the "no-go" on his income for that shift, the frustration which seethes within him, and his feelings of futility in dealing with his world.

This paper, then, is presented from the point of view of the cab driver, and is an examination of the major areas of his life which he sees as punitive. Relevant aspects of his work setting are examined, including problematic aspects of interaction with passengers, competition among cabbies, mechanisms of social control, the cabbie's equipment, and factors which are structured into the occupation that exert control over his life situation and lead him to work hard but to live in poverty.

THE CABBIE AND HIS PASSENGERS

The cab driver is constantly on the go, being dispatched throughout the city. He transports businessmen, shoppers, tourists, workers, drunks, prostitutes, and housewives to their destinations. As he deals with these people, the cabbie regularly confronts passengers who threaten his self, his routine, and sometimes his property or even his life.

The cabbie is frequently treated as a non-person, that is, people sometimes act as though he were not present. Passengers sometimes do not adjust their behavior for his presence—anymore than they would for the steering wheel of an auto. When intimate arguments are fought out in the cab between lovers, for example, it is as though the cab driver were merely a non-human extension of the steering wheel, a kind of machine which guides the cab. Such interaction in all its varied aspects—the tones and loudness of voice, the words used, the subjects spoken about—takes place as though the individuals were in private, with no third person present. The effect on the cabbie of some types of non-person treatment is a challenging of the self since others are not acknowledging his self but acting as though he did not exist.

The cabbie also regularly has passengers who in various ways challenge his control over the transaction. Some passengers berate him for not going fast enough or for missing a green light, while others withhold the tip as a sanction against something they did not like about the driver. The cabbie must also put up with persons who are "playing." (In "cabby-ese" this refers to those who call in and have a cab dispatched to a location where no one desires a cab.) Other callers are present when he arrives but refuse to enter the cab. Still others, "bucket loads," skip out without paying their fare. Other passengers demand services he is unwilling to provide, such as locating a prostitute or entering an area of the city which the driver considers to be unsafe after dark. To communicate some of the "flavor" of such problematic interactions, I shall illustrate the punitiveness of the belligerent and non-cooperative passenger. In an afterwork group, a driver related the following incident:

He picked up a passenger who said, "Take me to thirty-five." The driver asked, "Thirty-five what?" The passenger became somewhat angry and raised his voice, saying. "Just take me to thirty-five!" In exasperation, the driver said, "Well, thirty-five what?" The passenger then said, "Just start driving!" The driver began driving, and after he had driven a short while, the passenger told him to make a right turn, and the driver did so. A while later, the passenger asked, "Where in the hell do you think you're going?" The driver then said, "I don't know where I'm going." The passenger then said, "I told you to take me to thirty-five!"

At this point the driver covertly placed his hand on a hammer he carried in the cab and said, "Thirty-five hundred what? You just name me the street, and I'll show you what thirty-five hundred is on any street in St. Louis!" At this, the passenger finally named his street. When they arrived at his destination, the fare was $1.55, and the passenger handed two one dollar bills to the driver, who still had his hand on the hammer. He then tapped the driver on the shoulder, and said, "There you are, buddy. Take it easy."

In reaction to such passengers, cabbies frequently develop a veneer of hardness, an outward crust which helps deflect painful threats to the self. This veneer manifests itself in the commonly perceived belligerency of cab drivers—the shaking fist and the cursing mouth, or the "Don't-tell-me-how-to-get-there" attitude. These are part of the cabbies' attempt to maintain control over threatening passengers and a life situation over which he actually has little control.

The threat of danger is also a constant part of the cab driver's work. Each day he drives his cab he lives with the knowledge that he might be robbed or murdered. This uncertainty of safety is constantly in the back of his mind as he picks up strangers as a routine part of his job. In the privacy of the cab, with these strangers at his back, he is literally at their mercy for his very life. This fear for his own safety constantly gnaws at him, and because holdup men are disproportionately black, both black and white cabbies tend to avoid black neighborhoods and black passengers—especially at night . . .

Since the potential of danger is always present, many warning devices have been suggested. One was to install a mechanism to flash the cab's top lights when the cab driver stepped on a button. The flashing lights would supposedly alert pedestrians, motorists, and the police. But cabbies scoffed when the device was suggested, saying that the light would also alert the robber since he would be able to see its reflection as they drove past store windows. If this happened, the robber might retaliate physically, and cabbies felt that they would be in greater danger with this device than without it.

In spite of this continual and seemingly permanent danger of robbery and murder, cabbies are prevented by law from carrying weapons, even for self defense. Most drivers just take their chances, but some find substitute weapons:

> While we were waiting for the cabs to arrive, I noticed that one driver was carrying what looked like a small fishing tackle box. As he was putting something in this box, I saw a hammer and said, "Hey, watcha got that for?" The driver replied, "Ah ha! That's it! I use that! Cops can't get you for carrying a concealed weapon. And it will do the job. I just lay it right out on the front seat."

> Another driver picked up the small ball peen hammer, one with a regular flat nail-driving surface on one end but with a ball instead of the nail-pulling claw on the other, and hit the flat surface against his hand and said, "Yeah, that will do the job." The first driver took the hammer, gestured to the end with the ball, and said, "No. Hit 'em with this other end. It'll go way in."

Some drivers are not satisfied with weapons such as hammers or tire tools, and they run the risk of being arrested on a felony charge for carrying a gun. Cabbies, however, generally feel utter futility and defenselessness in the face of this danger. This is well expressed by the driver who said: "You got ten guns—that don't do a fucking thing when . . . son-of-a-bitch puts that fucking thing in the back of your neck, there's not a fucking thing you can do."

COMPETITION AND CONFLICT

Besides problems with passengers, cabbies also are problematic to one another. The major reason for this is the intense competitiveness of cabdriving. Each cabbie, if he is to survive financially, directly competes with all other cab drivers in the city—both those from rival companies and drivers from his own company

Intra-company competition regularly takes the simple but legitimate form of beating other drivers to a stand or getting one's own bid for "open" orders accepted by being faster at the mike than others. At other times competition with co-workers takes the more deviant form of being dissimulative when bidding for "open" orders, that is, lying about one's location in order to be eligible for the order. A more deviant form of intra-company competition, however, is "scooping" (stealing orders). It is possible to "scoop" or steal an order because all drivers can hear via their cab radio the location to which a driver is being dispatched. By also knowing the location of the stand from which the driver is being dispatched, a second driver can approximate the time it will take the first driver to arrive at the order. If he figures that he can get there first and still have enough time to pick up the passenger and be out of sight when the dispatched driver arrives, scooping is within his realm of possible action. The dispatched driver is then confronted with a "no-go." Since "no-goes" are punitive, scooping is a technique by which cabbies sometimes "pay back" or "get even with" other cabbies. Its use as a sanction is illustrated by the cabbie who said, "He's a son-of-a-bitch! Every chance I get, I scoop him!"

Inter-company competition is always keen, but it sometimes changes to conflict. Beatings, tire slashing, and other violence during periods of strikes and rate disputes are well-known. However, even during "times of peace" the "truce" is uneasy and regularly threatens to erupt in violence. For example, after work one Metro driver related:

I was drivin' in Forest Park, and these three women flagged me down. I pulled over, and as they was gettin' in the cab I saw this Red Top Cab come beatin' down the road and the last woman wasn't in yet and she said, "Look! There's our cab now!" Red Top is an air conditioned cab, and so they wanted to ride with him. The women got out, and I said, "You better pay me somethin' for my stoppin' or else this bastard's gonna get his windshield knocked in." One woman gave me a dollar, and I left.

SOCIAL CONTROL THROUGH SARCASM, CENSURE, AND THREATS

While he is on the job the cabbie needs to deal not only with problematic passengers and competitive co-workers, but he must also drive for an extremely punitive management. Management regularly uses biting verbal techniques in order to keep cabbies in line. For example, in the early morning hours some drivers park at stands with the motors running and their radios on, and then lie down on the front seat and sleep, keeping mentally "tuned" for their stand to be called. When their stand is called they sometimes awaken in time to answer the call, but they frequently respond more slowly than usual, or are perhaps a bit sluggish in their speech. The following, which took place at 4:45 a.m., illustrates the dispatcher's generous use of (1) sarcasm, (2) censure, and (3) threats:

Dispatcher: "DeBaliviere Delmar." (The dispatcher is calling a "stand," places where drivers park to await orders.)
Cabbie: ((Gives his cab number and stand.))[1]
Dispatcher: "5560 Waterman."
Cabbie: ((Probably says, "Clear," meaning that he understood the order.))
Dispatcher: (1) *Did I disturb you, junior?*
Cabbie: ((   ))
Dispatcher: "Well I'm glad to hear that."
Cabbie: ((   ))
Dispatcher: (2) *Then quit laying down,* (3) *or you won't get the order.*

To understand the punitory nature of this combined sarcasm, censure, and threats, keep in mind first of all that this occurs *publicly*. These statements are being broadcast to all drivers, making the violator's positive reference group knowledgeable of the problem. Secondly, the regular dispatcher on the shift I usually worked was a woman. This means that males, who are already being ordered about by anyone who has the price of a cab, must undergo scorn or berating by a female in the "audible presence" of their fellow drivers.

Cabbies have not found an effective recourse to this ill treatment. Some drivers attempt to "get even" with dispatchers by "tying up the air." They keep the button on their microphones depressed in order to make it difficult for the dispatcher to give out orders. Not only is this action seldom successful, but were a cabbie to succeed in "tying up the air," he would also be penalizing his fellow cabbies by preventing them from receiving orders. He would end up being punitive toward those with whom he strongly identifies. With neither a legitimate nor an effective recourse open to get back at a dispatcher with whom he is having problems, a driver will sometimes withdraw—sitting in his cab, but angrily refusing to answer his radio. This, of course, is also a most ineffective sanction because he ends up harming himself, further lowering his already depressed income.

THE CABBIE AND HIS EQUIPMENT

In analyzing negative aspects of cabdriving, I wish to broadly apply the concept of punishment. The common sense idea of punishment refers to more than just persons as punitive agents. People frequently apply the term punishment not only to persons who are either purposely or inadvertently punishing to them, but also to experiences with material objects in which they feel that they are in some way humiliated, degraded or frustrated. We shall now examine this broader approach to understanding punishment and cab drivers, looking at objects which are punishing to cabbies.

The cab is obviously of extreme importance to the cab driver. He is so strongly identified with this vehicle that his name is but a diminutive of it—"cabbie." Moreover, . . . the cabbie's vehicle is a sort of armed weapon with which he approaches a hostile world. However, even his cab, with its equipment, is in many ways inimical to the cabbie.

Although the cab driver is supposed to "check out" his cab before he begins driving, he soon finds that factors militate against doing so. First of all, checking the cab for mechanical problems means that the cabbie loses time when he could be taking his first order. Secondly, he soon learns to avoid the garage men who repair the cabs since they become surly and sarcastic when they see anyone bringing a cab to the garage. The garage men are salaried, so cabs needing repairs represent only additional work for them. Finally, since cabs sitting in the garage also represent a loss of income to management, there is little encouragement from this sector.

The typical attitude is that as long as the cab moves when the accelerator is pressed it should be on the road. These cabs are on the go twenty-four hours a day, with one driver turning a cab in at the end of his twelve hour shift and another driver immediately taking it out again. When a motor burns out, another is merely shoved into the old chassis. With the combination of not checking the cabs and running them continuously, cabs, at least in the City of St. Louis, are some of the most unsafe vehicles on the road.

A dysfunctional consequence is that it is not uncommon for a cabbie to find himself without such "niceties" as signal lights and properly working brakes. Additionally, with the condition of the cabs on the road, breakdowns are not infrequent. When a breakdown occurs, the cabbie is stuck. He must await "Metro Safety," whom the dispatcher sends to either make on-the-road repairs or to tow the cab away. Even such a small item as a flat tire means a breakdown for the cabbie since it is the practice of Metro Cab Company to send drivers out with neither a spare tire nor tire changing tools.

His cab can also prove physically dangerous to the cabbie. The air intake of the cab is unfortunately located in front of the vehicle. In bumper-to-bumper traffic it directly sucks in the exhaust of the car in front. Those who live in urban settings all experience short periods of such exposure when they drive in rush hour traffic, but the cabbie is frequently in such situations for extended periods of time. In protest against the location of the mounting of the air vent, one Chicago cabbie refused to return his taxi to the garage. For this defiant act, however, he was summarily fired.[2]

The other major part of a cabbie's equipment, his radio, is also a punitive source for the driver. He sometimes receives an electric shock, especially when he is perspiring and resting his arm on the cab's door as he presses the button on his microphone. His radio is also likely to "go bad" at any moment, and to do so without warning. The new driver soon learns by painful experience that a variety of factors will cause his transmission to be too fuzzy or too weak for the dispatcher to receive, such as having too little water in the cab battery, parking too close to the curb, not warming up the radio, and even driving in a low area of the city. These occupational facts are ordinarily learned only through frustrating personal experience.

Radio silence is also threatening to the cab driver. When his radio is silent, the cabbie does not know whether anything is being broadcast or whether his radio is malfunctioning. He can check the source of radio silence by pressing the button on his mike and listening for a click to indicate working order, or he can call the dispatcher. These checks, however, tell him only if his radio is working *at that moment*. Should there continue to be silence, as happens during slack periods, the driver is again made uncomfortable, thinking that he might not be receiving orders which are being broadcast. In periods of radio silence drivers nervously respond to this tension, as indicated by the dispatcher saying such things as, "There's nothing wrong with your radio, Driver. I just don't have any orders." But this only gives a momentary reassurance since his radio can begin malfunctioning at any time, without warning.

HARD WORK AND POVERTY

In the midst of these varied problems, the cabbie works hard to make a buck. Sometimes even the weather and climate appear to conspire against him. In summer the cabbie swelters in heat since none of the rental cabs are air-conditioned. It is only when his cab is moving that he has air circulating to cool him. In winter, on the other hand, he not only suffers from heaters which are less than adequate, but he must climb in and out of his cab as he searches for a house number or picks up a package. Consequently, he cannot wear clothing adequate for the situation, and he is either too warm in heavy clothing or too cold in lighter clothing.

Cabdriving does not even allow normal release of bladder tension. If he is to make any money at all, the cabbie must be constantly listening to his radio, and doing so does not give him time to urinate. If he takes time out to use the restroom of a gas station or restaurant (to use a dark street is to invite arrest), he runs the risk of missing orders and lowering his income. On the other hand, if he takes time to relieve his bladder after he has received an order, it takes longer to arrive at the order and greatly increases the chances of a "no-go." And, of course, after he picks up the passenger, it would be both humiliating and awkward to, in effect, "ask permission" of his passenger to go to the bathroom! Consequently, bladder tension is a routine part of the cabbie's job.

Another physical need which cabdriving cuts into is sleep. St. Louis cabbies work an eleven or twelve hour day, six days a week. Since this is required to make a living, and the cabbie must also allow for driving time to and from work, the cabbie must either cut down his sleep or cut down on the amount of time he spends in non-work activities such as his family or recreation. Judging from the haggardly tired appearance marking these cabbies, most seem to make the choice of cutting down on sleep.

Although they work full time, usually six days a week, eleven or twelve hours each day, cabbies in St. Louis still live in poverty. One cabbie, for example, goes to the City Hospital when he is sick since there he can receive the free treatment which the city provides for indigents. This full-time working man considers himself to be so poor that he is in need of public welfare. I have also seen a cabbie begging other drivers for a dollar with which to buy breakfast, and another cabbie who did not know where he was going to sleep that night after work. In a single issue of *Taxi Union News* (March 1967), which focuses primarily on cabbies in Chicago, it was reported that food and clothing had been given to one cabbie who along with eight children had been burned out of his home. Another cabbie had been put out of his home by the landlord. Still another cabbie had been placed in an industrial plant and his "family of five children were put back into their apartment after the furnishings had been placed in the street."

Above rental and gasoline expenses, St. Louis cabbies average approximately fifteen to eighteen dollars per twelve hour shift. From this pittance they must put away money for income taxes, which are not withheld since cabbies are "independent entrepreneurs." Nor do they even receive a check from which to withhold taxes. If they desire basic social security coverage, cabbies must pay at the higher "self-employed" rate since they are technically not employees of the company. Through this loophole in the law, their "employer" contributes nothing. In effect, cabbies are day laborers who end up with a variable but small amount of cash at the end of each working day. Cabbies struggle for existence without the benefits American workers have learned to take for granted: they do not enjoy employer-contributed pension plans, paid sick leaves, hospitalization, holidays, vacations, or even social security. Nor do they even have job security, but are subservient to the employment whims of management. Not surprisingly, this leads to a life situation which prevents cab drivers from planning ahead, giving them little security for either the present or the future.

There are indeed not many unionized occupations today where poverty characterizes workers who labor sixty-six to seventy-two hours per week under the punitive and degrading conditions I have outlined. How can this possibly be? How can a group of men be unionized and yet be so blatantly exploited?[3]

Cabbies themselves have not been in a good bargaining position. Alternative means of transportation are usually readily available, and if their collective demands bring too great an increase in fares, they may run out of passengers. More than this is involved, however. The major source of exploitation appears to be the capitalistic system under which these men labor. Management, regardless of any high-sounding ideological phraseology to the contrary concerning service to the public, has but one purpose—and that is profit. In order to turn the greatest profit, costs must be cut. Management, as we have seen, drastically cuts the amount it spends on the maintenance of its cabs. Safety features, also expensive, are almost non-existent. But the major source of cutting costs centers around the remuneration cabbies receive. By paying them little, management cuts its costs and remains competitive. By keeping them poverty-stricken and in physical need, management attempts to assure itself of a certain type of labor—a fawning, self-ingratiating type which is grateful for every "favor" it receives.

Central to management maintaining its dictatorial dominancy is the cooptation of the unions. Management has been able to manipulate cabbie unions to the point that union officials frequently appear to represent management more than they do workers. For example, management is able to successfully and regularly manipulate work rules to the detriment of workers. As a case in point, we can note "down time" refunds. During "down time" a driver is supposed to be refunded his cab rental for the period during which his cab is inoperable, being reimbursed about seventy-five cents an hour. This reimbursement is merely a negation of the amount which he would otherwise have had to pay during that period for an operable cab. It is not remuneration from management; nor does it represent a profit. Yet the cabbie ordinarily has to fight *as an individual* to get even this cancellation of rental fees.

When the interests of management and union officials coincide, it is ordinarily at the direct cost and detriment of cabbies. Collusion between the two does not appear to be uncommon, as one would infer from what took place in San Francisco in 1970. At that time a more dissident element of a major cabbie union attempted to vote its candidates into power. The establishment of the union refused to recognize the motion and hastily adjourned the meeting. In the following weeks the management of this cab company fired a dozen or so of its cabbies which of course included the dissident group who had attempted to gain control over the union.[4]

The nationally noted cab strike of 1970 in the City of New York was not, as commonly thought, an attempt to gain higher wages for cab drivers. It was, rather, a successful attempt to gain a higher fare structure for *employers*. Moreover, while higher profits were gained for the employer, wage *cuts* were "gained" for the cabbies. After the union's fifteen day strike, taxi fares went up from 45 cents for the first sixth of a mile to 60 cents for the first fifth of a mile, and from 10 cents for each additional one-third mile to 10 cents for each additional one-fifth mile. "Waiting time" charges were also increased at about the same proportion. But the drivers' commission on the total fare was actually reduced by 10 cents for each trip: 10 cents per trip is subtracted from the total bookings and held in "escrow" for "benefits" which no one has seen. Additionally, the commissions of "new" drivers were further reduced from 49 percent of "new" bookings to 42 percent . . .

CONCLUSION

If from my presentation the reader comes to the conclusion that almost everything about cabdriving appears to be punitive, this is not too far from the truth. Although there are indeed compensations to this occupation, the cabbie is enmeshed in a hostile, exploiting, threatening, and punitive world. Some of the punitive and exploitative aspects of cabdriving are willfully inflicted on the cabbie, but most are built into the structure of cabdriving. The source of this exploitation and punishment does not arise primarily from individuals, such as passengers, managers, and fellow cabbies, but it originates especially from the structuring of the profit system within which the cabbie works.

In order to understand man, one must study the structure which helps determine the elements present in his world, and the situations or contexts within which man lives out his life. Cabdriving is structured such that it is exploitative to cabbies. This centers especially around its capitalistic context and focuses specifically on the nature of cabbies' shift work and the forms and amounts of remuneration which he receives. These men live a hard, exploited life—a life in which they are filled with frustration and in which they are continually manipulated by both their physical and social environments. It is difficult to escape the view that cabbies are captives within an extremely exploitative and punishing system. It is probably not that the men directing the system are invidious. It is rather, that the system itself is invidious, pitting man against man for the sake of profit . . .

If sociologists desire to understand the everyday or common-sense experience of man, interaction in occupations should be a focal point since they demand such a huge part of the waking hours of people in our society. Man's everyday experiences in his occupations greatly structure his perception of the world. If, for example, we are to understand such a common thing in our society as why cabbies feel they are punished, we must understand both the structure of the occupation and the cabbie's reaction to or perception of his place in that structure.

NOTES

1. The cabbie's response to the dispatcher cannot be heard by other drivers. The double parenthesis indicates these responses. Where the responses are patterned, I have indicated the typical response, placing it within the double parenthesis.

2. It should be noted that in this case Yellow Cab Company was forced to pay the "offender" ten months' back wages. This decision was won through arbitration, and the union claimed that because of it they now had "greater protection and a higher degree of job security than ever before." (For details, see *Taxi Union News*, 3, January and April 1967.)

3. This situation may be different in other parts of the country, such as New York where the number of cabs allowed on the street is limited and where the demand for cabs is exceptionally high. New York cabbies are also exploited, however. See the relevant item in the conclusion to this paper.

4. My thanks to George Toussaint for this information.

Terry Mason
Studs Terkel

She has been an airline stewardess for six years. She is twenty-six years old, recently married. "The majority of airline stewardesses are from small towns. I myself am from Nebraska. It's supposed to be one of the nicest professions for a woman—if she can't be a model or in the movies. All the great benefits: flying around the world, meeting all those people. It is a nice status symbol.

"I have five older sisters and they were all married before they were twenty. The minute they got out of high school, they would end up getting married. That was the thing everybody did, was get married. When I told my parents I was going to the airlines, they got excited. They were so happy that one of the girls could go out and see the world and spend some time being single. I didn't get married until I was almost twenty-five. My mother especially thought it would be great that I could have the ambition, the nerve to go to the big city on my own and try to accomplish being a stewardess."

When people ask you what you're doing and you say stewardess, you're really proud, you think it's great. It's like a stepping stone. The first two months I started flying I had already been to London, Paris, and Rome. And me from Broken Bow, Nebraska. But after you start working, it's not as glamorous as you thought it was going to be.

They like girls that have a nice personality and that are pleasant to look at. If a woman has a problem with blemishes, they take her off. Until the appearance counselor thinks she's ready to go back on. One day this girl showed up, she had a very slight black eye. They took her off. Little things like that.

We had to go to stew school for five weeks. We'd go through a whole week of make-up and poise. I didn't like this. They make you feel like you've never been out in public. They showed you how to smoke a cigarette, when to smoke a cigarette, how to look at a man's eyes. Our teacher, she had this idea we had to be sexy. One day in class she was showing us how to accept a light for a cigarette from a man and never blow it out. When he lights it, just look in his eyes. It was really funny, all the girls laughed.

It's never proper for a woman to light her own cigarette. You hold it up and of course you're out with a guy who knows the right way to light the cigarette. You look into their eyes as they're lighting your cigarette and you're cupping his hand, but holding it just very light, so that he can feel your touch and your warmth. (Laughs.) You do not blow the match out. It used to be really great for a woman to blow the match out when she looked in his eyes, but she said now the man blows the match out.

The idea is not to be too obvious about it. They don't want you to look too forward. That's the whole thing, being a lady but still giving out that womanly appeal, like the body movement and the lips and the eyes. The guy's supposed to look in your eyes. You could be a real mean woman. You're a lady and doing all these evil things with your eyes.

She did try to promote people smoking. She said smoking can be part of your conversation. If you don't know what to say, you can always pull out a cigarette. She says it makes you more comfortable. I started smoking when I was on the airlines.

Our airline picks the girl-next-door type. At one time they wouldn't let us wear false eyelashes and false fingernails. Now it's required that you wear false eyelashes, and if you do not have the right length nails, you wear false nails. Everything is supposed to be becoming to the passenger.

That's the whole thing: meeting all these great men that either have great business backgrounds or good looking or different. You do meet a lot of movie stars and a lot of political people, but you don't get to really visit with them that much. You never really get to go out with these men. Stewardesses are impressed only by name people. But a normal millionaire that you don't know you're not impressed about. The only thing that really thrills a stewardess is a passenger like Kennedy or movie stars or somebody political. Celebrities.

I think our average age is twenty-six. But our supervisors tell us what kind of make-up to wear, what kind of lipstick to wear, if our hair is not the right style for us, if we're not smiling enough. They even tell us how to act when you're on a pass. Like last night I met my husband. I was in plain clothes. I wanted to kiss him. But I'm not supposed to kiss anybody at the terminal. You're not supposed to walk off with a passenger, hand in hand. After you get out of the terminal, that's all yours.

The majority of passengers do make passes. The ones that do make passes are married and are business people. When I tell them I'm married, they say, "I'm married and you're married and you're away from home and so am I and nobody's gonna find out." The majority of those who make passes at you, you wouldn't accept a date if they were friends of yours at home. . . .

They say you can spot a stewardess by the way she wears her make-up. At that time we all had short hair and everybody had it cut in stew school exactly alike. If there's two blondes that have their hair cut very short, wearing the same shade of make-up, and they get into uniform, people say, "Oh, you look like sisters." Wonder why? (Laughs.)

The majority of us were against it because they wouldn't let you say how *you'd* like your hair cut, they wouldn't let you have your own personality, *your* makeup, *your* clothes. They'd tell you what length skirts to wear. At one time they told us we couldn't wear anything one inch above the knees. And no pants at that time. It's different now.

Wigs used to be forbidden. Now it's the style. Now it's permissible for nice women to wear wigs, eyelashes, and false fingernails. Before it was the harder looking women that wore them. Women showing up in pants, it wasn't ladylike. Hot pants are in now. Most airlines change style every year. . . .

The other day I had fifty-five minutes to serve 101 coach passengers, a cocktail and full-meal service. You do it fast and terrible. You're very rude. You don't mean to be rude, you just don't have time to answer questions. You smile and you just ignore it. You get three drink orders in a hurry. There's been many times when you miss the glass, pouring, and you pour it in the man's lap. You just don't say I'm sorry. You give him a cloth and you keep going. That's the bad part of the job. . . .

I've never had the nerve to speak up to anybody that's pinched me or said something dirty. Because I've always been afraid of these onion letters. These are bad letters. If you get a certain amount of bad letters, you're fired. When you get a bad letter you have to go in and talk to the supervisor. Other girls now, there are many of 'em that are coming around and telling them what they feel. The passenger reacts: She's telling me off! He doesn't believe it. Sometimes the passenger needs it.

One guy got his steak and he said, "This is too medium, I want mine rarer." The girl said, "I'm sorry, I don't cook the food, it's precooked." He picked up the meal and threw it on the floor. She says, "If you don't pick the meal up right now, I'll make sure the crew members come back here and make you pick it up." (With awe) She's talking right back at him and loud, right in front of everybody. He really didn't think she would yell at him. Man, he picked up the meal . . . The younger girls don't take that guff any more, like we used to. When the passenger is giving you a bad time, you talk back to him.

It's always: the passenger is right. When a passenger says something mean, we're supposed to smile and say, "I understand." We're supposed to *really* smile because stewardesses' supervisors have been getting reports that the girls have been back-talking passengers. Even when they pinch us or say dirty things, we're supposed to smile at them. That's one thing they taught us at stew school. Like he's rubbing your body somewhere, you're supposed to just put his hand down and not say anything and smile at him. That's the main thing, smile.

When I first went to class, they told me I had a crooked smile. She showed me how to smile. She said, "Kinda press a little smile on"—which I did. "Oh, that's great," she said, "that's a *good* smile." But I couldn't do it. I didn't feel like I was doing it on my own. Even if we're sad, we're supposed to have a smile on our face.

I came in after a flight one day, my grandfather had died. Usually they call you up or meet you at the flight and say, "We have some bad news for you." I picked up this piece of paper in my mailbox and it says, "Mother called in. Your grandfather died today." It was written like, say, two cups of sugar. Was I mad! They wouldn't give me time off for the funeral. You can only have time off for your parents or somebody you have lived with. I had never lived with my grandparents. I went anyway. . . .

. . . I used to play bridge with passengers. But that doesn't happen any more. We're not supposed to be sitting down, or have a magazine or read a newspaper. If it's a flight from Boston to Los Angeles, you're supposed to have a half an hour talking to passengers. But the only time we can sit down is when we go to the cockpit. You're not supposed to spend any more than five minutes up there for a cigarette.

We could be sitting down on our jump seat and if you had a supervisor on board, she would write you up—for not mixing with the crowd. We're supposed to be told when she walks on board. Many times you don't know. They do have personnel that ride the flights that don't give their names—checking, and they don't tell you about it. Sometimes a girl gets caught smoking in the cabin. Say it's a long flight, maybe a night flight. You're playing cards with a passenger and you say, "Would it bother you if I smoke?" And he says no. She would write you up and get you fired for smoking in the airplane.

They have a limit on how far you can mix. They want you to be sociable, but if he offers you a cigarette, not to take it. When you're outside, they encourage you to take cigarettes.

You give your time to everybody, you share it, not too much with one passenger. Everybody else may be snoring away and there's three guys, maybe military, and they're awake 'cause they're going home and excited. So you're playing cards with 'em. If you have a supervisor on, that would be a no-no. They call a lot of things no-no's.

They call us professional people but they talk to us as very young, childishly. They check us all the time on appearance. They check our weight every month. Even though you've been flying twenty years, they check you and say that's a no-no. If you're not spreading yourself around passengers enough, that's a no-no. Not hanging up first-class passengers' coats, that's a no-no, even though there's no room in the coatroom. You're supposed to somehow make room. If you're a pound over, they can take you off flight until you get under.

False Promises
Stanley Aronowitz

The General Motors Assembly Division is a tough, no-nonsense outfit charged with the responsibility "of being able to meet foreign competition." GMAD "adopted 'get tough' tactics to cope with increased worker absenteeism and boost productivity." According to *Business Week*, the new division was set up in 1965 to tighten and revamp assembly operations. "The need for GMAD's belt-tightening role was underscored during the late 1960s when GM's profit margin dropped from 10 percent to 7 percent."[1]

At Lordstown, efficiency became the watchword. At 60 cars an hour, the pace of work had not been exactly leisurely, but after GMAD came in the number of cars produced almost doubled. Making one car a minute had been no picnic, especially on a constantly moving line. Assembly work fits the worker to the pace of the machine. Each work station is no more than 6 to 8 feet long. For example, within a minute on the line, a worker in the trim department had to walk about 20 feet to a conveyor belt transporting parts to the line, pick up a front seat weighing 30 pounds, carry it back to his work station, place the seat on the chassis, and put in four bolts to fasten it down by first hand-starting the bolts and then using an air gun to tighten them according to standard.

It was steady work when the line moved at 60 cars an hour. When it increased to more than 100 cars an hour, the number of operations on this job were not reduced and the pace became almost maddening. In 36 seconds the worker had to perform at least eight different operations, including walking, lifting, hauling, lifting the carpet, bending to fasten the bolts by hand, fastening them by air gun, replacing the carpet, and putting a sticker on the hood. Sometimes the bolts fail to fit into the holes; the gun refuses to function at the required torque; the seats are defective or the threads are bare on the bolt. But the line does not stop. Under these circumstances the workers often find themselves "in the hole," which means that they have fallen behind the line.

"You really have to run like hell to catch up, if you're gonna do the whole job right," one operator named Jerry told me when I interviewed him in the summer of 1972. "They had the wrong-sized bolt on the job for a whole year. A lot of times we just miss a bolt to keep up with the line."

In all plants workers try to make the work a little easier for themselves. At Lordstown, as in other automobile plants, there are many methods for making the work tolerable. Despite the already accelerated pace, workers still attempt to use the traditional relief mechanism of "doubling up." This method consists of two workers deciding that they will learn each other's operation. One worker performs both jobs while the other worker is spelled. At Lordstown, a half-hour "on" and a half-hour "off" is a fairly normal pattern. The worker who is on is obliged to do both jobs by superhuman effort. But workers would rather race to keep up with the line than work steadily—in anticipation of a half-hour off to read, lie down, go to the toilet, or roam the plant to talk to a buddy. Not all jobs lend themselves to this arrangement, especially those where a specific part like a front seat must be placed on all models; here the work is time consuming, and full of hassles. But there are many operations where doubling up is feasible, particularly light jobs which have few different movements. Fastening seat belts and putting on windshield wipers are examples.

"The only chance to keep from goin' nuts," said one worker, "is to double up on the job. It's the only way to survive in the plant. . . ."

The company claims that doubling up reduces quality. The method engenders a tendency for workers to miss operations, especially when they fall behind, according to one general foreman. Some workers believe that the company blames workers for doubling up as an excuse to explain its own quality control failures. There is a widespread feeling among the line workers that the doubling-up "issue" has more to do with the company's program of harrassment than the problem of quality control.

The tenure of the previous management at the Chevrolet division of

GM was characterized by a plethora of shop floor agreements between foremen and line workers on work rules. These agreements were not written down, but were passed from worker to worker as part of the lore of the job. As in many workplaces, a new line supervisor meant that these deals had to be "renegotiated."

When GMAD took over at Lordstown, management imposed new, universally applicable rules which, in fact, were applied selectively. On Mondays, "when there are not many people on the line," the company tolerates lateness. On Tuesdays, when young workers come back from their long weekends, "they throw you out the door" for the rest of the shift for coming in fifteen minutes or a half-hour late. "When the company gets a bug up its ass to improve quality, they come down on you for every little mistake. But then things start goin' good on the cars, so they start to work on other areas. Then you are not allowed to lay down—not allowed to read on the job; no talkin' (you can't talk anyway the noise is so terrific); no doubling up."

Efficiency meant imposing on workers the absolute power of management to control production. GMAD instituted a policy of compulsory overtime at the time of the model changeover. The "normal" shift became ten hours a day and there were no exceptions to the rule. Absenteeism and lateness became the objects of veritable holy crusades for the new management. Nurses refused to grant permission for workers to go home sick. The company began to consider a worker a voluntary quit if he stayed off for three days and failed to bring a doctor's note certifying his illness. Doctors were actually sent to workers' homes to check up on "phony" illnesses in an effort to curb absenteeism.

The average hourly rate for production line workers was $4.56 an hour in mid-1972. In addition, annual cost of living increases geared to the consumer price index had been incorporated into the contract. Gross base weekly earnings for ten hours a day were more than $195. With overtime, some workers had made more than $13,000 a year. Besides, GM workers have among the best pension, health insurance, and unemployment benefits programs in American industry. Certainly, there is no job in the Warren area whose terms compare with the high wages and benefits enjoyed by the GM workers. Equally significant, GM is among the few places in the area still hiring a large number of employees. The steel mills, electrical plants, and retail trades offer lower wages to unskilled workers and less steady employment to low-seniority people. For some, General Motors is "big mother." Many workers echo the sentiment of Joe, a forty-five-year-old assembly line worker who said that GM offered better wages and working conditions than he had ever enjoyed in his life—"I don't know how anybody who works for a living can do better than GM."

Compared to the steel mill where he did heavy dirty jobs, GM was "not near as hard."

Of course Joe has had differences with company policies. The job was "too confining." He didn't like to do the same thing every day. He objected to the company harrassment of the men and had actually voted for a strike to correct some of the injustices in the plant. But, like many others, Joe had "married the job" because he didn't know where else he could get a retirement plan which would give him substantial benefits after thirty years of service, full hospital benefits, and real job security.

GMAD likes workers like Joe too. They know Joe isn't going anywhere. They believe him when he says he is sick and, if he misses installing parts on a car he can "chalk it up." In such cases, he simply tells the foreman about the missing operation and the "repairmen will take care of it."

Yet high wages and substantial fringe benefits have not been sufficient to allay discontent among the young people working on the line. If other area employers paid wages competitive with GM wages, GM would have serious difficulty attracting a labor force. The wages are a tremendous initial attraction for workers and explain why many are reluctant to leave the shop. But even the substantial unemployment in the Warren and Youngstown areas has not succeeded in tempering the spirit of rebellion among young workers or preventing the persistence of turnover among them. The promise of high earnings has not reduced the absentee rate in the plant. One young worker, married with a child, earned a gross income of $10,900 in 1971, a year when overtime was offered regularly to employees. This was a gross pay at least $2,000 below his possible earnings. He had taken at least one day off a week and refused several offers of Saturday work.

GM acknowledges that absenteeism, particularly on Mondays and Fridays, constitutes its most distressing discipline problem. Workers report line shutdowns "for as much as a half hour" on Mondays because there are simply not enough people to perform the operations. But many young people are prepared to sacrifice higher earnings for a respite from the hassles of assembly line work, even for one day.

At Lordstown and other plants where youth constitute either a majority or significant minority of the work force there is concrete evidence that the inducements to hard work have weakened. Older workers in the plant as well as a minority of the youth admit that they have never seen this kind of money in their lives. But the young people are seeking something more from their labor than high wages, pensions, and job security. At Lordstown, they are looking for "a chance to use my brain" and a job "where my high school education counts for something." Even though workers resent the demanding pace of the line, no line job takes more than a half-hour to learn. Most workers achieve sufficient speed in their operation to keep up with the line in about a half a shift. The minute rationalization of assembly line operations to a few simple movements has been perfected by GMAD. One operator whose job was to put two clips on a hose all day long said, "I never think about my job. In fact, I try to do everything I can to forget it. If I concentrated on thinking about it, I'd go crazy. The trouble is I have to look at what I'm doing or else I'd fuck up every time." This worker spent some of his time figuring out ways to get off the line, especially ways to take days off. "I always try to get doctor's slips to take three days if I can." Another worker reported provoking a foreman to give him a disciplinary layoff (DLO) just to avoid the monotony of his tasks.

The drama of Lordstown is the conflict between the old goals of decent income and job security, which have lost their force but are by no means dead, and the new needs voiced by young people for more than mindless labor. The company and the union represent the promise that the old needs can be met on a scale never before imagined for many of the people on the line. The youth are saying that these benefits are not enough.

The picture is complicated by the fact that not all young people share the same attitudes. Even though the overwhelming majority of workers in the shop are between twenty and thirty years old, they are not all cut from the same cloth. The most disaffected group in the plant are the youth who were raised in the Warren-Youngstown area. Their fathers and mothers were industrial workers, or at least had been part of an urban environment for most of their lives. Since the area has had a long industrial tradition (it lies in the heart of the Ohio valley), high wages and traditional union protections and benefits are part of the taken-for-granted world of a generation brought up in the shadows of the steel mills and rubber factories. These workers share the same upbringing, went to the same schools, frequented the same neighborhood social centers, and speak the same symbolic languages. When they came to General Motors, they brought with them a set of unspoken expectations about their work and their future. Many were high school graduates; a smaller, but significant number were attending college. Although it cannot be denied that the "good money" paid by GM was an important inducement for these young people to choose to work there, few of them considered steady work and good wages sufficient to satisfy a life's ambition.

NOTE

1. *Business Week,* "A GM Reorganization Backfires," No. 2221, March 25, 1972, pp. 46–51.

The Management Monopoly
Robert Vaughn

After Ralph Nader announced that the Public Interest Research Group would be mounting a study of the Civil Service Commission, hundreds of federal employees were heard from. The complaints seemed to indicate not simply individual dislocations, but structural faults in the ways in which employees are disciplined.

The civil servant finds himself in an unpleasant position in which his relationship with his agency is marked by a lack of substantive rights. It is a relationship between superior and subordinate in which the superior has many opportunities to make discretionary judgments of considerable importance to the subordinate. The exercise of legal rights in such a relationship is often difficult and restrained.

Few organizations stress superior-subordinate relationships more than the federal government. Status differentiations are made clear by the general service (GS) ratings. The GS scale establishes the rate of pay for employees in the federal service. As of January 1974 salaries range from approximately $5,000 for a GS-1 to $40,000 for a GS-18 with several years of service. The system provides precise differentiation between grades one through eighteen and ten salary step levels within each. (As one indication of status, lower-grade employees are given small metal desks while higher-grade employees receive larger wooden desks. Even space is an indication of station; a GS-5 is allowed 60 square feet of work space while a GS-15 supervisory employee is allotted 225 square feet.)

All communication is made through layers of intermediaries. Each employee must be given performance and appraisal ratings for purposes of retention and promotion. Such appraisals are always made by superiors, and the goodwill of one's supervisor therefore becomes paramount. The work environment may be made friendly or hostile, open or repressive, tolerable or intolerable by the superior, who is equipped with a finely honed and calibrated set of sanctions to be used against subordinates. The granting of leave and the assignment of duties may be effective tools of discipline in the hands of the superior. We found that employee after employee believed that an agency could "get" any employee. Some of the personnel officers with whom we spoke believed that it was always possible "to remove an irritant."

Adapted and reprinted by permission from *The Spoiled System* by Robert Vaughn, copyright © 1975 by the Center for Study of Responsive Law. Reprinted by permission of Charterhouse Books, Publishers.

Several methods are available by which agencies may remove or restrain a troublesome employee.

THE DIRECT APPROACH

One of the myths surrounding federal employment is that it is difficult or impossible to remove a federal employee. Initial restraints upon removals—the reluctance of managers to confront employees and the time and effort required to build a case—may cause a manager to reassess what would be an arbitrary decision, but these restraints may not serve the purpose for which they are intended; they may discourage management from removing a marginal employee who, while inconvenient, poses no real threat to the perpetuation of the status quo within the agency, but they do not prevent moving against outspoken or unorthodox employees who do pose a threat.

In actuality, a removal is easy if one takes the proper procedural steps, and even procedural safeguards against unfair use of removal mechanisms are susceptible to manipulation. (One personnel director noted, "Thirty days notice is required for a dismissal, but no notice is required for a suspension. We give the removal notice and a thirty-day suspension notice at the same time.")

Finding grounds presents little difficulty for motivated management. If the difficulty of building a case against an employee is too great, or if the agency does not want to risk the review of the grounds of removal, other methods are available. When it is not possible to build a case on nonperformance, management has the discretion of selective enforcement of regulations.[1] Consider, for example, that almost all federal employees occasionally violate the thirty-minute lunch rule; indeed, many employees regularly take an hour. But management can select employees to be punished for this violation. Similarly, many employees are late for work and escape with impunity, yet lateness can be selected as grounds for dismissal.

LOVE IT OR LEAVE IT

Rather than bringing formal charges against an employee, an agency may choose to use the threat of charges to force his retirement or resignation.[2] Even when the threatened charges are improper or not clearly supportable, an employee may be tempted to capitulate. If he fights and loses, he has a dismissal on his record and loses his pension and insurance rights. If he feels that his appeal will not be evaluated fairly, he may decide to resign. The legal process appears lengthy and, if there is a possibility that the case may be appealed ultimately in court, expensive, during which time the employee is out of a job and the psychological pressures on him are great.

Some officials argue that the opportunity to resign or retire is an act of mercy to protect an employee's record. Such protestations, however, are belied by the behavior of many agencies. Rather than ending the matter, many an employee has found that his resignation only began a new ordeal. The resignation that goes into his personnel folder, to be referred to by potential employers, is marked "resigned under charges of dismissal." (Bernard Rosen indicated that this practice is no longer tolerated, but nothing prevents management from providing this information when consulted by potential employers.)[3]

LOST IN A RIF

When an agency is required by budget restraints or by reorganization to reduce its staff, it follows a process known as a Reduction in Force (RIF). A dismissal by RIF carries with it no stigma of nonperformance or inadequate performance, for it is the job that is being eliminated, and not the jobholder. Management can and does use RIFs to rid itself of employees against whom dismissal actions would not be sustained.

In theory, who will lose his job in a RIF is based on objective principles that center on retention ratings. (Retention ratings are based in large part upon length of service; veterans receive special consideration, and additional retention points are given to employees who have received awards for superior service.) An employee's right to challenge a RIF is limited to questions of whether his retention rating has been properly computed, whether his job was in the proper category, whether he has been placed in the proper competitive area, and whether certain procedural requirements have been followed. An employee whose job is abolished in a RIF may take over the job of another employee in the same competitive category, who then loses his job instead. While this "bumping" is done on the basis of retention points, management has considerable discretion in establishing the competitive categories. Thus, an employee with several years of service and with high performance ratings may find himself in a category where his seniority and performance count for little.

One of the more famous examples of RIFing was that of Ernest Fitzgerald. Mr. Fitzgerald, an air force civilian employee who exposed before the Joint Economic Committee in the fall of 1968 a $2.5 billion cost overrun on the C-5A transport plane, was shortly thereafter removed in a Reduction in Force, which the air force described as an "economy move." His retention rights were mooted because he was the only man in his competitive category—his was the one job abolished and no similar jobs existed in which he might exercise his retention rights. An air force memorandum of January 6, 1969 suggested a RIF as one of three ways to get rid of Fitzgerald. Fitzgerald appealed to the Civil Service Commission. After court action, he won in 1972 the right to an open hearing. The Commission's Appeals Examining Office recently ordered Fitzgerald's reinstatement. However, the Commission failed to find that Fitzgerald's dismissal was in retaliation for his congressional testimony but was rather the result of an "adversary relationship" which had been allowed to develop between Fitzgerald and the air force. Fitzgerald commented that he made the appeals system work only because he had received approximately $200,000 in donated legal services from the American Civil Liberties Union to wage his lengthy battle.

Reduction in force can prove an effective tool to silence troublesome employees as the following case shows:

Oscar Hoffman, a government inspector of pipe welds on combat ships being built for the navy, troubled his superiors by finding a great many defects. When he resisted pressure to ease up, he was threatened with a reprimand. When he filed a grievance against this threat, he was reprimanded and transferred shortly from Seattle to Tacoma, Washington, where he was RIFed in 1970 soon after his arrival. (Accidents involving faulty welds have occurred since on some of the ships about which Mr. Hoffman had expressed concern. Although his superior has been promoted, Mr. Hoffman has been unable to secure another job as a government inspector.)

Those who appeal RIF actions are not notably successful. In 1970, 62,720 Reductions in Force occurred. In 1971, 2,241 RIF appeals were processed at the Commission's first appellate level. The appellant was defeated in 90 percent of the actions. Statistics do not indicate precisely how many of the remainder were reversed on grounds of faulty procedure, but the Commission's ultimate appeals level, its Board of Appeals and Review, processed 1,147 RIF appeals in 1971.

The examples of Fitzgerald and Hoffman do not begin to exhaust the possibilities inherent in RIFing. An employee may, for example, be downgraded to a position soon to be abolished; an employee may be RIFed on the basis of lack of work, and a temporary employee hired soon after; an employee may find that employees he might "bump" have been placed in special training programs where they are not subject to RIF. A variant of RIFing gets the employee down to get him out—to exercise bumping rights he may have to accept a reduction in grade or a reassignment. In 1970, 25, 890 employees were downgraded and 17,350 were reassigned through reductions in force. Management has considerable discretion in determining what positions will be offered an employee who is RIFed, and many employees will leave rather than accept the offered job. Such rejection ends all rights that the employee has to appeal the RIF. Of course, demotion or reassignment may itself be an effective sanction, even if the employee does not leave.

EXILED TO SIBERIA

Some agencies have a Siberia—an unpleasant or professionally unproductive duty station, to which rebellious employees may be reassigned. Faced with Siberia, an employee may, of course, resign, but even if he accepts exile, he is effectively removed from the position in which he caused difficulty.

Reassignments may be either to a different geographical location or to a different division within the agency. Since the decision to reassign is considered to be a management prerogative, an employee may have difficulty proving that the reassignment is unnecessary or retaliatory.[4] Because an employee must accept reassignment in order to file a grievance challenging reassignment, he may have to go through the trouble and expense of relocating his family before he can begin his appeal.[5]

"You'd be surprised how many resignations we had when people discovered they had been reassigned to Anchorage," said one former Federal Aeronautics Administration official. A Colorado-stationed research scientist for the Agricultural Research Service who expressed concern about consultants for private industry using laboratory facilities found himself exiled to Alabama. H. Battle Hale, the Department of Agriculture official who questioned the propriety of the activities of Billy Sol Estes, was sent to Louisiana for a nonexistent "key job" before he was eventually reassigned to Kansas City. What is exile for a New Yorker is, of course, not necessarily exile for a Texan. Management is, however, able to tailor the geographical Siberia to the individual. In 1970, 1,960 employees were separated for refusal to relocate geographically.

But it is hardly necessary to send an employee far away to convince him to resign. For many government employees a rewarding and stimulating job assignment is important, and transfer to an agency dumping ground creates, particularly for a professional, great pressure to resign or retire. (Within the Federal Trade Commission, for example, the Division of Wools and Textiles functions as Siberia.)

In regulatory areas, these reassignments directly affect the consumer, since they either incline an aggressive employee to resign or, by discouraging aggressive behavior, they weaken an entire regulatory program. The consumer's "cops on the beat," such as meat and poultry inspectors, are particularly susceptible to this type of harassment.[6]

But perhaps the best example of the use of Siberia to leave the consumer out in the cold is found in a case within the Food and Drug Administration.

Crucial to the FDA's ability to protect the consumer from unsafe or inadequately tested prescription drugs are the medical officers within its Bureau of New Drugs. The medical officer must determine whether clinical trials of new drugs on animals are adequate to justify tests on man. Based on his evaluation of their safety and effectiveness, he must determine whether new drugs should be marketed and whether proposed labeling contains truthful claims and adequate directions. The history of John O. Nestor, M.D., board-certified in pediatrics and board-eligible in cardiology, shows that it is often the most diligent civil servant who is marked for Siberia.

In 1961, Dr. Nestor was enjoying a lucrative practice as a pediatric cardiologist in Arlington, Virginia. In the same year that the FDA was excusing its ineffectiveness before the Kefauver Committee by pleading an inability to attract specialists, Dr. Nestor, who himself had been the victim of an adverse drug reaction because of a faulty label warning, volunteered to work part time for the FDA. When the FDA indicated it would not accept part-time work, Dr. Nestor agreed to give up the greater part of his practice in order to work full time for the FDA.

Immediately after joining, Dr. Nestor attacked his job with a dedication and intensity that should, although it does not, characterize all those who hold a public trust. He was responsible for the withdrawal from the market of Entoquel, a White Laboratories product for the systematic treatment of diarrhea, after he uncovered erroneous test data submitted to the FDA. Dr. Bennet A. Robin, who had submitted the data and who had "tested" approximately forty-five drugs for twenty-two firms, pleaded no contest to charges of submitting erroneous reports. Dr. Nestor was instrumental in helping to block the marketing here of Thalidomide, a drug that caused hundreds of deformed babies in Europe. He was also responsible for the withdrawal from the market of MER/29, a cholesterol-lowering drug that posed a significant risk of producing cataracts in patients, while having doubtful therapeutic efficacy. Three officials of Richardson-Merrill, the manufacturers of MER/29, after pleading no contest to charges of withholding information concerning the drug, were placed on probation.

In the wake of the MER/29 scandal, Dr. Nestor raised issues of general FDA policy before congressional committees and in the form of memoranda to FDA officials. In March 1963, testifying before Senator Hubert Humphrey's Subcommittee on Reorganization, Dr. Nestor criticized the fact that there was "no internal appraisal to determine how a drug was allowed to clear New Drug Procedures."

Rather than being rewarded for his record of public service, Dr. Nestor's tenure at the FDA has been one of trial. At one point, when he questioned a supervisor about not having received a pay increase, he was asked, "Why are you acting the way you are acting?" After a session with the grand jury investigating the MER/29 incident, Dr. Nestor returned to find his office empty; without consulting him the FDA had reassigned Dr. Nestor to the Surveillance Division of the Bureau of Medicine, an undesirable post. This was not to be the last undesirable reassignment Dr. Nestor would receive. In 1965 he was transferred to the Case Review Branch of the Division of Medical Review, which collects evidence for prosecution. Some eighteen months later, as the result of White House inquiries, Dr. Nestor was returned to the Bureau of New Drugs.

On June 11, 1970, Dr. Nestor directed a special memorandum to Charles Edwards, commissioner of the Food and Drug Administration, warning him of the risks involved in existing FDA testing procedures. Although Dr. Henry Simmons, director of the Bureau of New Drugs, did not approve of this communication, Dr. Nestor used the FDA Critical Problem Report System, ostensibly established to cut red tape in communicating with top officials. In July, Dr. Nestor again wrote Commissioner Edwards discussing the morality and ethics of human experimentation encouraged by the FDA and reiterating the gravity of the situation.

Early in the week of August 17, 1970, Dr. Nestor was called into the office of Dr. Marian Finkel, the deputy director of the Bureau of New Drugs, and asked if he would be interested in working in the Division of Drug Advertising. Dr. Nestor responded that he was not at all interested and left, believing the matter closed. On September 1, 1970, however, Dr. Nestor was informed that he was being transferred to the Division of Drug Advertising.[7] He had not been consulted prior to the decision and it was not until September 4 that he learned from Commissioner Edwards that he would be detailed to the division for only four months. The detail placed Dr. Nestor, a GS-15, under the supervision of a GS-14 whom he had formerly supervised. Dr. Nestor believed that the action was a retaliatory one, motivated by his use of the Critical Problem Report System and by a desire to remove him from the sensitive drug applications with which he was dealing. He feared that he would be placed on other undesirable details when this one was completed or would eventually be reassigned from the bureau entirely. Dr. J. Marion Bryant, a fellow medical officer, commented in 1970 on Dr. Nestor's reassignment. "A large segment of the medical officers, in cluding myself, are of the opinion that it *is* retaliatory and intended to silence Dr. Nestor."

Articles by Morton Mintz in the *Washington Post* of September 7, 1970, and by Reginald W. Rhein in *U.S. Medicine* of September 15, 1970, and continuing congressional inquiry and support for Dr. Nestor may have aided his return to the Cardiopulmonary-Renal Division of the Bureau of New Drugs. Once back, he proceeded to pursue his responsibilities with his customary zeal. Along with several other doctors, including Dr. John W. Winkler, acting division director, Dr. Nestor had turned the Cardiopulmonary-Renal Division into one of the most effective units within the bureau, an effectiveness that distressed the drug industry, and, apparently, the hierarchy of the FDA.

On March 14, 1972, Dr. Nestor was called to the office of Dr. Henry

Simmons, director of the Bureau of New Drugs, and told that he was being reassigned to the Bureau of Compliance—effective in six days. Neither Dr. Nestor nor his supervisor had been consulted about the reassignment. When asked the reason for the transfer, Dr. Simmons answered that Dr. Nestor had done such a good job with other investigations that the Bureau of Compliance wanted him to work on Laetrile, an anticancer drug. Dr. Nestor pointed out that he was not a cancer specialist and that one drug investigation hardly justified a reassignment, since he could work on loan for that. The reassignment, furthermore, would be to a nonspecialist position and would remove Dr. Nestor from important current drug investigations. Dr. Nestor became more concerned about the reassignment when he spoke the next day with the director of the Bureau of Compliance. The director told of a conversation with Dr. Simmons the week before in which Dr. Simmons said that he intended to move Dr. Nestor, and asked if he could be used in the Bureau of Compliance. The director had responded by saying there were some problems, such as Laetrile, on which Dr. Nestor could work.

Dr. Nestor filed a formal grievance with the FDA and an appeal with the Civil Service Commission, contending that his assignment to a general medical position not requiring a specialty was an improper reduction in rank. According to him, much of the work he had been assigned could be handled by "a competent first year medical student."

Dr. Nestor had been reviewing an application for the proposed new use of a cholesterol-lowering drug, which had been reviewed previously and approved for use in human investigation by Dr. Finkel. At the time of his transfer he was raising serious questions about the adequacy of the previous tests. He was also raising embarrassing questions about the propriety of the FDA's use of medical consultants to review drug applications who had tested or were testing drugs for private industry.

Dr. Nestor's formal grievance to the Food and Drug Administration was ultimately denied. Today, Dr. Nestor remains in the Office of Compliance. His assignments have become more substantive and, as he put it, "There is always something a concerned individual can find to do."

Not all reassignments, of course, are punitive or coercive, but present policies provide management with a means to suppress and punish dissidents that poses dangers for the effective enforcement of regulatory programs.[8]

THE DEEP FREEZE

Sometimes an instant Siberia can be created without moving the objectionable employee at all. Separation from contact with other employees, physical isolation, and boredom are part of the deep freeze treatment.

One GS-13 employee in the Department of Agriculture was assigned nothing but the task of organizing departmental beauty contests. A GS-9 employee in the Department of Labor was deprived of a telephone and given no work assignment for several weeks. At first he found the resemblance to solitary confinement amusing, but after a while the lack of anything to do became distressing. He began to bring magazines to work with him, a diversion that was ended when a supervisor told him that he was not allowed to read magazines while working. When the employee had the temerity to ask what he was to be working at, his supervisor responded, "What you are assigned." This technique is particularly useful when the employee has violated no regulation.

The deep freeze is also particularly valuable when an employee has been complaining about agency malfeasance, and it appears that an attempt to remove the employee would lead to uncovering the mess. A scientist who worked for the National Institutes of Health complained about the safety of vaccines and found himself placed under "house arrest." First, his secretary was reassigned and not replaced. Then his phone was removed. Eventually, he was moved into an isolated office, the physical access to which was monitored by the agency.

The technique is not always so severe. Often an employee will simply be denied information about what happens to his work or whether his memoranda are accepted or rewritten. One high-ranking HEW employee described these practices as "being sent to Coventry." Rather than a deep freeze, a merely chilly reception is provided. Many employees simply do not like the cold and resign.

FORCED ACCULTURATION

It is important to keep in mind that dismissal is not only a means to get people out, but a means to keep people in line.

Probationary employees—those who will be appointed to or who have served for less than a year in career civil service positions—are particularly vulnerable to manipulation. If the employee is being removed for unsatisfactory performance, he need only be notified in writing of the effective date of his separation and the agency's very brief statement of his inadequacies. In 1970, 9,680 probationary employees were thus removed.

The probationary period can and does serve a valuable purpose, but the lack of standards and the lack of requirements for a meaningful statement of the reasons for removal means that removal can be made on emotion or caprice. Since almost any basis will support a removal, an employee must be very careful not only to perform adequately, but also to refrain from extensive criticism of the agency's performance. This procedure tends to breed timidity and to deny the agency the benefit of a fresh and unbiased perspective.

The histories of the immediate victims of unjustly applied sanctions—the psychologically and morally wounded, the economically and physically destroyed—do not tell all that needs to be told. The coal miner dead because of a failure to enforce safety regulations is a victim of the same lack of external accountability within the management structure of federal agencies. But even if unfair disciplinary actions had no impact beyond the affected personnel, the individual injustices themselves would require that the system of discipline be examined.

For every Ernest Fitzgerald—who had the intelligence and luck to marshal and direct his resources, who had the active support of congressmen, who survived the investigation of his personal life and the attempts to destroy his reputation—there are hundreds who have not survived. Of course, the employees who have chosen to resign rather than to be cast into the agency mold are those who find it easiest to get another job—the most able.

NOTES

1. Kenneth Culp Davis in *Discretionary Justice* indicates that selective enforcement of rules and regulations is widespread in the administrative process Professor Davis gives an excellent example:

> An Oakland ordinance, as interpreted officially by the district attorney, required holding every woman arrested for prostitution for eight days in jail for venereal testing. The ordinance conferred no discretionary power on the police. Even so, the police illegally assumed a discretionary power to be lenient to the girls who cooperated; only 38 percent of those arrested were held for venereal testing. One officer explained: "If a girl gives us a hard time . . . we'll put a hold on her. I guess we're actually supposed to put a hold on everybody so there's nothing wrong in putting a hold on her . . . but you know how it is, you get to know some of the girls, and you don't want to give them extra trouble." (1) The ordinance required holding every arrested woman, yet the police illegally assumed the power to be lenient. (2) The police converted the power to be lenient into an affirmative weapon: "if a girl gives us a hard time . . . we'll put a hold on her." (3) The innocent girl is more likely to resist and therefore less likely to cooperate and therefore more likely to be held. The discrimination seems clearly unjust. And the personal element as part of the motivation is even acknowledged: "You get to know some of the girls." (4) The usual specious reasoning that leniency for some is not unjust comes out with great clarity: "We're actually supposed to put a hold on everybody, so there's nothing wrong in putting a hold on her."

The dynamics of selective enforcement of personnel rules are quite similar. According to USDA regulations, for example, ready-to-cook products coming from meat and poultry plants are to be 100 percent free of processing errors. This standard, however, is not met in any poultry plant, and veterinarians who serve as inspectors-in-charge vary in the number of processing errors they allow. An inspector may, however, find himself faced with the charge that he is allowing excessive errors in the ready-to-cook product.

2. Commission regulations consider but fail to protect the employee effectively from the pressures that can be used to force resignation. F.P.M. Supplement S1-la(3) provides that an agency may give an employee a choice between leaving his position voluntarily or having the agency initiate formal action against him. "It is also proper for the agency in the course of the discussion to advise the employee which of the possible alternatives will be in his best interests. . . . However, if the agency uses deception, duress, time pressure, or intimidation to force him to choose a particular course of action, the action is involuntary."

3. F.P.M. Supplement S1-26c(i) provides that if, after an employee is influenced to separate voluntarily by his agency's assurance that the action will leave him with a clear record in his official personnel folder, the agency enters any unfavorable information on the separation form, the separation is faulty because the employee was deceived. An employee who accepts an agency offer to resign rather than face charges would be well advised to acquire letters of recommendation from his supervisors and the personnel officer *before* he submits his resignation.

4. Federal employees are asked on their employment applications about their willingness to change job locations after they are hired. This information is used, presumably, to evaluate the applicant for employment. If an employee is unwilling to accept geographical reassignments, this may well be a factor in deciding whether or not to hire. An employee who indicates his unwillingness to be reassigned on his application cannot be criticized, however, for feeling that the government has implicitly taken that to be a consideration of his employment. The Public Interest Research Group has received complaints indicating that employees who expressed an unwillingness to relocate on their job applications still face dismissal for refusing to do so.

5. In some agencies, employees are not necessarily faced with this Hobson's choice. For example, in the Department of Labor, Secretary's Order #2-62 provides that any proposed personnel action (transfer) which has been made the subject of a grievance shall not be taken pending settlement of the grievance. Such an action could be taken prior to the resolution of the grievance only if the Secretary determines that the action must be taken to prevent hazards to other employees, to preserve the reputation of the department, or for the best interests of the department.

6. This procedure is described in Harrison Wellford's *Sowing the Wind*, a Nader Task Force study of the Department of Agriculture published in 1972.

7. The FDA contended that the reassignment was to "beef up" the Division of Drug Advertising by placing an M.D. in it. This explanation, however, seemed somewhat bizarre—a recent reorganization of the Division of Drug Advertising specifically excluded medical personnel. (Both Commissioner Edwards and Elliot Richardson, then Secretary of Health, Education and Welfare, had justified the exclusion of physicians by emphasizing that the division could call on medical expertise within other divisions of the FDA.)

8. The federal courts rather than the Civil Service Commission have begun to restrict the ability of agencies to use reassignments to circumvent the appellate rights of an employee. A district court in Louisiana held that reassignments could not be used to force the resignation of an employee as an attempt to circumvent his appellate rights. *Motto* v. *G.S.A.*, 335 F. Supp. 694 (E.D. La. 1971).

Out of Their League
Dave Meggyesy

When a player is injured, he is sent to the team physician, who is usually more concerned with getting the athlete back into action than anything else. This reversal of priorities leads to unbelievable abuses. One of the most common is to "shoot" a player before a game to numb a painful injured area that would normally keep him out of action. He can play, but in so doing he can also get new injuries in that part of his body where he has no feeling.

When I spoke to a group of athletes at the University of California in the Spring of 1970, Jim Calkins, co-captain of the Cal football team, told me that the coaching staff and the team physician had put him on anabolic steroids. Both assured him such drugs would make him bigger and stronger, and this is true. But they didn't bother to tell him that there are potentially dangerous side-effects. "I gained a lot of weight like they told me I would, but after a month or so, those steroids really began to mess me up," Jim told me. "I went to the team physician and he admitted that there are possible dangers. I had complete faith in the coaches and medical staff before this, and I felt betrayed." And well he might, because steroids are known to have caused atrophied testes, blunting of sex drives, damage to liver and glands, and some physicians believe that they are the causal agent for cancer of the prostate. And they are widely used.

The violent and brutal player that television viewers marvel over on Saturdays and Sundays is often a synthetic product. When I got to the National Football League, I saw players taking not only steroids, but also amphetamines and barbiturates at an astonishing rate. Most NFL trainers do more dealing in these drugs than the average junky. I was glad when Houston Ridge, the San Diego Chargers' veteran defensive tackle, filed a huge suit last spring against his club, charging them with conspiracy and malpractice in the use of drugs. He charged that steroids, amphetamines, barbiturates and the like were used "not for purpose of treatment and cure, but for the purpose of stimulating mind and body so he (the player) would perform more violently as a professional . . . "

I don't mean that players are given drugs against their will. Like Calkins, most players have complete trust in their coaches and team doctors and in the pattern of authority they represent. Associated with this is the atmosphere of suspicion which surrounds any injured player unless his injury is a visible one, like a broken bone. Coaches constantly question the validity of a player's complaints, and give him the silent treatment when he has a "suspicious" injury. The coaches don't say, "We think you're faking, don't you want to play football?" They simply stop talking to a player and the message comes across very clearly. Most players want and need coaches' approval, especially when they are injured and can't perform, and it really tears them up when the coach won't even speak to them. This is especially true in college where the players are young and usually identify closely with the coach. After a few days of this treatment, many players become frantic. They will plead with the team physician to shoot them up so they can play. The player will totally disregard the risk of permanent injury.

Coaches love to recount examples of players who have played with serious injuries. Ben's* favorite story was about Jim Ringo. According to Ben, Ringo played one game his senior year with infected boils covering both legs. Ben would emphasize that both Ringo's legs were covered with pus and blood when he came into the locker room at half time. According to Ben, Ringo did not once speak of the pain. He simply bandaged the draining boils, put on a clean pair of pants and went back out to play a great second half. It's like the fictional American soldier played by John Wayne who fights on with crippling, fatal wounds. In the Catch-22 world of football, as in war, this passes for reasonable behavior. . . .

I must admit to mixed feelings about the athletic department's willingness to keep guys out of trouble since they kept me out of jail once when the police had a warrant out for my arrest, because of my collection of over fifty-five parking tickets. They handled the matter so well that I not only avoided jail or a fine, but I didn't even pay the original fines. I remember standing before the judge trying to look humble and contrite. I knew the athletic department had already worked things out because it was Ben who had told me when to show up in court. But the judge began to lecture me in a stern monotone: "The total for these tickets and accumulated fines is over $800 and you could spend up to six months in jail. Just because you are a football player, don't think you can get away with this kind of thing." He kept on for about five minutes, and I began to have visions of myself sitting in jail wondering how the hell I was going to get $800. Suddenly the judge looked up, half smiled, and asked, "Are you guys going to have a good football team this year?" I heaved a sigh of relief; everything

*Ben Schwartzwalder, former coach at Syracuse University—*Ed. Note.*

was all right. "We have a real dedicated bunch of guys," I told him with all the boyish modesty I could summon, "and I think we can go all the way." "I'm glad to hear that," he said. "All of us down here follow the team closely and are pulling for you." He quickly switched back to his judge's face and voice, informed me I was being fined $10 for court costs and called the next case.

I was elated at getting off so easily, especially after the temporary scare the judge had given me. But I was also thinking about how the judge had treated other people in court that morning. The shabbily-dressed defendants, many of them black, were given the harshest penalties while the more affluent looking, like me, usually paid no more than a nominal fine. With my background it was easy to identify with the poor defendants, for I knew if I was not a college football star, I would be in the same boat.

Taking care of $800 worth of parking tickets, of course, was trivial compared to the effort and expense the athletic department had to put out for many players. This sort of thing makes you see yourself as pretty important. With all the wheeling and dealing the athletic department does on your behalf, you get the feeling you're immune from normal responsibilities—which is possibly why some athletes act like animals all the time.

After years of this special treatment, ball players begin to lose sight of the fact that this immunity is only temporary. For those who don't make it to the pros, it usually expires along with their college reputation. There are few more pathetic sights than a former college football hero walking around campus unnoticed. The same university that used to fix his grades, bail him out of jail and give him money under the table has now turned its back on him. You see a lot of guys whose life actually stopped after their last college game. They hang on by becoming insurance salesmen and the like, selling their former image as a football player. . . .

[Ed. Note: The author now relates his pro football experiences.]

At eleven o'clock we had to be in our rooms in bed with the lights out. I'd lie in my bed with my door about six inches open to hear the coach coming by for bed check. He'd open the door, shine the flashlight directly in your eyes to make sure you were in bed, and mumble "Good night." Players never mess around with bed check because they realize if they're ever reported to the head coach for missing bed check they face—at least under Winner*—an automatic $500 fine.

---

*Charlie Winner, former St. Louis Cardinals coach—Ed. Note.

A guy would be in the bathroom taking a dump or brushing his teeth and you'd hear the coach open the door and holler to him, "Get to bed now, it's after eleven o'clock." But what really pissed me off in this enforced infantilization were the times I hadn't been able to reach the one phone in the dorm to call my family until close to 11:00. I'd be talking with Stacy and the coach would come down and yell "Hang up now and get to bed." It was worse than absurd. The guys being bed-checked were adults, pulling down an average of about $25,000 a year. Many of them are stockbrokers off season; a few have Ph.D. degrees. But you find yourself reacting like a kid. Some nights when I was really digging a book, I'd turn off the light when I heard the coach coming up the hall and pretend to be sleeping when he opened my door. He'd check the other rooms and when he left the floor, I'd put on the light and continue reading like a guilty kid who sneaks a book under the covers with a flashlight after his parents have told him to go to sleep.

The 1969 season was the first one that I was able to rent a house near the training camp and have Stacy and the kids with me; but the coaches still insisted I had to be in bed in the dormitory at eleven o'clock. This meant I'd drive over to the house after dinner and spend an hour and a half or so playing with the kids, then rush back in time for the eight o'clock meeting. After that, I could drive back and be with Stacy until 10:45 when I'd have to run to the dorm and be in the sack when the coach came around for bedcheck.

In pro football, as in high school and college, the only way the coaches can establish their authority is to treat their players as boys. After I'd decided to retire, I was talking to "Chip" Oliver, the Oakland Raider linebacker who'd also quit at the peak of his career. We were talking in the Bay Area commune where he's now living and one of his comments struck me as right on. He said he'd told Al Davis, general manager of the Raiders, that he still liked football and would happily come back to play again if the coaches would treat him like a man. We smiled because we both knew this meant permanent retirement as long as he stuck to this demand. . . .

My contract made it financially important to me to play as many defensive plays as possible during the regular season. At the same time, the team, including myself, was attempting to win a division championship. So, where I was able to pick up a particular tip on the opposition, I was confronted with the dilemma of whether or not to share it with the other linebackers. Coaches constantly talk about team spirit but I've always wondered how the hell there can be team spirit if I know that the more other linebackers screw up, the more I'll be able to play, and the more I play, the more money I make. Owners keep writing contracts with performance clauses such as the one I had, though these can only work to create divisiveness on the team, for these clauses create a situation where the amount of money a player gets is dependent on how badly his teammates at his position play. A second string player who will not get his bonus unless he plays at least 40 percent of the plays will not be upset if the guy ahead of him screws up badly. The owners introduced these bonuses with the idea that they would extract better performances from the players and result in more victories. In reality, just the opposite usually happens. Rumors began to spread around the league during the 1969 season that receivers who had bonus clauses for the number of passes they caught were paying kickbacks to the quarterbacks.

This dual level of competition is built into pro football. On one hand, the player is competing against his opponent, the guy across from him, and wants to do a good job to further the club's success. At the same time, I was constantly aware that my every move would be on movie film and would be scrutinized closely by the coaching staff the following Monday when they decided between me and my competitors on the team for the starting role. This competition involved not only linebackers, but also halfbacks that I had to cover in practice: if they looked good it meant that I wasn't doing my job and that could get me demoted to second team.

Players bullshit the press on how they help the various rookies. I have rarely seen this happen—certainly I received no help at all when I was a rookie. Quite the contrary, rookies generally received constant abuse from the vets, designed to intimidate them and break their confidence. The new player must not only prove himself on the field, he must also prove he can take their harrassment. It's survival of the fittest from beginning to end. . . .

The only thing I had going for me after my return from the Virgin Islands was being enrolled in graduate school at Washington University. I began my studies again, yet felt the university setting added less and less meaning to my life. Though I'd done a lot of thinking about who I was, I never seemed able to know my real feelings about many things. There was, in short, much ambivalence in my life. Then, in the last week of March '69 I attended a five day workshop at Esalen Institute led by Seymour Carter. My experience at Esalen was, to make an understatement, significant. I saw very acutely the contradiction between the feelings I had during my experiences at Esalen and the experiences I had working within my craft, which was football. Since high school, I had been using the mask of "football player" to confront the world. It was both my main line of defense and my main source of gaining approval and recognition. I also realized, paradoxically, how cut off and removed I was from my body. I knew my body more thoroughly than most men are ever able to, but I had used it and thought of it as a machine, a thing that had to be well-oiled, well-fed, and well-taken-care of, to do a specific job. My five days at Esalen left me with an immensely good feeling. I had glimpsed a bit of myself and realized that the "me" behind the face guard was alive and well and could feel and think.

5

(ONFLI(T, REJIJTAN(E TO (HANGE, AND (ONTROL

Part One:
Jource/ of (onflict and Re/i/tance

"Conflict resolution," "confronting conflict," and "overcoming resistance to change" are popular words among organizational behaviorists. Relative to many other elements of modern organizational behavior these phrases lead to the discussion of sources of tension and dispute in organizations.

As commonly used, these terms unfortunately have not directed attention to the many bitter struggles which occur within organizations. For example, confronting conflict has come to refer to the open verbal expression of interpersonal feelings. Overcoming resistance to change has become associated with inviting participation to reduce defensiveness and perceived threat. While open expression of feelings and the reduction of threat are important accomplishments, a great deal is missed if the treatment of conflict and resistance to change stops there.

The selections in this section attempt to recoup some of what organizational behaviorists have overlooked. In particular, they demonstrate that conflict is expressed in a number of forms. Some forms are subtle and almost unobtrusive; others are blatant and coercive. Moreover, the selections indicate that conflict and resistance are pervasive processes which involve struggles among people at different levels as well as among people of the same organizational rank. Finally, a number of the readings show that conflict and resistance result, at least in part, from individuals and groups seeking to protect and advance their selfish interests.

Frequently, conflict and resistance to change are rooted in mistrust and fears of various sorts. The first selection by Andrew Pettigrew describes the intricacies of intense organizational conflict which resulted from computerization in one business organization. Clearly, fear of loss of control, jobs and status played a major role in the conflict stemming from this change. The article by Benjamin

DeMott shows how the competition for scarce resources contributes to conflict within academia. The next selection shows how conflict over control can retard change within a trade union to the disadvantage of the union's membership. Melville Dalton's discussion of the ratebusting tactics of a saleswoman reveals how the pursuit of self-interest can be a source of conflict (in this case, latent conflict) within a work group. Together, the materials which comprise the first portion of this section reveal some of the sources and processes of conflict among groups and individuals within organizations.

The Politics of Organizational Decision-making

Andrew M. Pettigrew

From the programmers' point of view this ambiguity of place was compounded by ambiguity of function. They were clear about their task, to design a computer system for the Stock Control department of the clothing division and to program and implement it. They were much less clear about the roles to be played by other people in the Computer department. Morgan's dual role as Bell's* "number one man" and supervisor of the punch-room staff seemed acceptable. After all, "data preparation was a rather routine clerical job." The problem for the programmers was trying to justify the appearance of Bill Reilly and Tim Philby, the two recruits from the Work Study department. Bell and Morgan were much clearer about the role of these two gentlemen. Morgan remarked:

> Wilson [a company director] was most anxious we should recruit a couple of people into the team with specialist knowledge of the affected departments. In this way we came across Reilly and Philby. Both of them were more or less spies for Wilson.

Bell seemed equally sure:

> In fact Reilly and Philby were sent to spy on us. Philby used to report what we were doing to his old boss in the Work Study de-

*Harry Bell, head of the computer department—*Ed. Note.*

Pp. 85–99 from *The Politics of Organizational Decision-making* by Andrew M. Pettigrew. Copyright Andrew M. Pettigrew 1973. Reprinted by permission of Barnes & Noble Books, a Division of Harper & Row, Publishers, Inc. and Tavistock Publications, Ltd., Publishers.

partment. However, he was a great "detail" man and got so bogged down in detail that he could never see the wood for the trees. Also, Reilly's job was to police us, querying everything we did with the management.

Reilly's way of discussing this issue is significant. He says:

Bell and Morgan were recruited from the furniture side of the business. Two of us were appointed from the clothing side. Tim Philby and myself. Then started what, in some respects, was a part of my working life that I could do well with forgetting. At that time Mills was in charge of the furniture division and we were working for Wilson. Really it was a typical Brian Michaels situation. Philby was a real Wilson man, everybody knew it at the time. Wilson expected Philby and myself to report exactly what Bell and Morgan were finding out and telling Mills. Really it was a terrible predicament to be in. I'd rather forget about it altogether.

The spying episode clearly indicates competition at board level between the two divisions of the company. It also reveals one of the ways in which Michaels directors operate. Wilson was using "his men" to check on the activities of two other men from another division of the company. In addition, the case illuminates the strategy used by a Michaels director to monitor the behaviour of a strange new breed of men working with a mysterious piece of technology. The strategies employed by the Michaels board to try to control the computer technologists are a topic we shall return to later. For the present, it is significant to note that Reilly, in describing this episode eleven years later, calls it "a typical Brian Michaels situation."

In this environment the Computer department was formed and the first batch of programmers appeared with their honours degrees in mathematics.

THE PROGRAMMERS

The arrival of programmers in Brian Michaels produced a culture shock of some magnitude. Many Michaels employees have never got over the experience. The programmers who were interviewed in the course of this study have equally vivid memories. Bell has described Michaels as:

a quill-pen firm . . . which traditionally has employed low-quality people to do low-quality work. The result is that it's the hardest of all firms to introduce change into.

While fear of what they represented may have been a major factor in explaining some of the extreme reactions towards the programmers, there were other equally pertinent reasons.

In the first place, the programmers appeared to be aliens with no interest in the firm of Brian Michaels. Like many other specialist groups, they were driven by the immediate challenge of their work. One programmer commented:

In the early days we motivated ourselves. Getting the job on the computer was everything. The integration of the department in the company was very small indeed. As a group of people we were very independent. We had no sense of involvement in company affairs.

Another said:

As a team we worked for an academic rather than a business interest. This was certainly true of the technical people. We were all back-room boys.

This lack of involvement even excluded interest in long-term policy matters in their own department:

Bell never went beyond the short-term objectives. This was quite sufficient incentive for us. The major motivation was that this was a pioneering job. The problems of getting to the short-term objectives were fascinating enough.

Bell's rather closed managerial style brought praise from the programmers:

Harry really put up the drawbridge. He kept the wolves from the door and allowed the boys to get on with the job.

Even with Bell's style and their different work patterns, the programmers could not totally isolate themselves. In fact, their strange work timetable and casual dress attracted criticism. The computer operators were the first group to pick up this ill feeling. One operator, now a senior programmer, said:

It started off with the operators; they were the first people in the company to work odd hours. They had beards, used to dress roughly, and were going home at 8:30 in the morning when everybody else was arriving. One day one of the personnel people came up and told me off for wearing a roll-collar sweater. He said to me, "You're supposed to be a young executive, you should dress accordingly."

The programmers also disrupted the company rules about clocking on and off. This, together with the rewards their market position afforded them at such a comparatively young age, created problems with the company status system. Since the Personnel department had to deal with these issues it was the focus of a lot of the programmers' discontent. The Personnel department had a terrible reputation for being ruthless and inconsiderate. One senior programmer referred to its staff as the "gestapo." An operator commented:

They were always asking us why we were late. They didn't realize we'd probably been working half the previous night. We were on overtime—some of us were earning £1200 with a base of £800, at that time a good deal more than their young executives! The fact was they tried to, but couldn't, control us in the same way as the little girls. They had a standard 8-5 attitude to everybody. We answered back. This had never happened to them before.

The programmers were clearly a group apart from the rest of the company. As Gerald Lane said: "There wasn't a graduate in the company. We must have stood out." They differed in education, values, work patterns, dress, and rewards from the rest of Michaels employees. While it is understandable that a stock controller might refer to them as "long-haired, highly paid yobos," it is less clear that the conflict between the programmers and user departments was just over value differences. As Mumford and Banks (1967) have pointed out, when a man is faced with change, the first question he is likely to ask is: How will it affect me?

THE PROGRAMMERS AND THE USER DEPARTMENTS

To the programmers, the Personnel department embodied all they disliked about their work situation. For the stock controllers, the computer represented a similar threat. They had no wish to become the victims of a change apparently imposed on them by a group of outsiders who knew little of their work. A stock controller, later to join the Computer department, recalled:

I was very loath to join the computer set-up at first. There was a great deal of anti-feeling towards the programmers which was heartily reciprocated. They called the stock controllers idiots and took the attitude that it was the programmers' job to tell them what to do. The user departments used to say *the* computer when referring to the Computer department.

I remember Kahn, who was head of stock control at that time, going into a tirade about computers when I had to see him as part of my induction course. He used to say: "These people coming into the business with the machine aren't going to tell me how to run my department." I had scars on my memory about computers before I even got near them.

Harry Bell was later asked how he got on with the stock controllers:

I had enormous problems. Kahn was opposed to the whole system. Also, individual stock controllers were opposed to it. One man said to me: "It's taken all the interest out of the job." Another said, "Before the computer I was so overworked people would tolerate my mistakes. Now everyone expects me to be right." We were tightening the controls over these people.

Although they were being asked to accept output from people who symbolized a machine they did not trust, the stock controllers were still responsible for making the kinds of decision they had made in the past. One stock controller expressed their feelings like this:

> We put so many obstacles in its way in the form of nervous argument. We didn't believe it could give us all the things we needed. We were frightened the computer would wrongly calculate something for us and we wouldn't notice this.

Essentially the stock controllers felt that if they did not lose their jobs altogether, their skills would be diluted and their livelihood threatened. None of these things happened. In fact, the very opposite occurred. The computer eventually took much of the routine from their work and allowed them to utilize their merchandising skills more effectively. The status of the department has considerably improved since this time. Today the head stock controller acknowledges the changes in his department's fortunes but insists that in 1958-9 "it wasn't obvious that this was going to happen."

Many people in the company attribute the user departments' early fears to the programmers' style of operating. The programmers were said to be "domineering," "arrogant," and "outside the situation of the ordinary stock controller." Even when they organized lecture courses for the stock controllers, the latter could not understand what was going on. A stock controller said:

> In the early days the programmers would give us lectures on mathematics. What we really wanted to know was what the machine could do for us and *not* the mathematical formulas behind the operations!

What eventually happened is well characterized in the following quote:

> If someone comes along from outside and just walks in without consulting people in the department, then it's only natural that staff begin to pull down the blinds.

Early in 1959, then, the programmers had mastered what was for them at that time technically an extremely complex and challenging task. They were now producing computer output for the Stock Control department. The only problem was that the stock controllers refused to accept it. A very expensive piece of machinery was producing, from the company's point of view, irrelevant information. In this situation Jim Kenny arrived to set up an O & M department.

THE PROGRAMMERS AND THE O & M OFFICERS

Kenny was brought into Michaels with the encouragement of the chief personnel officer and Brian Michael himself. Somebody had to act as a link between the programmers and the stock controllers. Someone had to translate the company's needs into computer terms. O & M officers at that time were generally involved in redesigning clerical procedures. It was felt that eventually they could redefine the system of work in the Stock Control department, set it out in the form of flow charts and reports, and then leave the programmers to translate these flow charts into a form acceptable to the computer.

Bill Reilly and two liaison officers, Tom Reagan and Harvey Peters, considered that they had been trying to do just that from within the Computer department. They found it very difficult to convince the programmers of the value of their approach. I asked Tom Reagan how he and Bill Reilly got on with the programmers:

> Not too well. The programmers wanted to go their way. They regarded Bill's work as trivial and time-wasting. They more or less dismissed his O & M work.

Harvey Peters' attitude was part admiration, part contempt:

> As a group they were highly individualistic, and at the time they struck me as being brilliant, though I wouldn't think that so much now . . . they had a tremendously selfish attitude. Anybody who was not a programmer was less than human. They were so involved in their work. I suppose it was so demanding, they had to look down a very narrow path.

Reilly described the situation in 1957-9 as follows:

> The whole thing was a bit of a melting-pot. The only real distinction between us and the programmers was that they had no knowledge of commerce. . . . There was no doubt their mathematical training helped their logical abilities. . . . I suppose you'd expect differences between the two groups for they were down in London all the time. We were only down every other week. When they eventually came up to Wolverhampton, we had to shield them from the management.

The programmers who were interviewed did not take such an extreme stand towards Reilly, Peters, and Reagan as the latter thought that they did. The programmers' attitude was more a matter of: *we have the skills, what is all the fuss about?* Pete Taft, a senior programmer, commented:

> There was a bit of friction, but not because we couldn't talk each other's language. We were the systems analysts working with the O & M boys. The only real friction came when what we wanted and what they wanted in systems terms differed. There were no real technical arguments because we were involved in the actual systems design. They weren't in a position to argue over technical points anyway.

The analytical training the programmers had was important to them, as was the lack of this training in some of their co-workers:

Reilly didn't have this and was therefore much less objective in problem-solving than we were.

Gerald Lane expressed a similar view:

Reilly was nothing exceptional. He was persistent and keen, but when Bell left Reilly moved over to Jim Kenny's new O & M outfit.

In spite of these differences in background, training, and work orientation, both groups in the Computer department talked of a distinct feeling of group solidarity. Much of this was due to high involvement in their work. In 1957-8 there were only about a dozen computers on order in Britain. Michaels purchased the first SE 100. The members of the Computer department felt like pioneers. They were. A programmer remarked:

In the main, relations in the Computer department were very good. Morale was very high when we were really trying to get the system going. I can't remember a group with such high morale or of such high calibre since. They were the pioneers.

Reagan, after accusing the programmers of arrogance, noted:

There were these differences but not enough friction to really divide the department. There was an air of enthusiasm to get things through that meant there was no real split.

Harvey Peters, the other liaison officer, pointed out the existence of an outside threat to the department which united everybody. Neil Turner, at that time a senior programmer, agreed:

As I've said, we were very much a group. There was a slight split between the programmers and Ted Morgan's laddies but no real friction. Nobody else in the business was obviously backing computers. We were the only group interested in proving they were worthwhile. We were bound to be a close-knit group.

This feeling of group cohesiveness was well dramatized in their out-of-work activities. Reilly described the formation of a pub drinking club christened "The Fluids Society." When the team started to break up in 1960-1, quite a few went to the London area and a "London Fluids Society" was formed. There was a tendency for members of the team, when it disbanded, to join each other in a small number of firms. Six moved to two companies in the south of England.

THE ORGANIZATION AND METHODS DEPARTMENT
1959-61

Jim Kenny arrived in Michaels in March 1959. He recruited his first four O & M officers from within the company and then offered jobs (in 1960) to Bill Reilly and Tom Reagan. They both accepted the offers. The O & M department was situated in the company's head office in

Birmingham. The stock controllers were in the same building. The Computer department was twenty miles away in Wolverhampton.

Kenny was not impressed with the job the programmers had done:

The computer was doing nothing but printing out some simple information. My first step was to say "let's have a look what the stock-control problem really is." Before I joined Michaels the only people who had contacted the Stock Control department were programmers. I put in a systems team.

Kenny's early contact with the stock controllers was not trouble-free. He blamed this on the backlog of discontent that had built up between the Computer department and the stock controllers:

Any hostility was due to the way they (the Computer department) did things. They did them over the stock controllers' heads. Also, the stock controllers were afraid to let the records go. I remember Kahn telling me that the stock controllers used to hide on a Friday afternoon. The department was cutting down staff and they were afraid they'd be fired if they were seen by the management. The stock controllers regarded all their records as, if you like, acquiring evidence for the inquest.

However, the present head of stock control recalls a certain amount of ambivalence towards Kenny's own activities:

So the first thing that happened was that Mr. Kenny came in and decided he would do a complete study of stock control and determine what we really wanted and what we didn't. This is where the main arguments came.

The stock controllers were still very concerned about the restricted amount of information the computer was putting out compared with the manual system. There was also the issue that the output was in a different form and language from what they were accustomed to. Slowly they began to appreciate Kenny's style of operating. They began to draw comparisons with Bell's behaviour:

Bell and Co. really didn't know about stock control and they had no time to study it. But Mr. Kenny came and really studied stock control and we sat beside him and his team while they did this.

I think the O & M team were rather lenient here because what they did was to slowly but surely take away from us the information we thought was required but ultimately didn't require.

By the end of 1960 the computer system was, from everybody's point of view, an acknowledged success. A week's stock had been saved. The stock controllers now had the information they needed in time to start making decisions about future stock levels. Their job increased in status. They were relieved of much of the clerical drudgery and could now act like merchandisers. The chief stock controller recalled:

> I had always felt that the original system was like a man walking around in a street without really being able to see what was going on around him in other areas. Now with the new system it was like a man in a helicopter who had an enormous range of vision and could see for miles around.

The main task the O & M department performed in making the SE 100 computer system a viable one was to act as an intermediary between the Computer department and the stock controllers. Between 1959 and 1961 the O & M department had only minimal contact with the Computer department. This was largely because the programmers were still heavily committed on the technical problems of systems design and programming for the clothing stock-control operation. In addition, at the end of 1959, the programmers had begun a new project, computerizing the stock-control function of the furniture division. The head of the programming section recalled the heavy commitments of that period:

> The Computer department looked after clothing and furniture stock control. There was no time to do anything else. Up until 1959 we were trying to get something working. From 1959-60 we tried to make it operationally robust and from 1961 onwards we were trying to cut it down to size. It was a full-time job in 1959-60 just trying to get the thing going.

SUMMARY OF PROGRAMMER—O & M OFFICER RELATIONS 1957-61[1]

A content analysis was made of the history interviews with programmers and O & M officers. . . . Statements were coded into three categories, positive, negative, and neutral, and the inter-coder reliability score for the data was .91.

Table 1 substantiates the earlier conclusion about the ultimate balancing of attitudes between the two groups in time period 1957-61. Each group made nearly the same number of neutral comments about the other, twenty-seven as against twenty-six. As might be expected from the quotations given above, the groups showed consistently strong negative attitudes towards each other. The interesting point is that the ratio of negative to positive comments is nearly the same for each group. For the O & M officers the ratio is 1.8:1, and for the programmers it is 2.1:1. There is only the slightest indication that the programmers felt more negatively towards the O & M officers than vice versa. A χ^2 test revealed no significant differences in the direction of the attitudes. Clearly, the feeling of solidarity that had arisen between the two groups while they lived side by side in the Computer department had watered down somewhat when the O & M officers moved into their own department. The important point to note at this stage is the similarity of the ratio of negative to positive statements for the two occupational categories. This ratio was soon to change radically for reasons that will presently be discussed.

Table 1 Comparison of attitudes: O & M officers to
programmers and programmers to O & M officers:
1957–61

	Positive	Negative	Neutral
O & M officers	20	36	27
Programmers	14	29	26

No significant differences: positive-negative cells only.

While the two groups were alike in the proportion of negative attitudes they expressed towards one another, their negative feelings about Brian Michaels, its management, and user departments were not so balanced (see Table 2).

Table 2 Comparison of O & M officers' and
programmers' perceptions of Michaels, its
management, and user departments:
1957–61

	Positive	Negative	Neutral
O & M officers	38	71	46
Programmers	10	74	38

Significant beyond ·001 level with 1 degree of freedom:
positive-negative cells only.

Given the comments that the programmers and the user departments made about one another, it is hardly surprising that the accumulated feeling of the programmers is negative. It is a little more surprising that the O & M officers should also have negative things to say about Michaels, its management, and the user departments. This is especially so since the great majority of the early O & M officers were recruited from the Michaels Work Study or Stock Control departments. Some of the ill feeling expressed by the O & M officers was directed specifically at the company. These feelings would not have been echoed by everyone in the company. But one O & M officer said:

Michaels is a funny place. The previous ten years had seen all sorts of purges and passions. It wasn't the sort of place where people felt secure.

Another commented:

Michaels isn't the sort of place you'd want to retire into!

The day-to-day contacts the O & M officers had with the stock controllers brought home to them the stresses of being change agents. Reilly talked of his frequent encounters with the head stock controller, Kahn, in the following way:

Kahn was one of the biggest cursers I've ever come across. I wouldn't like to repeat any of it now; but his general approach was, "How are you going to do it?" He'd pick a difficult one like rainwear or swimsuits and say, "Tell us the answers." We'd say: "You tell us how you do it and we'll work out how to do it on the computer." We knew he didn't know how he got his figures. They were just based on experienced hunches but he wouldn't admit it. He refused to cooperate. Kahn was afraid of his position. He was afraid the computer would affect his position.

Eventually, the Michaels directors forced Kahn to cooperate—an early signal to the user departments of where the board's allegiances lay.

The large power differential between programmers and O & M officers was soon to change. A new generation of equipment appeared which offered faster, cheaper, and more reliable service. Research was going on all the time to simplify programming. A new occupational group appeared called systems analysts, who claimed an area of task jurisdiction and a body of skills. All these factors were to affect the level of perceived hostility and the distribution of power and status among those concerned with computers in Brian Michaels. It must have been difficult for Jim Kenny to foresee all these changes and their implications in 1961. His recollection of how he felt about the programmers at that time gives a clear indication of his future strategy towards them:

They were like a bunch of sixth-formers, sixth-form mathematicians. They were slick, witty in a sarcastic sort of way. They hid behind their technology. Trying to get to grips with them was extremely difficult. They were regarded as a lot of eggheads who lived in their own little world. The programmers were contemptuous of everybody in the business. Everybody had a nickname. They had their own language and all this was reflected in their out-of-work group they called The Fluids. They asked me to go out drinking with them but I refused. The whole thing was bloody infantile. I've no time for that sort of thing. I suppose a lot of their behaviour was partly defensive. They were an odd group. They had to protect themselves.

They were a little "in" group. They larked around at Wolverhampton like a bunch of school kids. I thought, I must get control
of them.

NOTE

1. Note that the summary data are presented for programmers versus O &
M officers and not for Computer department versus O & M department. The
implication is that people like Reilly, Reagan, and Morgan were seen to be, and
accepted that they were, doing O & M-type work within the Computer department prior to the creation of the O & M department.

REFERENCE

Mumford, E., and Banks, O. (1967). *The Computer and the Clerk.* London: Rout-
ledge and Kegan Paul.

Once More in Academe,
Purists vs. Utilitarians

Benjamin DeMott

Utilitarians and their enemies are at each other's throats again in
American colleges and universities.

Sometimes the dispute comes to the surface in genteel form, pitting
knowledge valued for its uses against knowledge valued "for its own
sake." Sometimes the focus is the large course versus the small course,
or the department with high enrollment versus the department starved
for students.

Sometimes contention centers on published data about student
preferences. Two months ago, the American Council on Education
released figures comparing the preferred fields of study of freshmen
who entered college in 1974 and 1975 with those of freshmen entering
in 1966. The data showed, among other things, a steady movement
toward "applied fields"—business, health professions, agriculture,
forestry and the like—and away from less immediately utilitarian subjects. One much discussed statistic disclosed that 22 percent of entering freshmen in 1966 intended to major in English, humanities, fine
arts or mathematics, while in 1975 the same subjects were chosen by
only 10 percent of the first-year students.

Whatever the focus of discussion in this area, the invariable byproducts seem to be bitterness, suspicion and anger.

This winter the faculty dean of a New England college asked individual faculty members to estimate the probable enrollments in the courses they planned to teach next year. "It may be necessary," the dean added blandly, "to ask some faculty to do additional teaching."

The roar of rage echoed through the faculty dining room and out into the student newspaper. The dean underwent a grilling from the faculty executive committee, wrote a two-page letter of clarification, and was obliged to place the "issue" high on the agenda of the next faculty meeting. The chairman of the college's special curriculum committee opined, in public, that faculty competition for students was causing grade inflation and a decline of standards. And one humanities professor was heard to refer, in faculty meeting, to teachers of large courses as "whores."

At the root of the rumble is—once more—the higher education money crisis. Post-Sputnik resentment about the imbalance in the allocation of resources was tempered by the brio of academic expansionism—salaries, research funds, and enrollment were almost universally up—and by the willingness of the Federal Government to grant a piece of the action even to disciplines lacking a visible utilitarian side.

In the mid-70's, the safety valves are gone, and one academician's success is perceived as another's imminent budget cut. Nowadays, money to pay extra hands for an ascendant department can only be found by stripping a discipline down the list.

Despite the bitterness it arouses, hard-edged utilitarianism is by no means all bad. Tenured loafers are not uncommon on university faculties. More than a few teachers confuse dullness with rigor, dismiss concern for the public contexts of higher learning as unscholarly, and regard a light teaching load as a gentleman's perquisite rather than as a challenge to a working professional's powers of creation. When the budget-obsessed utilitarian shoots a rocket into faculty self-indulgence and self-deception, he not only helps to curb rising tuition bills, he improves the over-all tone of academic life.

But the utilitarian does have weaknesses and blind spots. Among the worst are the following:

• Extravagant faith in the "hot-occupation." In accepting the tyranny of the market place, utilitarian planners promote career fads that inevitably cool off in time. The chill that touched other once-hot occupations—nuclear physicist, astrophysicist, sociologist—may one day reach the economist.

• Dimness about how to cope with the cycle of fashion. An error as common among utilitarians as the shutdown is the pindown, under which an academic department with currently low enrollment is fixed at a level of teaching personnel insufficient to enable it to energize and restructure itself in preparation for eventual resurgence. A recent City

University of New York planning paper omitted philosophy from a list of growth disciplines essential to future CUNY curricula—sign of a pindown, or worse, in process. (According to recent reports, this mistake has lately been rectified.)

• Faith in false parity. Utilitarian planners often ignore department variations in teaching practice that have a direct bearing on budget items. The treasurer of an eastern liberal arts institution recently proposed a two-thirds cut in his English department's budget request for multilithing and Xerox funds. His aim was to bring the budget item in line with that of other departments. As it happened, the bulk of the English department's copying money was spent in support of classroom work, while in departments cited as spending less, Xerox money went largely to reproduce learned papers for the private libraries of the instructors. Parity here was counter-productive.

As is obvious, both sides in the current quarrel could profit from fresh perspectives. Utilitarian academic administrators need a new negotiating stance—conversant with cycles of academic fashion but not terrorized by them, prepared to probe for the levels at which an out-of-fashion discipline can continue to be represented in a way that will assure the chance for a future, aware that there are values, ideas, bodies of work that the university has an obligation to keep in currency, regardless of ratings.

The opposition for its part needs a clear sense of economic reality, less hostility to successful teachers, and more curiosity about their methods, greater sympathy with the notion that when ratings decline, the proper response is not to criticize society but to seek grounds for revitalization.

None of these virtues is a substitute for money, and from this it follows that, whatever happens to the manners of utilitarians and their enemies, the tension between them will last for the duration.

Feuding Stifles UMW Reform

Political feuding on the 24-man executive board of the United Mine Workers has turned into a desperate struggle for control of the union and has brought the administration of President Arnold Miller to a standstill. It has stymied organizing in the West—where the soft coal industry is growing fastest—and delayed programs to reduce wildcat strikes and improve safety in the mines.

The executive board is now split into irreconcilable factions, with Miller's enemies in control by a 2-to-1 margin. They have raised no issues of substance against Miller, though they disapprove of the liberal, innovative cast of his administration. Their immediate aim is to strip Miller of his administrative powers or force him out as president. For coal industry management, the UMW's internal struggle can only portend a weakening of control over a strike-prone work force.

BITTER DIVISIONS

The conflict began when the Miners for Democracy ousted W. A. "Tony" Boyle, the former president, and his corrupt administration in 1972. The reformers had forced the union to grant rank-and-filers in the UMW's 21 districts the right to elect representatives to the policymaking board, which formerly had been largely an appointive body.

Predictably, the influx of rank-and-file miners—as well as many former Boyle staff men who retained political clout—resulted in what at first was a "healthy conflict" on the board. In recent months, however, old political loyalties have bred personal animosities. "The hatreds on the board are so intense," says a union insider, "that when Miller says something is black, his opponents say it's white."

The situation worsened last summer when Vice-President Mike Trbovich, who had run on the reform ticket with Miller and Secretary-Treasurer Harry Patrick, swung over to the opposition. Virtually all administrative decisions made by Miller and Patrick, including the hiring and firing of staff personnel, down to clerks and secretaries, are subject to rejection by their enemies on the board. Miller's staff appointees are especially threatened. "We spend so much time protecting ourselves from political attack, we don't have any time to work for the members," says one.

The board has also attempted to impeach Miller by calling a special convention (though the UMW's constitution contains no such recall provision). It has tried to set up its own staff separate from the union's and to dictate when the board should meet.

Taking over the union is clearly the intention of opposition board leaders such as Lee Roy Patterson, representing UMW District 23 in western Kentucky. He is Miller's most vocal opponent, though the most articulate is Andrew Morris, of District 31 in northern West Virginia. Both were Boyle staffers.

PROGRAMS AT STAKE

Miller and Patrick contend that the political bickering has prevented the union from implementing vital programs in organizing, safety, and education. "Ninety percent of the wildcat strikes could be stopped if our guys knew how to use the contract," Patrick says. "We need a rank-and-file education program, but the board's whole attitude makes us reluctant to propose it to them."

The anti-Miller forces have also tried to take control of organizing campaigns away from Miller's staff. As a result, the UMW's campaign to sign up miners on the big new stripping operations in the West—where output is expected to jump from 12% to 25% of total U.S. production by about 1980—is failing. The UMW has all but lost a crucial strike at the Gillette (Wyo.) mine of AMAX Inc., and if the Western mines remain outside the UMW, its national structure will be weakened.

Two months ago Miller—who is a weak administrator and frequently loses control of meetings—began to crack down on the "dictators," as he calls them, who oppose him on the board. His toughest action was suspending District 23's Patterson for refusing to undertake a data-gathering mission to Alaska. In the UMW, board members have no administrative function but are required to travel on troubleshooting missions at the president's direction. Patterson balked on grounds that Miller should have assigned someone to help him. Miller and an aide then made the trip.

At a board meeting two weeks ago a "spirit-of-unity" compromise was proposed under which Miller agreed to reinstate Patterson if the board would reaffirm his power to suspend members for insubordination. Instead, Patterson demanded "vindication" and the board voted 15-1 to uphold his reason for rejecting Miller's order.

Management in the coal industry, which lost 15 million to 16 million tons of production because of wildcat strikes last year, views the split in the union with growing alarm. "The union is losing influence and is being held up to ridicule," says an industry man who feels that a strong union is necessary to keep discipline in the work force.

COALFIELD UNREST

There is growing evidence that anger over the political bickering is welling up in the coalfields. Rank-and-file anger could force changes at a convention scheduled for late this year.

In the UMW's view, AFL-CIO President George Meany did not help matters recently when he said of the UMW: "I don't think they're any better off than they were three years ago." Meany's implication was that the coming of democracy has not changed the union. UMW officers considered this a gratuitous insult and asked Meany for an explanation. He has not replied.

Under Miller, the UMW has become stronger in some respects. But because Boyle stifled the rise of strong local leaders, there was virtually nobody with experience to step into top posts when democracy finally came. "We went from a dictatorship to a democracy overnight," says Patrick, "and it's been hard to handle. The tragedy is the rank-and-file isn't getting anything out of it."

The Ratebuster: The Case of the Saleswoman*
Melville Dalton

THE SALESWOMEN

Of the six people in the boys' department only the head was male, and he made sales only occasionally. Two of the women were high sellers—Mrs. White and Mrs. Brown. Mrs. White was fifty-nine years old, large physically and somewhat taciturn. She had worked at Lassiters for fourteen years. Mrs. Brown was a small active person, thirty-two and had been with the store for eight years. Masters told me that when she started in the store she was much taken with Mrs. White and copied and improved upon Mrs. White's selling techniques. Then, too, Mrs. Brown had the insights that came from close personal experience in outfitting her son. Over a period of several months they developed a rivalry. For the last six years or so, according to Masters [Mike Masters, head of the boys' department], they were coldly polite to each other

*The names of the individuals in this case and the department store (Lassiters) are fictional. The incidents described took place in the boys' department of Lassiters. The saleswomen in the department were all on commission.

As Dalton observed in a portion of this article which was omitted here, it is common for members of work groups who are on a commission or other system of incentive payments to avoid showing each other up. In other words, there are informal standards about what members of the group perceive to be a reasonable amount of work. Individuals who produce significantly above this level are often called "ratebusters" or "grabbers" by social scientists. Members of the work group often apply less complimentary labels and even sanctions to individuals who violate the output norms. At Lassiters, ratebusters were called "saleshogs" by their peers—Ed. note.

From Melville Dalton, "The Ratebuster: The Case of the Saleswoman," in Varieties of Work Experience: The Social Control of Occupational Groups and Roles, by P. L. Stewart and M. G. Cantor, eds., pp. 206–214. Copyright 1974 by Schenkman Publishing Co., Inc. Reprinted by permission.

when it was necessary to speak. Masters regarded existence of this hostility as one of his major problems. His professed ideal was that the women should all be circulating among the customers, busy all the time and cordial to each other.

The other three salesgirls were Mrs. Bonomo, thirty-five, a quiet amenable person, in the department for four years; Mrs. Selby, forty-eight, an employee for five years, who took things as they came without being much disturbed—though judging from her behavior and remarks she made, she disliked Mrs. White much more than she did Mrs. Brown. Mrs. Dawson, at twenty-two, was the youngest member of the department. She had dubbed Mrs. Brown and Mrs. White "saleshogs." She had worked there less than two years. She liked Mrs. Brown despite the epithet she had given her. Mrs. Dawson had two years of college, the most schooling in the department.

The saleswomen received from $1.75 to $2.25 per hour, depending on how long they had been in the department. Records of sales (dollar-volume) for the department were kept for the past year and varied from month to month. These records established the quota for the current year. Once this was equaled, the women started drawing commission pay at the rate of five percent. Commission was paid separately once a month.

Before describing the selling tactics of Mrs. Brown and Mrs. White, the ratebuster types, it is instructive to note the average daily sales established over a six month period[1] by the five saleswomen. Mrs. Brown with $227 average daily sales is over twice as much as Mrs. Dawson and Mrs. Selby, nearly twice as much as Mrs. Bonomo, and $74 more than the second ratebuster, Mrs. White. Masters assured me that Mrs. White had slowed up noticeably in her selling over the last two years, but in terms of dollar sales and her constant challenge to Mrs. Brown she should still be classified as a ratebuster, or a ratebuster in decline.

Saleswomen	Average Daily Dollar Sales
Mrs. Brown	227
Mrs. White	153
Mrs. Bonomo	119
Mrs. Selby	110
Mrs. Dawson	101

Lassiters had an employee credit union. Masters had access to the complete membership which was seventy-six. He gave me *rank only* of the five saleswomen based on the individual amounts deposited in the credit union. (He was so shocked when I requested the total savings of each of the saleswomen that I gladly accepted the partial data.) Mrs.

White stood third in the store, and Mrs. Brown was fourth. Mrs. Selby ranked forty-ninth and Mrs. Bonomo was sixty-sixth. Mrs. Dawson was not a member. These data alone do not tell much, but they do indicate that Mrs. White and Mrs. Brown were among the top investors, and that commission was important in their behavior.

RATEBUSTER TACTICS

Mrs. Brown apparently had more personal relations with customers than anyone in the boys' department. She learned from Masters when specially-priced merchandise was coming in. She telephoned customers she knew well and made arrangements to lay away items of given size and style that were scheduled to go on sale. When she had filled these private orders there was little of the merchandise left for the general public when the official sale day arrived. These sales by telephone constituted about fifteen percent of her total sales. Relatively new customers who bought heavily a time or two she filed in her retentive memory and took steps to acquaint them with her special services.

Among her repeat buyers was a working woman with four sons who treated their clothing roughly. Every six weeks this woman came in to buy nearly complete outfits for the boys. This included shirts, underwear, socks and blue jeans, which amounted to what the sales force called a "big ticket" of about $120.

Mrs. Brown had another woman customer who did not believe in having the younger boys of her five sons wear the older boys' outgrown clothing. She did not come in much oftener than once a year to buy complete outfits, usually just before Easter, which could run to two hundred dollars or more. Mrs. Brown acted as though she had an exclusive right[2] to these customers, and several others that she knew who had only two sons. When Mrs. Brown expected these people she would skip her lunch hour for fear she might miss them, or ask Masters to make the sale and ring it up on her cash drawer in case the woman came when she was out to lunch. He was glad to do this. When business was very good, whether she expected specific customers or not, she ignored the coffee breaks (ten minutes each morning and afternoon) and the lunch hour, leaving the selling floor only long enough to eat a sandwich in the dressing room.

She also had a practical monopoly on sales for boys on welfare. These boys had to be presented by an agent on the welfare organization the first time they did business with the store. Masters turned the welfare customer over to Mrs. Brown and forever afterwards[3] she made the sales. In some cases the welfare officer brought the boy, or boys, with their only clothes on their backs, to buy a complete outfit with extra socks, handkerchiefs and underwear. (Shoes were not sold in the boys' department.) In any case, Mrs. Brown took care of the sales then and afterwards.

Mrs. Brown's housekeeping area was just inside the entrance from the parking lot. She watched this approach closely. When she was not busy, or was talking to the other members of the department, she could break off instantly—even when she was telling a joke—and move toward the door. If she did not recognize the person she formed some judgment on him based on the affluence of his dress and his bearing. If the customer had a boy along, she judged whether he would be hard to fit. In her own words, she had a theory that "the kids who are tall and skinny or short and fat are hard to fit."[4] Thus she made quick appraisals of everybody who moved toward the department. If she approached a customer and learned that he was not as promising as he looked, she often brought the person to one of the other saleswomen and presented him with a statement of what he wanted as though— according to the women—she was giving them an assured sale. She made no revealing comment on the matter, but she seemed at the same time to be putting a restraint on her rivals.

Mrs. Brown's most galling behavior to the group was her practice of getting sale claims on as many prospective buyers as possible. She thus deprived the other saleswomen of a chance at the buyers. For instance, as she was serving one person, she would see another coming through the door—which she nearly always faced even when busiest. Quickly she would lay a number of items before the first person with the promise to be back in a moment, then hurry to capture the second customer. If the situation were right, she might get her claim on three or four buyers while two or more of the saleswomen were reduced to maintaining the show cases, and setting things in order so as not to appear idle. Mrs. Brown was able to do this because her own housekeeping and stocking area (assigned by Masters) lay between the entrance to the store and the other sections of the boys' department. Only Mrs. White would challenge her by intercepting a patron. The rivalry between them never came to a visible break. As noted earlier some of the other saleswomen resented Mrs. Brown's behavior and privately called her a "sales hog." She was not called that by Mrs. Bonomo and Mrs. Selby who thought—as they said—that Mrs. Brown in action was a "show in itself."

A standard device was used by Mrs. Brown, for ends not intended, with the understanding and collaboration of Masters. On very slack days she frequently left the store shortly after one or two o'clock to do "comparative shopping," that is, to compare the selling prices of items that Lassiters sold with the prices that other local stores charged for the same or similar items. Sometimes Mrs. Brown actually did this, but often she would attend a matinee, or go home to catch up with her housework, or just take a nap. (Her time card was punched out by

Masters at the official quitting time.) In any case, to the favorable implications of "comparative shopping," the further obvious inference was made that her absence from the store allowed the other salesgirls to make more commission. (Actually, business was so slow on some days, because of weather, etc., that it was not possible for any of the saleswomen to earn bonus pay.)

Mrs. Brown's conduct may suggest total indifference to the group. But possibly because she was a female in our society, she was not as nonconformist as the grim ratebusters in industry. Some of these could work for years without exchange of words with people, only a few feet away, that they knew hated them. To a degree Mrs. Brown was concerned about her group. Every week or so she would buy a two pound box of choice chocolates from a candy store near Lassiters and bring it in to share with the group. She could have bought a less expensive grade of candy at Lassiters. Sharing of the candy was almost certainly calculated (she ate little of it herself) but it appeared spontaneous and was received without hesitation. The saleswomen could not direct an unqualified hostility toward her.

She had another uncommon practice which made her stand apart from all of Lassiters' employees. Despite her determined assault on the commission system she did not use her right to a discount on items that she might buy for herself or members of her family. She took her fifteen-year-old son to a local independent department store to buy his clothes. She vigorously declared that "I don't want anything that [Lassiters] has." She was emphatic to the group—and implicitly condemned them—that she did not want to participate in the common practice of getting legal price reductions in addition to the regular employee discount by buying items at the end of a season. For example, an assortment of women's purses would be delivered to the selling floor. This was the "beginning of the season" for that batch of purses. The saleswomen with friends in the purse department would look at the display and select ones that appealed to them. These were laid away until the "end of the season" when they could be bought at the sale price which was further reduced by the regular discount. Mrs. Brown would have nothing to do with such items. She clearly did not want it said that she was taking advantage of her job.

A likely interpretation is that she sensed she was rejected and widely criticized for her methods and high bonus pay. She feared that some envious salesperson would report any borderline activity on her part to top management. Her own explanation implied that her esthetic taste could not be satisfied by the merchandise at Lassiters. In effect she downgraded the status of the store. As part of this complex she also implied that she was morally somewhat above the group. Also she may have been posing to hide her possible guilt feelings about her treatment of the group.

Although the aim of this paper is not to deal with morale problems, it was glaringly clear that Masters damaged group feeling by routing welfare customers to Mrs. Brown, and by ringing up some of his sales on her cash drawer. His tacit approval of her behavior discouraged the other saleswomen from attempting to control her.

NOTES

1. Masters gave me these figures based on an average of 44 hours a week and including the back-to-school buying months of August and September 1969.

2. Probably she was encouraged by the customers to think that way; certainly some customers waited for her to be free to serve them.

3. The other saleswomen knew about this and resented it. Grateful to Masters for allowing me to observe and talk with the saleswomen, I naturally did not ask him why there was no sharing of such sales among his force. I inquired, but there was no voiced conception of a "day's work" among the saleswomen. This general practice of informal rewarding is not uncommon in industry where it is sometimes done even with the knowledge and cooperation of individual officers of the union. (Lassiters was not unionized.)

4. Alteration of coats and trousers was done free by the store's tailor. But measuring and marking and the extra trying on were time-consuming. In the extreme cases this was futile. In any case Mrs. Brown avoided customers with "odd size" boys unless she knew them to be liberal buyers and worth her time.

Part Two: Control of Conflict and Tactics to Blunt Change

This second part of the section picks up a different general theme —the control of conflict and the tactics for "resistance to change" employed by the more powerful members of organizations and the barriers to change which are often embedded in the organization. Rory O'Day's paper on intimidation rituals provides a number of insights into this "resistance" process. Similarly, Robert Vaughn's discussion of the "Appellate Lemon" reveals how a system which is designed specifically to help lower level employees defend their rights in fact operates to make the organization almost invulnerable to individuals who feel their rights have been violated. Les Aspin concludes that even though there are laws designed to protect the jobs of employees engaged in union activity, those employees who do exercise their rights under the law to be reinstated find themselves mistreated by the organization when they return to work. The next two selections, Rex Hardesty's "Farah: The Union Struggle in the 70s" and "The Post Breaks a Union's Iron Grip," show convincingly that violence, the use of strikebreakers, and "no holds barred" conflict are still part of organizational life. Finally, the selection from Studs Terkel's Working about Steve Carmichael reveals that change is often blunted by wearing down a would-be change agent, albeit through nonspectacular devices.

Intimidation Rituals: Reactions to Reform

Rory O'Day

The reaction of authority in social systems to the reform initiatives of a subordinate is viewed as a series of intimidation rituals. These rituals divide into two major phases, each involving two distinct steps. The first phase, Indirect Intimidation, *includes the rituals of* nullification *and* isolation; *the second,* Direct Intimidation, *the rituals of* defamation *and* expulsion. *Why these rituals for protest-suppression in organizations are powerful tools in the hands of the middle manager is discussed. Attention is also given to various images projected by the organizational reformer and reasons for resistance to reform from within an organization.*

This paper characterizes the reactions of superiors in social systems to a reform-minded subordinate as a series of intimidation rituals. Each successive "ritual of control" represents an escalation in the efforts of authority to discourage an individual (and those who may support him or her) from continuing to seek reform.

MIDDLE MANAGEMENT'S MECHANISM OF CONTROL

The rituals of intimidation satisfy the two primary concerns of authorities confronted by a subordinate who appears not only able to articulate the grievances of a significant number of other system members but also capable of proposing solutions to them. Their first concern is, of course, to control the reformer so that he does not succeed in recruiting support. Their other concern is to exercise this control in ways that absolve them of any wrongdoing in the matter. The individual in question must be controlled in such a way that he neither continues to be an effective spokesman nor becomes a martyr. When superiors are confronted with a reform-minded subordinate, they want his silence or his absence, whichever is easier to achieve. The "authorities" must also preserve their carefully managed image of reasonableness, and would prefer that the reformer leave voluntarily rather than be removed officially.

For purposes of illustration, this presentation will describe intimidation rituals used by various organizations in the service of protest-suppression, for organizational authorities prefer to *intimidate* a reform-minded individual rather than commit organizational energy to the structural and personnel changes required to transform a "non-

Reproduced by special permission from *The Journal of Applied Behavioral Science*, "Intimidation Rituals: Reactions to Reform" by Rory O'Day, Vol. 10, No. 3, pp. 373–386. Copyright, NTL Institute, 1974.

conforming enclave" into a legitimate subunit.[1] It is further suggested that an organization undergoes major changes that incorporate and accommodate a group of dissidents only when the intimidation rituals do not succeed in silencing the individuals who constitute the "leading edges" of the reform movement.

In the discussion that follows, I will be concerned primarily with the reformer who emerges from the lower hierarchy in an organization and challenges the *middle hierarchy*. A reformer threatens middle management in three distinctly different ways. The first threat is a function of the validity of his accusations about the inadequacy of specific actions of middle-level members and his suggestions for correcting them. If the reformer is correct, those in the middle will fear that those at the top will punish them when they discover the truth. The second threat comes from the moral challenge presented by such a reformer, for his demand for action will reveal the strength or weakness of middle management's commitment to the organization. And thirdly, the reformer's challenge may indicate to people at the top that middle management is unable to maintain order in its own jurisdiction. To protect their interests, middle-level bureaucrats therefore feel their only defense against reform-minded subordinates is intimidation.[2]

The rituals of intimidation involve two phases: *Indirect Intimidation*, which has two steps, *nullification* and *isolation*; and *Direct Intimidation*, which also comprises two steps, *defamation* and *expulsion*.

PHASE I: INDIRECT INTIMIDATION

Step 1: Nullification

When a reformer first approaches his immediate superiors, they will assure him that his accusations or suggestions are invalid—the result of misunderstandings and misperceptions on his part. His superiors, in this phase, hope that the reformer will be so awed by authority that he will simply take their word that his initiative is based on error. If, however, the reformer insists, his superiors will often agree to conduct an "investigation." The results of such an investigation will convince the reformer that his accusations are groundless and that his suggestions for enhancing organizational effectiveness or revising organizational goals have been duly noted by the appropriate authorities.

Bureaucratic justification for this response usually rests on the argument that this method copes with the system's "crackpots" and "hot-heads," discouraging them from disturbing the smooth, routine functioning of the organization with their crazy ideas and their personal feuds. But middle management also uses these rituals of nullification to handle a potentially explosive (for them and others in the organization) situation quickly and quietly, in order to prevent unfavorable publicity, maintain the organization's state of pluralistic ignorance, and prevent the development of a sympathetic and concerned audience for the reformer's ideas. The explicit message is: "You don't know what you're talking about, but thank you anyway for telling us. We'll certainly look into the matter for you." Members of the middle hierarchy then proceed to cover up whatever embarrassing (for them) truth exists in the reformer's arguments.

The protest-absorption power of the ritual of nullification derives from an element inherent in bureaucracies: the always-attractive opportunity to avoid personal responsibility for one's actions. Thus, if people attempt reform at all, they generally do not proceed beyond the first ritual, which is a process designed to quash the reformer and allow his superiors to reaffirm the collective wisdom of the organization, while clearing their consciences of wrongdoing. Nullification even gets the would-be reformer off the hook—and he may remain grateful to the organization for this added convenience. This shedding of personal responsibility allows the reformer and the authorities alike to compromise in the belief that although it might not be a perfect organizational world, it is nevertheless a self-correcting one.

Repeated exposure to the nullification ritual (the "beating your head against the wall" phenomenon) is expected to convince any sane organizational member that a reformist voice or presence is unwelcome. He is expected to take the hint and stop pestering his superiors with his misguided opinions. Gestures of generosity on the part of the middle hierarchy are not unusual if he decides to leave the organization—and such concern is usually expressed by offering to help the individual find employment opportunities elsewhere.

Step 2: Isolation

If the reformer persists in his efforts, middle management will separate him from his peers, subordinates, and superiors, thereby softening his impact on the organization and making it extremely difficult for him to mobilize any support for his position.

Middle managers argue that these procedures represent the exercise of their rights of office in the service of protecting the organization. But these attempts to isolate the reformer can also be seen as a show of force, as a way of reassuring their own superiors (if they are paying attention), their subordinates, and perhaps themselves that they can maintain order in their own jurisdiction.

Attempts at isolating the reformer include closing his communication links, restricting his freedom of movement, and reducing his allocation of organization resources. If these do not neutralize the reformer, he will be transferred to a less visible position in the organization. In these rituals, the bureaucratic message is: "If you insist on talking about things which you do not understand, then we will have to prevent you from bothering other people with your nonsense."

Systematic unresponsiveness to a reformer's criticism and suggestions is a particularly interesting form of isolation. This lack of response is meant to convince the reformer of the invalidity of his position; but if he presses his right to be heard, it may be used to create a feeling of such impotence that the reformer overreacts in order to elicit a response from his superiors. This overreaction may then be used to demonstrate the reformer's psychological imperfections.

When subjected to organizational isolation, most people come to see the error of their ways or the handwriting on the wall. When an individual learns that there is still time to mend his ways, he usually steps back in line and becomes a silent participant in the organization. When he realizes his career in the organization is at a standstill, he may decide to leave as gracefully as possible while he can still leave under his own steam. Middle managers closest to him then often offer him assistance in finding a new job, with the assurance that "*we* only want what is best for *you*."

Most forms of isolation are designed to persuade the reformer of the futility of trying to initiate change until such time as he is instructed by his superiors to concern himself with change. The reformer practically guarantees his defeat if he reacts to systematic organizational unresponsiveness by confronting his superiors in ways that violate policy or law. The temptation to confront administrative unresponsiveness in dramatic and often self-defeating ways stems in large part from the intense frustration induced by the reformer's belief that systematic unresponsiveness violates his basic rights of freedom of expression and carries with it the implication that he is personally ineffectual (Turner, 1973). Administrative unresponsiveness to what the reformer believes are crucial issues both for himself and for the organization may be sufficiently frustrating to compel him to act, however rashly, in order to clarify the situation. From the administration's point of view, this can be seen as "flushing the rebels out into the open," "giving them enough rope to hang themselves," or, more formally, deviance-heresy conversion (Harshbarger, 1973).

PHASE II: DIRECT INTIMIDATION

Step 3: Defamation
Should the reformer refuse to remain silent, and instead mobilizes support for his position, middle management will begin to impugn his character and his motives. "When legitimate techniques fail—the middle hierarchy might resort to illegitimate or non-legitimate ones" (Leeds, 1964, p. 126). Middle managers will often distort events or even fabricate instances of misconduct in order to intimidate not only the reformer but also those who would listen to or believe him.

Defamation attempts to cut the reformer off from a potentially sympathetic following by attributing his attempts at reform to questionable motives, underlying psychopathology, or gross incompetence. This three-pronged attack is meant to blackmail the reformer into submission and to transform a sympathetic following into a mistrustful crowd of onlookers or an angry mob that feels resentful at having been deceived by the reformer.

From the vantage point of the reformer, the Kafkaesque or Alice-in-Wonderland quality of the rituals of intimidation becomes particularly evident at this time. The reformer finds himself faced with charges which only he and his accusers know are either false or irrelevant in relation to the value of his reform initiatives. The reformer is in a double bind. His superiors will use their offices and positions of trust and responsibility to create the impression in the minds of others in the organization that their accusations of incompetence, self-interest, or psychopathology are true. If the reformer continues in the face of these accusations, he risks being viewed as power-hungry or irrational. If he allows himself to be intimidated by the threat of lies, he allows his superiors to win by default.

One tactic of the superior is to accuse the reformer of acting out his Oedipal conflicts. Such a personalization of a subordinate's reform efforts (especially a younger subordinate) permits his superior to present himself as a harassed "father" faced with a troubled "son," and blocks any examination of his conduct that might reveal provocation on his part. In this way the bureaucrat hopes to persuade others in the organization to respond to the reformer as a sick person in need of therapy or as a child in need of nurturing—a stance that allows him to take on the role of "good father" in relation to other subordinates and to the reformer, if and when the latter capitulates and admits his need for help and guidance.

Rituals of defamation are undertaken by superiors in order to focus attention away from themselves and onto the reformer. The superiors hope that by casting enough doubt on the motives, intentions, and personality of the reformer, enough people in the organization will think that "where there is smoke, there must be fire." The message of this ritual is: "Don't listen to him (his message) because you can't trust a person like him."

Like the rituals of nullification and isolation, the ritual of defamation is both an end in itself and a preliminary to the final ritual of expulsion. The superiors hope by threatening to destroy the reformer's reputation and his character, he will retreat into silence and passivity or leave the organization for greener pastures; if, however, the reformer continues his efforts, his superiors have laid the groundwork for his expulsion.

If the ritual of defamation is undertaken, its target is usually indeed a reformer and not simply a nonconformist or a deviant. His superiors would not need to engage in public tactics of intimidation if there were no substance to his challenge. It is precisely the validity of his reform initiatives that leads his superiors to attempt to destroy his credibility. If this destruction of the reformer's credibility with his peers, subordinates, and top management is effectively conducted, others in the organization will desert his cause and he can be dismissed easily as an undesirable member of the intact organizational team.

Step 4: Expulsion

When neither nullification, isolation, nor defamation can silence the reformer or force his "voluntary withdrawal" from the organization, the middle hierarchy seeks an official decision for his dismissal.

If successful, at least three aims may be achieved thereby. Obviously, by expelling the reformer, his superiors will cut him off from any actual or potential following and weaken any opposition to their authority. An official dismissal also serves as a warning to other budding reformers that middle management has the necessary power and authority to expel troublemakers. Finally, the act of expulsion—a verdict of unfitness—supports the contention that the reformer is an immoral or irrational person.

Of course, the middle hierarchy would prefer the reformer to withdraw voluntarily. Managers want to avoid the public and formal proceedings that often accompany an official request for dismissal of an employee, for the accuser (superior) can often then be scrutinized as carefully as the accused, if the accused person wishes to avail himself of the opportunity. The expulsion ritual involves the formal submission of evidence, the keeping of records, the establishment of independent investigative bodies, and the right of cross-examination, which all function to threaten the image of managers as reasonable, honest, and hardworking servants of the organization. Formal dismissal proceedings are also avoided by middle management because in some fundamental sense they imply that the organization has failed and that they, in particular, have shown themselves unable to maintain order.

THE RITUAL CYCLE ABSORBS AND DESTROYS

Indirect Intimidation attempts to absorb the accusations and suggestions of the reformer, first by depriving him of effectiveness or validity, then by treating him as if he were an "invisible person." The object here is to define the reformer as "harmless." It also attempts to absorb protest by psychologically and physically exhausting the reformer so that he comes to doubt his own experience of reality, his abilities to accomplish the task he sets for himself, and its significance. The authorities hope that the reformer will come to believe the task he has set for himself is humanly impossible and that his fatigue and confusion are the result of his inability to accept human nature for what it is. Short of this, they hope that the reformer will come to feel so inadequate that he will be grateful for continued employment by the organization, in any capacity. ("You're welcome to stay aboard as long as you don't rock the boat.")

Direct Intimidation attempts to destroy protest through destruction of the *character* of the reformer (defamation) or, if necessary, of his *position* in the organization (expulsion). Direct Intimidation represents middle management's active attempt to destroy the reformer as a source of legitimate grievances and suggestions and to terrorize, if necessary, other organizational members. Successful rituals of defamation create a "bad" person, enabling the "good" organization to close ranks once again and benefit from the curative properties of solidarity when he is cast out of the system. In this sense, the ritual destruction of the person (Garfinkel, 1956) necessarily precedes the destruction of his place in the organization.

In sum, Figure 1 portrays the specific cycles of intimidation rituals. Cycle 1 is most preferred by all organizations, while Cycle 4 is the least preferred. Cycle 2 is preferred to Cycle 3.

FIGURE 1.

Cycles of Intimidation Rituals

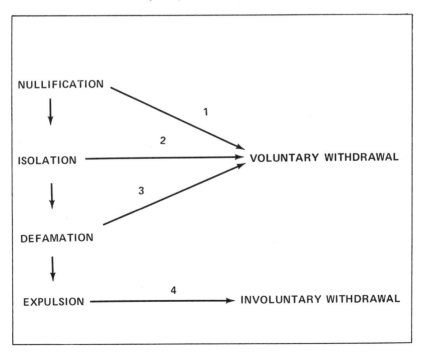

THE REFORMER IMAGE

Throughout this discussion, the individual subjected to the rituals of intimidation has been referred to as the *reformer*, a generic term for any organizational member who resorts to voice rather than to avoidance when faced with what *he* regards as a situation of organizational deterioration or imperfection. Voice is defined as

> . . . any attempt at all to change, rather than escape from, an objectionable state of affairs, whether through individual or collective petition to the management directly in charge, through appeal to a higher authority with the intention of forcing a change in management, or through various types of actions and protests, including those that are meant to mobilize public opinion (Hirschman, 1970, p. 30).

Therefore, in the sense in which it is being used here, "reformer" includes the various meanings contained in such labels as "internal muckraker" or "pure whistle-blower" (Peters & Branch, 1972), "innovator in innovation-resisting organizations" (Shepard, 1969), "crusader for corporate responsibility" (Heilbroner, 1972), "nonconforming individual" (Etzioni, 1961; Leeds, 1964), and "heretic" (Harshbarger, 1973); but it is not intended to include the various meanings inherent in the term "organizational change agent."[3] Thus *"reformer"* refers to any member who acts, in any way and for any reason, to alter the structure and functioning of the organization, when he has *not* been formally delegated authority to institute change.

Why Intimidation Works

From this definition we can see that it is the organization which has the power to define the "reformer" as such, and attaches the stigma to many a well-meaning individual who does not see himself in a protest role. It is often the case that a potential reformer initially thinks of himself or herself only as a hard-working and loyal member of the organization who is simply trying to make things "better" and wishes to be "understood" by busy but well-meaning superiors. However, by the time authorities begin the rituals of defamation, the most naive individual usually realizes that, at least in the eyes of his superiors, he poses a threat to the established order (Herbert, 1972).

The inside reformer is vulnerable to all the intimidation rituals that his particular organization has at its disposal. The reformer outside an organization is usually vulnerable only to the rituals of nullification, isolation (in the form of systematic unresponsiveness), and defamation, unless the organization he is challenging is able to pressure the parent organization into doing the intimidating for it (McCarry, 1972).

Authorities in formal organizations are rarely directly challenged by subordinates. As in the Hans Christian Andersen tale, most individuals do not presume to stand in public judgment of their organizational superiors. Belief in the wisdom and power of the people at the top serves to keep most individuals silent about their grievances concerning the status quo and their ideas (if they have any) for enhancing organizational effectiveness or revising organizational goals. Subordinates do not generally demand, as part of their organizational contractual arrangements, the power to hold their superiors accountable for actions in direct and continuing ways. So intimidation rituals are held to be a last resort—reserved for organizational members who resist, for whatever reason, the usual mechanisms of social control (Millham, Bullock, & Cherrett, 1972).

In their discussion of the obstacles to whistle-blowing, Peters and Branch (1972) include the "loyal-member-of-the-team" trap, the feeling that "going public" is unseemly and embarrassing, and the fear of current and future job vulnerability. Thompson (1968) and Peters and Branch (1972) also refer to the subconscious accommodative device of the "effectiveness trap," an organizational argument that permits its members to avoid conflict on an immediate issue in order to ensure "effectiveness" on some more important issue, at some future time. The curator mentality and emotional detachment generated by the bureaucratic role; the tendency to resort to wishful thinking that organizational deterioration and the consequences of bad policy must soon stop simply because they cannot go on; and the fear that one disagrees with a particular exercise of power only because one is too weak to handle it further contribute to inaction on the part of most "loyal" organizational members (Thompson, 1968).

Reformer as Bad Guy

In point of fact, the protest-absorbing and protest-destroying power of intimidation rituals derives, in large measure, from their infrequent use by organizations. Conversely, if more members were willing to turn their various dissatisfactions into reformist activities, intimidation rituals would lose much of their power.

To understand the effectiveness of organizational intimidation one must examine the reasons why peers and subordinates usually fail to support the reformer, withdraw support, or even actively resist his efforts. Their passive or active resistance may indicate an increased desire or struggle for an organization's scarce resources (material benefits or status, power or prestige—or even dependency). It may also indicate that they perceive themselves as cast in an unfavorable light by the reformer's enthusiasm and heightened activities in pursuing present or changed organizational goals. Members of the organization may secretly believe that the reformer's efforts will be successful, and fear its implication for their position in the organization. If the reformer is successful in convincing top management to investigate the organizational "engine," many may fear that close scrutiny of the performance of the parts will find them wanting. On the other hand, on the outside chance that the reformer manages to seize the reins of power, peers and subordinates may fear that if they do not match his zeal in pursuing new as well as old organizational goals he will turn them out of their present positions.

It frequently seems that practically everyone except the reformer has a personal stake in preserving the complicated fantasy of the organization, even though conditions in the organization are in fact unsatisfying to all but a few elite members. Bion (1959) has described a similar situation in therapy groups where members engage in a variety of neurotic attempts to resist and discourage changing the structure and functioning of a group that is obviously less than fully satisfying. It seems likely, then, that subordinates in an organization actively or passively resist a peer's reform initiatives because the pain of the status quo is less intense than their fear of the unknown.

In general, the reformer finds himself initially with little or no support because there is an implicit acceptance of the bureaucratic order in our society (Wilcox, 1968) and because most people find it difficult and improper to question the actions of authority (Milgram, 1965; Peters & Branch, 1972). There is also the well-ingrained reflex of flight in the face of crisis and change, which has characterized North American society since its colonial days (Hartz, 1955; Hirschman, 1970; Slater, 1970).

Most organizational members do not support the reformer at all, or they desert him at the first opportunity because they believe he will lose in his struggle with institutional authority—and they want to be on the winning side. Moreover, as Walzer (1969) has pointed out, most people accept nondemocratic organizational conditions on the basis of the argument of tacit consent and withhold or withdraw support from the reformer, saying that he is free to go someplace else if he does not like it where he is.

Peers and subordinates may also resist a reformer because they suspect that he is committing the unforgivable sin of pride (Slater, 1963). They may come to believe that in taking it upon himself to judge the organization and its leaders he is acting in a self-righteous manner (Peters & Branch, 1972). Those who wish to desert the reformer on this ground often use as supporting data the reformer's persistent efforts in the face of the rituals of defamation.

Since the reformer's departure is usually associated with an immediate reduction or elimination of overt conflict, which in turn relieves tension in the organization, members can wrap themselves in the organizational blanket and tell themselves that he was the source of the problem all along. When the emotional ruckus dies down, most members therefore experience a heightened commitment to the organization and return to their jobs with a renewed vigor. For those organizational members who continue to harbor some doubt about the reformer's guilt, the fear of retaliation against "sympathizers" usually dampens their enthusiasm for the reformer's cause and suppresses all but ritualistic expressions of concern for his plight.

SEIZE THE DAY

It is not possible here to do more than raise the issue of whether one should attempt to change organizations from within or whether one should create alternative organizations. Large formal organizations are going to be with us for a long time to come (Heilbroner, 1972), and their members are going to have to devise ways to make them more democratic, because there really is no place to run to anymore.

The serious reformer should be prepared to take advantage of organizational crises. He must learn how to recognize, expose, and make concrete those administratively designed arrangements that do not satisfactorily resolve critical problems. For it is in a time of crisis that an organization is open to solutions to the basic problem of survival. Organizational members will be eager to adopt new structures that promise to relieve the uncertainty and anxiety generated by a crisis (Shepard, 1969). If the organization has become weak internally, if it contains corruption and indolence at various levels, if the organization is beset by energy-consuming external pressures, and if the organizational elite lack the resources or the will to initiate changes essential for organizational survival, then the organization might well be ready for successful reform from within (Leeds, 1964). Such an organization might not be capable of successfully administering the intimidation rituals.

Internal organizational reform is a difficult process. The cause of reform as well as constructive revolution cannot be served by deluding ourselves as to the ease of restructuring human society (Heilbroner, 1972; Schon, 1973). The reformer's life is not an easy one. But neither need he feel doomed from the start by the inevitability of the success of intimidation rituals mobilized against him.

NOTES

1. "Nonconforming enclave" refers to the existence of a number of organizational members who, through collective effort, ". . . could potentially divert organization resources from their current commitments, undermine organizational effectiveness, or form a front capable of capturing control of the organization" (Leeds, 1964, p. 155).

2. In a related context, Etzioni (1961, p. 241) asserts, "Once deviant charisma has manifested itself, despite . . . elaborate preventive mechanisms, counter-processes are set into motion. These are of two kinds: those which attempt to eliminate the deviant charisma; and those which seek to limit its effect."

3. It is possible, however, that an organizational change agent might find himself undergoing the rituals of intimidation if he insists that effective action be taken on his proposals for change, particularly if such action would threaten certain organizational power arrangements.

REFERENCES

Bion, W. R. *Experiences in Groups*. New York: Basic Books, 1959.

Etzioni, A. *A Comparative Analysis of Complex Organizations*. New York: The Free Press, 1961.

Garfinkel, H. "Conditions of Successful Degradation Ceremonies," *American Journal of Sociology*, 1956, *61*, 420–424.

Harshbarger, D. "The Individual and the Social Order: Notes on the Management of Heresy and Deviance in Complex Organizations," *Human Relations*, 1973, *26*, 251–269.

Hartz, L., *The Liberal Tradition in America*. New York: Harcourt, Brace and World, 1955.

Heilbroner, R. L. *In the Name of Profit*. New York: Doubleday, 1972.

Herbert, A. *Soldier*. New York: Holt, Rinehart and Winston, 1972.

Hirschman, A. O. *Exit, Voice, and Loyalty*. Cambridge, Mass.: Harvard University Press, 1970.

Leeds, R. "The Absorption of Protest: a Working Paper," in W. W. Cooper, H. J. Leavitt, and M. W. Shelly, II (Eds.), *New Perspectives in Organization Research*. New York: Wiley, 1964.

McCarry, C. *Citizen Nader*. New York: Saturday Review Press, 1972.

Millham, S., Bullock, R., and Cherrett, P. "Social Control in Organizations," *The British Journal of Sociology*, 1972, *23*, 406–421.

Peters, C., and Branch, T. *Blowing the Whistle: Dissent in the Public Interest*. New York: Praeger, 1972.

Schon, D.S. *Beyond the Stable State*. New York: Norton, 1973.

Shepard, H. A. "Innovation-resisting and Innovation-producing Organizations, in W. G. Bennis, K. D. Benne, and R. Chin (Eds.), *The Planning of Change*, Rev. ed. New York: Holt, Rinehart and Winston, 1969. Pp.519–525.

Slater, P.E. "On Social Regression," *American Sociological Review*, 1963, *29*, 339–364.

Slater, P. E. *The Pursuit of Loneliness*. Boston: Beacon Press, 1970.

Thompson, J. C. "How Could Vietnam Happen? An Autopsy," *Atlantic Monthly*, April 1968, *221* (4), 47–53.

Turner, R. H. "Unresponsiveness as a Social Sanction," *Sociometry*, 1973, *36*, 1–19.

Walzer, M. "Corporate Responsibility and Civil Disobedience," *Dissent*, Sept.-Oct., 1969, pp. 395–406.

Wilcox, H. G. "The Cultural Trait of Hierarchy in Middle Class Children," *Public Administration Review*, 1968, *28*, 222–235.

The Appellate Lemon
Robert Vaughn

In exploring the ills of the appellate system, it is helpful to look, at the same time, at what is wrong with the Commission's handling of EEO discrimination complaints.

An employee must first have his complaint considered by an EEO counselor within his agency, who may attempt an "informal resolution" of the problem prior to the filing of a formal complaint. If the complainant remains dissatisfied with the informal resolution (if any), he may file a written complaint with an EEO officer of his agency.

The agency's director of EEO must then assign, for the "prompt" investigation of the complaint, a person who "shall occupy a position in the agency which is not, directly or indirectly, under the jurisdiction of the head of that part of the agency in which the complaint arose." After the complainant has reviewed an investigative file compiled by the agency, the agency again provides an opportunity for adjustment of the complaint on an informal basis.

If a satisfactory adjustment is not arrived at, the complainant may appeal to the Civil Service Commission, who will appoint a hearing examiner who must be an employee of another agency (usually a Commission EEO appeals examiner). The hearing is recorded and transcribed verbatim. The appeals examiner must then transmit (1) the complaint file (including the record of the hearing); (2) the appeals examiner's analysis of the matter which gave rise to the complaint and the general environment out of which the complaint arose; and (3) the recommended decision of the appeals examiner on the merits of the complaint, including recommended remedial action, where appropriate, to the head of the agency or his designee, who then makes the decision of the agency. . . .

Internally the Commission follows the pattern of the rest of the government in its handling of discrimination complaints and contacts with EEO counselors. One formal complaint was filed within the Commission in 1970 and three were filed in 1971. Contacts with counselors, however, greatly decreased, from seventy-two in 1970 to twenty-one (nineteen made by Commission employees, two by job applicants) in 1971. During the second half of 1970 and all of 1971, fifty-two employees contacted a counselor within the Commission. Twenty-one of the fifty-two contacts failed to result in an informal resolution of the employees' problems, but only the four formal complaints mentioned above were filed with the Commission. Therefore, for that period of a year and a half, seventeen employees contacted a Commission counselor but failed to receive an informal resolution and also failed to file a formal complaint.

Of the four formal complaints filed against the Commission for 1970-71, one complaint was closed because it was not filed in a timely manner by the employee. Mr. Clinton Smith, the Commission's internal director of EEO, claims that the complaint was filed six months after the incident at issue. . . .[1]

Information given by Irving Kator on October 20, 1971, to the Senate Subcommittee on Labor offers several other examples of what the Commission calls "corrective action." (Table 1.) None of the above "recommendations" of "corrective action" is inherently favorable to the complainant, and some are clearly less than what the complainant asked for.

Table 1 Agency "Corrective Actions"

Agency to reconsider two-day suspension	1 case
Supervisory training for supervisors	2 cases
Alleged discriminatory officials to take special training	1 case
Give career counseling to complainant	1 case
Renew offer to complainant of temporary 120-day promotion	1 case

In 1970, only 1,025 (8 percent) of 12,063 agency employees who were counseled filed formal complaints with the Commission. In the first nine months of 1971, counselors were contacted 10,628 times but only 989 formal complaints were filed. The Commission believes these figures demonstrate the success of the counseling program, because the number of formal complaints has dropped. A total of 3,615 (34 percent) employment problems were "informally resolved" at the counseling stage.

What casts doubt on the efficacy of the program is that 6,024 (57 percent) were not reported to have received either an "informal resolution" of their problem or to have filed a formal complaint. What happened to these 6,024 employees (a small number of whom may have been job applicants)?

Irving Kator answered:

The counseling system was not intended to guarantee that every employee who comes in would have corrective action taken. [Mr.

Kator is fond of referring to "informal resolution" as "corrective action," even though they are not strictly the same.] Counselors let people come to understand what their problems are, that they did not get promoted because they did not meet certain specified qualifications, and so forth. We don't know whether the man is satisfied or not. If he is not, he can file a complaint. I'm not surprised by the 57 percent who go away without filing a complaint.

Yet his answer still does not reveal what happened to the 57 percent. That they may have been told why they were not promoted—an explanation actually considered under Commission practice to be an "informal resolution"—ignores the possibility that counselors may turn away employees by misinforming or discouraging them. The lack of standards by which to judge "informal resolution" makes the unexplained fate of six thousand employee contacts even more significant. An "informal resolution" may be merely a counselor saying he did not think the employee had a valid grievance. It was unclear from the Commission's records how many "informal resolutions" were satisfactory to the employees involved.

When Kator was asked to distinguish between "informal resolutions" in which something less than "corrective action" was offered to the aggrieved employee and "informal resolutions" in which "corrective action" was taken, he wrote:

Inasmuch as EEO counseling is programmed to be informal, EEO counselors are not required to maintain any records other than certain basic ones needed to enable agencies to fulfill the reporting requirements outlined in Appendix C to Chapter 713 of the Federal Personnel Manual. Counselors do not report on their counseling of any individual unless the counsellee files a formal complaint of discrimination. For this reason, it is not known in how many counseling contacts there was an informal resolution without "corrective action," nor what types of "corrective action" were taken at the counseling stage. . . . Figures are not available on disciplinary action arising from a counseling session and there is no breakdown of corrective actions taken as a result of counseling.

In other words, what, if anything, was actually done for the 3,615 employees counseled in the first nine months of 1971 whom the agencies' counselors and the Commission allege received an "informal resolution" is as much a mystery to the Commission (and therefore to Congress and the public) as what eventually happened to the mysterious 6,024 who did not even receive the bureaucratic notation of an "informal resolution."[2]

Perhaps even if a complainant received no personal relief, he and others might benefit from the disciplining of supervisors guilty of discriminatory conduct. The deterrent effect might go far to assure adequate "affirmative action." In 1970 disciplinary action was taken in fifteen cases as follows:

- Five supervisors issued letter of warning.
- Five supervisors orally admonished.
- Letters of reprimand issued to three supervisors in one case.
- One discriminatory supervisor suspended.
- One foreman barred from supervisory duties.
- One supervisor reprimanded and reassigned to nonsupervisory work.
- One supervisor facing disciplinary action retired.

During the first half of 1971, disciplinary action was taken in fourteen cases as follows:

- Two supervisors orally reprimanded.
- Two supervisors in one case issued letters of warning.
- One supervisor cautioned regarding informal disciplining of employees.
- Two activity officials in one case orally admonished.
- One activity official admonished.
- Three discriminatory officials issued letters of reprimand.
- One military chief of staff relieved of position, given supervisory training.
- Two supervisors received "appropriate disciplinary action" [in two cases not further described].

It is hard to see how most of these penalties can be considered "disciplinary action," since no apparent financial, promotional, or positional losses seem to have been suffered by the "disciplined" supervisors.

Commission officials offer several explanations for the low percentage of supervisors disciplined. First, they claim that the source and/ or cause of discrimination is often "systemic"—institutional or historical—and discriminatory situations of this complexity and ambiguity cannot ordinarily be attributed to individual actions.

The Commission neither recommends nor suggests disciplinary action if the supervisor is not found to be directly responsible for discrimination, and this narrow view is the main reason for so small a percentage of disciplinary actions. But if direct accountability entails knowledge and intent, or knowledge and gross negligence, accountability through acquiescence entails knowledge and negligence through inaction, because of a duty to know and a failure to discover and eradicate practices over which one has power and authority.

Second, Commission officials are concerned that, if disciplinary action becomes common, supervisors may become too passive in their dealings with minority-group or female employees. As Irving Kator says, "If managers start 'going tiptoe'—that might be a problem."[3] This rests on the unconvincing and unsupported assumption that sensitivity to and accountability for EEO complaints result in passive management; on the contrary, *present* management is *passive* regarding an ineffective complaint processing system.

Third, Hampton, Rosen, and Kator were distressed about the possibility that the careers of managers or supervisors would be permanently ruined if a permanent record of the finding were maintained in their Official Personnel Folder. Similar solicitude has not been shown for careers ruined because of the injustices of the Commission's complaint system.

Fourth, if disciplinary actions become more prevalent, Commission officials fear a loss of agency cooperation and the concealment of evidence. Such fears hardly take into account the difficulties in hiding information from the Commission if it were willing to use its power.

Furthermore, the brand of "cooperation" the Commission is getting presently from the agencies is no bargain—as the long delays in complaint processing, to point to just one example, show.

Irving Kator said in a speech at an EEO conference in November 1970:

> It is not necessary to find a culprit in order to find discrimination. There will be few cases in which direct evidence of discrimination will be shown; most discrimination will be found by circumstantial evidence. Employment patterns are of significance in determining if there is discrimination and oftentimes there is no one person who can properly be charged with discrimination . . . but where a culprit is found, disciplinary action should follow. If it does not, the complaint system loses its credibility.

When Mr. Kator and his supervisors discuss disciplinary action or accountability for "system" discrimination, they assume that it is only reasonable or helpful to discipline a supervisor who is *directly responsible* or directly accountable for the discrimination. They fail to consider other forms of accountability, such as the possibilities of disciplining supervisors who are accountable *through acquiescence* to discriminatory practices, or supervisors or officials who can be held accountable *by virtue of their positions* for discriminatory practices, because of the affirmative duties inherent in their position of authority.

Better reporting and closer study of counseling activities are essential, for they will almost surely show that employees are being discouraged from filing complaints. James A. Scott, assistant director of the EEO office, said at an EEO conference in November 1970:

> Even with a present governmentwide cadre of over seven thousand EEO counselors, there are still some weak spots in this phase of the program. Some employees do not know that this EEO counseling service is available to them. Many counselors, particularly those who are infrequently called upon to perform in their EEO

roles, receive no follow-up or refresher training. EEO counselors often have no private place in which to interview aggrieved employees. Some ineffective counselors have been allowed to remain in their posts.

On February 23, 1971, the National Alliance of Postal and Federal Employees sent out a questionnaire to all EEO counselors in the Post Office and to some counselors in other agencies as well. Dr. Charles Thomas, head of EEO in the Post Office, directed EEO counselors not to respond to the questionnaire, yet many did. Among their comments were the following:

The EEO program is an appeasement action allowing itself to be a house organ.

A beautiful paper program.

Full-time counselors with true investigative authority and proper training are needed.

EEO is a token symbol, window dressing, and the EEO counselor a "flak-catcher" for management.

I face personnel roadblocks—my supervisor is the personnel office.

I am not doing a good job. I have since December 1970 been subjected to discrimination, harassment, and denied work in my area.

No line supervisors should be counselors. The hands of counselors are tied by "Uncle Toms." "Doc" Thomas has ordered all counselors not to make replies [to the Alliance's questionnaire]. No cooperation from management—if you call for help, they reply that you are too militant.

I have been refused permission to view personnel records by chief personnel officer.

I have received a directive that we are not to give a personal statement [to the Alliance questionnaire]. I am sometimes harassed.

Counselors may be concerned with future promotional opportunities.

I'm not given enough space and facilities; not given a proper conference room.

The counselor is on his own for information.

DESIGN DEFECTS

The failings of the appeal program should come as no surprise to the Commission. Numerous internal studies of the Board of Appeals and

Review and of the appeals process have been conducted and have pointed out these failings.[4]

Historically, appeals and review have been considered a part of the personnel administration function of the Commission. No attempt was made to review an action for more than procedural compliance until 1930, when the Commission created a Board of Appeals and Review. The BAR, however, was not seen as an independent adjudicatory body, but as an extension of the personnel office. The decisions of the Commission were considered advisory and subject to overrule by the agency director until the Veterans' Preference Act of 1944 was amended in 1948.

The perspective of the Commission's appeals system as part of its client-oriented personnel functions persists. Before a conference of appeals examiners in June 1969, Nicholas Oganavic, then executive director, said, "The appeals program is not an extension of an arm of Congress; nor is it a regulatory agency. The Commission is the central personnel agency of the President of the United States. . . . The Commission's appeals examiners are not hearing officers or hearing examiners, they are appeals examiners."[5]

Most of the activities of the Commission concern the provision of services to the management of federal agencies—executive manpower, training, testing, investigations, evaluations (inspections). The pervasiveness of this service approach seems, unfortunately, to extend to the appeals program.[6] The service approach focusing upon agency participation has extended to the EEO program.[7]

The training and career patterns of hearings examiners help to ensure that they will carry to their jobs a management perspective. Most examiners have spent time as investigators of employee suitability for the Bureau of Personnel Investigations, a job that stresses the view of agency as client.[8] In the case of examiners who hear discrimination complaints, a proper ethnic balance has not been achieved. Of eleven EEO examiners allotted to regional offices, eight do not belong to a minority group; one examiner is an Oriental; none is female. Examiners seem closely identified with management. In one agency installation with three counselors, one was dating someone in top management and a second was the director's secretary's brother. An obvious reason for employee suspicion is that an agency's EEO counselors are almost always appointed by management[9] and are often of so high a grade that employees feel uncomfortable about approaching them.[10]

All examiners are under the supervision and control of regional directors, and the problem of going against the bias of one's superior comes into question. In the regional offices of the Commission, appeals examiners are responsible to the regional director. The regional director is an operating official whose primary commitment is to the smooth functioning of all the Commission's programs, rather than solely to the appeals program. Concern for the Commission's good relationship with an agency and for the regional director's ability to cope with agency pressure may affect his outlook. Thus, appeals are influenced by the regional director, and in some areas they are even decided by him.

The participation of the regional director in the adjudication of cases varies. In the Philadelphia region, the regional director does not make an initial decision, but the appeals office does not have authority to issue a decision with which the regional director disagrees. In the Dallas region the regional director only reviews decisions of the appeals office. In the Boston region, however, the regional director not only reviews decisions but he also makes the decision itself when the examiner is "on the fence." This process means that some questions will be decided by persons who have had no contact with the presentation of evidence, who have had no opportunity to judge the demeanor of the witnesses, who may not have even examined the case materials. Indeed, policy positions that affect an appeal may already have been decided before a case reaches a Commission hearing or the Board of Appeals and Review. Both the hearing and the process are then pro forma. . . .

BEARING THE BURDEN

Once the appellant or complainant reaches the hearing arena, he has just begun to fight, and his weapons, compared with those of the agency, are slight. His lack of discovery or subpoena powers can hamper his ability to gather information essential to his case. In an EEO complaint the "leads" an investigator, an employee of the accused agency, fails to perceive, fails to follow up, or follows up inadequately may make the difference between success and failure for the appellant.

So long as the full burden of proof is placed upon the appellant and the assurance of impartial, aggressive investigators or examiners is lacking, adequate discovery procedures are not merely desirable, but essential.

Commission officials cite a regulation to show that no appellant or complainant has been harmed by the lack of subpoena power:

> The agency shall make its employees available as witnesses at a hearing on a complaint when requested to do so by the appeals examiner and *it is administratively practicable to comply with the request.* When it is not administratively practicable to comply with the request for a witness, the agency shall provide an explanation to the appeals examiner. If the explanation is inadequate, the appeals examiner shall so advise the agency and request it to make the employee available as a witness at the hearing. If the explanation is adequate, the appeals examiner shall . . . make arrangements to secure testimony through a written interrogatory. [emphasis added]

The inadequacies are obvious: no cross-examination of a hostile witness; no opportunity to pursue helpful, unclear, or surprising testimony; the possibility of a witness's artful preparation of answers; and the loss of the hearing examiner's chance to see a witness's attitude and demeanor. Placing the burden of proof on the appellant or complainant is particularly onerous, given the agency's full access to information. Further, the wide use of discretion allows an agency to structure its adverse action in such a way that it may obscure the real issues.

In determining whether an agency has properly disciplined an employee, there is no question more basic than whether or not the agency has proved its case. Yet the agency must sustain no precise burden of proof. Appeals staff members commented: "There is no more definite guide than each individual examiner's understanding." "My test is that they [the agencies] must convince me." "The action has to be reasonable." "There is no definition because there are no strict rules of evidence, but the appeals examiners use their best judgment."

In discrimination complaints, common sense is more just in its understanding of discrimination than is the Commission. Most people would think that if a supervisor treated Chicanos differently from the way in which he treated Caucasians, he should be considered discriminatory unless he could give sufficient reason. If the reason given were something nebulous like "lack of initiative," most people would still think the supervisor discriminatory unless he were able to point to actual situations in which Chicanos clearly showed "lack of initiative," compared to other employees. But the Commission's version is that the employee must show that the supervisor had a *motivation* to discriminate. The minority-group member, rather than the supervisor, is required to explain the supervisor's deviation from the norm.

It is quite correct for the Commission to require that the employee alleging discrimination show *something* has happened, but after such prima facie evidence, the supervisor or the agency should provide a convincing explanation for the unusual behavior. Placing the burden on the complainant to prove that dissimilar treatment is *clearly* discriminatory treatment results in the present system where "discrimination is difficult to prove."

The agency should rarely find the burden of proof as onerous since its managers and supervisors have access to personnel information to justify their actions. In many areas of the law, the party with the information necessary to prove a point is assigned the burden of presenting that evidence.

The situation for probationary employees is even worse. Those who file a complaint alleging a discriminatory dismissal do not receive a review of the substantive reasons for their separation.[11] The BAR at present cannot presume discrimination if the reasons for separation are found to be insufficient, because the BAR refuses even to examine the reasons for separation. "Discrimination is difficult to prove" when evidence that a probationer's dismissal was caused by discrimination is inadmissible.

The Civil Rights Commission's report on the Federal Civil Service Rights Reinforcement Effort in September 1970 stated: "Free legal aid should be provided on request to all lower-grade employees who require it. In this connection, CSC should take the lead in establishing a governmentwide pool of attorneys who are prepared to volunteer their services in discrimination complaint cases or adverse actions involving minority-group employees."

The Commission has not followed this sound recommendation. When Irving Kator was asked how many employees were represented in complaint processing at each stage, he replied, "We made a rough study when the issue came up with the U.S. Civil Rights Commission. We have not compiled statistics on this problem. Provisions for representation are under consideration now. The problem is not lack of representation, but the quality of representation, which could be better in some cases."

Kator provided the following information showing complainants' representation at EEO hearings between January and July 1971; no information on representation during investigation and appeal, or on how many of the complainants who did not request a hearing had representation, was provided (Table 2).

Because representation is necessary to protect the complainant's fundamental interests, the 13.6 percent rate of nonrepresentation at an EEO hearing seems too high. The high percentage for "private attorney" (22.2 percent) indicates that problems of quality of representation may be severe.

QUALITY UNCONTROL

John Hardesty, a member of the BAR, "doesn't think anyone has defined 'such cause as will promote the efficiency of the service' or ever will." One of the most serious failures of the Commission rests in its inability to develop standards by which to judge the actions of

Table 2 Representation at Hearings

Total Decisions Reviewed	117
Civil Rights Organization Representative	5 or 4.3%
Private Attorney	26 or 22.2%
Union Representatives	40 or 34.2%
Other Individual	30 or 25.6%
No Representative	16 or 13.6%

employees, causing judgments in its appeals system to be made on an ad hoc basis. The definition of aberrant behavior is left in the hands of the agency, which is unlikely to include in the definition such behavior as failure to enforce the laws, failure to pass along pertinent information, or failure of management officials to fulfill their personal responsibilities.

Commission officials argue that the complexity of the civil service and the fact that the aims of the federal agencies vary greatly prevent the development or application of uniform standards. They also counsel caution about doing anything that may interfere with agency performance. The very complexity and diversity of the civil service indicates the need for standards because the Commission's reliance on agency interpretation of unacceptable conduct, combined with increased complexity, may soon become abdication. The Commission has failed to participate meaningfully in the development of uniform agency codes of penalties that would bring some order.

NOTES

1. On October 7, 1971, for example, before the U.S. Senate Subcommittee on Labor of the Committee on Labor and Public Welfare, Mr. Kator testified on behalf of the Civil Service Commission, opposing removal of the EEO function from the Civil Service Commission to the Equal Employment Opportunity Commission. Mr. Kator was accompanied by Mr. Frazier, whom Mr. Kator introduced. Mr. Kator did all the talking before the subcommittee in defense of present Commission EEO programs. When the chairman of the subcommittee asked, "Now, Mr. Frazier, do you have anything to say?" Mr. Frazier replied, "No, sir." Several employees, technically on Frazier's staff, referred in interviews to Kator as their boss.

2. The poor performance of federal agencies in California in hiring Mexican-Americans is highlighted by a report of Public Advocates, Inc., undertaken under the sponsorship of the Mexican-American Legal Defense and Education Fund. The report found that the federal government is California's largest private or public employer. It employs 293,770 full-time civilians as of November 30, 1970. Only 16,506, or 5.6 percent, were Spanish-surnamed. The report also found that "Most Mexican-Americans employed by the federal government in California are in poverty-level jobs as defined for the U.S. Department of Labor for urban areas. For example, Spanish-surnamed persons constitute only *17.6 percent of all employees in the "Wage System" earning under $5,500 and only 0.6% of those earning $18,000 or more."* [Emphasis in original.]

3. The Commission's regulations also require each agency to develop plans, procedures, and regulations for affirmative action in EEO—including provision of sufficient resources; disciplinary actions against supervisors; maximization of the utilization of employee skills; maximization of on-the-job training and work-study programs; publicity of job opportunities to all sources of job candidates; cooperation with community groups to improve employment opportunities; evaluation, control, and training of managers and supervisors in regard to EEO programs; recognition of employees for superior accomplishment in EEO. The Commission also requires each agency to appraise, through

"self-evaluation," its overall EEO efforts at regular intervals to assure their conformity with Commission policies and programs; and to establish a system which provides statistical employment information by race and national origin.

4. The office of the general counsel has submitted reports to the executive director of the Commission. Two law professors working for the Commission during a summer program have submitted criticisms of the appeals program. Professor Egon Guttman's thorough work was published in volume 19 of the *American University Law Review*. Judge James A. Washington's thoughtful critique was submitted to the Commission in 1968.

5. At one time the appeals examiner did indeed provide direct services to the management of agencies. Appeals examiners—trial judges as it were—routinely provided advice on procedure to management in the same cases in which they later sat as examiners. In one case, in fact, the BAR altered the date of service of notice of adverse decision to make it comply with procedural rules. Although this practice appears to have ceased, members of the Appeals Examining Office still contact personnel offices before a decision is reached in a case that is procedurally defective to suggest that it be withdrawn. (This is as if a football coach were to serve as both coach and referee in a championship game, stopping the game to tell his offensive team that it is lined up improperly for the defensive formation it is facing.)

6. The Commission's perspective not only affects the adjudication of employee appeals, but the performance of the Commission. A young attorney, an associate of a prominent Washington law firm who represented an employee seeking a temporary restraining order on a matter submitted to the Commission, wrote to the research group:

> During argument the judges wanted to know what the status of proceedings before the Civil Service Commission is. Government counsel replied that proceedings have been stayed pending the Court of Appeals' decision. The Court wanted to know why the stay [delay] since the District Court's opinion did not preclude them from deciding, and, if they had decided, it would have mooted the issue. Government counsel agreed with that reading of [the] order and said the reason the Commission has stayed proceedings is that they [the Department of Justice] wanted to preserve the point for appeal. This business of the CSC taking action to accommodate the tactical needs of the Department of Justice did not sit very well with the court and didn't sit very well with me either. I am more than a little distressed at the idea that a quasi-judicial entity before which I am litigating an issue should be hand-in-glove with opposing counsel.

7. The Civil Rights Commission reports, regarding the IAG:

> During fiscal year 1969, Directors of Personnel and Equal Employment Opportunity Officers from the score of agencies comprising the Equal Employment Opportunity Committee met four times. . . . The group's attention was directed primarily to the revised discrimination complaint procedures. Although the group also made suggestions regarding the agency equal employment opportunity actions plans, *there is no way of determining the extent of its influence*. In the final analysis, governmentwide policy decisions on equal employment opportunity are made by the CSC. [emphasis added]

8. The dangers of such conflict of interest and the dangers of the imposition of management bias is exacerbated by the practice of regional directors of consulting with the executive staff of the Civil Service Commission before some appeals determinations are made. Both the Boston and Philadelphia regional directors said that such contacts were made. Although consistency in

the appeals program is desirable, this consistency is best supplied by the Board of Appeals and Review and by the Commission through the promulgation of regulations.

9. A small number of agencies have experimented with elected counselors, without the Commission's encouragement. Irving Kator, in an interview, stated views against *requiring* the election of counselors: "I've no objection to the election of counselors. The ultimate decision, though, I think ought to be a management decision. This is not a popularity contest. I've known people elected to such jobs that couldn't talk to management and that prevented a favorable case from getting an early resolution. It is important to have a guy who can do the job of counselor."

In a speech at an EEO conference, Kator also expressed the same viewpoint:

> An essential ingredient in an EEO counselor is his acceptability to employees as well as to management. He should be able to maintain the confidence and trust of all parties. Although it is management's responsibility to select the EEO counselor and to ensure that he is someone who can identify with all levels of the work force, unions and employees may have an input into nominating persons for counselors. Management, however, should make the final choice.

The fact that counselors are management-appointed and not employee-elected does not, of course, necessarily result in counselors able to "maintain the confidence and trust of all parties." Nor is it the case that any election of counselors need be what is called "a popularity contest."

10. Dr. Richard Weir, Professor of Political Science at Lindenwood College, St. Charles, Missouri, observed that "the EEO counselor usually has a relatively high grade. All of the EEO counselors encountered in this study [of upward mobility at two installations] had grades of either GS-9 or GS-11. Most complaints, however, come from employees from the lower grade ranges, with the bulk below GS-5. Thus the employee approaches an EEO counselor who, because of his relatively high grade, is identified with management, and it is management who is viewed by the complaining employee as responsible for his situation. The element of mutual trust, essential to any successful counseling situation, is, therefore, vitiated from the beginning by the selection of counselors with grades significantly higher than their clientele."

11. Judge Washington thinks that when a probationary employee has made out a prima facie case of discrimination, the agency should justify its reason for separation, which the agency is not required to do in adverse actions against a probationary employee who does not allege discrimination. Judge Washington writes:

> Probationers are entitled to a procedural review but not a merit review in separation cases. Hence the general view of the Board is that it will not inquire into the reasons for separation. This view should not be carried over into cases where the probationer alleges discrimination as the reason for separation. While it is arguable that the Board in any such procedural review is at least required to determine whether separation was unreasonable or capricious, it would seem manifest, when the charge is that separation is the product of discrimination, that the Board has an obligation to review the reasons given by the agency for the separation; and if BAR finds them unreasonable, it should conclude that discrimination was the basis for the discharge. It is inconceivable that in such a situation BAR can separate the validity of the agency's grounds for discharge from the probationer's allegation of discrimination. The same situation could arise in cases of suspensions for thirty days or less.

[Judge Washington appends a footnote:] Cf. In the Matters of . . . , decided 11/22/67, the Board, it appears, did examine the reasons assigned by the agency for the discharge. But see, in the Matter of . . . , decided 8/18/67—the sufficiency of the reasons for separation [is not for evaluation in this review]. Rather, the scope of the Board's review encompasses only the question of whether considerations of . . . race entered into, or influenced, the decision to separate him.

Reinstatement Isn't Enough

Les Aspin

Among the changes needed to make the National Labor Relations Act an effective law are improvements in the particularly weak sections of the law pertaining to the rights of individuals who are wrongly fired for union activity.

These conclusions were drawn from a study which I conducted in the New England area to attempt to find out what happens to individuals declared by the National Labor Relations Board to have been illegally fired.

Employes fired for exercising their rights to join and assist labor unions need more help than the law and the NLRB are now giving them. The law says they must be reinstated to their old job without loss of seniority or other benefits.

But the study found that this provision by itself is not enough.

These conclusions arose out of a study which began with the simple question: What happens to employes reinstated under the section of the National Labor Relations Act which prohibits a company from interfering with its employes' rights to organize, form or assist a labor union?

Typically, such a case will arise after a few employes make the initial steps toward unionization by gathering signatures on authorization cards. Shortly thereafter, the company fires these employes. The employes say they were fired for union activity—the company says they were fired for poor work—and a case under the NLRA is the result.

Abridged from Les Aspin, "Reinstatement Isn't Enough," *American Federationist* (September 1971), pp. 19–21. Reprinted by permission.

If the company is found guilty of violation, reinstatment is one of the remedies which the act prescribes. A person illegally fired for union activity must be offered reinstatement to the same or substantially equivalent position to the one held before he was fired.

But the NLRB has very little idea what happens to these reinstated employes. How many individuals accept reinstatement and how many refuse? If they go back to the company, do they stay or leave? If they leave, what is their reason? It was to get the answer to these kinds of questions that the study was undertaken.

The sample chosen for the study were the 71 cases between July 1, 1962, and July 1, 1964, handled by the NLRB's first region office in New England. The 71 cases covered a total of 194 employes who charged they had been discriminated against.

Of the 71 companies in which charges of violations were filed, 36 were in manufacturing, 21 in service and 14 in sales. Most of the cases—62 of the 71—rose out of union organizing drives and most of them—50 of the 71—were settled informally.

The study was not particularly concerned with the merits of the cases or whether the NLRB's findings were just. Rather it was concerned with the results—what ultimately happened to the 194 employes.

In 80 percent of the cases, it was possible to find a resolution from the first region office's "informal files" such as affidavits, field examiner's reports, inter-office memos or even short notes jotted on scraps of paper. In the remaining 20 percent of the cases, it was necessary to interview the NLRB agents, the employes themselves or other employes, both pro-union and anti-union.

What the study found was that initially most individuals wanted reinstatement with their former company. But the company definitely did not want them back. And very few of them were actually successfully reinstated.

As a matter of routine, the NLRB usually asks at the outset whether the individual wants reinstatement. Of those surveyed, 82 percent had responded in the affirmative.

But less than half of them ever went back. Among the varied reasons for refusing reinstatement, the three which stand out are 1) he already has a better job; 2) he waives reinstatement in order to get some backpay in a deal with the company; 3) he is afraid of company retaliation after he is reinstated.

For those who have a better job, there is clearly no problem. But others refuse reinstatement because they need the backpay. Under the law, the company must offer the individual backpay sufficient to make him "whole" for any loss of wages during the time that he was illegally

WHAT HAPPENS TO REINSTATED EMPLOYEES

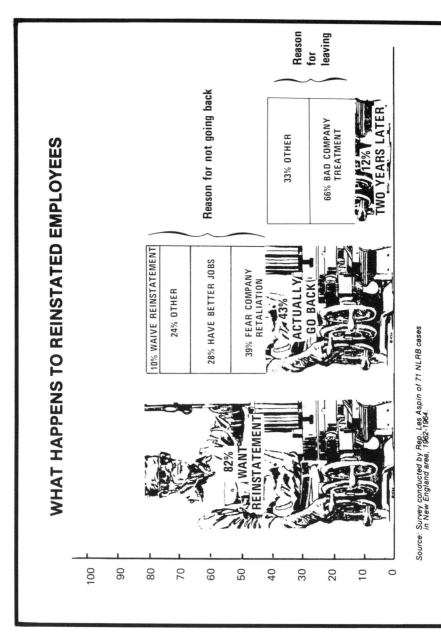

Reason for not going back

10% WAIVE REINSTATEMENT

24% OTHER

28% HAVE BETTER JOBS

39% FEAR COMPANY RETALIATION

82% WANT REINSTATEMENT

43% ACTUALLY GO BACK

Reason for leaving

33% OTHER

66% BAD COMPANY TREATMENT

12% TWO YEARS LATER

100
90
80
70
60
50
40
30
20
10
0

Source: Survey conducted by Rep. Les Aspin of 71 NLRB cases in New England area. 1962-1964.

fired. Depending on state law, the individual may not have received unemployment benefits while his case was being settled. So, faced with mounting bills, he is tempted when the company offers him perhaps several hundred dollars in backpay if he will settle the case and refuse reinstatement.

But the most frequent reason given for refusing reinstatement was the fear of company retaliation. During the settlement negotiations and during the union's organizing drive, the individual is able to observe the company's attitude. He begins to think about what it will be like to go back to work in that company. He knows that some jobs are heavier or dirtier than others and begins to wonder about how they will be assigned.

Thus the study found that the antagonistic attitude of the companies is a major reason so few accept reinstatement.

But the study also found that the individual's personal situation must also be taken into account. For instance, as one might expect, the more seniority an individual has the more he is interested in reinstatement. Also as might be expected, the individual's views toward reinstatement are colored by his ability to find other employment. This is true of others besides those who found a better job. Even if he has found a job which does not pay as well, he is less likely to press for reinstatement.

All of these were factors, the study found, in determining whether the individual went back: better job, needed backpay, fear of company retaliation, seniority, success in finding other employment. Of the 80 percent who originally wanted reinstatement, less than 50 percent actually went back after settlement.

The next question is what happened to those who were reinstated?

The study found that three-quarters of those actually reinstated were gone from the company within two years after reinstatement. Interviewing those, the study found that the story is not much different from those refused reinstatement in the first place. The most frequent reason given for leaving the company was "bad company treatment."

"Bad company treatment" usually involved a specific complaint: "They were always on my back," or "I always got the worst jobs." Sometimes the complaints were general: "It was really awful," or "I hope I never have to go through that again."

Farah: The Union Struggle in the 70s

Rex Hardesty

It's hot in Texas this time of year and there's a strike on—neither unusual for that state. But one strike, against the Farah Manufacturing Co. at eight plants in Texas and New Mexico, is unusual. It's being conducted by a group that is 98 percent Chicano and over 80 percent female and is being backed by a boycott of Farah clothing by the entire American labor movement. It includes the overtones of the changing South, runaway plants, immigrant labor laws and church indignation.

The strike started during a Clothing Workers organizing drive at Farah when six machinists were fired at San Antonio and the workers walked out in El Paso, site of four major Farah plants and the center of the activity that has followed. The strike is being fought over low wages, but also over the fundamental rights of a worker to bargain for wages, hours, production quotas, pensions, job security, promotions and a host of job conditions—rights that became negotiable for many Americans 40 years ago, but whose abrogation is still widespread in the U.S.

The struggle is vital for its ramifications for Texas, an industrialized state of great wealth, yet with a median family income $1,100 below the national average; for El Paso, a border town with innumerable green carders and illegals looming as potential strikebreakers; for women, who are joining the U.S. workforce in record-shattering numbers; and for the needle trades unions, which have struggled for decades for justice from employers in the South and Southwest.

But most of all, it is a strike by Latin Americans, the nation's second largest minority group which has a history of drudgery, disadvantage and poverty which is matched but not surpassed in American history.

The strike became a year old on May 9, 1973. On that same day, the AFL-CIO Executive Council was meeting in Washington, D.C., reemphasizing its support of the nationwide boycott of Farah clothing and also voting a special assessment to aid the United Farm Workers, a union as heavily Chicano as the Farah strikers are.

It also pledged the "wholehearted cooperation" of the U.S. trade union movement for the Labor Council for Latin American Advance-

From Rex Hardesty, "Farah: The Union Struggle in the 70s," *American Federationist* (June 1973), pp. 6–8. Reprinted with permission.

ment, a newly formed group that will coordinate the expanding activities of Latin American trade unionists, including voter registration and other political action. Leaders of the Labor Council for Latin American Advancement say it will be patterned after the A. Philip Randolph Institute, founded by black trade unionists in 1964.

It was in that era—now almost 10 years ago—that knowledgeable American Negro leaders began to redirect their efforts "from protest to politics," moving on from civil rights to economic advancement. "What good does it do to win the right to sit down in a lunch counter if you don't have the price of a hamburger?" became the motto of that strategy, with trade union action and political coalition replacing protest marches. That summation is descriptive for all workers in view of the price of ground beef in 1973.

In minority group history, the Farah strikers start somewhere in the middle of the same evolution—liberated from the old Texas, but still handicapped by language, education and employment practice barriers, as they are across the country.

The 1970 Census lists more than 10 million "Spanish-speaking" in the U.S., of whom about 6 million are of Mexican-American descent, 2 million Puerto Rican and 600,000 Cuban. They are outnumbered among U.S. minority groups only by the 22 million blacks.

In median family income, the Latin Americans fare slightly better than the U.S. Negro, $7,548 to $6,400, but both lag far behind the median family income of $10,285 for all Americans.

In educational level, the Latinos are worse off than blacks. Only 1 in 4 Chicanos over age 25 has finished high school; roughly 1 in 4 of all Latinos is illiterate in English. Twenty-nine percent of the Chicanos live in poverty, compared to 34 percent of blacks and 13 percent for all Americans.

The Latinos are even younger than Negroes. The median age for all Americans is 28.1; for Negros 22.4 and for Latinos 20.7, with 4.1 million of their official 10 million under age 18.

Farm labor migration has always moved Chicanos north and in the years since World War II, when their numbers have increased tremendously, so has their distribution. Chicanos are still heavily concentrated in four southwestern states, but there are now more Chicanos in Illinois than in Arizona.

In some regions, New Mexico particularly, Chicanos have been assimilated into the society as a whole for generations and are now a considerable political force. The Chicanos of the other states where they are heavily concentrated—3.1 million in California, 2.06 million in Texas, 407,000 in New Mexico, 364,000 in Illinois, 333,000 in Arizona and 286,000 in Colorado—have also made political headway, but they are plagued by the danger of having no effect except electing their enemies by draining votes from liberals.

If Willie Farah knew as much about men as he does about machines, he wouldn't be facing a nationwide boycott which brought his company losses in the millions of dollars last year.

Willie Farah is 53 now. With two Lear jets swirling buyers about the nation and Willie's own remarkable engineering ability directing the mechanical innovations which have made his company the envy of his competitors, the Farah Manufacturing Co. has come a long way since Willie's father ran a drygoods store when Willie was a toddler.

When the Farah company was first born in rented space in a downtown building, Willie's mother already was a sort of recreation director who installed radios around the workplace.

The Farahs expanded enough to take over their original building, but it wasn't until World War II and defense contracts that Farah's fortunes really soared. Farah was the first clothing contractor west of the Mississippi to win the Navy "E" for excellence in fulfilling its contracts. Willie was a fighter pilot during the war, a local figure of some dash, and when he came home, Farah really began to become a giant in men's and boys' clothing.

Ironically, it was soon afterward that another El Paso clothing firm, Hortex-Billy the Kid, signed a contract with the Clothing Workers, beginning a 20-year history of relatively smooth labor relations for a right-to-work state and a company whose competitors are overwhelmingly non-union. Subsequently, the El Paso Levi-Strauss plant has signed an ACWA contract and both have done quite well despite paying higher salaries than Farah. Last year, Billy the Kid's profits were up from $21 million to $30 million, the same period Farah was losing about $6 to $10 million.

Seemingly, Willie Farah doesn't equivocate. He is dead set against unions—they disturb the peace, butt in on decisions he has a divine right to make and give the rabble a voice in what his family worked hard to build up. So, too, is he dead set against foreign-made goods and Mexico's Border Industrialization Program of twin plants, which has brought over 240 plants to Juarez while their "twins" rapidly disappeared from the U.S. side. Willie once found a keg of Japanese-made nails at the construction site of his new home, the contractor told friends, and he not only ordered them off the job but also ordered a partially finished wall removed and rebuilt with American nails.

The Farah credo is evident from the radios of the 1920s to the paternalism of the 1970s: We take good care of "our" Chicanos; we know how to handle "them" and they would all be "happies" if it weren't for outside agitators.

The plants are modern, clean, and air-conditioned. A turkey is delivered to every Farah employe at Christmas time; a gala employes' Christmas party is held at the massive El Paso Civic Center; in short, anything for morale other than reasonable pay raises or a voice for the "happies" in their own destiny.

It is the classic closed mentality of the company town, an anach-
ronism in the national labor-management history, but an attitude
which still attracts considerable support in El Paso, Victoria, Las
Cruces and other locations of Farah plants.

Money attracts puppets and in El Paso, economic elitism has deep
roots—even some of the names have remained the same throughout
the long Farah history.

In the 1930s the El Paso National Bank was thriving in an era of
foreclosures on home mortgages and the bank's president, Sam D.
Young Sr., was instrumental in providing Farah the financing needed
to grow. Today, Willie Farah is on the board of directors of the El Paso
National Bank, as is Dorrance D. Roderick, publisher of the El Paso
Times. Directorships interlock easily in Texas.

It is useful in sustaining the status quo to treat the union and the
worker as separate entities. "We will talk to our employes, but not to
unions," said a letter from the mayor in the newspaper in nearby
Artesia, N.M. Farah's intention of solidifying that attitude in the public
mind was displayed recently in a covert attempt to get some of the
affiliates of the El Paso Building and Construction Trades Council interested in a jurisdiction in the Farah plants. "We don't mind unions so
much," it was said in the overture, "but we can't let any one union (the
Clothing Workers) have that much power."

The mastery of El Paso by the Farahs, Rodericks and Youngs
perhaps would not be challenged today if it were not for the indignant
Chicanos who walked out on Willie a year ago.

"They either have that rigged up to put a microphone in it, or else
they just say they do—it accomplishes the same thing," said one of the
pickets of the electric conduit which runs from somewhere in the in-
nards of Fortress Farah to the gates where the pickets walk.

The closed circuit television cameras are more evident. This sophisticated equipment hangs from special towers at the various Farah
plants, enabling a film record of all picket activities to be made easily.
And sound, possibly, can be matched with the film if the microphones
were installed.

Finally, security guards with hand cameras emerge on all the roofs
to photograph any unusual events in the parking lot or on the picket
line.

Barbed wire isn't enough. The barbed wire atop the high fences is in
turn topped by jagged metal spikes which appear to be the work of a
mad sadist cutting out designs in beer cans.

But the dogs that roamed the parking lots and brought fame to
Fortress Farah are gone—removed through a stipulation in which
Farah told the National Labor Relations Board that it didn't admit to
using dogs and won't do it anymore.

Also gone is the mass picketing law, which required that pickets be 50 feet apart and resulted in the arrest of 1,200 workers in the early days of the Farah strike. The Texas Supreme Court struck that law down, culminating a challenge to it that had been kicking around the Texas courts since the first attempts to organize farm workers there several years ago.

Gone also is the opportunity for the justices of the peace to collect $4 per head for handling the strikers' arrest process. The city auditor's unwillingness to pay that bounty cooled the ardor for arrests.

Today, Woody Briggs, a veteran of over 20 years of ACWA organizing drives and strikes in the South, still coordinates the residue of legal battles on behalf of the strikers—but the action isn't as furious as a year ago when he demanded jury trials for all 1,200 arrested strikers, thereby piling on a judicial load which aided the collapse of the house of cards of legal protections behind which Farah could hide.

But Fortress Farah is still impregnable.

The *Post* Breaks a Union's Iron Grip

An advertisement in the *Washington Post* this week may well mark the final decline of one of the country's major newspaper unions. "The *Washington Post* is now hiring experienced and inexperienced personnel to work in its pressroom," the ad said. " . . . Please be advised that we are seeking replacements for strikers." The *Post* offered wages of $5.24 to $9.52 an hour, and the flood of applicants raised the likelihood that Washington would soon join the growing list of cities where publishers have broken the once-iron grip of the International Printing & Graphic Communications Union.

Thanks first to borrowed press facilities and then to the use of management personnel to man its own presses, the *Post* has missed only one day of publication since the pressmen went on strike on Oct. 1. The *Post's* ability not only to continue operations but also to hire strikebreakers is certain to embolden publishers in other cities to take on the pressmen and other craft unions in work-rule disputes.

Reprinted from the December 29, 1975 issue of *Business Week* by special permission. © 1975 by McGraw-Hill, Inc.

The *Post* strike began in a spasm of violence. Negotiations had stalled over management's demands for changes in work rules that, the newspaper says, required excessive manpower and overtime and allowed some pressmen to earn as much as $30,000 a year. The night the contract expired, some pressmen went on a rampage, severely damaging the presses.

Officials of Pressmen's Local 6 claim that the *Post* intended to break the union from the beginning, a charge vehemently denied by Publisher Katharine Graham. After announcing plans to hire permanent replacements for the strikers, she still contended, "We are a union newspaper."

The violence, however, left the *Post* management determined to prove that it is the boss. That resolve was stiffened over the weekend when a union picketer appeared at the newspaper with a sign reading "Phil shot the wrong Graham," a reference to the 1963 suicide of Mrs. Graham's husband, Philip L. Graham.

RECURRING PATTERN

The *Post* was assured of victory over the pressmen this week when the Newspaper Guild, representing reporters and advertising workers, voted for the fourth time not to honor the craft union picket lines. Reporters and writers are harder to replace than mechanical workers, whose jobs increasingly are being automated. While some newspapers have continued publication during Guild strikes, the *Post* prides itself on editorial excellence and would be unable to maintain its standards if the reporters joined the strike.

Aside from the violence at the *Post*, which has cost the pressmen much public support, the strike has followed a pattern familiar to other cities. The pressmen have been driven out of newspapers in Miami, Portland (Ore.), Dallas, Kansas City, and New Haven, among other places, when they failed to accept work-rule changes. At the *Los Angeles Times*, the union won a representation election but was decertified as the bargaining agent before an initial contract could be negotiated. Only in St. Louis and Charlotte, N.C., have the pressmen negotiated contracts that accepted work-rule changes in exchange for job security arrangements.

The pressmen's history contrasts sharply with that of the International Typographical Union, which has belatedly recognized that rapid technological changes in printing will ultimately doom their typesetting craft. After a series of newspaper-killing strikes in the 1960s, the ITU has come to accept long-term agreements in New York, Washington, and other cities. In return for costly provisions, which protect the jobs and earnings of printers now on the job, the ITU has given up its fight against installation of electronic typesetting equipment that will drastically reduce the need for printers.

TIMES OF CHANGE

"The pressmen have always been a hard-line organization," says a long-time observer of newspaper labor relations. "In earlier years, they were so powerful that they could set their own working conditions. They had a sense that conditions would never really change, and, as a result, they refused to look squarely at the technological change that was occurring. I suppose it is really the difference between good leadership and counsel and the lack of it."

While not so dramatic as the changes in the composing room, where semi-skilled typists have replaced skilled typesetters, changes in pressroom technology have reduced the need for skilled pressmen. As soon as the initial damage was repaired, the *Post* began running papers on its own presses. With a cadre of skilled nonunion pressmen, the *Post* expects to be able to use locally hired personnel with no pressroom experience. This will probably mark a successful end to a long campaign by civil rights groups to get blacks into the virtually all-white craft.

Before the *Post* can resume normal operations, it must come to terms with other striking unions. The Photoengravers, Mailers, and the Stereotypers, who are members of Local 6 but have a separate agreement, also went on strike when their contracts expired Oct. 1. The ITU is in the middle of a five-year contract, but has honored the strike. Of the 800 members in the Guild unit, all but 150 have crossed the picket line.

Federal mediator Kenneth Moffett expects the strike to "slowly wind down." Negotiations will continue with the other unions, but talks with the pressmen came to a halt after the *Post* rejected two union concessions.

The *Post* strike is being watched with interest in New York City, where the *New York Times* and *Daily News* are negotiating with their pressmen's local union. The New York papers claim not to have the same work-rule problems as the *Post*, but both are trying to work out manning rules for new presses. "We are not looking to break the union," says a New York newspaper executive.

The apparent breaking of the *Post* strike is not the only trouble faced by Pressmen's Local 6. Federal officials who have reviewed photographs of the results of the Oct. 1 violence say there is no doubt that the damage to the presses was premeditated. A federal grand jury had been investigating the affair and is expected soon to indict several members and leaders of the union, including Local 6 President James Dugan.

Steve Carmichael
Studs Terkel

"I'm a coordinator. I'm project management." He works for the Neighborhood Youth Corps. Though it is federally funded through the OEO, he is employed by the city. "Two of our agencies were joined together about six months ago. A further step toward institutionalizing the poverty program." He heads a department of nine people. "We take young people of poverty income families and assist them through work experiences, those who've dropped out of school, and thereby better their potential of obtaining a job."

He is twenty-five, has a wife and one child.

When I was with VISTA my greatest frustration was dealing with administrators. I was working in a school and I saw the board of education as a big bureaucracy, which could not move. I was disdainful of bureaucrats in Washington, who set down rules without ever having been to places where those rules take effect. Red tape. I said I could replace a bureaucrat and conduct a program in relationship to people, not figures. I doubt seriously if three years from now I'll be involved in public administration. One reason is each day I find myself more and more like unto the people I wanted to replace.

I'll run into one administrator and try to institute a change and then I'll go to someone else and connive to get the change. Gradually your effectiveness wears down. Pretty soon you no longer identify as the bright guy with the ideas. You become the fly in the ointment. You're criticized by your superiors and subordinates. Not in a direct manner. Indirectly, by being ignored. They say I'm unrealistic. One of the fellas that works with me said, "It's a dream to believe this program will take sixteen-, seventeen-year-old dropouts and make something of their lives." This may well be true, but if I'm going to believe that I can't believe my job has any worth.

I may be rocking the boat, though I'm not accomplishing anything. As the criticism of me steps up, the security aspect of my job comes into play. I begin to say, "Okay, I got a recent promotion. I earned it." They couldn't deny anybody who made significant inputs. Now I'm at a plateau. As criticism continues, I find myself tempering my remarks, becoming more and more concerned about security.

I'm regarded as an upstart. I'm white and younger than they are. (Laughs.) They're between thirty and forty. They might rate me fair to middlin' as a person. They might give me a sixty percent range on a scale of a hundred percent. As a supervisor, I'd be down to about twenty percent. (Laughs.) I think I'm a better supervisor than they give me credit for. They criticize me for what criticism they may have of the entire program—which is about the way I criticized my supervisor when I was in their position. He became an ogre, the source of blame for the failings of the program. The difference is I don't patronize my staff the way he did. They make a recommendation to me and I try to carry it out, if I feel it's sound. I think it's built up some of their confidence in me.

My suggestions go through administrative channels. Ninety percent of it is filtered out by my immediate superior. I have been less than successful in terms of getting things I believe need to be done. It took me six months to convince my boss to make one obvious administrative change. It took her two days to deny that she had ever opposed the change.

We've got five or six young people who are burning to get into an automotive training program. Everybody says, "It takes signatures, it takes time." I follow up on these things because everybody else seems to forget there are people waiting. So I'll get that phone call, do some digging, find out nothing's happened, report that to my boss, and call back and make my apologies. And then deal with a couple of minor matters—Johnny ripped off a saw today . . . certain enrollees are protesting because they're getting gypped on their paychecks.

So we're about a quarter to five and I suddenly look at my desk and it's filled with papers—reports and memos. I have to sort them out before a secretary can file 'em. Everybody'll leave at five o'clock, except for me. Usually I'm there until six o'clock. If I did all the paper work I should, my sanity would go. Paper work I almost totally ignore. I make a lot of decisions over the phone. It hits you about two months later when somebody says, "Where's the report on such and such? Where's the documentation?"

The most frustrating thing for me is to know that what I'm doing does not have a positive impact on others. I don't see this work as meaning anything. I now treat my job disdainfully. The status of my job is totally internal. Who's your friend? Can you walk into this person's office and call him by his first name? It carries very little status to strangers who don't understand the job. People within the agency don't understand it. (Laughs.)

Success is to be in a position where I can make a decision. Now I have to wait around and see that what I say or do has any impact. I wonder how I'd function where people would say, "There's a hotshot. He knows what he's talking about." And what I say became golden. I don't know if it would be satisfying for me. (Laughs.) That might be more frustrating than fighting for everything you want. Right now I feel very unimportant.

POSTSCRIPT: *"While I was waiting for this job I was advised to see my ward committeeman. I was debating. My wife was pregnant. I had virtually no savings. I was gonna get a ten-thousand-dollar job. What was I gonna do? I was all set to work as a taxicab driver. Then I said, 'I'm going to be a bricklayer. Just come home at night, take a bath, relax.' I was prepared to call my uncle, who's a mason. I knew he could connect me, that's the irony. I was decrying a system that forced me to go to my ward committeeman to get a city job, but I was going to call my uncle to get me at the head of the line to get in the masons union. (Laughs.) One system was just as immoral as the other. By a stroke of luck, my application cleared city hall without my having to go through politics. To this day I'm politically unaffiliated. I don't know how long that will last. I may have to go to an alderman to get my promotion cleared.*

"My goal for the last two years is to be a university professor. He works only nine months a year. (Laughs.) He can supplement his income. What's a comfortable income? We started at fifteen thousand dollars—my wife and I—as our goal. We're up to about twenty-five thousand now. If I have another kid, the goal'll go to thirty thousand. The way I look at the university professor—aside from his capacity to influence other people—is that the business world often uses him as a consultant. Not bad."

6

THE POLITICS OF CONTROL IN ORGANIZATIONS

The Use and Abuse of Influence and Power

Textbook discussions on how people use influence and power to persuade or coerce others to do their bidding typically miss the breadth and the richness of these processes. They also fail to deal sufficiently with abuse of influence and power and the consequences of such abuses. Most individuals are not in a position to exert control without taking steps to acquire bases of influence and power; the concept of climbing to power is interesting, yet rarely is it the subject of serious study. Also intriguing is the question of cost. At what cost, if any, does an individual wield influence and power? The readings in this section are concerned with one or more of these issues.

People in control or those aspiring to increase control frequently harness and manipulate situations not normally considered avenues to influence and power. "How the Boss Stays in Touch With the Troops" (Meyer) describes tactics which leaders use to keep themselves on top of situations, events and people. "Campus Politico" (Kearns) provides a view of an individual (Lyndon Johnson) climbing the organization through intelligent use of a low-level position in a university organization.

The excerpts from *Boss* (Royko) provide interesting illustrations of tactics used by the late Mayor Richard Daley of Chicago to exert control over the decision-making process in city government and to maintain and increase the bases of his power and influence. A revealing glimpse of conflict among leaders, of the struggle to be leader of leaders, is given in an excerpt from *The Wreck of the Penn Central* (Daughen & Binzen). The clash of people in power is woven into the description of the decline and fall of the merged Penn Central Railway.

People aspiring to control use a wide variety of strategies in their pursuit of power and influence. It is sometimes recognized that leaders use emotions such as anger, fear, grief or love as tools to aid their efforts at control. Less obvious a means of control is the use of humor. Albert Speer describes the use which Goebbels made of jokes and pranks in maintaining his position in Hitler's government in "Inside the Third Reich."

Both Lyndon Johnson ("The Politics of Seduction," Kearns) and Vince Lombardi ("Winning is the Only Thing," Kramer) apparently had an ability to understand, and to be sensitive to, the needs and emotions of people. They were able to harness these talents to persuade or coerce others into following their wishes. The behavior of these two men is characterized in these pieces by the personalized attention which each man gave to the people with whom he interacted.

In the last selection, we glimpse some of the loneliness and stress associated with being in control in Eberhard Faber's account of his early days as a company president ("What Happened When I Gave Up the Good Life and Became President").

How the Boss Stays in Touch With the Troops

Herbert E. Meyer

There was a time, not long after World War II, when "communication" was a major preoccupation of top executives everywhere. The need for good communication in business, which today seems almost too obvious to mention, was then an arresting new idea. It was one of a number of ideas whose origins lay in academic research, and whose rapid dissemination gave many executives the sense that management —i.e., what they did all day—was developing into a real science.

In more recent years, a lot of top executives have been discovering that communication is also an art. Today everyone understands clearly that information has to flow in both directions in a large hierarchical organization. And everyone understands that, just as some Harvard Business School professors demonstrated years ago in those famous experiments at Western Electric, employees want a sense of participation—a feeling that they are members of the team. . . .

Adapted from material originally appearing in the June 1975 issue of *Fortune* Magazine by special permission; © 1975 Time Inc. □ Research associate: Wilton Woods.

THE ONLY QUESTION IS HOW

Chief executives have, it happens, developed some effective techniques, or gimmicks, for staying in touch. These techniques enable them to extend their reach beyond the dozen or so top managers with whom they deal every day and with whom staying in touch is relatively easy. Inevitably, all this communicating takes up a certain amount of time—it involves an evening now and then, or setting aside a half hour during an already crowded day, or finding a few moments for a chat en route to and from the office. But many chief executives believe that the techniques have become an important part of the job. In addition to providing lower-level executives with that sense of participation, they work in two different ways to strengthen the bottom line.

First, they enable the chief executive to acquire information he mightn't otherwise get. They help him avoid the situation in which everyone but the boss knows that an explosion is coming. "I cannot overemphasize the importance of getting out of your office and listening to what the employees are saying," says Richard M. Furlaud, chairman of Squibb Corp. "You listen for optimism, or you listen for a sense of pessimism which may be about something unreported to you. You listen for that quiet panic that can develop when some operation —or some individual—is not doing as well as the official reports would indicate."

Furlaud likes to keep his antennae beamed so as to pick up any changes in staff morale. He wants to be able to spot any decline in morale early, when there's time to get at the root of the problem before profits start to suffer. Why not wait for Squibb's formal reporting system to turn up the problem? Because, Furlaud says, it may take too long.

Chief executives' efforts to stay in touch support the bottom line in another way: by making sure that orders from the top are reaching the troops intact. Once again, Squibb's articulate Mr. Furlaud: "You want to be sure that your objectives are understood. The company has goals, and your objective is to meet those goals. But you don't want to do it by doing anything illegal or immoral. Top management should make sure that guys down the line know what the company's goals are."

DINING OUT ON THE ROAD

One chief executive who works hard and enthusiastically at talking with executives down the line is W. Michael Blumenthal, former professor of economics at Princeton, former Assistant Secretary of State, and now chairman of Bendix Corp. "You can't operate successfully in any organization if you're cut off from your people," says Blumenthal. "You've got to reach out toward them—out beyond the tight little group you work with daily—and let them know they can reach you when they feel they have to."

Blumenthal, who happens to be naturally ebullient and informal, has developed a variety of techniques for giving the troops at Bendix more access to the chief executive. Whenever he's in one of the hundred or so cities in which Bendix operates, Blumenthal makes certain to schedule lunches and dinners with divisional executives at all levels. "The conversations jump all over the place," he says. "One minute we're talking Bendix business, the next minute we're talking politics. Everybody learns."

LOOKING OVER THE OFFICE

When he's at company headquarters in Southfield, Michigan, Blumenthal works hard at staying in touch with lower-level executives. For example, when he writes a memorandum to someone in the same building, Blumenthal likes to deliver the memo himself. Usually, when he finds the recipient in his office, the chairman invites himself in for a chat. "It's a nice way to stay in touch," he explains cheerfully. "I like to see where a guy works—you know, what his desk looks like, and so on. It kind of rounds out my picture of the guy."

Blumenthal says that the actual content of the chat is apt to be of no great import on these occasions. Sometimes the conversation is quite unrelated to business; it may focus on the subordinate's personal life—e.g., his teenage son is just out of high school and trying to decide whether to start college or work for a year.

Sometimes, alternatively, the employee takes advantage of his few minutes with the chairman to tip him off to something that's going on in the company. "You'd be amazed how often I pick up information this way," says Blumenthal. "It's rarely anything earth-shattering. But it's often something I like to know about, something that gives me a feeling for what's going on. . . ."

The chairman of Pfizer Corp., Edmund T. Pratt Jr., has a different way of making off-hours contact. A lifelong tennis buff, Pratt noticed a few years ago that a number of Pfizer's other executives had also begun to play. So he rented time on one of Manhattan's indoor tennis courts, and invited company executives to use it during the reserved evening hours. A round-robin schedule was developed so that everyone, including Pratt, got to play with everyone else.

"Playing tennis with my people gives me a terrific opportunity to find out what's on their minds," Pratt says. "You'd be surprised at how much I learn. Changing in the locker room, or sitting around with the guys afterward, makes for a better atmosphere than the office. Besides, we all need the exercise."

Southland Corp. developed one effective way for the boss to communicate with his subordinates—though it wasn't really the boss's idea. When the executive vice president proposed that an executives' bar and lounge be opened on the top floor of the company's Dallas headquarters building, President Jere W. Thompson was against it at first. "I just didn't see the need for it," he recalls.

But the executive vice president kept pushing, and finally Thompson said to go ahead and build the thing. "It's great," he says now. "I'm a real strong believer in it. The lounge helps us get to know our people individually. Of course, you still have to balance your knowledge of the people against the usual reports of performance. But it gives us another view of the man. . . ."

A WORD WITH THE DESIGNER

Thompson's efforts to stay in touch with Southland's executives go beyond his biweekly foray into the company lounge. He also holds a two-hour, no-agenda staff meeting every other Monday morning to which about fifteen people are invited. Thompson believes these meetings provide a good forum for executives to say whatever is on their minds, about business in general, the company, or the work they're doing. It's also a good chance for everyone to gossip a little.

Meetings without agendas are also used by Richard B. Loynd, president of Eltra Corp., a New York-based producer of electrical products. Once a month he calls together about fifteen members of the headquarters staff (there are about fifty in all), ranging in rank from vice presidents to junior members of the financial department; secretaries are also included. Out-of-town Eltra executives who happen to be in New York are also invited. Loynd rotates the participants so that everybody gets a chance to attend at least a few times a year.

Communicating with subordinates is an especially difficult task for an executive who has not been promoted from within the company, but who has been brought in from outside. When Anthony J. A. Bryan arrived in Houston to become president of Cameron Iron Works two years ago (after a twenty-five-year career with Monsanto), he worked hard at getting acquainted with the Cameron staff. He scheduled a series of breakfasts and lunches at a restaurant near the company's headquarters, and over a period of fifteen months ate and spoke with more than 2,000 of Cameron's 4,500 Houston employees—including line foremen, engineers, and secretaries, as well as top managers. He told them a little about himself, about his plans for Cameron, and about his personal style of operation. Then he answered questions.

A STRANGER IN THE NIGHT

During the same period, Bryan made constant forays out of his own office and down to Cameron's production areas. Employees say that it was not unusual for them to look up from their work, even during the late night shifts, to see a slim, bespectacled stranger in a dark suit and a hard hat waiting patiently for a chance to shake their hands. Once, before he had an opportunity to introduce himself, the stranger was ordered to leave a restricted area.

Bryan told all of Cameron's employees that their president was available whenever they wanted to speak with him. He meant it, which is fortunate, because many Cameron workers took him at his word. At least twice a week, nowadays, an employee comes up to Bryan's office for a chat with the boss. Sometimes the man has a problem that isn't being satisfactorily handled via the usual channels. Sometimes he has a suggestion to offer, and doesn't quite know whom he should be telling about it. Not long ago an employee came to Bryan with a proposal for a special metal clamp he thought would increase the durability of the safety shoes workers must wear.

Bryan believes the time he puts in talking with company employees is extremely useful. "If one man comes in here with a personal problem of some sort, it's a good bet we have some other people with the same problem. By getting involved in one case, I learn how well, or how poorly, our regular machinery is equipped to deal with it. And our employees get to feel that their ideas, their own contributions to the company's productivity, matter to management."

THE CHAIRMAN TAKES THE LOCAL

Many chief executives have a variety of techniques for exposing themselves, more or less randomly, to the troops. Robert T. Quittmeyer, president of Amstar, leaves about two lunch hours a week unscheduled. On those days he goes to the company cafeteria and sits down with any group of employees, executive or clerical, whose table has an empty chair. Fletcher Byrom, the chairman of Koppers Co., has made it a practice always to take the local elevator, rather than the express, to and from his fifteenth-floor office "on the chance that someone will want to say something to me when he sees me."

Chief executives do a lot of traveling, and many of them are keenly aware of the opportunities to get to know other executives on trips. Ian MacGregor, chairman of AMAX Inc., has a custom of taking along one or two junior executives when he travels on business. "Two days in a plane going to Johannesburg," says MacGregor, "and you get to know a man pretty well."

Obviously, it is possible for chief executives to "overcommunicate." There are situations in which a boss who thinks he's just being friendly can leave a subordinate feeling that he's being watched or that his privacy is being invaded. Still, the desire to be communicated with is a powerful one, and the greater risks for morale would appear to be on the side of seeming unfriendly.

And, of course, the boss learns a lot by being "friendly." "You must discipline yourself to do these things," says Anthony Bryan. "If not, your isolation increases. You may think you know what you're doing, but you don't test yourself sufficiently. That's dangerous."

Campus Politico

Doris Kearns

From the beginning at San Marcos College (later Southwestern Texas State Teachers College), Johnson set out to win the friendship and respect of those people who would assist his rise within the community which composed San Marcos. Most obvious was the president of the college, Cecil Evans, whose favor would have a multiplier effect with the faculty and student body. But Johnson was not alone in the desire to have a special relationship with Evans. "I knew," Johnson later said, "there was only one way to get to know Evans and that was to work for him directly." He became special assistant to the president's personal secretary.

As special assistant, Johnson's assigned job was simply to carry messages from the president to the department heads and occasionally to other faculty members. Johnson saw that the rather limited function of messenger had possibilities for expansion; for example, encouraging recipients of the messages to transmit their own communications through him. He occupied a desk in the president's outer office, where he took it upon himself to announce the arrival of visitors. These added services evolved from a helpful convenience into an aspect of the normal process of presidential business. The messenger had become an appointments secretary, and, in time, faculty members came to think of Johnson as a funnel to the president. Using a technique which was later to serve him in achieving mastery over the Congress, Johnson turned a rather insubstantial service into a process through which power was exercised. By redefining the process, he had given power to himself.

Evans eventually broadened Johnson's responsibilities to include handling his political correspondence and preparing his reports for the

Abridged and adapted from "Lyndon Johnson and the American Dream" by Doris Kearns, as it appeared in *The Atlantic Monthly*. Copyright © 1976 by Doris Kearns. Reprinted by permission of Harper & Row, Publishers, Inc., and Andre Deutsch, Ltd., Publishers.

state agencies with jurisdiction over the college and its appropriations. The student was quick to explain that his father had been a member of the state legislature (from 1905 to 1909, and from 1918 to 1925), and Lyndon had often accompanied him to Austin where he had gained some familiarity with the workings of the legislature and the personalities of its leaders. This claim might have sounded almost ludicrous had it not come from someone who already must have seemed an inordinately political creature. Soon Johnson was accompanying Evans on his trips to the state capital in Austin, and, before long, Evans came to rely upon his young apprentice for political counsel. For Johnson was clearly at home in the state legislature; whether sitting in a committee room during hearings or standing on the floor talking with representatives, he could, in later reports to Evans, capture the mood of individual legislators and the legislative body with entertaining accuracy. The older man, on whose favor Johnson depended, now relied on him, or at least found him useful.

The world of San Marcos accommodated Lyndon Johnson's gifts. If some found him tiresome, and even his friends admitted that he was difficult, they were nonetheless bedazzled by his vitality, guile, and endurance, his powers of divination, and ability to appeal to the core interests of other people. In two years, he became a campus politician, a prizewinning debater, an honors student, and the editor of the college *Star*.

Boss: Richard J. Daley of Chicago
Mike Royko

If there is a council meeting, everybody marches downstairs at a few minutes before ten. Bush and the department heads and personal aides form a proud parade. The meeting begins when the seat of the mayor's pants touches the council president's chair, placed beneath the great seal of the city of Chicago and above the heads of the aldermen, who sit in a semi-bowl auditorium.

It is his council, and in all the years it has never once defied him as a body. Keane manages it for him, and most of its members do what they are told. In other eras, the aldermen ran the city and plundered it. In

From *Boss: Richard J. Daley of Chicago* by Mike Royko. Copyright © 1971 by Mike Royko. Reprinted by permission of the publishers, E. P. Dutton & Co., Inc.

his boyhood they were so constantly on the prowl that they were known as "the Gray Wolves." His council is known as "the Rubber Stamp."

He looks down at them, bestowing a nod or a benign smile on a few favorites, and they smile back gratefully. He seldom nods or smiles at the small minority of white and black independents. The independents anger him more than the Republicans do, because they accuse him of racism, fascism, and of being a dictator. The Republicans bluster about loafing payrollers, crumbling gutters, inflated budgets—traditional, comfortable accusations that don't stir the blood.

That is what Keane is for. When the minority goes on the attack, Keane himself, or one of the administration aldermen he has groomed for the purpose, will rise and answer the criticism by shouting that the critic is a fool, a hypocrite, ignorant, and misguided. Until his death, one alderman could be expected to leap to his feet at every meeting and cry, "God bless our mayor, the greatest mayor in the world."

But sometimes Keane and his trained orators can't shout down the minority, so Daley has to do it himself. If provoked, he'll break into a rambling, ranting speech, waving his arms, shaking his fists, defending his judgment, defending his administration, always with the familiar "It is easy to criticize . . . to find fault . . . but where are your programs . . . where are your ideas . . ."

If that doesn't shut off the critics, he will declare them to be out of order, threaten to have the sergeant at arms force them into their seats, and invoke *Robert's Rules of Order*, which, in the heat of debate, he once described as "the greatest book ever written."

All else failing, he will look toward a glass booth above the spectator's balcony and make a gesture known only to the man in the booth who operates the sound system that controls the microphones on each alderman's desk. The man in the booth will touch a switch and the offending critic's microphone will go dead and stay dead until he sinks into his chair and closes his mouth.

The meetings are seldom peaceful and orderly. The slightest criticism touches off shrill rebuttal, leading to louder criticism and finally an embarrassingly wild and vicious free-for-all. It can't be true, because Daley is a man who speaks highly of law and order, but sometimes it appears that he enjoys the chaos, and he seldom moves to end it until it has raged out of control.

Every word of criticism must be answered, every complaint must be disproved, every insult must be returned in kind. He doesn't take anything from anybody. While Daley was mediating negotiations between white trade unions and black groups who wanted the unions to accept blacks, a young militant angrily rejected one of his suggestions and concluded, "Up your ass!" Daley leaped to his feet and answered, "And up yours too." Would John Lindsay have become so involved?

Independent aldermen have been known to come up with a good

idea, such as providing food for the city's hungry, or starting day-care centers for children of ghetto women who want to work; Daley will acknowledge it, but in his own way. He'll let Keane appropriate the idea and rewrite and resubmit it as an administration measure. That way, the independent has the satisfaction of seeing his idea reach fruition and the administration has more glory. But most of the independents' proposals are sent to a special subcommittee that exists solely to allow their unwelcome ideas to die.

The council meetings seldom last beyond the lunch hour. Aldermen have much to do. Many are lawyers and have thriving practices, because Chicagoans know that a dumb lawyer who is an alderman can often perform greater legal miracles than a smart lawyer who isn't. . . .

The afternoon work moves with never a minute wasted. The engineers and planners come with their reports on public works projects. Something is always being built, concrete being poured, steel being riveted, contractors being enriched.

"When will it be completed?" he asks.

"Early February."

"It would be a good thing for the people if it could be completed by the end of October."

The engineers say it can be done, but it will mean putting on extra shifts, night work, overtime pay, a much higher cost than was planned.

"It would be a good thing for the people if it could be completed by the end of October."

Of course it would be a good thing for the people. It would also be a good thing for the Democratic candidates who are seeking election in early November to go out and cut a ribbon for a new expressway or a water filtration plant or, if nothing else is handy, another wing at the O'Hare terminal. What ribbons do their opponents cut?

The engineers and planners understand, and they set about getting it finished by October.

On a good afternoon, there will be no neighborhood organizations to see him, because if they get to Daley, it means they have been up the ladder of government and nobody has been able to solve their problem. And that usually means a conflict between the people and somebody else, such as a politician or a business, whom his aides don't want to ruffle. There are many things his department heads can't do. They can't cross swords with ward bosses or politically heavy businessmen. They can't make important decisions. Some can't even make petty decisions. He runs City Hall like a small family business and keeps everybody on a short rein. They do only that which they know is safe and that which he tells them to do. So many things that should logically be solved several rungs below finally come to him.

Because of this, he has many requests from neighborhood people.

And when a group is admitted to his office, most of them nervous and wide-eyed, he knows who they are, their leaders, their strength in the community. They have already been checked out by somebody. He must know everything. He doesn't like to be surprised. Just as he knows the name of every new worker, he must know what is going on in the various city offices. If the head of the office doesn't tell him, he has somebody there who will. In the office of other elected officials, he has trusted persons who will keep him informed. Out in the neighborhoods his precinct captains are reporting to the ward committeemen, and they in turn are reporting to him.

His police department's intelligence-gathering division gets bigger and bigger, its network of infiltrators, informers, and spies creating massive files on dissenters, street gangs, political enemies, newsmen, radicals, liberals, and anybody else who might be working against him. If one of his aides or handpicked officeholders is shacking up with a woman, he will know it. And if that man is married and a Catholic, his political career will wither and die. That is the greatest sin of all. You can make money under the table and move ahead, but you are forbidden to make secretaries under the sheets. He has dumped several party members for violating his personal moral standards. If something is leaked to the press, the bigmouth will be tracked down and punished. Scandals aren't public scandals if you get there before your enemies do.

So when the people come in, he knows what they want and whether it is possible. Not that it means they will get it. That often depends on how they act.

He will come out from behind his desk all smiles and handshakes and charm. Then he returns to his chair and sits very straight, hands folded on his immaculate desk, serious and attentive. To one side will be somebody from the appropriate city department.

Now it's up to the group. If they are respectful, he will express sympathy, ask encouraging questions, and finally tell them that everything possible will be done. And after they leave, he may say, "Take care of it." With that command, the royal seal, anything is possible, anybody's toes can be stepped on.

But if they are pushy, antagonistic, demanding instead of imploring, or bold enough to be critical of him, to tell him how he should do his job, to blame him for their problem, he will rub his hands together, harder and harder. In a long, difficult meeting, his hands will get raw. His voice gets lower, softer, and the corners of his mouth will turn down. At this point, those who know him will back off. They know what's next. But the unfamiliar, the militant, will mistake his lowered voice and nervousness for weakness. Then he'll blow, and it comes in a frantic roar:

"I want *you* to tell *me* what to do. *You* come up with the answers. *You* come up with the program. Are we perfect? Are *you* perfect? We all make mistakes. We all have faults. It's easy to criticize. It's easy to find fault. But *you* tell me what to do. This problem is all over the city. We didn't create these problems. We don't want them. But we are doing what we can. *You* tell me how to solve them. *You* give me a program." All of which leaves the petitioners dumb, since most people don't walk around with urban programs in their pockets. It can also leave them right back where they started.

They leave and the favor seekers come in. Half of the people he sees want a favor. They plead for promotions, something for their sons, a chance to do some business with the city, to get somebody in City Hall off their backs, a chance to return from political exile, a boon. They won't get an answer right there and then. It will be considered and he'll let them know. Later, sometimes much later, when he has considered the alternatives and the benefits, word will get back to them. Yes or no. Success or failure. Life or death.

Some jobseekers come directly to him. Complete outsiders, meaning those with with no family or political connections, will be sent to see their ward committeemen. That is protocol, and that is what he did to the tall young black man who came to see him a few years ago, bearing a letter from the governor of North Carolina, who wrote that the young black man was a rising political prospect in his state. Daley told him to see his ward committeeman, and if he did some precinct work, rang doorbells, hustled up some votes, there might be a government job for him. Maybe something like taking coins in a tollway booth. The Rev. Jesse Jackson, now the city's leading black civil rights leader, still hasn't stopped smarting over that.

Others come asking him to resolve a problem. He is the city's leading labor mediator and has prevented the kind of strikes that have crippled New York. His father was a union man, and he comes from a union neighborhood, and many of the union leaders were his boyhood friends. He knows what they want. And if it is in the city's treasury, they will get it. If it isn't there, he'll promise to find it. He has ended a teachers' strike by promising that the state legislature would find funds for them, which surprised the Republicans in Springfield, as well as put them on the spot. He is an effective mediator with the management side of labor disputes, because they respect his judgment, and because there are few industries that do not need some favors from City Hall. . . .

The Wreck of the Penn Central

Joseph R. Daughen
Peter Binzen

On Merger Day, February 1, 1968, three kinds of internal problems confronted the Penn Central: operational, financial and "people." These problems were interrelated, but of the three the most disruptive were the "people" problems.

When two railroads that had been bitter rivals for 100 years combined, human conflicts were inevitable. Yet they were never dealt with openly and honestly. They weren't even anticipated. One could read 40,000 pages of merger testimony before the ICC without encountering a hint of impending trouble in meshing "red" PRR people with "green" Central people.[1] Even after the collapse, Stuart Saunders considered reports of red-green feuding "greatly exaggerated." The reports, if anything, were understated. The differences were excruciatingly real. And the failure of Saunders, Alfred Perlman and David Bevan to work as a team and to inspire their subordinates to do so hastened Penn Central's collapse.

James Symes to the contrary, the PRR and Central were not like "two peas in a pod." In operating style, in marketing philosophy, in personnel, they differed sharply. The Pennsylvania, stolid, steady and traditional, carried ore over mountains. It was "volume oriented," and its operations were highly decentralized. It generally promoted from within its own ranks. The Central was smaller, scrappier, hungrier, more inclined to abandon the book and innovate. Perlman once said: "After you've done a thing the same way for two years, look it over carefully. After five years, look at it with suspicion. After ten years, throw it away and start all over again." The Central carried manufactured goods along its "water-level route." It was profit oriented and centralized. PRR critics conveyed the impression that the Central was run "out of Al Perlman's hat." But Perlman often went outside the company for promising executive talent.

In addition to major stylistic differences between the two rival railroads there were many minor operational ones. The Central, for example, used in-cab locomotive signals; the Pennsylvania used visual signals along its right-of-way. Central locomotives came equipped with cushioned armrests for engineers; Pennsylvania locomotives didn't. (Central engineers refused to operate PRR locomotives until the armrests were installed.) The two railroads even used different kinds of railroad spikes. And then there were the incompatible computers . . .

Not one of these operational problems was insuperable. But the problem of incompatible executives proved to be just that. "The most difficult part of the merger," William A. Lashley, Penn Central's perceptive vice president for public relations and advertising, said in an interview nine months before the bankruptcy, "is the human personality. You can combine tracks and stations but getting people together is something else." Another executive said it was "human nature" for the reds and the greens to fight it out. "Not that you'll find blood an inch thick on the floor. It's all been fairly gentlemanly. But I don't see the rivalry as having lessened at all lately. It's surprisingly deeprooted in the human psyche." And he was talking at a point seventeen months after the merger began. . . .

On his appointment as Pennsylvania Railroad board chairman in 1963, Stuart T. Saunders had moved to the Main Line. Where else? After virtually creating the Main Line in the 1870's and eighties, the PRR had more or less required its presidents, says Nathaniel Burt, the social historian, to "plunk their estates out there." Whether under duress or not and whether or not they rode the renowned Paoli Local commuter trains to work—Saunders never did—all PRR chief executives in the twentieth century lived in Philadelphia's plush western suburbs. The trains didn't always run on time—after World War II the service got plain awful—but a real estate mystique continued to hang over those tracks. "Nothing was so holy," rhymed Christopher Morley, "as the local to Paoli." And out in Oklahoma, people named three towns after the Main Line stations of Ardmore, Wynnewood and Wayne. . . .

Club-conscious Proper Philadelphia warmly welcomed Stuart Saunders. Within a few weeks of his arrival he was guest of honor at a gourmet dinner given by—and cooked by—members of the Rabbit, a very exclusive gentlemen's cooking club. Saunders quickly joined the Merion Cricket Club, the Racquet Club and the Gulph Mills Golf Club, as well as Merion Golf, and in two years he was taken into the city's most prestigious club, the Philadelphia Club. The Philadelphia Club, which claims to be the oldest private men's club in the country (founded in 1834), generally limits its membership to Old Philadelphians with impeccable social credentials and others who, over a period of years, have made major contributions to the community. While Saunders' early admission might not impress New Yorkers or Chicagoans, Proper Philadelphians considered it quite a feat. Even some eminently qualified citizens long resident in Philadelphia have had the devil of a time getting into this "Gibraltar of Social Order. . . ."[2]

The fact was that Saunders, both personally and professionally, had much to recommend him to the best clubs. After hours, he enjoyed martinis, fine wines, dancing (although his one social setback came when a select "Dancing Class" of couples at the Gulph Mills Golf Club blackballed him), poker (often with publisher Walter Annenberg) and the company of women. The "right people" found him a most attractive companion. But if he played hard he also worked hard. In the late 1960's, he drove Pennsylvania Railroad stock up, up, up, and in three years boosted its annual dividend payments from $6.8 million to nearly $32 million. For his fellow club members as well as for "widows and orphans" and Pennsylvania Railroad stockholders generally, these results meant money in the bank—literally. It was to put money in their banks and in their personal accounts that the bankers and other Establishment representatives on the PRR's board recruited Saunders in the first place. And for quite a while the short, bald, bouncy man in the vest with the watch chain of gold and the cigarette holder produced remarkable results—while also joining George and Peggy Cheston (he being president of the Philadelphia Art Museum board and she an heiress to the Dodge millions) at the opera, keeping up his memberships in Pittsburgh's Duquesne Club, New York's Links and Washington's Metropolitan Club, and engaging in cross-country high-stake poker with Walter Annenberg, John (Jackie) Dorrance of Campbell Soup and PRR's board, and a few other well-placed cronies.

With all that, Saunders somehow found time for outside directorships—U.S. Steel, Chase Manhattan Bank, Bell Telephone Company of Pennsylvania, First Pennsylvania Banking and Trust Company, among many others—and for corporate good works. He served on the high-level Business Council, the John F. Kennedy Library Corporation and the Philadelphia Bicentennial Commission. He advised President Lyndon B. Johnson on labor-management policy. He was vice chairman of the National Coal Policy Conference and Philadelphia metropolitan area chairman of the National Alliance of Businessmen. He was also chairman of the board of trustees at his alma mater, Roanoke College, in Virginia. And back home in Ardmore, the *Essays of Montaigne* was on his library shelf.

Small wonder that the *Saturday Review*, after a national poll of 300 business leaders, economists, business writers and others, picked Saunders as its "Businessman of the Year" for 1968. It hailed him as a hard-nosed, profits-oriented executive and as a railroad innovator. The PRR's consolidated earnings had tripled—from $31 million to $90 million—in Saunders' first three years in Philadelphia, said *SR*, and the railroad had spent nearly $600 million on capital improvements. *Saturday Review* termed Saunders "the best-known innovator and initiator of the modern railroad merger movement." It credited him with launching "a program of diversification to free the company from the cyclical swings and low rate of return, which unfortunately characterize the railroad industry."[3]

Despite all the publicity given Saunders, the PRR's record in the five years before the merger was almost identical to that of Alfred E. Perlman's New York Central. Penn Central reports to the ICC show that between 1963–1967 the PRR lost a total of $32.9 million from rail operations while the Central lost $48.8 million. From nonrail operations in that five-year period the Central made $175.6 million to the Pennsylvania's $164.3 million. Overall, the Pennsylvania showed earnings of $131.4 million and the Central $126.8 million, or just $4.6 million less. The PRR's capital spending for railroad improvements was more than double that of the Central, and its debt retirement was almost twice as great. Since the PRR was half again as large as the Central, these results were not far out of line.

But if the performances of Saunders' railroad and Perlman's railroad were not very different, the contrasts between the men themselves were great. "Personally, I like Perlman," Saunders was to say after the Penn Central's collapse. "I really do. And he's got a lovely wife. She's a nice woman. A real lady. And he's got nice children. I like Perlman. I really do."

Saunders may have liked Perlman but they weren't friends, really. They were never close. Perlman was, in the view of PRR executives, "a complicated fellow." Certainly, he was a rarity—a Jew who made it to the top in the railroad industry. Before the merger the highest-ranked Jew in the 60,000-employee Pennsylvania Railroad was an accountant. Roman Catholics also were notably absent from its upper echelons. The Central had a broader ethnic mix. An Irish executive at the Central was said to have complained: "I was brought up to hate Protestants and the Pennsylvania Railroad. After this [merger], I've got to love them both."[4]

Perlman's railroad experience differed sharply from Saunders'. Saunders had spent most of his career with the prosperous N&W. Perlman worked the other side of the tracks. In testimony in Washington after the bankruptcy, Perlman put it this way:

> I went through the depression of the 1930's, and all my experience has been with railroads that were in trouble. Mr. Saunders came from one of the wealthiest railroads in the country and his outlook on these railroad problems may be entirely different from mine. A lot of people say, "Well, here the two men have different philosophies." Well, sure, a man that comes from one side of the tracks may have a different philosophy than the other. I have always had to help out, every time a railroad got into trouble . . .This has been my whole experience. Mr. Saunders had an entirely different experience, you see. So we looked at things from different ways.

It seems clear that Perlman and Saunders were simply on different wavelengths. This was true professionally and it was also true socially. New York society was neither as compact nor as homogeneous as Philadelphia's but, in any event, Alfred Edward Perlman wasn't a part of it. He and other New York Central executives lived in posh Westchester County but they didn't "occupy" it as PRR executives did the Main Line. Few Central men had had time to sink their roots as deeply in the New York area as many PRR men had sunk theirs in Philadelphia. The Minnesota-born Perlman had moved around a good deal and J. R. Sullivan, his marketing vice president, to cite one example, had moved twenty-four times in his first thirty years as a railroader. (His twenty-fifth move was to Wayne, Pennsylvania, after the merger.)

Perlman's thirty lines (compared to Saunders' fifty-three) in the 1970 *Who's Who* listed membership in four clubs: the M.I.T. Club, the Economic Club of New York, the Sky Club (a businessmen's luncheon club in New York's Pan Am Building) and the Westchester Country Club. He wasn't a joiner. "My father," said Lee Perlman, one of Perlman's three children, a partner in a Philadelphia public-relations firm, "is not a big socialite. He liked to stay around home by the pool. He joined the Westchester Country Club—finally—when he took up golf. They wanted to put him on the [club's] board of directors but he wouldn't do it."

Perlman didn't pal around with New York's bluebloods but, as a railroad executive, he had close and continuing relations with some of the leaders of corporate finance. They never awed him. When he and Robert R. Young once disagreed on a major policy issue at the Central, Perlman recalled, "I put on my hat and coat and walked to the door." Whereupon his boss called him back and made him a director.

At an ICC hearing many years ago, Perlman was asked to identify A. P. Kirby, who was then on the Central's board. "Mr. A. P. Kirby," said Perlman, "is an industrialist or a financier or whatever the heck you want to call him. I don't know, he has got a lot of money anyway."

He was asked about another wealthy Central director, John Murchison, son of Clint, the late Texas oil tycoon. To commissioners who were trying to decide whether or not the PRR and Central should be merged, Perlman proceeded to tick off John Murchison's social graces: "He is a good fisherman. I have hunted with him. He is a good shot. He has a very nice-looking wife. He dances well." One can't imagine Saunders—or many executives—publicly discussing individual board members so flippantly.

At still another point, Perlman was asked if it were true that while heading the Central he was also president of a dozen or more affiliated railroads. He said it was. Each railroad was named; most were Toonerville trolley lines like the Indiana Harbor Belt Railroad Company and the Peoria and Eastern. The interrogation bored Perlman.

Q: You are president and director of the Troy Union Railroad?
PERLMAN: That is right. I don't know whether that is defunct yet, but I guess I am.

Not that Perlman was self-effacing or overly modest. Neither his friends nor his detractors accused him of that. "A man of sublime self-confidence." "Hard-headed." "A very personable, cultured, intelligent, persuasive guy of whom a lot of people are awfully afraid." "A fearsome antagonist." "Temperamental." "He's got human frailties." "His sarcasm slices like a frozen scalpel. . . ."

Not until Merger Day was the Penn Central's organization chart made public. Then a company press release identified the men chosen for the top jobs and gave their previous railroad affiliation. It read as though the red and green were neatly dovetailed. Beneath Saunders, Perlman and Bevan were three executive vice presidents—two from the old PRR and one from the Central—and two senior vice presidents—one from each of the former rivals. Beneath these officers were twenty vice presidents—eleven from the PRR and nine from the Central. Throughout the organization reds and greens seemed intermingled. An ex-PRR man, Richard Davis, was named Perlman's personal secretary in New York and an ex-Central man, Robert Lawson, was chosen as head of Penn Central's Philadelphia division. Of the nine newly named general managers, five were from the Pennsylvania and four from the Central. At Cleveland and Chicago, green (Central) assistants worked under red (PRR) general managers. At Indianapolis and Detroit, the reverse was true, with red assistants to green GMs.

In theory, this meshing of staff was fine. But an artist who mixes red and green gets brown. And that's what the corporate artists who blended Central's green and Pennsylvania's red got—a brownish, gooey mess. It was a mixture that pleased no one. Perlman's reaction has been widely publicized. To him, the Penn Central amalgamation "was not a merger, it was a [PRR] takeover." What is less well known is that the new table of organization enraged David Bevan. Actually, Bevan had been unhappy for a long time. He had hoped to succeed Symes as board chairman of the PRR. When the selection of Saunders was announced in 1963, Bevan threatened to resign. He made such a fuss that the press release announcing Saunder's appointment was delayed.

Even Bevan's foes—and they are legion—concede that he had done an impressive job tidying up the PRR's chaotic financial structure in the 1950's and reducing its debt. A graduate of Haverford College and the Harvard Business School, he had been junior officer of a Philadelphia bank and then treasurer of the New York Life Insurance Company before being named vice president-finance of the PRR in 1951. Under his direction, the railroad's debt was cut from $765 million in 1952 to $531 million in 1964. The number of subsidiary and affiliated companies was cut from 171 to a low of eighty-nine. Because of diversification, the number rose to 102 by 1968 and the merger itself brought in another eighty-four companies, making a new high of 186, but Bevan had begun reducing that total, too. With Bevan putting a brake on spending of all kinds, the PRR employment force tumbled from 137,765 in 1951 to 67,242 ten years later. All of these developments, coupled with what was for quite a while an extremely successful diversification program, suggested that Bevan, as chief financial officer of a railroad that didn't really want to run railroad trains, knew his job and did it well. And he also served as director and finance committee chairman of Saunders' Norfolk & Western, from 1952–1964.

But Bevan had this problem: Outside his own staff, nobody seemed to like him. "Very bright, egocentric, very difficult to work for, power hungry" is the way one PRR officer described Bevan. Another said: "He is his own worst enemy. He has an unfortunate manner. He's a centipede for putting his foot in his mouth." The head of one of Philadelphia's top-drawer banks rated Stuart Saunders "a genius" in putting the merger together and a man whom "I would hire tomorrow and give him the next job to mine." But for Bevan, this banker had nothing but contempt. "The favorite villain in the banking community," he said after the Penn Central's bankruptcy, "is Bevan."

Bevan and Saunders never seemed to have gotten along. Though their homes were only a few miles apart they never entertained one another. And at the office their relations were correct but cool. Bevan had less authority under Saunders than he had enjoyed under Symes. Tension between the two mounted as the merger time approached. "It was common talk before the merger," said a Saunders supporter, "that there were two Pennsylvania Railroads. There was Bevan's railroad and there was our railroad. Bevan wouldn't let his men talk to officers of other [PRR] departments."

Whatever Saunders may have thought of Bevan before the merger, he took no overt action against him. And in the merger shuffle Bevan retained his high-salaried post as finance committee chairman. But Bevan's wings were clipped. He'd been a director of the PRR; he was left off the twenty-five member merged board of directors. This was a shattering blow to a proud man. And it created an anomalous situation: Penn Central's finance committee consisted of seven members, six of whom were members of the policy-making board of directors. The seventh was not a director—yet he was the committee chairman. Penn Central's news release made no mention of the decision to drop

Bevan from the board. Instead, it played up his appointment to the finance committee chairmanship. But Bevan knew very well that his wings had been clipped. And he resented it. Furthermore, he resented the entire organization chart. He had three vice presidents reporting to him. But Perlman had ten—three executive vice presidents, two senior vice presidents, five vice presidents. And Bevan lost responsibility for the merged railroad's critical accounting system. It was turned over to a former Central man.

In an interview early in 1971, Bevan poured out his bitterness over the organizational setup:

> Perlman had ten people reporting to him, far too many. And seven of them were New York Central men. They gave Perlman Budget Administration, Data Processing, Accounting, Taxes and Insurance. I got Accounting in 1958 [with the PRR] and had it until the time of the merger.

> Practically everything was taken away from me. I said, "The hell with this." I called Dick Mellon, our senior director, and said, "I don't want anything, I can't live with this, I want out." He said, "The whole thing may blow up if you walk out. You've got an obligation to the stockholders and to the company." This was in January 1968, a couple of weeks before the merger. Mellon said he had been up till four o'clock that morning working on the organization chart. He said, "I want to ask you as a personal favor, and I've never asked you for anything, to stay on, grit your teeth and bear. I will change everything I can." He did change some things, but then he got sick.[5] I wasn't even going to have charge of the bank account.

Bevan left no doubt that the celebrated red-green feuding was actually a tricolor—red, green and Bevan. He attacked both Perlman and Saunders with equal ferocity.

> Perlman could ride around a small railroad like the D&RGW [Denver & Rio Grande Western] and keep on top of things. He wanted accounting done his way, not our way. I wanted an income budget where we would know what was coming in and where it was going. He said, "You can't run a railroad on an income budget." His budget was just a bunch of statistics. He had no budget.[6] He put his budget chief in over my budget chief. He put Mike Flannery,[7] a damn good operating guy, in charge of data processing. He didn't know a damn thing about it . . . We lost ten or twelve of the best young guys we had. They didn't want to work under Perlman or under people they thought were inferior, and they were.

> All Perlman wanted to do was build classification yards. He spent money like it was going out of style. At a meeting in June 1969, he was madder than hell. "I'm not a harbinger of gloom," he said. I

remember that phrase, "harbinger of gloom." "I don't care if we lose X dollars this year and X dollars next year. I'm building for the future."

On the subject of Saunders, Bevan had this to say:

When Symes went out the railroad was in very sound condition. Symes took my advice on financial matters. After Saunders came in . . . (Bevan shook his head.) Saunders said, "As soon as the merger takes place, I'll be the boss." But he never exercised authority. He seemed to be afraid of Perlman. Some of us thought he wanted to be in a position to say, "I'm not an operating man," if anything went wrong.

One board member came up to me and wanted to know what was going on. I told him Accounting and Budget Administration had been taken away from me. He said, "Well, they didn't let the word back to the board. The board didn't know anything about it." I said the board voted on it at the first meeting and he was there and had voted on it.

I had no control over expenditures. At every board meeting, I said, "Cash is tight, we've stretched this rubber band as far as it will stretch." In June 1969 I submitted my resignation to Saunders. I said, "You've got to accept it." Finally, Saunders got nervous. He said he wanted me back on the board. I said I wanted no part of it. I was electing early retirement and I wanted to be out no later than March 1, 1970. I said I would leave at the convenience of the board, that I would not embarrass anybody . . .

Saunders said, "You can't do this. You've got a responsibility to the banks and to the stockholders. You're the best man we've got." You'd never know we had a disagreement, the way he talked. He said he wanted me to keep it [the job] until after he got back from Europe. He was going on vacation. When he came back from Europe, he asked me to go on the board and I said, no. He went through an intermediary, a friend of mine, and my friend said, "Won't you at least talk to Stuart?" I said okay. Saunders said, "We've got to get a new president and I want you to help me find one. . . ." He said, "What do you want in compensation?" I said I didn't want to talk about that, that wasn't my aim in life. I helped him look for a new president. I got involved in that. Some of the directors were after me to stay. One director said, "If you walk out, the banks walk in."

Bevan never did walk out; he was pushed out, along with Perlman and Saunders. But the Penn Central tragedy is much like *Rashomon*; each witness has a different view of what happened. Who was running the railroad? Saunders is firm on this point. He told the subcommittee on surface transportation of the Senate Commerce Committee:

When Mr. Perlman was president, he was in charge of railroad operations and he had full authority. He may not agree completely with this, but he was given complete responsibility.

Saunders also told us:

I have the highest regard for Mr. Perlman and he had complete responsibility for running the railroad. That was his job and I believe in giving responsibility. He had authority . . . Never once was he denied any authority of any consequence. I can't recall a single instance where he was ever turned down.

We never had any disagreements to my knowledge about any officer. I gave no consideration, and I don't think Mr. Perlman did, to whether a man was a Pennsylvania man or a New York Central man. Considering the relative size of the two railroads the management was pretty well balanced and today a lot of your top officers are New York Central people.

Perlman is equally firm that he was *not* running the railroad. In his testimony before the same Senate subcommittee, he engaged in this exchange with Sen. Vance A. Hartke, Democrat, of Indiana, the subcommittee chairman:

SEN. HARTKE: Mr. Saunders . . . left the impression at least with this Senator that you had the complete authority to run the operation and you were given everything you needed to run it. Is that true or not?

PERLMAN: It was not true.

SEN. HARTKE: In other words, it was not true in personnel, was it?

PERLMAN: No, sir.

SEN. HARTKE: Was it true in regard to money for these projects you were talking about?

PERLMAN: No, sir.

SEN. HARTKE: Why not?

PERLMAN: Well, as an example, that budget never even was seen by the board of directors.

SEN. HARTKE: Why not?

PERLMAN: Well, it was held on his desk.

SEN. HARTKE: On Mr. Saunders' desk?

PERLMAN: Yes.

SEN. HARTKE: Why did he hold it?

PERLMAN: He said we had no money, so why show it to them. . . .

. . . Regarding red-green rivalries, the facts are that the "people" problems centered primarily on two departments: marketing and operations. Of the Penn Central's twenty-five top officers immediately below Saunders, Perlman and Bevan, eleven, as indicated earlier, came from the Central and fourteen from the PRR. But veteran PRR executives were named to head both operations and marketing. Perlman didn't like either one of them. They were two big reasons why he answered "no" to the Senate subcommittee's question whether he thought the best men were placed in the best jobs. What was not disclosed is that Saunders also was dissatisfied with the performance of these two officers. And he joined Perlman in working to replace them. . . .

Our investigation suggests the following timetable of events:

Almost from the opening day, Perlman was out to get his two executive vice presidents. He considered them incompetent and told them so. At a meeting of executive staff in Tarrytown, New York, he delivered a two-hour diatribe against Large that stunned the ex-PRR witnesses. They had never heard anything like it. Large, by birth, breeding and career, was a pillar of the Philadelphia Establishment; he was such a decent fellow that it was hard to imagine anybody wanting to throw him out, and Perlman's brass-knuckles methods simply weren't those of the old Pennsy. Beyond all that, Henry Large had spent decades building up contacts and he was a close friend of more big shippers than anyone else in railroading.

Saunders' initial inclination was to mediate the differences between the green president and the red executive vice presidents. He sought to "work things out" through compromise. Trying to "work things out" was a mark of the chairman. One of Saunders' closest associates at Penn Central said: "Perlman had been after Saunders to let him get rid of Smucker.* Saunders wouldn't do it. He wanted a compromise. The feud between Perlman and Smucker did more than anything else to set up the red-green rivalry." This official, viewing the contretemps from a vantagepoint of almost two years, said that Perlman "could never adjust to being number two," suffered from megalomania and conducted a "personal vendetta" to oust both Smucker and Large. Saunders, faced with Perlman's demands, vacillated and compromised and didn't make the tough decisions that were needed, said this observer, himself a member of Penn Central's executive suite.

Despite these delays, not too many months passed before Saunders concluded that Perlman was right: Smucker and Large had to go. Indeed, Saunders actually wanted Perlman to replace Smucker with Mike Flannery when the merger was less than one year old. But Flannery was gradually making sense of the nightmarish computer operations, and Perlman delayed the switch. Finally, on February 23, 1969, Penn Central announced that Smucker was being "freed from his day-to-day administrative duties in order to fill . . . [a] position on the

---

*David E. Smucker was Pennsylvania Railroad's Vice-President of Operations. He had spent 40 years with the Pennsylvania Railroad. —Ed. Note.

chairman's staff and will handle special projects for the chief executive officer." Smucker soon retired to his home, "Green Meadows," in Villanova, on the Main Line. Mike Flannery took over operations. Saunders and Perlman also agreed to seek a replacement for Henry Large. . . .

While these major changes were taking place in Penn Central's badly divided executive suite, Stuart Saunders was doing something that Alfred Perlman knew nothing about: Saunders was secretly hunting for a man to replace Perlman. Perlman had reached sixty-five, the normal retirement age, in December 1967, three months before the merger. His contract with Penn Central continued him in office as president until December 1, 1970, when he would be sixty-eight.

Saunders believed the railroad could not afford Perlman's leadership for that length of time. It would be cheaper to force his retirement, even though it meant Perlman, whose salary had been raised to $220,000 a year on February 1, 1968, would receive at least $170,000 until November 30, 1970, and would be paid $50,000 annually for ten years and eight months after that by the Penn Central.

One of the things that bothered Saunders and several board members was that Perlman, despite his advanced years, had groomed no one to succeed him.[8]

Late in 1968 or early in 1969, Saunders quietly obtained the approval of key board members to purge Perlman. Then he searched for a successor. The hunt was top secret. It appears that none of Penn Central's other officers knew of it and possibly only two or three of the directors closest to Saunders did. Saunders first approached Louis W. Menk, who was chief executive of the Northern Pacific Railroad. Menk, dynamic, aggressive, occasionally volatile, was one of the nation's most respected railroad executives. At Saunders' invitation, the fifty-year-old Menk flew to Philadelphia early in 1969 for talks with the chairman. His wife accompanied him. They were entertained by Saunders and his wife, Dorothy, at the Saunders' Ardmore home. The Menks even did some preliminary house hunting—along the Main Line, of course.

Under the offer by Saunders, Menk apparently would have joined Penn Central as chief executive officer or as presdient with the promise of prompt elevation to the top post. In March 1969, Menk turned down the offer. . . .

Finally, in September 1969, Saunders found the man to succeed Perlman: Paul A. Gorman, just retired as president of the Western Electric Co. Gorman, though a stranger to railroading, knew how to run a big corporation. At this critical moment, Saunders thought, maybe a hard-nosed businessman could turn the railroad around. Gorman's appointment, at $250,000 a year, took effect in December. When Perlman was informed of the decision just before the September meeting at which Gorman was named, he was very unhappy. He had not intended to quit and did not want to step down. But lacking the votes on Penn Central's board of directors, he could not fight back. However, he insisted that his contract, which provided that he should remain as a top officer for three years beyond the normal retirement age of sixty-five, be honored. He also insisted that all the incidental benefits specified in his contract, such as office space in both New York and Philadelphia, a secretary and a car, continue in force. And this was done. But when Perlman became vice chairman his influence in decision making diminished. After that, he was relatively inactive for the final seven months until he was finally dropped, along with Saunders and Bevan.[9]

When Gorman arrived in December 1969, the eastern United States was engulfed in its most severe winter in decades. With switches frozen, yards frozen, snow and ice causing delays everywhere, railroad expenses rose calamitously and revenues sank. Mike Flannery's rescue mission suffered a fatal blow.[10]

Saunders and Bevan were in a race against time. As Penn Central's outside investments went sour, they borrowed desperately for what one of their associates termed "this money-consuming monster, the railroad." Nothing seemed to work. Service slipped, deficits grew and morale worsened. Making matters even more chaotic was the fact that, by this time, these two men, who bore such heavy responsibility for keeping the nation's largest railroad running, were barely on speaking terms. Bevan jealously guarded information concerning his own activities and swore his staff to secrecy. . . .

Infighting at the top permeated the entire railroad organization. High-salaried executives, both red and green, left in a steady stream. In two years, all five principal associates of Saunders, Perlman and Bevan either had been eased out or had quit. Eight of the original twenty vice presidents were gone. Gone, too were more than 100 of the Central's former marketing staff. . . .

As the end drew near, Stuart Thomas Saunders, the man in charge of the entire $6.5 billion conglomerate—the railroad, the hotels, the real estate, the pipelines, the trucks, and on and on—withdrew into himself. "In his last months in office," said a close associate, "Saunders changed from an outgoing, self-confident man to a frightened man. He ceased communicating with everybody. I wouldn't see him for weeks at a time, where before we had been in touch almost daily. He knew the countdown was on. The question was whether he could keep borrowing until the railroad started making money."

He couldn't. Nobody could. Time and money ran out. How the mighty fell: Stuart Saunders, businessman of the year in 1968, business bankrupt of the year in 1970. Hailed as a genius for getting the merger on the track, he couldn't make it run. A great advocate of "working things out," he never really worked anything out. Of the three top executives, he had the greatest faith in the merger even though he had nothing to do with the original concept. Unlike so many of his associates, he never gave up on it. And when the crash came he lost the most—close to $1 million in Penn Central stock which he had purchased on options and then held until the bitter end while Bevan and other executives were unloading theirs through insider trading that was later questioned. The end came on June 8, 1970, when Saunders, his dream shattered, was thrown out.

His manicurist was one of those who noticed a change in the chairman after he was fired. In the weeks before June 8, when Saunders went downtown for his manicure, his hands shook as though they were palsied. But shortly after that terrible day he went back. And now his hands were firm and steady and he seemed self-assured again. Only Stuart Saunders would know how much of a relief it was to have the nightmare end.

NOTES

1. So designated because of the color of their respective boxcars. The Pennsylvania's were red and the Central's were green.

2. Richardson Dilworth, former Philadelphia mayor who is widely regarded as the city's outstanding citizen of this century, was made to wait many years before being taken into the Philadelphia Club. His membership became a political issue in Pennsylvania's 1962 gubernatorial election. His opponent, William W. Scranton, said the Philadelphia Club had no Jewish or Negro members (which was true). Dilworth delights in recalling that Scranton, shortly after winning the election, joined the Philadelphia Club himself.

3. Although the diversification program began just after Saunders' arrival, Bevan was the driving force behind it. Since he is now blamed for its failure he should have been more closely identified with its bright beginning.

4. Largely because of Saunders' involvement in the National Alliance of Businessmen, the PRR employed many more Negroes than the Central. On both railroads blacks were employed only at the lower work levels.

5. Mellon died in June 1970, a week before Bevan was fired.

6. Bevan wasn't the first to express surprise at some of Perlman's operating methods. Back in 1962, an ICC lawyer was shocked at the way in which Perlman went about studying the proposed merger.

Q: And so, from November 1957 to January 8, 1958, you had under active exploration the possibility of merger between the Pennsylvania and the New York Central and you never got a written report on it?

PERLMAN: That is just what I said three times before.

Q: Mr. Perlman, I must apologize. I don't like to ask questions over again. The statement is so amazing that I must admit I have some very great difficulties believing it.

7. Robert G. Flannery, ex-Central.

8. Under the original merger agreement of 1962, Perlman was to become vice chairman of Penn Central's board and serve in only an advisory capacity. When the merger finally came, six years later, the board decided that the New York Central had no one else capable of assuming the presidency and so gave it to Perlman.

9. In December 1970, Perlman became president of the Western Pacific Railroad, with headquarters in San Francisco. The Western Pacific gave up its last passenger train several months before Perlman took over. It now carries only freight.

10. Flannery, after being named Penn Central's executive vice president for operations, left at the end of 1970 to work under Perlman at the Western Pacific.

Inside the Third Reich
Albert Speer

Hitler had no humor. He left joking to others, although he could laugh loudly, abandonedly, sometimes literally writhing with laughter. Often he would wipe tears from his eyes during such spasms. He liked laughing, but it was always laughter at the expense of others.

Goebbels was skilled at entertaining Hitler with jokes while at the same time demolishing any rivals in the internal struggle for power. "You know," he once related, "the Hitler Youth asked us to issue a press release for the twenty-fifth birthday of its staff chief, Lauterbacher. So I sent along a draft of the text to the effect that he had celebrated this birthday 'enjoying full physical and mental vigor.' We heard no more from him." Hitler doubled up with laughter, and Goebbels had achieved his end of cutting the conceited youth leader down to size.

To the dinner guests in Berlin, Hitler repeatedly talked about his youth, emphasizing the strictness of his upbringing. "My father often dealt me hard blows. Moreover, I think that was necessary and helped me." Wilhelm Frick, the Minister of the Interior, interjected in his bleating voice: "As we can see today, it certainly did you good, *mein Führer*." A numb, horrified silence around the table. Frick tried to save the situation, "I mean, *mein Führer*, that is why you have come so far." Goebbels, who considered Frick a hopeless fool, commented sarcastically: "I would guess you never received a beating in your youth, Frick."

Walter Funk, who was both Minister of Economics and president of the Reichsbank, told stories about the outlandish pranks that his vice president, Brinkmann, had gone on performing for months, until it was finally realized that he was mentally ill. In telling such stories Funk not only wanted to amuse Hitler but to inform him in this casual way of events which would sooner or later reach his ears. Brinkmann, it seemed, had invited the cleaning women and messenger boys of the Reichsbank to a grand dinner in the ballroom of the Hotel Bristol, one of the best hotels in Berlin, where he played the violin for them. This sort of thing rather fitted in with the regime's propaganda of all Germans forming one "folk community." But as everyone at table laughed, Funk continued: "Recently he stood in front of the Ministry of Economics on Unter den Linden, took a large package of newly printed banknotes from his briefcase—as you know, the notes bear my signature—and gave them out to passers-by, saying: 'Who wants some of the new Funks?'"* Shortly afterward, Funk continued, the poor man's insanity had become plain for all to see. He called together all the employees of the Reichsbank. "Everyone older than fifty to the left side, the younger employees to the right." Then, to one man on the right side: "'How old are you?'—'Forty-nine, sir.'—'You go to the left too. Well now, all on the left side are dismissed at once, and what is more with a double pension.'"

Hitler's eyes filled with tears of laughter. When he had recovered, he launched into a monologue on how hard it sometimes is to recognize a madman. In this roundabout way Funk was also accomplishing another end. Hitler did not yet know that the Reischsbank vice president in his irresponsible state had given Goering a check for several million marks. Goering cashed the check without a qualm. Later on, of course, Goering vehemently objected to the thesis that Brinkmann did not know what he was doing. Funk could expect him to present this point of view to Hitler. Experience had shown that the person who first managed to suggest a particular version of an affair to Hitler had virtually won his point, for Hitler never liked to alter a view he had once expressed. Even so, Funk had difficulties recovering those millions of marks from Goering. . . .

Many jokes were carefully prepared, tied up as they were with actual events, so that Hitler was kept abreast of interparty developments under the guise of foolery. Again, Goebbels was far better at this than all the others, and Hitler gave him further encouragement by showing that he was very much amused.

An old party member, Eugen Hadamowski, had obtained a key position as Reichssendeleiter (Head of Broadcasting for the Reich), but now he was longing to be promoted to Leiter des Reichsrundfunks (Head of the Reich Radio System). The Propaganda Minister, who had another candidate, was afraid that Hitler might back Hadamowski

*A pun in German; *Funken* = sparks.—*Translators' note.*

because he had skillfully organized the public address systems for the election campaigns before 1933. He had Hanke, state secretary in the Propaganda Ministry, send for the man and officially informed him that Hitler had just appointed him Reichsintendant (General Director) for radio. At the table Hitler was given an account of how Hadamowski had gone wild with joy at this news. The description was, no doubt, highly colored and exaggerated, so that Hitler took the whole affair as a great joke. Next day Goebbels had a few copies of a newspaper printed reporting on the sham appointment and praising the new appointee in excessive terms. He outlined the article for Hitler, with all its ridiculous phrases, and acted out Hadamowski's rapture upon reading these things about himself. Once more Hitler and the whole table with him was convulsed. That same day Hanke asked the newly appointed Reichsintendant to make a speech into a dead microphone, and once again there was endless merriment at Hitler's table when the story was told. After this, Goebbels no longer had to worry that Hitler would intervene in favor of Hadamowski. It was a diabolic game; the ridiculed man did not have the slightest opportunity to defend himself and probably never realized that the practical joke was carefully plotted to make him unacceptable to Hitler. No one could even know whether what Goebbels was describing was true or whether he was giving his imagination free rein.

From one point of view, Hitler was the real dupe of these intrigues. As far as I could observe, Hitler was in fact no match for Goebbels in such matters; with his more direct temperament he did not understand this sort of cunning. But it certainly should have given one pause that Hitler allowed this nasty game to go on and even encouraged it. One word of displeasure would certainly have stopped this sort of thing for a long while to come.

I often asked myself whether Hitler was open to influence. He surely could be swayed by those who knew how to manage him. Hitler was mistrustful, to be sure. But he was so in a cruder sense, it often seemed to me; for he did not see through clever chess moves or subtle manipulation of his opinions. He had apparently no sense for methodical deceit. Among the masters of that art were Goering, Goebbels, Bormann, and, within limits, Himmler. Since those who spoke out in candid terms on the important questions usually could not make Hitler change his mind, the cunning men naturally gained more and more power.

The Politics of Seduction
Doris Kearns

The authority that Johnson inherited as Senate Democratic majority leader had been rendered ineffective by the Senate's inner club. Johnson set about to change all that, and before long he had transformed the instruments at hand—the steering committee, which determined committee assignments, and a hitherto unimportant Democratic Policy Committee—into mechanisms of influence and patronage in his relations with his Democratic colleagues and of control in the scheduling of legislations.

From facts, gossip, observation—a multitude of disparate elements—he shaped a composite mental portrait of every senator: his strengths and his weaknesses: his place in the political spectrum; his aspirations in the Senate, and perhaps beyond the Senate; how far he could be pushed in what direction, and by what means; how he liked his liquor; how he felt about his wife and his family; and, most important, how he felt about himself. For Johnson understood that the most important decision each senator made, often obscurely, was what kind of senator he wanted to be; whether he wanted to be a national leader in education, a regional leader in civil rights, a social magnate in Washington, an agent of the oil industry, a wheel horse of the party, a President of the United States. Yet his entrepreneurial spirit encompassed not simply the satisfaction of present needs but the development of new and expanding ones. He would, for instance, explain to a senator that "although five other senators are clamoring for this one remaining seat on the congressional delegation to Tokyo, I just might be able to swing it for you since I know how much you really want it. . . . It'll be tough but let me see what I can do." The joys of visiting Tokyo may never have occurred to the senator, but he was unlikely to deny Johnson's description of his desire—after all, it might be interesting, a relaxing change, even fun; and perhaps some of the businesses in his state had expressed concern about Japanese competition. By creating consumer needs in this fashion, and by then defining the terms of their realization, Johnson was able to expand the base of benefits upon which power could be built.

Johnson's capacities for control and domination found their consummate manifestation during his private meetings with individual senators. Face to face, behind office doors, Johnson could strike a different pose, a different form of behavior and argument. He would try to make each senator feel that his support in some particular matter was the critical element that would affect the well-being of the nation, the Senate, and the party leader; and would also serve the practical and political interests of the senator. . . .

The arrangements that preceded a private meeting were elaborate indeed. A meeting with a colleague might seem like an accidental encounter in a Senate corridor, but Johnson was not a man who roamed through halls in aimless fashion; when he began to wander he knew who it was he would find.

After the coincidental encounter and casual greetings, Johnson would remember that he had something he would like to talk about. The two men would walk down the corridor, ride the elevator, and enter an office where they would begin their conversation with small talk over Scotch. As the conversation progressed, Johnson would display an overwhelming combination of praise, scorn, rage, and friendship. His voice would rise and fall, moving from the thunder of an orator to the whisper reminiscent of a lover inviting physical touch. Transitions were abrupt. He responded to hostility with a disconcerting glance of indignation; the next minute he would evoke a smile by the warmth of his expression and a playful brush of his hand. Variations in pitch, stress, and gesture reflected the importance which he attached to certain words. His appeal would abound with illustration, anecdote, and hyperbole. He knew how to make his listeners see things he was describing, make them tangible to the senses. And he knew how to sustain a sense of uninterrupted flow by parallel structure and a stream of conjunctions.

From his own insistent energy, Johnson would create an illusion that the outcome, and thus the responsibility, rested on the decision of this one senator; refusing to permit any implication of the reality they both knew (but which in this office began to seem increasingly more uncertain), that the decisions of many other senators would also affect the results.

Then too, Johnson was that rare American man who felt free to display intimacy with another man, through expressions of feeling and also in physical closeness. In an empty room he would stand or sit next to a man as if all that were available was a three-foot space. He could flatter men with sentiments of love and touch their bodies with gestures of affection. The intimacy was all the more excusable because it seemed genuine and without menace. Yet it was also the product of meticulous calculation. And it worked. To the ardor and the bearing of this extraordinary man, the ordinary senator would almost invariably succumb.

Johnson was often able to use the same behavior with the press as he did with his colleagues, dividing it into separate components, and carving out a special relationship with each of the reporters.

"You learn," he said, "that Stewart Alsop cares a lot about appearing to be an intellectual and a historian—he strives to match his brother's intellectual attainments—so whenever you talk to him, play down the gold cufflinks which you play up with *Time* magazine, and to him, emphasize your relationship with FDR and your roots in Texas, so much so that even when it doesn't fit the conversation you make sure to bring in maxims from your father and stories from the Old West. You learn that Evans and Novak love to traffic in backroom politics and political intrigue, so that when you're with them you make sure to bring in lots of details and colorful description of personality. You learn that Mary McGrory likes dominant personalities and Doris Fleeson cares only about issues, so that when you're with McGrory you come on strong and with Fleeson you make yourself sound like some impractical red-hot liberal."

Winning Is the Only Thing
Jerry Kramer

FRANK GIFFORD: "I WAS ALWAYS TRYING TO PLEASE HIM"

When Vince joined the New York Giants in 1954, he walked into a disaster area. Their defense was a shambles; their offense was worse. The year before, they had lost nine out of twelve games and had scored only 179 points, the fewest of any team in the league. Vince immediately molded a new offense and, in the process, created a superstar: Frank Gifford, a halfback who could run, block, pass and catch passes.

An All-American at the University of Southern California, Gifford had been used almost exclusively on defense in 1952, his rookie season. Under

Vince, he became the most exciting offensive halfback in the National Football League. In each of the five years he played for Vince, Gifford was nominated for the Pro Bowl. In those five years, the Giants never had a losing record, never scored fewer than 246 points. . . .

In the spring of 1970, before we knew of Vince's illness, I sat down with Frank Gifford in his office at CBS. After thirteen seasons with the Giants, Frank is now a highly successful television sportscaster, covering everything from the Masters to the Super Bowl. . . .

To be honest, very few of the guys liked him at first. For one thing, he had us running like we had never run before. But the main thing was that we resented a guy coming in from college and telling us what to do. And he was completely in charge. Jim Lee never interfered; he left the offense entirely to Vinny and the defense entirely to Tom Landry. As Jim Lee himself said many times, "I'm just here to take the roll and blow up the balls."

The first two or three weeks, we weren't too impressed by Vinny's Here's-how-we-did-it-at-St.-Cecilia-High-or-at-Army attitude. . . .

But it didn't take us long to realize that even though Vinny's approach to football was very basic—fundamentals: hit, block and tackle—he was somebody special. His enthusiasm, his spirit, was infectious. We really began to dig him when he started coming up to our rooms at night after he'd put in a new play during a chalk talk. I was rooming with Charlie, and Vinny'd come to our room, after putting in an off-tackle play, and say, "Well, what do you think? Will it work?" He was very honest. When he put in the power sweep, he'd ask, "Can the halfback get down and hold that defensive end and stop the penetration?" That was my job on one side and Alex Webster's on the other. We'd say, "Oh, sure, Coach, we can do it." And then he'd just drill the hell out of us.

I can remember sneaking out some nights after curfew in Oregon, and sometimes I'd come back in pretty late, and the lights would still be on in his room. I realized then the kind of work he was putting in. He had to be exhausted, but he never showed it. He'd be out on the field the next day, going full speed, driving himself every minute.

We never feared Vinny in New York. It wasn't like in Green Bay later, when he came in with you guys as a winner, as an established person. To us, he was just an assistant coach from Army and St. Cecilia High. There are maybe twelve or fifteen of us who were the core of the offense, and we were kind of a clique, and Vinny liked to hang around with us. He'd eat dinner with us on the road and laugh with us when we won and die with us when we lost. We used to tease him and raise hell with him. We'd hide his baseball cap, things like that, just to see him get his emotions worked up. When he was showing us films, we used to bait him, lead him on to the point where he'd smash a table or throw an eraser at the blackboard. He'd break two or three projectors a year when he got angry. . . .

He was always a great psychologist, great at analyzing individuals, knowing which players needed to be driven and which ones needed a friendly pat on the fanny. When he was with us, we had a few players who needed driving. One was Mel Triplett. Mel used to exasperate Vinny. He could've been a great player—he had a fantastic year in 1956—but he never played up to his potential, except on certain occasions, like against the Cleveland Browns after they got Jimmy Brown. Mel always felt that he was better than Jimmy. You and I both know that he wasn't, but he was a fine football player.

Vinny used to ride Mel pretty good, especially in the movies. You know how he is with that projector. You could miss a block, and he'd never say a word sometimes, but he'd run the film back and forth, back and forth, till every guy in the room felt like he'd done something wrong. It was sort of like going to a revival meeting. A preacher will fire some buckshot out there, and everybody is going to feel it. Everybody is the guilty party.

Well, Mel used to think that Vinny was persecuting him something awful. All he really was trying to do was help Mel along. But one time he went a little too far with Mel, who was kind of a frightening guy when he got hot. Vinny kept running this one play back and forth, back and forth, back and forth—with Mel missing a block—and about the eighth or tenth time, Mel said, loud and hard, "Move on with that projector."

You could have heard a pin drop. We all wondered what was going to happen. Mel had told the rest of us a few times what he intended to do to Mr. Lombardi someday. And Mel was the kind of guy who was emotional and might do just what he said he would. He was at the breaking point right then. Vince didn't say a word. He went on to the next play. He read Mel just right. They never did have a confrontation. I heard a lot of guys over the years say they were going to punch Vinny out at the end of the season, but no one ever did. You've got to end up loving a guy who can build a team, put it all together—and you share in the rewards. But Vinny walked a very dangerous line at times.

He ruled us all equally—with one exception. He loved Charlie Conerly. He never said a harsh word to Charlie. And, again, he was really getting the proper reading, because Charlie didn't need it. You couldn't fire Charlie up with a branding iron. But you couldn't cool him off, either. Charlie was his own person.

When Charlie used to throw a couple of interceptions or blow an automatic—which really fried Vinny—Vinny wouldn't say a word. He'd get on Don Heinrich—Don was our other quarterback, and he was a little younger and a little wilder than Charlie—but never to the point where he got totally angry. I think he has a special fondness for his quarterbacks. A quarterback is his own extension on the field. I think he looked at Bart Starr as Vinny Lombardi out there. I think he feels the same way about Sonny Jurgensen.

But the rest of us got equal treatment. I remember when he put in the nutcracker drill: A defensive lineman sets himself in between two big bags, and an offensive lineman tries to lead a ballcarrier through. Everybody always used to say, "Oh, that poor offensive lineman." Nobody ever thought about the poor offensive back, who was just getting the hell knocked out of him. After an hour of banging heads, those defensive linemen were so hot and so mad they didn't care what they did to you. Maybe you were a star, or thought you were a star, but you ran the nutcracker as often as the rookie trying to make the team. Vinny kept track of it, close track, and if you tried to get out of one run at it, his teeth'd be grinning at you, and he'd be yelling. "Get in here, get in here," and there'd be no way you could escape. . . .

And Vinny could put his finger on these elements in a personality. He knew exactly how to motivate. He knew just what buttons to push. You see, I didn't hide anything from him. I was always just as open as I could be with him, because I liked him so much. I know that after a while it got to the point where I was playing football for just one reason: I was always trying to please him. When we played a game, I could care less about the headlines on Monday. All I wanted was to be able to walk into the meeting Tuesday morning and have Vinny give me that big grin and pat me on the fanny and let me know that I was doing what he wanted me to do. A lot of our guys felt that way. We had guys who would run through a stadium wall for him—and then maybe cuss him in the next breath. . . .

I can remember very clearly the happiest I've ever seen Vinny. It wasn't after a game. It was in the middle of a week during the 1956 season. We'd gotten up over .500 in 1954 and 1955, but we hadn't finished first or second in our division. Then, in 1956, we won four of our first five games, and on a Wednesday—we were getting ready to play Pittsburgh—he called us all around him, the whole offense. He just couldn't restrain himself. He was bubbling. He was bursting with pride. "By God," he said, "we've really got something going." His eyes were shining. He just felt that we were going to win everything, and he knew it was his baby, and he had to tell us, and, of course, he was right. We did go on to win everything that year. . . .

People are always asking me what makes Vince Lombardi different from other coaches, and I've got one answer: He can get that extra ten percent out of an individual. Multiply ten percent times forty men on a team times fourteen games a season—and you're going to win. He proved that last year at Washington. That's not a talented team, and, my God, they hadn't had a winning team since 1955. But he made them winners. He made them believe they could win. Sonny Jurgensen loved him. He had no right to succeed in Washington. There are twenty-six teams now, not twelve like there were when he went to Green Bay. It's a hell of a lot harder to find good ballplayers. You can't trade the way you used to; you can't draft the way you could. There just isn't the same material available for every team. And the quality of coaching has been upgraded throughout the league. And, still, he did it. Nobody else could've done it. There are four or five coaches that know as much strategically and tactically as Lombardi, but they don't get that extra ten percent.

Vinny believes in the Spartan life, the total self-sacrifice, and to succeed and reach the pinnacle that he has, you've got to be that way. You've got to have total dedication. The hours you put in on a job can't even be considered. The job is to be done, and if it takes a hundred hours, you give it a hundred hours. If it takes fifteen minutes, you give it fifteen minutes. I saw the movie, *Patton*, and it was Vince Lombardi. The situation was different, but the thought was the same: We're here to do a job, and each and every one of us will put everything we've got into getting the job done. That was Vince. . . .

KYLE ROTE: "HE WAS SEARCHING FOR A RELATIONSHIP WITH US

During Vince's years with the New York Giants, Kyle Rote was more than one of his stars: He was Vince's kind of ballplayer. Kyle had a bad left knee that forced him, after a few pro seasons, to forget about playing halfback, to give up the brilliant running and passing that had made him college football's most spectacular All-American in 1950. He became a flanker instead and, through hard work and despite his painful knee, made himself one of the finest receivers in the league.

You may find this hard to believe, but Vince Lombardi impressed me as a shy person when he first came to the Giants.

When I look back at those days now, I suppose that I mistook caution for shyness. Vinny was a perfectionist, and to his credit, I think he wanted to make sure his feet were on solid ground before he asserted himself. He was feeling his way until he was positive of what he was doing.

His previous experience had been limited to high school and college football, and in his first exhibition season with the pros, Vinny was rather careful in his dealings with the players, especially the older players. I don't mean he was timid, but I do think he was searching for a relationship with us that would make us both feel acceptable to each other. He was perceptive enough to sense that, because of the absence of any arena for physical give and take, it's often more difficult for a rookie coach to be accepted by the veterans than it is for a rookie player.

Some of us tested Vinny in his first few weeks. Charlie Conerly and I were not above trying to play as little as possible in the preseason games, and I can recall Vinny, during one exhibition, coming to Conerly and me on the sidelines and asking if we thought we'd like to get in a little work. "Maybe in a couple of more series, Coach," we replied.

What Vinny didn't realize—or, at least, what we thought he didn't realize—was that Charlie and I were trying to pick our spot. We knew that before the game was over, we'd have to go in, and we were studying the opposing team's rookie defensive backs, trying to find one with a weakness we could take advantage of.

Fortunately for Charlie and me, we were usually able to find what we were looking for, and when we felt our club was in good field position, we'd tell Vinny we were ready. In we'd go, and more times than not, we were able to complete a pass on the rookie we'd been watching.

I honestly think Vinny, at the beginning, held most of the older players in slight awe, and when we'd pull off a stunt like that, it enhanced his image of us.

Of course, that was only the first few weeks. After a while, Vinny would turn to us and say, "You and Charlie ready to go in now?"

"Give us just a few more downs," I'd say.

"Go in there now," he'd say.

The shyness or the cautiousness wore off quickly, and as Vinny began to realize that pro ball is actually a less complicated game than college ball—that the tactics and skills of the opposition are much more predictable—the Lombardi confidence began to emerge. And in direct ratio to the emergence of his confidence, our little "confidence game" submerged. . . .

One year, when we were training at Bear Mountain, New York, we lost most of our exhibition games, and Vinny decided that we were too tight. So just before our opening game, when Jim Lee Howell, our head coach, was off scouting or something, Vinny threw a beer blast for the whole team in the basement of the Bear Mountain Inn. We all loosened up, and we went on to win the Eastern championship.

Kyle's mention of the beer blast and of how much Vince enjoyed being with the Giant players made me think of how difficult it must have been for him to divorce himself from the players in Green Bay. I think he really would have liked to have been close to us—I think he felt, as I did, that the special appeal of football was the camaraderie among men with a common goal—but he knew he couldn't allow himself that luxury. To fulfill his commitment to victory, he had to go against his nature and stay aloof from us.

I remember how much he enjoyed Rookie Night, the one night when we all really relaxed together, when the rookies staged a show and made fun of training camp in general and of Vince in particular. They could be pretty rough in their caricatures, and they portrayed Vince as a dictator, and they ridiculed his manner and his physical appearance, and he sat and watched and laughed as heartily as anyone. It took a big man, and a strong man, to see himself through others' eyes, to see his foibles exposed and attacked, but Vince seemed to love it. He would have liked more opportunities to relax and laugh with his players, but he knew, in Green Bay, he couldn't be one of the boys anymore. He wasn't an assistant coach anymore. He had to be a leader.

WILLIE DAVIS: "HE MADE ME FEEL IMPORTANT"

When I first saw Willie Davis, with his big torso and his relatively slender legs —his "getaway sticks," we called them —I was skeptical about his reputation for speed. I challenged him to a race. We both got down in three-point stances, and someone yelled, "Go," and he jumped and just beat me. We did it again, and I jumped and just beat him. That was enough for me; I didn't race Willie anymore.

Willie broke into our starting lineup right away, and by 1962, he was an All-Pro defensive end. Willie made All-Pro five out of six years and, in 1966, became captain of our defensive team, by then the toughest defensive unit in pro football.

Football is a game of emotion, and what the old man excels at is motivation. I maintain that there are two driving forces in football, and one is anger, and the other is fear, and he capitalized on both of them. Either he got us so mad we wanted to prove something to him or we were fearful of being singled out as the one guy who didn't do the job.

In the first place, he worked so hard that I always felt the old man was really putting more into the game on a day-to-day basis than I was. I felt obligated to put something extra into it on Sunday; I had to, just to be even with him.

Another thing was the way he made you a believer. He told you what the other team was going to do, and he told you what you had to do to beat them, and invariably he was right. He made us believe that all we had to do was follow his theories on how to get ready for each game and we'd win.

I knew we were going to win every game we played. Even if we were behind by two touchdowns in the fourth quarter, I just believed that somehow we were going to pull it out. I didn't know exactly how or when, but I knew that sooner or later, we'd get the break we needed— the interception or the fumble or something. And the more important it was for us to win, the more certain I was we would win. . . .

Probably the best job I can remember of him motivating us was when we played the Los Angeles Rams the next-to-last game of 1967. We had already clinched our divisional title, and the game didn't mean anything to us, and he was worried about us just going through the motions. He was on us all week, and in the locker room before the game, he was trembling like a leaf. I could see his leg shaking. "I wish I didn't have to ask you boys to go out there today and do the job," he said. "I wish I could go out and do it myself. Boy, this is one game I'd really like to be playing in. This is a game that you're playing for your pride." He went on like that and he got me so worked up that if he hadn't opened that locker-room door quick, I was going to make a hole in it, I was so eager.

And we played a helluva game. We had nothing to gain, and the Rams were fighting for their lives, and they just did manage to beat us. They won by three points when they blocked a punt right near the end. . . .

You never could predict how he was going to act. The days you really expected him to go through the ceiling, he'd come in and be very soft. He'd say something like, "You're a better football team than you showed today." Or he'd blame himself and the other coaches for not preparing us properly. He'd never let us slip into a defeatist attitude. But then sometimes, when you figured you'd played pretty decent— maybe you'd lived up to what you thought he expected of you—he'd come in and drop the bomb on you. Like one time we beat Minnesota, and didn't play all that bad even though they scored a lot of points, and he walked into the locker room and said, "I'd like our front four to apologize to the rest of the team. You cheated on us today. You should apologize. You didn't play the kind of football you're capable of playing." His words kind of froze me. I felt awful.

One time, when we thought we'd played a good game, he started in on us, "Who the hell do you think you are? The Green Bay Packers? The Green Bay Nothings, that's who you are. You're only a good football team when you play well together. Individually, none of you could make up a team. You'd be nothing without me. I made you, mister."

How about the day we beat the Rams, 6–3, in Milwaukee in 1965? We'd broken a two-game losing streak, and we were all kind of happy and clowning around, and he came in and you saw his face and you knew nothing was funny anymore. He kicked a bench and hurt his foot, and he had to take something out on somebody, so he started challenging us. "Nobody wants to pay the price," he said. "I'm the only one here that's willing to pay the price. You guys don't care. You don't want to win."

We were stunned. Nobody knew what to do, and, finally, Forrest Gregg stood up and said, "My God, I want to win," and then somebody else said, "Yeah, I want to win," and pretty soon there were forty guys standing, all of us shouting, "I want to win." If we had played any football team in the world during the next two hours, we'd have beaten them by ten touchdowns. The old man had us feeling so ashamed and angry. That was his greatest asset: His ability to motivate people.

He never got me too upset personally. Of course, I had pretty thick skin by the time I got to Green Bay. Paul Brown had chewed on me so much in Cleveland that when I got to the Packers, Vince was a welcome sight. Vince and Paul Brown were similar in the way they could cut you with words and make you want to rise up to prove something to them.

I think Vince got on me sharp maybe twice in eight years. I remember once, after the Colts had been hooking me on the sweep, he ate me up, and Max McGee said, "Well, I've seen everything: Vince got on Willie Davis."

Maybe he wasn't as tough on me as he was on some people, but, I'll tell you, I hated to have him tell me I was fat. I hated to have him tell me I didn't have the desire anymore. He'd just say those things to the whole team—"You're all fat; you don't want to win anymore"—and I'd get so angry I couldn't wait till I got out on the field.

I guess maybe my worst days in football were the days I tried to negotiate my contracts with the old man. I'd get myself all worked up before I went in to see him. I'd drive up from my home in Chicago, and all the way, I'd keep building up my anger, telling myself I was going to draw a hard line and get just as much money as I deserved.

One year, I walked into his office feeling cocky, you know, "Roll out the cash, Jack, I got no time for small change." All he had to do was say one harsh word, and I was really going to let him have it. I never got a word in. Soon as he saw me, he jumped up and began hugging me and patting me and telling me, "Willie, Willie, Willie, it's so great to see you. You're the best trade I ever made. You're a leader. We couldn't have won without you, Willie. You had a beautiful year. And, Willie, I need your help. You see, I've got this budget problem . . ."

He got me so off-balance, I started feeling sorry for him. He had me thinking, "Yeah, he's right, he's gotta save some money for the Kramers and the Greggs and the Jordans," and the next thing I knew, I was saying, "Yes, sir, that's fine with me," and I ended up signing for about half what I was going to demand. When I got out of that office and started driving back to Chicago, I was so mad at myself, I was about to drive off the highway.

The next year, finally, I got him. I went into his office and I said, "Coach, you're quite a guy. I got to be very frank, Coach, I just can't argue with you. You know, you just overwhelm me. So I've jotted down a few things I want to tell you." And I handed him a letter I'd written.

He started reading the letter—and I'd put a lot of stuff in it, like how I felt about the fans and what he'd done for me and how many years I had left—and, at first, he gave me that "heh . . . heh . . . heh" of his. Then, when he got around to how much money I wanted, he put his frown on me. He looked at me and said, "I can't argue with what you say here, Willie, but I can't pay you that much money."

"Well, Coach," I said, "I really feel that way."

He thought it over a little and said, "I'll tell you what I'll give you," and named a figure not too much below what I was willing to settle for.

"You'd be one of the highest-paid linemen in the whole league," he whispered, like he was afraid somebody might hear him.

"Look, Coach," I said, "I really thought hard about this, and I got to have a thousand dollars more than that. It's only a thousand dollars, but it's the difference between me driving back to Chicago today feeling real good and driving back to Chicago wanting to go head-on into somebody. It's really what I feel like I'm worth."

"If it's that important to you," he said, "you got it."

I felt good. I had my letter in my hand and I started to walk out, and he said, "Hey, wait a minute. Let me have that letter. Let me keep it. I don't want you giving it to anybody else."

What Happened When I Gave Up the Good Life and Became President

Eberhard Faber

A rather extraordinary thing happened to me this year. Last spring I was without a job—I'd been without one for two years, in fact—and on the whole was enjoying life immensely. In June, however, I had to go back to work. Since working is a common enough experience among adults, and since I'm thirty-five, I don't expect any special sympathy over my reappearance in the U.S. labor force. But the job I got was something special. I became president and chief executive of a $20-million enterprise in deep trouble. . . .

The company I've now gone to work for is Eberhard Faber Inc., the family business. It was founded by my great-grandfather in 1849, and is one of the oldest, and I think the best, manufacturer of pencils and other stationery supplies in the U.S. Its domestic operations are based in a plant at Mountaintop, outside Wilkes-Barre, Pennsylvania, but it also has subsidiaries in Germany and Canada, partnerships in Venezuela and Colombia, and licensees in Brazil, Argentina, Peru, El Salvador, Turkey, and the Philippines. The company seemed to be thriving when I was growing up, and it occurred to me at a fairly early age that, if I wanted to, I could run it one day.

Reprinted from material originally appearing in the December 1971 issue of *Fortune* Magazine. Copyright © 1971 by Eberhard Faber. Reprinted by permission of the author.

THE VIEW FROM GREENPOINT

Actually, I have been somewhat ambivalent about this prospect over the years. I remember that in the summer of 1953, just before I went off to college at Princeton, I worked as a stock boy in the shipping department. The company was then located in a sprawling thirteen-building complex in the Greenpoint section of Brooklyn. I used to take my lunch up to the roof, sit under the huge letters of the Eberhard Faber sign there, and gaze across the East River at the United Nations Building, trying to decide what to make of my life. At that point I was inclined to be a man of letters. In college I edited the *Daily Princetonian*. Later I won a Fulbright Teaching Fellowship, under which I taught American literature at the University of Caen in Normandy. And later still I spent two years in Paris writing fiction.

However, I also kept my hand in at the company. In 1960–61, I worked as an executive trainee (unpaid) at the new Mountaintop offices. In the spring of 1965, I came back for another, somewhat longer tour of duty: I worked as assistant treasurer, then assistant secretary, and finally secretary of the corporation. I'd been attending board meetings of the company since I was twenty-one, and in 1966, when I was twenty-nine, I became a director.

Then, in 1969, I decided to leave the company. I was bored with my duties, the enterprise seemed to run perfectly well without me, and I wanted to write. Besides, I felt that I wanted to extract more fun out of life than I'd been doing. . . .

Anyway, in March, 1969, I quit the company and took up the good life in Belle Mead. Unfortunately, the company began running into trouble at about the same time. There was, I'm afraid, no connection between my departure and the company's new problems.

HARD TIMES IN THE PENCIL GAME

Some of the problems were built into the industry. The pencil business itself, which represents almost 40 percent of our revenues, had been substantially depressed during much of the postwar period. It is plagued by overcapacity, the result of seventeen companies sharing a market of only about $40 million, and chronically afflicted by ruinous price wars. The ball-point pen and increased computerization of many office operations have held down the market growth that might have been expected with a rising population. Efforts to diversify have not been entirely successful. In addition to pencils, Eberhard Faber Inc. now makes erasers, rubber bands, felt and porous-tipped markers, a "whiteboard" visual-aid panel for schools, several kinds of adhesives, type cleaners, and more: and profit margins on quite a few of the lines are low.

But some of the company's problems in 1969 went beyond those of the industry. Labor relations deteriorated that year and there was an eleven-week strike. When the dust settled, the company had lost a lot of business, some of it permanently. The size of the final settlement further reduced profit margins on the bulk of the product line. Worst of all, there were indications that, even after the settlement, the union's relations with management were hostile and communication was bad. The directors were not surprised when 1969 turned out to be a loss year. They were shaken when the losses continued, and in fact deepened, during 1970.

Later, when it began to look as though 1971 would be even worse, the company called in Goggi & Race, a New York consulting firm, to get an outside appraisal of the problems. Specifically, the firm was asked what Eberhard Faber Inc. should do to straighten out its labor problems. After a long, hard look at the company, Paul Goggi reported to the board that the real problem wasn't labor—it was management. He went on to make some specific suggestions for improving the company's materials management and sales forecasting, reshaping the organizational structure, using our machinery and space more efficiently. Later, when the suggestions were not implemented rapidly enough, Goggi indicated forcibly that the company needed some executive changes.

For almost a century after it was founded, Eberhard Faber Inc. was run by, as well as owned by, members of the family. But a series of tragedies some three decades ago interrupted the family's managerial role. In 1945 my father and one of his brothers were drowned while trying to rescue me in the rough surf off the New Jersey shore; I was eventually rescued by another uncle, my mother's brother Duncan. Not long afterward, my grandfather died. My father had been the company's executive vice president; my grandfather had been president. In an effort to fill this large management vacuum, my great-uncle John took over as president—although he was in his nineties! Not surprisingly, Uncle John never did get a very firm grip on the company, and when he died in 1949 it was pretty much out of control.

KEEPING IT IN THE FAMILY

At this point, all logic pointed to selling the company, but my mother insisted that it stay in the family. She continued to insist on family control even after she had received some attractive offers for the company, and she stuck to this position after she was stricken by cancer and had to undergo major surgery. One potential buyer actually got a representative into her room at the hospital, when her condition was still critical, and attempted to do business right there. It is another cherished family tradition that my Uncle Duncan finally got rid of the man by brandishing a revolver at him. Luckily, my mother has the constitution of a Texas steer and the fighting spirit of an Irish terrier. She recovered, held on to the company, and became a vice president (for many years she handled public relations). She did not attempt to run the company, however, and no other Faber was available in the years after Uncle John's death.

I mention all these details because they help to explain why, when Paul Goggi said the company needed new management, I decided to offer my services as president. I had, of course, some large material reasons for being concerned about the company's future. Almost all my family's resources are tied up in the business. If it fails, the family is in trouble. But I wasn't just making an investment decision; a lot of family history and traditions were fed into the decision too. On top of everything else, I felt an obligation to try to do something for the company's employees, hundreds of whom I knew personally. I thought I could actually help the company.

A BEGINNING IN THE CAFETERIA

The board accepted my offer, and I took over as president on June 8. The first few hours were fairly rugged. I'd been up almost until dawn the night before I showed up at the office, working on a speech I had to deliver to the employees of Eberhard Faber Inc. I knew that the employees would be tense when they assembled for the meeting. They didn't know what they were going to be told, or even by whom. When they saw me appear at the podium of our cafeteria—it's the largest room available at Mountaintop, and it has to be used for meetings— they would realize the occasion was an important one, possibly an announcement that the company would be sold or moved elsewhere. The first thing I had to tell them, therefore, was that I was speaking to them as president of an ongoing enterprise. That would reassure them to some extent; however, there was no getting around the company's massive problems, and so I also had to let them know about the company's deteriorating financial position. Finally, I wanted to inspire them—to give them a feeling that they could turn the company around.

At Eberhard Faber, Inc., the factory gets to work at seven, the office at eight. It was seven-thirty on an outrageously beautiful June morning when I pulled into the parking lot. I had an hour before the speech was to be delivered, and I didn't want to be seen, and start all sorts of rumors, during that hour. I scurried quickly up the stairs to the executive offices, feeling somewhat conspiratorial, and spent the ensuing hour with several other executives, trying to smile through the terror. Paul Mailloux, our new executive vice president, kept assuring me that arrangements for the meeting would go smoothly; I noticed, however, that he seemed unable to light his pipe.

Actually, there was a large complication about speaking to all the employees of our company. There were 523 of them at Mountaintop and the production workers were on two different shifts. The cafeteria, furthermore, holds only about seventy-five. In the end, my speech to the employees had to be delivered *eight times*.

I thought that the first session,which was for the management group, went fairly well. I could feel the sweat coursing down my arms and chest as I prepared for the second session, which was for the union committee. But that one seemed to go fairly well too, and when it was over the union president, Paul Butchko, came over and said. "As long as you play fair with us, we'll play fair with you." He had the same husky tone in his voice that I'd heard in mine during parts of the speech, and I suddenly realized that Butchko, who was about my own age, had a lot of new responsibilities to deal with too.

The speeches went on all through the day, which just got hotter every hour. By the time I'd finished Speech No. 8, for the night shift, I was completely exhausted. It was a Wednesday, and I briefly considered dropping by at the Westmoreland Club in downtown Wilkes-Barre to relax in the club's weekly poker game. But the evening papers were carrying our story, and I just didn't feel strong enough to face a crowd of well-wishers and answer questions about my new situation. I went home and slept like a log. . . .

CAGING THE PAPER TIGER

Obviously, I had a lot to learn about running the company, but I did have some advantages when I started out. I had, of course, a lot of help from our management team and from Goggi & Race. Because of my previous tours of duty in the company, I knew where the men's room was, so to speak. I was reasonably familiar with the plant operation, the sales distribution patterns, the organizational structure, and the daily routines. And, of course, I knew the people.

The first thing I had to learn about running the company concerned the mounds of paper that were now dumped on my desk—larger mounds than I'd ever seen in my life. Enormous, incomprehensible data-processing runs arrived daily. Tickler files, based on miscellaneous memoranda of past years, appeared promptly every Thursday, often leaving me mystified about whom to tickle, how to tickle them, and whether it really mattered. Job applications and résumés, acquisition and merger inquiries, advertising and sales bulletins, association newsletters, results from our test labs, interoffice memos, travel schedules of other executives, letters of congratulation on my appointment, brochures on the advantages of alternate plant sites, news about our community services, were all in the mound. Also, it seemed as though everyone in the company thought it prudent to send the new president a copy of every letter he wrote, if only as evidence of hard work.

I let this avalanche pour over me for a while; but finally, guided by a powerful instinct for survival, I took a deep breath, prayerfully apologized to the puritan God of Hard Work, and instructed my secretary to hide most of it in the closet. She now screens my mail ruthlessly. Sometimes letters don't get answered for a week, or at all, and sometimes an important document gets buried in the great mound, but I can't really believe it's affecting the bottom line.

The company's major problem at the time I took over was, of course, to stem the accelerating flow of losses and get onto a breakeven basis, at least. This meant, inevitably, that the operating budget had to be trimmed severely. There was also an urgent need to get a grip on our inventories, which were far too large in several product lines. Thus far, we've reduced the budget by 18 percent and reduced the total inventory by about 25 percent. The inventory cutback enabled us to pay off our short-term loan and, in general, lower the pressures represented by our friendly bankers.

SELLING THE WHITEBOARD

The single most important business decision we faced concerned our "whiteboard" operations in Lansing, Michigan. We had acquired the Lansing operation in 1967, and it was losing money at a frightening rate. The product itself, which we call the Eberhard Faber-Board visual-aid panel, is a white panel that has some substantial advantages over ordinary composition or slate blackboards. It uses water and xylene-based markers as writing instruments, and the writing is a lot easier to read than anything chalked on blackboards; in addition, there's less glare and no smudging when you erase. Finally, the panel can be used as a projection screen.

Unfortunately, we badly misjudged the market for it. We had felt that its principal use would be in schools and colleges, and that it could easily ride on the coattails of our regular line, much of which is sold through school-supply houses and other educational distributors. We failed to see one large difficulty about selling it, however. The panel would be a capital item for the school, which meant that administrators who wanted to buy it would have to go through a quite different and more complicated approval process than they go through when they buy our pencils and erasers. Given the financial crisis that schools generally have been in recently, there just wasn't much heart to take on new lines. A few schools and colleges—one is the Massachusetts Institute of Technology—have been good customers, but in general we haven't had nearly as many educational sales as we'd counted on. The market has thus far turned out to be in industry and architects. We've sold the board to just about every major corporation in the U.S., and many have been repeat buyers. The whiteboard was even bought by Grumman for use in planning the production and testing of the lunar modules. (Grumman had the panels on tracks, and used groups of them to keep its people informed about the status of the modules as they went through the production process.)

The fact remained, however, that our total sales volume was not high enough to justify the kind of costs we were running up in the Lansing facility. And so I asked our management committee to meet and ponder three alternatives: sell the whiteboard operation to another company; liquidate it; or move it into the Mountaintop plant (which would reduce total corporate overhead charges). I indicated that the one option we did *not* have was doing nothing—that is, leaving the operation as it was.

At the first meeting the management committee was somewhat disposed to move the operation to Mountaintop. For one thing, moving it would be far less costly than liquidating it. For another, we still felt that the product had an exciting sales potential. At this point, however, we found ourselves confronting a question to which we had no answer: what kind of profit margin could we expect on the product if we did move it to Mountaintop? We asked George Flower, our treasurer, for an answer, and I adjourned the meeting.

At a second meeting on the whiteboard, we had Mr. Flower's projections in front of us. They showed a fair enough margin between our production costs and the selling price; the gross margin was close to the necessary minimum for product at Mountaintop. But it occurred to me to ask about the cost of selling the panels, and Mr. Mailloux's off-the-cuff reply indicated that it was far higher than our average. Suddenly everyone was scribbling numbers on his pad. I have a lot to learn about management, but I know, at least, that you're supposed to do your homework before meetings, not during them. Somewhat exasperated, principally at myself, I adjourned this meeting too and asked George Flower to project his figures all the way to the bottom line. When the new figures came in, they were clearly unsatisfactory.

The reason our selling expenses were so high was that many of our dealers hadn't been willing to devote much time to selling the panel. Therefore we'd had to direct our own sales and promotion effort directly to the ultimate consumer; on many orders we ended up doing all the selling ourselves. That wouldn't have been so bad except that, after we'd done the work, we were letting the dealers write up the orders— and take their standard commissions. With George Flower's new figures in front of him, our sales manager, Walt Krieger, proposed a selling program that was a lot more equitable. The program produced a projected net profit that seemed to make some sense. The decision to move the Lansing operation to Mountaintop was approved.

The moral I drew from this sequence of events was not to worship the false God of Gross Profit Margin. We now base all our product decisions on models that project to the bottom line. . . .

WAITING FOR A VERDICT

One morning a few weeks back, I was driving to my office and thinking about the day's business. Its main feature was a management-committee meeting with a lot of important business on the agenda—one entry was the future of the whiteboard. Brooding about the potential for big trouble in each of the situations, I suddenly felt that it might be a good idea to pull over to the side of the road. I opened the car door and parted with my breakfast. I was weak and found, to my dismay, that I couldn't stop trembling.

At any previous point in my life, I would have felt that the symptoms justified going home and getting into bed. This time, however, it seemed that the management-committee meeting absolutely had to take place, and that I had to be there for it. I drove to the drugstore, bought a bottle of mouthwash, and went to work.

As the story might indicate, I'm still not entirely at ease in my new way of life. Nevertheless, I'm actually having a lot of fun in the job. The prospect of turning our company around, of succeeding at that challenging task, has exhilarated me, just as it has the people working with me. Thus far we have met our short-term objectives; I believe that we'll meet our long-range ones as well, though it certainly will not be easy. I just hope I don't completely lose the ability to loaf.

7

GETTING
RE/ULT/

Means and Consequences

Getting people to work hard, to perform well and to strive for intended outcomes is frequently subsumed under the topic of motivation in textbooks on organizational behavior. Concern with getting results and accomplishing desired outcomes requires allocating incentives and rewards specifically to those result and outcome areas, recognizing that people will direct their efforts to where the payoff is high. The articles by Kerr ("On the Folly of Rewarding A, While Hoping for B") and by Faltermayer ("Who Will Do the Dirty Work Tomorrow?") provide excellent illustrations of this point.

How are motivated people conceptualized? Two sides of the coin apparently exist. "Young Top Management" (*Business Week*) provides profiles of three hardworking and productive company presidents. The rosiness of this picture of motivated behavior fades, however, as the article on workaholism illustrates ("Workaholics: This Land of Ours Has to Have Them," by Oates). A further blemish, the potential costs of a competitive push for results and outcomes, is contained in the brief excerpt from "A Body With Many Heads" by Peter Cohen.

On the Folly of Rewarding A, While Hoping for B

Steven Kerr

Illustrations are presented from society in general, and from organizations in particular, of reward systems that "pay-off" for one behavior even though the rewarder hopes dearly for another. Portions of the reward systems of a manufacturing company and an insurance firm are examined and the consequences discussed.

Whether dealing with monkeys, rats, or human beings, it is hardly controversial to state that most organisms seek information concerning what activities are rewarded, and then seek to do (or at least pretend to do) those things, often to the virtual exclusion of activities not rewarded. The extent to which this occurs of course will depend on the perceived attractiveness of the rewards offered, but neither operant nor expectancy theorists would quarrel with the essence of this notion.

Nevertheless, numerous examples exist of reward systems that are fouled up in that behaviors which are rewarded are those which the rewarder is trying to *discourage*, while the behavior he desires is not being rewarded at all.

In an effort to understand and explain this phenomenon, this paper presents examples from society, from organizations in general, and from profit making firms in particular. Data from a manufacturing company and information from an insurance firm are examined to demonstrate the consequences of such reward systems for the organizations involved, and possible reasons why such reward systems continue to exist are considered.

SOCIETAL EXAMPLES

Politics

Official goals are "purposely vague and general and do not indicate . . . the host of decisions that must be made among alternative ways of achieving official goals and the priority of multiple goals . . . " (8, p. 66). They usually may be relied on to offend absolutely no one, and in this sense can be considered high acceptance, low quality goals. An example might be "build better schools." Operative goals are higher in quality but lower in acceptance, since they specify where the money will come from, what alternative goals will be ignored, etc.

Reprinted from the *Academy of Management Journals* (December 1975), pp. 769–783. Reproduced by permission of the publisher and author.

The American citizenry supposedly wants its candidates for public office to set forth operative goals, making their proposed programs "perfectly clear," specifying sources and uses of funds, etc. However, since operative goals are lower in acceptance, and since aspirants to public office need acceptance (from at least 50.1 percent of the people), most politicians prefer to speak only of official goals, at least until after the election. They of course would agree to speak at the operative level if "punished" for not doing so. The electorate could do this by refusing to support candidates who do not speak at the operative level.

Instead, however, the American voter typically punishes (withholds support from) candidates who frankly discuss where the money will come from, rewards politicans who speak only of official goals, but hopes that candidates (despite the reward system) will discuss the issues operatively. It is academic whether it was moral for Nixon, for example, to refuse to discuss his 1968 "secret plan" to end the Vietnam war, his 1972 operative goals concerning the lifting of price controls, the reshuffling of his cabinet, etc. The point is that the reward system made such refusal rational.

It seems worth mentioning that no manuscript can adequately define what is "moral" and what is not. However, examination of costs and benefits, combined with knowledge of what motivates a particular individual, often will suffice to determine what for him is "rational."[1] If the reward system is so designed that it is irrational to be moral, this does not necessarily mean that immorality will result. But is this not asking for trouble?

War

If some oversimplification may be permitted, let it be assumed that the primary goal of the organization (Pentagon, Luftwaffe, or whatever) is to win. Let it be assumed further that the primary goal of most individuals on the front lines is to get home alive. Then there appears to be an important conflict in goals—personally rational behavior by those at the bottom will endanger goal attainment by those at the top.

But not necessarily! It depends on how the reward system is set up. The Vietnam War was indeed a study of disobedience and rebellion, with terms such as "fragging" (killing one's own commanding officer) and "search and evade" becoming part of the military vocabulary. The difference in subordinates' acceptance of authority between World War II and Vietnam is reported to be considerable, and veterans of the Second World War often have been quoted as being outraged at the mutinous actions of many American soldiers in Vietnam.

Consider, however, some critical differences in the reward system in use during the two conflicts. What did the GI in World War II want? To go home. And when did he get to go home? When the war was won! If he disobeyed the orders to clean out the trenches and take the hills, the war would not be won and he would not go home. Furthermore, what were his chances of attaining his goal (getting home alive) if he obeyed the orders compared to his chances if he did not? What is being suggested is that the rational soldier in World War II, *whether patriotic or not*, probably found it expedient to obey.

Consider the reward system in use in Vietnam. What did the man at the bottom want? To go home. And when did he get to go home? When his tour of duty was over! This was the case *whether or not* the war was won. Furthermore, concerning the relative chance of getting home alive by obeying orders compared to the chance if they were disobeyed, it is worth noting that a mutineer in Vietnam was far more likely to be assigned rest and rehabilitation (on the assumption that fatigue was the cause) than he was to suffer any negative consequence.

In his description of the "zone of indifference," Barnard stated that "a person can and will accept a communication as authoritative only when . . . . at the time of his decision, he believes it to be compatible with his personal interests as a whole" (1, p. 165). In light of the reward system used in Vietnam, would it not have been personally irrational for some orders to have been obeyed? Was not the military implementing a system which *rewarded* disobedience, while *hoping* that soldiers (despite the reward system) would obey orders?

Medicine

Theoretically, a physician can make either of two types of error, and intuitively one seems as bad as the other. A doctor can pronounce a patient sick when he is actually well, thus causing him needless anxiety and expense, curtailment of enjoyable foods and activities, and even physical danger by subjecting him to needless medication and surgery. Alternately, a doctor can label a sick person well, and thus avoid treating what may be a serious, even fatal ailment. It might be natural to conclude that physicians seek to minimize both types of error.

Such a conclusion would be wrong.[2] It is estimated that numerous Americans are presently afflicted with iatrogenic (physician *caused*) illnesses (9). This occurs when the doctor is approached by someone complaining of a few stray symptoms. The doctor classifies and organizes these symptoms, gives them a name, and obligingly tells the patient what further symptoms may be expected. This information often acts as a self-fulfilling prophecy, with the result that from that day on the patient for all practical purposes is sick.

Why does this happen? Why are physicians so reluctant to sustain a type 2 error (pronouncing a sick person well) that they will tolerate many type 1 errors? Again, a look at the reward system is needed. The punishments for a type 2 error are real: guilt, embarrassment, and the threat of lawsuit and scandal. On the other hand, a type 1 error (labeling a well person sick) "is sometimes seen as sound clinical practice, indicating a healthy conservative approach to medicine" (9, p. 69). Type 1 errors also are likely to generate increased income and a stream of steady customers who, being well in a limited physiological sense, will not embarrass the doctor by dying abruptly.

Fellow physicians and the general public therefore are really *rewarding* type 1 errors and at the same time *hoping* fervently that doctors will try not to make them.

GENERAL ORGANIZATIONAL EXAMPLES

Rehabilitation Centers and Orphanages

In terms of the prime beneficiary classification (2, p. 42) organizations such as these are supposed to exist for the "public-in-contact," that is, clients. The orphanage therefore theoretically is interested in placing as many children as possible in good homes. However, often orphanages surround themselves with so many rules concerning adoption that it is nearly impossible to pry a child out of the place. Orphanages may deny adoption unless the applicants are a married couple, both of the same religion as the child, without history of emotional or vocational instability, with a specified minimum income and a private room for the child, etc.

If the primary goal is to place children in good homes, then the rules ought to constitute means toward that goal. Goal displacement results when these "means become ends-in-themselves that displace the original goals" (2, p. 229).

To some extent these rules are required by law. But the influence of the reward system on the orphanage's management should not be ignored. Consider, for example, that the:

1. Number of children enrolled often is the most important determinant of the size of the allocated budget.
2. Number of children under the director's care also will affect the size of his staff.
3. Total organizational size will determine largely the director's prestige at the annual conventions, in the community, etc.

Therefore, to the extent that staff size, total budget, and personal prestige are valued by the orphanage's executive personnel, it becomes rational for them to make it difficult for children to be adopted. After all, who wants to be the director of the smallest orphanage in the state?

If the reward system errs in the opposite direction, paying off only for placements, extensive goal displacement again is likely to result. A common example of vocational rehabilitation in many states, for example, consists of placing someone in a job for which he has little interest and few qualifications, for two months or so, and then "rehabilitating" him again in another position. Such behavior is quite consistent with the prevailing reward system, which pays off for the number of individuals placed in any position for 60 days or more.

Rehabilitation counselors also confess to competing with one another to place relatively skilled clients, sometimes ignoring persons with few skills who would be harder to place. Extensively disabled clients find that counselors often prefer to work with those whose disabilities are less severe.[3]

Universities

Society *hopes* that teachers will not neglect their teaching responsibilities but *rewards* them almost entirely for research and publications. This is most true at the large and prestigious universities. Cliches such as "good research and good teaching go together" notwithstanding, professors often find that they must choose between teaching and research oriented activities when allocating their time. Rewards for good teaching usually are limited to outstanding teacher awards, which are given to only a small percentage of good teachers and which usually bestow little money and fleeting prestige. Punishments for poor teaching also are rare.

Rewards for research and publications, on the other hand, and punishments for failure to accomplish these, are commonly administered by universities at which teachers are employed. Furthermore, publication oriented resumés usually will be well received at other universities, whereas teaching credentials, harder to document and quantify, are much less transferable. Consequently it is rational for university teachers to concentrate on research, even if to the detriment of teaching and at the expense of their students.

By the same token, it is rational for students to act based upon the goal displacement which has occurred within universities concerning what they are rewarded for. If it is assumed that a primary goal of a university is to transfer knowledge from teacher to student, then grades become identifiable as a means toward that goal, serving as motivational, control, and feedback devices to expedite the knowledge transfer. Instead, however, the grades themselves have become much more important for entrance to graduate school, successful employment, tuition refunds, parental respect, etc., than the knowledge or lack of knowledge they are supposed to signify.

It therefore should come as no surprise that information has surfaced in recent years concerning fraternity files for examinations, term paper writing services, organized cheating at the service academies, and the like. Such activities constitute a personally rational response to a reward system which pays off for grades rather than knowledge.

BUSINESS RELATED EXAMPLES

Ecology

Assume that the president of XYZ Corporation is confronted with the following alternatives:

1. Spend $11 million for antipollution equipment to keep from poisoning fish in the river adjacent to the plant; or
2. Do nothing, in violation of the law, and assume a one in ten chance of being caught, with a resultant $1 million fine plus the necessity of buying the equipment.

Under this not unrealistic set of choices it requires no linear program to determine that XYZ Corporation can maximize its probabilities by flouting the law. Add the fact that XYZ's president is probably being rewarded (by creditors, stockholders, and other salient parts of his task environment) according to criteria totally unrelated to the number of fish poisoned, and his probable course of action becomes clear.

Evaluation of Training

It is axiomatic that those who care about a firm's well-being should insist that the organization get fair value for its expenditures. Yet it is commonly known that firms seldom bother to evaluate a new GRID, MBO, job enrichment program, or whatever, to see if the company is getting its money's worth. Why? Certainly it is not because people have not pointed out that this situation exists; numerous practitioner oriented articles are written each year to just this point.

The individuals (whether in personnel, manpower planning, or wherever) who normally would be responsible for conducting such evaluations are the same ones often charged with introducing the change effort in the first place. Having convinced top management to spend the money, they usually are quite animated afterwards in collecting arigorous vignettes and anecdotes about how successful the program was. The last thing many desire is a formal, systematic, and revealing evaluation. Although members of top management may actually *hope* for such systematic evaluation, their reward systems continue to *reward* ignorance in this area. And if the personnel department abdicates its responsibility, who is to step into the breach? The change agent himself? Hardly! He is likely to be too busy collecting anecdotal "evidence" of his own, for use with his next client.

Miscellaneous

Many additional examples could be cited of systems which in fact are rewarding behaviors other than those supposedly desired by the rewarder. A few of these are described briefly below.

Most coaches disdain to discuss individual accomplishments, preferring to speak of teamwork, proper attitude, and a one-for-all spirit. Usually, however, rewards are distributed according to individual performance. The college basketball player who feeds his teammates instead of shooting will not compile impressive scoring statistics and is less likely to be drafted by the pros. The ballplayer who hits to right field to advance the runners will win neither the batting nor home run titles, and will be offered smaller raises. It therefore is rational for players to think of themselves first, and the team second.

In business organizations where rewards are dispensed for unit performance or for individual goals achieved, without regard for overall effectiveness, similar attitudes often are observed. Under most Management by Objectives (MBO) systems, goals in areas where quantification is difficult often go unspecified. The organization therefore often is in a position where it *hopes* for employee effort in the areas of team building, interpersonal relations, creativity, etc., but it formally *rewards* none of these. In cases where promotions and raises are formally tied to MBO, the system itself contains a paradox in that it "asks employees to set challenging, risky goals, only to face smaller paychecks and possibly damaged careers if these goals are not accomplished" (5, p. 40).

It is *hoped* that administrators will pay attention to long run costs and opportunities and will institute programs which will bear fruit later on. However, many organizational reward systems pay off for short run sales and earnings only. Under such circumstances it is personally rational for officials to sacrifice long term growth and profit (by selling off equipment and property, or by stifling research and development) for short term advantages. This probably is most pertinent in the public sector, with the result that many public officials are unwilling to implement programs which will not show benefits by election time.

As a final, clear-cut example of a fouled-up reward system, consider the cost-plus contract or its next of kin, the allocation of next year's budget as a direct function of this year's expenditures. It probably is conceivable that those who award such budgets and contracts really hope for economy and prudence in spending. It is obvious, however, that adopting the proverb "to him who spends shall more be given," rewards not economy, but spending itself.

TWO COMPANIES' EXPERIENCES

A Manufacturing Organization

A midwest manufacturer of industrial goods had been troubled for some time by aspects of its organizational climate it believed dysfunctional. For research purposes, interviews were conducted with many employees and a questionnaire was administered on a companywide basis, including plants and offices in several American and Canadian locations. The company strongly encouraged employee participation in the survey, and made available time and space during the workday for completion of the instrument. All employees in attendance during the day of the survey completed the questionnaire. All instruments were collected directly by the researcher, who personally administered each session. Since no one employed by the firm handled the questionnaires, and since respondent names were not asked for, it seems likely that the pledge of anonymity given was believed.

A modified version of the Expect Approval scale (7) was included as part of the questionnaire. The instrument asked respondents to indicate the degree of approval or disapproval they could expect if they performed each of the described actions. A seven point Likert scale was used, with one indicating that the action would probably bring strong disapproval and seven signifying likely strong approval.

Although normative data for this scale from studies of other organizations are unavailable, it is possible to examine fruitfully the data obtained from this survey in several ways. First, it may be worth noting that the questionnaire data corresponded closely to information gathered through interviews. Furthermore, as can be seen from the results summarized in Table 1, sizable differences between various work units, and between employees at different job levels within the same work unit, were obtained. This suggests that response bias ef-

Table 1

Summary of Two Divisions' Data Relevant to Conforming and Risk-Avoidance Behaviors (Extent to Which Subjects Expect Approval)

Dimension	Item	Division and Sample	Total Responses	Percentage of Workers Responding		
				1, 2, or 3 Disapproval	4	5, 6, or 7 Approval
Risk Avoidance	Making a risky decision based on the best information available at the time, but which turns out wrong.	A, levels 1-4 (lowest)	127	61	25	14
		A, levels 5-8	172	46	31	23
		A, levels 9 and above	17	41	30	30
		B, levels 1-4 (lowest)	31	58	26	16
		B, levels 5-8	19	42	42	16
		B, levels 9 and above	10	50	20	30
	Setting extremely high and challenging standards and goals, and then narrowly failing to make them.	A, levels 1-4	122	47	28	25
		A, levels 5-8	168	33	26	41
		A, levels 9+	17	24	6	70
		B, levels 1-4	31	48	23	29
		B, levels 5-8	18	17	33	50
		B, levels 9+	10	30	0	70

Table 1 (continued)

		Division and Sample	Total Responses	Percentage of Workers Responding		
				1, 2, or 3 Disapproval	4	5, 6, or 7 Approval
Risk Avoidance (Continued)	Setting goals which are extremely easy to make and then making them.	A, levels 1-4	124	35	30	35
		A, levels 5-8	171	47	27	26
		A, levels 9+	17	70	24	6
		B, levels 1-4	31	58	26	16
		B, levels 5-8	19	63	16	21
		B, levels 9+	10	80	0	20
Conformity	Being a "yes man" and always agreeing with the boss.	A, levels 1-4	126	46	17	37
		A, levels 5-8	180	54	14	31
		A, levels 9+	17	88	12	0
		B, levels 1-4	32	53	28	19
		B, levels 5-8	19	68	21	11
		B, levels 9+	10	80	10	10
	Always going along with the majority.	A, levels 1-4	125	40	25	35
		A, levels 5-8	173	47	21	32
		A, levels 9+	17	70	12	18
		B, levels 1-4	31	61	23	16
		B, levels 5-8	19	68	11	21
		B, levels 9+	10	80	10	10
	Being careful to stay on the good side of everyone, so that everyone agrees that you are a great guy.	A, levels 1-4	124	45	18	37
		A, levels 5-8	173	45	22	33
		A, levels 9+	17	64	6	30
		B, levels 1-4	31	54	23	23
		B, levels 5-8	19	73	11	16
		B, levels 9+	10	80	10	10

fects (socially desirability in particular loomed as a potential concern) are not likely to be severe.

Most importantly, comparisons between scores obtained on the Expect Approval scale and a statement of problems which were the reason for the survey revealed that the same behaviors which managers in each division thought dysfunctional were those which lower level employees claimed were rewarded. As compared to job levels 1 to 8 in Division B (see Table 1), those in Division A claimed a much higher acceptance by management of "conforming" activities. Between 31 and 37 percent of Division A employees at levels 1-8 stated that going along with the majority, agreeing with the boss, and staying on everyone's good side brought approval; only once (level 5-8 responses to one of the three items) did a majority suggest that such actions would generate disapproval.

Furthermore, responses from Division A workers at levels 1-4 indicate that behaviors geared toward risk avoidance were as likely to be rewarded as to be punished. Only at job levels 9 and above was it apparent that the reward system was positively reinforcing behaviors desired by top management. Overall, the same "tendencies toward conservatism and apple-polishing at the lower levels" which divisional management had complained about during the interviews were those claimed by subordinates to be the most rational course of action in light of the existing reward system. Management apparently was not getting the behaviors it was *hoping* for, but it certainly was getting the behaviors it was perceived by subordinates to be *rewarding*.

An Insurance Firm

The Group Health Claims Division of a large eastern insurance company provides another rich illustration of a reward system which reinforces behaviors not desired by top management.

Attempting to measure and reward accuracy in paying surgical claims, the firm systematically keeps track of the number of returned checks and letters of complaint received from policyholders. However, underpayments are likely to provoke cries of outrage from the insured, while overpayments often are accepted in courteous silence. Since it often is impossible to tell from the physician's statement which of two surgical procedures, with different allowable benefits, was performed, and since writing for clarifications will interfere with other standards used by the firm concerning "percentage of claims paid within two days of receipt," the new hire in more than one claims section is soon acquainted with the informal norm: "When in doubt, pay it out!"

The situation would be even worse were it not for the fact that other features of the firm's reward system tend to neutralize those described. For example, annual "merit" increases are given to all employees, in one of the following three amounts:

1. If the worker is "outstanding" (a select category, into which no more than two employees per section may be placed): 5 percent
2. If the worker is "above average" (normally all workers not "outstanding" are so rated): 4 percent
3. If the worker commits gross acts of negligence and irresponsibility for which he might be discharged in many other companies: 3 percent

Now, since (a) the difference between the 5 percent theoretically attainable through hard work and the 4 percent attainable merely by living until the review date is small and (b) since insurance firms seldom dispense much of a salary increase in cash (rather, the worker's insurance benefits increase, causing him to be further overinsured), many employees are rather indifferent to the possibility of obtaining the extra one percent reward and therefore tend to ignore the norm concerning indiscriminant payments.

However, most employees are not indifferent to the rule which states that, should absences or latenesses total three or more in any six-month period, the entire 4 or 5 percent due at the next "merit" review must be forfeited. In this sense the firm may be described as *hoping* for performance, while *rewarding* attendance. What it gets, of course, is attendance. (If the absence-lateness rule appears to the reader to be stringent, it really is not. The company counts "times" rather than "days" absent, and a ten-day absence therefore counts the same as one lasting two days. A worker in danger of accumulating a third absence within six months merely has to remain ill (away from work) during his second absence until his first absence is more than six months old. The limiting factor is that at some point his salary ceases, and his sickness benefits take over. This usually is sufficient to get the younger workers to return, but for those with 20 or more years' service, the company provides sickness benefits of 90 percent of normal salary, tax-free! Therefore . . . .)

CAUSES

Extremely diverse instances of systems which reward behavior A although the rewarder apparently hopes for behavior B have been given. These are useful to illustrate the breadth and magnitude of the phenomenon, but the diversity increases the difficulty of determining commonalities and establishing causes. However, four general factors may be pertinent to an explanation of why fouled up reward systems seem to be so prevalent.

Fascination with an "Objective" Criterion
It has been mentioned elsewhere that:

Most "objective" measures of productivity are objective only in that their subjective elements are a) determined in advance, rather than coming into play at the time of the formal evaluation, and b) well concealed on the rating instrument itself. Thus industrial firms seeking to devise objective rating systems first decide, in an arbitrary manner, what dimensions are to be rated, . . . usually including some items having little to do with organizational effectiveness while excluding others that do. Only then does Personnel Division churn out official-looking documents on which all dimensions cho-sen to be rated are assigned point values, categories, or whatever (6, p. 92).

Nonetheless, many individuals seek to establish simple, quanti-fiable standards against which to measure and reward performance. Such efforts may be successful in highly predictable areas within an organization, but are likely to cause goal displacement when applied anywhere else. Overconcern with attendance and lateness in the in-surance firm and with number of people placed in the vocational re-habilitation division may have been largely responsible for the prob-lems described in those organizations.

Overemphasis on Highly Visible Behaviors

Difficulties often stem from the fact that some parts of the task are highly visible while other parts are not. For example, publications are easier to demonstrate than teaching, and scoring baskets and hitting home runs are more readily observable than feeding teammates and advancing base runners. Similarly, the adverse consequences of pro-nouncing a sick person well are more visible than those sustained by labeling a well person sick. Team-building and creativity are other examples of behaviors which may not be rewarded simply because they are hard to observe.

Hypocrisy

In some of the instances described the rewarder may have been getting the desired behavior, notwithstanding claims that the behavior was not desired. This may be true, for example, of management's attitude toward apple-polishing in the manufacturing firm (a behavior which subordinates felt was rewarded, despite management's avowed dislike of the practice). This also may explain politicians' unwillingness to revise the penalties for disobedience of ecology laws, and the failure of top management to devise reward systems which would cause sys-tematic evaluation of training and development programs.

Emphasis on Morality or Equity Rather than Efficiency

Sometimes consideration of other factors prevents the establishment of a system which rewards behaviors desired by the rewarder. The felt obligation of many Americans to vote for one candidate or another, for example, may impair their ability to withhold support from politicians who refuse to discuss the issues. Similarly, the concern for spreading the risk and costs of wartime military service may outweigh the advan-tage to be obtained by commiting personnel to combat until the war is over.

It should be noted that only with respect to the first two causes are reward systems really paying off for other than desired behaviors. In the case of the third and fourth causes the system *is* rewarding behaviors desired by the rewarder, and the systems are fouled up only from the standpoints of those who believe the rewarder's public statements (cause 3), or those who seek to maximize efficiency rather than other outcomes (cause 4).

CONCLUSIONS

Modern organization theory requires a recognition that the members of organizations and society possess divergent goals and motives. It therefore is unlikely that managers and their subordinates will seek the same outcomes. Three possible remedies for this potential problem are suggested.

Selection

It is theoretically possible for organizations to employ only those individuals whose goals and motives are wholly consonant with those of management. In such cases the same behaviors judged by subordinates to be rational would be perceived by management as desirable. State-of-the-art reviews of selection techniques, however, provide scant grounds for hope that such an approach would be successful (for example, see 12).

Training

Another theoretical alternative is for the organization to admit those employees whose goals are not consonant with those of management and then, through training, socialization, or whatever, alter employee goals to make them consonant. However, research on the effectiveness of such training programs, though limited, provides further grounds for pessimism (for example, see 3).

Altering the Reward System

What would have been the result if:
1. Nixon had been assured by his advisors that he could not win re-election except by discussing the issues in detail?
2. Physicians' conduct was subjected to regular examination by review boards for type 1 errors (calling healthy people ill) and to penalties (fines, censure, etc.) for errors of either type?
3. The President of XYZ Corporation had to choose between (a) spending $11 million dollars for antipollution equipment, and (b) incurring a fifty-fifty chance of going to jail for five years?

Managers who complain that their workers are not motivated might do well to consider the possibility that they have installed reward systems which are paying off for behaviors other than those they are seeking. This, in part, is what happened in Vietnam, and this is what regularly frustrates societal efforts to bring about honest politicians, civic-minded managers, etc. This certainly is what happened in both the manufacturing and the insurance companies.

A first step for such managers might be to find out what behaviors currently are being rewarded. Perhaps an instrument similar to that used in the manufacturing firm could be useful for this purpose. Chances are excellent that these managers will be surprised by what they find—that their firms are not rewarding what they assume they are. In fact, such undesirable behavior by organizational members as they have observed may be explained largely by the reward systems in use.

This is not to say that all organizational behavior is determined by formal rewards and punishments. Certainly it is true that in the absence of formal reinforcement some soldiers will be patriotic, some presidents will be ecology minded, and some orphanage directors will care about children. The point, however, is that in such cases the rewarder is not *causing* the behaviors desired but is only a fortunate bystander. For an organization to *act* upon its members, the formal reward system should positively reinforce desired behaviors, not constitute an obstacle to be overcome.

It might be wise to underscore the obvious fact that there is nothing really new in what has been said. In both theory and practice these matters have been mentioned before. Thus in many states Good Samaritan laws have been installed to protect doctors who stop to assist a stricken motorist. In states without such laws it is commonplace for doctors to refuse to stop, for fear of involvement in a subsequent lawsuit. In college basketball additional penalties have been instituted against players who foul their opponents deliberately. It has long been argued by Milton Friedman and others that penalties should be altered so as to make it irrational to disobey the ecology laws, and so on.

By altering the reward system the organization escapes the necessity of selecting only desirable people or of trying to alter undesirable ones. In Skinnerian terms (as described in 11, p. 704), "As for responsibility and goodness—as commonly defined—no one . . . would want or need them. They refer to a man's behaving well despite the absence of positive reinforcement that is obviously sufficient to explain it. Where such reinforcement exists, 'no one needs goodness.'"

NOTES

1. In Simon's (10, pp. 76–77) terms, a decision is "subjectively rational" if it maximizes an individual's valued outcomes so far as his knowledge permits. A decision is "personally rational" if it is oriented toward the individual's goals.

2. In one study (4) of 14,867 films for signs of tuberculosis, 1,216 positive readings turned out to be clinically negative; only 24 negative readings proved clinically active, a ratio of 50 to 1.

3. Personal interviews conducted during 1972-1973.

REFERENCES

1. Barnard, Chester I. *The Functions of the Executive* (Cambridge, Mass.: Harvard University Press, 1964).

2. Blau, Peter M., and W. Richard Scott. *Formal Organizations* (San Francisco: Chandler, 1962).

3. Fiedler, Fred E. "Predicting the Effects of Leadership Training and Experience from the Contingency Model," *Journal of Applied Psychology,* Vol. 56 (1972), 114–119.

4. Garland, L. H. "Studies of the Accuracy of Diagnostic Procedures," *American Journal Roentgenological, Radium Therapy Nuclear Medicine,* Vol. 82 (1959), 25–38.

5. Kerr, Steven. "Some Modifications in MBO as an OD Strategy," *Academy of Management Proceedings,* 1973, pp. 39–42.

6. Kerr, Steven. "What Price Objectivity?" *American Sociologist,* Vol. 8 (1973), 92–93.

7. Litwin, G. H., and R. A. Stringer, Jr. *Motivation and Organizational Climate* (Boston: Harvard University Press, 1968).

8. Perrow, Charles. "The Analysis of Goals in Complex Organizations," in A. Etzioni (Ed.), *Readings on Modern Organizations* (Englewood Cliffs, N.J.: Prentice-Hall, 1969).

9. Scheff, Thomas J. "Decision Rules, Types of Error, and Their Consequences in Medical Diagnosis," in F. Massarik and P. Ratoosh (Eds.), *Mathematical Explorations in Behavioral Science* (Homewood, Ill.: Irwin, 1965).

10. Simon, Herbert A. *Administrative Behavior* (New York: Free Press, 1957).

11. Swanson, G. E. "Review Symposium: Beyond Freedom and Dignity," *American Journal of Sociology,* Vol. 78 (1972), 702–705.

12. Webster, E. *Decision Making in the Employment Interview* (Montreal: Industrial Relations Center, McGill University, 1964).

Who Will Do the Dirty Work Tomorrow?

Edmund Faltermayer

In the computer age, millions of men and women still earn wages by carrying food trays, pushing brooms, shoveling dirt, and performing countless other menial tasks in ways that haven't changed much in centuries. Traditionally, these jobs have been taken by people with no

Reprinted from material originally appearing in the January 1974 issue of *Fortune* Magazine by special permission; © 1974 Time Inc. □ Research associate: Alexander Stack.

choice: high-school dropouts, immigrants with language difficulties, members of racial minorities, women, and young people (as well as unemployed family heads in desperate straits and disproportionate numbers of ex-convicts, alcoholics, the mentally retarded, and people with personality disorders). But various currents of change—including egalitarianism, rising expectations, and ever-more-generous government programs of support for nonworkers—are tending to make it harder to fill such jobs as time goes by. Some observers, indeed, foresee an eventual drying up of the pool of labor available to do menial work.

Yet many of these "jobs of last resort," as they have been called, involve essential tasks that it would be difficult to dispense with or to mechanize. Under the pressure of rising wages, the U.S. has traveled far down the road of reducing menial labor, which currently engages somewhere between 10 and 15 percent of the working population. But we are approaching the limits of how far we can go, or wish to go.

NO REPLACEMENT FOR ELBOW GREASE

On farms, for example, machines have replaced most manual toil. But a visit to California's Imperial Valley, one of the most efficient agricultural regions in the U.S., reveals that a surprising amount of "stoop" labor still survives. At construction sites, machines now do most of the heavy digging, but men with shovels still must work behind them. Much of the restaurant industry has shifted to self-service and throwaways, but growing numbers of Americans want to dine out in conventional fashion, with the food served on china plates.

In an effort to simplify cleaning, developers have modified the design of new office buildings, stores, and hotels, and industry now supplies improved chemicals and equipment. But Daniel Fraad Jr., chairman of Allied Maintenance Corp., which cleans offices, factories, and passenger terminals across the U.S., sees few remaining breakthroughs in productivity. Years ago, he says, his company abandoned a mechanical wall-washing device after it was found to be less efficient than a man with a sponge. Says Fraad, himself a former window washer: "In the final analysis, cleaning is elbow grease."

All this helps explain why the century-long process in which Americans have been moving out of low-status jobs is decelerating and may even be reversing. Productivity in the remaining menial occupations is growing more slowly than in most other fields, and shorter working hours often necessitate larger working staffs even where the amount of work remains the same. According to the Department of Labor, the percentage of Americans who were either "nonfarm laborers" or "service workers" was higher in 1972 than in 1960.

Declines in some menial jobs, most notably maids and housekeepers, have been more than offset by increases in other occupations. The 1970 census showed 1,250,000 "janitors" at work in the U.S., up from 750,000 a decade earlier. In the same period the ranks of unskilled hospital workers, i.e., "nursing aides, orderlies and attendants," rose by nearly 80 percent to 720,000, and the number of "garbage collectors" doubled. And the trend seems likely to continue. Between now and 1985, the Bureau of Labor Statistics has predicted, openings in many low-status jobs will increase faster than total employment.

DESPERATION IN DALLAS

But who, in this era when the Army feels compelled to abolish K.P., will want to wait on tables, empty bedpans or, for that matter, bury the dead? In some cities it's already hard to keep menial jobs filled. In the booming Dallas region, with its unemployment rate of only 2.1 percent, jobs for waitresses, private guards, trash collectors, and busboys were recently going begging.

One restaurant owner who is short of "bus help" revealed that his current roster consists of an illiterate black man in his fifties, a white girl who is somewhat retarded, a divorced white man in his sixties with personality problems, and an unattached white man in his forties "who goes out and gets drunk each day after he finishes his shift."

In slack labor markets such as Boston, where the unemployment rate has been running above the recent national figure of 4.7 percent, employers are experiencing troubles of a different sort. There seem to be enough people to fill most menial jobs, but they just don't stay around.

At the popular Sheraton-Boston Hotel, the turnover among chambermaids is about 150 percent a year. On pleasant weekends, when absenteeism runs high, the hotel hurriedly telephones local college students on a standby list. Down in the kitchens, turnover among dishwashers on the night shift exceeds a phenomenal 400 percent a year. Sometimes, the hotel has to ask the local U.S.O. to send over Navy men on shore leave who want to earn some extra money by helping out in the kitchens.

THE INCENTIVES *NOT* TO WORK

In Boston, as in many other cities outside the South, liberal welfare benefits make it possible for a great many people to stay out of the labor market if they don't like the work and wages available. Stricter administration of welfare, currently being attempted in a number of states, may remove some cheaters and induce some other recipients to work. Under a 1971 provision of federal law, welfare mothers with no preschool children are required to register for work. But it would be unrealistic to expect a tightening effective enough to make any large number of welfare recipients take menial jobs.

A number of factors besides increasingly generous welfare have been eroding the supply of people available for menial work. Perhaps the leading expert on this subject is economist Harold Wool of the National Planning Association. Wool points out that during the Sixties society's efforts to keep young people in school reduced the number of dropouts entering the labor force. At the same time, he says, the U.S. drew down much of its remaining "reserve" of rural labor migrating to cities.

Most important of all, minority groups, especially blacks, began pushing in earnest toward equality in employment. According to Wool's reckoning, black young men with at least one year of college (but not teen-agers or young women) have actually achieved occupational parity with their white counterparts. This remarkable social achievement has been too little noticed.

Today a great many young black people refuse to take jobs they consider demeaning. Wool observes that while a decade ago 20 percent of the black young women who had graduated from high school worked as domestics, only 3 percent were settling for that kind of work in 1970. "The service-type job," he says, "has become anathema to many blacks, even on a temporary basis." This helps explain why some service jobs are hard to fill even in cities where unemployment among young black people runs at dismayingly high rates.

It seems clear, then, that in years ahead the traditional supply of menial workers will not meet the demand. Some work will go undone. Many prosperous families whose counterparts even a decade ago would have employed household help now get along without any. Corners are clipped in services. Some restaurants, for example, have reduced the number of items on their menus, which among other things trims the customer's decision-making time and enables the waitress to move along faster.

THE $12,886-A-YEAR TRASHMEN

But a lot of menial work will have to be done, one way or another. Society will have to respond to the tightening of the labor supply by improving pay and working conditions. Right now there are many places where the federal minimum wage of $1.60 an hour cannot buy work. In northern cities, even members of the so-called "secondary labor force"—women and young people whose pay supplements a family's principal source of income—are usually not willing to work for $1.60. For those groups, $2 to $2.50 is the real market "minimum" needed to balance supply and demand.

It may be a portent of things to come that New York City now pays its unionized sanitation men $12,886 a year (plus an ultraliberal pension). Hardly anybody ever quits, and thousands of men are on a waiting list for future job openings. At Chrysler Corp., unskilled "material handlers," whose job includes pushing carts around the plant floor by hand, get $4.90 an hour, which draws plenty of young married men, both white and black.

At Boston's Massachusetts General Hospital, the minimum starting pay for "dietary service aides" and "building service aides" is $2.78, more than local hotels pay busboys and chambermaids. But even so, few native Bostonians, black or white, are entering such jobs these days. Most of the hospital's recent hires for entry-level jobs are immigrants from Jamaica and other Carribean islands, or recent black arrivals from the rural south.

HIGH STANDARDS FOR SWABBING DOWN

Higher pay, if it's high enough, clearly helps improve the status of menial work. Another way to improve its status is to raise the quality and complexity of the work itself. Some of the credit for a fairly low turnover rate at Massachusetts General Hospital goes to a training program begun in 1968 for those "building service aides," who previously had gone by the relatively servile titles of "maid" and "houseman."

The one-month program, which involves eighty hours in a classroom and a loose-leaf manual resembling one used by higher-skilled workers at the hospital, is not mere industrial-relations gimmickry. "Janitorial work in a hospital is different than in an office building," says Ruth MacRobert, the hospital's personnel director. "Here they need to learn aseptic techniques, and the fact that they can't use slippery compounds that might cause a patient to trip and fall. If there's a spill, they can't leave broken glass lying around. It's a lot different than swabbing down a deserted office. Who cares if the John Hancock Building is wet and slippery after hours?"

A pleasanter work climate can also help make low-status work less lowly. Lack of amenity on the job is particularly noticeable in the clangorous kitchens where some of the country's 2,860,000 food service workers earn their living. Jan Lovell, president of the Dallas Restaurant Association, believes his industry is improving the work atmosphere but will have to do more in order to survive. In the most menial jobs, he says, "we used to have a tradition of taking the dregs of society off the street and working them twelve hours a day." This, he says, was bad for management as well as the worker.

"A few years ago it wasn't unusual for a restaurant to buy a $12,000 dishwashing machine and then hire two drunks or wetbacks at $75 a week who might forget to turn the water on. Today you pay one guy $150 a week who does the work of two. But maybe we also need to put in a radio and a rug on the floor. The restaurant business has been hot, dirty, and sweaty. Who needs it?"

TO REPLACE A "VANISHING BREED"

Still another strategy is to make menial jobs a stepping-stone to something better. Texas Instruments, for example, offers a prospect of advancement to anyone who signs on to push a broom. Six years ago, in an effort to get better-quality work (and save money too), T.I. terminated contracts with outside cleaning firms and created a staff of its own to clean its factories and offices in the Dallas area. As in so many menial occupations, the staff has a nucleus of mature people who never aimed much higher in life, a majority of them black men in their fifties and sixties who in one supervisor's words are "a vanishing breed."

To lure younger replacements, the company offers a starting wage of $2.43 an hour, exactly the same as in production, and allows anyone to seek a transfer after six months. And like other T.I. employees, the sweepers are entitled to an exceptional fringe benefit: 90 percent of the cost of part-time education.

In a way, though, "promotability" makes it even harder to maintain a staff. Over the course of a year about 40 percent of T.I.'s "cleaning service attendants" move on to other jobs within the company, in addition to the 36 percent who quit or retire. One recently arrived janitor who is already looking around is Willie Gibson, a soft-spoken, twenty-year-old high-school graduate. Willie has been talking to "the head man in the machine shop" about the possibilities of a transfer. "There ain't nothing wrong with cleaning," he says, "It's got to be done. But me, I feel I can do better."

Texas Instruments is forced to search ceaselessly for replacements, who these days include Mexican-Americans and a few whites as well as blacks. Recruiting methods have included the announcement of janitorial vacancies from the pulpit of a black church.

A MAGNET FOR ILLEGALS

Until the early 1920's, immigration provided an abundant supply of menial workers. And recent years have seen something of a resurgence. Legal immigration has grown to 400,000 a year and now accounts for a fifth of the country's population growth. While many of the newcomers are professionals from the Philippines and India, the ranks also include a great many unskilled men and women from Mexico, the West Indies, and South America.

In addition, it is estimated that between one million and two million illegal aliens are at large in the U.S., mostly employed in low-status jobs. And the number of illegal aliens, whatever it may be, is undoubtedly growing. "Suddenly, in the last few months, there have been more of the illegals," says an official of the Texas Employment Commission in Dallas. The hiring of illegal immigrants is against the law in Texas, and the federal Immigration and Naturalization Service periodically rounds some of them up and deports them. But the very low unemployment rate in Dallas, the official says, acts as a magnet pulling in the illegals, who work mainly in small enterprises that are not scrupulous about observing the law.

In northern cities, illegal immigration began to increase during the late 1960's. New York City alone may have as many as 250,000 illegals, including Chinese and Greeks as well as Haitians, Dominicans, and other Latin Americans. Such people can be an employer's dream. Often they have no welfare or unemployment compensation to fall back on, since applying for such assistance could reveal their existence to the authorities. In an era of liberal income-maintenance programs for the native population, says New York State Industrial Commissioner Louis Levine, such people "have a total incentive to work."

TOWARD SELF-SUFFICIENCY IN DIRTY WORK

To rely on increasing numbers of immigrants to perform menial jobs, however, is to put off true long-range solutions to the problem. Sooner or later, every mature nation intent upon keeping its cultural identity will have to figure out a way to get most of the work done with its own native-born.

The U.S. cannot, and should not, close the door to all immigration, but a crackdown on illegal immigrants seems overdue. In addition to penalties against employers who hire illegal immigrants, an effective crackdown might require some device such as identity cards for all citizens. While repugnant to many Americans, such controls have long been a fact of life in France.

The U.S. is in a better position than most countries to move toward a state of "self-sufficiency in dirty work." Americans are generally free of Europe's ingrained class consciousness, and under certain conditions are rather flexible about the jobs they will take. And in recent years, in fact, white Americans have been moving into low-status jobs as black Americans move out. Most of these native-born recruits to menial work are women or young people.

In view of all the attention given to the women's liberation movement in recent years, it may seem paradoxical that many women have been moving into the lower end of the occupational scale. But there is not really any paradox. The desire of *some* women to pursue careers in managerial and professional fields should certainly not preclude employment of a different kind of woman in a different kind of situation—the woman who is not a breadwinner and does not want a career, but who does want the freedom to divide her life between housekeeping and periods of work that entail no encumbering commitments between employer and employee.

A lot of these women are in jobs that are fairly pleasant, and whose "menialness" has more to do with society's prevailing view than the nature of the work itself. Some restaurant work falls into this category. That is the opinion, for example, of Peggy Easter, a middle-aged white woman who waits on tables at Jan's Restaurant, a moderate-priced but clean and well-run establishment in a Dallas suburb. "Some people look down on this kind of work," she says. "But there's an art to this, and I like the hectic, fast pace because I have lots of nervous energy."

Like many waiters and waitresses, Mrs. Easter works only part time, coming in for three and a half hours each day during lunchtime. Her only child is married and her husband works full time as a diesel mechanic. With growing numbers of married women wanting to get out of the house, it is reasonable to expect that more Peggy Easters will turn up in the years ahead.

A BULGE FROM THE BABY BOOM

Young white people have moved into low-status jobs in even greater numbers than women. In 1960, according to census data, only 8 percent of the country's janitors were young whites under twenty-five. By 1970 that figure had jumped to 22 percent. Some of the movement of white young men *down* the occupational status scale (which partly accounts for that "parity" between blacks and whites who went to college) is a result of the postwar baby boom. Many of the young janitors, kitchen workers, and construction laborers are part-time workers from the ballooning population of high-school and college students. Others are full-time employees who, meeting heavy competition for jobs from their numerous contemporaries, have taken menial jobs until they can find something better. Another factor here is that many young whites live in the suburbs, where fast-food and other service jobs have grown more rapidly than in the cities.

Because the baby boom began waning in the late 1950's, the bulge in the number of employable young people will begin to recede during the middle and late 1970's. During the current decade as a whole, the sixteen to twenty-four age group will increase by 16 percent—somewhat less than the entire labor force, and far less than the phenomenal 48 percent growth during the Sixties.

To some extent, however, this demographic slowdown could be offset by a reduction in school hours, particularly in the high-school years. A growing number of educators and sociologists favor more part-time exposure of teen-agers to the working world, where they can benefit by rubbing shoulders with adults. One principal at a high school in the Northeast confided not long ago that all the basic material in his three-year curriculum, including the courses necessary for entering college, could be given in half the time. Not many principals, perhaps, would go that far, but certainly high-school education is now a very inefficient process. Any reduction in classroom time, of course, would make more teen-agers available for work, and much of that would be work generally considered menial.

AGAINST THE GRAIN

In any event, it seems reasonable to expect that young people will be taking on more of those dirty jobs. According to a well-entrenched American tradition, almost unthinkable in much of Europe, it is healthy for sons and daughters of the middle class to wait on tables, scrub pots, and even clean toilets as part of their "rites of initiation" into the world of work. Late in the nineteenth century, the American author Edward Bellamy, in the Utopian novel *Looking Backward*, foresaw a day when all the onerous tasks of society would be performed by young people during a three-year period of obligatory service.

A formal period of "national youth service," a proposal that has been revived in recent years, runs against the American grain. But less extreme policies to encourage the employment of more young people would be a step in the right direction. Lots of young people might welcome earlier introduction to the world of work, especially high-school students, who these days seem increasingly inclined to work anyway.

"DIRTY WORK CAN BE FUN"

Charles Muer, who operates a chain of restaurants headquartered in Detroit, employs young part-time workers extensively and considers it entirely feasible that they could take over most of the kitchen work. "You might have to pay them more," he says, "but productivity would be high. Kids are strong and enthusiastic, and dirty work can be fun, especially if you enjoy your co-workers and the management is nice."

Others are skeptical. "You've got to screen young people," says a hospital administrator, "and you can't leave them off by themselves where they'll goof off." Some tasks cannot and should not be performed by the young, particularly those involving nighttime shifts or long commuting distances. And some parents, of course, would object to their children's taking jobs they consider demeaning. John R. Coleman, the president of Haverford College whose experiences last year as an incognito ditchdigger and trash collector are described in his book *Time Out,* advises many of his students to get a taste of menial work. The parents most likely to be upset by such an idea, Coleman says, are "people unsure of their own status."

There's another and perhaps more formidable impediment. Until now the large number of young people bumping from one job to another as they slowly settle into careers has provided much of the labor pool for temporary dead-end work. (See "A Better Way to Deal with Unemployment," *Fortune,* June, 1973.) But some of the desirable education reforms now being tested are designed to enable high-school graduates to jump right into jobs with career ladders. If "career education" or something like it becomes widespread, it may become necessary to get that menial work out of students *before* they graduate. That would entail new social arrangements of some kind.

In an ideal world, all menial work would be a passing thing, whether for adults seeking a temporary change from their normal routine or for young people who can count on better jobs later on. It won't turn out quite that way, of course. Some people, because of limited ability or sheer inclination, will mop floors or wait on tables throughout their working lives. If recent trends continue, however, their pay will rise and with it their self-esteem—and, of course, the costs of their labor, at a time when lots of other things are also getting costlier.

THE AIRLINE ROUTE

An indication of the direction things will move in can be seen in the way some airlines get their planes cleaned up between runs. The American Airlines system, for example, embodies nearly all of the features that society will probably have to incorporate into its low-status jobs. At New York's LaGuardia Airport a force of 185 "cabin service clerks" (an old designation rather than a recent euphemism) cleans floors, scrubs lavatories, and empties the ashtrays into which airline passengers grind their cigarettes. The men go about their work briskly, with no indication that they consider it demeaning. Two-thirds of them are white, the rest black and Puerto Rican. Their pay starts at $4.57 an hour, with a maximum of $5.15.

The job is not a dead end. Some recent hires are college graduates who, in the words of H. Lee Nichols, the staff's black manager, "get a foot in the door with an airline by taking a job like this." Most of these workers move on, replaced by a steady supply of new men attracted by the pay and the prospects for advancement. After all, Nichols says, "five years of cleaning ashtrays, if you have any drive, can get to you."

Young Top Management: the New Goals, Rewards, Lifestyles

A BANKING INTELLECTUAL WHO "RAMRODS THINGS THROUGH"

In an organization where the early morning talk over coffee generally revolves around last night's Phillies' baseball score or the skills of the Philadelphia Flyers hockey team, Richard S. Ravenscroft stands a bit apart. The 36-year-old president of Philadelphia National Corp., parent of the $4-billion Philadelphia National Bank, is more likely to be in his office, earphones on his head, listening to softly played classical music while he thinks about interest rates or the effect of regulation on the future of bank holding companies.

Ravenscroft earns $89,718 a year as the youngest president of a bank holding company in the U.S., and he is a fascinating study in contrasts. He is very much the bookish, pipe-smoking intellectual—whose quick mind frequently leaves co-workers miles behind—in an industry that is not much known for intellectual managers. He came to the bank 15 years ago, fresh out of Yale. But his college major was American studies, not business, though he has since taken finance courses at the Wharton School. He lives on Philadelphia's Main Line but in a house that is decidedly modest. He shuns such traditional sports as golf for cycling on his 10-speed bike, and jogging.

But Ravenscroft has pushed hard since he joined PNB in 1960 to help launch Philadelphia International Investment Corp., an Edge Act subsidiary set up to invest in foreign banks and industrial companies. By 1966 he was president of PHC, and in early 1974 he was named president of Philadelphia National Corp. "The corporation was always two steps ahead of me in new assignments and responsibilities," says Ravenscroft. "I was like a greyhound chasing a rabbit."

He has been and continues to be a brusque and demanding manager, pushing authority far down the chain of command and leaving it to lower-level managers to sell their ideas all the way to the top. Ravenscroft thrived in that sort of environment and expects his subordinates to do so today.

Nowadays, Ravenscroft is busy trying to expand the holding company's nonbanking business and to cut the losses of the businesses it is already in, including an assortment of ailing mortgage and consumer finance companies and a factoring firm. Last year PNB earned $26.8 million over-all, but lost $1.1 million, or 19 cents a share, on its four nonbank subsidiaries.

Forcing Decisions

Ravenscroft's career at the bank was briefly interrupted by a year's stint in government. In 1969, he served as director of the policy division in the Office of Foreign Direct Investments. He returned to the bank in 1970, and under the sponsorship of both departing chairman John McDowell and the new chairman, G. Morris Dorrance, Jr., became executive vice-president with responsibility for the investment division, personnel, public relations, national, and correspondent banking. Last year, a shuffle handed Ravenscroft the presidency of the holding company.

As at most banks, work is often performed by, and credited to, committees rather than individuals, and Ravenscroft seems to accentuate the method. In a deceptively humble way, he constantly speaks in the collective "we" when referring to his own performance. "Ravenscroft never seems to make decisions," says one insider. "He forces decisions on others."

A Close Watcher

Ravenscroft freely admits that he leaves decisions to others. "That's what they're paid for," he says. "I try to give people more than they think they can handle, then watch them very closely."

But Ravenscroft is not always the understanding teacher. "He has no patience for stupidity," says one employee. "If you don't do your homework, he knows. You can't snow him. He even dresses people down publicly." To subordinates, Chairman Dorrance is aloof, Ravenscroft direct and sometimes brutal. "Ravenscroft ramrods things through," says one man.

Casual

Ravenscroft, who works from 8:30 a.m. to 5 p.m., pursues hobbies with the same intensity he shows at the office. A serious amateur photographer, he has shown and sold some of his work. Free time is jealously guarded for his wife and two children, the younger born just last spring. But Ravenscroft still takes home a full briefcase of work, which he reads to music from his eclectic collection of records and tapes.

At the office, Ravenscroft may be hard-driving, but his management still is distinctly casual. He is a bit irreverent about organizational trappings, frequently canceling his weekly staff meetings and dispensing with memos. "I like things to be out in the open," says Ravenscroft. "I'd much rather go see someone in his office. I can see the picture of his new dog, the amount of work on his desk. I like to see people in their lair."

"CREATIVE TENSION" IN A GROWTH COMPANY

Steering his sleek, silver $14,000 Jensen Interceptor into his reserved parking stall at Fairchild Camera & Instrument Corp. in Mountain View, Calif., Wilfred J. Corrigan has definitely "arrived." At 37, he is president and chief executive of a $385-million-a-year company, the third largest in the semi-conductor industry behind only Texas Instruments, Inc., and Motorola, Inc. With 16,300 employees and 20 manufacturing facilities in four states and seven countries under his tight command, Corrigan claims that his is "a fun-sized company," and for the first time in his fast-paced 15-year career he is comfortable in a job and not edgy about moving on to something "bigger and better."

For one thing, Corrigan is well paid for his 60-hour average work week. His annual salary, bonuses, and fees total $174,384. In addition, there is $58,580 in annual pension contributions and rights to purchase 60,000 shares of Fairchild stock at $18.38 to $28.41 per share. The company's stock has recently been trading at over $50, but Corrigan, who owned 6,250 shares last January, says that in the cyclical electronics industry, executives become blasé about the actual value of their holdings. "We've all felt wealthy at some point," he says.

In the semiconductor industry, salaries and incentives are often dazzling enough to both attract executive talent and keep it. "Once you are through the middle-management level and as your tax base goes up," says Corrigan, "material rewards become less of a driving factor." Far more important to this supremely self-confident chief executive is running a growth company and "managing change."

Keep Moving

Corrigan successfully steered Fairchild through the 1974-75 recession after becoming chief operating officer in 1973 and president in July, 1974. This summer he led the company from making just components to making end products when he announced a Fairchild line of electronic watches, and he has even grander plans for the company over the coming decade. Within those 10 years he expects it to move into the $1-billion class. "Whether a company or a country, you go either forward or backward; there is no way of standing still," he says.

That certainly has been Corrigan's personal and business philosophy. The son of a dockworker in Liverpool, England, Wilf (as he is still known to first- and second-tier Fairchild managers) knew from the age of 10 that he was going to leave England. One summer, between semesters spent earning a chemical engineering degree from the Imperial College of Science in London, Corrigan hitchhiked around the U.S. Favorably impressed, he later accepted a $7,000-a-year job as a product-line engineer in a Boston electronics plant over offers from a chemical plant in Germany and a gunpowder factory in Australia. Today about the only things Corrigan has from England are his Liverpool accent, his two-year-old sports car, and his wardrobe of $400 Savile Row suits.

Corrigan was recruited in 1961 by C. Lester Hogan, then executive vice-president of Motorola, as a junior-level engineer in the company's Phoenix semiconductor division. From his early Motorola days, Corrigan recalls, "I knew I wanted to be president of something." When Hogan resigned in 1968 to become president of Fairchild, seven of his lieutenants—including Corrigan—were quick to follow. Corrigan's title was group director of discrete devices. Says Hogan: "I knew he would be general manager of semiconductor component operations [Fairchild's largest division], but I felt Wilf had to earn his stripes first." Although Corrigan was cocky and occasionally insensitive to people's feelings, Hogan maintains that he had all the attributes of a top executive: "no-nonsense" toughness, stamina, a "mind like a sponge," and the uncanny ability to "always make the right decision." Corrigan became vice-president in charge of semiconductor operations in 1971 and chief operating officer in 1973. "I was grooming him for the top spot from the moment he arrived," says Hogan.

But it was Corrigan who finally took the initiative that actually put him in the presidency. He went over Hogan's head to Fairchild's Walter Burke, former chairman of the company and still president of a foundation that controls 13% of the company's stock, and threatened to resign if he were not named to Hogan's post. He got the job, and Hogan was moved upstairs to vice-chairman.

Stiff Payments

Corrigan's meteoric rise had its price. In 1970, when Fairchild was facing a recession, an internal liquidity crisis, and plunging sales and profits, Corrigan says he was working "literally all the time." He rarely saw his two sons and two daughters (now aged 7 to 13), and his Norwegian wife, Sigrun, was as "uptight" as he was. "When you're a workaholic," Corrigan recalls, "you tend to lose your mental equilibrium and go through periods when you feel persecuted." So Corrigan decided to put into Fairchild "whatever it takes" during the week but to save weekends for his family. With this two-dimensional view of life, Corrigan does not have time for the "trivia" of outside directorships, but he usually does manage to keep his weekend date with the family.

Although his wife has little doubt that work is the most important thing in Wilf's life, and Corrigan concedes that "it probably is," he still enjoys the time he spends at his seven-bedroom $200,000 home, an "English country cottage" in fashionable Los Altos Hills, Calif., where he takes an occasional swim in his new pool.

At the office, where Corrigan still spends long days, he feels he is adept at delegating authority without abandoning it and at maintaining an efficient and responsive organization. There is a monthly review of the objectives of each of the 11 divisions, each product line, and each individual product, and Corrigan spends fully a quarter of his time in financial and planning reviews. He also devotes considerable attention to listening to customers, distributors, competitors, and lower-level managers. "It's dangerous when you hear just what you want to hear," he says.

A Tough Style

Corrigan has strong feelings about which management techniques work and which do not. One he rejects is "the Noah's Ark philosophy, where there are two managers in every chair." When a company is overly concerned about what happens when an officer leaves and "puts an organizational safety belt on everything," he says, it builds in political pressure and high overhead. "I don't believe in redundancy. We don't carry safety parachutes," he says.

What he does believe in is "creative tension," a state in which workers are under enough pressure to get their jobs done but not so much that it panics them. "I want to create enough tension to keep the adrenalin flowing, but I don't want to overdo it," says Corrigan. Says Vice-President Thomas A. Longo: "Wilf makes sure people don't get comfortable in their jobs."

A half-dozen vice-presidents and other top executives left in various shakeups and resignations during Corrigan's rise to power, and only one other of "Hogan's heroes" still remains. One former division vice-president was fired without warning at 9:15 one morning and told to be out of Fairchild's headquarters by noon. He claims that Corrigan is not only bright and gutsy but also "very calculating and ambitiously ruthless—he is effective in cutting costs and people, but there is icewater in his veins."

With penetrating eyes, shortish hair combed straight back from his receding hairline, and a somewhat brittle manner, Corrigan does not exude warmth. Another former vice-president suggests that the "hard shell" might be a way Corrigan compensates for his youth. And Hogan thinks Corrigan is mellowing, no longer moving managers in and out as quickly as he was.

Not everyone agrees. In the past seven years there have been five managers of metal oxide semiconductors (MOS) products at Fairchild, and one former executive suggests, "If Corrigan doesn't see results in 18 months, he assumes it must be the guy who's running it rather than the fact that MOS is a long-term investment."

Industry analyst James R. Berdell of the San Francisco brokerage house of Robertson, Colman, Siebel & Weisel agrees that MOS is Fairchild's "Achilles heel" and adds that although Corrigan did well in the recession, "the jury is still out on how effectively he can run the company during an upturn."

Corrigan talks as though he expects a more or less unlimited upturn in his own business, which he grandly calls "the heartland of the universe." He says component companies like his will dominate the watch market and that sales of microprocessors—used in computers, auto and industrial controls, and cash registers—will grow from last year's $45 million to $300 million by 1980. He sees microprocessors being used in products as diverse as voice-activated typewriters and industrial robots. "Integrated circuitry is making possible products Flash Gordon would have ridiculed," says Corrigan. With such an electronic-oriented view of the world, it is no wonder Corrigan is happy in his job. "Why diddle around with things that aren't mainstream?" he asks. "There is no status quo in this business."

TAKING OVER AT NATE CUMMINGS' CONGLOMERATE

In business school, at the University of Virginia, professors accused John H. Bryan, Jr., of not being aggressive enough. Even after graduation, Bryan says, he set no conscious goals for himself. Indeed, since his family is well off, Bryan has never worried about salary and did not even discuss compensation for his present job until after he had taken it.

That may sound like a formula for going nowhere in today's competitive business world, but a year ago the 38-year-old Bryan was promoted from the presidency of Bryan Packing Co., the $160-million West Point (Miss.) meat-packing company founded by his father, to president and chief executive officer of its parent company, the $2.5-billion conglomerate, Consolidated Foods Corp. of Chicago.

The job, which carries a salary of $200,000 plus bonus, would have been a challenge to an executive with twice the experience of Bryan. Although sales have advanced steadily the past few years, earnings have sagged badly, dropping from a lackluster $72 million in the fiscal year ended June 30, 1974, to $50.6 million in fiscal year 1975. And waiting in the wings, presumably ready to reassert himself if Bryan should falter, is the 78-year-old Nathan Cummings, Con Foods' founder and still honorary chairman, who until Bryan came along seemed altogether reluctant to let anyone else really manage the company.

"I have made it abundantly clear to him [Cummings] that I feel the charge of running the corporation and will do so," says Bryan. "But there was no point at which I felt compelled to say 'sit down, let's get this straight that I'm running the company.' You just begin doing it."

Early Experience

Already Bryan is refurbishing the troubled conglomerate. He ordered unprofitable operations such as Fuller Brush Co. and a furniture group sold, reorganized Con Foods' toy and home furnishing subsidiaries, and strengthened management controls throughout the company. He also has made a major effort to remake the board. Five outsiders are being added to Con Foods' 15-man board, including Paul W. McCracken, who was chairman of the President's Council of Economic Advisers in the Nixon years.

Despite his relative youth, Bryan had already piled up 16 years of experience in running a sizable company before he came to Consolidated Foods. Although his record was made in the meatpacking company founded by this father, it was impressive enough to catch the attention of the officers and directors of Con Foods, which acquired the company in 1968. That was the year Bryan formally became president of Bryan Packing, though he had been running the company for nine years before that.

"He's calm, deliberate, and has an excellent manner in dealing with people," says Tilden Cummings, a Con Foods' director, retired president of Chicago's Continental Illinois Corp., and no relation to Nathan Cummings. "He's not timid about facing problems."

Most of Bryan's management maturity can be traced back to the unique upbringing he received in his father's business. The oldest of four children, Bryan was born the day his father opened a small slaughtering plant next door to the family home in West Point, Miss., a town of 8,000.

"I grew up with the business, it was my playground," recalls Bryan. "My father was a very driving, determined person who just never suspected I might not be totally interested in the business." Yet Bryan was undecided about what he wanted to do, and after earning an economics degree at Southwestern at Memphis, he refused his father's entreaties to come back and run the store. Instead, he entered the business school at the University of Virginia to buy more time. A year later he gave in, and while finishing work for his MBA degree at Mississippi State University, took over operating control of the company.

"My father seemed instinctively to have confidence in me," says Bryan. "He wouldn't let me have any other office than his. He just left when I came in and got into other businesses."

Reorganizing

Working a 12-hour day that began at 7 a.m., Bryan boosted sales from $18 million when he took over to $160 million when he left last year. When he could not buy the company from other family members who shared in the ownership, he arranged the merger with Con Foods.

Today, Bryan still works 12-hour days. Taking the 7 a.m. train from his suburban Kenilworth, Ill., home, he is in his office by 7:45 and does not arrive home until about 8 p.m., sometimes by train, sometimes by limousine if he has missed the hourly train. He admits he is concerned that he does not spend as much time with his family—his four children range up to 15—as he did in Mississippi.

At home each night, Bryan plans his next day, breaking his activities into categories: what has to be done absolutely that day, and things to keep in mind. "I like to know what's coming up long- and short-term," says Bryan, who combats tension with spates of organizing.

Not surprisingly, Bryan began reorganizing Con Foods in the same meticulous way. At his first board meeting he listed six goals to be accomplished in his first months in office, including a review of the role of the corporate staff and a long-term expense reduction program.

Need for Controls

Bryan has a simple theory of management that involves three characteristics: leadership, financial control, and planning.

"The most important is the leadership aspect, the ability to select, organize, and motivate employees," he says. "You do that by having a genuine respect for people you work with."

Bryan has also installed financial controls and audit procedures the company was conspicuously lacking. "There is great strength in de-centralization because of the motivation it fosters," he says. "But busi-nesses are fragile things and you have to know what's going on. When several Con Foods' companies ran into trouble, the need for controls became evident." In the third quarter of fiscal 1975 Con Foods actually showed a net loss from continuing operations of $913,000 on sales of $570 million, compared with earnings a year earlier of $18 million on sales of $552 million. In the same quarter the company also provided for an estimated loss of $28.9 million on the disposition of Fuller Brush and four furniture companies.

But Bryan predicts that earnings in the current fiscal year—the first full year under the new management—will be "more respectable." He will not make projections, but some analysts forecast that earnings will rise from 1975's $1.63 per share to between $2 and $2.25. For a company the size of Con Foods, that still leaves a lot of room for progress. "It's a great company that got into trouble, and we had to take some correc-tive steps," he says. "But there is clearly optimism in the corporation today."

Workaholics: This Land of Ours Has to Have Them

Wayne Oates

WORKAHOLISM: THE ORGANIZATION MAN'S NECESSITY

The organizational life of business, industry, or the church tends to call for the workaholic. One asks whether this syndrome of effort-riddenness is not spawned by a bureaucratic culture. There are certain identifiable cultural factors in alcoholic addiction and drug addiction which produce an "alcoholic culture" or a "drug culture," and my point here is that this is true of work addiction also. One kind of person that an organization must have is the man or woman who has *no* value that is not subordinated to the "good of the organization." He idolizes his outfit. If he celebrates his wedding anniversary, he feels he has to do it in such a way as to be good public relations for the organization. If he takes a vacation, it must be used in a way to make progress for the company, the school, or the plant.

Furthermore, this man does not work a given number of hours. He is always on call for the company. As William H. Whyte describes him and his kind, "they are never at leisure than when they are at leisure." This person is one who "is so completely involved in his work that he cannot distinguish between work and the rest of his life—and he is happy that he cannot."* This is rarely a salaried man who works so many days a month and year for his income, nor the nine-to-five man who when he finishes his daily stint forgets about work until his shift comes up again. This is a person who works around the clock. Let us take a look at his typical day.

He awakens at a specific time each morning without being called or without an alarm. He lies in bed for a few minutes and arranges in his mind every known detail of the schedule for that day. He ritualistically dresses and eats breakfast. He then moves through a day in which every moment is scheduled, except the time of leaving the office. At the

The Organization Man (New York: Doubleday, 1957), p. 164.

end of the day—usually after everyone else has gone home—he never heads for home until he has gathered materials for work at night. He eats his dinner, and his work is the main topic of the conversation at the table. He then retreats to his workroom to make the best of the remaining hours of the day. He retires and spends the time just before he drops off to sleep in trying once again to solve the problems that defied solution during the day, rehearsing accounts of conflicts he has had with other people during the day, and experiencing considerable anxiety about the amount of work he has to do the next day, week, or month.

I recall a businessman telling me of an experience which changed his whole life. He decided that he was going to quit taking work home at night. He first did so by staying at the office until he finished, gradually reducing the length of time he stayed at the office. Then he disciplined himself to have all his work done by 5:30 P.M. He tells of the first evening he went home when the rest of the office force did. He stood outside the office building and watched each one go by on his way home. Then he went through an "almost physical agony" as he resisted the temptation to go back upstairs to work or to get his briefcase to take work home. He finally made a break for home and has neither worked late nor taken work home since.

My central point in this section is: the organization *needs* a few workaholics to prosper as an organization. Culture as we have it calls for this kind of devotee to his work—workaholics who live by a sweephand watch and dream of ways to give more time than twenty-four hours each day.

WORKAHOLISM IN THE NINE-TO-FIVE MAN

The impression I have left thus far would seem to suggest that the work addict is an upper-middle-class and lower-upper-class phenomenon. He is not. The recent concern about "law and order" has called attention to the wages of policemen and firemen. Because of their relatively low pay these persons are forced to take additional jobs as security policemen, night watchmen, fire wardens, etc., for private companies in order to supplement their income.

The same need is felt also by public school teachers, and even university and college professors. I recently found one schoolteacher who worked in the evenings as a motel clerk, a job in which he could be paid extra and still have time to grade papers and prepare for classes the next day. During the Christmas holidays, he, being overweight, served as a Santa Claus in a nearby department store. These are persons with fixed-hour schedules who nevertheless moonlight in order to make additional money.

At first, the basic factor in overwork by people on fixed-schedule jobs seems to be purely financial. They need to make more money, which is not forthcoming from the public budgets out of which their initial salaries are paid. Usually they are in types of work where labor unions, and thus strikes for higher wages, etc., are taboo. Consequently the need for more income can only be met by taking extra work. On the surface, this seems to be *the* reason for moonlighting. However, closer inspection reveals other more subtle factors.

One of them is social prestige. These persons want their families to have what other families have, notably education. They and their wives both work in order to send their children to college. They themselves had to work long hours in order to get a college education. They do not want their sons and daughters to have to work as they did but to be able to give *all* their time to study. They want to have two cars so their wives can get around as they wish and so the children can have "wheels." They want to move to a better neighborhood so their children will have a chance to better themselves through the prestige of the kinds of friends they associate with, and marry.

As we probe underneath these social factors, we find the element of competition. In the Ten Commandments, we are told not to be covetous, but tradition approves all forms of competition. The ambiguous condition of the workaholic is that he works hard to get the things and the place in society that other men envy. At the same time he isolates himself from the very people whose approval he thinks he can get by outdoing them. The salty brine of competition is exciting to swim in, cooling to the skin as one revels in it, but does not satisfy the thirst for companionship and communion with others. As Samuel Johnson said in 1775, "That is the happiest conversation where there is no competition, no vanity, but a calm, quiet interchange of sentiments."

As we probe underneath the competitive factor, we find other causes of overwork. We find men who no longer can *see* the results of their labors. Even the assembly worker on the line does not *see* the total design of what he is doing. He has to assume that by doing his particular operation he has accomplished a great deal. The assembly line has removed the artisan from our culture; rarely today can one man in business for himself create enough pieces of furniture, jewelry, pottery, etc., to earn a living by direct sale of what he produces. There is a poignancy in the situation of a man who cannot invest his identity in the *substantive things he produces* rather than in the intangible of money. He has trouble communicating to his family the *worthwhileness* of what he is doing because he cannot show them the fruits of his hands except in the form of money. He cannot teach them his skill, but can only prove his manhood by bringing money home. It is little wonder that he seeks to work more and more in order to bring more and more money home. Yet all he gets as his reward is loneliness. Money creates a mythology of power in his family's mind; it also isolates him from them. He cannot easily teach his own children how to work, or communicate with his wife about what *his* work is really like. Little wonder that he solves the problem by returning to work! When he is gone and at work, he feels that they understand a *little*. When he is at home with *nothing to do*, they have no place for him because they have organized their lives on the assumption of his absence.

AGE AND WORKAHOLISM

One of the things that our culture is doing for us and to us at the same time is enabling us to live longer. Even a full generation ago retirement for people of certain social classes was unknown. Social security has changed all this.

The middle-aged person approaching retirement begins to feel the pangs of his workaholism just when he has earned enough money to have the right to a certain amount of leisure because he doesn't know how to use that leisure. Also, unwillingness to spend money for recreational or creative purposes may actually express the fear of spending money without doing a sufficient amount of work to punish oneself for it. For example, one doctor told me that when he went on vacation he always borrowed the money because he would have to punish himself with work to pay it back, and this was just penance for the pleasure of not working!

The middle-aged person, furthermore, often feels the need to redouble his efforts in order to get ready for retirement. He continues to do repetitious tasks in order to have something in reserve for a "rainy day." He then may become severely depressed. Fortunately, excellent methods of treatment for "middle-aged depressions" are available, and a professional person can be of real assistance to someone who is suffering in this way. They have the "know-how" to help him decide things he hitherto has had no support in deciding. They can even intervene directly and decide a few things for him, such as specific changes in his work habits. Thus, although middle-aged depression is very painful, it can often lead the middle-aged work addict to do what he should have done in the first place without becoming depressed and feeling guilty about it: interrupt his routine of work, do something for a while that he really enjoys doing, and stop driving himself like a slave.

Today culture has created the possibility of more leisure time for us through a shorter work week. As a people, we have more of this world's goods at an earlier age. We are lengthening life; we can retire. Yet we have not escaped the compulsion about work that defies external efforts to make life easier. We have not found the answer to the covetousness that makes men compete with each other in their work all out of proportion to their needs. We have not found the secret of rest in the midst of plenty, renewal in the midst of work, and companionship in the atmosphere of loneliness that tarrying too long at the job produces. Our culture produces the workaholic. We need to attend to the nature of a society that needs such slaves to work, and at the same time to struggle against our individual compulsions to work.

A Body With Many Heads
Peter Cohen

April 8: The scene was all too familiar. First the police and then the dean and then, a couple of hours later—when people were having dinner—the little black wagon came. There were two men in the wagon with a two-wheeled cart—the kind used to move heavy crates up and down staircases—they took the cart into one of the wings of the dorm, and when they came out, there was this thing strapped to the cart. Something the size and shape of a bag of golf clubs, only taller maybe—wrapped in dark tarpaulin.

They moved it quickly, and one of the men jumped and opened the rear of the wagon and they swung the cart around and lifted it in. The wagon was plain black, with no markings, and it drove away in a hurry.

That's how James Hinman left his first year at the Harvard Business School—dead of poison.

This is the third guy now, leaving like that, without knowing, without caring, where he is going to be five or a hundred or a couple of thousand years from now.

God knows how many times you have been told that competition is the American way and the only way; how you have heard it from lecterns and pulpits, and how you have almost come to believe it. And then you see a little cart wheel away what could have been a lifetime of laughter and tenderness and bright ideas. Suddenly you see the problems of it, the cost, and you wonder whether there *really* is no other way.

Because, when you come down to it, all competition is, is behavior. A piece of behavior that builds on the need of individuals to be faster, cleverer, richer than the next guy. And, undeniably, this need to be unequal is of great value to society. Because one way of getting things done is to get everybody to outdo each other.

So society encourages that kind of behavior by reward structures where the guy who ends up fastest or smartest gets everything, the others nothing. Suddenly it forgets that people have needs other than wanting to be unequal. That some groups and types of people, that everybody at certain times in his life, want very much to be *like*, not unlike, other types or groups of people. That progress doesn't just depend on people setting new and higher standards, but that, just as often, progress is a matter of attaining existing standards consistently.

Everybody forgets that despite its undeniable advantages competition is a wasteful process. That every winner comes at the cost of a hundred, a thousand, a hundred thousand losers. And that one ought to consider the cost of it, before one starts advocating indiscriminate competition.

And this is where the American society is at; it talks of *competition* as if it had never heard the word "co-operation." It refuses to see that too much pressure doesn't move people; it kills them. Instead, everybody pushes and pushes each other, and they call the other a lazy bastard, if one of them happens to break down.

No, Coach—winning isn't everything. It's only a thing.

8

ORGANIZATIONAL STRESS

The stress imposed on people in organizations is dealt with in traditional texts in terms of topics such as role conflict and ambiguity, interdepartmental conflict and the management of conflict. Rarely is even a partial inventory provided of the pressures which individuals are subjected to as part of their organizational lives. While stress and frustration are themes that are present throughout this book, the selections included in this section focus directly on some of the psychological and physical costs that organizations extract from their members.

In the excerpt from *Death of a Salesman*, Miller eloquently expresses the agony experienced by an aging salesman and his family over the realization of his obsolescence—and his employer's subsequent reactions.

Tiger comments on the practice of frequent corporate transfers and their effect on the wives and the families of the upward mobile manager and on the manager himself. He argues that while the children are undoubtedly most seriously affected, transfers seriously handicap the career-oriented wife, limiting her opportunities to become established and progress in her own work.

Meyer examines another fact of organizational life, the inability or unwillingness of executives to take vacations consonant with the maintenance of adequate health. While he blames this fundamentally on the scope and pace of today's business world, Meyer and others see this trend as symptomatic of the executive as either a driven man tied to his work or basically insecure about his job.

The selection from Arthur Hailey's *Wheels* takes us to another and much less rarified level of organizational reality. Here we visit the operating level of management in a large automobile factory and witness some of the pressures and trade-offs that must be dealt with routinely in large-scale, mass-production industry.

The preceding selections graphically illustrate a variety of stressful situations. The concluding piece in this section summarizes the evidence from both physicians and psychologists concerning the cumulative effects of occupational stress. Thus, the reader can readily extrapolate to other aspects of organizational life.

Death of a Salesman
Arthur Miller

From the right, Willy Loman, the Salesman, enters, carrying two large sample cases. The flute plays on. He hears but is not aware of it. He is past sixty years of age, dressed quietly. Even as he crosses the stage to the doorway of the house, his exhaustion is apparent. He unlocks the door, comes into the kitchen, and thankfully lets his burden down, feeling the soreness of his palms. A word-sigh escapes his lips—it might be "Oh, boy, oh, boy." He closes the door, then carries his cases out into the living-room, through the draped kitchen doorway.

Linda, his wife, has stirred in her bed at the right. She gets out and puts on a robe, listening. Most often jovial, she has developed an iron repression of her exceptions to Willy's behavior—she more than loves him, she admires him, as though his mercurial nature, his temper, his massive dreams and little cruelties, served her only as sharp reminders of the turbulent longings within him, longings which she shares but lacks the temperament to utter and follow to their end.

LINDA, *hearing Willy outside the bedroom, calls with some trepidation:* Willy!

WILLY: It's all right. I came back.

LINDA: Why? What happened? *Slight pause.* Did something happen, Willy?

WILLY: No, nothing happened.

LINDA: You didn't smash the car, did you?

WILLY, *with casual irritation:* I said nothing happened. Didn't you hear me?

LINDA: Don't you feel well?

WILLY: I'm tired to the death. *The flute has faded away. He sits on the bed beside her, a little numb.* I couldn't make it. I just couldn't make it, Linda.

LINDA, *very carefully, delicately:* Where were you all day? You look terrible.

WILLY: I got as far as a little above Yonkers. I stopped for a cup of coffee. Maybe it was the coffee.

LINDA: What?

WILLY, *after a pause:* I suddenly couldn't drive any more. The car kept going off onto the shoulder, y'know?

LINDA, *helpfully:* Oh. Maybe it was the steering again. I don't think Angelo knows the Studebaker.

WILLY: No, it's me, it's me. Suddenly I realize I'm goin' sixty miles an hour and I don't remember the last five minutes. I'm—I can't seem to—keep my mind to it.

LINDA: Maybe it's your glasses. You never went for your new glasses.

WILLY: No, I see everything. I came back ten miles an hour. It took me nearly four hours from Yonkers.

LINDA, *resigned:* Well, you'll just have to take a rest, Willy, you can't continue this way.

WILLY: I just got back from Florida.

LINDA: But you didn't rest your mind. Your mind is overactive, and the mind is what counts, dear.

WILLY: I'll start out in the morning. Maybe I'll feel better in the morning. *She is taking off his shoes.* These goddam arch supports are killing me.

LINDA: Take an aspirin. Should I get you an aspirin? It'll soothe you.

WILLY, *with wonder:* I was driving along, you understand? And I was fine. I was even observing the scenery. You can imagine, me looking at scenery, on the road every week of my life. But it's so beautiful up there, Linda, the trees are so thick, and the sun is warm. I opened the windshield and just let the warm air bathe over me. And then all of a sudden I'm goin' off the road! I'm tellin' ya, I absolutely forgot I was driving. If I'd've gone the other way over the white line I might've killed somebody. So I went on again—and five minutes later I'm dreamin' again, and I nearly— *He presses two fingers against his eyes.* I have such thoughts, I have such strange thoughts.

LINDA: Willy, dear. Talk to them again. There's no reason why you can't work in New York.

WILLY: They don't need me in New York. I'm the New England man. I'm vital in New England.

LINDA: But you're sixty years old. They can't expect you to keep traveling every week.

WILLY: I'll have to send a wire to Portland. I'm supposed to see Brown and Morrison tomorrow morning at ten o'clock to show the line. Goddammit, I could sell them! *He starts putting on his jacket.*

LINDA, *taking the jacket from him:* Why don't you go down to the place tomorrow and tell Howard you've simply got to work in New York? You're too accommodating, dear.

WILLY: If old man Wagner was alive I'd a been in charge of New York now! That man was a prince; he was a masterful man. But that boy of his, that Howard, he don't appreciate. When I went north the first time, the Wagner Company didn't know where New England was!

LINDA: Why don't you tell those things to Howard, dear?

WILLY, *encouraged:* I will, I definitely will. Is there any cheese?

LINDA: I'll make you a sandwich.

WILLY: No, go to sleep. I'll take some milk. I'll be up right away. . . .

[*Editor's note:* The scene shifts to Howard Wagner's office the following day.]

WILLY: Pst! Pst!

HOWARD: Hello, Willy, come in.

WILLY: Like to have a little talk with you, Howard.

HOWARD: Sorry to keep you waiting. I'll be with you in a minute.

WILLY: What's that, Howard?

HOWARD: Didn't you ever see one of these? Wire recorder.

WILLY: Oh. Can we talk a minute?

HOWARD: Records things. Just got delivery yesterday. Been driving me crazy, the most terrific machine I ever saw in my life. I was up all night with it.

WILLY: What do you do with it?

HOWARD: I bought it for dictation, but you can do anything with it. Listen to this. I had it home last night. Listen to what I picked up. The first one is my daughter. Get this. *He flicks the switch and "Roll out the Barrel" is heard being whistled.* Listen to that kid whistle.

WILLY: That is lifelike, isn't it?

HOWARD: Seven years old. Get that tone.

WILLY: Ts, ts. Like to ask a little favor if you . . .

The whistling breaks off, and the voice of Howard's daughter is heard.

HIS DAUGHTER: "Now you, Daddy."

HOWARD: She's crazy for me! *Again the same song is whistled.* That's me! Ha! *He winks.*

WILLY: You're very good!

The whistling breaks off again. The machine runs silent for a moment.

HOWARD: Sh! Get this now, this is my son.

HIS SON: "The capital of Alabama is Montgomery; the capital of Arizona is Phoenix; the capital of Arkansas is Little Rock; the capital of California is Sacramento . . ." *and on, and on.*

HOWARD, *holding up five fingers:* Five years old, Willy!

WILLY: He'll make an announcer some day!

HIS SON, *continuing:* "The capital . . ."

HOWARD: Get that—alphabetical order! *The machine breaks off suddenly.* Wait a minute. The maid kicked the plug out.

WILLY: It certainly is a—

HOWARD: Sh, for God's sake!

HIS SON: "It's nine o'clock, Bulova watch time. So I have to go to sleep."

WILLY: That really is—

HOWARD: Wait a minute! The next is my wife.

They wait.

HOWARD'S VOICE: "Go on, say something." *Pause.* "Well, you gonna talk?"

HIS WIFE: "I can't think of anything."

HOWARD'S VOICE: "Well, talk—it's turning."

HIS WIFE, *shyly, beaten:* "Hello." *Silence.* "Oh, Howard, I can't talk into this . . ."

HOWARD, *snapping the machine off:* That was my wife.

WILLY: That is a wonderful machine. Can we—

HOWARD: I tell you, Willy, I'm gonna take my camera, and my bandsaw, and all my hobbies, and out they go. This is the most fascinating relaxation I ever found.

WILLY: I think I'll get one myself.

HOWARD: Sure, they're only a hundred and a half. You can't do without it. Supposing you wanna hear Jack Benny, see? But you can't be at home at that hour. So you tell the maid to turn the radio on when Jack Benny comes on, and this automatically goes on with the radio . . .

WILLY: And when you come home you . . .

HOWARD: You can come home twelve o'clock, one o'clock, any time you like, and you get yourself a Coke and sit yourself down, throw the switch, and there's Jack Benny's program in the middle of the night!

WILLY: I'm definitely going to get one. Because lots of time I'm on the road, and I think to myself, what I must be missing on the radio!

HOWARD: Don't you have a radio in the car?

WILLY: Well, yeah, but who ever thinks of turning it on?

HOWARD: Say, aren't you supposed to be in Boston?

WILLY: That's what I want to talk to you about, Howard. You got a minute? *He draws a chair in from the wing.*

HOWARD: What happened? What're you doing here?

WILLY: Well . . .

HOWARD: You didn't crack up again, did you?

WILLY: Oh, no. No . . .

HOWARD: Geez, you had me worried there for a minute. What's the trouble?

WILLY: Well, tell you the truth, Howard. I've come to the decision that I'd rather not travel any more.

HOWARD: Not travel! Well, what'll you do?

WILLY: Remember, Christmas time, when you had the party here? You said you'd try to think of some spot for me here in town.

HOWARD: With us?

WILLY: Well, sure.

HOWARD: Oh, yeah, yeah. I remember. Well, I couldn't think of anything for you, Willy.

WILLY: I tell ya, Howard. The kids are all grown up, y'know. I don't need much any more. If I could take home—well, sixty-five dollars a week, I could swing it.

HOWARD: Yeah, but Willy, see I—

WILLY: I tell ya why, Howard. Speaking frankly and between the two of us, y'know—I'm just a little tired.

HOWARD: Oh, I could understand that, Willy. But you're a road man, Willy, and we do a road business. We've only got a half-dozen salesmen on the floor here.

WILLY: God knows, Howard, I never asked a favor of any man. But I was with the firm when your father used to carry you in here in his arms.

HOWARD: I know that, Willy, but—

WILLY: Your father came to me the day you were born and asked me what I thought of the name of Howard, may he rest in peace.

HOWARD: I appreciate that, Willy, but there just is no spot here for you. If I had a spot I'd slam you right in, but I just don't have a single solitary spot.

He looks for his lighter. Willy has picked it up and gives it to him. Pause.

WILLY, *with increasing anger:* Howard, all I need to set my table is fifty dollars a week.

HOWARD: But where am I going to put you, kid?

WILLY: Look, it isn't a question of whether I can sell merchandise, is it?

HOWARD: No, but it's a business, kid, and everybody's gotta pull his own weight.

WILLY, *desperately:* Just let me tell you a story, Howard—

HOWARD: 'Cause you gotta admit, business is business.

WILLY, *angrily:* Business is definitely business, but just listen for a minute. You don't understand this. When I was a boy—eighteen, nineteen—I was already on the road. And there was a question in my mind as to whether selling had a future for me. Because in those days I had a yearning to go to Alaska. See, there were three gold strikes in one month in Alaska, and I felt like going out. Just for the ride, you might say.

HOWARD, *barely interested:* Don't say.

WILLY: Oh, yeah, my father lived many years in Alaska. He was an adventurous man. We've got quite a little streak of self-reliance in our family. I thought I'd go out with my older brother and try to locate him, and maybe settle in the North with the old man. And I was almost decided to go, when I met a salesman in the Parker House. His name was Dave Singleman. And he was eighty-four years old, and he'd drummed merchandise in thirty-one states. And old Dave, he'd go up to his room, y'understand, put on his green velvet slippers—I'll never forget—and pick up his phone and call the buyers, and without ever leaving his room, at the age of eighty-four, he made his living. And when I saw that, I realized that selling was the greatest career a man could want. 'Cause what could be more satisfying than to be able to go, at the age of eighty-four, into twenty or thirty different cities, and pick up a phone, and be remembered and loved and helped by so many different people? Do you know? when he died—and by the way he died the death of a salesman, in his green velvet slippers in the smoker of the New York, New Haven and Hartford, going into Boston—when he died, hundreds of salesmen and buyers were at his funeral. Things were sad on a lotta trains for months after that. *He stands up. Howard has not looked at him.* In those days there was personality in it, Howard. There was respect, and comradeship, and gratitude in it. Today, it's all cut and dried, and there's no chance for bringing friendship to bear— or personality. You see what I mean? They don't know me any more.

HOWARD, *moving away, to the right:* That's just the thing, Willy.

WILLY: If I had forty dollars a week—that's all I'd need. Forty dollars, Howard.

HOWARD: Kid, I can't take blood from a stone, I—

WILLY, *desperation is on him now:* Howard, the year Al Smith was nominated, your father came to me and—

HOWARD, *starting to go off:* I've got to see some people, kid.

WILLY, *stopping him:* I'm talking about your father! There were promises made across this desk! You mustn't tell me you've got people to see—I put thirty-four years into this firm, Howard, and now I can't pay my insurance! You can't eat the orange and throw the peel away—a man is not a piece of fruit! *After a pause:* Now pay attention. Your father—in 1928 I had a big year. I averaged a hundred and seventy dollars a week in commissions.

HOWARD, *impatiently:* Now, Willy, you never averaged—

WILLY, *banging his hand on the desk:* I averaged a hundred and seventy dollars a week in the year of 1928! And your father came to me—or rather, I was in the office here—it was right over this desk—and he put his hand on my shoulder—

HOWARD, *getting up:* You'll have to excuse me, Willy, I gotta see some people. Pull yourself together. *Going out:* I'll be back in a little while.

On Howard's exit, the light on his chair grows very bright and strange.

WILLY: Pull myself together! What the hell did I say to him? My God, I was yelling at him! How could I! *Willy breaks off, staring at the light, which occupies the chair, animating it. He approaches this chair, standing across the desk from it.* Frank, Frank, don't you remember what you told me that time? How you put your hand on my shoulder, and Frank . . . *He leans on the desk and as he speaks the dead man's name he accidentally switches on the recorder, and instantly*

HOWARD'S SON: ". . . of New York is Albany. The capital of Ohio is Cincinnati, the capital of Rhode Island is . . ." *The recitation continues.*

WILLY, *leaping away with fright, shouting:* Ha! Howard! Howard! Howard!

HOWARD, *rushing in:* What happened?

WILLY, *pointing at the machine, which continues nasally, childishly, with the capital cities:* Shut it off! Shut it off!

HOWARD, *pulling the plug out:* Look, Willy . . .

WILLY, *pressing his hands to his eyes:* I gotta get myself some coffee. I'll get some coffee . . .

Willy starts to walk out. Howard stops him.

HOWARD, *rolling up the cord:* Willy, look . . .

WILLY: I'll go to Boston.

HOWARD: Willy, you can't go to Boston for us.

WILLY: Why can't I go?

HOWARD: I don't want you to represent us. I've been meaning to tell you for a long time now.

WILLY: Howard, are you firing me?

HOWARD: I think you need a good long rest, Willy.

WILLY: Howard—

HOWARD: And when you feel better, come back, and we'll see if we can work something out.

WILLY: But I gotta earn money, Howard. I'm in no position to—

HOWARD: Where are your sons? Why don't your sons give you a hand?

WILLY: They're working on a very big deal.

HOWARD: This is no time for false pride, Willy. You go to your sons and you tell them that you're tired. You've got two great boys, haven't you?

WILLY: Oh, no question, no question, but in the meantime . . .

HOWARD: Then that's that, heh?

WILLY: All right, I'll go to Boston tomorrow.

HOWARD: No, no.

WILLY: I can't throw myself on my sons. I'm not a cripple!

HOWARD: Look, kid, I'm busy this morning.

WILLY, *grasping Howard's arm:* Howard, you've got to let me go to Boston!

HOWARD, *hard, keeping himself under control:* I've got a line of people to see this morning. Sit down, take five minutes, and pull yourself to-gether, and then go home, will ya? I need the office, Willy. *He starts to go, turns, remembering the recorder, starts to push off the table holding the recorder.* Oh, yeah. Whenever you can this week, stop by and drop off the samples. You'll feel better, Willy, and then come back and we'll talk. Pull yourself together, kid, there's people outside. . . .

REQUIEM

[*Editor's note:* Biff & Charley are Willy's sons.]

CHARLEY: It's getting dark, Linda.

Linda doesn't react. She stares at the grave.

BIFF: How about it, Mom? Better get some rest, heh? They'll be closing the gate soon.

Linda makes no move. Pause.

HAPPY, *deeply angered:* He had no right to do that. There was no necessity for it. We would've helped him.

CHARLEY, *grunting:* Hmmm.

BIFF: Come along, Mom.

LINDA: Why didn't anybody come?

CHARLEY: It was a very nice funeral.

LINDA: But where are all the people he knew? Maybe they blame him.

CHARLEY: Naa. It's a rough world, Linda. They wouldn't blame him.

LINDA: I can't understand it. At this time especially. First time in thirty-five years we were just about free and clear. He only needed a little salary. He was even finished with the dentist.

CHARLEY: No man only needs a little salary.

LINDA: I can't understand it.

BIFF: There were a lot of nice days. When he'd come home from a trip; or on Sundays, making the stoop; finishing the cellar; putting on the new porch; when he built the extra bathroom; and put up the garage. You know something, Charley, there's more of him in that front stoop than in all the sales he ever made.

CHARLEY: Yeah. He was a happy man with a batch of cement.

LINDA: He was so wonderful with his hands.

BIFF: He had the wrong dreams. All, all, wrong.

HAPPY, *almost ready to fight Biff:* Don't say that!

BIFF: He never knew who he was.

CHARLEY, *stopping Happy's movement and reply. To Biff:* Nobody dast blame this man. You don't understand: Willy was a salesman. And for a salesman, there is no rock bottom to the life. He don't put a bolt to a nut, he don't tell you the law or give you medicine. He's a man way out there in the blue, riding on a smile and a shoeshine. And when they start not smiling back—that's an earthquake. And then you get yourself a couple of spots on your hat, and you're finished. Nobody dast blame this man. A salesman is got to dream, boy. It comes with the territory.

BIFF: Charley, the man didn't know who he was.

HAPPY, *infuriated:* Don't say that!

BIFF: Why don't you come with me, Happy?

HAPPY: I'm not licked that easily. I'm staying right in this city, and I'm gonna beat this racket! *He looks at Biff, his chin set.* The Loman Brothers!

BIFF: I know who I am, kid.

HAPPY: All right, boy. I'm gonna show you and everybody else that Willy Loman did not die in vain. He had a good dream. It's the only dream you can have—to come out number one man. He fought it out here, and this is where I'm gonna win it for him.

BIFF, *with a hopeless glance at Happy, bends toward his mother:* Let's go, Mom.

LINDA: I'll be with you in a minute. Go on, Charley. *He hesitates.* I want to, just for a minute. I never had a chance to say good-by.

Charley moves away, followed by Happy. Biff remains a slight distance up and left of Linda. She sits there, summoning herself. The flute begins, not far away, playing behind her speech.

LINDA: Forgive me, dear. I can't cry. I don't know what it is, but I can't cry. I don't understand it. Why did you ever do that? Help me, Willy, I can't cry. It seems to me that you're just on another trip. I keep expecting you. Willy, dear, I can't cry. Why did you do it? I search and search and I search, and I can't understand it, Willy. I made the last payment on the house today. Today, dear. And there'll be nobody home. *A sob rises in her throat.* We're free and clear. *Sobbing more fully, released:* We're free. *Biff comes slowly toward her.* We're free . . . We're free . . .

Biff lifts her to her feet and moves out up right with her in his arms. Linda sobs quietly. Bernard and Charley come together and follow them, followed by Happy. Only the music of the flute is left on the darkening stage as over the house the hard towers of the apartment buildings rise into sharp focus, and
The Curtain Falls

Is This Trip Necessary?
The Heavy Human Costs
of Moving Executives Around
Lionel Tiger

In the late 1960's, I wrote a book called *Men in Groups* that sought to describe how and why males controlled the powerful organizations in all human societies, and what consequences this had for themselves, for their wives and children, and for the communities themselves. Even though I began working on it long before the present controversy about male dominance surfaced, the book's entry into the world coincided with the beginnings of the female liberation movement, and it was a very controversial book indeed. I reaped a lot of letters. One in particular struck me as an extraordinarily powerful statement of the condition I would like to explore in this article.

The writer of the letter had been married for twenty-five years to an executive of a large U.S.-based chemical company. She said that she agreed with my description of how things were. However, she wanted to tell me that in the twenty-five years of her marriage she had moved seventeen times with her husband and family. Each time she moved, she said, her husband was able to work with colleagues whom he had met before, at least through correspondence or over the telephone. But she had to construct, each time, a new life and a new personal community for herself and her children. Then she made this remarkably chilling statement: "Only my husband knows and cares about my past and future."

There occurred to me the image of her husband's brain as the museum of her existence. Only her husband knew what she was like

Reprinted from material originally appearing in the September 1974 issue of *Fortune* Magazine by special permission; © 1974 Time Inc.

when she was newly married and how she responded to her first child. Only her husband cared about her middle age and her concern about her body. Only her husband would have a perspective within which she could expect to live with some sense of continuity. And when he died, as he would some seven or eight years before her (if the statistics applied to this couple), she would become a peculiar kind of psychologically homeless person.

Even Gypsies move in groups. The nomads of the African drought region, facing starvation, still travel in groups, with friends, with relatives, with persons who are part of the web of their lives. When ours was a new and poor continent, it is true, people homesteaded, moved as single families; many lived at a great distance from their neighbors. But the wagon trains of the settlers provided a gregarious context, a community within which the complicated business of moving one's body, one's mind, one's symbols, and one's possessions could proceed.

In the rich society we boast of, however, such a commodity of friendship and familiarity may not be available to the manager of a powerful chemical company, nor to thousands upon thousands of men and women who each year are moved around, pulled around, pushed around—choose your own term. What happens to the wives and children (or, increasingly perhaps, husbands and children) of the employees who receive marching orders, however elegantly they are framed and however persuasively they are issued? And what kinds of businessmen and citizens do the managers become who live in symbolic mobile homes?

DISENCHANTING THE CHILDREN

I would like to suggest that an important consequence of the corporate commitment to moving managers around is that their wives and children are deprived of the fundamental human requirement of social continuity and personal stability; that the managers are debarred from becoming effective members of the communities in which they find themselves; and that by forcing people to adapt to the company's scheme, rather than adapting the company to the people who work in it, American business is disenchanting the sons and daughters of its own executives, and in some degree impairing the potential effectiveness of the executives themselves. Now let me examine these contentions.

Some time ago I participated in a course for up-and-coming middle managers, given at Rutgers University, where I work. During one session I raised the matter of executive mobility, and the room exploded with emotions, anecdotes, and a large amount of baffled bitterness. One man said he had made major moves every eighteen to twenty-four months. That was the only way he could be promoted, he added, because that was how his company organized itself. Another said that if he had been unwilling to move as requested, his income would be substantially lower than it was. A woman said she expected difficulty in her company because if she and her husband could not receive good transfers together, her promising career might be hindered.

Especially memorable were the words of a man who said that he had been offered a considerable improvement in his job, but that when he presented the possibility to his family, his two oldest children refused to go. The girl was seventeen and had been in no less than eleven schools; the boy was fifteen and had been in eight different schools. They had had enough, or too much. Their father pointed out to them what they could be losing should he reject the offer. But the increased income they might share and the greater sense of power and accomplishment their father might enjoy interested them not at all. That particular family stayed put.

The discussion continued in a similar vein. None of the companies involved was a bush-league operation. Each was a leader in its field; each routinely bought full-page ads to describe its commitment to the communities it served. However, their own highly valued employees, and the families of those employees, were forced to endure on a regular basis a migration uprooting them as formidably as if there had been a natural catastrophe in their towns. These most elegant and rewarded of migrants could see their lives only in terms of a procession of more or less identical suburbs designed for interchangeable people.

The loss of social continuity involves serious costs. Human beings have a great need for intimate and regular social experience. The prototypical relationship is that of the child with its parents—we are creatures who require a long period of close contact and dependency between parents and children. In social terms, children are very tender creatures; the shy child hiding behind its parent as a stranger approaches is reflecting a deeply conservative conception of what the social world is like and how unpredictable it can be.

HAVE THE TUMULTS BEEN FORGOTTEN?

While it is obviously important for children to encounter new experiences and come to know a variety of people, it is also important that there be a set of social certainties and continuities, providing a definite sense of place and identity and a confidence that even if things do change, not everything changes at once. Have the managers of companies promoting their executives from one side of this continent to another forgotten the tumults of their own childhoods, when they moved to a new house or a new town? Are they unaware of the problems of children who must establish themselves in a new school, with new friends, new bullies, new teams, new loyalties, and new challenges? Are the large numbers of affluent dropouts, the children of the most privileged members of the community, rebelling in part against a special form of deprivation—the lack of continuity and stability? Are they reflecting an unwillingness to be exiles in their own country?

While children are undoubtedly the most severely affected persons in this joyless game of musical chairs—sometimes called "executive development"—wives are surely not spared from fundamental disruption. Moreover, they are to a great extent deprived of the possibility of sustained involvement in a rewarding career. Feminist pressures for long-term careers for women have exposed, and will more starkly expose, the disability suffered by talented women whose careers are dependent on their husbands' jobs. On the principle of last hired, first fired, the wife of the mobile executive is always vulnerable to adjustments in the economy. She is very unlikely to be a serious candidate for senior posts, because she will lack seniority and will be unable to provide her employers the continuity they may seek in their higher management.

AN EXPENSIVE PATTERN

There is a vicious circle here. Since husbands by and large earn more money than their wives, job choices are made in terms of male careers; and since wives must move with their husbands, they are unable to become senior enough to earn the high salaries that might alter a male-centered pattern of mobility. The circle is not only vicious, but also expensive, for it condemns thousands of well-educated women to episodic employment rather than serious careers, and must induce them to trivialize their work in their own minds and lose confidence in its economic and social meaning.

This is by no means to be taken as an argument that wives *should* enter the labor force—what I am arguing for is increased freedom and opportunity. Some wives, of course, do not want to enter the labor force. And while the matter is controversial, it is not clear that the absence of working mothers from the home is without costs to the healthy development of preschool children. The lot of the working wife herself, of course, is not always a happy one. While what has been graphically described as "the captive housewife" may suffer social and intellectual deprivation, the wife with both demanding job and demanding young family may experience an overabundance of demands on her energy and time.

Certainly, however, there is now too little opportunity for wives who do want to pursue careers. It is well to see this in perspective. From the time of the hunting-gathering phase of our evolution, through the pastoral and agricultural phases, females were involved in

extra-domestic activities of considerable variety and of major significance for the prosperity and well-being of their communities. The
idle heroines of John Cheever and J. P. Marquand, with nothing but
golf, adultery, couture, and martinis on their minds, are decidedly not
the crowning glory of female evolution, but rather a special product of
the displacements of the industrial revolution and the very specialized
demands of a highly mobile work force.

Another kind of perspective has to do with demographic changes.
Toward the end of the last century, a woman might well die by the age
of forty-five; her adult life would have been totally involved with sustaining the existence of her children and her husband. But the situation
now is radically different. Women marry early, typically at twenty or
twenty-one, and they have relatively few children, who in any event
are absorbed in school by the time their mothers are in their early or
middle thirties. And then a woman has more than half her life to lead
even though the challenges of her traditional biological career have
been successfully met.

"I'VE BEEN MOVED"

I would not be at all surprised if before long there is growing and
effective pressure on companies to assure spouses of reasonable employment when executives are moved—or at least some respectable
opportunity to acquire skills, perhaps even in the companies involved.
Nor will it be altogether unexpected if women begin to demand some
more formal role in decision making about executive mobility, other
than to pack their bags and then smile somewhat weakly at yet another
Welcome Wagon in yet another town.

Of course, it is not solely executive mobility that causes this waste of
women's abilities, and perhaps it is not even the primary factor.
Nonetheless, the difficulties women face as they seek productive
careers are magnified in a major way by the mobility of their husbands.
Even if wives are willing and able to try something more than volunteer
work or sporadic employment, both their prospective employers and
they themselves have to consider that once they're in position for a
major job, it'll be time to call the movers once again.

This situation not only deprives women of opportunities and satis-
factions, but also deprives communities of the long-run participation
of educated wives of effective husbands. In this and other ways, the
practice of moving executives around reduces the useful connection of
business groups with the wider society.

About a year ago I was with a realtor showing me some country
cottages in the Hudson Valley, north of New York City, in an area
where a large I.B.M. facility had been established. In commenting on
the pattern of life in the region, he recalled the bitter, oft repeated joke

that I.B.M. stands for "I've Been Moved." The company's employees, he said, had little to do with the community except help cause the tax rates to increase. He appeared to perceive the company as a group of foreign creatures living off his territory, interested only in themselves, and lacking serious connection with the place where he lived. While it has become clear to multinational companies that there are great advantages, both political and functional, in having local managers as leading figures in their foreign operations, this principle has scarcely penetrated the domestic operations of U.S. companies whose executives live the mobile life.

Now, it would plainly be absurd to suggest that members of management should work only in the region in which they were born or raised—the North American pattern of education, if nothing else, would make that unlikely. But this is all a matter of degree. It seems very plausible that to the extent they move executives rapidly from place to place, businesses lose the fruits of the individual's ability to form connections and commitments in the community. They also lose what happens when the community has an opportunity to come to know business practice and particular companies through the people who work in them, and not solely through commercial interchange.

Even at the level of local politics, a high-mobility pattern among executives condemns business organizations to try to protect their interests through formal public relations and crude economic clout rather than through sets of personal friendships, allegiances, and understandings, and the involvements of their own employees in the life and politics of the community. I would scarcely wish to suggest that this lack of local and detailed social connection is the principal reason for the decline in the prestige of business as a career and the increase in suspicion of business among both consumers and public officials. Nonetheless, moods and attitudes cannot but be affected by the network of human relationships—or lack of them in this case—that in part determine an organization's stature in its environment.

A SCORCHED-EARTH POLICY

In the very simplest kind of matter, an executive's effort to convince a local planning authority that the plant his company wants to build will have no severe ecological impact will hardly be helped if experience makes it seem reasonably certain that by the time the installation is at work, this particular executive and his family will no longer be around. While perhaps it is unfair, it is not unrealistic for local people to see corporate representatives as practitioners of a scorched-earth policy: get your orders, follow them unswervingly, make your mark, collect your reward money, and let your successor live with the consequences, and the smell. While national citizenship has been accepted as an important factor in securing a reasonable climate for business operations, that is far less so when it comes to local citizenship. The complex and subtle consequences appear to be inadequately understood by proponents of the mobile organizational style.

Now let me turn briefly to what may be the higher inefficiency of that style. Certainly there are losses of various kinds when the executive who has just moved from another community must enter a new work situation with little or no experience of the people involved in it and the human problems it presents. The newcomer has to learn not only a new job but also a new social and physical environment for the job. His peers, superiors, and subordinates must likewise adapt to an unknown, or little-known, set of qualities. While the costs in time and energy of this sociological retooling are difficult to calculate, there is reason on the face of it to think the costs are considerable.

TO IDENTIFY THOSE OF STERNER STUFF

Not that all this is without apparent benefits to the organization. One important benefit is that by demanding frequent moves from young executives, the system extracts them from the social networks they create for themselves, or from their regional affinities, and links them increasingly to their professional roles rather than social preferences. It is part of the folklore of this particular group—though becoming less important as more executives rebel—that unwillingness to move for a company implies a suspicious lack of loyalty to it.

Frequent moves, then, may serve as part of a process of initiation and testing. On this model, an important function of mobility is to identify those who can take it well, those of the sterner stuff of potential higher management. The result of all the moving and shaking, all the posting and reposting, is the selection of the elite. It is almost as if all the moiling motions of the company exist to choose the chief.

An additional advantage for companies with diverse branches and units is that over time mobility of executives provides select employees with a detailed understanding of the diversity of the companies and the special character of each area. There is plainly no substitute, in the development of broad administrative perspectives, for the experience of varied places and social patterns.

VOWS OF PSYCHOLOGICAL SILENCE

Yet the question may be asked: is repeated migration the only way to achieve such a perspective? Is it impossible to develop programs of orientation and expansion-of-perspectives that do not depend on moving the body but can rely instead on the adaptability and receptivity of the human brain?

It is well worthwhile for corporations to seek answers to these questions. For apart from the effects upon wives and children, and upon the image of the corporation, mobility does subtle damage to the executives themselves.

One important consequence of their form of lucrative exile is that it becomes almost necessary to cultivate a "cool" social style. The easy informality and congeniality of American corporate life may reflect an innovative attitude and a democratic ethic, but may also mask a lack of concern with, and even isolation from, strong relationships with colleagues and friends—detachment as a matter of personal psychological survival. When one's social network will be destroyed every few years, there is little gain and considerable cost in trying to establish the complex mixture of trust, commitment, self-exposure, and freedom that is essential to serious friendships.

Almost like monks who are vowed to silence yet live in close contact with each other, mobile executives must in a sense take vows of "psychological silence" and keep their lives, fears, and enthusiasms to themselves. Perhaps only during conventions and office parties and only under the permissive influence of alcohol is the glad-handing impersonality of corporate society broken by the jagged utterances and actions of people with a private story to tell.

As they glide from Darien to Palo Alto and from Grosse Point to Princeton, the managers of business may be helping to establish themselves as a form of quasi-religious priesthood—men who are unconcerned with local political and social affairs but are devoted instead to the larger impersonal forces of the particular system of rules they have allowed to govern their actions. Like monks, they become devout proponents of a higher order of things, a more coercive plan, than concerns other men. And yet, unlike monks, who if they avoid blotting their copybooks are ensured a lifetime (and maybe more) of security and usefulness, executives bear the personal costs with few of the guarantees.

WHAT THEY TAKE FOR GRANTED

This has been an effort to look at one aspect of the tribal behavior of corporate executives, and to suggest some implications. Needless to say, I have drawn a rather angular and severe picture. I have done so in the hope of providing perspectives on a situation that might otherwise be unrecognizable to people who are actively living within it.

A research rule that anthropologists bear in mind when studying a community runs, "The most important thing to know is what they take for granted." Corporate executives take it for granted that to do their work they have to move around a lot. Perhaps they must. But it may be worthwhile for them to ask, "Is this trip necessary?"—to ask what they're leaving and where they're going, and to try to determine why the system moves their bodies instead of enhancing their skills.

The Boss Ought to Take More Time Off

Herbert E. Meyer

This is the time of year when many Americans are poring over travel brochures, negotiating final details with rental agents at Cape Cod or Lake Tahoe, airing out last year's camping gear, and starting to worry about whether the family station wagon can survive another trip. But one conspicuous class of Americans is, by and large, missing out on all the fun. Senior corporate executives, who can afford the best vacations and who probably need vacations the most, seem to be taking less and less time off.

Thirty or forty years ago, successful businessmen would slice out a large part of July or August for golf, fishing, traveling, or just relaxing and socializing at the family estate in Bar Harbor, Colorado Springs, or some other hallowed haven. Nowadays, the variety of things to do is greater, and so is the ease of getting there. More executives than ever before have built comfortable—sometimes elegant—second homes.

But executives have been turning away from extended, uninterrupted rest periods. Many of them are not even taking their full allotment of vacation. And what little time off they do take is gulped in small doses—by adding an extra day or two on to weekends and holidays, or tacking a day or two on to their myriad business trips. Mentally, they are never away from the office.

A PSYCHOLOGICAL BARRIER

There are still some holdouts who . . . believe the new style of shorter vacations is deplorable, or at the very least uncivilized. But most businessmen say that they take short vacations because they prefer them. Rodney D. Strong, chairman and chief executive of Sonoma Vineyards, has an attitude that is fairly common among senior corporate officials. "I like my work," he says simply, "and I really hate

Adapted from material originally appearing in the June 1974 issue of *Fortune* Magazine by special permission; © 1974 Time Inc.

to be away too long." John R. Beckett, chairman and president of Transamerica Corp., points out a practical reason for limiting his vacations to just one week at a time. He says the work piling up in his absence forms "an almost psychological barrier" to staying away any longer.

Whether this devotion to duty is entirely wise for corporate managers is very much open to question. A number of doctors who specialize in caring for businessmen state quite emphatically that truncated vacations are decidedly unhealthy for executives and so, in the long run, for their companies. Dr. Richard Call, medical director at Union Oil Co., believes regular vacations of at least two weeks' duration are "absolutely necessary to break the pace." Executives who fail to take enough time out, he adds, "run a serious risk of ruining their health."

NO RESPITE FROM CRISES

The scope and pace of business itself are probably the most fundamental reasons for the new vacation style. Today's executive is by far the busiest in history. The sheer growth of so many companies, the increasingly multinational nature of business, the new social responsibilities pressing on corporations, and the constantly proliferating web of government regulation have placed a larger load on top executives than their predecessors had to bear. So it has become harder and harder for them to find time for long vacations, however much they'd like to have them. . . .

CLIMBING THE WALLS

It would be tempting to conclude from today's style of abbreviated vacations that the rush and tumble of world events have dragged executives kicking and screaming back to their offices. And one might easily suppose that such amenities as company jets and meetings in sunny spas are ingenious corporate devices to keep executives chained to their work. But it would be wrong. Many executives say they really like the high-speed, more or less nonstop pace of modern business. It is, after all, exciting.

Sonoma Vineyards' Rodney Strong says that long vacations drive him nuts. "After the fifth day," he claims, "I start climbing the walls. A friend of mine just left on a six-week cruise. I'd have to be drugged to do that." Instead, Strong takes some long weekends and extra days throughout the year. And usually he takes along some paper work he says he can't ever get done in the office.

Some executives say they don't need extended vacations to get the rest their minds and bodies require. William A. Marquard, the chairman of American Standard Inc., takes long weekends and sometimes a one-week vacation devoted mostly to tennis and golf. "I can relax fairly quickly," he insists. "A four-day weekend is great, and if I can do that three times each summer it's enough. After the fourth day I start to get itchy."

Like many executives, Marquard travels extensively on business—he's in Europe once every other month, and calculates that he spends fully one-third of his time away from company headquarters—so the urge to take a long vacation to go traveling somewhere is not strong. Marquard often takes his wife along on business trips, and they try to arrange a free day at the end of them.

Curiously, many chief executives express little interest in how their subordinates take their vacations, or even whether they take them at all. Strong, Marquard, Transamerica's John Beckett, and others in similar positions say they are concerned only that their underlings get their work done on time.

Fletcher Byrom, the chairman of Koppers Co., takes a fairly typical approach to the subject of subordinates' vacations. "I urge them to take all of their officially allotted time," he says, "but I don't think they ever do. Most of us enjoy our work so much we don't feel the need for it." Byron isn't sure whether as chairman he is "officially" allowed four or five weeks of annual vacation, but he says he's never come close to taking that much time off.

WORKING WITH A GIN AND TONIC

Many chief executives justify their inattention to their lieutenants' vacations on the grounds that there is no reason for them to become involved. At many companies the policy is based on seniority, rather than on the nature and responsibilities of the job itself. Thus a middle manager who has been employed by his firm for many years may be entitled to more time off than a newly hired president. At Du Pont, for example, some executives are entitled to more vacation than the new chairman, Irving Shapiro.

Some executives question the wisdom of this arrangement. They argue that at a time of increasing executive mobility, when young men often ascend to jobs with heavy responsibility, rank as well as seniority should count toward vacation allotments.

However they regard vacations, today's corporate chairmen seem to have a far more flexible attitude than those of a generation ago toward how the people under them use their working time. Now more than ever, it is acceptable for an executive to work at home, or on his boat, or even to sift those inescapable piles of papers while nursing a gin and tonic at a resort far from company headquarters. What counts is results.

THE EXECUTIVE AS WARRIOR

The emphasis on results goes a long way toward explaining the shrinking executive vacation. And so do such influences as the perquisites of travel and the increasing pace of business. But the phenomenon can also be traced to another factor that keeps businessmen from getting the rest and relaxation they need. Its roots lie buried deep and silent within the mind and character of the American executive.

He is, as the sociologists and psychiatrists have long been telling us, a driven man. His work dominates his life; indeed, it often *is* his life. To be away from work is to be cut off from living. So a holiday or vacation is not so much a welcome respite as it is a boring pause to be endured until the battle can again be joined. Like any natural warrior, the executive is more comfortable at the front, however exhausted or exposed to danger he may be, than he would be if safe behind the lines. He would rather fight than rest.

A less noble explanation, but one subscribed to in varying degrees by virtually every professional observer of the species, is that like any driven man or women the executive suffers from a gnawing sense of insecurity. He lives in constant fear of losing his job or, much worse, his reputation. And since the surest way to protect one's interests is to be constantly on guard, an extended vacation represents a kind of threat.

How can one relax at some resort if he believes, perhaps with justification, that his colleagues may use his absence to commit all manner of office atrocities—stealing his secretary, unfairly pinning the blame on him for someone's else's error, reorganizing him out of his job, or even moving corporate headquarters to another city? Proximity to one's interests is power; distance is impotence. So an executive may consider lengthy vacations to be dangerous to his career. . . .

AN EXECUTIVE'S INVISIBLE LABOR

Yet all of this reflects a dangerously lopsided concern among executives—particularly chief executives, who set the tone for others —about the two essential functions of all executives: acting and thinking. Corporations have succeeded brilliantly in providing executives with all the paraphernalia necessary to act efficiently. They get limousines, private jets, elegant offices, competent secretaries, and telephones with rows of square plastic buttons that can put a man in contact with the world at a touch. But corporations have been far less successful at providing executives with the conditions necessary for efficient thinking: regular, extended, and uninterrupted periods of peace and quiet.

The French author Victor Hugo wrote in his novel *Les Misérables* that "a man is not idle because he is absorbed in thought. There is a visible labor and there is an invisible labor." As the world of business grows ever more complex, and as businessmen's responsibilities become ever broader, the product of this invisible labor increasingly will determine the fate of companies and even entire industries.

Nothing so enhances a man's ability to think productively as a period of relaxation or a simple, but extended, change of pace. So vacations are not a luxury but rather a necessity for any businessman who wants to remain truly effective over a period of years and decades. Companies that value their executives, and executives who value themselves, will see that the vacations are taken.

Wheels

Arthur Hailey

At a car assembly plant north of the Fisher Freeway, Matt Zaleski, assistant plant manager and a graying veteran of the auto industry, was glad that today was Wednesday.

Not that the day would be free from urgent problems and exercises in survival—no day ever was. Tonight, like any night, he would go homeward wearily, feeling older than his fifty-three years and convinced he had spent another day of his life inside a pressure cooker. Matt Zaleski sometimes wished he could summon back the energy he had had as a young man, either when he was new to auto production or as an Air Force bombardier in World War II. He also thought sometimes, looking back, that the years of war—even though he was in Europe in the thick of things, with an impressive combat record—were less crisis-filled than his civil occupation now.

Already, in the few minutes he had been in his glass-paneled office on a mezzanine above the assembly plant floor, even while removing his coat, he had skimmed through a red-tabbed memo on the desk—a union grievance which he realized immediately could cause a plant-wide walkout if it wasn't dealt with properly and promptly. There was undoubtedly still more to worry about in an adjoining pile of papers—other headaches, including critical material shortages (there were always some, each day), or quality control demands, or machinery failures, or some new conundrum which no one had thought of before, any or all of which could halt the assembly line and stop production.

Zaleski threw his stocky figure into the chair at his gray metal desk, moving in short, jerky movements, as he always had. He heard the chair protest—a reminder of his growing overweight and the big belly he carried around nowadays. He thought ashamedly: he could never squeeze it now into the cramped nose dome of a B-17. He wished that worry would take off pounds; instead, it seemed to put them on, especially since Freda died and loneliness at night drove him to the refrigerator, nibbling, for lack of something else to do.

But at least today was Wednesday.

First things first. He hit the intercom switch for the general office; his secretary wasn't in yet. A timekeeper answered.

"I want Parkland and the union committeeman," the assistant plant manager commanded. "Get them in here fast."

Parkland was a foreman. And outside they would be well aware which union committeeman he meant because they would know about the red-tabbed memo on his desk. In a plant, bad news traveled like burning gasoline.

The pile of papers—still untouched, though he would have to get to them soon—reminded Zaleski he had been thinking gloomily of the many causes which could halt an assembly line.

Halting the line, stopping production for whatever reason, was like a sword in the side to Matt Zaleski. The function of his job, his personal *raison d'être*, was to keep the line moving, with finished cars being driven off the end at the rate of one car a minute, no matter how the trick was done or if, at times, he felt like a juggler with fifteen balls in the air at once. Senior management wasn't interested in the juggling act, or excuses either. Results were what counted: quotas, daily production, manufacturing costs. But if the line stopped he heard about it soon enough. Each single minute of lost time meant that an entire car didn't get produced, and the loss would never be made up. Thus, even a two- or three-minute stoppage cost thousands of dollars because, while an assembly line stood still, wages and other costs went rollicking on.

But at least today was Wednesday.

The intercom clicked. "They're on their way, Mr. Zaleski."

He acknowledged curtly.

The reason Matt Zaleski liked Wednesday was simple. Wednesday was two days removed from Monday, and Friday was two more days away.

Mondays and Fridays in auto plants were management's most harrowing days because of absenteeism. Each Monday, more hourly paid

employees failed to report for work than on any other normal week-
day; Friday ran a close second. It happened because after paychecks
were handed out, usually on Thursday, many workers began a long
boozy or drugged weekend, and afterward, Monday was a day for
catching up on sleep or nursing hangovers.

Thus, on Mondays and Fridays, other problems were eclipsed by
one enormous problem of keeping production going despite a critical
shortage of people. Men were moved around like marbles in a game of
Chinese checkers. Some were removed from tasks they were accustomed to and given jobs they had never done before. A worker who
normally tightened wheel nuts might find himself fitting front fenders,
often with the briefest of instruction or sometimes none at all. Others,
pulled in hastily from labor pools or less skilled duties—such as loading trucks or sweeping—would be put to work wherever gaps remained. Sometimes they caught on quickly in their temporary roles; at
other times they might spend an entire shift installing heater hose
clamps, or something similar—upside down.

The result was inevitable. Many of Monday's and Friday's cars were
shoddily put together, with built-in legacies of trouble for their owners, and those in the know avoided them like contaminated meat. A
few big city dealers, aware of the problem and with influence at factories because of volume sales, insisted that cars for more valued customers be built on Tuesday, Wednesday, or Thursday, and customers
who knew the ropes sometimes went to big dealers with this objective.
Cars for company executives and their friends were invariably
scheduled for one of the midweek days.

The door of the assistant plant manager's office flung open abruptly.
The foreman he had sent for, Parkland, stroke in, not bothering to
knock.

Parkland was a broad-shouldered, big-boned man in his late thirties, about fifteen years younger than Matt Zaleski. He might have
been a football fullback if he had gone to college, and, unlike many
foremen nowadays, looked as if he could handle authority. He also
looked, at the moment, as if he expected trouble and was prepared to
meet it. The foreman's face was glowering. There was a darkening
bruise, Zaleski noted, beneath his right cheekbone.

Ignoring the mode of entry, Zaleski motioned him to a chair. "Take
the weight off your feet, then simmer down."

They faced each other across the desk.

"I'm willing to hear your version of what happened," the assistant
plant chief said, "but don't waste time because the way this reads"—
he fingered the red-tabbed grievance report—"you've cooked us all a
hot potato."

"The hell I cooked it!" Parkland glared at his superior; above the bruise his face flushed red. "I fired a guy because he slugged me. What's more, I'm gonna make it stick, and if you've got any guts or justice you'd better back me up."

Matt Zaleski raised his voice to the bull roar he had learned on a factory floor. "Knock off that goddam nonsense, right now!" He had no intention of letting this get out of hand. More reasonably, he growled, "I said simmer down, and meant it. When the time comes I'll decide who to back and why. And there'll be no more crap from you about guts and justice. Understand?"

Their eyes locked together. Parkland's dropped first.

"All right, Frank," Matt said. "Let's start over, and this time give it to me straight, from the beginning."

He had known Frank Parkland a long time. The foreman's record was good and he was usually fair with men who worked under him. It had taken something exceptional to get him as riled as this.

"There was a job out of position," Parkland said. "It was steering column bolts, and there was this kid doing it; he's new, I guess. He was crowding the next guy. I wanted the job put back."

Zaleski nodded. It happened often enough. A worker with a specific assignment took a few seconds longer than he should on each operation. As successive cars moved by on the assembly line, his position gradually changed, so that soon he was intruding on the area of the next operation. When a foreman saw it happen he made it his business to help the worker back to his correct, original place.

Zaleski said impatiently, "Get on with it."

Before they could continue, the office door opened again and the union committeeman came in. He was a small, pink-faced man, with thick-lensed glasses and a fussy manner. His name was Illas and, until a union election a few months ago, had been an assembly line worker himself.

"Good morning," the union man said to Zaleski. He nodded curtly to Parkland, without speaking.

Matt Zaleski waved the newcomer to a chair. "We're just getting to the meat."

"You could save a lot of time," Illas said, "if you read the grievance report."

"I've read it. But sometimes I like to hear the other side." Zaleski motioned Parkland to go on.

"All I did," the foreman said, "was call another guy over and say, 'Help me get this man's job back in position.'"

"And I say you're a liar!" The union man hunched forward accusingly; now he swung toward Zaleski. "What he really said was 'get this *boy's* job back.' And it so happened that the person he was speaking of, and calling, 'boy,' was one of our black brothers to whom that word is a very offensive term."

"Oh, for God's sake!" Parkland's voice combined anger with disgust. "D'you think I don't know that? D'you think I haven't been around here long enough to know better than to use that word that way?"

"But you *did* use it, didn't you?"

"Maybe, just maybe, I did. I'm not saying yes, because I don't remember, and that's the truth. But if it happened, there was nothing meant. It was a slip, that's all."

The union man shrugged. "That's your story now."

"It's no story, you son-of-a-bitch!"

Illas stood up. "Mr. Zaleski, I'm here officially, representing the United Auto Workers. If that's the kind of language . . . "

"There'll be no more of it," the assistant plant manager said. "Sit down, please, and while we're on the subject, I suggest you be less free yourself with the word 'liar.'"

Parkland slammed a beefy fist in frustration on the desk top. "I said it was no story, and it isn't. What's more, the guy I was talking about didn't even give a thought to what I said, at least before all the fuss was made."

"That's not the way *he* tells it," Illas said.

"Maybe not now." Parkland appealed to Zaleski. "Listen, Matt, the guy who was out of position is just a kid. A black kid, maybe seventeen. I've got nothing against him; he's slow, but he was doing his job. I've got a kid brother his age. I go home, I say, 'Where's the boy?' Nobody thinks twice about it. That's the way it was with this thing until this other guy, Newkirk, cut in."

Illas persisted, "But you're admitting you used the word 'boy.'"

Matt Zaleski said wearily, "Okay, okay, he used it. Let's all concede that."

Zaleski was holding himself in, as he always had to do when racial issues erupted in the plant. His own prejudices were deep-rooted and largely anti-black, and he had learned them in the heavily Polish suburb of Wyandotte where he was born. There, the families of Polish origin looked on Negroes with contempt, as shiftless and troublemakers. In return, the black people hated Poles, and even nowadays, throughout Detroit, the ancient enmities persisted. Zaleski, through necessity, had learned to curb his instinct; you couldn't run a plant with as much black labor as this one and let your prejudices show, at least not often. Just now, after the last remark of Illas, Matt Zaleski had been tempted to inject: *So what if he did call him "boy"? What the hell difference does it make? When a foreman tells him to, let the bastard get back to work.* But Zaleski knew it would be repeated and maybe cause more trouble than before. Instead, he growled, "What matters is what came after."

"Well," Parkland said, "I thought we'd never get to that. We almost had the job back in place, then this heavyweight, Newkirk, showed up."

"He's another black brother," Illas said.

"Newkirk'd been working down the line. He didn't even hear what happened; somebody else told him. He came up, called me a racist pig, and slugged me." The foreman fingered his bruised face which had swollen even more since he came in.

Zaleski asked sharply, "Did you hit him back?"

"No."

"I'm glad you showed a little sense."

"I had sense, all right," Parkland said. "I fired Newkirk. On the spot. Nobody slugs a foreman around here and gets away with it."

"We'll see about that," Illas said. "A lot depends on circumstances and provocation."

Matt Zaleski thrust a hand through his hair; there were days when he marveled that there was any left. This whole stinking situation was something which McKernon, the plant manager, should handle, but McKernon wasn't here. He was ten miles away at staff headquarters, attending a conference about the new Orion, a super-secret car the plant would be producing soon. Sometimes it seemed to Matt Zaleski as if McKernon had already begun his retirement, officially six months away.

Matt Zaleski was holding the baby now, as he had before, and it was a lousy deal. Zaleski wasn't even going to succeed McKernon, and he knew it. He'd already been called in and shown the official assessment of himself, the assessment which appeared in a loose-leaf, leather-bound book which sat permanently on the desk of the Vice-president, Manufacturing. The book was there so that the vice-president could turn its pages whenever new appointments or promotions were considered. The entry for Matt Zaleski, along with his photo and other details, read: "This individual is well placed at his present level of management."

Everybody in the company who mattered knew that the formal, unctious statement was a "kiss off." What it really meant was: *This man has gone as high as he's going. He will probably serve his time out in his present spot, but will receive no more promotions.*

The rules said that whoever received that deadly summation on his docket had to be told; he was entitled to that much, and it was the reason Matt Zaleski had known for the past several months that he would never rise beyond his present role of assistant manager. Initially the news had been a bitter disappointment, but now that he had grown used to the idea, he also knew why: He was old shoe, the hind end of a disappearing breed which management and boards of directors didn't want any more in the top critical posts. Zaleski had risen by a route which few senior plant people followed nowadays—factory worker, inspector, foreman, superintendent, assistant plant manager. He hadn't had an engineering degree to start, having been a high school dropout before World War II. But after the war he had armed himself with a degree, using night school and GI credits, and after that had started climbing, being ambitious, as most of his generation were who had survived *Festung Europa* and other perils. But, as Zaleski recognized later, he had lost too much time; his real start came too late. The strong comers, the top echelon material of the auto companies—then as now—were the bright youngsters who arrived fresh and eager through the direct college-to-front office route.

But that was no reason why McKernon, who was still plant boss, should sidestep this entire situation, even if unintentionally. The assistant manager hesitated. He would be within his rights to send for McKernon and could do it here and now by picking up a phone.

Two things stopped him. One, he admitted to himself, was pride; Zaleski knew he could handle this as well as McKernon, if not better. The other: His instinct told him there simply wasn't time.

Abruptly, Zaleski asked Illas, "What's the union asking?"

"Well, I've talked with the president of our local . . . "

"Let's save all that," Zaleski said. "We both know we have to start somewhere, so what is it you want?"

"Very well," the committeeman said. "We insist on three things. First, immediate reinstatement of Brother Newkirk, with compensation for time lost. Second, an apology to both men involved. Third, Parkland to be removed from his post as foreman."

Parkland, who had slumped back in his chair, shot upright. "By Christ! You don't want much." He inquired sarcastically, "As a matter of interest, am I supposed to apologize before I'm fired, or after?"

"The apology would be an official one from the company," Illas answered. "Whether you had the decency to add your own would be up to you."

"I'll say it'd be up to me. Just don't anyone hold their breath waiting."

Matt Zaleski snapped, "If you'd held your own breath a little longer, we wouldn't be in this mess."

"Are you trying to tell me you'll go along with all that?" The foreman motioned angrily to Illas.

"I'm not telling anybody anything yet. I'm trying to think, and I need more information than has come from you two." Zaleski reached behind him for a telephone. Interposing his body between the phone and the other two, he dialed a number and waited.

When the man he wanted answered, Zaleski asked simply, "How are things down there?"

The voice at the other end spoke softly. "Matt?"

"Yeah."

In the background behind the other's guarded response, Zaleski could hear a cacophony of noise from the factory floor. He always marveled how men could live with that noise every day of their working lives. Even in the years he had worked on an assembly line himself, before removal to an office shielded him from most of the din, he had never grown used to it.

His informant said, "The situation's real bad, Matt."

"How bad?"

"The hopheads are in the saddle. Don't quote me."

"I never do," the assistant plant manager said. "You know that."

He had swung partially around and was aware of the other two in the office watching his face. They might guess, but couldn't know, that he was speaking to a black foreman, Stan Lathruppe, one of the half dozen men in the plant whom Matt Zaleski respected most. It was a strange, even paradoxical, relationship because, away from the plant, Lathruppe was an active militant who had once been a follower of Malcolm X. But here he took his responsibility seriously, believing that in the auto world he could achieve more for his race through reason than by anarchy. It was this second attitude which Zaleski—originally hostile to Lathruppe—had eventually come to respect.

Unfortunately for the company, in the present state of race relations, it had comparatively few black foremen or managers. There ought to be more, many more, and everybody knew it, but right now many of the black workers didn't want responsibility, or were afraid of it because of young militants in their ranks, or simply weren't ready. Sometimes Matt Zaleski, in his less prejudiced moments, thought that if the industry's top brass had looked ahead a few years, the way senior executives were supposed to do, and had launched a meaningful training program for black workers in the 1940s and '50s, there would be more Stan Lathruppes now. It was everybody's loss that there were not.

Zaleski asked, "What's being planned?"

"I think, a walkout."

"When?"

"Probably at break time. It could be before, but I don't believe so."

The black foreman's voice was so low Zaleski had to strain to hear. He knew the other man's problem, added to by the fact that the telephone he was using was alongside the assembly line where others were working. Lathruppe was already labeled a "white nigger" by some fellow blacks who resented even their own race when in authority, and it made no difference that the charge was untrue. Except for a couple more questions, Zaleski had no intention of making Stan Lathruppe's life more difficult.

He asked, "Is there any reason for the delay?"

"Yes. The hopheads want to take the whole plant out."

"Is word going around?"

"So fast you'd think we still used jungle drums."

"Has anyone pointed out the whole thing's illegal?"

"You got any more jokes like that?" Lathruppe said.

"No." Zaleski sighed. "But thanks." He hung up.

So his first instinct had been right. There wasn't any time to spare, and hadn't been from the beginning, because a racial labor dispute always burned with a short fuse. Now, if a walkout happened, it could take days to settle and get everybody back at work; and even if only black workers became involved, and maybe not all of them, the effect would still be enough to halt production. Matt Zaleski's job was to keep production going.

As if Parkland had read his thoughts, the foreman urged, "Matt, don't let them push you! So a few may walk off the job, and we'll have trouble. But a principle's worth standing up for, sometimes, isn't it?"

"Sometimes," Zaleski said. "The trick is to know which principle, and when."

"Being fair is a good way to start," Parkland said, "and fairness works two ways—up and down." He leaned forward over the desk, speaking earnestly to Matt Zaleski, glancing now and then to the union committeeman, Illas. "Okay, I've been tough with guys on the line because I've had to be. A foreman's in the middle, catching crap from all directions. From up here, Matt, you and your people are on our necks every day for production, production, more production; and if it isn't you it's Quality Control who say, build 'em better, even though you're building faster. Then there are those who are working, doing the jobs—including some like Newkirk, and others—and a foreman has to cope with them, along with the union as well if he puts a foot wrong, and sometimes when he doesn't. So it's a tough business, and I've been tough; it's the way to survive. But I've been fair, too. I've never treated a guy who worked for me differently because he was black, and I'm no plantation overseer with a whip. As for what we're talking about now, all I did—so I'm told—is call a black man 'boy.' I didn't ask him to pick cotton, or ride Jim Crow, or shine shoes, or any other thing that's supposed to go with that word. What I did was help him with his job. And I'll say another thing: if I did call him 'boy'—so help me, by a slip!—I'll say I'm sorry for that, because I am. But not to Newkirk. Brother Newkirk stays fired. Because if he doesn't, if he gets away with slugging a foreman without reason, you can stuff a surrender flag up your ass and wave goodbye to any discipline around this place from this day on. That's what I mean when I say be fair."

"You've got a point or two there," Zaleski said. Ironically, he thought, Frank Parkland *had* been fair with black workers, maybe fairer than a good many others around the plant. He asked Illas, "How do you feel about all that?"

The union man looked blandly through his thick-lensed glasses. "I've already stated the union's position, Mr. Zaleski."

"So if I turn you down, if I decide to back up Frank the way he just said I should, what then?"

Illas said stiffly, "We'd be obliged to go through further grievance procedure."

"Okay." The assistant plant manager nodded. "That's your privilege. Except, if we go through a full grievance drill it can mean thirty days or more. In the meantime, does everybody keep working?"

"Naturally. The collective bargaining agreement specifies . . . "

Zaleski flared, "I don't need you to tell me what the agreement says! It says everybody stays on the job while we negotiate. But right now a good many of your men are getting ready to walk off their jobs in violation of the contract."

For the first time, Illas looked uneasy. "The UAW does not condone illegal strikes."

"Goddamit, then! Stop this one!"

"If what you say is true, I'll talk to some of our people."

"Talking won't do any good. You know it, and I know it." Zaleski eyed the union committeeman whose pink face had paled slightly; obviously Illas didn't relish the thought of arguing with some of the black militants in their present mood.

The union—as Matt Zaleski was shrewdly aware—was in a tight dilemma in situations of this kind. If the union failed to support its black militants at all, the militants would charge union leaders with racial prejudice and being "management lackeys." Yet if the union went too far with its support, it could find itself in an untenable position legally, as party to a wildcat strike. Illegal strikes were anathema to UAW leaders like Woodcock, Fraser, Greathouse, Bannon, and others, who had built reputations for tough negotiating, but also for honoring agreements once made, and settling grievances through due process. Wildcatting debased the union's word and undermined its bargaining strength.

"They're not going to thank you at Solidarity House if we let this thing get away from us," Matt Zaleski persisted. "There's only one thing can stop a walkout, and that's for us to make a decision here, then go down on the floor and announce it."

Illas said, "That depends on the decision." But it was plain that the union man was weighing Zaleski's words.

Matt Zaleski had already decided what the ruling had to be, and he knew that nobody would like it entirely, including himself. He thought sourly: these were lousy times, when a man had to shove his convictions in his pocket along with pride—at least, if he figured to keep an automobile plant running.

He announced brusquely, "Nobody gets fired. Newkirk goes back to his job, but from now on he uses his fists for working, nothing else." The assistant plant manager fixed his eyes on Illas. "I want it clearly understood by you and by Newkirk—one more time, he's out. And before he goes back, I'll talk to him myself."

"He'll be paid for lost time?" The union man had a slight smile of triumph.

"Is he still at the plant?"

"Yes."

Zaleski hesitated, then nodded reluctantly. "Okay, providing he finishes the shift. But there'll be no more talk about anybody replacing Frank." He swung to face Parkland. "And you'll do what you said you would—talk to the young guy. Tell him what was said was a mistake."

"An apology is what it's known as," Illas said.

Frank Parkland glared at them both. "Of all the crummy, sleazy backdowns!"

"Take it easy!" Zaleski warned.

"Like hell I'll take it easy!" The burly foreman was on his feet, towering over the assistant plant manager. He spat words across the desk between them. "You're the one taking it easy—the easy out because you're too much a goddam coward to stand up for what you know is right."

His face flushing deep red, Zaleski roared, "I don't have to take that from you! That'll be enough! You hear?"

"I hear." Contempt filled Parkland's voice and eyes. "But I don't like what I hear, or what I smell."

"In that case, maybe you'd like to be fired!"

"Maybe," the foreman said. "Maybe the air'd be cleaner some place else."

There was a silence between them, then Zaleski growled, "It's no cleaner. Some days it stinks everywhere."

What Stress Can Do to You
Walter McQuade

It has long been a matter of common intuition that bottled-up anger can crack the bottle, prolonged strain can make people sick. This old folklore now has considerable scientific support. Working independently, several groups of medical researchers—both physicians and psychologists—have collected impressive evidence that emotional factors are primarily responsible for many of the chronic diseases that have been hitting American males hard in middle age, notably the big one, heart disease. Challenging medical dogma, these doctors deny that fatty diet, cigarette smoking, and lack of proper exercise pose the main perils to men in their working prime. Much more important, they say, is stress. Stress might be defined as the body's involuntary reactions to the demanding life that we Americans choose—or that chooses us.

These reactions are rooted deep in the prehistory of the human species. Early man survived in a brutal world because, along with an elaborate brain, he had the mechanisms of instantaneous, unthinking physical response when in danger. Picture a primitive man, many thousands of years ago, lying in the sun in front of his cave after the hunt, digesting. Suddenly, he felt the cool shadow of a predatory carnivore, stalking. Without thinking, he reacted with a mighty surge of bodily resources. Into his blood flashed adrenal secretions that mustered strength in the form of both sugar and stored fats to his muscles and brain, instantly mobilizing full energy, and stimulating pulse, respiration, and blood pressure. His digestive processes turned off at once so that no energy was diverted from meeting the threat. His coagulation chemistry immediately prepared to resist wounds with quick clotting. Red cells poured from the spleen into the stepped-up blood circulation to help the respiratory system take in oxygen and cast off carbon dioxide as this ancestral man clubbed at the prowling beast, or scuttled safely back into his cave.

A COOL MEMO FROM A V.P.

Today, say stress researchers, a man in a business suit still reacts, within his skin, in much the same chemical way. He does so although

Adapted from material originally appearing in the January 1972 issue of *Fortune* Magazine by special permission; © 1971 Time Inc. □ Research associate: Varian Ayers Knisely.

today's threat is more likely to be in the abstract, for example, a cool memo from a vice president of the corporation: "The chairman wants a study of the savings possible in merging your division with warehousing and relocating to South Carolina."

Flash go the hormones into the blood; up goes the pulse beat—but the manager who receives the memo can neither fight physically nor flee. Instead his first tendency is to stall, which only induces guilt, before he plunges into a battle fought with no tangible weapons heavier than paper clips. Under his forced calm builds repressed rage without any adequate target—except himself.

If he is the kind of hard-driving, competitive perfectionist whom many corporations prize, and if this kind of stress pattern is chronic, the stress experts will tell you that he is a prime candidate for an early coronary (an even likelier candidate than American men in general, whose chances of having a heart attack before age sixty are one in five). If not a coronary, it may be migraine, ulcers, asthma, ulcerative colitis, or even the kind of scalp itch James V. Forrestal developed as he began to give way to interior pressure. Or perhaps a collision on the road— stressed people are more accident-prone.

Chronic strain is so common that there are conventional ways of fighting back. Millions of pills repose in desk drawers, ready to foster calmness or energy. The trouble with them, say the doctors, is that after the calm or the uplift there usually comes a period of depression. Martinis may be better, although they too involve dangers. Some people under stress try to vent their repressed anger in polite violence at a driving range or bowling alley, or by chopping wood or throwing themselves at ocean waves breaking on the beach. But the violent exercisers had better be careful of contracting another common stress symptom, low back pain.

Marriages have to accept a lot of stress, both in hurtful words and yet another symptom, temporary impotence. If a man coming under job stress has been on an anti-cholesterol diet he had better stay on it, but the competitive strain on him will be upping his serum cholesterol, whatever he eats. In broad terms, man the victorious predator now preys internally on himself.

LOST CONSOLATIONS

. . . Particularly destructive of the individual's sense of security have been the side effects of one of the industrial world's most precious products—social mobility. This bright trophy of our times has its deeply etched dark side. Social mobility has weakened the sense of belonging to a class, the sense of having a place in the social order. More important, social mobility implies that success depends on merit alone, and to the extent that a society believes in such correlation, individual bread-winners are thrust into an endless competition in which losing or lagging can be interpreted as a sign of personal inadequacy. . . .

DISCOVERING THE UBIQUITOUS – *existing or being every where at the same time*

A pioneer investigator into the implications of stress was Dr. Hans Selye, a Canadian who has become the world's acknowledged authority on his subject. Selye, now sixty-four, defines stress as the non-specific response of the body to any demand made on it. He maintains that stress went unstudied in detail for centuries simply because it had always been so common. "Stress is ubiquitous, and it is hard to *discover* something ubiquitous."

Selye recalls that an intimation of his future specialty came to him in his youth. "I was a second-year medical student in Prague in 1926 when my professor brought in five patients for the students to diagnose—one with cancer, one with gastric ulcer, etc. It struck me that the professor never spoke about what was common to them all, only about what were the specifics of the diagnosis. All these patients had lost weight, lost energy, and lost their appetites."

Ten years later, as an assistant professor at McGill in Montreal, Selye observed that various kinds of insults to the bodies and nervous sytems of laboratory animals had lasting effects in making them vulnerable to subsequent stress. "I was trying to isolate a hormone in the laboratory. I was working with extracts of cow ovaries and injecting them into rats. All of them, when later subjected to stress, had the same reaction—adrenal overaction, duodenal and gastric ulcers, and shrinking thymus, spleen, and lymph nodes. The worse the stress, the stronger the reaction. Then I tried injecting other materials, even simple dirt. I even tried electric shock, and got the same results." When he tried inducing fear and rage, results were again similar.

WHEN ALL THE RATS DIED

One of Selye's most significant breakthroughs came when he realized he could take two similar groups of rats and predispose one group to heart disease, uncommon in animals, by injecting an excess of sodium and certain types of hormones. Then he would expose both groups of rats to stress. None of the control group suffered. *All* the rats in the predisposed group died of heart disease.

In time, Selye came to the conviction that the endocrine glands, particularly the adrenals, were the body's prime reactors to stress. "They are the only organs which do not shrink under stress; they thrive and enlarge. If you remove them, and subject an animal to stress, it can't live. But if you then inject extract of cattle adrenals, stress resistance will vary in direct proportion to the amount of the injection, and can even be put back to normal."

Selye explains that when the brain signals the attack of a stressor—which could be either a predatory beast or a threatening memorandum—the adrenal and pituitary glands produce the hormones ACTH, cortisone, and cortisol, which stimulate protective bodily reactions. If the stress is a fresh wound, the blood rushes irritants to seal it off; if the stress is a broken bone, swelling occurs around the break. The pro-inflammatory hormones are balanced by anti-inflammatory hormones, which prevent the body from reacting so strongly that the reaction causes more harm than the invasion.

ENERGY THAT CAN'T BE REPLENISHED

So the initial reaction to any kind of stress is alarm. It is followed by an instantaneous rallying of the body's defenses. The fight is on—even if the body, in effect, is just fighting the mind. If the threat recedes or is overcome, stability returns. But if the attack is prolonged, deterioration sets in, as the defense system gradually wears down. Selye calls this process the General Adaptation Syndrome, and it is recognized in the field as a brilliant concept.

Stress is not only a killer, Selye teaches, but also a drastic aging force. Different men have different hereditary capacities to withstand stress, but once each man's "adaptation energy" has been expended, there is no way yet known to replenish it. Selye believes that some time in the future it may be possible to produce from the tissues of young animals a substance that could replenish human stress energy. "But that is for the Jules Verne future—soft research, like soft news, that *may* happen."

Selye likens each man's supply of life energy to deep deposits of oil; once the man has summoned it up and burned it in the form of adaptation energy, it is gone—and so, soon, is he. If he picks a high-stress career, he spends his portion fast and ages fast. "There are two ages," says Selye, "one which is chronological, an absolute, and the other which is biologic and is your effective age. It is astonishing how the two can differ. . . ."

A QUEERLY CONTEMPORARY QUALITY

Stress research in the U.S. centers on heart disease, and for good reason. Cardiovascular ailments such as coronary heart disease now take an appalling annual toll in lives of American men in vigorous middle age. Of the 700,000 people who died from coronary heart disease in the U.S. last year, almost 200,000 were under sixty-five.

Yet until this century heart disease was virtually unknown anywhere in the world, and as late as the 1920's it was still fairly rare in the

U.S. Dr. Paul Dudley White, the eminent cardiologist, recalls that in the first two years after he set up his practice in 1912 he saw only three or four coronary patients. The queerly contemporary quality of heart disease cannot be attributed to the ignorance of earlier doctors. As far back as the time of Hippocrates, most afflictions were described well enough to be recognizable today from surviving records. A convincing description of heart disease, however, was not entered in medical records until late in the eighteenth century.

Some of the most important research on the effects of occupational stress in the U.S. has been carried out by the University of Michigan's Institute for Social Research, and the experts there are not impressed with the conventional medical wisdom regarding coronaries. Professor John R. P. French Jr., an austere and plainspoken psychologist at the institute, says that the known risk factors do not come close to accounting for the incidence of the disease. He maintains that "if you could perfectly control cholesterol, blood pressure, smoking, glucose level, serum uric acid, and so on, you would have controlled only about one-fourth of the coronary heart disease." There is little solid evidence, he adds, "to show that programs of exercise substantially reduce the incidence of coronary heart disease or substantially reduce some of the risk factors."

To a great extent, argues French, the problem is the job. "The stresses of today's organizations can pose serious threats to the physical and psychological well-being of organization members. When a man dies or becomes disabled by a heart attack, the organization may be as much to blame as is the man and his family." A nationwide survey directed by French's colleague Robert L. Kahn found evidence of widespread occupational stress in the U.S. The results indicated that 35 percent of the employees had complaints about job ambiguity, meaning a lack of clarity about the scope and responsibilities of the work they were supposed to be doing. Nearly half—48 percent—often found themselves trapped in situations of conflict on the job, caught in the middle between people who wanted different things from them. Some 45 percent of the sample complained of overload, either more work than they would possibly finish during an ordinary working day, or more than they could do well enough to preserve their "self-esteem."

Other occupational stresses found by the survey included insecurity associated with having to venture outside normal job boundaries; difficult bosses or subordinates; worry over carrying responsibility for other people; the lack of a feeling of participation in decisions governing their jobs—a malaise, adds Dr. French, that distinctly lowers productivity.

Management jobs carry higher risks than most. In a detailed study done for NASA at the Goddard Space Flight Center, the investigators from Ann Arbor found that administrators were much more subject to stress than engineers or scientists. Responsibility for people, French explains, always causes more stress than responsibilities for things—equipment, budgets, etc. The rise in serum cholesterol, blood sugar, and blood pressure among ground managers is much greater during manned space flights than during flights of unmanned satellites. Whatever their assignment, the administrators at Goddard, as a group, had higher pulse rates and blood pressure, and smoked more, than the engineers or scientists. Medical records revealed that administrators also had suffered almost three times as many heart attacks as either the scientists or the engineers.

THE CORONARY TYPE

In any occupation, though, people vary a great deal in the amounts of stress they can handle. Some researchers at the institute hope psychologists will be able to work out methods of screening employees for their tolerance of stress. There may even prove to be physiological methods of selection. Dr. French and his associates have discovered a direct correlation between "achievement orientation" and high readings of uric acid in the blood—regarded in the past principally as a sign of susceptibility to gout. "High serum uric acid persons," French reported, "tend not to see the external environment as a source of pressure. [They] tend to master their external environment, while high cholesterol persons are typified by the perception that the external environment is mastering them."

It is not a new observation that some people are more subject to stress than others. Sir William Osler lived too early to see many coronary cases, but he left a shrewd description of the angina type. "It is not the delicate, neurotic person who is prone to angina," he commented, "but the robust, the vigorous in mind and body, the keen and ambitious man, the indicator of whose engine is always at 'full speed ahead' . . . the well set man of from forty-five to fifty-five years of age, with military bearing, iron gray hair, and florid complexion."

This Osler quotation is a favorite of two California cardiologists, Meyer Friedman and Ray H. Rosenman, who are among the country's leading students of stress. In the past seventeen years they and their staff at the Harold Brunn Institute of Mount Zion Hospital in San Francisco have spent thousands of hours and hundreds of thousands of research dollars building up an impressive case that behavior patterns and stress are principal culprits in the high incidence of coronary heart attacks among middle-aged Americans—and that personality differences are of vital importance.

Until 1955, Friedman and Rosenman were conventional cardiologists, doing research in the standard heart risk factors: serum cholesterol, cigarette smoking, blood pressure, diet, and obesity. They also gave half their time to practice, however, and, says Friedman, "We finally began to look at the individuals. They were signaling us. More than 90 percent showed signs of struggle. An upholsterer came in to redo our waiting room, and pointed out that the only place the chairs were worn was at the front edge."

In studying reactions to stress, Friedman and Rosenman gradually came to the conviction that people can be divided into two major types, which they designate A and B. Type A, the coronary-prone type, is characterized by intense drive, aggressiveness, ambition, competitiveness, pressure for getting things done, and the habit of pitting himself against the clock. He also exhibits visible restlessness. Type B may be equally serious, but is more easygoing in manner, seldom becomes impatient, and takes more time to enjoy leisure. He does not feel driven by the clock. He is not preoccupied with social achievement, is less competitive, and even speaks in a more modulated style. Most people are mixtures of Type A and Type B characteristics, but a trained interviewer can spot one pattern or the other as predominant.

A RATHER GRIM CHUCKLE

The extreme Type A is a tremendously hard worker, a perfectionist, filled with brisk self-confidence, decisiveness, resolution. He never evades. He is the man who, while waiting in the office of his cardiologist or dentist, is on the telephone making business calls. His wife is certain he drives himself too hard, and she may be a little in awe of him. The world is a deadly serious game, and he is out to amass points enough to win.

He speaks in staccato, and has a tendency to end his sentences in a rush. He frequently sighs faintly between words, but never in anxiety, because that state is strange to him. He is seldom out sick. He rarely goes to doctors, almost never to psychiatrists. He is unlikely to get an ulcer. He is rarely interested in money except as a token of a game, but the higher he climbs, the more he considers himself underpaid.

On the debit side, he is often a little hard to get along with. His chuckle is rather grim. He does not drive people who work under him as hard as he drives himself, but he has little time to waste with them. He wants their respect, not their affection. Yet in some ways he is more sensitive than the milder Type B. He hates to fire anyone and will go to great lengths to avoid it. Sometimes the only way he can resolve such a situation is by mounting a crisis. If he himself has ever been fired, it was probably after a personality clash.

Type A, surprisingly, probably goes to bed earlier most nights than Type B, who will get interested in something irrelevant to his career and sit up late, or simply socialize. Type A is precisely on time for appointments and expects the same from other people. He smokes cigarettes, never a pipe. Headwaiters learn not to keep him waiting for a table reservation; if they do, they lose him. They like him because he doesn't linger over his meals, and doesn't complain about quality. He will usually salt the meal before he tastes it. He's never sent a bottle of wine back in his life. Driving a car, Type A is not reckless, but does reveal anger when a slower driver ahead delays him.

Type A's are not much for exercise; they claim they have too little time for it. When they do play golf, it is fast through. They never return late from vacation. Their desk tops are clean when they leave the office at the end of each day.

AN UNRECOGNIZED SICKNESS

But in the competition for the top jobs in their companies, says Dr. Friedman, A's often lose out to B's. They lose because they are too competitive. They are so obsessed with the office that they have attention for nothing else, including their families. They make decisions too fast—in minutes, rather than days—and so may make serious business mistakes. They are intoxicated by numerical competition: how many units were sold in Phoenix, how many miles were traveled last month. Also, says Friedman, Type A's frequently have about them an "existential" miasma of hostility, which makes others nervous.

Type B's differ little in background or ability from A's, and may be quietly urgent, but they are more reasonable men. Unlike Type A, Type B is hard to needle into anger. Friedman says, "A's have no respect for B's, but the smart B uses an A. The great salesmen are A's. The corporation presidents are usually B's."

What is most tragic of all in this picture of hopeful, driving, distorting energy is that the Type A's are from two to three times more likely than the Type B's to get coronary heart disease in middle age. In all of Sinclair Lewis' pitiless characterizations of the go-getting American businessman of another era, there is nothing so devastating as these doctors' cool, clinical statistics. Says Rosenman about the Type A condition: "It is a sickness, although it is not yet recognized as such."

The test program that Friedman and Rosenman offer as their strongest body of evidence was undertaken in 1960 with substantial backing from the National Institutes of Health. A total of 3,500 male subjects aged thirty-nine to fifty-nine, with no known history of heart disease, were interviewed and classified as Type A or Type B. Then came complete physical examinations, which are still being performed on a regular basis as the program continues to accumulate data. So far, 257 of the test group—who are roughly half A's and half B's—have developed coronary heart disease. Seventy percent of the victims have been Type A's.

Even more emphatic is the picture that emerged when A's and B's were evaluated with respect to the generally accepted risk factors for heart trouble. As a group the A's had higher cholesterol levels than the

B's. But it was found that even A's whom the conventional wisdom would have rated safer in blood pressure, parental history, or any combination of the usual risk factors were more likely to develop coronary heart disease. Conversely, B's could show adverse ratings in blood pressure and other factors and still be relatively safe. Dr. Rosenman reported that any B whose level of cholesterol and other fatty acids was within normal limits "had complete immunity to coronary heart disease, irrespective of his high-fat, cholesterol diet, family history, or his habits of smoking or his lack of exercising."

What creates a Type B or Type A? These cardiologists do not profess to know the complete answer yet. But to them it is obvious that both heredity and environment are involved. A's are naturally attracted toward careers of aggressiveness and deadline pressure. American life today, Friedman and Rosenman observe, offers plenty of these. What Type A's need but cannot easily achieve is restraint, says Dr. Friedman, who himself suffered a heart attack in 1967.

The medical debate that the Brunn Institute and the other stress researchers have joined is a bitter one, with deeply entrenched positions. The most emphatic opponents of the stress theory are those nutrition experts who, over the past twenty years, have virtually convinced the nation that a diet high in saturated fat and cholesterol is responsible for the epidemic of heart trouble. One pointed criticism that opponents make against the Friedman-Rosenman studies is that their method of classifying individuals into Type A or Type B is subjective, relying heavily on signs of tension as observed by the interviewer. The two cardiologists do not deny this, but point out that a good deal of all medical analysis is subjective. Their independent appraisals of Type A's or Type B's agree, they say, at least as much as doctors' readings of identical x-ray films. Says Rosenman: "Most epidemiologists are incapable of thinking of anything that cannot be qualified. There are no positive links between diet or exercise and heart disease, either. A migraine is subjective, too."

LAST WORDS OF A GREAT MAN

Studies of stress and its effects are now under way around the world. In 1950 Hans Selye's pioneering work was the sole technical treatise published on stress; last year there were close to 6,000 separate reports on stress research. At the Brunn Institute, Dr. Rosenman says, "we can't keep up with the requests from all over the world to train people here." During recent years, courts of law in the U.S., in a highly significant switch, have begun to favor plaintiffs seeking compensation for damage related to heart attacks caused by alleged stress on the job.

Now that even cardiologists are beginning to believe heart disease can be traced to unrelenting competitiveness and baffled fury, will a wave of concern over stress sweep over this hypochondriacal country, to match the widespread interest in jogging and polyunsaturated oils? Quite likely. There is nothing more fascinating to the layman than folklore finally validated by reputable scientists. A murmur of assent rises faintly from the past. When the great Pasteur lay in terminal illness, in 1895, he reflected once again on his long scientific disagreement with Claude Bernard. Pasteur's dying words were: "Bernard was right. The microbe is nothing, the terrain is everything."

9

ORGANIZATIONAL EFFECTIVENESS-INEFFECTIVENESS

Organizational effectiveness is a "bottomline measure." It is a term which is used to summarize the overall success of an organization in acquiring, transforming and using resources to establish favorable reactions with its important constituents. Of course, bottomline measures often interfere with understanding underlying dynamic processes. So it has been with effectiveness.

Almost all books on management, whether they are written by presidents, accountants, economists, engineers or behavioral scientists, place the goal of organizational effectiveness (or some related goal such as efficiency) at the core of their analysis. Most writers stress some set of rational designs, decisions, controls, policies, models and so on which organizations use or ought to use in the pursuit of effectiveness. However correct these ideas may be as normative approaches, they provide only limited insight into what organizations actually do to achieve "effectiveness" and provide little insight into the social processes which are major determinants of effectiveness.

Frequently, writers have failed to realize that "organizational effectiveness" is more than a pervasive goal of almost all organizations; it is also a constraint upon how organizational members use resources. Members most frequently define, justify and defend their decisions and actions in terms of "effectiveness." Moreover, members use effectiveness as a weapon to control others. Individuals who are ineffective in demonstrating how their preferred actions can be reconciled with organizational effectiveness are apt to be continually frustrated in achieving their goals.

Of course, it is a mistake to conclude that the explicit concern with effectiveness leads directly to well-run organizations which are internally well managed and efficient. In fact, as these first selections will show, the quest for effectiveness often has exactly the opposite consequences. Examples of the dysfunctional consequences of rationally based attempts to improve the operation of organizations elicit chuckles when we read about them in newspapers almost every day.

The article by Andrew Glass provides a typical example. The selection by Robert D. McFadden reveals how attempts to monitor effectiveness may become almost totally removed from the actual requirements of effective performance. The humorous story by Joanne Greenberg reveals another aspect of the latent consequences of attempts to design effective organizations—systems which are well equipped to deal routinely and efficiently with one set of circumstances are incapable of coping with a different set of events. Together, these selections demonstrate that the attempts to design effective organizations often go awry. However, the dynamics of effectiveness-ineffectiveness are more complex than such examples of unanticipated consequences suggest.

The next set of readings suggest a number of additional aspects of tensions within organizations which limit effectiveness of individuals and of whole organizations. The selection by Antony Jay reveals that the relationship of individuals to corporations is such that effectiveness is a minor concern in the everyday concerns of organizational members. Samuel Culbert focuses on a different aspect of individual-organizational relations and effectiveness. He suggests that ineffectiveness is an outgrowth of tensions arising from the human need for acceptance, organization practices and interpersonal behavior. Yet another aspect of the interrelationship of pressures experienced by individuals and organizational effectiveness is revealed by the testimony of Kermit Vandivier about the behavior of employees at B.F. Goodrich. There, behavior was such that it had, at least, the appearance of being effective.

Often it is assumed that the causes of ineffectiveness lie in the behavior of lower-level members of the organizational hierarchy. In many ways, the selections in this section which have been discussed so far give support to this point of view. However, the actions of people at the top are frequently far less compatible with effectiveness than we assume. Max Ways's managerial analysis of Watergate shows how the actions of "top management" contributed to tragic blunders. The article by Ben Heineman reveals that even boards of directors are unlikely to act as checks on ineffective behavior. The report by Tom Alexander, noting that it took a crisis before U.S. Borax discovered how much slack existed in its operation, indicates how far an organization can deviate from effective behavior without top management even being aware of it. The stimulus for greater effectiveness there was a crisis, not the rational behavior of management at any level.

The final reading points to some nontraditional aspects of the effectiveness of organizations in dealing with their environments. Based on the dominance that economic thinking has had on our paradigms of organizations, we frequently think of the relationships of organizations to their environments very narrowly. We look at organizations as systems which transform inputs into goods and services to serve the wants of certain consumers or clients. However, as the final selection reveals, this perspective, while true, is seriously incomplete. Organizations are active in creating their environments. "The Corporate Rush to Confess All" shows how bribes, kickbacks and other illegal practices are used by organizations to shape the environment they confront in ways which will help their firms to achieve their goals.

Other ways not reported here in which organizations shape their environments include using the media to modify behavior (for example, see Thomas Griffith's "Must Business Fight the Press?" *Fortune,* June 1974) and influencing the legal environment of similar organizations through concerted political action (for example, Robert Fendell's "Auto Dealer's Fund Will Sort Friends from Enemies," The *New York Times*, 1976).

Clearly, the selections in this section give only a glimpse of some of the processes which influence the effectiveness of organizations. Most of these processes have been given little attention by students of management, who have sought to understand effectiveness through traditional economic, management and behavioral science models. We hope that the direct look at the behavior of organizations themselves provides the reader with a greater understanding of the actual dynamics of processes which influence organizational effectiveness.

Paperwork Bogs Down Paperwork Probe

Andrew Glass

A presidential move to investigate the spread of paperwork in government has been stalled for five months by voluminous White House paperwork.

Last December, while on a ski vacation, President Ford signed into law a bill creating a high-level bipartisan commission to suggest ways of reducing the $36 billion annual paperwork crunch imposed by the government on Americans.

The law calls for a 14-member panel to probe all facets of the growing paperwork burden and to report within two years. It will cost $6 million to produce the report.

Throughout the winter and spring, White House officials claimed that the new Commission on Federal Paperwork soon would be digging into thousands of bureaucratic data-gathering programs, seeking to determine which were truly needed.

But the White House personnel office has yet to advise the President on who should be named to the Commission. By all accounts, Ford's personnel staff has been so engulfed in political clearances, security forms, inter-agency memorandums and the like that it hasn't been able to produce a slate of commissioners for the President's review and approval.

"For a variety of reasons, the system isn't working," said a congres-

From Andrew Glass, "Paperwork Bogs Down Paperwork Probe," *The Miami News* (May 31, 1975), p. 1. Reprinted with permission.

sional source who deals regularly with the White House personnel office. "That place is a shambles."

The source noted that the White House personnel chief, William Walker, was nominated last month as a U.S. trade envoy and that no one has been chosen to replace him.

"It looks like we'll be getting off the ground in the near future," a White House official said last week when asked about the long delay. The official said the target date for a White House proclamation on paperwork was "only a couple of weeks away."

The commission's task, if and when it gets going, will be to examine the reasons behind the 15 billion federal forms that were printed in 1974.

The National Association of Public Accountants recently found that more than 10 billion sheets of paper pass each year between bureaucrats and citizens. It costs U.S. business about $18 billion annually to fill them out and, according to the General Accounting Office, nearly as much in taxpayers' dollars to pay people to process them.

Federal forms cost $1 billion to produce in 1974. Official directives cost another $1 billion and various reports cost $1.3 billion. To that must be added the $1.7 billion spent to file and store these records.

"Naturally, you recognize, that your story will be cited in the daily (presidential) news summary," a White House source said. "I think some people who read it will have questions and (the personnel office) will have to put something on paper."

"Audit of an Audit" Spoofs Levitt's Staff as Liability

Robert D. McFadden

With barbs, broadsides and a parody of the bookkeeper mentality, a state hospital in Queens has answered an audit of its operations by State Comptroller Arthur Levitt by issuing a pseudo-scientific report entitled, "Audit of an Audit."

Among the hundreds of tax-supported agencies that quake at the auditor's call, this was the first in memory that has dared to turn the tables on the Comptroller and audit the auditor.

"How valid is the auditing mystique?" asks the Queens Children's Psychiatric Center in Bellerose, which posed other embarrassing questions:

"Is there a mortal behind those glinting steel-rimmed glasses, prone to fatigue, subject to error, perhaps afflicted with a hangover?

"Do those ominous attaché cases, with their shiny snaplocks and their aura of omniscience, sometimes contain only a salami sandwich?"

Stapled between pointedly blood-red cardboard covers, the satirical 16-page report nips at the Comptroller's heels for what it calls the bumbling, incompetence and unfairness of his auditing agents. And it describes his as-yet-unpublished report as largely a waste of the taxpayers' money.

As an example of its genre, the report is both zany and cutting and its tone is a blend of mock-serious and seriously mocking.

It is set in the numbered-paragraph, lettered-subparagraph format of the audit reports that emerge with regularity from Mr. Levitt's office, focusing the glare of publicity—normally on quiet weekends—on the faults and foibles of taxpayer-supported agencies and organizations.

The report is laced with accounting jargon and tables of impenetrable statistics to back it up. There are chapters called "First, the Bad News" and "Now the Good News." There are recommendations and appendices and an epilogue entitled, "Dam the Torrents of Paper."

CONCLUSION LEADS

Appraised of the report, a spokesman for the Comptroller's office said: "We're not going to dignify this with a response. The audit will speak for itself. The auditors are human beings who can make mistakes, but they're well-trained and supervised and are working in teams to make mistakes less likely."

Prepared by Dr. Gloria Faretra, the director of the psychiatric center, and Dr. Abbas D. Nabas, the center's director of research, the hospital report, which accused the state's auditors of unbending bias, began with its conclusion:

"There is no more validity in employing an auditor to evaluate the treatment of programs of a hospital than there would be in employing a physician to audit the financial affairs of a bank."

Noting that there were no medical or clinical personnel on the team that audited the hospital's operations from May 12 to Aug. 19, 1975, the report declared: "In the area of clinical evaluations and recommendations, the audit was found useless, time- and money-wasting, duplicative, unnecessary and counter-therapeutic."

"SOME VALUE" FOUND

It said some recommendations in the areas of accounting, receipts, disbursements, payroll procedures and voucher and inventory systems were of "some value," and either had been or were being implemented.

But the bulk of the auditors' work came in for some harsh criticism—"a startling measure of fancy," "impressions overruling arithmetic," "bias instead of objectivity" and "virtually an effort to practice medicine without a license," were some of the characterizations in an accompanying news release.

The report's litany of findings included the following:

• The longer that hospital staff members worked with the auditors, the more they became convinced that the auditors were incompetent.

• "Auditors' 'biases' were unaffected by on-site information."

• While the auditors reported a "stable" census of about 300 children at the hospital from 1970 to 1975, the actual numbers dropped 45 percent during that period, from 480 to 275.

• The auditors compared the resident population of patients with the hospital's operating budget and concluded that the better (or longer or more detailed) the records kept on patients, "the shorter the patient's hospital stay," a leap of reasoning that prompted this response: "We have found neither professional opinion nor research results to validate this questionable comparison, but we are still searching."

"STILL MORE PAPERWORK"

The report's epilogue focused on paperwork, noting that a study two years ago had found that the professional staff at the hospital spent 40 or 50 percent of its time on it. The report said:

"Virtually every recommendation of the auditors, each suggested solution to a problem, each 'answer' to a question, calls directly or indirectly for still more forms, still more paperwork.

"It seems increasingly obvious that the conscious or unconscious goal of the auditor is the Perfect Form—something that can substitute for medical training, clinical field experience and medical judgment, something which can be fed into a computer for an instant readout with all the answers."

Rites of Passage
Joanne Greenberg

It was a bright green day. Big trees on the side streets were raining seeds and the wind stirred in its second sleep. A long flatbed truck came rattling down one of the streets and stopped by the new steel, chrome, and glass building. The building's lines were so "functional" it made Cephas wonder if anyone actually worked in it. Then he saw some women going in. Good.

He checked his appearance by hitching up to the rearview mirror. He was wearing a clean white shirt and a bow tie and his thin gray hair had been slicked down with water. When he was sure he was presentable, he got down out of the cab of the truck, dusted himself off, and began to walk slowly toward the building.

It had been many years . . . perhaps they had moved. No, there was the sign: BOONE COUNTY DEPARTMENT OF PUBLIC WELFARE. The last time he had been here the building had been a temporary shed and people had been lined up outside waiting for the relief trucks to come. That had been in 1934, in the winter. His father had been proud of holding out until '34.

Cephas stopped and looked at the building again. Some secretaries came out, laughing and talking. They didn't look at him, being used to seeing people who came hesitantly to their offices to acknowledge failure in life.

Cephas checked himself again in the big glass door and then went in. There was a large booth with a woman behind it and eight or nine rows of benches facing it. People were sitting quietly, staring at nothing waiting. To the right there were a series of chutes with numbers over them. Cephas went up to the booth.

"Take a number," the woman said without looking at him.

"Ma'am?"

"You take a number and wait your turn. We'll call you."

He took one of the plastic number cards. It said 15. He sat down and waited.

"Five," the woman called. A heavy woman got up slowly and went to the booth and then to one of the chutes.

Cephas waited. Minutes were born, ripened, aged, and died without issue.

"Number six." Around him the springtime asthmatics whistled and gasped in their season. He looked at the cracks in his fingers.

"Number seven." An hour went by; another. He was afraid to go out and check his truck lest the line speed up and he lose his place.

"Number thirteen," the woman called. . . .

They came to his number at last and he went up to the desk, gave back the plastic card, and was directed to his chute. Another woman was there at another desk. She took his name, Cephas Ribble, and his age, sixty-eight.

Had he been given aid before?

Yes.

Had he been on General Assistance, Aid to the Needy, Disabled or Tuberculosis Aid?

"It was what they called Relief."

"But under what category was it?"

"It was for people that was off their farms or else didn't have nothin' to eat. They called it 'goin' on the county'. It was back in nineteen and thirty-four. We held out 'till thirty-four."

"I see. . . . Now you are applying for the old-age pension?"

He said he wasn't.

"Are you married, Mr. Ribble?" She sighed.

"Never had the pleasure," he said.

"Are you without funds, in emergency status?"

He said he wasn't.

"Then take this card and go to Room Eleven, to your left." She pressed a little light or something and he felt the people shifting their weight behind him, Number 16, he supposed. He made his way to Room Eleven.

The lady there was nice; he could see it right off. She told him about the different requirements for what they called "Aid," and then she had him sign some forms: permission to inquire into his bank account, acceptance of surplus or donated food, release of medical information, and several others. Then she said sympathetically, "In what way are you disabled?"

He thought about all the ways a man might be disabled and checked each one off. It was a proud moment, a man sixty-eight without one thing in the world to complain of in his health.

"I ain't disabled no way. I am pleased you asked me, though. A man don't take time to be grateful for things like his health. If the shoe don't pinch, you don't take notice, do you?" He sat back, contented. Then he realized that the sun was getting hotter, and what with everything in the truck, he'd better get on.

The woman had put down her ball-point pen. "Mr. Ribble, if you aren't disabled or without funds, what kind of aid do you want?" A shadow of irritation crossed her face.

"No aid at all," he said. "It's about somethin' different." He tried to hold down his excitement. This was his special day, a day for which he had waited for over a decade, but it was no use bragging and playing the boy, so he said no more.

The woman was very annoyed. "Then why didn't you tell the worker at the desk?"

"She didn't give me no chance, ma'am, an' neither did that other lady. I bet you don't have many repair men comin' in here to fix things—not above once, anyway except them gets paid by the hour."

"Well, Mr. Ribble, what is it you want?" She heard the noise of co-workers leaving or returning on their coffee breaks. She sighed and began to drum her fingers, but Cephas wasn't aware of her impatience. He was beginning back in 1934. Good God, she thought, he's senile. She knew that she would have to listen to all of it. In his time, in his way.

"'Thirty-four cleaned us out—cleaned us bare. You wonder how *farmers* could go hungry. I don't know, but we did. After the drought hit, there was nothin' to do but come in town an' sign up on the County. Twice a month my pa would come in an' bring back food. Sometimes I came with him. I seen them lines of hungry men just standin' out there like they was pole-axed an' hadn't fallen yet. I tell you, them days was pitiful, *pitiful*." He glanced at her and then smiled. "I'm glad to see *you* done good since—a new buildin' an' all. Yes, you come right up." He looked around with approval at the progress they had made.

"Mr. Ribble . . . ?"

He returned. "See, we taken the Relief, but we never got to tell nobody the good it done for us. After that year, things got a little better, and soon we was on toward bein' a payin' farm again. In 'forty-six we built us a new house—every convenience—an' in 'fifty-two we got some of them automated units for cattle care. Two years ago we dug out of debt, an' last year, I knew it was time to think about my plan for real. It was time to thank the Welfare."

"Mr. Ribble, thanks are not necessary————"

"Don't you mind, ma'am, you just get your men an' come with me."

"I beg your pardon. . . . "

"I don't just talk, ma'am; I act. You just bring your men."

Mr. Morrissey had come back from his coffee break and was standing in the hall.

The woman signaled him with her eyes as she followed Cephas Ribble, now walking proud and sure out the door to his truck. Mr.

Morrissey sighed and followed, wondering why he was always around when somebody needed to make a madness plain. Why did it never happen to McFarland?

Cephas reached into his pocket and both of the welfare people thought: *Gun*. He took out a piece of paper and turned to them as they stood transfixed and pale, thinking of death. "I got it all here, all of what's in the truck. Get your men, ma'am, no use wastin' time. It's all in the truck and if it don't get unloaded soon, it's gonna spoil."

"What is this *about*, Mr. Ribble?"

"My gift, ma'am; my donation. I'm giving the Relief four hundred chickens, thirty barrels of tomatoes, thirty barrels of apricots—I figured, for variety. Don't you think the apricots was a good idea—ten barrels Eyetalian beans, six firkins of butter. . . . Ma'am, you better get the chickens out—it don't do to keep 'em in the sun. I thought about milk, so I give two cans—that's a hundred gallons of milk in case there's hungry babies."

They were dumbfounded. Cephas could see that. He wanted to tell them that it wasn't a case of trying to be big. He'd figured that everybody gave when they could. He'd even signed a form right there in the office about promising to accept donated food and clothing. Their amazement at his gift embarrassed him. Then he realized that it was probably the only way they could thank him—by making a fuss. People on the State payroll must have to walk a pretty narrow line. They'd have to be on the lookout for people taking advantage. That was it. It was deep work, that Welfare—mighty deep work.

"What are we supposed to do with all that food?" Mr. Morrissey asked.

Cephas knew that the man was just making sure that it wasn't a bribe. "Why, give it to the poor. Call 'em in an let 'em get it. You can have your men unload it right now, an' I'd do it quick if I was you. Like I said, it won't be long 'till it starts to turn in all this heat."

Mr. Morrissey tried to explain that modern welfare methods were different than those in 1934. Even then, the food had been U.S. surplus, not privately donated. It had come from government warehouses.

Cephas spoke of the stupidity and waste of Government in Farming, and rained invective on the Soil Bank.

Mr. Morrissey tried again to make his point. "We don't *give* out any food. There hasn't been any food *donated* since nineteen sixteen!"

No doubt of it, these Welfare people had to be awful careful. Cephas nodded. "The others do what they can—don't blame 'em if it don't seem like much," he said sympathetically. "I signed that slip in there about the donated food, so there must *be* a lot of donated food."

"It's an old law," Morrissey argued tiredly. "It's one of the old Poor Laws that never got taken off the books."

"'An here you folks are followin' it, right today," Cephas mused. "It must make you mighty proud."

"Mr. Ribble, *we have no place to store all this!*"

Cephas found his throat tightening with happiness. He had come in humility, waited all morning just so he could show his small gratitude and be gone, and everyone was thunderstruck at the plenty. "Mister," he said, "I pay my taxes without complainin', but I never knowed how hard you people was workin' for your money. You got to guard against every kind of bribes an' invitations to break the law; you got to find ways to get this food to the poor people so fast, you can't even store it! By God, Mister, you make me proud to be an American!"

A policeman had stopped by the truck and was tranquilly writing a ticket. Cephas excused himself modestly and strode off to defend his situation. The two Welfare workers stood staring after him as he engaged the officer.

It was, after all, State law that food could be donated. Were there no loading ramps, no men attending them? Had the department no parking place for donors? The policeman began to look at the two stunned bearers of the State's trust. He had stopped writing.

"Could that truck fit in the workers' parking lot?" Morrissey murmured.

"What are we going to *do* with it all?" Mrs. Traphagen whimpered.

"All those chickens—four hundred chickens!"

Mrs. Traphagen sighed. "The poor will never stand for it."

"First things first," Mr. Morrissey decided, and he went to confront the policeman.

Cephas' truck in the workers' parking lot blocked all their cars. As a consequence, the aid applications of eight families were held pending investigation. Six discharged inmates of the State hospital remained incarcerated for a week longer pending home checkups. Thirty-seven women washed floors and children's faces in the expectation of home visits which did not come about. A Venereal Disease meeting at the Midtown Hotel was one speaker short, and high-school students who had been scheduled to hear a lecture entitled "Social Work, Career of Tomorrow," remained unedified. Applicants who came to apply for aid that afternoon were turned away. There was no trade in little plastic cards and the hive of offices were empty. But the people of the Boone County Department of Public Welfare were not idle. It was only that the action had moved from the desks and files and chutes to the workers' parking lot and into the hands of its glad tyrant, Cephas Ribble.

All afternoon Cephas lifted huge baskets of apricots and tomatoes into the arms of the Welfare workers. All afternoon they went from his truck to their cars, carrying baskets, or with chickens festooned limply over their arms. When they complained to Mr. Unger, the head of the department, he waved them off. Were they to go to every home and deliver the food? He said he didn't care—they were to get rid of it. Were big families to get the same amount as small families? He said that the stuff was political dynamite and that all he wanted was to be rid of it before anybody noticed.

Cephas, from the back of his flat-bed, was a titan. He lifted, smiling and loaded with a strong hand. He never stopped to rest or take a drink. The truck steamed in the hot spring light, but he was living at height, unbothered by the heat, or the closeness, or the increasing rankness of his chickens. Of course he saw that the Welfare people weren't dressed for loading food. They were dressed for church, looked like. It was deep work, very deep, working for the State. You had to set a good example. You had to dress up and talk very educated so as to give the poor a moral uplift. You had to be honest. A poor man could lie; Cephas had been poor himself, so he knew; but it must be a torment to deal with people free to lie and not be able to do it yourself.

By three thirty the truck had been unloaded and Cephas was free to go home and take up his daily life again. He shook hands with the director and the case-work supervisor, the head bookkeeper and the statistician. To them he presented his itemized list, with weights carefully noted and items given the market value as of yesterday, in case they needed it for their records. Then he carefully turned the truck out of the parking lot, waved good-bye to the sweating group, nosed into the sluggish mass of afternoon traffic, and began to head home.

A cacophony of high-pitched voices erupted in the lot behind him:

"I've got three mothers of drop-outs to visit!"

"What am I going to *do* with all this stuff?"

"Who do we give this to? . . . My people won't take the Lady Bountiful bit!"

"Does it count on their food allowance? Do we go down Vandalia and hand out apricots to every kid we see?"

"I don't have the time!"

"Which families get it?"

"Do we take the value off next month's check?"

"It's hopeless to try to distribute this fairly," the supervisor said.

"It will cost us close to a thousand dollars to distribute it at all," the statistician said.

"It would cost us close to two thousand dollars to alter next month's checks," the bookkeeper said, "and the law specifies that we have to take extra income-in-kind off the monthly allowance."

"If I were you," the director said, "I would take all this home and eat it, and not let anyone know about it."

"Mr. Morrissey!" Mrs. Traphagen's face paled away the red of her exertion, "that is fraud! You know as well as I do what would happen if it got out that we had diverted Welfare Commodities to our own use! Can you imagine what the Mayor would say? The Governor? The State Department of Health? The HEW, The National Association of Social Workers?!'' She had begun to tremble and the two chickens that were hanging limply over her arm nodded to each other with slow decorum, their eyes closed righteously against the thought.

Cars began to clot the exit of the parking lot. The air was redolent.

But many of the workers didn't take the food home. The wolf of hunger was patient in shadowing the poor, even in summer, even on Welfare. As the afternoon wore on, apricots began to appear in the hands of children from Sixteenth and Vandalia Street all the way to the Boulevard. Tomatoes flamed briefly on the windowsills of the Negro ghetto between Fourteenth and Kirk, and on one block, there was a chicken in every pot.

The complaints began early the next day. Sixteen Negroes called the Mayor's Committee on Racial Harmony, claiming that chickens, fruit, and vegetables had been given to the White Disadvantaged, while they had received tomatoes, half of them rotten. A rumor began that the food had been impregnated with contraceptive medicine to test on the poor and that three people had died from it. The Health Department denied this, but its word was not believed.

There were eighteen calls at the Department of Welfare protesting a tomato fight which had taken place on Fourteenth and Vandalia, in which passers-by had been pelted with tomatoes. The callers demanded that the families of those involved be stricken from the Welfare rolls as Relief cheaters, encouraging waste and damaging the moral fiber of working people.

Eighteen mothers on the Aid to Dependent Children program picketed the Governor's mansion, carrying placards that read: *Hope, Not Handouts* and *Jobs, Not Charity*.

Sixty-eight welfare clients called to say that they had received no food at all and demanded equal service. When they heard that the Vandalia Street mothers were picketing, a group of them went down as counter-pickets. Words were exchanged between the two groups and a riot ensued in which sixteen people were hospitalized for injuries, including six members of the city's riot squad. Seven of the leaders were arrested and jailed pending investigation. The FBI was called into the case in the evening to ascertain if the riot was Communist-inspired.

At ten o'clock the Mayor appeared on TV with a plea for reason and patience. He stated that the riot was a reflection of the general decline in American morals and a lack of respect for the law. He ordered a six-man commission to be set up to hear testimony and make recommendations. A political opponent demanded a thorough investigation of the county Welfare System, the War on Poverty, and the local university's radicals.

The following day, Mrs. Traphagen was unable to go to work at the Welfare office, having been badly scalded on the hand while canning a bushel of apricots.

Cephas Ribble remembered everyone at the Welfare Office in his prayers. After work, he would think about the day he had spent in the city, and of his various triumphs: the surprise and wonder on the faces of the workers; the open awe of the lady who had said, "You don't need to thank us." How everyone had dropped the work they were doing and run to unload the truck. It had been a wonderful day. He had given his plenty unto the poor, the plenty and nourishment of his own farm. He rose refreshed to do his work, marveling at the meaning and grandeur with which his chores were suddenly invested.

"By God," he said, as he checked the chickens and noted their need for more calcium in the feed," a man has his good to do. I'm gonna do it every year. I'm gonna have a day for the poor. Yessir, every year." And he smiled genially on the chickens, the outbuildings, and the ripening fields of a generous land.

The Evolution of Corporation Man

Antony Jay

One of the most important discoveries of my working life was made between 8:30 a.m. and 6:00 p.m. on Thursday, April 9th, 1964.

On Wednesday, April 8th, I left the British Broadcasting Corporation, which I had joined more or less straight from university and military service nine years earlier. At BBC I had been a trainee, a production assistant, a producer, a program editor, a head of department. But at 8:30 a.m. on April 9th I was just me, sitting at my desk at home with a number of writing assignments which I had prudently contracted before giving in my notice. The discovery I had made by 6:00 p.m., to express it the way it appeared at the time, was the enormous amount of work that could be done in a day. Nine years in a great corporation had obliterated the memory of how much time there was if you had no telephone calls, correspondence, minutes, routine meet-

ings, departmental meetings, budget reviews, requests for authorization, annual interviews, policy documents, appointments with visitors, and all the rest of that endless succession of events and non-
events that compose the manager's day, and his year, and his life.

But the discovery can be expressed in the opposite way: that the
corporation day is absurdly, ludicrously short. Only a week before I left
I had spent a whole morning at a meeting with the head of my group,
my three fellow departmental heads, and the group administrative
officer. Our problem had what the Caliph in *Hassan* called "the monstrous beauty of the hindquarters of an elephant." In the past year we
had recruited a large number of trainee producers to prepare for the
opening of the BBC's second channel. In a few more months, when we
thought the trainees were ready, we would be inviting them to make
formal applications for permanent posts in our group. But—horror!—
the head of a rival group in the BBC was advertising his vacancies
already, and the trainees in our group wanted to apply for them. What
could we do? There was a BBC staff agreement saying that every
employee must be free to apply for any advertised vacancy. Did this
mean we had to stand by and watch him cream off all our best trainees,
the young men and women we had spent a year selecting and training
to work on our own programs? Should we privately warn them that
applications would bring our displeasure? Should we put up a case to
the head of personnel to suspend the normal ruling? Should we put up
a case to the director of programs to impose simultaneity on all groups'
advertisements? There were many possibilities, and six of us to discuss
them, so it is not surprising that the meeting lasted nearly three hours.

The important point about the problem was that it was the corporation itself that created it. It had nothing to do with producing good
programs or controlling their costs or developing new people or ideas.
It was entirely concerned with, and consequent upon, the corporation's internal organization, and yet it took half a day—10 percent of
a week—of the time of six senior managers to resolve it.

The next morning I had one of my producers on the phone in a
panic. The planning department wanted to take away his staff film
editor and get him to put his work out to a free lance. For several
reasons this was impossible, but the planners did not seem to understand why. I spent most of that day in a telephone battle, arguing with
planning, appealing to the head of programs, going back to the producer for more ammunition, drafting powerful memos, consulting the
film department, proposing alternatives. By the end of the day I had
won. The planning department had seen reason, they had withdrawn
the proposal, and my producer and his program were safe. But what
had I actually achieved in positive terms? I had merely stopped a silly
mistake from being made.

It is pointless (though it would be easy) to multiply these instances.

Everyone who has ever worked in or with large corporations has his own parallel experiences. I wish I had spent a week noting how much of my time was spent doing my real job—the job determined by the needs of our market, the television audience—and how much in administrative machine maintenance, stopping the corporation from grinding to a halt. The ratio would have been impressive.

But it is not only time that evaporates in large corporations. Money evaporates as well. Just before I left, I went into a stationery shop to buy typing paper, carbons, paper clips, and so on. I actually paid money over the counter for them. Real money, the sort that gets you into theaters and out of restaurants, and buys groceries and furniture and presents for the children. Previously, all stationery was bought for me with corporation money, which bore no relation to human money. It was a purely notional currency that appeared on forms and memos, but never passed through pockets or wallets. Indeed, the budget for a single edition of a weekly program might be more than the producer's annual salary. Dealing with such large sums, it was only worth a very limited effort to save a thousand dollars of corporation money on a fifty-thousand-dollar program budget, even if there were any incentive to do so. By contrast, a thousand dollars of human money could take a year's hard and conscious saving to accumulate. Equally, you could save five dollars by shooting twelve seconds' less film, and five dollars was the difference between a glass of beer and a bottle of wine for supper. But it was impossible to make the connection: corporation money, like corporation time, was simply something that was there. It had to be used up somehow, and each of us was allocated separate quantities of it to achieve various objectives. There was a certain professional pride about keeping to your own budget, but a great deal of corporation money was not on your own budget: carpets, curtains, offices, and any number of other central facilities. These we wheedled and cajoled and argued and fought for without any compunction at all, and if we finished up with more research assistants or film units or studio time than we needed we would not have dreamed of handing any back: we could always use them in some way.

An illuminating manifestation of this attitude toward money appeared when I was discussing with a top executive a proposal which might earn a considerable profit. He was not very interested (it would have meant more work for him) and more or less terminated the discussion by saying, "You realize that even if it made a million dollars a year, that's still only one percent of our gross revenue?" So it was; but it was also a million dollars, which if offered to him privately, in human money instead of corporation money, would have been worth almost any effort or sacrifice. But for all the relationship he felt between it and the money in his wallet, he might as well have been playing Monopoly. But the classic case was the one hundred pounds that the BBC advanced to the comedy writers Frank Muir and Denis Norden for a program that was ultimately canceled. Some time later they received a request from the BBC to send it back, and they replied, "We regret we have no machinery for returning money." This apparently was a completely satisfactory answer, and they never heard about the one hundred pounds again. No individual human would accept such a reason for surrendering one hundred pounds of his own money—but obviously the rules for corporation money are totally different.

Even while I was a member of the BBC I wondered if this attitude to time and money was unique or unusual among corporations. After leaving, I worked with quite a number of big organizations, and realized that in fact the BBC was rather good. (I ought in fairness to point out that the present BBC, after an almost complete change of top management and a going-over from McKinsey's, bears little relationship to the corporation I knew: but even the old BBC would have shuddered at some of the examples of corporate behavior I have since collected.) My favorite instance happened to a friend who was also a free-lance writer. He had worked out a series of comedy commercials for a detergent firm, and the agency was so delighted they fixed up a day-long conference with him and the client at a London hotel. A dozen of them met in a room with pads and pencils and blotters at each place. Around the walls were waiters and waitresses manning three tables, one with urns full of coffee and milk, another groaning under bottles of every conceivable drink, the third piled high with plates of cold ham and chicken and tongue, salads, trifles and cakes, ready for the marathon session. The clients opened the proceedings by saying they thought comedy diminished the dignity of cleanliness. The agency men turned and stared at my friend. He agreed that it might well be so—he was a writer, not a market researcher. They thereupon agreed it was better not to risk it, and the meeting was over. They all trooped out into the London street, but my friend is convinced that he was the only one who was haunted for the rest of the day by the thought of the empty room, spread with a vast banquet which no one was going to eat. But then I suppose it was corporation food.

Outside the BBC I found that the corporations' incredible unreality about time and money also extended to people. Time and time again the best and most logical person for a job was passed over in favor of some unlikely and unsuitable candidate from outside, who proceeded to make a mess of it. Often the passed-over manager would leave and discover to his astonishment that he could quadruple his income outside, and devote to his new private enterprise ten times more energy and productivity than the corporation was ever able to release or harness. I found horrifying schemes for reporting on staff that tried to turn every manager into a cross between God and a consulting psychiatrist.

I found people treated with an indulgent softness that in ordinary life no one would show to a plumber or car mechanic who had fallen down on the job a quarter as badly, or with an inhuman callousness that the same people would privately not inflict on a stray dog.

But once you start judging big organizations, not by other big organizations, but by the simple standards of an ordinary human community, there is a phenomenon that is even more extraordinary than all these. By organization standards, of course, it is quite common, not in the least extraordinary: it is the absence of a sense of belonging to the corporation. Of course, in all corporations there are some people who feel part of it, and in some corporations almost everyone feels part of it. They are the ones who say "we" when talking about what the corporation makes or sells or plans to do. But "they" seems to be the more common expression, and as mergers and takeovers create fewer larger units, the "they"-to-"we" ratio increases. And yet the individual members of the corporations nearly all like to belong to some organization, to feel part of it, to be proud when it succeeds or depressed when it is going through a bad stretch. The focus of their loyalty may be a football team or a golf club or a social club or a rose-growing association, but it is not the corporation which occupies by far the largest part of their waking life.

Of course, the corporations are aware that something is wrong: over the years this awareness shifts from one symptom to another, and each shift calls into being a new branch of management consulting and stimulates scores of postgraduate theses in management or social studies. If money-wasting is the focus, there is cost accountancy, management accountancy and all manner of stock and budgetary control procedures. If it is the use of time, the organization and methods and operational research men are standing by to help. If it is the misuse or alienation of people, there are shelves full of books on personnel recruitment and motivation, bonus schemes and personality tests, and management development programs. What they all have in common is that they do not go to the heart of the problem: they are like ointment for spots, fine if you have one or two spots, but if you have chicken pox you will not cure it by putting ointment on every spot; the disease has to be attacked at the root. The most recent corporation anxiety focus is "communication," and no doubt we shall soon be seeing a troop of communication consultants come galloping over the horizon, blowing their bugles and brandishing a score of lengthy comparative studies of vertical and lateral communication in General Motors, IBM and du Pont. They will serve up the usual compound of common sense, jargon and nonsense in the name of Claude Lévi-Strauss or Marshall McLuhan or that professor from Harvard Business School or M.I.T. whose name I didn't quite catch, and the corporations will set up internal communication programs and send managers off to communication courses, and one more spot will be covered with ointment. But the disease will not be cured.

Perhaps the most significant objective finding about large corporations was published a year or two ago in *Economica*, the quarterly review published by the London School of Economics. It showed how the average profitability of companies increased up to two or three million dollars employed capital, and then descended steadily as the amount of capital employed rose higher and higher. And yet the tendency of all industrial countries is toward larger and larger industrial units. And of course it is this very largeness that is at the root of all the other problems: small private companies of twenty or thirty people, even companies of a few hundred, do not spend ages sorting out their own managerial muddles; they do not spend money as if it were a centrally provided facility; they do not tolerate continuing incompetence or behave with impersonal cruelty; and the people who work there usually feel they belong. When the Lotus sports car company was flooded out, the 600 employees heard about it on television and came in late that night to help mop up. That sort of loyalty at Ford or British Leyland would make headline news across the nation.

Does it have to be so? Do we have to accept that this is more and more the nature of the industrial world in which we shall spend the rest of the century? I am convinced we do not, and there are enough corporate exceptions to the rule to show that large does not have to mean impersonal, inefficient, and inhuman. But in that case, have the exceptional few found corporate success by accident, or is there some factor at work which can perhaps be isolated and used to help us improve the vast clumsy modern corporation not only as a place for humans to work in but also as a profit-making industrial unit? I believe there is; all these problems spring from a single root, and the root is deep in our own natures. The truth about how a great corporation should be organized is a personal truth which each of us can recognize in himself. But the scientific knowledge which enables us to relate our personal experience to scientifically authenticated fact is only now beginning to be published. It has already caused a revolution in science, and it is hard to see how it can avoid causing an even greater revolution in the corporation.

The name of the revolution is the New Biology. Its findings and theories are scattered over thousands of papers, books, theses, and learned articles published over the past twenty years and more, and most of them concern particular discoveries and observations, and experiments with individual species of animal. But in the past few years a handful of writers, bolder than the rest, have begun to arrange all these separate mosaic pieces into a new picture of the origins and nature of man. The best known are Konrad Lorenz, Desmond Morris and Robert Ardrey: and it was above all Ardrey's three books, *African Genesis, The Territorial Imperative* and *The Social Contract,* which started off the various trains of thought that have come together in this book. The New Biology is still very new, but before it is much older it will bring as profound a change in our thinking as Freud and his successors brought a century ago. Indeed, there is a sense in which the New Biology, although it compels the most profound revision of Freud's theories, is nevertheless the completion of his work. Hard though many of Freud's explanations were to accept, there was one element in them that struck a sympathetic chord in the minds of most of Freud's readers, and that was his assertion that the spring of human action was not the controlled logical working of the reason, but the uncontrollable surge of much deeper subconscious or unconscious emotional drives. There is nothing in the New Biology to conflict with that insight, though there is a great deal to modify our views on what those drives are, and where they come from.

The basis of the New Biology is evolution. Ever since Darwin we have understood the operation of evolution and natural selection on physical characteristics: we know that giraffes have long necks because somewhere back in time there was not enough food on the lower branches of trees, with the result that the longer-necked of each generation survived to breed, and the shorter-necked died without issue; we know that tigers are striped because the unstriped varieties stood out from the dappled shadows with the result that their breakfast saw them in time and escaped, while their better camouflaged brothers and sisters ate and survived. But the New Biology takes Darwin a whole stage further: it shows animal behavior, and human behavior, as the consequence of the same evolutionary pressures that produced claws and teeth, feathers and fur, or hooves and horns. Status-seeking emerges not as an unworthy failing of jealous executives, but as an immutable ingredient in man's make-up—an ingredient he shares with many other species including the jackdaw, the baboon and the domestic hen. The same is true of exploring, and aggressive behavior, and defense of territory, and protection of young: they are deep in our nature because our predecessors who lacked these qualities died, while our ancestors who had them survived.

It would be very tempting to lead off at this stage into a book on the fundamental nature of man. After all, I have now read some ten or a dozen fairly respectable books on the subject, which have started off any number of exciting ideas. And since I have not actually studied in detail any of the relevant sciences, the free flight of those ideas is not weighed down by any inconvenient facts or restricted by the disciplines of scholarship. But the temptation must be resisted; in the words of Donald McRae, professor of sociology at the London School of Economics, the trouble with Darwinism is that it explains too much.

The Darwinian principle, coupled with an intoxicating absence of concrete evidence, can be used to prove almost any theory you choose. And so its importance to this book is not for the new ideas it provides, but for the unity it gives to a whole range of ideas, discoveries and observations recorded by many people over many years. Its particular importance to me is for the sense it makes of my own personal experience of the corporation, reinforced by the experiences of friends and colleagues discussed obsessively over many years. I feel as if I have spent the past ten years working at a jigsaw puzzle. The pieces have been assembled from my own experience and memory, from observation and consultation, from discussion and interview, from books and articles on history, politics, management, behavioral science, and a number of related subjects. The New Biology has not provided any more pieces: what it has done is to reveal the picture on the front of the puzzle box.

The subject only took off when scientists realized that observations of animal behavior, and especially primate behavior, ultimately depended on observations made in the wild. And so for the past thirty years or more they have tramped over mountains and through jungles, across swamp and savannah, and lurked inconspicuously in silent discomfort to try and observe the natural behavior of their quarry. My own field work may have been less systematic but it has been a good deal more comfortable, since the species I have been studying—*Homo sapiens corporalis*, Corporation Man—flourishes in a much more accessible and agreeable habitat. I have also had the advantage that in contrast with other species, this one has been abundantly observed and recorded; accounts of its behavior have come in from every country in the world and stretch back over thousands of years.

There is one other unique factor which has operated in my favor. I have been able to do something which is impossible with any other species in the animal kingdom, namely to be accepted so completely by the objects of my study that my presence in no way inhibited or modified their behavior. Indeed, there were times when I could honestly say that I felt I was one of them myself.

How the Organization Exploits Our Need for Acceptance

Samuel A. Culbert

Our needs for external affirmation are so great that we are willing to subordinate our independently based pictures of reality to the prevailing view of the system. Because we would rather reject our own experience than risk being denied this acceptance, we are highly vulnerable to exploitation by the organization system. The effects of such exploitation can be seen in any number of work practices that impose artificial limitations on our personal styles. They are seen in the moral judgments we impose on ourselves and heap upon others, in the ways work problems get defined and dealt with, and in the paternalistic practices we accept as characterizing a benevolent management. Let's look at these practices in more detail to see what we're up against and what must be changed if we're to exert greater control over our organization life.

MORALISTIC JUDGMENTS

Our dependence on external affirmation leads us to judge ourselves and others against standards which are not really ours. The values of the organization system become our own. In fact, these values become implanted in our minds as if they constituted a moral code that we must observe. We worship competence, results, and dedication to the job. We seldom tell someone above us in the hierarchy that what he wants can wait, is not all that important, or isn't worth the pressure it creates. We attend meetings religiously, even when we know in advance that we'll be bored. In our efforts to meet organization standards, we are unable to act on values that are truly our own.

As with any moral code, there are violations. But because our beliefs result from conditioning, we cling to them more rigidly than we would if they came directly from experience. When their validity is questioned, we get defensive precisely because we have no rationale to support our position. The effect is similar to one of those experiments where a subject is hypnotized into voicing an attitude that's inconsis-

From *The Organization Trap and How to Get Out of It*, by Samuel A. Culbert, © 1974 by Basic Books, Inc., Publishers, New York.

tent with all the other things he believes. When he is awakened and these inconsistencies are brought out into the open, he will get defensive, and stretch and distort common logic in order to make incompatible assumptions fit with one another. We see similar distorted logic at work when we take home empty briefcases lest someone get the impression that we've stopped taking our job seriously.

The rigidity with which we hold organizationally imposed standards makes it difficult for us to analyze a violation without getting emotional. Violations feel like moral transgressions. When we're the violator, we feel guilty. We confess to crimes we didn't commit just to get past the punishment. We prefer to agree, "Yes, I made a mistake by not going through channels," rather than argue whether going through channels was necessary in the first place. When someone else is the violator, we allow ourselves to get righteous about actions in which we ourselves indulge. We criticize a colleague for knocking off early for a round of golf or for fooling around with Miss Whatshername with the great knees. Yet we are likely to feel puzzled by the intensity of the emotion we display. How often has a co-worker suddenly become very serious after we've said something flip like "I'm only in this job for the money." And then, much to our surprise, we find ourselves saluting every standard of commitment and allegiance to the organization as if we had said something for which we needed to atone.

The tendency to levy moral judgments is a prime contributor to the almost constant stream of criticism, backbiting, put downs, and negative judgments one hears around some organizations. Everyone tries to avoid guilt and censure by blaming others for ineffective performances and human acts that violate organization standards. For instance, there's the boss who says, "The trouble with Ed is that he never comes to me with his half-baked ideas." And Ed says, "My boss always appears too busy for me to raise the philosophical questions we need to discuss." Inevitably, our judgments prove to be little more than uninformed interpretations about why others act the way they do. Like Ed and his boss, we shall continue to blame and bypass one another until we sit down and openly contrast our individual pictures of what's going on.

When someone acts differently than we think he should, we seldom have an accurate understanding of what's happening; yet we're often critical of his motivations or abilities. We see this in the district manager who is constantly criticized behind his back for not being human with the people working for him. Because he's so technically competent, it never occurs to anyone that he's actually quite shy and doesn't know how to make social conversation with people. We see this in the animosity we direct toward the guy who spends the day making personal telephone calls, until we find out that he's in the throes of marital difficulties.

It's so easy to discover someone else's frame of reference; we merely have to ask him. But, instead, we turn part of our organization life into a combat zone by judging others before the facts are in. We immediately react with anger when someone misses an important meeting or makes an independent decision on which we feel we should have been consulted. Not only do we fail to take into account conditions that might justify such deviations but we refuse to consider whether or not the organization might be better off if our expectations were challenged more often.

By continuing in our moralistic ways, we defend and perpetuate actions that interfere with our real effectiveness. Our moral judgments create tensions between us and the very people we need to help us change unsuitable procedures. We are involved in a terrible irony here: although we are the ones who have the most to gain by the organization system becoming less moralistic, we are the ones who keep things going the way they are.

PROBLEM-SOLVING STYLES

Our need for external affirmation excessively influences how we define and solve problems. Thus, in large organizations, it's commonplace for problems to be defined at one organization level and solved by people at the next lower level. This results in people at each successive lower level receiving a narrower definition of a problem than the people above them. Take the hospital administrator who is concerned about the lack of responsibility shown by the staff for the overall operation of the hospital. He focuses on the problem of phones that aren't being answered during the lunch hour. Then the supervisor to whom he complained installed a time clock to make sure the schedule for lunch breaks worked. Thus, we wind up basing our solutions on parameters set down by a "problem identifier." Perhaps a supervisor with a different boss would find a less coercive means for insuring telephone coverage and improving people's identification with the running of the hospital.

As a general rule, the people identifying a problem have more organization power than the people assigned to solve it. And while the problem identifier is almost always formally charged with evaluating the problem solver's work, only rarely does a problem solver evaluate the person telling him what to do. Lacking such parity in evaluation, the problem solver has little recourse but to do the job he thinks has been defined for him, which usually means suppressing some of his own ideas. This helps explain why people who have been highly successful on previous assignments often muff their first assignment for a new boss.

Not only do problem solvers lack the power to help define the problems and tasks but their problem-solving mandate doesn't demand that they come up with the best possible solution. In the first place, most organization problems are little more than someone's arbitrary decision that something needs to be done. In the same situation, different people will see different problems. For instance, the problem faced by the new recruits who never met with the plant manager could be termed the recruits' hang-up with authority, their immediate supervisors' inability to manage, or the system's overreliance on hierarchy. Because there is no statement of the problem everyone would agree that what needs to be done is usually a particular person's idea of what will put order in a turbulent organization world.

Second, when problems are arbitrarily defined, it's hard to tell the best answer from an adequate one. For instance, what do we say when the company president asks us how we can best meet community demands for corporate responsibility? We tell him what makes sense for him, not necessarily for the community. In trying to put order into someone else's unique picture of the world, we're very dependent on which criteria *he* feels need to be met.

Third, the types of problems people work on these days are usually so complex that it is difficult to envision how a solution will stack up against all the criteria on which it is being assessed. Consider, for example, the dilemmas faced by the personnel man who was asked to prepare a report on the best way for his company to staff its new overseas operations. He had to examine everything from national politics to the fatigue factors of overseas travel.

Thus, in most organizations, our problem-solving techniques are ultimately judged according to whether or not we follow the methods and procedures that our evaluators are convinced will lead to a proper solution. In order to get a good rating, it's usually more important to show that we took the required steps than to come up with the best result possible. We go through *all* the steps and just-in-case procedures so that we can justify our position when problems arise. (Indeed, we learn to tell people how we've gone about solving the problem before we give them the answer.) Thus, we can get good grades for questionable solutions like the following classic memo: "We're going to have a meeting to discuss duplication in the department. It will be held Tuesday afternoon at one, two, three, and four." Such problem solving also allows us to promise solutions to problems that don't even exist. One manager told me, "I'm willing to guarantee anything with a time limit beyond six months because I know they'll change their minds before then."

In effect, the way to work successfully on a problem that somebody else has presented to us is to identify the assumptions that that person is making about which methods will lead to a good solution. Because our problem identifier is a problem solver for someone else higher up, we can expect that in time everyone in the organization is going to become enculturated with a similar set of assumptions. To the extent that we're not conscious of the discrepancies between our experience and the problem-solving style preferred by the system, we're vulnerable to taking on the organization's style as if it were our own.

It's problem-solving conditions like these that cause us to become more absorbed with issues of "What do I need to do to be successful?" than with issues of "What do I know that will produce a successful solution?" We rely on external acceptance at the expense of the self-acceptance we might gain from drawing more fully on our own expertise and experience. We might reason, though, that doing what other people want can also result in our being successful, which is what *we* want. When someone thinks like this, he's a tough person to argue with, because he fails to see the traps inherent in bypassing his own experience.

Of course, the above is somewhat exaggerated. Each of us has had the experience of trying to persuade someone who has given us an assignment that "This doesn't make sense!" But how many times will he answer us before he's even heard our reasons out? Even if he does listen, how often does he pass the buck by confiding that, although he agrees with us, this is the way the boss wants it? And because his boss is at least two steps above us in the hierarchy, we agree. Only afterward does it occur to us that if we're confronting him, and he's our boss, then why can't he confront his boss?

The range of problems a person is allowed to formulate and solve is also limited by his position in the hierarchy. For instance, I know any number of large corporations where first-level personnel are given latitude in the way they work on a project but not in choosing which project they work on; low-level managers are given latitude in who they assign to a project, but not on which projects need to be accomplished; middle-level managers are given latitude in determining which projects best direct organization resources toward established goals, but do not have much voice in determining what the goals ought to be; while upper-level managers reserve the right to determine organization policies and declare which goals best achieve these policies.

Notwithstanding these various constraints, all organization workers are allowed some areas where they're permitted to define problems. However, the way a person formulates a problem is usually biased to require his unique and special talents for solving it. Thus, a manager with expertise for shuffling people and work loads might respond to numerous client complaints by seeing the main problem as a mismatch between people and jobs. Another manager will respond to the same client complaints by focusing on problems in team coordination and communications. Coincidentally, he just happens to be an expert in using group techniques that improve communications and assist members in redesigning organization procedures.

In some ways, having an area where we can define the problem is as good for the organization as it is for us. The organization gets its job done expertly, and we get the chance to exercise authority. But there are also drawbacks. Because we are constantly on our guard against the jurisdictional challenges of others, we define power as our ability to get others to accept our definition of the problem. Yet if we were really in control, we might modify our definition of power to include the personal power that allows us to accept new ways of defining problems, especially in areas where we have ultimate authority. Concern over how to keep others out of our territory would then be replaced with concern over how to include others and incorporate valid suggestions.

PATERNALISTIC PRACTICES

Our needs for external affirmation keep us from demanding the information and perspectives we need in order to manage our organization life intelligently. Instead of finding out for ourselves what is going on in the organization and how we are seen, we allow others who claim to have this information, usually our bosses, to make it available to us as they see fit. However, their unconscious needs to keep us under control stop them from giving us this information directly. Instead, they leak it to us in a form that accentuates their benevolence and our dependency.

Management gives us some facts, but seldom enough for us to make our own decisions. This puts them in the parent's role of advising us what to do, and it places us in the child's role of trying to guess what they're implying we ought to do. Of course, everyone involved is sufficiently ambivalent to keep the situation from becoming too blatant. We say something like, "I'd like to get your thoughts on the matter, although I know it's my decision to make" and they respond, "I don't know anything for certain, all I can tell you is what I would do in your situation." This type of paternalism pervades today's organization system and strangely enough, is positively received by most of the people controlled by it. Indeed, such fatherly advice becomes proof of management's concern and interest in us as people.

This kind of paternalistic practice begins either when someone with information gives us unsolicited advice or makes decisions for us, or when we feel out of control and take comfort in believing that someone who is benevolent and powerful will watch out for us. It's shown when the department head tells us "Just in case you haven't read all the signals, the task force you've been asked to volunteer for is being closely watched by top management," but then refuses to give us more details.

A paternalistic pact is made when people with complementary assumptions—"I know what's good for you" and "He can help me"—find one another. When the person with the superior perspective also occupies a position of greater organization power, the paternalistic pact expands to include his offering of privileges, or rights, that we don't feel we could take without the sanction of someone with more authority. Thus, we drag ourselves into the office hoping that our boss will notice and say, "You look beat. Why not take a day of compensatory leave to make up for all the traveling you've been doing."

Paternalistic advice carries with it the implicit message that, if only we had a better perspective on ourselves and the organization, we would make the same decisions, follow the prescribed action, or be entitled to the same privileges. But the authority of the person who gives it implies that the limits of time, organizational confidentiality, and our lack of self-objectivity make it difficult for him to tell us the facts and, thus, put his superior perspective to the test.

Paternalism induces feelings of dependency, passivity, and helplessness in us. Probably because most of us didn't get enough benevolent fathering when we were children, we seem to linger with the dream that some day someone whom we can trust will come along with a better perspective on our life than we can provide for ourselves. We are setups for anyone whose actions imply that he's authoritative and knowledgeable. We see him as the *mavin*, the expert whose advice we should follow. And we know better. We know this person lacks information about crucial aspects of our life without which he can't possibly be smarter than we are about ourselves.

In the short run, an organization where this type of paternalism is widespread will enjoy a number of benefits. Its management can expect obedience, predictability, and coordination. However, over the longer run, this order is accomplished at the expense of our assertiveness, autonomy, risk-taking, and complexity. Paternalistic practices give rise to a sort of self-fulfilling prophecy whereby we are dependent on the advice of management and management interprets our dependence as a request for more direction. They then make more decisions and take additional action on our behalf. But by withholding the information on which their decisions are based, they leave us feeling even less on top of things and more in need of managerial counsel than before.

REFLECTION

In this chapter, we have considered some of the ways in which the organization system, as we live it, exploits our dependence on external affirmation. We will eliminate much of the seaminess of organization life once we learn to form pictures of reality without constraining what we see by what we think will be acceptable.

Each of us seeks a life-style and benefits that are only possible when we pool our efforts within some type of organization system. A greater degree of self-acceptance and independence would allow for a more open-ended examination of some crucial questions, such as, "What alternative ways of organizing involve fewer—and less critical— compromises than we're currently making?" and "What goals should we abandon and what should we replace them with in our quest to live a self-fulfilling organization life?"

While these questions are fairly practical, they are also existential. All of us will spend a major portion of our lives trying to bring about the resolutions we have reached today. Ultimately, we will settle for the life we lead. However, there are some things we can do to further enrich our lives before we accept what we have achieved, and these will occur to us as we develop greater skills in learning the tacit lessons contained in our experience. . . .

Air Force A-7D Brake Problem

Mr. VANDIVIER. In the early part of 1967, the B. F. Goodrich Wheel & Brake Plant at Troy, Ohio, received an order from the Ling-Temco-Vought Co. of Dallas, Tex., to supply wheels and brakes for the A–7D aircraft, built by LTV for the Air Force.

The tests on the wheels and brakes were to be conducted in accordance with the requirements of military specification Mil–W–5013G as prepared and issued by the U.S. Air Force and to the requirements set forth by LTV Specification Document 204–16–37D.

The wheels were successfully tested to the specified requirements, but the brake, manufactured by Goodrich under BEG part No. 2–1162–3, was unable to meet the required tests.

The laboratory tests specified for the brake were divided into two categories: dynamic brake tests and static brake tests.

The dynamic brake tests basically consisted of 45 simulated normal energy stops, 5 overload energy stops and one worn-brake maximum energy stop, sometimes called a rejected take-off, or RTO.

These simulated stops were to be conducted on one brake assembly with no change in brake lining to be allowed during the test.

In addition, a maximum energy brake stop (or RTO) was to be con-

From the Hearing before the Subcommittee on Economy in Government of the Joint Economic Committee of the Congress of the United States, Ninety-first Congress, August 13, 1969.

ducted on a brake containing new linings and still another series of tests called a turnaround capability test was to be performed.

The turnaround capability test consisted of a series of taxis, simulated takeoffs, flight periods and landings, and time schedule for the turnaround test was supplied by LTV to coincide with conditions under which the A–7D brake might operate on a typical mission.

Generally speaking, the brake successfully passed all the static brakes tests, but the brake could not and did not pass any of the dynamic tests I have just described with the exception of the new brake maximum energy stop.

During the first few attempts to qualify the brake to the dynamic tests, the brake ran out of lining material after a few stops had been completed and the tests were terminated. Attempts were made to secure a lining material that would hold up during the grueling 51-stop test, but to no avail.

Although I had been aware for several months that great difficulty was being experienced with the A–7D brake, it was not until April 11, 1968, almost a full year after qualification testing had begun, that I became aware of how these tests were being conducted.

The 13th attempt at qualification was being conducted under B. F. Goodrich Internal Test No. T–1867.

On the morning of April 11, Richard Gloor, who was the test engineer assigned to the A–7D project, came to me and told me he had discovered that some time during the previous 24 hours, instrumentation used to record brake pressure had *deliberately* been miscalibrated so that while the instrumentation showed that a pressure of 1,000 pounds per square inch had been used to conduct brake stops No. 46 and 47 (two overload energy stops) 1,100 p.s.i. had actually been applied to the brakes. Maximum pressure available on the A–7D is 1,000 p.s.i.

Mr. Gloor further told me he had questioned instrumentation personnel about the miscalibration and had been told they were asked to do so by Searle Lawson, a design engineer on the A–7D.

Chairman PROXMIRE. Is this the gentleman who is with you now, Mr. Vandivier?

Mr. VANDIVIER. That is correct. I subsequently questioned Lawson who admitted he had ordered the instruments miscalibrated at the direction of a superior.

Upon examining the log sheets kept by laboratory personnel I found that other violations of the test specifications had occurred.

For example, after some of the overload stops, the brake had been disassembled and the three stators or stationary members of the brake had been taken to the plant toolroom for rework and during an earlier part of the test, the position of elements within the brake had been reversed in order to more evenly distribute the lining wear.

Additionally, instead of braking the dynamometer to a complete stop as required by military specifications, pressure was relased when the wheel and brake speed had decelerated to 10 miles per hour.

The reason for this, I was later told, was that the brakes were experiencing severe vibrations near the end of the stops, causing excessive lining wear and general deterioration of the brake.

All of these incidents were in clear violation of military specifications and general industry practice.

I reported these violations to the test lab supervisor. Mr. Ralph Gretzinger, who reprimanded instrumentation personnel and stated that under no circumstance would intentional miscalibration of instruments be tolerated.

As for the other discrepancies noted in test procedures, he said he was aware they were happening but that as far as he was concerned the tests could not, in view of the way they were being conducted, be classified as qualification tests.

Later that same day, the worn-brake, maximum energy stop was conducted on the brake. The brake was landed at a speed of 161 m.p.h. and the pressure was applied. The dynamometer rolled a distance 16,800 *feet* before coming to rest. The elapsed stopping *time was 141 seconds.* By computation, this stop time shows the aircraft would have traveled over 3 miles before stopping.

Within a few days, a typewritten copy of the test logs of test T–1867 was sent to LTV in order to assure LTV that a qualified brake was almost ready for delivery.

Virtually every entry in this so-called copy of the test logs was drastically altered. As an example, the stop time for the worn brake maximum energy stop was changed from 141 seconds to a mere 46.8 seconds.

On May 2, 1968 the 14th attempt to qualify the brakes was begun, and Mr. Lawson told me that he had been informed by both Mr. Robert Sink, project manager at Goodrich—I am sorry, Mr. Sink is project manager—and Mr. Russell Van Horn, projects manager at Goodrich, that "Regardless of what the brake does on test, we're going to qualify it."

Chairman PROXMIRE. What was that?

Mr. VANDIVIER. The statement was, "Regardless of what the brake does on test, we're going to qualify it."

He also said that the latest instructions he had received were to the effect that if the data from this latest test turned out worse than did test T–1867, then we would write our report based on T–1867.

Chairman PROXMIRE. The statement was made by whom?

Mr. VANDIVIER. Mr. Lawson told me this statement was made to him by Mr. Robert Sink, projects manager and Mr. Russell Van Horn, project manager.

During this latest and final attempt to qualify the four rotor brake, the same illegal procedures were used as had been used on attempt No. 13. Again after 30 stops had been completed, the positions of the friction members of the brake were reversed in order to more evenly distribute wear.

After each stop, the wheel was removed from the brake and the accumulated dust was blown out.

During each stop, pressure was released when the deceleration had reached 10 miles per hour.

By these and other irregular procedures the brake was nursed along until the 45 normal energy stops had been completed but by this time the friction surfaces of the brakes were almost bare, that is, there was virtually no lining left on the brake.

This lack of lining material introduced another problem.

The pistons which actuate the brake by forcing the friction surfaces together were almost at the end of their allowable travel and it was feared that during the overload stops the pistons might actually pop out of their sockets within the brake, allowing brake fluid to spray the hot surfaces, resulting in fire.

Therefore, a metal spacer was inserted in the brake between the pressure plate and the piston housing.

This spacer served to make up for the lack of friction material and to keep the pistons in place.

In order to provide room for the spacer, the adjuster assemblies were removed from the brake.

The five overload stops were conducted without the adjuster assemblies and with the spacer in place.

After stop number 48—the third overload stop—temperatures in the brake were so high that the fuse plug, a safety device which allows air to escape from the tire to prevent blowout, melted and allowed the tire to deflate.

The same thing happened after stop number 49—the fourth overload stop. Both of these occurrences were highly irregular and in direct conflict with the performance criteria of the military requirements.

Chairman PROXMIRE. I understand you have a picture of this that might help us see it.

Mr. VANDIVIER. Yes.

Mr. PROXMIRE. Do you want to show that to us now?

Mr. VANDIVIER. I was going to show it here just a little bit later.

Chairman PROXMIRE. Go ahead.

Mr. VANDIVIER. For the worn brake maximum energy stop the adjusters were replaced in the brake and a different spacer was used between the pressure plate and the piston housing.

Now I have a copy, a picture of this brake just before it went on the maximum energy test, and here you may see at the top is the additional spacer that has been added in order to get sufficient braking action on the brake.

Chairman PROXMIRE. Who took that picture?

Mr. VANDIVIER. That was taken with a Polaroid camera. I am not sure————

Chairman PROXMIRE. I think it is only fair to the committee, Mr. Conable and the committee, to ask you about it later. You go ahead and we will ask questions.

Mr. VANDIVIER. All right.

In addition to these highly questionable practices, a turnaround capability test, or simulated mission test, was conducted incorrectly due to a human error. When the error was later discovered, no corrections were made.

While these tests were being conducted, I was asked by Mr. Lawson to begin writing a qualification report for the brake. I flatly refused and told Mr. Gretzinger, the lab supervisor, who was my superior, that I could not write such a report because the brake had not been qualified.

He agreed and he said that no one in the laboratory was going to issue such a report unless a brake was actually qualified in accordance with the specification and using standard operating procedures.

He said that he would speak to his own supervisor, the manager of the technical services section, Mr. Russell Line, and get the matter settled at once.

He consulted Mr. Line and assured me that both had concurred in the decision not to write a qualification report.

I explained to Lawson that I had been told not to write the report, and that the only way such a report could be written was to falsify test data.

Mr. Lawson said he was well aware of what was required, but that he had been ordered to get a report written, regardless of how or what had to be done.

He stated if I would not write the report he would have to, and he asked if I would help him gather the test data and draw up the various engineering curves and graphic displays which are normally included in a report.

I asked Mr. Gretzinger, my superior, if this was all right and he agreed as long as I was only assisting in the preparation of the data, it would be permissible.

Both Lawson and I worked on the elaborate curves and logs in the report for nearly a month. During this time we both frankly discussed the moral aspects of what we were doing and we agreed that our actions were unethical and probably illegal.

Several times during that month I discussed the A–7D testing with Mr. Line, and asked him to consult his superiors in Akron, in order to prevent a false qualification report from being issued.

Mr. Line declined to do so and advised me that it would be wise to just do my work and keep quiet.

I told him of the extensive irregularities during testing and suggested that the brake was actually dangerous and if allowed to be installed on an aircraft, might cause an accident.

Mr. Line said he thought I was worrying too much about things which did not really concern me and advised me to just "do what you're told."

About the first of June————

Chairman PROXMIRE. You skipped one line here.

Mr. VANDIVIER. Yes.

Chairman PROXMIRE. You said "I asked him"————

Mr. VANDIVIER. Yes. I asked Mr. Line if his conscience would hurt him if such a thing caused the death of a pilot and this is when he replied I was worrying about too many things that did not concern me and advised me to "do what you're told."

About the first of June 1968, Mr. Gretzinger asked if I were finished with the graphic data and said he had been advised by the chief engineer, Mr. H. C. Sunderman, that when the data was finished it was to be delivered to him—Sunderman—and he would instruct someone in the engineering department to actually write the report.

Accordingly, when I had finished with the data, I gave it to Mr. Gretzinger who immediately took it from the room. Within a few minutes, he was back and was obviously angry.

He said that Mr. Sunderman had told him no one in the engineering department had time to write the report and that we would have to do it ourselves.

At this point, Mr. Line came into the room demanding to know "What the hell is going on." Mr. Gretzinger explained the situation again and said he would not allow such a report to be issued by the lab.

Mr. Line then turned to me and said he was "sick of hearing about this damned report. Write the ————thing and shut up about it."

Chairman PROXMIRE. Let me ask you, you had this in quotes. Did you make a note of this at the time?

Mr. VANDIVIER. Yes.

Chairman PROXMIRE. Do you have your notes with you?

Mr. VANDIVIER. No. I have notes with me, yes. I am not sure if I have this note or not, but I have notes with me.

Chairman PROXMIRE. All right.

Mr. VANDIVIER. When he had left, Mr. Gretzinger and I discussed the position we were in and Mr. Gretzinger said that we both should have resigned a long time ago. He added that there was little to do now except write the report.

Accordingly, I wrote the report, but in the conclusion, I stated that the brake had "not" met either the intent or the requirements of the specifications and was therefore "not" qualified.

When the final report was typewritten and ready for publication, the two "nots" in the conclusion had been eliminated, thereby changing the entire meaning of the conclusion.

I would like to point out at this time the various discrepancies between the military standards and procedures and the qualification tests actually conducted:

1. Brake pressure was cut on all stops at 10 miles per hour and the wheel allowed to coast to a stop.

2. The five overload stops were conducted with a spacer between the pressure plate and the piston housing.

3. The lining carriers used for the test were specially made with an additional 0.030 of an inch lining material. This was done to assure sufficient lining material on the carriers.

4. Stators in the brake were physically reversed after stop 30 and remained in those positions throughout the test.

Mr. Chairman, the next two sentences of my printed statement contain a typographical error, words have been omitted and I would like to insert those in at this time.

5. The worn brake RTO was conducted with an additional pressure plate between the original pressure plate and piston housing. This was done because allowable piston travel had been exceeded and without the additional pressure plate the brakes could not have been applied.

6. Prior to the worn brake RTO (maximum energy stop), the inside diameter of the lining carriers was increased by 0.120 of an inch to alleviate the severe shrinkage of the lining carriers on the torque tube caused by overheating.

7. On stops 48 and 49 (overload stops 3 and 4) the fuse plug eutectic material—material designed to melt at a specified temperature—melted, allowing the tire to deflate.

8. The torque plate and keyway inserts for the wheel had their drive surfaces chromeplated, because of extreme wear. This was not a production process on this brake.

9. Before the start of the tests and at teardowns the keyway inserts were sprayed with molybdenum disulfate (a lubricant).

10. After every stop the wheel and tire assembly were removed from the brake, the brake was blown out with high-velocity air and the keyway inserts and heat shield were wiped clean.

11. After stops Nos. 10, 20, 30, 40, 45, and 50 the brake was disassembled and the expansion slots in the lining carriers were cleaned of excess lining material and opened. Excess materials removed from between the segments in the rotors and the lugs and links on the rotors were cleaned and radiused by machining processes. This in a sense is equivalent to a minor overhaul in the brake linings.

In addition there were at least four other major irregularities in the test procedure.

These, gentlemen, are only irregularities which occurred during the testing. As for the report itself more than 80 false entries were made in the body of the report and in the logs.

Many, many of the elaborate engineering curves attached to the report were complete and total fabrications, based not on what had actually occurred, but on information which would fool both LTV and the Air Force.

I have already mentioned that the turn-around capability test which was supposed to determine what temperatures might be experienced by the brake during a typical flight mission, had been misconducted through a human error on the part of the test lab operator.

Rather than rerun this very important test, which would have taken only some 6 hours to complete, it was decided to manufacture the data.

This we did, and the result was some very convincing graphic curves. These curves were supposed to demonstrate to LTV and the Air Force exactly what the temperatures in the brakes had been during each minute of the simulated mission.

They were completely false and based only on data which would be acceptable to the customers.

I could spend the entire day here discussing the various elaborate falsifications that went into this report but I feel that, by now, the picture is clear.

The report was finally issued on June 5, 1968, and almost immediately, flight tests on the brake were begun at Edwards Air Force Base in California.

Mr. Lawson was sent by Goodrich to witness these tests and when he returned, he described various mishaps which had occurred during the flight tests and he expressed the opinion to me that the brake was dangerous.

That same afternoon, I contacted my attorney and after describing the situation to him, asked for his advice.

He advised me that, while I was technically not guilty of committing a fraud, I was certainly part of a conspiracy to defraud.

He further suggested a meeting with U.S. Attorney Roger Makely in Dayton, Ohio.

I agreed to this and my attorney said he would arrange an appointment with the Federal attorney.

I discussed my attorney's appraisal of our situation with Mr. Lawson, but I did not, at this time, tell him of the forthcoming visit with Mr. Makely.

Mr. Lawson said he would like to consult with my attorney and I agreed to arrange this.

Shortly thereafter, Mr. Lawson went to the Dallas offices of LTV and, while he was gone, my attorney called and said that, upon advice of the U.S. attorney, he had arranged an interview with the Dayton office of the FBI.

I related the details of the A-7D qualification to Mr. Joseph Hathaway, of the FBI.

He asked if I could get Mr. Lawson to confirm my story and I replied that I felt Mr. Lawson would surely do this.

Upon Mr. Lawson's return from Dallas, I asked him if he still wished to consult my attorney and he answered "I most certainly do."

Mr. Lawson and I went to the attorney's office, and Mr. Lawson was persuaded to speak to the FBI.

I wish to emphasize that at no time prior to Mr. Lawson's decision to speak to the FBI was he aware that I had already done so. His decision and mine were both the result of our individual actions.

Mr. Lawson related his own story to Mr. Hathaway, who advised us to keep our jobs and to tell no one that we had been to see him.

I might add here that he advised us that an investigation would be made.

About this time the Air Force demanded that Goodrich produce its raw data from the tests.

This Goodrich refused to do, claiming that the raw data was proprietary information.

Goodrich management decided that, since pressure was being applied by the Air Force, a conference should be arranged with LTV management and engineering staff.

A preconference meeting was set for Goodrich personnel in order to go over the questionable points in the report.

On Saturday, July 27, 1968, Mr. Robert Sink, Mr. Lawson, Mr. John Warren—A–7D project engineer—and I met and went over the discrepant items contained in the qualification report.

Each point was discussed at great length and a list of approximately 40 separate discrepancies was compiled.

These, we were told by Mr. Sink, would be revealed to LTV personnel the following week.

However, by the time of the meeting with LTV, only a few days later, the list of discrepancies had been cut by Mr. Sink from 43 items to a mere three.

Mr. Chairman, during this meeting Mr. Lawson took from the blackboard at the Goodrich conference room word for word listing of all these discrepancies. This contains the 43 items I have just mentioned.

I would like to enter this into the record, and also enter the subsequent list of three major discrepancies which later came out of this meeting.

Chairman PROXMIRE. Do you have copies of those documents?

Mr. VANDIVIER. Yes, I do have.

Mr. VANDIVIER. The following 2-month period was one of a constant running battle with LTV and the Air Force, during which time the Air Force refused final approval of the qualification report and demanded a confrontation with Goodrich about supplying raw data.

On October 8, another meeting was held, again with Mr. Sink, Mr. Lawson, Mr. Warren, and myself present.

This was only 1 day prior to a meeting with Air Force personnel and Mr. Sink said he had called the meeting "so that we are all coordinated and tell the same story."

Mr. Sink said that LTV personnel would be present at the meeting with the Air Force and our policy would be to "Let LTV carry the ball." Mr. Sink appeared to be especially concerned because Mr. Bruce Tremblay, the Air Force engineer most intimate with A–7D brake would be present at the meeting and it was felt at B. F. Goodrich that Mr. Tremblay was already suspicious.

Mr. Sink warned us that "Mr. Tremblay will probably be at his antagonistic best."

He added that the Air Force had wanted to meet at the Goodrich plant, but that we—Goodrich—couldn't risk having them that close to the raw data.

"We don't want those guys in the plant," Mr. Sink said.

What happened at the meeting with the Air Force, I do not know. I did not attend.

On October 18, I submitted my resignation to Goodrich effective November 1.

I would like to read that resignation. This is addressed to Russell Line, manager of technical services:

> In May of this year I was directed to participate in the preparation of qualification report for the A7D, 26031. As you are aware this report contained numerous deliberate and wilful misrepresentations which according to legal counsel constitutes fraud and therefore exposes both myself and others to criminal charges of conspiracy to defraud. In view of this fact, I must terminate my employment with the B. F. Goodrich Company effective November 1, 1968. I regret that this decision must be made, but I am sure that you will agree that events of the past seven months have created an atmosphere of deceit and distrust in which it is impossible to work effectively and productively.

On October 25 I was told that my resignation was to be accepted immediately, and within 20 minutes I had left the Goodrich Co.

Gentlemen, I am well aware that the B. F. Goodrich Co. is a well-known and well-respected firm with an almost impeccable reputation.

I am equally aware that the charges I have made are serious.

However, everything I have said to you is completely true and I can prove my statements with documentary evidence.

The unfortunate part of a situation such as this is that, invariably, many innocent persons are made to suffer along with the guilty.

Therefore, I should like to emphasize that three people whom I have mentioned here are, I feel, completely blameless and were implicated in this situation through no fault of their own.

Mr. Ralph Gretzinger from the very start fought this situation and tried very hard to use his influence to stop the issuance of the false report.

Mr. Richard Gloor, in his own handwriting, listed the irregularities occurring during the test and was outspoken in his opposition to the report.

This list was shown to B. F. Goodrich management.

Mr. Lawson, of course, was in a position similar to mine and the fact that he voluntarily disclosed the details of the A–7D test program to the FBI and GAO should stand upon its own merits. Thank you.

Chairman PROXMIRE. Thank you, Mr. Vandivier.

Mr. Lawson, you have heard the statement as read and I take it you have had a chance to see the full statement?

Mr. LAWSON. No, I have not.

Chairman PROXMIRE. You have not?

Mr. LAWSON. No, I have not.

Chairman PROXMIRE. The statement you have just heard read by Mr. Vandivier, do you agree with it fully or in part or do you disagree and can you tell us your reaction to it?

Mr. LAWSON. The factual data that Mr. Vandivier has presented is correct, to the best of my knowledge.

Chairman PROXMIRE. There is no statement that you heard him read with which you would disagree in any part?

Mr. LAWSON. I really don't know. I haven't read the complete text.

Chairman PROXMIRE. Would you disagree with any part of what you heard him read right now in your presence?

Mr. LAWSON. No. I don't believe there is.

Chairman PROXMIRE. Now I would like to ask you, Mr. Vandivier, you gave us a picture which we may want to ask other witnesses about, so I want to qualify that picture. As far as we know, it is a picture which you say was taken of the brake that was tested?

Mr. VANDIVIER. That is correct.

Chairman PROXMIRE. But we would like to make sure that we qualify that, because it is going to be used later.

Now would you describe again, tell us how you came to have that, when the picture was taken and so forth?

Mr. VANDIVIER. Yes. This was taken just approximately an hour and a half or 2 hours before the worn brake RTO was conducted. This was for the qualification test, and I asked the plant photographer if he would take a Polaroid picture of this for me. He did so, and I took the Polaroid shot and I had it enlarged. I have a certification on this. I had the original Polaroid negative. I have the negatives that the photographer used.

Chairman PROXMIRE. Will you give us the date, the time that was taken, if you have that?

Mr. VANDIVIER. If you will give me just a moment, I can.

Chairman PROXMIRE. Meanwhile, may I ask Mr. Lawson, while Mr. Vandivier is looking up that, if you can confirm that this is in fact the picture of the A–7D brake that was undergoing qualification?

Mr. LAWSON. Yes, it appears to be.

Chairman PROXMIRE. It appears to be?

Mr. LAWSON. I would say it is.

Chairman PROXMIRE. It is. All right. Well, you can supply that a little later for the record, Mr. Vandivier.

Mr. VANDIVIER. All right.

Chairman PROXMIRE. Let me ask you this. You say you worked for Goodrich for 6 years?

Mr. VANDIVIER. That is correct.

Chairman PROXMIRE. What was your previous employment before you were hired by Goodrich?

Mr. VANDIVIER. I worked for the Food Machinery and Chemical Corp. at their Newport, Ind. plant.

Chairman PROXMIRE. Technical writer is a professional position that requires considerable competence and ability. What experience did you have that would qualify you to be a technical writer?

Mr. VANDIVIER. I had none.

Chairman PROXMIRE. Did you immediately go into this or did they give you a training course?

Mr. VANDIVIER. No. I had no training course. I kind of worked into the job I guess. It was—

Chairman PROXMIRE. You were not hired to be a technical—

Mr. VANDIVIER. No, I was actually hired as an instrumentation technician, and Goodrich engaged in a mass changeover of instrumentation techniques, and they wanted degreed people for this kind of work so I was switched over to the technical writing section.

Chairman PROXMIRE. How long did you work as a technical writer?

Mr. VANDIVIER. Approximately 3 years.

Chairman PROXMIRE. Three years. How many reports did you prepare for B. F. Goodrich?

Mr. VANDIVIER. At least 100, possibly 150.

Chairman PROXMIRE. Were any of these reports questioned in any way?

Mr. VANDIVIER. No, they were not.

Chairman PROXMIRE. Were they accepted? Did you get any reaction at all favorable or unfavorable in these reports that you wrote?

Mr. VANDIVIER. Occasionally we would get a question from the manufacturer about a wording or a clarification, and these would be supplied.

Chairman PROXMIRE. Was there any question as to the accuracy or competence of the report?

Mr. VANDIVIER. No, none whatsoever.

Chairman PROXMIRE. Were you criticized at any time that the reports were not adequate?

Mr. VANDIVIER. No; I was not.

Chairman PROXMIRE. In your statement, you say "Accordingly I wrote the report but in the conclusion I stated that the brake had 'not' met either the intent or the requirement of the specification and therefore was 'not' qualified." Then you add "When the final report was typewritten and ready for publication the two 'nots' in the conclusion had been eliminated, thereby changing the entire meaning of the conclusion."

Now it seems to me that you have testified before this that you and Mr. Lawson constructed this report based on your instructions from your superiors, and that this report was false in many ways that you knew, and that the report seemed to qualify the brakes, at least that was the impression I got, and yet you concluded, and I quote, "I stated the brake had not met either the intent or the requirement of the specifications and therefore was not qualified."

Doesn't it seem on the basis of your testimony that this is somewhat inconsistent? In other words, you had written a report that would qualify the brake and then you come in with a one-sentence conclusion in which you say it was not qualified? Do you see what I am getting at?

Mr. VANDIVIER. Yes. Mr. Chairman, this was probably one final gesture of defiance. I was so aggravated and sick at having to write this thing. I knew the words "not" would be taken out, but I put them in to show that, I do not know, that they had bent me to their will but they had not broken me yet. It was a foolish thing perhaps to do, but it was showing that I still had a little spirit left. At least this is how I felt.

Chairman PROXMIRE. What did you think your superiors at B. F. Goodrich would do when they found the "not qualified" in your report, when you had been told to show the brake qualified?

Mr. VANDIVIER. I knew it would be changed probably without question. I was not worried if you are trying—I was not worried at being called on the carpet for this. I knew they would just merely change it.

Chairman PROXMIRE. Was this the only time in the 3 years you worked as a technical writer with Goodrich the only time that you made false entries into a report of manufacture?

Mr. VANDIVIER. Yes, it was.

Chairman PROXMIRE. So as far as you know B. F. Goodrich's record is clean in every other respect with your experience?

Mr. VANDIVIER. With me—

Chairman PROXMIRE. With this single incidence being an exception?

Mr. VANDIVIER. That is right; that is correct.

Chairman PROXMIRE. They had never before asked you to do this?

Mr. VANDIVIER. No.

Chairman PROXMIRE. Do you know of any other technical writer you worked with, in which Goodrich had instructed them to take this kind of action?

Mr. VANDIVIER. If they had done this, I would know nothing of it. I could not say.

Chairman PROXMIRE. This was the only incident?

Mr. VANDIVIER. Yes, as far as I know, the only incident which I was asked to do this.

Chairman PROXMIRE. What was the normal procedure at Goodrich when a brake failed to meet all of the requirements or when normal procedures were not followed?

Mr. VANDIVIER. If for some reason or other the normal procedure was not followed or the brake simply could not meet a particular requirement, the report was written and a deviation was requested from the manufacturer, which in other words is a request to allow him to accept the brake with these noted deviations from the procedure.

I might add that there are many times that a brake just could not meet a certain requirement specified by the manufacturer, and it was always the customary procedure to ask for a deviation, and many times it was granted or some sort of a compromise was reached between the manufacturer and Goodrich.

Chairman PROXMIRE. I cannot understand what was going through the minds of Goodrich's management the way you have told the story. I cannot see what they have to gain by passing on a brake that would not meet qualifications. Somewhere along the line this is going to be shown as an unqualified brake. As you pointed out, it might be under disastrous circumstances, but in any event Goodrich would suffer and suffer badly by passing on a brake to LTV or the Air Force that was not going to work. What is their motivation?

Mr. VANDIVIER. I cannot tell you what their motivation is. I can tell you what I feel was behind this.

Chairman PROXMIRE. All right.

Mr. VANDIVIER. I feel in the beginning stages of this program someone made a mistake, and refused to admit that mistake, and in order to hide his stupidity or his ignorance, or his pride, or whatever it was, he simply covered up, you know, with more false statements, false information, and at the time it came time to deliver this brake, Goodrich was so far down the road there was nothing else to do.

They had no time to start over, I think it was a matter not of company policy but of company politics. I think that probably three or four persons within the Goodrich organization at Troy were responsible for this. I do not believe for a moment that the corporate officials in Akron knew that this was going on.

Watergate as a
Case Study
In Management
Max Ways

Watergate will not become, as some of those hurt by it have suggested, a mere footnote to history. For generations ahead, political scientists, lawyers, and moralists will be sorting out this jumble of facts, quasi-facts, confessions, lies, and accusations. Since it involves organized activity, Watergate can also be approached as a study in management.

The prime measure of management is effectiveness—often expressed as a relation of benefit to cost. Although neither benefits nor costs need be monetary, effectiveness is a frankly pragmatic test, separated from larger considerations of legality and morality. Speaking managerially, one gang of assassins may be judged "better" than a rival gang. One monastery may be judged "better" than another although both pursue high ends with equal ardor. A well-run gang of assassins may even be "better"—managerially—than a sloppy monastery.

That kind of statement does not imply that management in real life has nothing to do with morality. Like any other specialized approach, a managerial analysis is incapable of expressing the whole truth about a messy mass of phenomena from which the material under study has been selected. A look at Watergate as management, then, is not meant to evade or supersede judgments made from political or legal or moral viewpoints. On the contrary, a management analysis may throw some peripheral light on larger issues, and vice versa.

AN EXECUTIVE'S NIGHTMARE

Managerially, Watergate is an obvious disaster area. Its participants—whoever they may be assumed to be—incurred "costs" so much larger than "benefits" that it would be hard to think of an organized peacetime operation with an effectiveness rating farther on the wrong side of zero. Bad luck will not begin to explain the Watergate calamity. No matter which of many possible assumptions is adopted

Adapted from material originally appearing in the November 1973 issue of *Fortune* Magazine by special permission; © 1973 Time Inc. □ Research associate: Alice Siegel Arvan.

about how much Nixon knew at what "points in time," Watergate from its start to the present reeks of mismanagement.

Especially conspicuous are defects in the lifeblood of organizations: accurate communication. . . . The assumption that Nixon knew as little as he says he did, represents a manager's nightmare: the wishes (or presumed wishes) of the chief executive are magnified and distorted as they move down through his hierarchy to the plane of action; on the other hand, information about what is actually going on is diminished as it moves toward the chief executive. The well-known management malady called constipated feedback seems to have been especially severe in the White House during the period of the cover-up when the President, on his own version of events, was isolated from both the activities of his aides and from rising public concern.

No doubt the universal managerial problem of communication is particularly difficult in the White House, where awe of presidential power can foster both overkill in efforts to serve and undue reticence in reporting unpleasant information. Such tendencies must be countered by presidential vigilance. After all, the essence of any President's job is to stay in touch with the people. The main function of his staff is to help him do that. When the staff became more of a barrier than a conduit, failure in a central responsibility occurred.

AN OVERCAPITALIZED ENTERPRISE

But this is only one of a hundred managerial flaws that can be identified in the Watergate record. Organizational objectives were ill selected and ill defined. Choice of people, that key management function, was poor, not so much in terms of their over-all quality but rather in the casting for the particular roles they played; somewhere a personnel manual must exist that warns against slotting the likes of Liddy, Hunt, and Dean in the operational spots they came to occupy. Coordination was weak. Cooperators, who needed to communicate, didn't. The enterprise was so overcapitalized that money was recklessly sloshed around in a way that facilitated detection. The burglaries were overmanned; nobody can argue with the judgment of the former New York cop, Anthony Ulasewicz, that professionals "would not have walked in with an army." Indeed, analysis of Watergate can be discouraged or misled by the very richness of its pathology. So many people at so many levels in and around the White House made so many different kinds of mistakes that the observer is first tempted to say that this was the stupidest lot of managers ever assembled.

That lazy hypothesis is demolished by the plain fact that neither Richard Nixon nor the men around him are stupid—managerially or otherwise. Nixon is believed by some shrewd observers of government to be the most management-minded of recent Presidents. Those who viewed the parade of witnesses before the Ervin committee knew they were listening to intelligent men. Management analysis of Watergate, then, must turn upon the question of why officials, whose ability ranged from average to very high, made so many mistakes.

Much of the answer must lie in the ambience of the group, the cognitive and emotional patterns that permeated and shaped its organizational style. Such a collective atmosphere is not necessarily the exact sum of the attitudes, ideas, suppositions, desires, and values of the individuals who make up the group. Every organization has its own character, its own way of acting and reacting, and this quality powerfully colors what its members feel, think, say, and do within the organization. We will dig around in some Watergate material, starting at the bottom with the burglaries themselves, in an attempt to find the poisoned spring from which so much error flowed.

Hindsight makes it perfectly clear that nobody in or around the White House should have dabbled in burglary. But one of the attributes of management is supposed to be foresight. The quality of the decision to embark upon burglary must be appraised on the basis of what the deciders knew—or could have known—at the time of decision. The question may be cast in a strictly managerial form, leaving aside consideration of legality and morality: should an organization, not usually in the burglary business, diversify its activities in that direction?

THE BASIC ECONOMY OF BURGLARY

Superficially, the prospect may seem inviting, just as people who pay restaurant checks are often seduced into believing that the restaurateur has an automatic and infallible surplus of benefits over costs. (A little research would show that more than half of new restaurants fail within a year.) White House staffers (no career burglars among them) were, like most of us, victims or potential victims of burglary. From that viewpoint, the burglar's profit seems easy and assured. Again, a little research into the burglary industry would have disclosed a repellent picture.

Though the number of burglaries in the U.S. is high and rising (2,345,000 in 1972), the curve of growth has been flattening out—and no wonder. Total cost to the victims was an impressive $722 million (or $308 per job). But burglars, because of the severe markdown traditional in thieves' markets, do not gain nearly as much as their victims lose. The actual take is probably closer to $200 per job, and this often has to be split among two or more perpetrators.

In the vast majority of burglaries, operating costs are so low as to be negligible. But risks, which are costs *in posse*, are formidable. While an individual netting $150 per job would have to commit fifty burglaries a year to achieve a modest income of $7,500 (tax-free, to be sure), the basic risk statistics of the industry indicate that one burglary in every five ends up with an arrest. Among adults arrested, half of those charged with burglary are convicted. Consequent unemployment and other costs reinforce the conclusion that burglary is not an activity that commends itself to mature and prudent people. No doubt that explains why half of all those arrested for burglary are under eighteen years old; the other half includes a high proportion of drug addicts, school drop-outs, and persons otherwise disadvantaged and/or disturbed.

TARGET SELECTION: POOR

As every manager knows, attractive "special situations" sometimes appear in even those industries that are statistically most bleak. In the case of the Watergate sequence of burglaries, we have to ask whether the specific rewards that could reasonably be expected were so great or the specific risks so low as to overbalance the general probability that shows burglary to be a game for losers.

The sad truth is that the Watergate burglaries were "special situations" only in a negative sense: their prospective rewards were lower and their operating costs and contingent costs (risks) were both very much higher than in the modal U.S. burglary. The highest expectable benefit that could have been gained from the break-in at the office of Daniel Ellsberg's psychiatrist would have been a file containing otherwise unobtainable personal information about him, information that might have been used (although it isn't clear how) to discredit him or to stop leaks. None of the White House deciders paused to note: (1) that the Pentagon papers case turned on legal and political issues to which Ellsberg's personality and motives were largely irrelevant; (2) that knowledge of Ellsberg's emotional make-up would not have contributed to solving the general problem of Washington leaks, which derive from many different kinds of people, few of whom bear a psychological resemblance to Ellsberg; (3) that since Ellsberg is not a notably secretive man, lots of personal information about him, for what it was worth, could have been gathered, free of risk, around Harvard Yard, around the Pentagon, and around the Rand Corp. From the burglary at the psychiatrist's office that promised such meager rewards, the burglars got, in fact, precisely nothing.

Nevertheless, the same team with some unhelpful additions was retooled to break into the Democratic National Committee. Once again, target selection was deplorable. Here the main mission was to bug the phone of Lawrence O'Brien, a man of probity and circumspection, two qualities often found together—although some barefoot moralizers insist virtue has no need of prudence. Public officials and politicians have been wary of telephones ever since 1876 when Alexander Graham Bell, demonstrating his gadget in Philadelphia, unwittingly startled the visiting Emperor of Brazil. An O'Brien friend says: "If you had a verbatim transcript of every telephone conversation Larry has engaged in since he was nineteen years old, you wouldn't have enough to embarrass him." In short, the break-in at the Watergate office building had an expectable reward very close to zero.

THE PREVALENCE OF OGRES

These footless ventures would remain forever incomprehensible unless we turned to the beliefs and emotional patterns of the participants. Their attitudes were shaped in part by the general ambience that enveloped the White House and the Committee to Re-elect the President, and that ambience included a lot of fear, suspicion, and hostility. Although the word "paranoia," used by many people, is too strong, it is correct to say that a high level of self-pity influenced the style of the Nixon White House.

The seeds of this attitude were sown long before Watergate. Self-pity was evident, though excusable, in many of Nixon's periods of adversity, and it had not melted away in the warm sun of ambition fulfilled. The public utterances of President Nixon, and those he encouraged Vice President Agnew to make in the early years of their first terms, often contained a strong theme of complaint against the unfairness of adversaries. The internal atmosphere of the White House was even more marked by this air of hostility and suspicion toward such outside bodies as Congress, the federal bureaucracy, and the press. All Presidents have had adversaries, but no other White House institutionalized its hostility by keeping, as Nixon's did, an "enemies list."

The U.S. organizes its political life, as well as its business life, through competition. Not only do we have competing parties, but government has many separate elements that are simultaneously in cooperation and competition with one another. Among the people themselves we don't expect—and don't want—a placid homogeneity of outlook and aims. In our kind of pluralist politics, a degree of combativeness, an awareness of adversaries, is inevitable and constructive. But there's a line, blurred but real, beyond which a normal self-assertion in the face of opposition can move over into either arrogance or self-pity.

Many business managers have seen in their own sphere examples of the damage that can be done when this blurred line is crossed. It is desirable, for instance, that a sales force be on its toes, alert to spot and to counter moves by its opposition. A given sales force can become too proud of its competitive ability and be made vulnerable by overconfidence. Or it can become demoralized by the pressure of competition. A sensitive executive would worry if his salesmen were constantly telling him and one another about the perfidy of their competitors, dwelling on their dirty tricks, exaggerating their unfairness. In that ambience his own salesmen would have a built-in excuse for poor performance, or they might goad themselves into foolish and imprudent acts.

The nearest business equivalent of the Watergate folly was the great electrical price-fixing conspiracy uncovered in 1962. The question that then ran through the business world was: how could experienced executives in well-run companies do anything so stupid? Much of the answer lay in the ambience of the conspirators. They felt overpressured—by their bosses, by rising costs, by government regulations they considered unfair. One executive in the industry, trying to explain his colleagues' gross misjudgment, told a *Fortune* reporter at the time that the conspirators did what they did because they were "distressed men."

The distress, of course, was not visible in their objective condition of opulence and success. The distress was in their minds. So, too, powerful men in the White House came to think of themselves as inhabitants of a beleaguered and distressed city, surrounded by enemies whose strength and malice they exaggerated. An intense will to win, coupled with the belief that the situation is desperate, can release a lot of energizing adrenalin. If it goes too far, such a state of mind can also trigger reckless misjudgments. Whom the gods would destroy they first make unduly sorry for themselves.

A SURPLUS OF SINCERITY

Nixon's White House, of course, was not the first to overstress the power and menace of its adversaries. Franklin Roosevelt had depicted himself as standing, along with the weak, against the "economic royalists" who, he implied, were really in charge of the country. This tactic was so brilliantly successful that all subsequent Presidents have flirted with it. But in Roosevelt's underdog posture there was always a saving measure of insincerity. He never really believed his histrionic pretense that the dragons he opposed were all that monstrous. Nor did the men around him, cheerfully manipulating the reins of power, lose themselves in the dramatic myth he had created. Nixon's aides, unfortunately, seem to have let the role of victim capture their hearts and minds.

In a culture that prizes justice, fears power, and roots for underdogs, the temptation to cast oneself as a victim is ever present. The average American, when looking privately at his own situation, resists this temptation rather effectively; he knows—most of the time—that he is not doing too badly. But in any public discourse or in any capacity where he represents others, the contemporary American tends toward donning the victim's robe.

Listening to the speeches of businessmen, with their frequent emphasis on the abuse of government and labor-union power, an observer may worry lest their self-pity blind them to the ever expanding scope of action that beckons to business. Spokesmen for blacks or women can express real grievances in terms so extravagant that their followers will not perceive actual opportunities; the result can be stagnation or angry, self-destructive action. This unhappy pattern even extends to sports. One September night this year in Baltimore the managers of both baseball teams were thrown out of the same game for protesting too raucously against the injustice of the umpires. Passionate complaint is the almost unvarying tone of those man-in-the-street interviews cherished by producers of TV news programs. If Americans ever became, in fact, as sorry for themselves as they sound in public discourse, the country as a whole might begin to act as foolishly as the "distressed" men who blindly stumbled into Watergate.

Nixon early recognized the danger in protest run wild. It was he who laudably set out to "bring us together" and admonished us to "lower our voices." One of the deepest ironies of Watergate is the public demoralization that has occurred because the Nixon White House got carried away by its own agonized indignation toward the "unfairness" of its adversaries. The public in 1973 would never have had occasion to "wallow in Watergate" (as the President expressed it) had not the White House, years before, wallowed in self-pity.

ARISTOTLE WOULD UNDERSTAND

Watergate is often referred to as a "tragedy," as indeed it is in the sense that it blasted lives and caused suffering. But Watergate imitates in many other ways the structure of classic tragedy as Aristotle described it. The action of the plot, he said, proceeds from a "flaw" (*hamartia*). This may be either a defect of knowledge (e.g., Oedipus didn't know that his wife, Jocasta, was his mother) or an emotional imbalance (e.g., Medea, filled with woe-is-me, overreacted to Jason's infidelity by killing their children). Sometimes the tragic flaw is a mingling of cognitive and emotional imperfections.

From the flaw emerges *hubris*, which has long been translated as pride or arrogance. But recent scholarship pushes toward a different understanding of *hubris*. Walter Kaufmann in *Tragedy and Philosophy* argues persuasively that *hubris* refers to the quality of the action that proceeds from the flaw; it is not the internal flaw itself. Greek writers used the word *hubris* in referring to rivers that overflow their banks. They applied *hubris* to armies that run riot, indulging in wanton behavior, or to anything—human, animal, vegetable, or inanimate—that rankly transgresses the usual order of its nature.

In the Watergate case, the flaw obviously was not pride, which scorns to slink about by night in other people's offices. If we think of self-pity as the tragic flaw in Watergate, then all the wild imprudence of the consequent actions, the *hubris*, becomes less baffling. The literary analogy may illuminate details of a problem in management analysis.

Act I, Scene I occurs in the summer of 1971, in the ruler's room of state. He is giving urgent orders to members of his staff. The precise content of his instruction is not known to us, but its tone and general import are clear. His government is bedeviled by leaks of information to a press deemed hostile. He invokes his highest responsibility, that in respect to the national security, as he tells them he wants his government sealed against leaks.

So far, there is nothing irrational about the ruler's attitude or the gist of his instruction. Leaks are no trivial matter. They can impair national security—and some have done so. More often they are devices employed by a government official to support a policy he favors, to hurt a rival, or advance his own career. Such leaks sow distrust among officials, inhibit frank discussion, and demoralize government. Now, publication of the Pentagon Papers, a veritable Niagara of a leak, requires drastic and immediate remedy.

At first the plumbers' unit interprets its responsibility in a normal and harmless way. Its members start to carry out a staff assignment to needle the chiefs of line departments and the regular investigatory agencies into greater vigilance against leaks. But progress, if any, is too slow. At this point, the tragic flaw in the spiritual ambience of the White House group begins to manifest itself.

In and around the plumbers' unit, deviation from organizational normality takes two forms. The atmosphere of a besieged city over-motivates the staffers involved. They wish so intensely to succeed in their assigned task that restraints of ordinary prudence drop away. The second manifestation of the flaw is more specifically managerial: they transform a staff function into a line operation. They decide that they themselves will gather the evidence that will retard leaks.

Their master, the President, deploys under his hand the largest, most expensive, and most professional array of investigatory agencies this side of the Soviet border. Yet these agencies are bypassed when the plumbers' unit decides to go into clandestine operations—which is no woods for babes. Neither Egil Krogh nor David Young, who headed the plumbers, had relevant experience in this line of work. Their immediate superior, John Ehrlichman, had no investigatory experience. Liddy, who had worked for the FBI, and Hunt, who had worked for the CIA, did have relevant experience. But many instances are known where individuals can render valuable service within a large professionalized organization and yet be helpless or harmful when working without professional supervision and organized support. In the plumbers' unit, Liddy and Hunt plainly lacked the competence, restraint, and judgment to be found (one hopes) in the organizations that had previously girdled their exuberance.

A former aide to a different President believes that all White House staffs, becoming impatient with the regular line agencies of government, are from time to time tempted to get into operations themselves. They hardly ever do so, however, partly because of what he called "the danger of involving the President." He was talking about possible interventions far less dangerous to the presidential reputation than burglary. Why, then, was the Nixon White House so incautiously willing to bypass the regular agencies and place its honor in the hands of people who knew so little about what they were doing?

SHOULD BUREAUCRATS OBEY?

The decision was almost certainly influenced by an attitude of distrust toward the whole federal bureaucracy. This was one of the areas where members of the Nixon circle felt most sorry for themselves. One expert on government structure remembers a long meeting of Nixon staff men at San Clemente devoted to the question of how to make the bureaucracy more obedient.

A familiar management problem is involved here, as anybody knows who has taken over the top spot in a corporation, or a division, or even a small office. He is likely to have found there men and women who took their own responsibilities seriously and who are entrenched by their specialized competence. A wise executive does not try to command the servile obedience of such people. His responsibility for coordinating their efforts and changing the over-all direction of the organization can only be achieved through the patient arts of leadership. He has to talk, to listen, to persuade and be persuaded.

But from the first the Nixon inner circle seems to have misunderstood the nature of the difficulty. It saw bureaucratic resistance as arising from political philosophy. No doubt, most civil servants are Democrats and maybe even "liberals." But this is not as important a truth as the Nixon people thought it. Presidents Kennedy and Johnson also had trouble with the bureaucracy. A Nixon official who has been most effective in his leadership of civil servants is Secretary of the Treasury George Shultz, whose own political philosophy happens to be most remote from the presumed liberalism of the bureaucrats. Shultz talks and listens to his experts. Shultz does not withdraw into injured and persecuted silence because they won't obey him. In short, Shultz follows a pattern widespread among managers of corporations who anticipate resistance from their experts. They do not perceive it as disloyalty or hostility. They know that dealing with such resistance is just what they are hired to do.

WHEN THE BIG SCENE WAS BUNGLED

But the Nixon Administration, with some distinguished exceptions, had never been notable for strong, independent personalities, secure enough to listen to the experts below and speak candidly to the chief above. The White House staff, the citadel of the beleaguered city, seems to have been chosen more for its zeal to protect the boss than for ability to serve him with information and argument. This criterion owed part of its origin to the tragic flaw, and it resulted in disaster at a crucial decision time.

Classic tragedy moves toward a point of "recognition," the scene where the flaw in all its horror is revealed to the audience and the dramatis personae. In the Watergate sequence, that point was reached in the summer of 1972 after the arrests, after the disclosure that large sums of money had been "laundered" in Mexico. Clearly, these were no ordinary burglars. They had backing at high levels.

If at that point the President or his former Attorney General had publicly recognized that a serious error had occurred, Watergate would never have grown to anything approaching its ultimate proportions. Such a public recognition would have been painful, but it almost certainly would not have cost Nixon either the election or the respect of several millions of Americans who lost confidence in him this year.

Nixon and the men around him bungled the recognition scene. Or to put the same thought in business terms, they failed to face the hard decision to cut their losses. Exactly what went on in the White House in the year following June, 1972, is still far from clear. But on any assumption about those months, there was serious managerial trouble in two big areas: personnel and communications.

In the most unlikely case, that Nixon knew exactly what was going on at every step, he was picking the wrong people to do the wrong things. On the much more likely assumption that Nixon didn't know much about the cover-up efforts, then those who were involved in it badly needed some coordinator—and they needed one with more authority, prudence, experience, and fiber than John Dean.

As a group, the White House staff contained too few men of the caliber and courage to make Nixon face the situation that the public, Nixon's audience, had long since recognized. On one version of events, it was not until April 15, 1973, that anybody told Nixon just how bad the situation was and what immediate steps he had to take. That messenger was Henry Petersen, not a member of Nixon's staff but one of the despised careerists, who had never spoken to the President until he stood before him in tennis shoes and old clothes on a Sunday afternoon and finally got the bad news across.

Nixon understands organizational information systems better, perhaps, than any previous President. But he showed in the Watergate sequence no sign that he grasped the most important fact about such systems: they are all far short of perfect. A prudent executive keeps testing his organization's ability to tell him what he needs to know about its own activities. A classical management story on this point goes back to 1924 and its hero is Alfred P. Sloan. In the spring of that year General Motors plants were turning out cars much faster than salesmen were getting rid of them. The established channels of information failed to bring this bad news to corporate headquarters. Corporate calamity was averted only because Sloan visited dealers in St. Louis, Kansas City, and Los Angeles, and himself counted the cars that had piled up in their lots. Nixon, on his version of what happened during the cover-up, never got down to personal investigation of widely published reports of what was being done in his name.

THE PRESS *IS* UNFAIR

It is quite possible that Nixon simply did not believe what the media were reporting concerning the cover-up because he had grown so accustomed to considering himself the victim of a press hostile to him.

The press is unfair to Nixon in a sense more fundamental than he knows. It has been unfair to all recent Presidents. It is unfair to businessmen, labor leaders, and everybody else responsible for carrying out action in a world whose complexity makes for dull writing. The inadequacy of the press in explaining to the public the actual working of government processes may be one of the most serious defects in contemporary democracy. Compared to this problem, the additional fact that many influential journalists don't much like Richard Nixon pales toward insignificance.

The Nixon White House diminishes its chances of constructive coverage by its attitude of pained withdrawal from the media. The exceptions demonstrate this general point. Henry Kissinger, who talks frequently and (relatively) frankly with reporters, manages to get through the media to the public. Nixon himself, on the rare occasions when he endures face-to-face contact with the media, handles press conferences with verve. His San Clemente press conference of August 22 was one of the few effective White House moves in the long Watergate sequence.

Nixon's relations with Congress also have that hurt and withdrawn look. Before he came to office, Congress was already becoming restless under what many of its members considered the undue power of the executive branch. Nixon was bound to have trouble with Congress, no matter what its political coloration might have been. But Nixon seems to have taken congressional opposition as a personal affront. In its day-to-day contact with individual Congressmen, the Nixon White House has been less active, less persuasively communicative than previous Administrations, including Eisenhower's. In public Nixon has, as a President must, often summarized what was wrong about the record of Congress and what was right about his own record. But in his relations with Congress he has not, as they say in Seville, worked close to the bull.

WHY WE REMEMBER HANNIBAL

Deplorable tendencies in Congress, in the bureaucracy, and in the media are easier to denounce than to overcome. A President, nevertheless, will be appraised by how much headway he makes against such objective difficulties. Hannibal is remembered for actually crossing the Alps, not for whatever Carthaginian maledictions that he, frustrated in Gaul, might have hurled at the "unfair" gradients confronting him.

The flaw that mars Nixon's style in domestic affairs becomes the more glaring when it is limned against his foreign-policy successes. In dealing with Red China and the Soviet Union he has brilliantly demonstrated that he can rise above self-pity. He has studied these offshore adversaries so long and so intently that he can handle the problems they represent much more coolly, objectively, and effectively than he handles the onshore problems represented by Daniel Ellsberg or Larry O'Brien or the fedeal bureaucracy or the *Washington Post*. Nixon isn't thrown off stride by Peking's or Moscow's "dirty tricks." It never seems to occur to him that Brezhnev or Mao is "unfair." He manages his relations with them like a manager, not with the mien of a wounded deer.

Excessive self-pity is, of course, an emotional and moral flaw. It is often found entwined with an inaccurate cognitive picture of reality. Individuals or groups marked by such a flaw may be handicapped in practical affairs, even in those activities that are put in such specialized pigeonholes as politics or economics or management.

Machiavelli taught the world that politics, for instance, has rules of success that are independent of moral strictures. But he never taught that men who act in politics are to be considered unbound by moral law. Twenty years ago Professor Charles Singleton in a memorable lecture called "The Perspective of Art" pointed to a passage in Machiavelli's *Discourses* as a corrective to the popular view of what the Florentine believed. Machiavelli, in one of those typical passages about what a ruler must do to grasp and hold power, gives an example of some morally horrible but politically effective policies carried out by Philip of Macedon. Then Machiavelli says: "Doubtless these means are cruel and destructive of all civilized life, and neither Christian nor human, and should be avoided by everyone."

Now that politics is clearly recognized as an independent art, any practitioner faces a double hurdle. What he does must be good as politics, but must not be bad as morals. The point is even clearer in the relation of morals to economics. When Alfred Sloan, in the example given above, learned that unsold cars were piling up, he shut down the production lines. As a compassionate man, he regretted the consequent unemployment and suffering. But in the economic circumstances his decision was not immoral. On the contrary, once he knew the facts any other decision would have been economically, managerially, and morally irresponsible.

Allen Dulles, when he was head of the CIA, once told a group of journalists that anyone entering upon his job must leave all moral considerations outside the door. This dangerous proposition is an example of the vulgar misreading of the Machiavellian view. The head of the CIA works in circumstances that ordinary citizens do not encounter. Circumstances change cases, and the head of the CIA may morally do things which an ordinary citizen would have no compelling occasion and no moral right to do. But the head of the CIA must nevertheless weigh the morality of any such act by whatever standards are appropriate to the circumstances.

John Ehrlichman in his testimony indicated that he could think of circumstances involving, say, the threat of nuclear attack, in which a President could justifiably order a burglary. But does this mean that a President, by invoking the name of national security, can order *any* burglary? A weighing of circumstances becomes critical in government morality, as indeed it is in private morality. It is not only managerially shocking but morally shocking that so serious an offense as the Beverly Hills break-in was undertaken in circumstances that did not come within miles of requiring it.

MELANCHOLY EXAMPLE

The moral standards of political life are, indeed, often more strict than those of private life. "Dirty tricks" that may be merely tasteless in undergraduate elections are seriously offensive when plotted by people on a White House staff. All that useless Dick-Tuckery revealed by the Ervin committee is one of the most appalling aspects of the Watergate disclosures. Another, and more melancholy, example is brought to mind by Spiro Agnew's resignation. Many people may not regard an ordinary citizen's failure to report taxable income as one of the graver moral offenses. But when a Vice President of the United States is exposed as having done that, we are all—quite logically—horrified.

In the Watergate sequence, self-pity blinded the participants to dangers that were political, managerial, legal, and moral. As their retribution unfolds, the rest of us may from time to time ask whether our own legitimate resentment against our share of the injustices that all men experience might not be making us so sorry for ourselves that we mismanage our practical affairs.

What Does and Doesn't Go On in the Boardroom

Ben W. Heineman

After years of studying the actions and inactions of corporate directors, Professor Myles L. Mace of the Harvard Business School concluded that there was "a considerable gap between what professors
and business executives have stated boards of directors should do and
what in fact they do." As he describes it in *Directors: Myth and Reality*
(Division of Research, Harvard Business School), the gap is wide indeed.

Seen through Professor Mace's eyes, directors are not a particularly
attractive lot. Not attractive, that is, if the ordinary stockholder relies
upon them to represent and protect his interests. Directors are far more
likely to identify with and protect the interests of the chief executive,
who in fact selects them, than the interests of the stockholders, who
technically elect them and to whom they are legally responsible. Even
if an individual director, or a group of directors, becomes convinced
that the president is unsatisfactory, only rarely is the president asked
to resign. The typical response is for the directors themselves to resign
on innocuous grounds that will not embarrass either the company or
its president.

None of this should be surprising if one accepts Mace's explanation
of how and why directors are chosen, and why they agree to serve. In
the publicly held enterprise, powers of control in fact rest in the president, and he selects the directors. He wants them to be holders of
prestigious positions, to be "attractive ornaments on the corporate
Christmas tree." He also wants them to be congenial with himself and
the other directors, and understanding of his problems. Controversial
or abrasive figures need not apply.

The outside director agrees to serve principally for prestige, but also
to learn how other companies are run. He rationalizes his passivity and
lack of involvement by measuring his contributions against the relatively small director's fee he receives, and the far smaller portion that
he retains. Unless the outside director is a major stockholder, or represents one, his primary motivation in coming on a board is seldom, if
ever, to produce a better company or to safeguard the stockholders'
interests.

From Ben W. Heineman, "What Does and Doesn't Go On in the Boardroom,"
Fortune (February, 1972), pp. 157–158. Reprinted with permission of author.

Contrary to conventional belief—or myth, as Professor Mace would have it—boards of directors do not establish corporate strategies or broad policy. This would require a degree of knowledge and effort impossible for a board of directors meeting monthly or quarterly. Inevitably, the powers of control possessed by the chief executive and the confidence usually reposed in him require that his proposals be approved. Most chief executives do not believe in management by committee, nor would they lightly accept it if attempted by a board of directors.

Nor do most chief executives welcome discerning questions from board members. Challenging questions, Mace finds, are regarded as showing a lack of confidence in the president, often to his embarrassment before his subordinates who have been invited to attend the meeting. Only under crisis conditions are such questions regarded as appropriate. Otherwise, to ask such questions is a breach of professional courtesy and a violation of good corporate manners.

What directors really do, according to Professor Mace, is to give advice and counsel when asked, and, by the mere fact of their presence, serve as a discipline for presidents and subordinate management. For even when reasonably sure that they will not ask embarrassing questions, the chief executive seeks the approval of the board members as respected peers in the business world. But it is accepted that this role is advisory only.

A SHELTERED ENVIRONMENT

Directors: Myth and Reality may be taken as a fair description of the workings of the board system in publicly held companies of relatively large size. Mace recognizes that there are exceptional chief executives who seek out and welcome discerning questions, who take pains to educate their boards of directors, and who regard their boards as responsible, jointly with them, for the conduct of the company's business. These chief executives constitute a distinct minority. There are also exceptional directors who do not hesitate to question and challenge. But essentially, Mace's picture of boards of directors of medium and large-size corporations is, to borrow another author's description, a picture of "cronyism, elitism, and do-nothingism."

Fair description though the book may be, it is deficient in important respects. It does not evaluate the system, nor does it consider important new trends. Out of Professor Mace's wide experience and extensive research (he himself has served on a number of boards of directors), one would have had reason to hope for significant contributions to both of these areas.

The board system as it exists buffers and protects the chief executive and provides him and his subordinate management with a sheltered and supportive environment in which to function. With a superior chief executive, the system works well. When disaster is threatening, however, the realities of the board system frequently result in corporate impotence.

In the case of Penn Central, for example, it seems reasonably clear that the board of directors acquiesced over a long period of time in not being given adequate information, dealt only with the superficialities of the situation, and failed to challenge the increasingly ominous results. Only as the company tottered into bankruptcy were the officers removed. At United Air lines (another crisis situation), the board of directors moved to change chief executives, but only with much pain and trauma. There is probably no other genuinely effective remedy available to a board; it is prescribed too seldom, and often too late.

But far more dangerous than the general ineffectiveness of boards in disaster situations—which are uncommon, after all—is the lack of any mechanism for identifying and eliminating mediocrity of management. The principal virtue of the present board system, when teamed with superior management, now becomes its principal vice. The sheltering instinct remains strong even though with mediocre management its justification has disappeared. Being friends and busy people, and not themselves large stockholders, directors are far more likely to "go along," or resign, than to demand changes because of mediocre performance. Because the chief executive controls the agenda as well as the data he presents, a board often does not have the facts to determine that results are mediocre, or to challenge the president's explanation that unsatisfactory results are due to circumstances beyond his control.

Mediocrity, when it exists, is often transmitted through successive generations of management. It requires no extensive familiarity with the behavioral sciences to understand and believe that mediocre chief executives attract, retain, and promote mediocre subordinates. A board of directors in a noncrisis situation has very little choice but to accept a mediocre successor, selected from among his principal subordinates.

Since boards of directors, by virtue of their selection and traditions, cannot be counted on to change mediocre managements, stockholders themselves, either through the proxy fight or the take-over bid, have on occasion sought to get this power into their own hands. Almost universally, boards of directors have closed ranks to protect, not the stockholders, but the management. Because of the difficulties outsiders have in identifying mediocrity, the rallying around of prestigious members of a board of directors to protect the chief executive has frequently influenced members of Congress, the media, and the public. Corporate democracy and the best interests of the stockholders have often been the losers.

The defects that Professor Mace describes in his book are not at issue in much of the current disaffection with boards of directors, as evidenced most visibly by Campaign G.M. The stir arises not so much from dissatisfaction with the boards themselves as from a differing perception of the role of the business corporation in our society. There is a peculiar love-hate relationship between the corporation and the liberal reformer. He both hates it as the socially indifferent money machine he thinks it to be, and loves it as the force for social progress he thinks it can become. The demands for board representation of blacks, consumers, women, environmentalists, and the public generally, reflect this new thinking about the nature and responsibilities of corporations.

VIEWED AS THE CUTTING EDGE

Increasingly there is public discussion of the social responsibilities and the "quasi-public" nature of the largest corporations. As political mechanisms fall short of achieving social, environmental, or other public goals, the business corporation is viewed by some as the cutting edge of change. Large corporations having important consumer constituencies may be regarded as more vulnerable and more quickly responsive to such pressure than the political system generally. But in seeking to bring about change through representation on boards of directors, reformers are almost certainly accepting the myth, rather than the reality, of board power.

Last-ditch resistance on the part of corporate managers is not necessarily inevitable. In the last few years many black Americans—and the number is increasing almost daily—have been elected to the boards of directors of major U.S. corporations. Women are also becoming visible in walnut-paneled boardrooms. The time is not too far distant when major corporations to whom the approbation of consumers or environmentalists is necessary will add representatives of these groups to their boards.

The best corporate managements are self-confident and pragmatic; in other words, adaptable to change. And this adaptability applies not only to changing markets and new technology but also to new congressional and public attitudes. Responsiveness to changing attitudes can be demonstrated not only by action on how and what one manufactures and sells but also by action in the boardroom itself. The ultimate goal of the business corporation, of course, must be the maximizing of profits over time. Moreover, since management by committee is demonstrably unsound, control will continue to reside with the chief executive. But the new board members will be important contributors to the traditional board role of providing advice and consultation. They will also add measurably to the vital board role of providing management with protective coloration against an increasingly hostile outside world.

How the Tenderfeet Toughened Up U.S. Borax

Tom Alexander

Over the past few months, an extraordinary drama of labor-management conflict has been playing itself out in the California desert. A company got shoved a little too hard and shoved back. As a result, its white-collar employees found themselves toiling away in a singularly hellish mine and refinery in the middle of the Mojave.

The mine in question produces about 60 percent of the free world's borax and is owned by U.S. Borax & Chemical Corp., a subsidiary of the giant British mining company, Rio Tinto Zinc. While just about everybody associates the company's product with old-fashioned cleansing agents, Death Valley Days, and twenty-mule teams, it turns out that borax—otherwise known as sodium borate—is one of those all-around whizzer chemicals of the new industrial age. A lot of borax still goes into soap, but it also finds its way into everything from agriculture to atomic energy (where it controls the rate of nuclear reactions). The biggest use of all, though, is in making certain kinds of glass, including glass fiber.

Well before its contract with the International Longshoremen's and Warehousemen's Union expired last June, U.S. Borax was in an odd kind of trouble: largely because of the huge increase in demand for glass-fiber insulation, the world wanted more borax than Borax could provide. At the same time, the company was discovering that its automated plant, two miles north of the tiny town of Boron, was apparently incapable of producing as much borax as it was designed to. When demand surged last year, the managers of the plant tried to go to full production but were seldom able to exceed about 80 percent of the nominal capacity. Instead of increasing, in fact, plant output had been dropping for the last year. So customers were put on allocation, shipments were delayed, and by last June, the borax stockpiles had dwindled to nothing.

YOU DARE NOT LET IT COOL

The company's president, Carl Randolph, now says that because of the inventory bind, Borax entered the negotiations all prepared to buy a

Reprinted from material originally appearing in the December 1974 issue of *Fortune* Magazine by special permission; © 1974 Time, Inc.

costly settlement from the I.L.W.U. locals that represent the hourly workers at Boron and at a smaller plant in Wilmington, California. Initially, the union demands included an immediate 25 percent boost in hourly pay—which then averaged $5.02. The company countered by offering a 10 percent immediate increase and 7 percent rises in each of the two subsequent years. But what put management's back up were union demands that would infringe upon management prerogatives; for example, the Boron local wanted to review new construction projects with an eye to doing the work themselves. U.S. Borax was planning a $60-million refinery-expansion program, aimed at increasing output by a third. The company wanted the new construction done by outside contractors and decided that it would take a strike rather than give in to this and other union demands. Management resolved, however, to try to keep the two plants operating with supervisory personnel plus salaried employees brought in from elsewhere.

The problem with that idea was that Borax is not really all that big a company. While an annual sales figure of more than $130 million is scarcely trivial, the company has only about 2,000 employees. Nearly 1,200 of these were members of the striking I.L.W.U. locals. The rest are mainly white-collar people—managers, secretaries, clerks, salesmen, computer specialists, engineers, and scientific researchers— hardly the kind of people that one would judge to possess the requisite skills and toughness to operate a borax mine and a technically complex refining plant in a mid-Mojave summer.

Furthermore, once you get a borax refinery in operation, you have to keep it going twenty-four hours a day. The basic refining process consists mainly of dumping crushed ore into hot water, which extracts the soluble borax from the insoluble clay. Then the concentrated solution is piped to various parts of the plant to be turned into various kinds of borax products. Once the solution is in the pipelines, you dare not let it cool, or else the borax will crystallize and solidify inside the pipes.

BAGGIES IN THE GAS TANKS

The drifts of borax were symptomatic of the complex troubles at Boron. Some company men say that one of the problems was that the plant was ill-designed in the first place. But foremen and managers contend that a major source of trouble was worker intransigence, slowdowns, and a lot of outright sabotage, including the plastic Baggies that someone dropped into the fuel tanks of trucks and earthmoving machines. In any case, everybody agrees that labor relations had been deteriorating for a number of years. In its effort to get production up, the company had kept hiring more men. But the newcomers, no matter how eager, soon came under pressure from older hands to slow down.

Over the years, the powdery fallout had accumulated waist-deep throughout many portions of the mine and plant, with drifts running much higher. Plant workers were confined to narrow paths shoveled through the Lower Slobbovian whiteness. Foremen, under pressure to increase production, neglected day-to-day cleanup chores, and in any case could usually count on foot-dragging when they ordered workers to shovel borax. The foremen felt all but powerless in the face of this resistance because of the many regulations and guarantees of job security that had crept into the union contracts over the years.

It's little wonder, then, that the foremen's eyes gleamed when the white-collar men stepped off the planes. The job assignments were made by refinery manager Ken Barnhill without much attention to normal company rank or occupation. "We used the Army system," said Barnhill, "and tried not to let a man's background influence his placement." Inevitably, however, the new men's inexperience meant that they wound up with most of the grubby laboring jobs—the toting, oiling, refueling, and the eternal shoveling and cleaning. The more skilled and technical tasks were done by the foremen and resident supervisors. Once the makeshift crew had mastered the routine of keeping the plant running, the foremen seized the opportunity to set the newcomers to digging the plant out from under all that borax. Shovels were handed out and when the men asked where they should start digging, the foremen replied, "Anywhere."

After looking over its roster, the company concluded that at best it could muster only about 450 able-bodied people to run the two plants that normally employ over 1,400. The 450 included the plant supervisors, virtually the entire sales and research staffs, together with clerks, managers, and so forth, all the way up to vice presidents.

A week or two prior to the expiration of the union contract, the prospective strikebreakers were given a chance to volunteer for the duty, although few were under much illusion that there was anything particularly voluntary about it. Aside from the obvious fact that unless the plants kept going, the salesmen would have nothing to sell and the managers nothing to manage, the only inducements were peer pressure and unverified rumors that the company would pay its salaried scabs $60 a day as a bonus. Ultimately such a bonus was declared, but only after the strike was already under way.

In view of the company's intentions, management seems to have been oddly surprised by the violence that ensued. Within minutes after the walkout on midnight of June 14, several hundred I.L.W.U. men massed outside the Boron plant gates. A group of strikers broke through the gates, roughing up several plant guards. Railroad cars, an automobile, and a small building were burned.

The white-collar "volunteers" assembled early the next day in U.S. Borax's Los Angeles parking garage to be bused to Fox Field Airport.

From there they were flown in company planes to the plant's airstrip where they confronted—many of them for the first time—the vast whiteness of an operating borax mine.

It must have been a sobering sight. Automated the refinery may be, but it is scarcely any paragon of industrial efficiency or cleanliness. It's an eighty-acre complex of furnaces, calciners, centrifuges, vibrators, scrubbers, and baggers, all interconnected by an overhead network of what must be some of the leakiest conveyors ever built. Day and night, the plant—and the sagebrush for miles downwind—are dusted with a warm, unremitting outfall of borax, white as snow, fine as flour, and gritty as sand.

In the presence of moisture, the stuff dissolves and recrystallizes in solid lumps. Without constant application of brooms, shovels, sledgehammers, and sometimes even dynamite, the machines and furnaces clog up and stop working. All the more delicate pieces of machinery are labeled "Do Not Beat."

At the same time, though, the presence of all those great big vehicles and other machines standing idle aroused small-boy instincts in the shovelers. They discovered that if they wanted to jump into some mechanical monster and try to run it, why, there was no one to discourage them. Soon, the plant and the mine were aswarm with bucket loaders and Lectra Haul dump trucks careening around with dangerous enthusiasm.

For the first two and a half months of the strike, most of the out-of-towners worked eighteen days straight and then got four days off to return home. Aside from their "R. and R.," they virtually never left the heavily guarded plant compound—no one had any enthusiasm for crossing the sporadically violent line of picketers. The company had scattered cots throughout the plant—in rented trailers, offices, conference rooms, even the ladies' rest rooms. A cafeteria was set up in a large storeroom, manned by one of the catering services that specialize in feeding on-location motion-picture crews. The strikebreakers ate well; steak and lobster appeared regularly on the menu. Twice a week—on Wednesdays and Saturdays—each man was issued precisely two cans of beer. Work clothes and boots, snacks, and other items were handed out free in a "goody room," as it was called. It bore a sign: "Through these doors pass the best damn scabs in the world."

They worked twelve-hour shifts, ate, and tumbled into bed. Throughout the night, helicopters with spotlights flew round and round the plant perimeter.

GLOOM IN THE SONIC BOOM CAPITAL

Beyond that perimeter was a grimmer world, without steaks and lobsters and $60 bonuses. Since the mine opened in 1926, it has existed in a tight but infrequently abrasive symbiosis with the small town that was swept together on the desert floor for the miners to live in. Boron, as it is now called, is a tough town in a tough place. More than a thousand of its inhabitants work—*used to work*, that is—at the mine and refinery. In a quest for other distinction, the Boron Chamber of Commerce has claimed for the town the title "Sonic Boom Capital of the World," but even that comes courtesy of the test pilots of Edwards Air Force Base, thirty miles away, who try out experimental aircraft overhead.

The town's average wage earner has been working at the Borax mine for about fifteen years, and some families have three generations employed there. Many of the families came there years ago from the coal fields in Kentucky, West Virginia, and Oklahoma, bringing with them the coal miners' traditional refractoriness.

For the first thirty years, the borax deposits were worked through conventional underground mining techniques, calling upon the special skills and psychological immunities of the coal miners. The raw ore was shipped by rail to the refining plant in Wilmington. In 1957, however, the company elected to convert the underground mine to an open pit. Among other economies, this would permit utilization of the 40 to 50 percent of ore that is normally wasted in the form of pillars to hold up the roof of an underground mine. The borax emerges from open-pit operations mixed with a lot of contaminating clay, so Borax built the refining plant near the rim of the pit.

The change in mining techniques and the coming of the refinery specialists from outside naturally disturbed the restive, captive population of Boron. Miners and their descendants saw their skills rendered beside the point as the machines stripped away the hundred-foot-thick overburden to expose the gleaming borax lode riddled with the ants'-nest handiwork of old shafts and chambers. Many of the higher-paid men proved less adept with the new machines than younger men and outsiders; they often wound up in lowlier jobs and worried for their future.

Isolated together with their troubled work force and under little competitive pressure, the plant managers made some attempts to placate their men over the years. They established special pay categories for the displaced workers, paying them at their old rate even when they worked in lower categories. Such special treatment, of course, only antagonized other workers. In addition, the company accumulated all kinds of overmanned shop practices and featherbedding. Skilled laborers, plumbers, and electricians admit to sitting idly for hours, waiting for a laborer to finish preparatory work under union rules.

Over the years, the insecurities, jealousies, and militance fermented. In 1964 the plant workers voted to switch from the A.F.L.-C.I.O. International Chemical Workers Union to the more radical

I.L.W.U. Four years later, the union's tough negotiations plus a violent strike ended with the company's buckling under and the workers getting pretty much what they demanded.

The success in 1968 and subsequent gains in 1970 encouraged the I.L.W.U. locals at Boron and Wilmington to ask for more this year. Since the company had a big backlog of orders, and virtually no reserves of refined borax, the timing seemed highly favorable.

Once the strike was under way, however, confidence began to evaporate. The locals had accumulated nothing in the way of strike funds and as the payless weeks went by, workers' savings disappeared. Some got part-time jobs, some had working wives, some got food stamps. Other I.L.W.U. locals contributed a little. Banks and finance companies extended loan contracts on cars and furniture, but unpaid bills accumulated, and utilities shut off services.

The social fabric of the close-knit little town began unraveling. Plant managers and foremen crossed the picket lines each morning and evening, setting neighbor against neighbor, and in some cases, foreman father against union son. The foremen's cars were regularly stoned and occasionally shot at, families received threatening phone calls, windows were broken, one or two houses were bombed. A few union men broke ranks and returned to work. The house trailer of one was firebombed when no one was home. A bundle of dynamite was thrown under another returnee's house when the family *was* at home, but the fuse went out and the family was spared.

"THEY CAN'T BE PRODUCING MUCH"

In mid-August, the Wilmington local voted to accept the company's terms and go back to work, but the Boron local held on. Local 30's leaders told the members that if only they stuck it out, they could bring U.S. Borax to its knees. The leaders claimed they were being kept informed about what was going on in the plant by people who were crossing the picket lines. The leaders told the workers that the plant, which could be seen belching its familiar clouds of dust and sending out its strings of railroad cars, was really producing only 15 percent of normal output. This estimate was backed up, it is said, by one union member who was allowed into the plant to collect his tools. When he emerged, he told his fellow strikers, "They can't be producing much borax in there. The place is *clean*."

In fact, however, the plant had rarely ever done so well. The skimpy, undertrained work force of 325 scabs (not counting about fifty hired guards and helicopter pilots) was regularly shipping out more borax than the normal work force of more than a thousand. Prior to the strike, the plant had averaged about 3,100 tons of borax a day; during the strike months of July and September, output averaged around

3,600 tons a day, and on a few days reached an all-time record of 4,000 tons. Production dropped off a little in August because several days of heavy rain hobbled operations in the pit and a storm knocked out the electric power. All told, the plants' managers calculated that output per man-hour averaged between two and three times that of the pre-strike force.

As the implications of this began to sink in, U.S. Borax management gained a new perspective on their old labor practices. Company President Randolph traces many of the problems to the company's posture in the 1968 strike. "It was easy to make concessions that seemed small at the time, but they grew into major problems. We only realized the magnitude of it after we began operating with the temporary people—and began producing more than we had before."

Plant managers ascribed the high output to the strong motivation of the salaried men. "They didn't need any supervision," marveled mine superintendent Lowell Page. "They would just run the mine until they knew they had enough to keep the refinery going, and then they'd look around for additional jobs to do." Randolph traces the high motivation to anger over union violence. "It created a cause for them to rally around."

A STIFFENING STAND

One of the implications, of course, was that the Boron facility should be able to get along with a lot fewer people—750 to 800 instead of more than a thousand. After they had learned the ropes, many members of the tiny force of scabs wondered how the regular workers had occupied their time. One of those who wondered was Al Ertel, who left his regular job as a computer-systems designer in Los Angeles and served as an oiler at the Boron plant. "I'd like to be here when there were eight or nine hundred hourly workers in this place," he said. "They'd be crawling all over each other."

U.S. Borax began taking a stiffer stand in its labor negotiations. In August the company offered to up the pay boost from 10 to 11 percent. In return, however, it demanded a number of major concessions. They included reserving to the company the right to contract out not only new capital construction, but also a lot of major repairs and other work. The company also demanded that new job categories be created, consolidating several old ones. For example, a new "millwright" category would include former mechanics, welders, and pipefitters. The union negotiating committee predictably refused the offer, though it did reduce its wage-increase demand from 25 to 20 percent.

A month later, Borax addressed a letter to the strikers, warning them that it would begin hiring permanent replacements to fill the jobs of employees who were not back at work by September 23. Twenty-four employees returned by the deadline, despite a lot of intimidation and some violence by militant union members. The frustration of those who stayed out manifested itself in a major escalation of violence. On the morning of September 23, strikers lined the roads to the plant, stoning every car going in or out, and injuring several people.

DESERT CARAVANS

But two developments put the seal on the strike's outcome. The first was the refusal of various A.F.L.-C.I.O. craft unions that were slated to perform the contract work at Boron to agree to observe the I.L.W.U. picket lines. The second was the unexpectedly large response to the company's prominent help-wanted ads in several California cities. Unemployment in the state was then averaging around 7.5 percent, and within days after the ads appeared in late September, hundreds of eager applicants showed up, despite the traditional reluctance of many people to cross a union's picket line. The company claimed that the newly hired workers often turned out to be far more willing hands than the old ones. It suddenly saw that it had within its grasp not only the chance to reduce its plant manpower but, if it chose, to rid itself of all its ingrained Boron labor troubles and start afresh.

The newcomers commuted in from such towns as Mojave, Barstow, and Lancaster, thirty to fifty miles away. Every morning and evening, they gathered into hundred-car convoys. Guarded by police cars, led by a helicopter, the caravans made their way across the hostile desert.

By then, the union had begun to cave in. It had reduced its wage-increase demand to a face-saving 13 percent. Among the remaining sticking points was the issue of amnesty. The company had made clear its intention of firing or suspending about ten individuals who had been identified in acts of violence. The union wanted the company to drop all charges and disciplinary action.

U.S. Borax refused to make even this concession. In its final offer, possibly made to convince the National Labor Relations Board that it was still bargaining in good faith, the company said it would take back all strikers except those under discipline. Most of the supervisors and the now-toughened tenderfeet in the Boron plant hoped that the union would turn down the offer.

A SIGH HEARD ALL OVER

The union met on the night of October 7. After a quick show of hands, the leaders ruled that no formal vote would be taken, the effect of this being that the company offer was rejected. When the news reached the plant the next morning, "the sigh of relief," as one man put it, "could be heard all over the place." The company immediately began large-scale hiring from cities as far away as San Diego and Tucson.

On October 24, the union finally voted 332 to 86 to go back to work, accepting all the company's terms. By that time, though, 250 people had already been hired. And since the company was by then contemplating a workforce reduction of another 200 to 300, a substantial proportion of Boron's breadwinners would be looking for work in a bad and worsening job market. Many owned houses that they would have a hard time selling if they decided to move; for a long time to come, no doubt, most of the newly hired plant workers would rather commute a long way than move to a resentful community where life would be uncomfortable at best and possibly dangerous. So, it appeared that the dusty plant and the little town would continue in uneasy coexistence side by side—one in improved health, the other sorely ailing, both wiser than they were before.

The Corporate Rush to Confess All

Scandals over foreign kickbacks, bribes, and questionable payments by U.S. multinational companies are becoming a domestic and foreign policy problem for the Ford Administration. After fresh disclosures of overseas payoffs by Lockheed Aircraft Corp. the President this week ordered a full Cabinet-level review of illegal corporate practices. And the Securities & Exchange Commission is working to keep up with the reports of dozens of companies who are disclosing their misdeeds voluntarily. Last July the SEC suggested that companies in violation of disclosure laws might "lessen the need for SEC enforcement action" by confessing bribes and kickbacks and cooperating with the SEC. Now, as the season of proxy solicitations and annual meetings approaches, companies are indeed rushing to confess. When the dust settles, say SEC sources, corporate wrongdoing, especially involving foreign operations, will be shown to be far more pervasive than suspected.

SEC officials say their voluntary disclosure program "has only just begun," yet an unexpectedly large sampling of companies are admitting misdeeds.

Without citing any names, SEC Chairman Roderick M. Hills told Congress last month that 15 companies had confessed to the agency.

Reprinted from the February 23, 1976 issue of *Business Week* by special permission. © 1976 by McGraw-Hill, Inc.

Cities Service Co., among the first, also told its shareholders last September about questionable payments. Santa Fe International Corp. was another. Last month it said that, among other things, it had participated in the Arab-led economic boycott of Israel.

Richard H. Rowe, an associate director of corporation finance at the SEC, says the number of corporate confessions is now around 30 and "climbing so rapidly no one has time to count."

SOME OF THE BEST

Of the cases being volunteered, none yet involves illegal payments of a magnitude publicly revealed by such companies as Gulf Oil Corp. or Lockheed. "But," says one SEC official, "we now see corporate misdeeds being carried on in business to an extent that is sickening."

The SEC is interested in the companies' tales mainly for two reasons. Bribes and kickbacks frequently involve falsification of records, a violation of SEC law. Then, too, the SEC requires companies to inform investors of material facts concerning their business.

"The bribery of a foreign official," says Commissioner Irving M. Pollack, "is per se a material fact." In most of the cases thus far, companies may get off simply by disclosing some of the facts and taking strong corrective remedies. But for others, there is the possibility of an SEC suit or referral to the Justice Dept. for criminal proceedings. "What we really don't like," says an SEC official, "is to have a company coming back in here with the line: 'It appears that we forgot to tell you about a little matter . . . '"

"After coming to us," adds Rowe, "most companies trot right down to the IRS." Treasury Secretary William E. Simon this week ordered the Internal Revenue Service to "intensify and broaden" its own investigations of companies suspected of illegal actions.

CAUGHT UNAWARE

The wrongdoing being confessed to the SEC is difficult to characterize. So far, public attention has been focused on huge payments to sales agents and on schemes directly involving top management. But this "may be misleading as to the nature of the over-all problem," says one official. It appears that in a great many of the volunteered cases, top management was unaware of what was going on until fairly recently. Then the disclosures by Lockheed and others caused management, and in some cases the accountants, to take a harder look at what was going on. Some middle-level managers and other employees had set up illegal deals either to improve their own "performance" or, in a few cases, to line their pockets.

An example offered by the SEC that may, with variations, be common is the case of a company whose officials wished to transfer funds from one country to another while avoiding taxes or currency restrictions. They simply found another company with a like amount of funds in the desired currency and bribed bank officers to switch ownership of the accounts. Another ploy that the SEC says may be common is to help foreign suppliers cheat on their income taxes by making payments for goods and services to Swiss bank accounts.

DIVERTING STAFFERS

The new revelations are causing unexpected problems for the SEC. Bribery and kickbacks in international business appear so extensive that the agency could investigate indefinitely. Some agency officials, including Commissioner A. A. Sommer Jr., fear the SEC is close to exceeding its own mandate. "At some point," says Sommer, "we end up trying to enforce everyone else's law, which is not our job to do."

On the other hand, the confessions are causing the SEC, as one staffer puts it, "to question the integrity of the entire corporate record-keeping and disclosure system." What has everybody shocked, this official says, "is that in many instances, such schemes have been going on for years with apparently nobody knowing about it."

Many important questions remain unanswered, including the role of accountants. "Accountants," an enforcement official says, "argue they are not responsible for detecting fraud. But you have to wonder in some cases where they have been all these years."

Epilogue

The material presented in this book provides, we feel, an interesting view of life and death in organizations. It is different in many ways from what is encountered in academic treatments of formal organization. One might question why material such as is described in this book is not dealt with typically in teaching and research within the organizational behavior and management field. We have concluded that this is so in part because scholars in these fields treat the material as aberrational, as something which doesn't fit the traditional or conventional views of formal organization. The material is thus ignored or discarded. We feel that to the extent such material is not seriously examined for its potential contribution to the field, so our current academic perspectives on organizations are incomplete.

Clearly, organizations and their members survive and prosper in the midst of and, at times, apparently because of conflict-ridden, manipulative, spontaneous and even serendipitous behaviors and processes. Equally clear from a reading of the material in this book is the inference that organizations and their members suffer, are injured and, on occasion, die under the same sets of conditions and events. The principles, models and ideals described in some organizational behavior and management texts may in fact cushion the extremes of failure, pain and decline in organizations. We feel they succeed only partially, and often not at all, because of their development in ignorance of, or without reference to, the kinds of behaviors and situations presented in this book.

We are reminded of the story of the somewhat inebriated young man who, one dark night, was found peering at the ground around a lighted lamppost by a passing patroller. When the officer of the law asked him what he was doing, he replied he was looking for his car keys. "Where did you lose them?" the patroller inquired. "Over there, around the corner," replied the man. "Then why look here?" asked the cop, somewhat surprised. "Because there's a light here and I can't see anything there at all."

Perhaps we need to look around the corner in our search for a deeper understanding of organization. There may be organizational phenomena "over there" which are being described consistently by others but which we don't regard typically as sources of light, and so we perceive only a dark corner, if we see anything there at all.

We have found our own thinking greatly stimulated and our own models of organization much in need of revision as a result of our encounter with the material in this book. We suspect there is in such literature a rich source of questions to be explored, ideas to be investigated and challenges to be met in building new models to better describe and explain formal organization.

Perhaps our visitor to Earth from planet Utopia, arriving ten years from now, will take back documents from academia and documents from periodicals, newspapers and other sources which reflect a steady flow of ideas and applications between the theoretical and the so-called "real world" of organizational behavior. We look forward to such a development!